Records of the Grand Historian of China

TRANSLATED FROM THE *Shih chi* OF SSU-MA CH'IEN

IN TWO VOLUMES

PREPARED FOR THE COLUMBIA COLLEGE PROGRAM
OF TRANSLATIONS FROM THE ORIENTAL CLASSICS
WM. THEODORE DE BARY, EDITOR

NUMBER LXV OF THE
RECORDS OF CIVILIZATION: SOURCES AND STUDIES
EDITED UNDER THE AUSPICES OF THE
DEPARTMENT OF HISTORY, COLUMBIA UNIVERSITY

Records of the Grand Historian of China TRANSLATED FROM THE *Shih chi* OF SSU-MA CH'IEN BY BURTON WATSON

VOLUME I:

EARLY YEARS OF THE HAN DYNASTY

209 TO 141 B.C.

COLUMBIA UNIVERSITY PRESS

NEW YORK AND LONDON

Copyright © 1961 Columbia University Press
First printing 1961
Third printing 1968
Library of Congress Catalog Card Number: 60-13348
Printed in the United States of America

The addition to the "Records of Civilization:
Sources and Studies" of a group of translations
of Oriental historical materials, of which this
volume is one, was made possible by funds granted
by Carnegie Corporation of New York. That Corporation
is not, however, the author, owner, publisher, or
proprietor of this publication, and is not to be
understood as approving by virtue of its grant
any of the statements made or views expressed therein.

UNESCO COLLECTION OF REPRESENTATIVE WORKS
CHINESE SERIES
This work has been accepted in the Chinese Translations
Series of the United Nations Educational, Scientific
and Cultural Organization (UNESCO).

RECORDS OF CIVILIZATION
SOURCES AND STUDIES

EDITED UNDER THE AUSPICES OF THE
DEPARTMENT OF HISTORY, COLUMBIA UNIVERSITY

GENERAL EDITOR

JACQUES BARZUN, *Seth Low Professor of History*

EDITORS EMERITI

JAMES T. SHOTWELL, *Bryce Professor Emeritus of the History of International Relations*

AUSTIN P. EVANS, *Professor Emeritus of History*

EDITOR: EUROPEAN RECORDS

JOHN H. MUNDY, *Associate Professor of History*

EDITORS: ORIENTAL RECORDS

C. MARTIN WILBUR, *Professor of Chinese History*

WM. THEODORE DE BARY, *Professor of Chinese and Japanese*

CONSULTING EDITORS

SALO W. BARON, *Professor of Jewish History, Literature, and Institutions on the Miller Foundation*

GILBERT HIGHET, *Anthon Professor of the Latin Language and Literature*

DONALD KEENE, *Professor of Japanese*

PAUL O. KRISTELLER, *Professor of Philosophy*

GARRETT MATTINGLY, *William R. Shepherd Professor of European History*

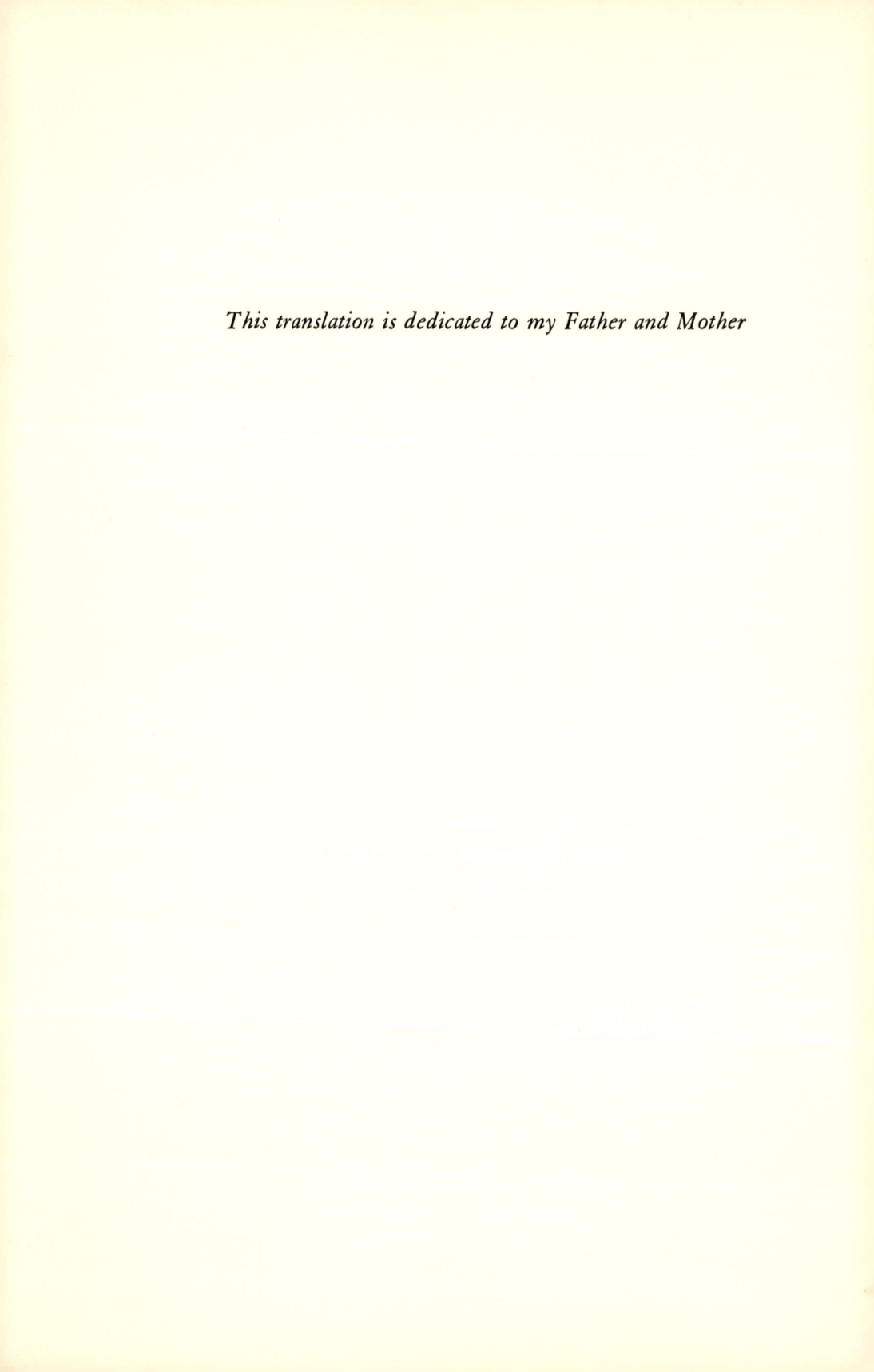

This translation is dedicated to my Father and Mother

FOREWORD

This translation has been undertaken for the Columbia College program of Translations from the Oriental Classics in the belief that Ssu-ma Ch'ien's monumental *Shih chi* (Records of the Historian) can be read not only as history but as literature, and not by the China specialist alone but by the educated reader in general. Generations of scholars—Chinese, Japanese, and Korean—have studied and commented upon the *Shih chi* as the most important historical source for a knowledge of ancient China. Had Dr. Watson a lifetime to give to it, he might have attempted to recapitulate this massive scholarship for the Western student, and it would have been no more than the *Shih chi* deserved. But the heirs of the Chinese tradition have also loved this book as a literary classic, and if Dr. Watson has provided a translation which permits us to enjoy it that way, much as it came from the hands of Ssu-ma Ch'ien himself, this too the *Shih chi* well deserves.

It is a mark of the Chinese tradition, in contrast to other Asian civilizations, that it gave a high place to historical writing. This would have been so if only because Confucius and his followers considered history to have such a great didactic value. But its importance might still have been purely academic or official had not Ssu-ma Ch'ien transcended the limitations of his role as court historian and produced a book which helped to form people's tastes in literature from that time on. Certainly if those touched by Confucian culture tended to read history as today we read fiction, it was because Ssu-ma Ch'ien's work made them feel in a special way the fascination of history. Thus when Lady Murasaki's famous *Tale of Genji* appeared in Japan, many people thought she had taken the *Shih chi* as her model, because its author, uniquely among earlier writers, had portrayed individual human lives as intimately as she had, in all their grandeur and pathos and variety. This the reader of Dr. Watson's translation will also soon appreciate.

Wm. Theodore de Bary

Kyoto, 1960

CONTENTS

Foreword *by* Wm. Theodore de Bary	vii
General Introduction	3
Translator's Note on the Text	10
The Founding of the Han Dynasty (Parts I–VI)	13
Part I. The Beginning of the Revolt	17
The Hereditary House of Ch'en She (*Shih chi* 48)	19
Part II. The Vanquished	35
The Basic Annals of Hsiang Yü (*Shih chi* 7)	37
Part III. The Victor	75
The Basic Annals of Emperor Kao-tsu (*Shih chi* 8)	77
Reflections on the Rise of Emperor Kao-tsu (*Shih chi* 16, excerpt)	120
Part IV. The Great Ministers	123
The Hereditary House of Prime Minister Hsiao (*Shih chi* 53)	125
The Hereditary House of the Marquis of Liu (*Chang Liang*) (*Shih chi* 55)	134
The Hereditary House of Prime Minister Ch'en (*Shih chi* 56)	152
Part V. The Disaffected	169
The Biographies of Chang Erh and Ch'en Yü (*Shih chi* 89)	171
The Biographies of Wei Pao and P'eng Yüeh (*Shih chi* 90)	189
The Biography of Ch'ing Pu (*Shih chi* 91)	196
The Biography of the Marquis of Huai-yin (Han Hsin) (*Shih chi* 92)	208
The Biographies of Hann Hsin and Lu Wan (*Shih chi* 93)	233
The Biography of T'ien Tan (*Shih chi* 94)	245

Contents

Part VI. The Loyal Followers	253
The Biographies of Fan K'uai, Li Shang, Lord T'eng, and Kuan Ying: Concluding Remarks (*Shih chi* 95)	255
The Biography of Chancellor Chang (*Shih chi* 96)	257
The Biographies of Li I-chi and Lu Chia (*Shih chi* 97)	269
The Biographies of Fu K'uan, Chin Hsi, and the Marquis of K'uai-ch'eng: Concluding Remarks (*Shih chi* 98)	284
The Biographies of Liu Ching and Shu-sun T'ung (*Shih chi* 99)	285
The Biographies of Chi Pu and Lüan Pu (*Shih chi* 100)	299
The Second Era of Han History (Parts VII–XI)	309
Part VII. The Rulers	319
The Basic Annals of Empress Lü (*Shih chi* 9)	321
The Basic Annals of Emperor Wen the Filial (*Shih chi* 10)	341
The Basic Annals of Emperor Ching the Filial (*Shih chi* 11)	367
The Basic Annals of Emperor Wu (fragment) (*Shih chi* 12)	375
Part VIII. The Empresses	377
The Hereditary Houses of the Families Related to the Emperors by Marriage (*Shih chi* 49)	379
Part IX. The Great Families	393
The Hereditary House of King Yüan of Ch'u (*Shih chi* 50)	395
The Hereditary Houses of Ching and Yen (*Shih chi* 51)	399
The Hereditary House of King Tao-hui of Ch'i (*Shih chi* 52)	405
The Hereditary House of Prime Minister Ts'ao (excerpt) (*Shih chi* 54)	421
The Hereditary House of Chou P'o, the Marquis of Chiang (*Shih chi* 57)	427
The Hereditary House of King Hsiao of Liang (*Shih chi* 58)	441
The Hereditary Houses of the Five Families (*Shih chi* 59)	450
Part X. The Leader of the Revolt	463
The Biography of Liu P'i, the King of Wu (*Shih chi* 106)	465
Some Remarks on the Han Peers (*Shih chi* 17, 18, 19)	487

Contents xi

Part XI. The Eminent Officials 497
   The Biographies of Ch'ü Yüan and Master Chia (*Shih chi* 84) 499
   The Biographies of Yüan Ang and Ch'ao Ts'o (*Shih chi* 101) 517
   The Biographies of Chang Shih-chih and Feng T'ang (*Shih chi* 102) 533
   The Biographies of Lord Wan-shih and Chang Shu (*Shih chi* 103) 543
   The Biography of T'ien Shu (*Shih chi* 104) 556

Finding List of Chapters of the *Shih chi* 562

MAPS

The Topography of Han China 25
Principal Feudal Kingdoms of Late Chou and Early Han Times 57
Principal Cities and Areas Mentioned in the Text 92

Ssu-ma Ch'ien to his friend Jen An

A man has only one death. That death may be as weighty as Mount T'ai, or it may be as light as a goose feather. It all depends upon the way he uses it. . . .

It is the nature of every man to love life and hate death, to think of his relatives and look after his wife and children. Only when a man is moved by higher principles is this not so. Then there are things which he must do. . . .

Yet the brave man does not necessarily die for honor, while even the coward may fulfill his duty. Each takes a different way to exert himself. Though I might be weak and cowardly and seek shamelessly to prolong my life, yet I know full well the difference between what course ought to be followed and what rejected. How could I bring myself to sink into the shame of ropes and bonds? If even the lowest slave and scullion maid can bear to commit suicide, why should not one like myself be able to do what has to be done? But the reason I have not refused to bear these ills and have continued to live, dwelling in vileness and disgrace without taking my leave, is that I grieve that I have things in my heart which I have not been able to express fully, and I am shamed to think that after I am gone my writings will not be known to posterity. . . .

Before I had finished my rough manuscript, I met with this calamity. It is because I regretted that it had not been completed that I submitted to the extreme penalty without rancor. When I have truly completed this work, I shall deposit it in the Famous Mountain archives. If it may be handed down to men who will appreciate it, and penetrate to the villages and great cities, then though I should suffer a thousand mutilations, what regret would I have?

VOLUME I

Early Years of the Han Dynasty
209 to 141 B.C.

GENERAL INTRODUCTION

Not much is known about the life of the Chinese historian Ssu-ma Ch'ien outside of the little information he gives us in the autobiography appearing at the end of his life work, the *Shih chi,* or *Records of the Historian*. Most scholars place his birth in 145 B.C. and agree that he died around 90 B.C., so that his lifetime more or less parallels that of Emperor Wu, the vigorous, strong-willed ruler who brought the Han dynasty to its peak of power and at whose court Ssu-ma Ch'ien spent most of his life.

Ssu-ma Ch'ien's father, Ssu-ma T'an, was given the position of grand historian at the court of Emperor Wu shortly after that ruler's accession in 141 B.C., and at Ssu-ma T'an's death in 110 B.C., Ssu-ma Ch'ien succeeded to the post. The official duties of the grand historian seem to have been largely connected with astrology and divination, though Ssu-ma T'an, perhaps on his own initiative, planned to write a work of history and began to collect material for it. In accordance with his father's dying request, Ssu-ma Ch'ien took up the task when he became grand historian and spent the next twenty-some years bringing it to completion. Midway in his work he aroused the ire of Emperor Wu and was condemned to suffer castration. Although it was customary under such circumstances for men of honor to commit suicide, Ssu-ma Ch'ien chose to bear the indignity in order to complete his manuscript and justify himself in the eyes of posterity. Two thousand years of admiring readers have amply rewarded his bitter decision.

The result of his labors is a monumental work in 130 chapters covering the history of the Chinese people, as well as of the foreign peoples known to China, from the earliest times down to the lifetime of the historian. In our present version of the work, at least one chapter is missing altogether and several others appear to be fragmentary or incomplete. Compared to the sad state in which the works of some of

Ssu-ma Ch'ien's Western contemporaries such as Polybius or Livy have come down to us, however, we can only marvel at the excellent condition of the text.

The *Shih chi* is divided into five large sections. The first section, entitled "Basic Annals," comprises twelve chapters devoted to the histories of the earlier dynastic houses or, in the case of the reigning Han dynasty, to the lives of individual emperors. These are followed by ten "Chronological Tables" listing in graph form the important events of the past with their dates. Next come eight "Treatises" on such subjects as rites, music, astronomy, religious affairs, and economics. These are followed by thirty chapters entitled "Hereditary Houses," which for the most part deal with the histories of the various feudal states of pre-Ch'in China. The work ends with seventy chapters entitled "Biographies" or "Accounts," devoted to the lives of famous men of history, or to the foreign peoples and countries with which China had contact. Within each section the chapters are arranged chronologically, but the grouping of the material into sections and the essentially biographical approach of most of the chapters necessitates considerable scattering of the data pertaining to any given period, as well as frequent recapitulation in the narrative.

Early histories in chronicle form, notably the famous *Spring and Autumn Annals* of the state of Lu, traditionally supposed to have been edited by Confucius, as well as collections of speeches and historical anecdotes, had existed before the time of Ssu-ma Ch'ien. But the form of the *Shih chi,* with its division of material into "Annals," "Treatises," "Biographies," etc., seems to have been Ssu-ma Ch'ien's own creation. In spite of certain obvious drawbacks, it has been regarded by Chinese historians as a masterpiece of form, and was adopted in the twenty-four "Dynastic Histories," the official accounts compiled to cover all of the dynasties from the time of Ssu-ma Ch'ien to the present century.

According to tradition, Chinese rulers employed historiographers at their courts as early as a thousand years before the time of Ssu-ma Ch'ien, and no doubt a vast number of chronicles and similar historical materials came into existence during this early period. Unfortunately, most of these were lost in the wars and uprisings that accompanied the unification of China under the Ch'in dynasty, and its successor, the Han, or were deliberately destroyed by the Ch'in's notorious "burning of the books." As a result, Ssu-ma Ch'ien in his account of pre-Ch'in history was forced to rely heavily on two or three well-known sources, such as the *Tso chuan,* or the *Intrigues of the Warring States,* and in places had to piece out his narrative with legend and popular romance. With the treatment of Ch'in and Han times, however, Ssu-ma Ch'ien's narrative takes on depth and verisimilitude; his characters cease to be moral stereotypes and become fully rounded personalities. These chapters, dealing with events close to or contemporary with his own lifetime, form the heart of his history and display the most original and important aspects of his genius. Accordingly it is these later sections which I have chosen to translate here.

The exploits of mankind being basically much the same in any age or clime, the English reader, I expect, will find little in Ssu-ma Ch'ien's account of the emperors, generals, and statesmen of the Han dynasty that is not already familiar to him from the history of the Classical West. Indeed, Ssu-ma Ch'ien's whole approach to history—his concern with the didactic import of his story, his emphasis upon the life and importance of the individual, his skepticism and relative lack of interest in the supernatural—show a striking similarity to that of the historians of ancient Greece and Rome. Even the literary devices which he uses to create his dramatic effects resemble those of his Western contemporaries. Though there is no evidence that he intended his work to be declaimed in public as did the Greek or Roman historians, he was hardly less concerned than they with rhetoric and questions of style. Like Thucydides or Tacitus, he relies heavily upon elaborate and probably fictitious speeches put into the mouths of his characters to explain and advance the action and to delineate personality, speeches composed with the same balanced periods, the hyperboles, the erudite allusions and homely metaphors familiar to us in the Western rhetorician's art.

In addition to these formal speeches, however, the Chinese historian makes very free use of direct discourse. The past is visualized as a series of dramatic episodes in which, instead of describing the action, the historian makes his characters speak aloud. Repeatedly we find the narrative serving only to set the scene, while the burden of the story is carried forward by the discourse of the participants. If, in the pages that follow, the reader from time to time has a distinct impression that he is reading a novel rather than a work of history, it is because of this characteristic Chinese fondness for direct speech.

Classical Chinese, it should be noted, is capable of a breathtaking economy and vigor of expression. Chinese historians in particular prize terseness above almost any other quality of style, and though the *Shih chi* is relatively verbose compared to other early historical works, its narrative still maintains a swiftness and leanness that can seldom be reproduced in another language. There are few passages of pure description, few of the digressions and leisurely asides we are accustomed to in the works of Greek and Roman historians. All is speech and action, the two traditional components of Chinese history.

In the two thousand years since its appearance, the *Shih chi* has been widely and affectionately read not only by educated Chinese but by men of learning in Korea and Japan, as well. The reason for its continued popularity and the incalculable influence it has had upon the literatures of these countries lies undoubtedly in its moving portraits of the great men of the past, its dramatic episodes and deft anecdotes. Accordingly, it is these aspects of the *Shih chi*—giving it interest as a collection of good stories—which I have been most concerned to reproduce in the translation.

I have avoided the use of Chinese technical terms or titles which might prove distracting, or of awkward sounding translations of such titles and terms, no matter how faithfully they might reproduce the meaning of the originals. Again, I have used as few Chinese weights and measures as possible, employing English substitutes in cases where the exact value of the measurement did not seem of great importance to the sense of the narrative. I have occasionally translated place names, such as White Horse Ford, where the original meaning of the name is still immediately apparent in the Chinese.

In another important respect I have sacrificed strict fidelity to readability. Most of the major figures appearing in the *Shih chi* have two given names, a familiar and a polite one, and a variety of military, official, and noble titles by which they are referred to at various times. Some commentators insist that Ssu-ma Ch'ien, by the particular way he chooses to refer to his characters at particular times, is attempting to convey subtle moral judgments on their worth and dignity. I have grave doubts about this theory, but, however valid it may be, I have felt compelled to sacrifice such subtleties to considerations of intelligibility. The Western reader, to whom the profusion of unfamiliar names which follows will be trial enough, can hardly be expected to carry in his head a complicated set of titles and ranks, while continual bracketing to assist identification would prove tiresome. As far as possible I have therefore chosen one name to refer to a person and used it throughout, regardless of how the original reads. The one exception is the hero of this volume, Liu Chi, the founder of the Han dynasty, who in the course of his rise to power is variously known as "governor of P'ei," "king of Han," and finally "Emperor Kao-tsu."

In addition to such titles, the Chinese language employs an elaborate set of pronouns and polite terms of address in direct discourse. English, to be sure, possesses acceptable equivalents such as "Your Majesty" or "Your Lordship." But too frequent use of such terms would, I fear, give a labored and archaic tone to the translation, and nothing could be farther from the style of the original. I have consequently used honorific expressions only occasionally to set the tone of a discourse, and hope that the reader will imagine that the appropriate air of humility is sustained throughout. Again I have attempted to vary in the translation some of the set formulas of the original, such as the ubiquitous "he said" or "he asked saying." Good Chinese permits such formulas where good English demands variety, and it seems pointless, merely for the sake of literalness, to make Ssu-ma Ch'ien sound like a clumsy schoolboy. Where proper names or historical allusions are used metaphorically, I have, as Robert Graves would say, "brought up" into the translation whatever information is necessary to make their meaning comprehensible. I have avoided footnotes wherever possible; in most cases what is not clear at first will, I believe, become so as the reader proceeds to later chapters. I have occasionally enclosed in parentheses one or two sentences of the original which appear to be in the nature of an aside.

I am aware that some of these practices may render the translation unsatisfactory to specialists who are interested in the *Shih chi* as a source for historical data, rather than as a unified work of literature. Yet any attempt to please all readers, specialists and non-specialists alike, would almost certainly end by pleasing none. Michael Grant, in the introduction to his translation of Tacitus' *Annals,* states his opinion that "except as a mere crib, an unreadable translation is useless."[1] Though the wording is perhaps a bit drastic, I fully agree with this dictum in principle, and ask the reader to keep it in mind in judging what follows.[2]

The maps which have been provided will, I hope, assist the reader in locating the various feudal kingdoms and principal cities mentioned. The China of this time is centered in the north, along the Yellow River valley. In the west, surrounded by a barrier of mountains and rivers, are the capital city of Hsien-yang and the heartland of Ch'in. South of the river is the area of Ch'u, whose people bear the house of Ch'in a bitter hatred and cherish the memory of their former kings. To the north are the areas of Wei, Chao, Tai, and Yen, and near the river's mouth on the Shantung Peninsula the sites of the states of Ch'i and Lu. Scattered about the plain stand hundreds of walled cities within which the people live, emerging from their gates during the day to till the fields, and before whose walls the armies of the rebellion and the contending forces of the rivals, Hsiang Yü and Liu Chi, fight and die. Between lie swamps and mountain wastes, the home of fugitives and outlaws.

The Table of Contents may serve as a guide to the main actors in the drama, since the chapters are titled by the names of the men whose biographies they recount. In addition, there appear in the narrative a number of minor characters who, as Addison says, "have sounding names given them for no other reason but that they may be killed, and are celebrated for nothing but being knocked on the head." I trust that as the reader continues he will become familiar with the important

[1] *Tactitus on Imperial Rome,* trans. by Michael Grant (Penguin Classics), p. 24.
[2] For a much fuller account of early Chinese historiography and of the life and work of Ssu-ma Ch'ien, the reader is referred to the translator's study, *Ssu-ma Ch'ien: Grand Historian of China* (New York, Columbia University Press, 1957).

General Introduction

characters, and that these others will not distract him. In particular I would warn him not to be taken aback by the profusion of petty generals and revolutionaries appearing in the first chapter. Outside of a few like Chang Erh and Ch'en Yü, who are the subjects of a later chapter, most of these men play little part in what follows. The rebellion of Ch'en She loosed upon the empire a flood of confusion and revolt, and if the reader finds himself confused as well, this is probably the precise effect which Ssu-ma Ch'ien was aiming at. It is one of those periods of political chaos which the Chinese call a "muddy age." But let not the reader be dismayed. As he proceeds, the water will clear.

TRANSLATOR'S NOTE ON THE TEXT

On the whole I have followed the text of the *Shih chi* as it appears in the edition entitled *Shiki kaichū kōshō* (Tokyo, 1934), edited and with a commentary in Chinese by Takikawa Kametarō, which has recently been reprinted. This I have found to be the most readable and convenient edition, though I have had occasion to differ with the punctuation at numerous points and have in places adopted what appear to be better readings from the *Po-na-pen* edition, or from parallel passages in the *Han shu*. The more important variant readings adopted are noted in footnotes. For the chapters on Hsiang Yü and Kao-tsu I have consulted with great profit the French translation of these chapters by Edouard Chavannes in *Les Mémoires historiques de Se-ma Ts'ien* (Paris, E. Leroux, 1895–1905), Vol. I, as well as the translation of the parallel *Han shu* text, the "Annals of Kao-tsu," by Homer H. Dubs, in *The History of the Former Han by Pan Ku* (London, Waverly Press, 1939–44), Vol. I. For the chapter on Han Hsin I am indebted to the English translation by John De Francis, "Biography of the Marquis of Huai-yin," *Harvard Journal of Asiatic Studies*, X (1947), 179–215. I have also consulted the Japanese translation by Kuda Rentarō in the *Kokuyaku kambun taisei* series; the new modern-language Japanese translation by Otake Fumio and Otake Takeo, *Shiki* (Tokyo, Kōbundō, 1957–58); that by Noguchi Sadao and others, *Shiki* (Tokyo, Heibonsha, 1958–59); and the selected translations in *Shiki, So-kan-hen*, by Tanaka Kenji and Ikkai Tomoyoshi, *Chūgoku-kotensen* series (Tokyo, 1958). In preparing the maps I have been greatly aided by the maps appearing in these works, particularly those in the Dubs and De Francis translations. Finally, I am deeply grateful to Professors Yoshikawa Kōjirō and Tanaka Kenji of Kyoto University for their frequent help and guidance, though they are in no way responsible for the shortcomings of my work.

The Founding of the Han Dynasty
(*PARTS I–VI*)

Ssu-ma Ch'ien begins his account of Chinese history in the *Shih chi* with a description of the marvelous deeds and reigns of the legendary "Five Emperors," of whom the last two, Yao and Shun, are so often cited as paragons of political virtue. This is followed by an account of the Hsia, Shang or Yin, and Chou dynasties, the so-called Three Dynasties of antiquity. Archeological evidence has so far confirmed the existence of only the last two of these, and it is still uncertain how much actual authority the Shang and early Chou rulers wielded over the area of North China as a whole. The *Shih chi* and other Han works tend to depict these early dynasties as widespread and unified empires ruled by a universally revered "Son of Heaven," though in fact they were probably more often loose confederations of city-states. Certainly by the time of Confucius in the sixth century B.C. the Chou kings had become powerless figureheads and China was divided into a number of autonomous states engaged in a constant struggle for expansion or survival. The number of these states eventually narrowed to half a dozen, among which the most powerful were Ch'i in the northeast, Ch'u in the south, and Ch'in in the west. This last, with its capital in the so-called area within the Pass, near present-day Sian in Shensi, continued to grow in size and power until, under the leadership of the famous Ch'in Shih-huang-ti, or First Emperor of the Ch'in, it succeeded in 221 B.C. in conquering the other states and uniting China under one rule.

The First Emperor in the course of his long and vigorous reign did all he could to stamp out the memory of the states which he had overthrown and to weld their people into a single nation, dividing the area of China into thirty-six provinces ruled by governors and magistrates appointed by the central government. But the violence of the changes he wrought and the harshness of his rule aroused widespread discontent. His successor, the Second Emperor, was an incompetent weakling who was completely dominated by his eunuch chamberlain,

Chao Kao. In the very first year of his reign, 209 B.C., the unrest broke out in open revolt, an uprising in the area of the old kingdom of Ch'u led by a peasant upstart named Ch'en She. Although Ch'en She was soon defeated, he had set an example, and soon leaders arose in other states, all determined either to become petty kings themselves or to restore to power the royal families of the extinct kingdoms. It appeared that China was destined to return to its former state of disunity and strife.

But the memory of Ch'in's unified empire and the idealized empires of the ancient past, which was not forgotten, in the end proved stronger than local loyalties. Under the leadership of a second peasant adventurer, Liu Pang or Liu Chi, China was once again conquered and brought beneath the rule of a single house. Because he had at one stage in his rise to power been granted the title "King of Han," Liu Chi called his new dynasty the Han and set about securing its position and organizing its government in such a way as to avoid the fatal harshness of the Ch'in. He and his ministers did their work well, and the Han dynasty, except for one brief period of eclipse in the middle, maintained its rule for four hundred years, from its founding in 206 B.C. until its final collapse in A.D. 221.

The present volume begins with the founding of the Han; the main events of this period take place during the years from the beginnings of the rebellion against the Ch'in dynasty in 209 B.C. to the death of Liu Chi, or Kao-tsu, in 195 B.C. The chapters translated have been selected from various sections of the *Shih chi* and arranged in such a way as to present, as nearly as possible, a connected picture. As I have mentioned, however, most of the chapters of the *Shih chi* are centered about the lives of great men. What follows, therefore, is not a continuous narrative but a series of biographies of the major figures in the drama of the founding of the Han, arranged so that they dovetail into each other and into the earlier chapters devoted to the history of the Ch'in dynasty, which are not presented here. The first chapter is a biography of the leader of the first revolt, Ch'en She. This is followed by the biography of Hsiang Yü, the tragic hero of Ch'u who succeeded Ch'en She as the leader of the rebellion and for a while had his way with the whole empire until Liu Chi, the king of Han, rose to challenge

The Founding of the Han Dynasty

his power and eventually defeat him. Completing the period of revolt and the ensuing struggle between the forces of Ch'u and Han is the biography of the final victor, Liu Chi, posthumously titled Emperor Kao-tsu of the Han. This is followed by a long series of biographies of the men who aided Kao-tsu in establishing the new dynasty or who contended unsuccessfully with him for rule. Because of the biographical nature of each chapter, the reader will at times find himself carried forward into the reigns of Kao-tsu's successors, his son Emperor Hui, his wife Empress Lü, and the rulers who followed them, Emperors Wen and Ching, whose reigns will be dealt with more fully later. He will also discover that, since all these men were more or less contemporaries, the same events are touched upon again and again in successive chapters, sometimes described in more detail than previously, sometimes drastically abbreviated, but each time presented from a slightly different point of view because of the way in which they affect the life of the subject of the chapter. Much of the beauty and interest of the *Shih chi* lies in this subtle division and disposition of material, this technique of viewing a single event or figure through the eyes of a succession of different characters. The personality of the hero, Emperor Kao-tsu, in particular, is carefully and effectively built up through dozens of scenes and anecdotes revealed chapter by chapter until in the end we have seen every facet of his peasant wiliness, his generosity, his notorious bad manners, and the melancholy splendor of his last years. It is a technique which makes considerable demands upon the attention of the reader and may seem more appropriate to a novel than to a work of history, but it will perhaps help to explain why the *Shih chi* has had such a great appeal to the imagination and literary sensibilities of the Chinese and other East Asian peoples. The events of this period are stirring and significant enough, but more than the events it is the men themselves, as they are revealed in the colorful, incisive portraits which Ssu-ma Ch'ien has created, that remain in the memory of the reader.

Part I

THE BEGINNING OF THE REVOLT

Shih chi 48: The Hereditary House of Ch'en She

When Chieh and Chou sank into evil, T'ang and Wu rose to replace them. When the way of Chou faltered, the *Spring and Autumn Annals* were made. When Ch'in's rule failed, Ch'en She marched forth. The lords sprang to revolt like a great wind rising, like clouds that cover the sky, until the house of Ch'in at last crumbled. All the world took its cue from Ch'en She's rebellion. Thus I made The Hereditary House of Ch'en She.[1]

Ch'en Sheng, whose polite name was Ch'en She, was a native of Yang-ch'eng; Wu Kuang, or Wu Shu, was from Yang-hsia. When Ch'en She was young, he was working one day in the fields with the other hired men. Suddenly he stopped his plowing and went and stood on a hillock, wearing a look of profound discontent. After a long while he announced, "If I become rich and famous, I will not forget the rest of you!"

The other farm hands laughed and answered, "You are nothing but a hired laborer. How could you ever become rich and famous?"

Ch'en She gave a great sigh. "Oh, well," he said, "how could you little sparrows be expected to understand the ambitions of a swan?"

During the first year of the Second Emperor of Ch'in [209 B.C.],[2] in the seventh month, an order came for a force of nine hundred men from the poor side of the town to be sent to garrison Yü-yang. Ch'en She and Wu Kuang were among those whose turn it was to go, and they were appointed heads of the levy of men.[3] When the group had

---

[1] This and the summaries which head the other chapters of the translation are taken from Ssu-ma Ch'ien's table of contents in *Shih chi* 130, unless otherwise noted.

[2] Chinese historians customarily record dates by the year of the reigning monarch. Hence we have here the years of the Second Emperor of Ch'in, which will be followed by the years of Han, i.e., of Emperor Kao-tsu of the Han. The Ch'in dynasty began its new year with the tenth month, around our November, a custom continued in the early Han, so that the months run 10, 11, 12, 1, 2, 3, 4, 5, 6, 7, 8, and 9, with occasional intercalary months.

[3] I.e., they were chosen from among the men of the group to be its leaders;

got as far as Ta-tse County, they encountered such heavy rain that the road became impassable. It was apparent that the men would be unable to reach the appointed place on time, an offense punishable by death. Ch'en She and Wu Kuang accordingly began to plot together. "As things stand, we face death whether we stay or run away," they said, "while if we were to start a revolt we would likewise face death. Since we must die in any case, would it not be better to die fighting for our country?" [4]

"The world has long suffered under Ch'in," said Ch'en She. "From what I have heard, the Second Emperor was a younger son and ought never to have succeeded to the throne. The one who should have been made ruler was Prince Fu-su. But because Fu-su several times remonstrated with the former emperor, he was sent to lead the armies in the field. Someone has told me that, though Fu-su was guilty of no crime, he has been murdered by the Second Emperor. The common people have heard much of Fu-su's worth, but they do not know that he is dead. Hsiang Yen was a general of Ch'u who many times distinguished himself in battle. He took good care of his troops and the people of Ch'u thought fondly of him. Some say that he is dead, but others say that he is only in hiding. Now with the group we have, if we could deceive people into thinking that I am Fu-su and you are Hsiang Yen, we could lead the world in our own tune, and there are sure to be many who will join in the chorus!"

Wu Kuang approved of this idea, and they went to consult a diviner. The diviner guessed what the two were planning, and replied, "Your undertakings will all meet with success. But might you not seek your fortune with the spirits?" [5]

Ch'en She and Wu Kuang were delighted with the idea of enlisting supernatural aid in their scheme. "It must mean that we should first do

---

the group as a whole was in turn commanded by officers of the Ch'in government.

[4] I.e., die fighting for the restoration of the former state of Ch'u. Another interpretation would have it mean "die fighting to win a kingdom."

[5] Like all good diviners, this one is careful to answer ambiguously. His remark may be interpreted to mean, "Though your plan may succeed, will you not find yourselves among the spirits of the dead?" But Ch'en She and Wu Kuang prefer to interpret him differently.

something to overawe the men in our group!" they declared, and proceeded to write with cinnabar on a piece of silk: "Ch'en She shall be a king." They stuffed the silk into the belly of a fish someone had caught in a net. When one of the soldiers bought the fish and boiled it for his dinner, he discovered the message in the fish's belly and was greatly astonished. Also Ch'en She secretly sent Wu Kuang to a grove of trees surrounding a shrine which was close to the place where the men were making camp. When night fell, Wu Kuang lit a torch and, partly concealing it under a basket, began to wail like a fox [6] and cry, "Great Ch'u shall rise again! Ch'en She shall be a king!"

The soldiers were filled with alarm, and when dawn came they talked here and there among themselves, pointing and staring at Ch'en She.

Wu Kuang had always been kind to others and many of the soldiers would do anything for him. When the officer in command of the group was drunk, Wu Kuang made a point of openly announcing several times that he was going to run away. In this way Wu Kuang hoped to arouse the commander's anger, get him to punish him, and so stir up the men's ire and resentment. As Wu Kuang had expected, the commander began to beat him, when the commander's sword slipped out of its scabbard. Wu Kuang sprang up, seized the sword, and killed the commander. Ch'en She rushed to his assistance and they proceeded to kill the other two commanding officers as well. Then they called together all the men of the group and announced: "Because of the rain we encountered, we cannot reach our rendezvous on time. And anyone who misses a rendezvous has his head cut off! Even if you should somehow escape with your heads, six or seven out of every ten of you are bound to die in the course of garrison duty. Now, my brave fellows, if you are unwilling to die, we have nothing more to say. But if you would risk death, then let us risk it for the sake of fame and glory! Kings and nobles, generals and ministers—such men are made, not born!"

The men of the garrison all replied, "We are with you!" Then, in order to win the loyalty of the people, Ch'en She and Wu Kuang falsely proclaimed themselves to be Prince Fu-su and Hsiang Yen. Baring

[6] The fox in China and Japan is closely associated with the supernatural.

their right shoulders, they raised the cry of "Great Ch'u!" and built an altar and swore an oath before it, offering as a sacrifice the heads of the commanding officers. Ch'en She set himself up as commander of the army, with Wu Kuang as his colonel, and together they attacked Ta-tse County. After capturing Ta-tse County, they proceeded to attack and capture Chi. They dispatched Ko Ying, a man of Fu-li, with a force to seize control of the area east of Chi, while they themselves attacked Chih, Tsuan, K'u, Che, and Ch'iao, all of which submitted. Recruiting soldiers as they went along, they were able by the time they reached the city of Ch'en to build up a force of six or seven hundred chariots, over a thousand horsemen, and twenty or thirty thousand infantry.

When they attacked Ch'en, neither the governor of the province nor any of the magistrates of the districts under him were in the city. Only one of the governor's aides was present, who engaged them in battle at the Ch'iao Gate but was defeated and killed. They entered the city and quartered there for several days, sending out an order summoning all the village heads and important men of the region to meet with them and plan a course of action. To this the village heads and distinguished men replied, "The general has buckled on armor and taken up his weapons to attack the unrighteous and punish the violence of Ch'in, that he may restore once more the sacred altars of the state of Ch'u. Because of the glory he has won, he deserves to be made a king."

Ch'en She accordingly was made king and given the title "Magnifier of Ch'u," whereupon men in many of the other provinces and districts who had suffered under the Ch'in officials overpowered and murdered their governors and magistrates and allied themselves with Ch'en She.

Ch'en She made Wu Kuang an acting king with supervision over the other leaders of their band, and sent him west to attack Jung-yang. Ch'en She ordered Chang Erh, Ch'en Yü, and Wu Ch'en, a man of Ch'en, to seize the region of Chao, while he sent Teng Tsung, a native of Ju-yin, to seize the province of Chiu-chiang. By this time a countless number of bands consisting of several thousand men each had been formed throughout Ch'u.

When Ko Ying, who had been sent by Ch'en She to seize the land east of Chi, reached Tung-ch'eng, he set up Hsiang Ch'iang as king of Ch'u. Later, hearing that Ch'en She had already become king himself, he murdered Hsiang Ch'iang and returned to report what he had done to Ch'en She. Ch'en She executed him, and dispatched Chou Shih, a native of Wei, to march north and seize the region of Wei.

Meanwhile Wu Kuang surrounded the city of Jung-yang, but Li Yu, the governor of San-ch'uan, held the city, and Wu Kuang was unable to conquer it.

Ch'en She summoned the distinguished men of the state of Ch'u to meet with him and plan the next move. He appointed Ts'ai Tz'u, the lord of Fang, a man of Shang-ts'ai, as his chief minister. Chou Wen, a man of some distinction in Ch'en, had formerly been diviner of auspicious days in the army of Hsiang Yen and had also served under the lord of Ch'un-shen. When he declared himself adept in military affairs, Ch'en She presented him with the seals of a general and sent him west to attack Ch'in. Gathering troops as he went along, he entered the Pass [7] with a force of a thousand chariots and twenty or thirty thousand infantry and camped at Hsi. Ch'in ordered its privy treasurer, Chang Han, to free all conscript laborers at Mount Li,[8] and the children of household slaves, and lead them forth in an attack upon the army of Ch'u. They succeeded in routing it, whereupon Chou Wen fled back through the Pass in defeat, halting and camping at Ts'ao-yang for several months. Chang Han pursued him and defeated him again, and Chou Wen once more fled, camping at Min-ch'ih for ten days or more. Here Chang Han inflicted a final defeat. Chou Wen cut his throat, and his army ceased all further resistance.

When Wu Ch'en reached Han-tan in Chao, he set himself up as king of Chao, making Ch'en Yü his commanding general and Chang Erh and Shao Sao his prime ministers of the left and right. Ch'en She was enraged at this and seized and bound the members of their families, preparing to execute them. But the chief minister, Ts'ai Tz'u, interceded, saying, "Ch'in, our great enemy, has not yet been destroyed. Now if you execute the families of the king of Chao and his ministers,

[7] The heartland of Ch'in, with its capital, Hsien-yang, lay in the northwest, surrounded by rivers and mountains, the so-called land within the Passes. The two principal approaches to it were through the Wu Pass in the south and the Han-ku Pass in the east. Unless otherwise stated, "the Pass" refers to the latter.

[8] Where they had been assembled to work on the great mausoleum of the First Emperor of Ch'in.

you will only create a second Ch'in to plague us. It would be better to comply with what Wu Ch'en and the others have done and confirm their positions."

Ch'en She accordingly dispatched an envoy to congratulate Wu Ch'en on his new position as king of Chao, but the families of Wu Ch'en and the others he had transferred to his own palace and kept under guard. Chang Erh's son, Chang Ao, he enfeoffed as lord of Ch'eng-tu.

Ch'en She urged the troops of Chao to proceed with all haste to the area within the Pass, but Chao's generals and ministers plotted with their king, saying, "It was not Ch'en She's intention that you should become king of Chao. When he has finished conquering Ch'in, he will assuredly turn his forces against us. The best plan, therefore, would be for us not to dispatch troops west, but instead to send a force north to seize the region of Yen and broaden the territory under your command. With the Yellow River to protect Chao in the south, and Yen and Tai to the north in our possession, Ch'en She in Ch'u will not dare try to impose his will upon us, even if he is victorious over Ch'in. And if Ch'en She should fail to conquer Ch'in, he will be forced to rely more heavily than ever upon us. At that point we can take advantage of the damage already inflicted upon Ch'in by Ch'en She and have our way with the whole empire!"

The king of Chao approved their suggestion and sent no troops west, but instead dispatched Han Kuang, a former troop commander of the province of Shang-ku, to lead an army north and seize the region of Yen.

The former nobles and leaders of Yen addressed Han Kuang, saying, "Ch'u has already set up a king, and so has Chao. Although Yen is rather small, it still deserves to be called, as the old phrase has it, 'a kingdom of a myriad chariots.' We would like therefore to make you king of Yen."

Han Kuang, however, objected. "My mother is still in Chao," he said. "I am afraid it would not do!" But the men of Yen replied, "Chao at the present time has all it can do to worry about Ch'in in the west and Ch'u to the south. It has no strength left to interfere with what we do. Ch'en She, in spite of all his power, did not dare to harm the

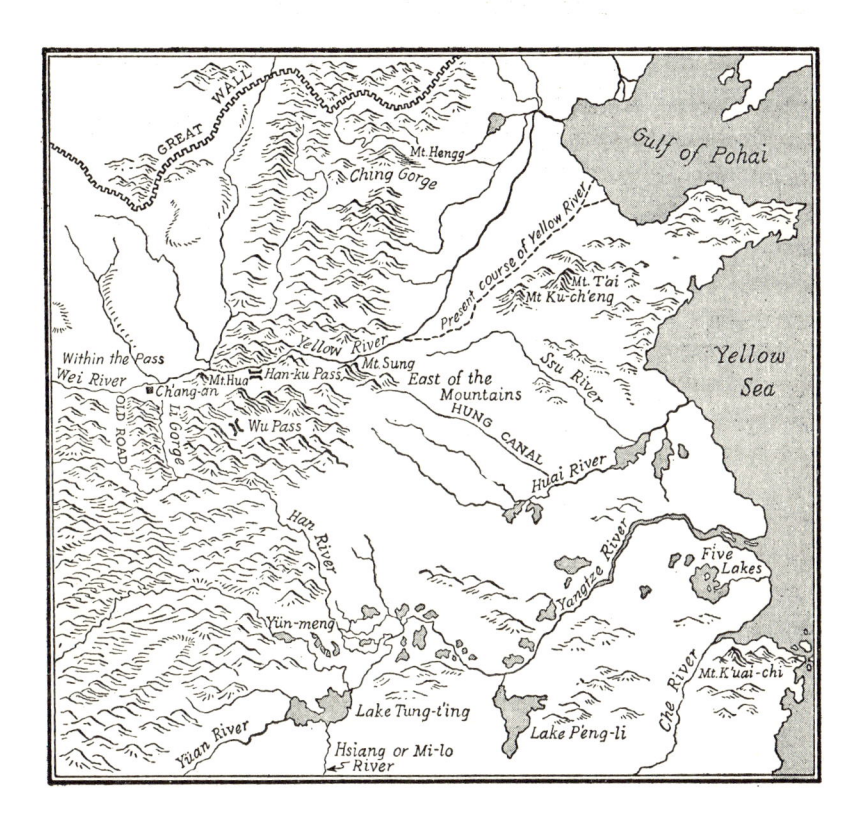

THE TOPOGRAPHY OF HAN CHINA

families of the king and ministers of Chao. How should Chao dare to do any harm to your family?"

Han Kuang, considering that what they said was true, declared himself king of Yen. After a few months Chao with all due respect sent his mother and the rest of his family to him in Yen.

By this time there were any number of leaders of the revolt attempting to win control of different regions of the empire. Chou Shih raided the north as far as Ti in Ch'i. T'ien Tan, a native of Ti, murdered the magistrate of the district of Ti and declared himself king of Ch'i. He then proceeded to lead the forces of Ch'i in an attack on Chou Shih. Chou Shih's army scattered before him, turned back, and retreated to the region of Wei. Chou Shih wanted to set up Wei Chiu, the former lord of Ning-ling, who was a descendant of the royal family of Wei, as king of Wei, but Chiu was at the time with Ch'en She and so was not able to come to Wei. After Chou Shih's men had conquered the region of Wei, they wanted to join the people of Wei in setting up Chou Shih himself as king, but Chou Shih refused to consent. Five times envoys were sent back and forth between Wei and Ch'en She in an attempt to reach a solution, until finally Ch'en She agreed to make Chiu the king of Wei, and sent him to his new kingdom. Chou Shih in the end became his prime minister.

T'ien Tsang, one of Ch'en She's generals, plotted with his fellow officers, saying, "Since Chou Wen's army has been defeated, Ch'in's soldiers day and night draw nearer. Now we have encircled the city of Jung-yang, but we have been unable to take it. When the armies of Ch'in reach us we are sure to suffer a great defeat. It would be better to leave a small number of troops behind, sufficient to keep watch on Jung-yang, and lead our best men west to meet the Ch'in armies. Our leader, Wu Kuang, who has been made an acting king, is too arrogant and knows nothing of military tactics. He is not worth consulting with on matters of strategy. If we do not do away with him our whole undertaking will be in danger of collapse!" Accordingly they joined in forging orders from Ch'en She and proceeded to execute Wu Kuang and send his head to Ch'en She. Ch'en She in turn sent an envoy to reward T'ien Tsang with the official seals of prime minister of Ch'u, making him commanding general.

T'ien Tsang then ordered Li Kuei and some of his other generals to guard the city of Jung-yang, while he himself led his best troops west to meet the army of Ch'in at the Ao Granary and join in battle. T'ien Tsang was killed and his army defeated. The Ch'in commander Chang Han advanced with his troops and attacked Li Kuei and the others before the walls of Jung-yang, defeating and killing them.

A man of Yang-ch'eng named Teng Yüeh was at this time in charge of a force of men in T'an. Chang Han dispatched an expeditionary force to attack and crush him, whereupon Teng Yüeh's army scattered and fled to Ch'en. Wu Hsü, a man of Chih, held command of a force at Hsü, but when attacked by Chang Han his army, too, scattered and fled to Ch'en. Ch'en She executed Teng Yüeh.

At the time when Ch'en She first set himself up as a king a group of men, including Ch'in Chia of Ling, Tung Hsieh of Chih, Chu Chi-shih of Fu-li, Cheng Pu of Ch'ü-lu, and Ting Chi, started an uprising of their own, leading a band of troops to surround Ch'ing, the governor of Tung-hai, at T'an. When Ch'en She received word of this he dispatched P'an, the lord of Wu-p'ing, to act as their commander and take charge of their forces, which were camped outside the walls of T'an. Ch'in Chia, however, declined to accept these orders, but instead declared himself a grand marshal and refused to put himself under the lord of Wu-p'ing's command. "The lord of Wu-p'ing is too young and knows nothing of military affairs," he advised his officers. "Do not listen to what he says!" Accordingly they forged an order from Ch'en She and executed the lord of Wu-p'ing.

After Chang Han had defeated Wu Hsü he marched to attack the city of Ch'en, killing Ts'ai Tz'u, the chief minister. He then advanced and attacked the army of Chang Chia west of Ch'en. Ch'en She came out to observe the battle, but the army was defeated and Chang Chia killed. In the twelfth month, at the time of the winter sacrifice, Ch'en She journeyed to Ju-yin and from there withdrew to Hsia-ch'eng-fu, where he was murdered by his carriage driver, Chuang Chia, who declared Ch'en loyal to the Ch'in government. Ch'en She was buried at Tang with the posthumous title of "The Melancholy King."

General Lü Ch'en, former master of purification under Ch'en She, formed a band of men known as the Blue Heads and started an uprising in Hsin-yang. They attacked and conquered the city of Ch'en, killed Chuang Chia, and declared Ch'en loyal to Ch'u once more.

When Ch'en She first marched on Ch'en he dispatched Sung Liu, a man of Chih, with orders to lead a force of troops west to conquer the region of Nan-yang and enter the Wu Pass. Sung Liu had already gained control of Nan-yang, but when news of Ch'en She's death spread abroad, Nan-yang declared itself loyal again to Ch'in. Sung Liu was therefore unable to enter the Wu Pass, but instead marched back east as far as Hsin-ts'ai, where he encountered the Ch'in army and surrendered to it. The Ch'in government had him brought back to the capital by relay carriage, where he was tied to two carts and torn apart to serve as a warning to the populace.

When Ch'in Chia and his band heard that Ch'en She's army had been defeated and was in flight they set up Ching Chü as king of Ch'u and led their troops to Fang-yü, planning to attack the Ch'in army outside the walls of Ting-t'ao. In the meantime they dispatched Kung-sun Ch'ing as their envoy to T'ien Tan, the king of Ch'i, requesting that Ch'i join with them in the attack.

"Though word has come that Ch'en She has been defeated, no one knows whether he is still alive or not," said the king of Ch'i. "What do you mean by setting up a new king of Ch'u without consulting me?"

"You did not consult Ch'u when you set yourself up as king of Ch'i," responded Kung-sun Ch'ing. "Why should Ch'u consult Ch'i when it sets up its own king? Ch'u is the leader of the uprising. It is only proper that she should give orders to the rest of the empire!" The king of Ch'i executed Kung-sun Ch'ing.

Ch'in's colonels of the left and right again attacked Ch'en and recaptured it. Lü Ch'en's army fled, but soon recruited more men and reformed. Ch'ing Pu, the lord of Tang-yang, a bandit leader of P'o, recruited a force of men and joined Lü Ch'en in another attack on the colonels of Ch'in, defeating them at Ch'ing-p'o. With this, the city of Ch'en once more became an ally of Ch'u. It was at this time that Hsiang Liang set up Hsin, the grandson of the former King Huai, as the new king of Ch'u.

All in all, Ch'en She was a king for six months. When he had be-

Ch'en She

come king and was ruling the region of Ch'en, one of his old friends who had once worked as a hired hand with him in the fields heard of his success and went and knocked upon the palace gate of Ch'en, saying, "I want to see She!" The gatekeeper was about to order him arrested, but he managed to convince the keeper that he was an old friend of Ch'en She. The gatekeeper let him go, but refused to allow him to enter the palace.

When the king emerged from the palace, the man stood by the roadside and shouted "She!" Hearing his voice, Ch'en She ordered that he be brought forward and, inviting him to ride in his carriage, returned with him to the palace. When the man entered the palace and saw all its great halls with their curtains and trappings he said, "Oh, a heap of stuff you have, She, now you're a king! Such a big place!" (The people of Ch'u say "a heap" when they mean a lot.) Eventually the story spread all over the empire, so that from this incident with Ch'en She originated the saying "Even 'heap-of-She' got to be king."

After this the old friend came often to visit Ch'en She, making himself more and more at home in the palace and telling people about Ch'en She's life in the old days. Someone warned Ch'en She about this, saying, "This guest of yours is ignorant and ill-bred, and his idle chatter serves only to degrade your dignity!" Ch'en She had his old friend's head cut off. Thereafter all of Ch'en She's former acquaintances withdrew of their own accord, and no one attempted to be on intimate terms with him.

Ch'en She appointed Chu Fang as rectifier and Hu Wu as director of faults, putting them in charge of his other ministers and officials. When any of the various generals returned from expeditions to seize territory, if it appeared that they had not carried out their orders exactly, these two officials believed it their duty to bind them like criminals and subject them to the severest examination. If any fault was found in their behavior, their case was not submitted to the lesser officials for trial, but was settled summarily by Chu Fang and Hu Wu themselves. Ch'en She entrusted everything to these two men with the fullest confidence, and for this reason his generals felt no personal attachment to him. This is why he failed.

Although Ch'en She himself died very early, the various rulers and commanders whom he set up and dispatched on expeditions eventually succeeded in overthrowing the Ch'in. Thus it was he who actually began the uprising. In the time of Emperor Kao-tsu of the Han, thirty families were established to take care of Ch'en She's grave at Tang, so that down to the present day he has continued to enjoy the blood and flesh of sacrifices.[9]

It is by the lay of the land and its strategic fastnesses that one's position is made secure, and by the force of arms and law that one executes his rule. And yet these alone cannot be relied upon. The kings of antiquity made humanity and righteousness the root of their rule, and considered strategic power, laws, and regulations as no more than its branches. Was this not a just view? Chia I, discussing the history of the Ch'in dynasty, has written as follows:

Duke Hsiao of Ch'in [fourth century B.C.], relying upon the strength of the Han-ku Pass and basing himself in the area of Yung-chou, with his ministers held fast to his land and eyed the house of Chou, for he cherished a desire to roll up the empire like a mat, to bind into one the whole world, to bag all the land within the four seas; he had it in his heart to swallow up everything in the eight directions. At this time he was aided by the Legalist philosopher Lord Shang, who set up laws for him, encouraged agriculture and weaving, built up the instruments of war, contracted military alliances, and attacked the other feudal lords. Thus the men of Ch'in were able with ease to acquire territory east of the upper reaches of the Yellow River.

After the death of Duke Hsiao, Kings Hui-wen, Wu, and Chao carried on the undertakings of their predecessor and, following the plans he had laid, seized Han-chung in the south and Pa and Shu in the west, and acquired rich land in the east and provinces of strategic value. The other feudal lords in alarm came together in council to devise some plan to weaken Ch'in, sparing nothing in gifts of precious objects and rich lands to induce men from all over the empire to come and join with them in a "vertical alliance,"

[9] This chapter lacks the customary closing remarks of the Grand Historian. The section which follows in present texts is introduced by the words "Master Ch'u remarks." Master Ch'u, or Ch'u Shao-sun, was a scholar who, some time after Ssu-ma Ch'ien's death, took it upon himself to make additions to the historian's work. However it is quite possible that this closing section, with its long quotation from the poet Chia I's famous essay "The Faults of Ch'in," describing the rise and fall of the Ch'in empire, was actually added by Ssu-ma Ch'ien himself, since in other chapters he quotes from the same essay or other works of Chia I.

and pool their strength. At this time there were Lord Meng-ch'ang in Ch'i, Lord P'ing-yüan in Chao, Lord Ch'un-shen in Ch'u, and Lord Hsin-ling in Wei. These four lords were all men of intelligence and loyalty, generous and kind to others, who honored worthy men and took good care of their followers. They rejected the Horizontal Alliance and instead formed the Vertical Alliance, which united all the forces of the states of Hann,[10] Wei, Yen, Ch'u, Ch'i, Chao, Sung, Wei, and Chung-shan. At this time among the distinguished men of the Six States were men like Ning Yüeh, Hsü Shang, Su Ch'in, and She Ho, who laid the plans; Ch'i Ming, Chou Chü, Ch'en Chen, Shao Hua, Lou Huan, Ti Ching, Su Li, Yüeh I, and their followers, who carried out these plans; and Wu Ch'i, Sun Pin, Tai T'o, Erh Liang, Wang Liao, T'ien Chi, Lien P'o, and Chao She, who commanded the troops. With a force of a million soldiers drawn from an area ten times that of Ch'in they beat upon the Pass and pressed forward toward Ch'in. But the men of Ch'in opened the Pass and went out to meet the enemy, and the armies of the Nine States fled and did not dare to advance. Ch'in, without expending a single arrow or losing a single arrowhead, threatened the fate of the whole empire.

With this, the Vertical Alliance collapsed, its treaties came to naught, and the various states hastened to present Ch'in with parts of their territories as bribes for peace. With its superior strength Ch'in pressed the crumbling forces of its rivals, pursued those who had fled in defeat, and overwhelmed and slaughtered the army of a million until their shields floated upon a river of blood. Following up the advantages of its victory, Ch'in gained mastery over the empire and divided up its mountains and rivers. The powerful states begged to submit to its sovereignty and the weaker ones paid homage at its court.

Then followed Kings Hsiao-wen and Chuang-hsiang, whose reigns were short and uneventful. After this came the First Emperor who, carrying on the glorious spirit of his six predecessors, cracked his long whip and drove the universe before him, swallowed up the eastern and western Chou, and overthrew the feudal lords. He ascended the throne of honor and ruled the six directions, scourging the world with his rod, and his might shook the four seas. In the south he seized the land of the hundred tribes of Yüeh and made of it Kuei-lin and Hsiang provinces, and the lords of the hundred Yüeh bowed their heads, hung halters from their necks, and pleaded for their lives with the lowest officials of Ch'in. Then he sent Meng T'ien to

[10] A state in north-central China, just south of the Yellow River. I have romanized it with two *n*'s throughout to distinguish it from the other state of Han, in the west, which gave its name to the Han dynasty.

build the Great Wall and defend the borders, driving back the Hsiung-nu over seven hundred *li*,[11] so that the barbarians no longer ventured to come south to pasture their horses and their men dared not take up their bows to vent their hatred.

Thereupon he discarded the ways of the former kings and burned the books of the hundred schools of philosophy in order to make the people ignorant. He destroyed the walls of the great cities, assassinated the powerful leaders, and collected all the arms of the empire, which he had brought to his capital at Hsien-yang, where the spears and arrowheads were melted down and cast to make twelve human statues. All this he did in order to weaken the people of the empire. After this he ascended and fortified Mount Hua, set up fords along the Yellow River, and strengthened the heights and precipices overlooking the fathomless valleys, in order to secure his position. He garrisoned the strategic points with skilled generals and strong crossbowmen and stationed trusted ministers and well-trained soldiers to guard the land with arms and question all who passed back and forth. When he had thus pacified the empire, the First Emperor believed in his heart that, with the strength of his capital within the Pass and his walls of metal extending a thousand miles, he had established a rule that would be enjoyed by his sons and grandsons for ten thousand generations.

For a while after the death of the First Emperor the memory of his might continued to awe the common people. Yet Ch'en She, born in a humble hut with tiny windows and a wattle door, a day laborer in the fields and a garrison conscript, whose abilities could not match even the average, who had neither the worth of Confucius and Mo Tzu nor the wealth of T'ao Chu or I Tun, stepped from the ranks of the common soldiers, rose up from the paths of the fields, and led a band of some hundred poor, weary soldiers in revolt against Ch'in. They cut down trees to make their weapons and raised their flags on garden poles, and the whole world gathered like a cloud, answered like an echo to a sound, brought them provisions, and followed after them as shadows follow a form. In the end the leaders east of the mountains rose up together and destroyed the house of Ch'in.

Now the empire of Ch'in at this time was by no means small or feeble. Its base in Yung-chou, its stronghold within the Pass, were the same as before. The position of Ch'en She could not compare in dignity with the lords of Ch'i, Ch'u, Yen, Chao, Hann, Wei, Sung, Wei,[12] and Chung-shan. The

[11] The nomadic people who occupied the area north of China. They are often identified with the Huns. The Chinese *li* is about one third of an English mile.

[12] There were two states named Wei.

weapons which he improvised from hoes and tree branches could not match the sharpness of spears and battle pikes; his little band of garrison conscripts was nothing beside the armies of the Nine States. In deep plotting and far-reaching stratagems, in methods of warfare, he was far inferior to the men of earlier times. And yet Ch'en She succeeded in his undertaking where they had failed, though in ability, size, power, and strength his forces could in no way compare to those of the states east of the mountains that had formerly opposed Ch'in. Ch'in, beginning with an insignificant amount of territory, reached the power of a great kingdom and for a hundred years made the ancient eight provinces pay homage at its court. Yet, after it had become master of the six directions and established its palaces within the Pass, a single commoner opposed it and its seven ancestral temples toppled, its ruler died by the hands of men, and it became the laughing stock of the world. Why? Because it failed to rule with humanity and righteousness, and did not realize that the power to attack and the power to retain what one has thereby won are not the same.[13]

[13] Other texts of this famous essay, appearing in *Shih chi* 6, *Hsin shu* 1, *Wen hsüan* 51, and elsewhere, have been consulted and occasional variant readings adopted.

Part II
THE VANQUISHED

Shih chi 7: The Basic Annals of Hsiang Yü

Ch'in failed in goodness and the great leaders rose to vex it. Hsiang Liang began the task and his nephew, Yü, carried it on. When the latter killed Sung I and rescued Chao, the feudal leaders made him their ruler; but when he executed Tzu-ying and rebelled against King Huai, the world joined in censuring him. Thus I made The Basic Annals of Hsiang Yü.

Hsiang Chi, whose polite name was Yü, was a native of Hsia-hsiang. He was twenty-four when he first took up arms. His father's youngest brother was Hsiang Liang. Hsiang Liang's father, Hsiang Yen, was a general of Ch'u who was driven to suicide by the Ch'in general Wang Chien. The Hsiang family for generations were generals of Ch'u and were enfeoffed in Hsiang; hence they took the family name Hsiang.

When Hsiang Yü was a boy he studied the art of writing. Failing to master this, he abandoned it and took up swordsmanship. When he failed at this also, his uncle, Hsiang Liang, grew angry with him, but Hsiang Yü declared, "Writing is good only for keeping records of people's names. Swordsmanship is useful only for attacking a single enemy and is likewise not worth studying. What I want to learn is the art of attacking ten thousand enemies!" With this, Hsiang Liang began to teach his nephew the art of warfare, which pleased Yü greatly. On the whole Yü understood the essentials of the art, but here again he was unwilling to pursue the study in detail.

Hsiang Liang was once implicated in some crime in Yüeh-yang but, obtaining a letter on his behalf from the prison warden of Chi, Ts'ao Chiu, he presented it to Ssu-ma Hsin, the prison warden of Yüeh-yang, and was released from the charge.

Later Hsiang Liang killed a man and, with Hsiang Yü, fled to the region of Wu to escape the vengeance of the man's family. All the worthy and renowned men of the region of Wu acknowledged Hsiang Liang as their superior and, whenever there was some major government construction work or a funeral in the area, Hsiang Liang was put in charge of the proceedings. In secret he formed a band of guests and retainers and trained them in the art of war so that he came to know the abilities of each.

Once the First Emperor of Ch'in came on a visit to K'uai-chi. When he was crossing the Che River, Hsiang Liang and Hsiang Yü went to watch the procession. "This fellow could be deposed and replaced!" Hsiang Yü remarked. Hsiang Liang clapped his hand over his nephew's mouth. "Don't speak such nonsense," he cautioned, "or we and all our family will be executed!" After this incident Hsiang Liang treated his nephew with peculiar respect.

Hsiang Yü was over eight feet tall[1] and so strong that with his two hands he could lift a bronze cauldron. In ability and spirit he far surpassed others, so that all the young men of the region of Wu were afraid of him.

In the first year of the Second Emperor of Ch'in [209 B.C.], during the seventh month, Ch'en She and his band began their uprising in the region of Ta-tse. In the ninth month T'ung, the governor of K'uai-chi, announced to Hsiang Liang, "All the region west of the Yangtze is in revolt. The time has come when Heaven will destroy the house of Ch'in. I have heard it said that he who takes the lead may rule others, but he who lags behind will be ruled by others. I would like to dispatch an army with you and Huan Ch'u at the head." (Huan Ch'u was at this time in hiding in the swamps.)

Hsiang Liang replied, "Huan Ch'u is in hiding and no one knows where he is. Only Hsiang Yü knows the place." Hsiang Liang left the room and went to give instructions to Hsiang Yü, telling him to hold his sword in readiness and wait outside. Then he returned and sat down again with the governor. "I beg leave to call in my nephew Yü, so that he may receive your order to summon Huan Ch'u," said Hsiang Liang. The governor consented, and Hsiang Liang sent for Hsiang Yü to come in. After some time, Hsiang Liang winked at his nephew and said, "You may proceed!" With this, Hsiang Yü drew his sword and cut off the governor's head. Hsiang Liang picked up the governor's head and hung the seals of office from his own belt. The governor's

[1] I.e., over six feet. The Han foot is about three fourths of our foot.

office was thrown into utter panic and confusion. After Hsiang Yü had attacked and killed several dozen attendants the entire staff submitted in terror, not a man daring to offer resistance.

Hsiang Liang then summoned a number of high officials whom he had known in the past and informed them of his reasons for starting a revolt. He called out all the troops of the region of Wu, sending men to recruit them from the various districts under his jurisdiction, until he had obtained a force of eight thousand picked men, and he assigned various distinguished and powerful men of Wu as his commanders, lieutenants, and marshals. One man, to whom no post had been assigned, went to Hsiang Liang and asked the reason. "In the past," replied Hsiang Liang, "at the time of So-and-so's funeral, I put you in charge of certain affairs, but you were unable to handle them properly. For this reason I have not assigned you a post." After this everyone accepted his assignments without argument. Hsiang Liang became governor of K'uai-chi and Hsiang Yü was made lieutenant general with the task of subduing the districts under the governor's jurisdiction.

Chao P'ing, a man of Kuang-ling, had been sent by Ch'en She to seize the district of Kuang-ling, but the district had not yet submitted. When Chao P'ing heard that Ch'en She had been defeated and fled and that the Ch'in forces were on their way, he crossed the Yangtze and, pretending that he was acting on orders from Ch'en She, conferred on Hsiang Liang the title of chief minister to the king of Ch'u. "Now that this region east of the Yangtze is under control," he said, "you must with all speed lead your troops west and attack Ch'in!"

Hsiang Liang took his eight thousand men, crossed the Yangtze, and proceeded west. When he heard that Ch'en Ying had already conquered Tung-yang he sent an envoy suggesting that the two of them join forces and proceed west together. Ch'en Ying had formerly been secretary to the district magistrate of Tung-yang. He was unfailingly honest and circumspect in all his duties in the district and was known as a man of exceptional worth. Some of the young men of Tung-yang had murdered the district magistrate and, gathering together a force of several thousand men, were looking for a leader. Failing to find anyone suitable, they asked Ch'en Ying. He refused, saying that he was unsuited for the job, but they finally forced him to become their leader.

When they had gathered a force of twenty thousand men from the district they decided to make Ch'en Ying a king, mark their forces off from the other rebel groups by wearing blue caps, and start their own uprising.

Ch'en Ying's mother advised him, saying, "From the time I first came into your household as a bride I have never heard of any of your ancestors who were noblemen. Now if you should suddenly acquire a great title, I fear it would bring ill luck. It would be better for you to place yourself under the command of someone else. If the undertaking is successful, you will still be made a marquis. And should the undertaking fail, it will be easy for you to go into hiding, for the world will not point you out by name."

As a result Ch'en Ying did not venture to become a king. Instead he told the leaders of his army, "The Hsiang family have for generations been generals, and are well known in Ch'u. If we wish now to begin a revolt, it is imperative that we have one of them as our general. If we put our trust in a family of such renown, there is no doubt that Ch'in can be destroyed." All agreed to follow his advice and put their troops under Hsiang Liang's command. When Hsiang Liang crossed the Huai River, both Ch'ing Pu and General P'u, as well, placed their troops under his command. In all he had a force of sixty or seventy thousand men, which he encamped at Hsia-p'ei.

At this time Ch'in Chia had already set up Ching Chü as king of Ch'u and was himself camped east of P'eng-ch'eng, intending to block Hsiang Liang's advance. Hsiang Liang addressed his officers, saying "Ch'en She, king of Ch'u, was formerly the leader of the uprising, but he was unsuccessful in battle and we do not know at present where he is. Now Ch'in Chia, acting in defiance of Ch'en She, has set up Ching Chü as king. This is a most outrageous act of treason!" Then he led his troops to attack Ch'in Chia, who fled in defeat. Hsiang Liang pursued him as far as Hu-ling, where Ch'in Chia turned and engaged in battle. At the end of the day Ch'in Chia was dead and his army had surrendered. Ching Chü fled to the region of Liang, where he died. Hsiang Liang then joined Ch'in Chia's army to his own and camped at Hu-ling, preparing to march west.

At this time the Ch'in army led by Chang Han had reached Li.

Hsiang Yü

Hsiang Liang sent Chu Chi-shih and Yü Fan-chün as special generals to attack him there, but Yü Fan-chün was killed in battle and the army of Chu Chi-shih, defeated, fled back to Hu-ling. Hsiang Liang then led his forces into Hsieh and executed Chu Chi-shih.

Earlier, Hsiang Liang had sent Hsiang Yü with a special force to attack the city of Hsiang-ch'eng, but the city was strongly defended and would not submit. When he at last succeeded in capturing it Hsiang Yü had all the defenders butchered. He then returned and reported to Hsiang Liang. When Hsiang Liang received definite news that Ch'en She was dead he summoned all his various generals to a meeting at Hsieh to plan his next move. At this time Liu Chi, the governor of P'ei, who had also begun an uprising in P'ei, attended the meeting.

Also present was Fan Tseng of Chü-ch'ao, a man of seventy who lived in retirement and took no part in public affairs. He was very fond of peculiar plans and stratagems, and counseled Hsiang Liang, saying, "It is altogether natural and proper that Ch'en She should have met with defeat. Among all the six great kingdoms which Ch'in destroyed Ch'u was least deserving of its fate. Ever since the time when King Huai of Ch'u went to visit Ch'in and failed to return to his own land the people of Ch'u have never ceased to grieve. Therefore Master Nan, the seer of Ch'u, has said: 'Though but three houses be left in Ch'u, it is she who will destroy Ch'in!' When Ch'en She was head of the uprising he did not set up the heir to the royal house of Ch'u, but made himself king instead, and thus his power quickly waned. Now, since you have risen east of the Yangtze, the leaders of Ch'u swarm forth like bees, vying with one another to place themselves at your disposal. This is because the men of your family have for generations been generals of Ch'u and you have it in your power to reestablish the royal line of Ch'u."

Hsiang Liang, acknowledging the truth of his words, sought out Hsin, the grandson of the late King Huai of Ch'u, who was living among the common people, herding sheep in the hire of another man, and set him up as King Huai of Ch'u in accordance with the wishes of the people. Ch'en Ying he made prime minister of Ch'u, with a fief of five districts, and sent him with King Huai to establish the capital at Hsü-i. Hsiang Liang himself took the title of lord of Wu-hsin.

After several months he led his troops to attack K'ang-fu. Joining with the armies of T'ien Jung of Ch'i and Marshal Lung Ch'ieh, he went to the rescue of Tung-a, which was besieged by Ch'in, and there inflicted a major defeat upon the Ch'in army. T'ien Jung led his troops back to Ch'i and deposed T'ien Chia, the king of Ch'i. T'ien Chia fled to Ch'u and his prime minister, T'ien Chüeh, fled to Chao, where his younger brother, T'ien Chien, a former general of Ch'i, was living, afraid to return to Ch'i. T'ien Jung set up Shih, the son of T'ien Tan, as king of Ch'i. Hsiang Liang, having already defeated the army at Tung-a, was in pursuit of the Ch'in forces, and several times sent envoys to urge the forces of Ch'i to join him in proceeding west. T'ien Jung announced: "If Ch'u will kill T'ien Chia and Chao will kill T'ien Chüeh and T'ien Chien, then I will dispatch my troops." Hsiang Liang replied, "T'ien Chia is the king of an allied state. He has come to me in distress and placed himself under my care. I cannot bring myself to kill him." Chao likewise declared that it would not kill T'ien Chüeh and T'ien Chien for the sake of buying favor with Ch'i. As a result, Ch'i was unwilling to dispatch troops to aid Ch'u.

Hsiang Liang sent the governor of P'ei and Hsiang Yü with a special force to attack the city of Ch'eng-yang and massacre its inhabitants. After accomplishing this they proceeded west and defeated the Ch'in forces east of P'u-yang. When the Ch'in forces withdrew to cover in P'u-yang the governor of P'ei and Hsiang Yü attacked Ting-t'ao. Failing to capture Ting-t'ao, they withdrew and seized the land to the west until they reached Yung-ch'iu, where they inflicted a major defeat on the Ch'in forces and decapitated Li Yu. Then they turned back and attacked Wai-huang. Before Wai-huang had submitted, Hsiang Liang marched out of Tung-a and proceeded west until he reached Ting-t'ao, where he inflicted a second defeat upon the Ch'in army.

Because of this, and because Hsiang Yü and his men in the meantime had succeeded in decapitating Li Yu, Hsiang Liang became increasingly contemptuous of the Ch'in forces and began to grow proud and overbearing. Sung I warned him, saying "If, because of victory in battle, a general becomes proud and his soldiers unwary, defeat is sure to follow. Now your soldiers have begun to grow rather lazy, while the Ch'in forces increase day by day. I am afraid of what may happen to you!" Hsiang Liang, however, refused to listen to Sung I's counsel, but dispatched him as his envoy to Ch'i. On the way there, Sung I happened to meet the envoy from Ch'i, Hsien, the lord of Kao-ling. "Are you on your way to see Hsiang Liang, the lord of Wu-ling?" he inquired, to which the other replied "I am." "I can tell you," said Sung I, "that the lord of Wu-ling is sure to meet with defeat. If you proceed on your way slowly enough, you may escape death. But if you hurry you will only encounter misfortune!"

As Sung I had foreseen, Ch'in gathered together all its forces and sent them to aid Chang Han, who attacked the Ch'u army at Ting-t'ao, inflicted a decisive defeat, and killed Hsiang Liang.

The governor of P'ei and Hsiang Yü withdrew from Wai-huang and attacked Ch'en-liu, but Ch'en-liu was stoutly defended and they could not conquer it. They discussed what their best plan would be and decided that, since Hsiang Liang's army had been defeated and their soldiers were filled with terror, they had better join with the army of Lü Ch'en and withdraw to the east. Accordingly they retreated, and Lü Ch'en camped east of P'eng-ch'eng, Hsiang Yü west of P'eng-ch'eng, and the governor of P'ei at Tang.

Chang Han, the Ch'in commander, having defeated Hsiang Liang's army, considered that the forces of the Ch'u area were no longer worth worrying about. Therefore he crossed the Yellow River and attacked Chao, inflicting a severe defeat. At this time Chao Hsieh was king of Chao, Ch'en Yü was in command of the army, and Chang Erh was prime minister. All fled and took refuge within the walls of Chü-lu. Chang Han ordered Wang Li and She Chien to encircle the city, while he himself camped to the south and constructed a walled road along which to transport supplies of grain. Ch'en Yü, the Chao general, with a force of some twenty or thirty thousand men, camped north of Chü-lu. This was the so-called Army North of the River.

With the forces of Ch'u already defeated at Ting-t'ao, King Huai grew fearful and moved from Hsü-i to P'eng-ch'eng, where he combined the armies of Hsiang Yü and Lü Ch'en and himself took command. He appointed Lü Ch'en as minister of instruction and his father, Lü Ch'ing, as prime minister. The governor of P'ei he made head of Tang Province, enfeoffed him as marquis of Wu-an, and put him in command of the troops of Tang.

Hsien, the lord of Kao-ling, the envoy from Ch'i whom Sung I had formerly chanced to meet on his way, was at this time with the Ch'u army, and went to see the king of Ch'u. "Sung I," he said, "warned me that Hsiang Liang would surely meet defeat, and after a few days he was in fact defeated. He who can read the signs of defeat before the armies have even engaged in battle may indeed be said to understand the art of warfare." The king thereupon summoned Sung I and discussed affairs of strategy with him. He was delighted with Sung I and made him supreme general of the army. Hsiang Yü, with the title of "Duke of Lu," he made second general, and Tseng Fan third general, and sent them to relieve Chao. All of the other special commanders were placed under the command of Sung I, who was given the title of "His Lordship, the Commander of the Armies."

The armies advanced as far as An-yang, where they halted for forty-six days without proceeding further. Hsiang Yü conferred with Sung I, saying, "News has come that the Ch'in army has besieged the king of Chao at Chü-lu. If we lead our troops across the Yellow River at once, we can attack them with our forces from outside, Chao will respond by attacking from the city, and we are sure to defeat the Ch'in army."

"Not so," replied Sung I. "He who merely slaps at the gadfly on the cow's back will never succeed in killing the pesky lice.[2] Ch'in is now attacking Chao. If she is victorious in battle, then her troops will be weary and we can take advantage of their weakness. And if she is defeated, then we may lead our forces openly and without fear to the west, assured of victory over Ch'in. Therefore it is better for us to let Ch'in and Chao fight it out first. In buckling on armor and wielding a weapon I may be no match for you, but in sitting down and working out problems of strategy you are no match for me!" After this Sung I circulated an order throughout the army reading: "Fierce as a tiger, recalcitrant as a ram, greedy as a wolf, so headstrong they will not

[2] I.e., the Ch'in forces, deployed in small groups all over the empire, cannot be defeated by a single local victory, no matter how spectacular.

submit to orders—if there are any such men, let them all be decapitated."[3]

Sung I dispatched his son, Sung Hsiang, to be prime minister of Ch'i, accompanying him along the way as far as Wu-yen, where he held a great drinking party. The day was cold, a heavy rain was falling, and the soldiers were chilled and starving.

"We joined forces for the purpose of attacking Ch'in," Hsiang Yü declared, "but instead we have sat here all this time without advancing. The year is lean, the people are poor, and our men eat nothing but taro root and pulse. We have no provisions for our army, and yet Sung I holds a great drinking party. He will not lead the troops across the river so that we may live off the food of Chao and join forces with Chao in attacking Ch'in, but instead tells us to 'take advantage of Ch'in's weakness.' Now if Ch'in in all her strength attacks the newly founded state of Chao, she is sure to be powerful enough to defeat Chao. And if Chao is defeated and Ch'in is left as strong as ever, what sort of weakness will there be for us to take advantage of? Our troops were only lately defeated and the king sits uneasy on his throne, yet all the men within our borders are swept up together under Sung I's sole command, so that the entire safety of our state depends upon this one move. Now he takes no thought for our soldiers, but attends only to his personal affairs. He is a traitor to the altars of our soil and grain!"

Early the next day Hsiang Yü went to make his morning report to the supreme general, Sung I, and, when he had entered the tent, he cut off Sung I's head. Then he went outside and issued an order to the army, saying: "Sung I was plotting with Ch'i against Ch'u. The king of Ch'u secretly ordered me to execute him." All the other generals submitted in fear, none daring to raise any objection. "It was General Hsiang's family who first set up the royal family of Ch'u," they declared, "and now the general has executed this traitor!" By mutual assent they set up Hsiang Yü as acting supreme general. Someone was sent to pursue Sung I's son and murder him when he reached Ch'i, while Huan Ch'u was dispatched to report what had happened to King Huai, who confirmed Hsiang Yü's title of supreme general. Ch'ing

---

[3] A hint that he would welcome the assassination of Hsiang Yü.

Pu, the lord of Tang-yang, and General P'u both placed their armies under Hsiang Yü's command.

Hsiang Yü had already killed "His Lordship, the Commander of the Armies"; his might now shook the whole land of Ch'u and his fame reached the ears of all the leaders of the other states. He then dispatched Ch'ing Pu and General P'u at the head of a force of twenty thousand soldiers to cross the Yellow River and bring aid to the city of Chü-lu, but they succeeded in winning only slight success. Ch'en Yü, the Chao commander, sent a request for more troops. With this Hsiang Yü led his entire force across the river. Once across, he sank all his boats, smashed the cooking pots and vessels, and set fire to his huts, taking with him only three days' rations, to make clear to his soldiers that they must fight to the death, for he had no intention of returning. This done, he proceeded to surround the Ch'in general Wang Li and engage his army. After nine battles he managed to cut the supply road and inflict a major defeat, killing the Ch'in general, Su Chüeh, and taking Wang Li prisoner. A third Ch'in general, She Chien, refused to surrender to Ch'u and burned himself to death.

At this time the troops of Ch'u took the lead before those of all the other states. The armies of ten or more of the other states who had come to aid Chü-lu were camped in fortifications outside the city, but none of them dared send forth their troops. When the Ch'u army arrived and set upon Ch'in the leaders of the other armies all stood upon the ramparts of their camps and watched. Of the fighting men of Ch'u there was none who was not a match for ten of the enemy; the war cry of Ch'u shook the heavens and the men of the other armies all trembled with fear.

After Hsiang Yü had defeated the Ch'in army he summoned the leaders of the armies of the other states to audience. Entering the "carriage gates,"[4] they all crawled forward on their knees and none dared look up. With this, Hsiang Yü for the first time became supreme commander of the leaders of the various states, and all of them were under his jurisdiction.

Chang Han's army was at this time camped at Chi-yüan and Hsiang Yü's army south of the Chang River, both holding their positions with-

[4] Formed by Ch'u's war chariots drawn up in array.

out engaging in battle. The Ch'in armies had several times been forced to retreat, and the Second Emperor sent an envoy to reprimand Chang Han for this. Chang Han grew fearful and dispatched his chief secretary, Ssu-ma Hsin, to plead on his behalf. When Ssu-ma Hsin reached the capital, he waited outside the palace gate for three days, but Chao Kao [5] refused to grant him audience on the grounds that he could not be trusted. Ssu-ma Hsin, filled with apprehension, hastened with all speed back to the army, not daring to take the road by which he had come. As he had feared, Chao Kao sent someone to pursue him, but the man failed to overtake him, and Ssu-ma Hsin succeeded in reaching the army and making his report: "Chao Kao is in complete control of the government and the officials under him can do nothing. If we manage to win victory now, Chao Kao is sure to be jealous of our merit, while if we are not victorious we will never escape the death penalty. I beg you to lay plans with the gravest care!"

Ch'en Yü, commander of the Chao forces, also sent a letter to Chang Han, stating:

Po Ch'i was once a general of Ch'in. In the south he conquered Yen and Ying; in the north he annihilated Ma-fu's army. Countless were the cities he attacked and the lands he seized, but at last he was condemned to death. Meng T'ien, too, was a general of Ch'in. In the north he drove out the barbarians and opened up thousands of miles of border land. But in the end his head was cut off at Yang-chou. Why was this? Because these men had won great merit and Ch'in could not reward them sufficiently with fiefs of land. So it invented some legal excuse to condemn and execute them instead.

Now you have been a general of Ch'in for three years, and while you have lost some hundred thousand troops, the leaders of the other states have risen up in ever increasing numbers. This man Chao Kao has for a long time flattered and deceived the Second Emperor, and now that affairs have reached a crisis he is afraid that the emperor will punish him. Therefore he hopes to use the law to punish you, in order to divert responsibility, and to send someone to take your place so that he may avoid disaster to himself.

You have been in the field for a long time, General, and you have many enemies at court. Regardless of whether you win glory or not, you are sure to be executed. The time has come when Heaven will destroy Ch'in and

---

[5] The eunuch who controlled the Second Emperor of the Ch'in and wielded the real power in the government.

every man, wise or foolish, knows it. Powerless to speak the truth openly to the court, camping in the fields as the leader of a doomed nation, would it not be pitiful if you were to try to drag out your days thus alone and friendless? Why do you not lead your troops and join with the other leaders of the Vertical Alliance? [6] We will take an oath to attack Ch'in together, divide up the land into kingdoms, face south [7] and call ourselves sovereigns. Would this not be better than bowing your body beneath the executioner's axe and seeing your wife and children slaughtered?

Chang Han was deeply perplexed and secretly sent his lieutenant Shih-ch'eng to Hsiang Yü, requesting an alliance. But before the alliance was concluded Hsiang Yü dispatched General P'u who, marching day and night, led his troops across the Chang River at the ford called Three Houses and camped south of the river, where he fought with the Ch'in army and defeated it again. Hsiang Yü then led all his troops in an attack upon the Ch'in army on the banks of the Yü River and inflicted a major defeat.

Chang Han again sent one of his men to see Hsiang Yü. Hsiang Yü summoned his officers into council and announced, "Our provisions are running low. I think we had better listen to his request for an alliance." When his officers all agreed Hsiang Yü set a date for a meeting with Chang Han at the site of the old capital of Yin south of the Yüan River. After the oaths of alliance had been concluded Chang Han came to Hsiang Yü, the tears streaming from his eyes, and informed him of Chao Kao's behavior. Hsiang Yü made Chang Han the king of Yung and quartered him with his own army. The chief secretary Ssu-ma Hsin he made supreme commander of the Ch'in armies with orders to lead them in an advance march as far as Hsin-an.

The officers and soldiers of the armies of the other states had in the past from time to time been sent to work on construction projects or on garrison duty and, when they had passed through the capital area of Ch'in, had often been ruthlessly treated by the officers and men of Ch'in. Now that the Ch'in army had surrendered to the other leaders they and their men took advantage of their victory to treat the Ch'in

---

[6] The alliance of states along the eastern coast who were traditionally opposed to Ch'in.

[7] The Chinese sovereign when he sits upon his throne faces south; hence, to "face south" means to become an independent ruler.

soldiers like slaves or prisoners and insult and abuse them with impunity. Many of the Ch'in officers and men whispered among themselves in secret, saying, "General Chang and the rest have tricked us into surrendering to the other leaders. Now if we succeed in entering the Pass and defeating Ch'in, all will be well. But if we are not successful, the other leaders will make prisoners of us and take us east with them, and Ch'in will most certainly execute all our parents and wives and children."

The generals of the army, hearing rumors of these plottings, reported them to Hsiang Yü, who summoned Ch'ing Pu and General P'u and announced to them this plan: "The officers and men of Ch'in are still very numerous, and in their hearts they have not surrendered. If, after we reach the land within the Pass, they should prove disloyal, we will be in a very dangerous situation. It would be better to attack and kill them, sparing only Chang Han, the chief secretary Ssu-ma Hsin, and Colonel Tung I to go with us to invade Ch'in." Accordingly the Ch'u army attacked by night and butchered over 200,000 soldiers of Ch'in south of the city of Hsin-an.

Then they proceeded on their way, overrunning and seizing control of the territory of Ch'in, until they reached the Han-ku Pass. But the Pass was guarded by soldiers, and they could not enter. When news came that the governor of P'ei had already conquered the capital city of Hsien-yang, Hsiang Yü was enraged, and sent Ch'ing Pu and others to attack the Pass. Hsiang Yü was finally able to enter, and proceeded as far as the west side of the Hsi River.

The governor of P'ei was camped at Pa-shang and had not yet had an opportunity to meet with Hsiang Yü. Ts'ao Wu-shang, marshal of the left to the governor of P'ei, sent a messenger to report to Hsiang Yü, saying, "The governor of P'ei is planning to become king of the area within the Pass, employ Tzu-ying [8] as his prime minister, and keep possession of all the precious articles and treasures of the capital." Hsiang Yü was in a rage. "Tomorrow," he announced, "I shall feast my soldiers and then we will attack and crush the governor of P'ei."

At this time Hsiang Yü had a force of 400,000 men encamped at Hung-men in Hsin-feng. The governor of P'ei, with a force of 100,000,

---

[8] The last ruler of Ch'in, who had already surrendered to the governor of P'ei.

was at Pa-shang. Fan Tseng counseled Hsiang Yü, saying, "When the governor of P'ei was living east of the mountains he was greedy for possessions and delighted in beautiful girls. But now that he has entered the Pass he has not taken a single thing, nor has he dallied with any of the wives or maidens. This proves that his mind is not set upon minor joys. I have sent men to observe the sky over the place where he is encamped, and they all found it full of shapes like dragons and tigers and colored with five colors. These are the signs of a Son of Heaven. You must attack him at once and not lose this chance!"

Hsiang Po, the Ch'u commander of the left, was an uncle of Hsiang Yü and for a long time had been good friends with Chang Liang, the marquis of Liu. Chang Liang was at this time serving under the governor of P'ei. That night Hsiang Po galloped on horse to the camp of the governor of P'ei and visited Chang Liang in secret, telling him of Hsiang Yü's plans and begging Chang Liang to come away with him. "Do not throw your life away along with all the others!" he urged.

"I have been sent by the king of Hann to accompany the governor of P'ei," Chang Liang replied. "Now when he is faced with these difficulties, it would not be right for me to run away and leave him. I must report to him what you have told me."

Chang Liang then went and reported the situation in full to the governor of P'ei. "What shall we do?" exclaimed the governor in great consternation.

"Who was it who thought up this plan of action for you?" asked Chang Liang.

"Some fool advised me that if I guarded the Pass and did not let the other leaders enter, I could rule the entire region of Ch'in, and so I followed his plan," he replied.

"Do you believe that you have enough soldiers to stand up against Hsiang Yü?" Chang Liang asked.

The governor was silent for a while, and then said, "No, certainly not. But what should we do now?"

"You must let me go and explain to Hsiang Po," said Chang Liang, "and tell him that you would not dare to be disloyal to Hsiang Yü."

"How do you happen to be friends with Hsiang Po?" asked the governor.

"We knew each other in the time of Ch'in," replied Chang Liang, "and once when Hsiang Po killed a man I saved his life. Now that we are in trouble, he has for that reason been good enough to come and report to me."

"Is he older or younger than you?" asked the governor.

"He is older than I," replied Chang Liang.

"Call him in for me," said the governor, "and I will treat him as I would an elder brother."

Chang Liang went out and urged Hsiang Po to enter. Hsiang Po came in to see the governor of P'ei, who offered him a cup of wine and drank to his long life, swearing an oath of friendship. "Since I entered the Pass," he said, "I have not dared to lay a finger on a single thing. I have preserved the registers of the officials and people and sealed up the storehouses, awaiting the arrival of General Hsiang Yü. The reason I sent officers to guard the Pass was to prevent thieves from getting in and to prepare for any emergency. Day and night I have looked forward to the arrival of the general. How would I dare be disloyal to him? I beg you to report to him in full and tell him that I would not think of turning my back upon his kindness!"

Hsiang Po agreed to do so, adding, "You must come early tomorrow and apologize in person to General Hsiang." "I shall," promised the governor, and with this Hsiang Po went back out into the night.

When he reached his own camp, he reported to Hsiang Yü all that the governor had said. "If the governor of P'ei had not first conquered the land within the Pass how would you have dared to enter?" he said. "When a man has done you a great service it would not be right to attack him. It is better to treat him as a friend." Hsiang Yü agreed to this.

The next day the governor of P'ei, accompanied by a hundred some horsemen, came to visit Hsiang Yu. When he reached Hsiang Yü's camp at Hung-men, he made his apologies, saying, "You and I have joined forces to attack Ch'in, you fighting north of the Yellow River, I fighting south. Quite beyond my expectation it happened that I was able to enter the Pass first, conquer Ch'in, and meet with you again here. Now it seems that some worthless person has been spreading talk and trying to cause dissension between us."

"It is your own marshal of the left, Ts'ao Wu-shang, who has been doing the talking," replied Hsiang Yü. "If it were not for him, how would I ever have doubted you?"

On the same day Hsiang Yü invited the governor of P'ei to remain and drink with him. Hsiang Yü and Hsiang Po as hosts sat facing east. Fan Tseng (whose other name was Ya-fu) took the place of honor facing south, while the governor of P'ei sat facing north with Chang Liang, as his attendant, facing west. Fan Tseng from time to time eyed Hsiang Yü and three times lifted up the jade pendant in the form of a broken ring which he wore and showed it to Yü, hinting that he should "break" once and for all with the governor, but Hsiang Yü sat silent and did not respond. Fan Tseng then rose and left the tent and, summoning Hsiang Yü's cousin, Hsiang Chuang, said to him, "Our lord is too kind-heated a man. Go back in and ask to propose a toast, and when the toast is finished, request to be allowed to perform a sword dance. Then attack the governor of P'ei and kill him where he sits. If you don't, you and all of us will end up as his prisoners!"

Hsiang Chuang entered and proposed a toast. When the toast was finished he said, "Our lord and the governor of P'ei are pleased to drink together but I fear that, this being an army camp, we have nothing to offer by way of entertainment. I beg therefore to be allowed to present a sword dance." "Proceed," said Hsiang Yü, whereupon Hsiang Chuang drew his sword and began to dance. But Hsiang Po also rose and danced, constantly shielding and protecting the governor of P'ei with his own body so that Hsiang Chuang could not attack him.

With this, Chang Liang left and went to the gate of the camp to see Fan K'uai. "How are things proceeding today?" asked Fan K'uai.

"The situation is very grave," replied Chang Liang. "Now Hsiang Chuang has drawn his sword and is dancing, always with his eyes set on the governor of P'ei!"

"This is serious indeed!" said Fan K'uai. "I beg you to let me go in and share the fate of the rest!" Fan K'uai buckled on his sword, grasped his shield, and entered the gate of the camp. The sentries standing with crossed spears tried to stop him from entering but, tipping his shield to either side, he knocked the men to the ground. Entering the camp, he went and pulled back the curtain of the tent and stood facing west, glaring fixedly at Hsiang Yü. His hair stood on end and his eyes blazed with fire.

Hsiang Yü put his hand on his sword and raised himself up on one knee.[9] "Who is our guest?" he asked.

"Fan K'uai, the carriage attendant of the governor of P'ei," announced Chang Liang.

"He is a stouthearted fellow," said Hsiang Yü. "Give him a cup of wine!" A large cup of wine was passed to Fan K'uai, who knelt and accepted it, and then rose again and drank it standing up. "Give him a shoulder of pork," ordered Hsiang Yü, and he was given a piece of parboiled pork shoulder. Fan K'uai placed his shield upside down on the ground, put the pork shoulder on top of it, drew his sword, and began to cut and eat the meat.

"You are a brave man," said Hsiang Yü. "Can you drink some more?"

"I would not hesitate if you offered me death! Why should I refuse a cup of wine?" he replied. "The king of Ch'in [10] had the heart of a tiger and a wolf. He killed men as though he thought he could never finish, he punished men as though he were afraid he would never get around to them all, and the whole world revolted against him. King Huai of Ch'u made a promise with all the leaders that whoever defeated Ch'in first and entered the capital of Hsien-yang should become its king. Now the governor of P'ei has defeated Ch'in and entered Hsien-yang ahead of all others. He has not dared to lay a finger on the slightest thing, but has closed up and sealed the palace rooms and returned to Pa-shang to encamp and await your arrival. The reason he sent officers to guard the Pass was to prevent thieves from getting in and to prepare for an emergency. After suffering great hardship and winning such merit, he has not been rewarded by the grant of a fief and title. Instead you have listened to some worthless talk and are

---

[9] The Chinese of this age had no chairs, but sat on mats on the floor.
[10] I.e., the First Emperor of Ch'in.

about to punish a man of merit. This is no more than a repetition of the fated Ch'in. If I may be so bold, I advise you not to go through with it!"

Hsiang Yü, having no answer to this, said "Sit down!" Fan K'uai took a seat next to Chang Liang. After they had been seated for a while, the governor of P'ei got up and went to the toilet, summoning Fan K'uai to go with him. When they had been outside for a while, Hsiang Yü sent Colonel Ch'en P'ing to call the governor back in. "When I left just now," said the governor, "I failed to say good-by. What should I do?"

"Great deeds do not wait on petty caution; great courtesy does not need little niceties," replied Fan K'uai. "This fellow is about to get out his carving knife and platter and make mincemeat of us! Why should you say good-by to him?"

With this, the governor of P'ei left, ordering Chang Liang to stay behind and make some excuse for him. "What did you bring as gifts?" asked Chang Liang.

"I have a pair of white jade discs which I intended to give to Hsiang Yü," replied the governor, "and a pair of jade wine dippers for Fan Tseng, but when I found that they were angry I did not dare to present them. You must present them for me." "I will do my best," said Chang Liang.

At this time Hsiang Yü's camp was at Hung-men, and the governor of P'ei's camp at Pa-shang some forty *li* away. The governor of P'ei left his carriages and horsemen where they were and slipped away from the camp on horseback, accompanied by only four men, Fan K'uai, Lord T'eng, Chin Ch'iang, and Chi Hsin, who bore swords and shields and hastened on foot. Following the foot of Mount Li, they returned by a secret way through Chih-yang.

When the governor left the camp he told Chang Liang, "By the road I will take it is no more than twenty *li* back to our camp. When you think I have had time to reach the camp, then go back and join the party." After the governor of P'ei had left and enough time had elapsed for him to reach camp, Chang Liang went in and made apologies. "The governor of P'ei was regrettably rather far gone in his cups and was unable to say good-by. He has respectfully requested me on his behalf to present this pair of white jade discs to Your Lordship with his humblest salutation, and to General Fan Tseng this pair of jade wine dippers."

"Where is the governor of P'ei?" asked Hsiang Yü.

"He perceived that Your Lordship was likely to reprove him for his shortcomings," replied Chang Liang, "and so he slipped away alone and returned to his camp."

Hsiang Yü accepted the jade discs and placed them beside him on his mat, but Fan Tseng put the dippers on the ground, drew his sword and smashed them to pieces. "Ah!" he said, "it does not do to lay plans with an idiot! It is the governor of P'ei who will snatch the world out of our hands, and on that day all of us will become his prisoners."

When the governor of P'ei got back to his camp he immediately had Ts'ao Wu-shang seized and executed.

A few days later Hsiang Yü led his troops west and massacred the inhabitants of Hsien-yang, the capital city, killing Tzu-ying, the king of Ch'in, who had already surrendered, and setting fire to the palaces of Ch'in; the fire burned for three months before it went out. Then he gathered up all the goods, treasures, and waiting women, and started east.

Someone advised Hsiang Yü, saying, "The area within the Pass is protected on all four sides by barriers of mountains and rivers, and the land is rich and fertile. This is the place to make your capital and rule as a dictator." But Hsiang Yü saw that the palaces of Ch'in had all been burned and destroyed, and he remembered his native land and longed only to return east. "To become rich and famous and then not go back to your old home is like putting on an embroidered coat and going out walking in the night," he said. "Who is to know about it?"

Later the man who had advised him remarked, "People say that the men of Ch'u are nothing but monkeys with hats on, and now I know what they mean!" Hsiang Yü heard about the remark and had the adviser boiled alive.

Hsiang Yü sent an envoy to report to King Huai of Ch'u. "Let all be done according to the agreement," the king replied. Hsiang Yü then honored King Huai with the title of "Righteous Emperor." Wishing to make himself a king, he first conferred titles on his generals and ministers, telling them, "When the rebellion broke out in the empire, I temporarily set up the heirs of the former feudal rulers, so that they would attack Ch'in. But it was you, my generals, and I who actually donned armor, took up our weapons, and led the undertaking, camping for three years in the open fields, until our might at last destroyed Ch'in and brought peace to the world. As for the Righteous Emperor, though he has done nothing to win merit, it is for various reasons fitting that we assign him a portion of the territory to rule." The generals all expressing agreement, Hsiang Yü accordingly divided the empire and set up the generals as marquises and kings.

Hsiang Yü and Fan Tseng suspected that the governor of P'ei had ambitions to seize the whole empire. But since they had already made their peace with him, and hesitated to go back on the agreement to make him ruler of the land within the Pass, for fear that the other leaders would revolt, they plotted together in secret, saying, "The area of Pa and Shu is cut off by mountains and inhabited largely by settlers sent by Ch'in. Thus we can say that it too is a 'land within the pass.'" With this as an excuse they set up the governor of P'ei as king of Han, ruling over the area of Pa, Shu, and Han,[11] with his capital at Nan-cheng. The real land within the Pass they divided into three parts, and they made kings of the Ch'in generals who had surrendered, so that the latter could block any advance of the king of Han. Thus Hsiang Yü made Chang Han the king of Yung, ruling over the land west of the city of Hsien-yang, with his capital at Fei-ch'iu. The chief secretary Ssu-ma Hsin had formerly been prison warden of Yüeh-yang and had done a great kindness for Hsiang Liang, while Colonel Tung I was the one who had originally urged Chang Han to surrender to the Ch'u army. Therefore Hsiang Yü made Ssu-ma Hsin the king of Sai, ruling the area from Hsien-yang east to the Yellow River, with his capital at Yüeh-yang, and made Tung I the king of Ti, ruling the province of Shang, with his capital at Kao-nu. Pao, the king of Wei, he transferred to the position of king of Western Wei, ruling Ho-tung, with his capital at P'ing-yang. Shen Yang, governor of Hsia-ch'iu, a

[11] The area southwest of the Ch'in capital, on the far western border of China.

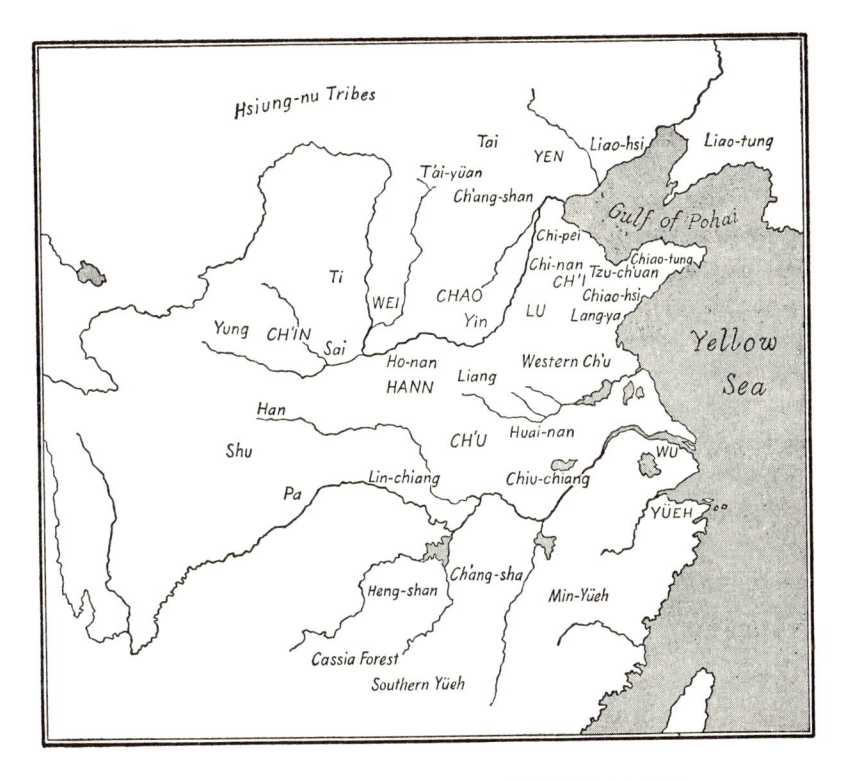

PRINCIPAL FEUDAL KINGDOMS OF
LATE CHOU AND EARLY HAN TIMES

favorite minister of Chang Erh, had formerly conquered the province of Ho-nan and gone to welcome the Ch'u army on the banks of the Yellow River. Therefore Hsiang Yü set up Shen Yang as king of Ho-nan, with his capital at Lo-yang. Ch'eng, the king of Hann, remained at his former capital, Yang-ti. Ssu-ma Ang, general of Chao, had pacified the area of Ho-nei and several times distinguished himself, so he was set up as king of Yin, ruling Ho-nei, with his capital at Chao-ko. Hsieh, the king of Chao, was removed and made king of Tai. The prime minister of Chao, Chang Erh, was a man of worthy character and had, moreover, followed Hsiang Yü in his march through the Pass. Therefore he was made king of Ch'ang-shan, ruling the land of Chao, with his capital at Hsiang-kuo. The lord of Tang-yang, Ch'ing Pu, as a general of Ch'u had repeatedly won the highest distinction in battle and therefore was made king of Chiu-chiang, his capital at Liu. Wu Jui, the lord of P'o, had led the forces of the hundred Yüeh to aid the other leaders and had also followed Hsiang Yü within the Pass. Therefore he was made king of Heng-shan, his capital at Chu. Kung Ao, chief minister to the Righteous Emperor, had led troops in attacking the Nan district and had won great merit; accordingly he was made king of Lin-chiang, his capital at Chiang-ling. Han Kuang, the king of Yen, was moved to the position of king of Liao-tung. Tsang Tu, general of Yen, had joined the Ch'u forces in rescuing Chao and afterwards had accompanied Hsiang Yü through the Pass, so Hsiang Yü made him king of Yen, his capital at Chi. T'ien Shih, the king of Ch'i, was moved to the position of king of Chiao-tung. T'ien Tu, general of Ch'i, because he had joined Ch'u in rescuing Chao and entering the Pass, was made king of Ch'i, with his capital at Lin-tzu. T'ien An was the grandson of King Chien of Ch'i whom Ch'in had deposed. At the time when Hsiang Yü crossed the Yellow River and went to the aid of Chao, T'ien An had captured several cities of Chi-pei and had led his troops and surrendered to Hsiang Yü. Therefore he was made king of Chi-pei, his capital at Po-yang. T'ien Jung, because he had several times betrayed Hsiang Liang and refused to send troops to join Ch'u in its attack on Ch'in, was not enfeoffed. Ch'en Yü, the lord of Ch'eng-an, had discarded his seals of authority as a general and fled, refusing to follow Hsiang Yü through the Pass.

But Hsiang Yü learned of his reputation as a man of worth and of his services to Chao and, hearing that he was living in Nan-p'i, enfeoffed him with the three surrounding districts. Mei Hsüan, general of Wu Jui, the lord of P'o, because of his many services, was enfeoffed as a marquis with a hundred thousand households. Hsiang Yü made himself "Dictator King of Western Ch'u," ruling nine provinces, with his capital at P'eng-ch'eng.

In the first year of Han [206 B.C.],[12] the fourth month, the various leaders left the command of Hsiang Yü and proceeded to their own countries. Hsiang Yü also departed and went to his kingdom. He then sent an envoy to transfer the residence of the Righteous Emperor, announcing that "the emperors of ancient times, who ruled over an area a thousand miles on each side, invariably resided on the upper reaches of a river." The envoy accordingly moved the Righteous Emperor to the district of Ch'en in Ch'ang-sha, pressing him to hurry on his way. The emperor's ministers became increasingly disillusioned and turned their backs on him. Hsiang Yü then secretly ordered the kings of Heng-shan and Lin-chiang to attack and murder the Righteous Emperor in the region of the Yangtze.

Ch'eng, the king of Hann, had won no merit in battle, so Hsiang Yü did not send him to his kingdom but instead took him with him to P'eng-ch'eng. There he deprived him of his title, made him a marquis, and later murdered him. Tsang Tu, the new king of Yen, proceeded to his realm and attempted to drive out the former king, Han Kuang, and send him to Liao-tung, the territory newly assigned to him. But Han Kuang refused to obey, so Tsang Tu attacked and killed him at Wu-chung and made himself king of Liao-tung as well. When T'ien Jung heard that Hsiang Yü had moved Shih, the king of Ch'i, to Chiao-tung, and set up T'ien Tu, a general of Ch'i, as the new king of Ch'i, he was very angry and refused to send Shih to Chiao-tung. Instead he declared Ch'i to be in revolt, and marched forth to attack T'ien Tu. T'ien Tu fled to Ch'u. T'ien Shih, king of Ch'i, fearful of Hsiang Yü, fled to Chiao-tung, thus reaching his new realm.

[12] The Han dynasty counted its years from the time when its founder, Liu Chi, first became king of Han, though it was not until 202 B.C. that he actually gained control of the whole empire.

T'ien Jung, in a rage, pursued and attacked him, killing him at Chi-mo. T'ien Jung then set himself up as king of Ch'i, marched west, and attacked and killed T'ien An, the new king of Chi-pei. Thus he became ruler of the three areas of Ch'i, Chi-pei, and Chiao-tung. He then presented P'eng Yüeh with the seals of office of a general and sent him to lead a revolt in the region of Liang.

Ch'en Yü, the former general of Chao, secretly sent Chang T'ung and Hsia Yüeh to advise T'ien Jung, saying, "Hsiang Yü's actions as ruler of the empire have been completely unjust. All the former kings he has made rulers of poor territories, giving the best lands to his own ministers and generals to rule. He has expelled the king of Chao, my former lord, and sent him north to live in Tai. I consider such actions inexcusable. I have heard that, as king of Ch'i, you have taken up arms and refused to bow to such unrighteousness. I beg that you will send troops to aid me so that I may attack Chang Erh, the new king of Ch'ang-shan, who is now ruling the land of Chao, and restore the former king of Chao. Then his kingdom may act as a protective barrier for you."

The king of Ch'i approved this suggestion, and dispatched troops to Chao. Ch'en Yü called up all the troops from the three districts under his command and, joining forces with Ch'i, attacked Chang Erh, the king of Ch'ang-shan, inflicting a severe defeat. Chang Erh fled and joined the king of Han. Ch'en Yü proceeded to Tai and escorted Hsieh, the former king of Chao, back to Chao. In turn, the king of Chao set up Ch'en Yü as king of Tai.

It was at this time that the king of Han returned from his fief and reconquered the three new territories of Ch'in. When Hsiang Yü received word that the king of Han had united all the area within the Pass under his rule and was about to proceed east, and that Ch'i and Liang were in revolt against him, he was enraged. He made Cheng Ch'ang, the former district magistrate of Wu, the king of Hann in order to block the advance of the Han armies, and dispatched Chüeh, the lord of Hsiao, and others, with orders to attack P'eng Yüeh, but P'eng Yüeh defeated them.

The king of Han sent Chang Liang to seize the region of Hann. Chang Liang sent a letter to Hsiang Yü, saying, "The king of Han has been deprived of the position which was rightly his. He desires to be given the territory within the Pass according to the original agreement. If this is done he will halt and proceed no farther east." He also sent to Hsiang Yü rebellious letters from Ch'i and Liang, proving that Ch'i intended to join with Liang in destroying Ch'u. As a result, Hsiang Yü for the moment gave up the idea of marching west and instead proceeded north to attack Ch'i. He sent an order for troops to Ch'ing Pu, the king of Chiu-chiang. Ch'ing Pu, pleading illness, refused to go in person, but instead sent his general with a force of several thousand men. Because of this incident, Hsiang Yü came to hate Ch'ing Pu.

In the winter of the second year of Han [205 B.C.] Hsiang Yü proceeded north as far as Ch'eng-yang. T'ien Jung led his troops to meet him there in battle, but failed to win a victory and fled to P'ing-yüan. Hsiang Yü marched north, firing and leveling the fortifications and dwellings of Ch'i, butchering all the soldiers of T'ien Jung who surrendered to him, and binding and taking prisoner the old people, women, and children. Thus he seized control of Ch'i as far as the northern sea, inflicting great damage and destruction. The people of Ch'i once more banded together in revolt. With this, T'ien Jung's younger brother, T'ien Heng, gathered a force of twenty or thirty thousand men from among the soldiers of Ch'i who had fled into hiding, and raised a revolt in Ch'eng-yang. Hsiang Yü was thus forced to remain in the area and continue fighting, but he was not able to put down the rebels.

In the spring the king of Han, with the forces of five of the other feudal leaders numbering 560,000 men under his command, marched east and attacked Ch'u. When Hsiang Yü received word of this, he ordered his subordinate generals to continue the assault on Ch'i, while he himself led a force of thirty thousand picked men south through Lu to Hu-ling.

In the fourth month the king of Han had already entered P'eng-ch'eng, the capital of Ch'u, had seized possession of its treasures and beautiful women, and was spending his days in feasting and revelry. Hsiang Yü marched west through Hsiao and at dawn attacked the Han army, fighting his way back east as far as P'eng-ch'eng, and in the course of the day inflicted a major defeat. When the Han army fled, he pursued it to the Ssu and Ku Rivers, killing over a hundred thousand Han soldiers. The remainder all fled south to the mountains, where Hsiang Yü once more pursued and attacked them on the Sui River east of Ling-pi. Thus in its retreat the Han army was constantly pressed by the Ch'u forces and many of its men killed. Some hundred thousand Han soldiers were driven into the Sui River, so that the flow of the river was blocked. Hsiang Yü had surrounded the king of Han with a threefold line of troops, when a great wind arose and began to blow from the northwest, breaking down trees, toppling roofs, and raising clouds of sand, so that the sky grew dark and the day turned to night. As the storm advanced and bore down upon the forces of Ch'u, they were thrown into great confusion and their lines crumbled. The king of Han was thus able to slip through with twenty or thirty horsemen and escape.

The king of Han hoped to pass through his old home of P'ei and gather up his family before proceeding west. But Hsiang Yü had in the meantime sent men to pursue him to P'ei and seize the members of his family, so that they had all fled into hiding and he could not find them. Along the road, however, he happened to encounter his son (later Emperor Hui) and daughter (later Princess Yüan of Lu). Putting them in the carriage, he hastened on his way.

The horsemen of Ch'u were in close pursuit, and the king of Han in desperation several times pushed his little son and daughter out of the carriage, but each time Lord T'eng, who was with him, got out, picked them up, and put them back in the carriage.[13] This had happened three times when Lord T'eng said, "No matter how sorely we are pressed in chase it will not do to abandon the children!"

The king of Han at last managed to elude his pursuers and went in search of his father and wife, but could find them nowhere. They, in the meantime, accompanied by Shen I-chi, had fled by a secret route and were searching for the king, but instead of finding him they stumbled into the Ch'u army and were seized and led back to the

---

[13] According to the much more plausible account of this incident in the biography of Lord T'eng (*Shih chi* 95) the king did not actually push the children out of the carriage, but only attempted to do so by kicking them with his foot, whereupon Lord T'eng each time pulled them back to safety.

camp. When their capture was reported to Hsiang Yü, he ordered them to be kept under guard in the midst of his army.

At this time Lü Tse, the marquis of Chou-lü, elder brother of the king of Han's wife, was in Hsia-i with a force of troops loyal to the king. The king secretly made his way there and joined him. Gathering his soldiers together bit by bit, he proceeded to Jung-yang, where he held a rendezvous of all his defeated divisions. In addition, Hsiao Ho dispatched all the old men and underaged youths from the area within the Pass to Jung-yang, so that the Han army again reached sizable strength.

Hsiang Yü, after his initial victory at P'eng-ch'eng, had taken advantage of his supremacy to pursue the Han forces north. Now, however, he fought with the Han army once more in the area of So in Ching, south of Jung-yang, and was defeated. Thus Hsiang Yü was unable to proceed west of Jung-yang. While Hsiang Yü was recapturing P'eng-ch'eng from the king of Han and pursuing him to Jung-yang, T'ien Heng managed to gain control of Ch'i and set up T'ien Jung's son Kuang as king of Ch'i. When the king of Han was defeated at P'eng-ch'eng, the other feudal lords all deserted him and went over to the side of Ch'u. The king camped at Jung-yang and constructed a walled supply road along the banks of the Yellow River in order to transport grain from the Ao Granary.

In the third year of Han [204 B.C.] Hsiang Yü several times attacked and cut off the Han supply road so that the king of Han grew short of provisions. Afraid of what might happen, he made a bid for peace, asking that he be allowed to retain all the territory west of Jung-yang as part of Han. Hsiang Yü was in favor of listening to the suggestion, but Fan Tseng (now marquis of Li-yang) advised him against it. "It is easy enough to make concessions to Han, but if you let him go this time and do not seize him, you are bound to regret it later!" Hsiang Yü and Fan Tseng then joined in pressing the siege of Jung-yang.

The king of Han was in great distress but, employing a strategy suggested by Ch'en P'ing, he managed to cause dissension between his two enemies. An envoy having arrived from Hsiang Yü, the king ordered a great feast prepared and brought in to be served to him. When the king saw the envoy, however, he pretended to be thoroughly startled and said, "Oh, I supposed you were the envoy from Fan Tseng, but I see on the contrary you have come from Hsiang Yü!" He then had the feast taken away and a poor meal brought and served to the man. When the envoy returned and reported this, Hsiang Yü began to suspect that Fan Tseng had made some secret alliance with Han and was trying gradually to usurp his own authority. Fan Tseng, deeply angered, announced, "The affairs of the world have been largely settled. My lord must now manage things for himself. For my part, I beg to be relieved of my duties and returned to the ranks of a common soldier." Hsiang Yü granted his request and Fan Tseng departed, but before he had got as far as P'eng-ch'eng an ulcerous sore broke out on his back and he died.

The Han general Chi Hsin advised the king, saying, "The situation is very grave. I beg you to let me deceive Ch'u for you by taking your place as king. In this way you will be able to slip away in secret." Accordingly, the king of Han dressed two thousand women of Jung-yang in armor and, when night fell, sent them out by the eastern gate of the city. The soldiers of Ch'u rushed to attack them from all sides. Chi Hsin then rode forth in the yellow-canopied royal carriage with its plumes attached to the left side and announced, "The food in the city is exhausted. The king of Han surrenders!" While the army of Ch'u joined in cheers of victory, the king of Han with twenty or thirty horsemen slipped out by the western gate and fled to Ch'eng-kao.

When Hsiang Yü saw Chi Hsin he demanded to know where the king of Han was. "The king of Han," replied Chi Hsin, "has already left the city!" Hsiang Yü had Chi Hsin burned alive.

The king of Han left the grand secretary Chou K'o, Lord Ts'ung, and Wei Pao, the former king of Wei, to guard Jung-yang. But Chou K'o and Lord Ts'ung plotted together, saying, "It is hard to guard a city with the king of a country that has once revolted,"[14] and so together they murdered Wei Pao.

Hsiang Yü captured Jung-yang and took Chou K'o alive. "If you will be my general, I will make you supreme commander and enfeoff you with thirty thousand households," said Hsiang Yü, but Chou K'o

---

[14] Wei Pao had formerly revolted against the king of Han and had been taken prisoner.

only cursed him, saying, "If you do not hurry and surrender to the king of Han, you will be taken prisoner! You are no match for him!" Hsiang Yü, enraged, boiled Chou K'o alive and at the same time executed Lord Ts'ung.

After the king of Han escaped from Jung-yang, he fled south to Yüan and She, and joined Ch'ing Pu, the king of Chiu-chiang. Gathering soldiers as he went, he returned and guarded Ch'eng-kao.

In the fourth year of Han [203 B.C.] Hsiang Yü advanced with his forces and surrounded Ch'eng-kao. The king of Han escaped alone from the northern gate of Ch'eng-kao, accompanied only by Lord T'eng, crossed the Yellow River, and fled to Hsiu-wu, where he joined the armies of Chang Erh and Han Hsin. His subordinate generals one by one managed to escape from Ch'eng-kao and join him there. Hsiang Yü finally captured Ch'eng-kao and was about to proceed west, but Han sent troops to block him at Kung so he could go no further west. At the same time P'eng Yüeh crossed the Yellow River and attacked part of the Ch'u army at Tung-a, killing the Ch'u general Lord Hsieh. Hsiang Yü then marched east in person and attacked P'eng Yüeh.

The king of Han, having obtained command of the soldiers of Han Hsin, wished to cross the Yellow River and proceed south. On the advice of Cheng Chung, however, he abandoned this idea and instead stopped at Ho-nei and built a walled camp, sending Liu Chia to lead a band of men to aid P'eng Yüeh and to burn Ch'u's stores and provisions. Hsiang Yü proceeded east and attacked them, forcing P'eng Yüeh to flee.

The king of Han then led his troops back across the Yellow River and retook Ch'eng-kao, camped at Kuang-wu, and again began to draw provisions from the Ao Granary. Hsiang Yü, having pacified the eastern seaboard, returned west and camped opposite the Han forces at Kuang-wu, and thus the two armies remained, each in its own camp, for several months.

Meanwhile P'eng Yüeh continued to foment rebellion in the region of Liang, and from time to time cut off Ch'u's supply lines. Hsiang Yü, much troubled by this, constructed a sacrificial altar and, placing the "Venerable Sire," the king of Han's father, on it, he announced to the king, "If you do not surrender to me at once, I shall boil your 'Venerable Sire' alive!"

"When you and I bowed together before King Huai and acknowledged our allegiance to him, we took a vow to be brothers," replied the king of Han. "Therefore my father is your father, too. If you insist now upon boiling your own father, I hope you will be good enough to send me a cup of the soup!"

Hsiang Yü, in a rage, was about to kill the old man, but Hsiang Po intervened: "No one knows yet how the affairs of the world will turn out. A man like the king of Han who has his eyes set upon the rulership of the world will hardly bother about a member of his family. Even if you kill his father, it will bring you no advantage, but only increase your misfortunes." Following his advice, Hsiang Yü desisted.

For a long time Ch'u and Han held their respective positions without making a decisive move, while their fighting men suffered the hardships of camp life and their old men and boys wore themselves out transporting provisions by land and water. Hsiang Yü sent word to the king of Han, saying, "The world has been in strife and confusion for several years now, solely because of the two of us. I would like to invite the king of Han to a personal combat to decide who is the better man. Let us bring no more needless suffering to the fathers and sons of the rest of the world." The king of Han scorned the offer with a laugh, saying, "Since I am no match for you in strength, I prefer to fight you with brains!"

Hsiang Yü then sent out one of his bravest men to challenge Han to combat. In the Han army there was a man who was very skillful at shooting from horseback, a so-called *lou-fan*.[15] Ch'u three times sent out men to challenge Han to combat, and each time this man shot and killed them on the spot. Hsiang Yü, enraged, buckled on his armor, took up a lance, and went out himself to deliver the challenge. The *lou-fan* was about to shoot when Hsiang Yü shouted and glared so fiercely at him that the man had not the courage to raise his eyes or lift a hand, but finally fled back within the walls and did not dare venture

---

[15] The men of the barbarian tribe of Lou-fan being famous for their skill in archery, the word *lou-fan* came to mean an expert bowman.

forth again. The king of Han secretly sent someone to find out who the new challenger was, and when he learned that it was Hsiang Yü himself he was greatly astonished. Hsiang Yü approached the place where the king of Han was standing, and the two of them talked back and forth across the ravine of Kuang-wu. The king berated Hsiang Yü for his crimes, while Hsiang Yü angrily demanded a single combat. When the king of Han refused to agree, Hsiang Yü shot him with a crossbow which he had concealed, and the king, wounded, fled into the city of Ch'eng-kao.

Hsiang Yü, receiving word that Han Hsin had already conquered the area north of the Yellow River, defeating Ch'i and Chao, and was about to attack Ch'u, sent Lung Chü to attack him. Han Hsin, joined by the cavalry general Kuan Ying, met his attack and defeated the Ch'u army, killing Lung Chü. Han Hsin then proceeded to set himself up as king of Ch'i. When Hsiang Yü heard that Lung Chü's army had been defeated, he was fearful and sent Wu She, a man of Hsü-i, to attempt to bargain with Han Hsin, but Han Hsin refused to listen.

At this time P'eng Yüeh had once more raised a revolt in the region of Liang, conquered it, and cut off Ch'u's sources of supply. Hsiang Yü summoned the marquis of Hai-ch'un, the grand marshal Ts'ao Chiu, and others and said to them, "Hold fast to the city of Ch'eng-kao. Even if the king of Han challenges you to a battle, take care and do not fight with him! You must not let him advance eastward! In fifteen days I can surely do away with P'eng Yüeh and bring the region of Liang under control once again. Then I will return and join you."

Hsiang Yü marched east and attacked Ch'en-liu and Wai-huang. Wai-huang held out for several days before it finally surrendered. Enraged, Hsiang Yü ordered all the men over the age of fifteen to be brought to a place east of the city, where he planned to butcher them. One of the retainers of the head of the district, a lad of thirteen, went and spoke to Hsiang Yü. "Wai-huang, oppressed by the might of P'eng Yüeh, was fearful and surrendered to him, hopeful that Your Majesty would come to the rescue," he said. "But now that you have arrived, if you butcher all the men, how can you hope to win the hearts of the common people? East of here there are still a dozen cities of Liang, but all will be filled with terror and will not dare to surrender."

Hsiang Yü, acknowledging the reason of his words, pardoned all the men of Wai-huang who were marked for execution and proceeded east to Sui-yang. Hearing what had happened, the other cities made all haste to submit to him.

The king of Han meanwhile several times challenged the Ch'u army to a battle, but the Ch'u generals refused to send out their forces. Then he sent men to taunt and insult them for five or six days, until at last the grand marshal Ts'ao Chiu, in a rage, led his soldiers across the Ssu River. When the troops were halfway across the river, the Han force fell upon them and inflicted a severe defeat on the Ch'u army, seizing all the wealth of the country of Ch'u. Grand marshal Ts'ao Chiu, the chief secretary Tung I, and Ssu-ma Hsin, the king of Sai, all cut their throats on the banks of the Ssu. (Ts'ao Chiu, former prison warden of Chi, and Ssu-ma Hsin, former prison warden of Yüeh-yang, had both done favors for Hsiang Liang, and so had been trusted and employed by Hsiang Yü.)

Hsiang Yü was at this time in Sui-yang but, hearing of the defeat of the grand marshal's army, he led his troops back. The Han army had at the moment surrounded Chung-li Mo at Jung-yang, but when Hsiang Yü arrived, the Han forces, fearful of Ch'u, all fled to positions of safety in the mountains. At this time the Han troops were strong and had plenty of food, but Hsiang Yü's men were worn out and their provisions were exhausted.

The king of Han dispatched Lu Chia to bargain with Hsiang Yü for the return of his father, but Hsiang Yü refused to listen. The king then sent Lord Hou to bargain. This time Hsiang Yü agreed to make an alliance with Han to divide the empire between them, Han to have all the land west of the Hung Canal and Ch'u all the land to the east. In addition, upon Hsiang Yü's consent, the king of Han's father, mother, and wife were returned to him amid cheers of "Long life!" from the Han army. The king of Han enfeoffed Lord Hou as "Lord Who Pacifies the Nation." (Lord Hou retired and was unwilling to show himself again. Someone remarked, "This man is the most eloquent pleader in the world. Wherever he goes he turns the whole nation on its head. Perhaps that is why he has been given the title 'Lord Who Pacifies the Nation.'") [16]

After concluding the alliance, Hsiang Yü led his troops away to the east and the king of Han prepared to return west, but Chang Liang and Ch'en P'ing advised him, saying, "Han now possesses over half the empire, and all the feudal lords are on our side, while the soldiers of Ch'u are weary and out of food. The time has come when Heaven will destroy Ch'u. It would be best to take advantage of Hsiang Yü's lack of food and seize him once for all. If we were to let him get away now without attacking him, it would be like nursing a tiger that will return to vex us later!"

The king of Han, approving their advice, in the fifth year of Han [202 B.C.] pursued Hsiang Yü as far as the south of Yang-hsia, where he halted and made camp. There he set a date for Han Hsin and P'eng Yüeh to meet him and join in attacking the Ch'u army. But when he reached Ku-ling, the troops of Han Hsin and P'eng Yüeh failed to appear for the rendezvous, and Hsiang Yü attacked him and inflicted a severe defeat. The king of Han withdrew behind his walls, deepened his moats, and guarded his position.

"The other leaders have not kept their promise. What shall I do?" he asked Chang Liang.

"The Ch'u army is on the point of being destroyed," Chang Liang replied, "but Han Hsin and P'eng Yüeh have not yet been granted any territory.[17] It is not surprising that they do not come when summoned. If you will consent to share a part of the empire with them, they will surely come without a moment's hesitation. If this is impossible, I do not know what will happen. If you could assign to Han Hsin all the land from Ch'en east to the sea, and to P'eng Yüeh the land from Sui-yang north to Ku-ch'eng, so that each would feel he

---

[16] The passage in parentheses, the meaning of which is far from certain, does not appear in the parallel passage in *Han shu* 31, and may well be a later addition.

[17] Although they had received impressive titles—Han Hsin was "king of Ch'i," P'eng Yüeh was "prime minister of Wei"—no specific grants of territory had as yet been awarded them.

was actually fighting for his own good, then Ch'u could easily be defeated."

The king of Han, approving this suggestion, sent envoys to Han Hsin and P'eng Yüeh, saying, "Let us join our forces in attacking Ch'u. When Ch'u has been defeated, I will give the land from Ch'en east to the sea to the king of Ch'i, and that from Sui-yang north to Ku-ch'eng to Prime Minister P'eng." When the envoys arrived and reported this to Han Hsin and P'eng Yüeh, both replied, "We beg leave to proceed with our troops." Han Hsin then marched out of Ch'i. Liu Chia led his army from Shou-ch'un to join in attacking and massacring the men of Ch'eng-fu; from there he proceeded to Kai-hsia. The grand marshal Chou Yin revolted against Ch'u, using the men of Shu to massacre the inhabitants of Liu, gained control of the army of Chiu-chiang, and followed after Liu Chia and P'eng Yüeh. All met at Kai-hsia and made their way toward Hsiang Yü.

Hsiang Yü's army had built a walled camp at Kai-hsia, but his soldiers were few and his supplies exhausted. The Han army, joined by the forces of the other leaders, surrounded them with several lines of troops. In the night Hsiang Yü heard the Han armies all about him singing the songs of Ch'u. "Has Han already conquered Ch'u?" he exclaimed in astonishment. "How many men of Ch'u they have with them!" Then he rose in the night and drank within the curtains of his tent. With him were the beautiful lady Yü, who enjoyed his favor and followed wherever he went, and his famous steed Dapple, which he always rode. Hsiang Yü, filled with passionate sorrow, began to sing sadly, composing this song:

> My strength plucked up the hills,
> My might shadowed the world;
> But the times were against me,
> And Dapple runs no more.
> When Dapple runs no more,
> What then can I do?
> Ah, Yü, my Yü,
> What will your fate be?

He sang the the song several times through, and Lady Yü joined her voice with his. Tears streamed down his face, while all those about him wept and were unable to lift their eyes from the ground. Then he mounted his horse and, with some eight hundred brave horsemen under his banner, rode into the night, burst through the encirclement to the south, and galloped away.

Next morning, when the king of Han became aware of what had happened, he ordered his cavalry general Kuan Ying to lead a force of five thousand horsemen in pursuit. Hsiang Yü crossed the Huai River, though by now he had only a hundred or so horsemen still with him. Reaching Yin-ling, he lost his way, and stopped to ask an old farmer for directions. But the farmer deceived him, saying, "Go left!", and when he rode to the left he stumbled into a great swamp, so that the Han troops were able to pursue and overtake him.

Hsiang Yü once more led his men east until they reached Tung-ch'eng. By this time he had only twenty-eight horsemen, while the Han cavalry pursuing him numbered several thousand.

Hsiang Yü, realizing that he could not escape, addressed his horsemen, saying, "It has been eight years since I first led my army forth. In that time I have fought over seventy battles. Every enemy I faced was destroyed, everyone I attacked submitted. Never once did I suffer defeat, until at last I became dictator of the world. But now suddenly I am driven to this desperate position! It is because Heaven would destroy me, not because I have committed any fault in battle. I have resolved to die today. But before I die, I beg to fight bravely and win for you three victories. For your sake I shall break through the enemy's encirclements, cut down their leaders, and sever their banners, that you may know it is Heaven which has destroyed me and no fault of mine in arms!" Then he divided his horsemen into four bands and faced them in four directions.

When the Han army had surrounded them several layers deep, Hsiang Yü said to his horsemen, "I will get one of those generals for you!" He ordered his men to gallop in all four directions down the hill on which they were standing, with instructions to meet again on the east side of the hill and divide into three groups. He himself gave a great shout and galloped down the hill. The Han troops scattered before him and he succeeded in cutting down one of their generals. At this time Yang Hsi was leader of the cavalry pursuing Hsiang Yü, but Hsiang Yü roared and glared so fiercely at him that all his men and horses fled in terror some distance to the rear.

Hsiang Yü rejoined his men, who had formed into three groups. The Han army, uncertain which group Hsiang Yü was with, likewise divided into three groups and again surrounded them. Hsiang Yü once more galloped forth and cut down a Han colonel, killing some fifty to a hundred men. When he had gathered his horsemen together a second time, he found that he had lost only two of them. "Did I tell you the truth?" he asked. His men all bowed and replied, "You have done all you said."

Hsiang Yü, who by this time had reached Wu-chiang, was considering whether to cross over to the east side of the Yangtze. The village head of Wu-chiang, who was waiting with a boat on the bank of the river, said to him, "Although the area east of the Yellow River is small, it is some thousand miles in breadth and has a population of thirty or forty thousand. It would still be worth ruling. I beg you to make haste and cross over. I am the only one who has a boat, so that when the Han army arrives they will have no way to get across!"

Hsiang Yü laughed and replied, "It is Heaven that is destroying me. What good would it do me to cross the river? Once, with eight thousand sons from the land east of the river, I crossed over and marched west, but today not a single man of them returns. Although their fathers and brothers east of the river should take pity on me and make me their king, how could I bear to face them again? Though they said nothing of it, could I help but feel shame in my heart?" Then he added, "I can see that you are a worthy man. For five years I have ridden this horse, and I have never seen his equal. Again and again he has borne me hundreds of miles in a single day. Since I cannot bear to kill him, I give him to you."

Hsiang Yü then ordered all his men to dismount and proceed on foot, and with their short swords to close in hand-to-hand combat with the enemy. Hsiang Yü alone killed several hundred of the Han men, until he had suffered a dozen wounds. Looking about him, he spied the Han cavalry marshal Lü Ma-t'ung. "We are old friends, are we not?" he asked. Lü Ma-t'ung eyed him carefully and then, pointing him out to Wang I, said, "This is Hsiang Yü!"

Hsiang Yü 73

"I have heard that Han has offered a reward of a thousand catties of gold and a fief of ten thousand households for my head," said Hsiang Yü. "I will do you the favor!" And with this he cut his own throat and died.

Wang I seized his head, while the other horsemen trampled over each other in a struggle to get at Hsiang Yü's body, so that twenty or thirty of them were killed. In the end the cavalry attendant Yang Hsi, the cavalry marshal Lü Ma-t'ung, and the attendants Lü Sheng and Yang Wu each succeeded in seizing a limb. When the five of them fitted together the limbs and head, it was found that they were indeed those of Hsiang Yü. Therefore the fief was divided five ways, Lü Ma-t'ung being enfeoffed as marquis of Chung-shui, Wang I as marquis of Tu-yen, Yang Hsi as marquis of Ch'ih-ch'üan, Yang Wu as marquis of Wu-fang, and Lü Sheng as marquis of Nieh-yang.

With the death of Hsiang Yü, the entire region of Ch'u surrendered to Han, only Lu refusing to submit. The king of Han set out with the troops of the empire and was about to massacre the inhabitants of Lu. But because Lu had so strictly obeyed the code of honor and had shown its willingness to fight to the death for its acknowledged sovereign, he bore with him the head of Hsiang Yü and, when he showed it to the men of Lu, they forthwith surrendered.

King Huai of Ch'u had first enfeoffed Hsiang Yü as duke of Lu, and Lu was the last place to surrender. Therefore, the king of Han buried Hsiang Yü at Ku-ch'eng with the ceremony appropriate to a duke of Lu. The king proclaimed a period of mourning for him, wept, and then departed. All the various branches of the Hsiang family he spared from execution, and he enfeoffed Hsiang Po as marquis of She-yang. The marquises of T'ao, P'ing-kao, and Hsüan-wu were all members of the Hsiang family who were granted the imperial surname Liu.

The Grand Historian remarks: I have heard Master Chou say that Emperor Shun had eyes with double pupils. I have also heard that Hsiang Yü, too, had eyes with double pupils. Could it be that Hsiang Yü was a descendant of Emperor Shun? How sudden was his rise to power! When the rule of Ch'in floundered and Ch'en She led his revolt, local heroes and leaders arose like bees, struggling with each other for power in numbers too great to be counted. Hsiang Yü did not have so much as an inch of territory to begin with, but by taking advantage of the times he raised himself in the space of three years from a commoner in the fields to the position of commander of five armies of feudal lords. He overthrew Ch'in, divided up the empire, and parceled it out in fiefs to the various kings and marquises; but all power of government proceeded from Hsiang Yü and he was hailed as a dictator king. Though he was not able to hold this position to his death, yet from ancient times to the present there has never before been such a thing!

But when he went so far as to turn his back on the Pass and return to his native Ch'u, banishing the Righteous Emperor and setting himself up in his place, it was hardly surprising that the feudal lords revolted against him. He boasted and made a show of his own achievements. He was obstinate in his own opinions and did not abide by established ways. He thought to make himself a dictator, hoping to attack and rule the empire by force. Yet within five years he was dead and his kingdom lost. He met death at Tung-ch'eng, but even at that time he did not wake to or accept responsibility for his errors. "It is Heaven," he declared, "which has destroyed me, and no fault of mine in the use of arms!" Was he not indeed deluded?

Part III
THE VICTOR

Shih chi 8: The Basic Annals of Emperor Kao-tsu

Hsiang Yü was violent and tyrannical, while the king of Han practiced goodness and virtue. In anger he marched forth from Shu and Han, returning to conquer the three kingdoms of Ch'in. He executed Hsiang Yü and became an emperor, and all the world was brought to peace. He changed the statutes and reformed the ways of the people. Thus I made The Basic Annals of Emperor Kao-tsu.

Kao-tsu[1] was a native of the community of Chung-yang in the city of Feng, the district of P'ei. His family name was Liu and his polite name Chi. His father was known as the "Venerable Sire" and his mother as "Dame Liu."

Before he was born, Dame Liu was one day resting on the bank of a large pond when she dreamed that she encountered a god. At this time the sky grew dark and was filled with thunder and lightning. When Kao-tsu's father went to look for her, he saw a scaly dragon over the place where she was lying. After this she became pregnant and gave birth to Kao-tsu.

Kao-tsu had a prominent nose and a dragonlike face, with beautiful whiskers on his chin and cheeks; on his left thigh he had seventy-two black moles.[2] He was kind and affectionate with others, liked to help people, and was very understanding. He always had great ideas and paid little attention to the business the rest of his family was engaged in.

When he grew up he took the examination to become an official

[1] Kao-tsu, meaning "Exalted Ancestor," is the posthumous title of Liu Chi, founder of the Han dynasty. Liu Chi's familiar name, Pang, was tabooed during the Han and is never mentioned in the *Shih chi*. Since Ssu-ma Ch'ien was writing during the Han, he often refers to members of the imperial family by the titles they later acquired. Hence Kao-tsu's wife is called Empress Lü, though this is often anachronistic from the point of view of the narrative.

[2] Seventy-two, the multiple of eight and nine, is a mystic number in Chinese thought.

and was made village head of Ssu River. He treated all the other officials in the office with familiarity and disdain. He was fond of wine and women and often used to go to Dame Wang's or old lady Wu's and drink on credit. When he got drunk and lay down to sleep, the old women, to their great wonder, would always see something like a dragon over the place where he was sleeping. Also, whenever he would drink and stay at their shops, they would sell several times as much wine as usual. Because of these strange happenings, when the end of the year came around the old women would always destroy Kao-tsu's credit slips and clear his account.

Kao-tsu was once sent on *corvée* labor to the capital city of Hsien-yang and happened to have an opportunity to see the First Emperor of Ch'in. When he saw him he sighed and said, "Ah, this is the way a great man should be."

There was a man of Shan-fu, one Master Lü, who was a friend of the magistrate of P'ei. In order to avoid the consequences of a feud, he accepted the hospitality of the magistrate and made his home in P'ei. When the officials and the wealthy and influential people of P'ei heard that the magistrate had a distinguished guest, they all came to pay their respects. Hsiao Ho, being the director of officials, was in charge of gifts and informed those who came to call that anyone bringing a gift of less than one thousand cash would be seated below the main hall. Kao-tsu, who as a village head was in the habit of treating the other officials with contempt, falsely wrote on his calling card: "With respects—ten thousand cash," though in fact he did not have a single cash. When his card was sent in, Master Lü was very surprised and got up and came to the gate to greet him. Master Lü was very good at reading people's faces and when he saw Kao-tsu's features he treated him with great honor and respect and led him in to a seat. "Liu Chi," remarked Hsiao Ho, "does a good deal of fine talking, but so far has accomplished very little." But Kao-tsu, disdaining the other guests, proceeded to take a seat of honor without further ado.

When the drinking was nearly over, Master Lü glanced at Kao-tsu in such a way as to indicate that he should stay a while longer, and so Kao-tsu dawdled over his wine. "Since my youth," said Master Lü, "I have been fond of reading faces. I have read many faces, but none with signs like yours. You must take good care of yourself, I beg you. I have a daughter whom I hope you will do me the honor of accepting as your wife."

When the party was over, Dame Lü was very angry with her husband. "You have always idolized this girl and planned to marry her to some person of distinction," she said. "The magistrate of P'ei is a friend of yours and has asked for her, but you would not give your consent. How can you be so insane as to give her to Liu Chi?"

"This is not the sort of thing women and children can understand!" replied Master Lü. Eventually he married the girl to Kao-tsu, and it was this daughter of Master Lü who became Empress Lü and gave birth to Emperor Hui and Princess Yüan of Lu.

When Kao-tsu was acting as village head he once asked for leave to go home and visit his fields. Empress Lü at the time was in the fields weeding with her two children. When an old man passed by and asked for something to drink, Empress Lü accordingly gave him some food. The old man examined her face and said, "Madam will become the most honored woman in the world." She asked him to examine her children. Looking at her son, he said, "It is because of this boy that madam will obtain honor," and when he examined the girl, he said that she too would be honored.

After the old man had gone on, Kao-tsu happened to appear from an outhouse nearby. Empress Lü told him all about how the traveler had passed by and, examining her and her children, had predicted great honor for all of them. When Kao-tsu inquired where the man was, she replied, "He cannot have gone very far away!"

Kao-tsu ran after the old man and, overtaking him, questioned him. "The lady and the little children I examined a while ago," he replied, "all resemble you. But when I examine your face, I find such worth that I cannot express it in words!"

Kao-tsu thanked him, saying "If it is really as you say, I will surely not forget your kindness!" But when Kao-tsu finally became honored he could never find out where the old man had gone.

When Kao-tsu was acting as village head, he fashioned a kind of hat out of sheaths of bamboo and sent his "thief-seeker"[3] to the district of Hsieh to have some made up for him, which he wore from time to time. Even after he became famous he continued to wear these hats. These are the so-called Liu family hats.

As village head Kao-tsu was ordered to escort a group of forced laborers from the district of P'ei to Mount Li.[4] On the way, however, so many of the laborers ran away that Kao-tsu began to suspect that by the time he reached his destination they would all have disappeared. When they had reached a place in the midst of a swamp west of Feng, Kao-tsu halted and began to drink. That night he loosened the bonds of the laborers he was escorting and freed them, saying, "Go, all of you! I too shall go my own way from here."

Among the laborers were ten or so brave men who asked to go with him. Kao-tsu, full of wine, led the men in the night along a path through the swamp, sending one of them to walk ahead. The man who had gone ahead returned and reported, "There is a great snake lying across the path ahead. I beg you to turn back!"

"Where a brave man marches what is there to fear?" replied Kao-tsu drunkenly and, advancing, drew his sword and slashed at the snake. After he had cut the snake in two and cleared the path, he walked on a mile or so and then lay down to sleep off his drunkenness.

When one of the men who had lagged behind came to the place where the snake lay, he found an old woman crying in the night. He asked her why she was crying and she answered, "I am crying because someone has killed my son."

"How did your son come to be killed?" he asked.

"My son was the son of the White Emperor," said the old woman. "He had changed himself into a snake and was lying across the road. Now he has been cut in two by the son of the Red Emperor, and therefore I weep."

The man did not believe the old woman and was about to accuse her of lying, when suddenly she disappeared. When the man caught up with Kao-tsu, he found him already awake and reported what

---

[3] A subordinate official in the local administration.
[4] Where the First Emperor of Ch'in was building his mausoleum.

had happened. Kao-tsu was very pleased in his heart and set great store by the incident, while his followers day by day regarded him with greater awe.

The First Emperor of Ch'in, repeatedly declaring that there were signs in the southeastern sky indicating the presence of a "Son of Heaven," decided to journey east to suppress the threat to his power. Kao-tsu, suspecting that he himself was the cause of the visit, fled into hiding among the rocky wastes of the mountains and swamps between Mang and Tang. Empress Lü and others who went with her to look for him, however, were always able to find him. Kao-tsu, wondering how she could do this, asked her and she replied, "There are always signs in the clouds over the place where you are. By following these we manage to find you every time." Kao-tsu was very pleased in his heart. When word of this circulated among the young men of the district of P'ei, many of them sought to become his followers.

In the autumn of the first year of the reign of the Second Emperor of Ch'in [209] Ch'en She and his band arose in Chi. When Ch'en She had reached the area of Ch'en and made himself a king with the title of "Magnifier of Ch'u," many of the provinces and districts murdered their head officials and joined in the rebellion.

The magistrate of P'ei, fearful of what might happen, wished to declare P'ei a party to the rebellion, but his chief officials Hsiao Ho and Ts'ao Ts'an said, "You are an official of Ch'in. Now, though you hope to turn your back on Ch'in and lead the men of P'ei, we fear they will not listen to you. We would suggest that you summon all the various men who have fled and are in hiding elsewhere. You should be able to obtain several hundred men, and with these you can threaten the rest of the people and force them to obey you."

Accordingly the magistrate sent Fan K'uai to summon Kao-tsu, who by this time had almost a hundred followers. Kao-tsu came with Fan K'uai, but the magistrate, repenting his action and fearing a move against himself, closed the gates and guarded the city, preparing to execute Hsiao Ho and Ts'ao Ts'an. Hsiao Ho and Ts'ao Ts'an in fear climbed over the wall and fled to Kao-tsu's protection. Kao-tsu then wrote a message on a piece of silk and shot it over the city walls saying, "The world has long suffered beneath Ch'in. Now, though you men of P'ei should guard the city for the sake of the magistrate, the other nobles who have risen in rebellion will join in massacring the inhabitants of the city. If you will unite and do away with the magistrate, select from among your sons a worthy man to be your leader, and declare yourselves with the other nobles, then your homes and families shall all be spared. But if you do not, you will all be massacred without further ado!"

The elders then led the young men and together they murdered the magistrate of P'ei, opened the city gates, and welcomed Kao-tsu. They wished to make him magistrate, but Kao-tsu announced, "The world today is in chaos with the nobles rising up everywhere. If you do not make a wise choice of a leader now, you will be cut down in one stroke and your blood will drench the earth. It is not that I care for my own safety, but only that I fear my abilities are not sufficient to insure your welfare. This is a most serious business. I beg you to consult once more among yourselves and select someone who is truly worthy."

Hsiao Ho, Ts'ao Ts'an, and the other civil officials were concerned for their own safety and, fearful that if they assumed leadership and the undertaking proved unsuccessful, Ch'in would exterminate their families, they all yielded in favor of Kao-tsu. Then all the elders announced. "For a long time we have heard of the strange and wonderful happenings and the predictions of greatness concerning Liu Chi. Moreover, when we divine by the tortoise and milfoil, we find that no one receives such responses as Liu Chi!" With this, Kao-tsu declined several times but, since no one else dared to accept the position, he allowed himself to be made governor of P'ei. He then performed sacrifices to the Yellow Emperor and to the ancient warrior Ch'ih Yu in the district office of P'ei and anointed his drums with the blood of the sacrifice. All his flags and banners he had made of red. Because the old woman had said that it was the son of the Red Emperor who had killed the snake, the son of the White Emperor, he decided to honor the color red in this fashion.

The young men and distinguished officials such as Hsiao Ho, Ts'ao Ts'an, Fan K'uai, and others gathered together for him a band of two or three thousand men of P'ei and attacked Hu-ling and Fang-yü. They then returned and guarded the city of Feng.

In the second year of the Second Emperor [208 B.C.] Ch'en She's general Chou Wen marched west with his army as far as Hsi and then returned. Yen, Chao, Ch'i, and Wei all set up their own kings and Hsiang Liang and Hsiang Yü began their uprising in Wu.

Ch'in's overseer in the province of Ssu River, a man named P'ing, led a force of troops and surrounded Feng for two days. The governor of P'ei marched out of the city and fought and defeated him. Then, ordering Yung Ch'ih to guard Feng, he led his troops to Hsieh. The magistrate of Ssu River, Chuang, was defeated at Hsieh and fled to Ch'i, where the governor P'ei's marshal of the left captured and killed him. The governor of P'ei returned and camped in the district of K'ang-fu, proceeding as far as Fang-yü. Chou Shih had arrived to attack Fang-yü, but had not yet engaged in battle. (Chou Shih was a man of Wei who had been sent by Ch'en She to seize the area.)

Chou Shih sent an envoy to Yung Ch'ih, who was guarding Feng, saying, "Feng was originally a colony of Liang, which was part of Wei. Now we have captured more than ten cities of Wei. If you will submit to Wei, Wei will make you a marquis. But if you persist in holding Feng and refuse to surrender, we will massacre the inhabitants."

Yung Ch'ih had originally had no desire to ally himself with the governor of P'ei and, when he was thus invited by Wei, he revolted and held the city of Feng in Wei's name. The governor of P'ei led his troops in an attack on Feng, but was unable to take it. Falling ill, he returned to P'ei.

The governor of P'ei was bitter because Yung Ch'ih and the men of Feng had turned against him. When he heard that Lord Ning of Tung-yang and Ch'in Chia had set up Ching Chü as acting king of Ch'u in Liu, he made his way there and joined them, requesting that they give him soldiers to attack Feng. At this time the Ch'in general Chang Han, pursuing Ch'en She's special general Ssu-ma I, led his troops north to pacify the region of Ch'u, massacring the inhabitants of Hsiang and marching as far as Tang. Lord Ning of Tung-yang and the governor of P'ei led their troops west and fought with him west of Hsiao, but they could win no advantage. Returning, they gathered together their troops in Liu and led them in an attack on Tang. After three days they seized Tang and, adding to their forces some five or six thousand men captured at Tang, attacked and overcame Hsia-i. Then they returned and camped near Feng.

Hearing that Hsiang Liang was in Hsieh, the governor of P'ei, accompanied by some hundred horsemen, went to see him. Hsiang Liang gave him five thousand foot soldiers and ten generals of the rank of fifth lord. The governor of P'ei then returned and led his troops in an attack on Feng.

A month or so after the governor of P'ei had allied himself with Hsiang Liang, Hsiang Yü captured the city of Hsiang-ch'eng and returned. Hsiang Liang then summoned all his various generals to come to Hsieh. Here, having received positive news that Ch'en She was dead, he set up Hsin, grandson of the former King Huai of Ch'u, as king of Ch'u, with his capital at Hsü-i. Hsiang Liang himself took the title of lord of Wu-hsin. After several months he marched north to attack K'ang-fu, rescued the city of Tung-a, and defeated the Ch'in army. Then, while Ch'i led its troops back to its own territory, Hsiang Liang alone pursued the defeated Ch'in army north, dispatching the governor of P'ei and Hsiang Yü with a special force to attack Ch'eng-yang. After massacring the inhabitants of Ch'eng-yang, they camped east of P'u-yang, where they fought with the Ch'in forces and defeated them.

The Ch'in army, recovering from this blow, defended its position at P'u-yang by encircling it with water. The Ch'u army then withdrew and attacked Ting-t'ao, but was unable to conquer it. The governor of P'ei and Hsiang Yü seized the area to the west. Arriving before the walls of Yung-ch'iu, they again engaged the Ch'in forces and gravely defeated them, cutting down the Ch'in general Li Yu. They returned and attacked Wai-huang, but were unable to conquer it. Hsiang Liang in the meantime had inflicted another defeat on Ch'in and began to grow proud and boastful. Sung I cautioned him about this, but he would not listen. Ch'in then sent reinforcements to aid Chang Han. Putting gags in the mouths of his men,[5] Chang Han made a night

[5] To prevent them from talking or shouting during the surprise attack.

attack on Hsiang Liang and inflicted a crushing defeat. Hsiang Liang was killed in the battle.

The governor of P'ei and Hsiang Yü were at the time attacking Ch'en-liu but, hearing of Hsiang Liang's death, they joined forces with General Lü Ch'en and marched east. Lü Ch'en camped east of P'eng-ch'eng, Hsiang Yü to the west, and the governor of P'ei at Tang.

Chang Han, having defeated Hsiang Liang, felt that he had nothing more to worry about from the soldiers of the region of Ch'u. Therefore he crossed the Yellow River and marched north to attack Chao, inflicting a severe defeat. At this time the Ch'in general Wang Li surrounded Chao Hsieh, the king of Chao, in the city of Chü-lu. This was the so-called Army North of the River.

In the third year of the Second Emperor [207 B.C.], when King Huai of Ch'u saw that Hsiang Liang's army had been defeated, he grew fearful and moved his capital from Hsü-i to P'eng-ch'eng, where he combined the armies of Lü Ch'en and Hsiang Yü, and himself took command of the troops. He made the governor of P'ei head of Tang Province, enfeoffed him as marquis of Wu-an, and put him in command of the troops of Tang. Hsiang Yü he enfeoffed as marquis of Ch'ang-an with the title of "Duke of Lu." Lü Ch'en was appointed minister of instruction and his father, Lü Ch'ing, was made prime minister.

Since Chao had several times sent pleas for aid, King Huai made Sung I supreme general, Hsiang Yü second general, and Fan Tseng third general, and sent them north to rescue Chao. The governor of P'ei he ordered to seize the region to the west and enter the Pass, making a promise with the various leaders that whoever should enter the Pass first and conquer the area within should become king of the region.

At this time the Ch'in forces were still very strong and took advantage of their supremacy to pursue those they had defeated, so that none of the leaders of the rebellion was anxious to be the first to enter the Pass. But Hsiang Yü, embittered over the defeat of Hsiang Liang's army by Ch'in, angrily demanded to be allowed to go west with the governor of P'ei and attempt to enter the Pass.

King Huai's elder generals all advised him, saying, "Hsiang Yü is by nature extremely impetuous and cruel. When he attacked and conquered the city of Hsiang-ch'eng, he butchered every one of the inhabitants without mercy. Wherever he has passed he has left behind him destruction and death. The armies of Ch'u have several times in the past advanced and won gains, but Ch'en She and Hsiang Liang were both in the end defeated. This time it would be better to send a man of true moral worth who, relying upon righteousness, will proceed west and make a proclamation to the elders of Ch'in. The men of Ch'in have long suffered under their rulers. Now if we can send a truly worthy man who will not come to them with rapine and violence in his heart, we can surely persuade them to submit. Hsiang Yü is far too impetuous to be sent. Only the governor of P'ei, who from the first has shown himself to be a man of tolerance and moral stature, is worthy to go."

In the end King Huai refused to grant Hsiang Yü's request, but dispatched only the governor of P'ei who, gathering up the scattered remnants of Ch'en She's and Hsiang Liang's armies, marched out of Tang to seize the region to the west. Proceeding to Ch'eng-yang and Chiang-li, he threw his weight against the Ch'in fortifications there and defeated both garrisons. (In the meantime the Ch'u forces under Hsiang Yü had attacked the Ch'in general Wang Li at Chü-lu and severely defeated him.)

The governor of P'ei led his forces west and joined P'eng Yüeh at Ch'ang-i. Together they attacked the Ch'in forces but, failing to achieve a victory, retreated to Li. Here they met the marquis of Kang-wu, seized the troops under his command amounting to about four thousand men, and added them to their own forces. Then, joining the armies of the Wei general Huang Hsin and the Wei minister of works Wu P'u, they attacked Ch'ang-i again but, being unable to capture it, proceeded west past Kao-yang.

Li I-chi, the village gatekeeper,[6] remarked, "Many generals have passed through this region, but I can see that the governor of P'ei is the most magnanimous and worthy of them all." Then he requested to be allowed to meet the governor of P'ei and speak with him. At the

[6] Following the *Han shu* reading.

time the governor was sitting sprawled upon a couch with two servant girls washing his feet. When Master Li [7] entered, he did not make the customary prostration but instead gave a very deep bow and said, "If you truly desire to punish the evil rulers of Ch'in, it is hardly proper to receive one who is your elder in this slovenly fashion!"

With this the governor arose, straightened his clothes, and apologized, showing Master Li to a seat of honor. Master Li then explained to him how to assault Ch'en-liu and capture the stores of grain which Ch'in had there. The governor of P'ei gave Li I-chi the title of "Lord of Kuang-yeh" and made his brother Li Shang a general, putting him in command of the troops of Ch'en-liu. Together they attacked K'ai-feng but, failing to capture it, proceeded west and engaged the Ch'in general Yang Hsiung in battle at Po-ma and again east of Ch'ü-yung, severely defeating him. Yang Hsiung fled to Jung-yang where, in order to serve as a warning to the rest of the army, he was executed by an envoy sent from the Second Emperor.

The governor of P'ei attacked Ying-yang, massacring its defenders, and then, relying upon the guidance of Chang Liang, proceeded to seize the area of Huan-yüan in the region of Hann. At this time Ssu-ma Ang, a general dispatched by Chao, was about to cross the Yellow River in hopes of entering the Pass. In order to prevent him, the governor of P'ei marched north to attack P'ing-yin, destroyed the fording place across the Yellow River, and then continued south to battle with the Ch'in forces east of Lo-yang. Being unsuccessful here, he withdrew to Yang-ch'eng, gathered together all his horsemen, and attacked and defeated I, the governor of Nan-yang Province, east of Ch'ou. He seized the province of Nan-yang while the governor, I, fled to the city of Yüan for protection.

The governor of P'ei was about to lead his troops on to the west, but Chang Liang cautioned him, saying, "Although you wish to enter the Pass as soon as possible, there are a great many soldiers of Ch'in holding the strong points. Now if you march on without seizing the city of Yüan, Yüan will attack you from behind. With the power of Ch'in awaiting you ahead, your way will be fraught with danger!" Accordingly the governor of P'ei led his troops back by another road

---

[7] So called because he was a Confucian scholar.

at night, changed his flags and pennants, and just before dawn encircled the city of Yüan with several bands of troops. The governor of Nan-yang was about to cut his throat when one of his followers, Ch'en Hui, stopped him, saying, "There is still plenty of time to die." Then he climbed over the city wall and appeared before the governor of P'ei. "I have heard," he said, "that Your Lordship has made an agreement that whoever shall enter the capital city of Hsien-yang first will become its king. But now you have stayed your march in order to invest the city of Yüan. Yüan is the capital of a great province, with twenty or thirty cities under its control. Its people are numerous and its stores of provisions plentiful. Our officers believe that if they surrender they will certainly be put to death and therefore they have all mounted the walls and are firmly guarding their city. Now if you wear out your days remaining here attacking the city, many of your men are bound to suffer injury and death, while if you lead your troops away from Yüan, Yüan will surely pursue you from behind. Should you choose the former course you will never reach Hsien-yang in time to take advantage of the agreement, while should you choose the latter you will be bedeviled by the power of Yüan. If I were to suggest a plan for you, I would say it is best to promise to enfeoff the governor if he surrenders. Then you may leave him behind to guard the city for you while you lead his troops with you to the west. When the other cities that have not submitted hear of your action, they will hasten to open their gates and await your coming, so that your passage will be freed from all hindrance."

The governor of P'ei approved this idea and accordingly made the governor of Yüan marquis of Yin and enfeoffed Ch'en Hui with a thousand households. Then he led his troops west, and all the cities without exception submitted to him. When he reached the Tan River, Sai, the marquis of Kao-wu, and Wang Ling, the marquis of Hsiang, surrendered the area of Hsi-ling to him. Then he turned back and attacked Hu-yang where he met Mei Hsüan, special general of Wu Jui, the lord of P'o, and together they conquered Hsi and Li.

The governor of P'ei dispatched Ning Ch'ang, a man of Wei, as his envoy to the court of Ch'in. But he had not yet returned when Chang Han surrendered his army to Hsiang Yü at Chao. (Earlier, Hsiang Yü and Sung I had marched north to rescue Chao from the Ch'in attack. Later, when Hsiang Yü murdered Sung I and took his place as supreme general, Ch'ing Pu and the other leaders joined with him. He then defeated the army of the Ch'in general Wang Li, received the surrender of Chang Han, and secured command over all the other leaders.)

After Chao Kao had murdered the Second Emperor, the governor of P'ei's envoy returned with a promise from Ch'in to divide the area within the Pass and make the governor a king over part of it. Believing this to be a trick, however, the governor followed the strategy suggested by Chang Liang and sent Master Li and Lu Chia to go and bargain with the Ch'in generals and tempt them to treason with offers of profit, while he himself proceeded to attack the Wu Pass and capture it. He also fought with the Ch'in armies at Lan-t'ien, disposing his soldiers and increasing the number of his flags and pennants in such a way as to make his forces appear greater than they actually were. Wherever he passed, he forbade his men to plunder or seize prisoners. The people of Ch'in were delighted at this mildness and the Ch'in armies grew unwary so that they suffered great defeat. He also fought to the north of Lan-t'ien and inflicted a major defeat. Taking advantage of these victories, he was able at last to destroy the Ch'in armies.

In the tenth month of the first year of Han [November–December, 207 B.C.] the governor of P'ei finally succeeded in reaching Pa-shang ahead of the other leaders. Tzu-ying, the king of Ch'in, came in a plain carriage drawn by a white horse, wearing a rope about his neck,[8] and surrendered the imperial seals and credentials by the side of Chih Road. Some of the generals asked that the king of Ch'in be executed, but the governor of P'ei replied, "The reason King Huai first sent me upon this mission was that he sincerely believed I was capable of showing tolerance and mercy. Now to kill a man who has already surrendered would only bring bad luck!" With this he turned the king of Ch'in over to the care of his officials. Then he proceeded west

---

[8] White is the color of mourning, while the rope indicated total submission. Tzu-ying had succeeded the Second Emperor as ruler of Ch'in, but because of the wobbly state of his empire had ventured only to call himself "king."

and entered Hsien-yang. He hoped to stay and rest for a while in the palaces of Ch'in, but Fan K'uai and Chang Liang advised him against this. Therefore he sealed up the storehouses containing Ch'in's treasures and wealth and returned to camp at Pa-shang. There he summoned all the distinguished and powerful men of the districts and addressed them, saying:

"Gentlemen, for a long time you have suffered beneath the harsh laws of Ch'in. Those who criticized the government were wiped out along with their families; those who gathered to talk in private were executed in the public market. I and the other nobles have made an agreement that he who first enters the Pass shall rule over the area within. Accordingly I am now king of this territory within the Pass. I hereby promise you a code of laws consisting of three articles only: He who kills anyone shall suffer death; he who wounds another or steals shall be punished according to the gravity of the offense; for the rest I hereby abolish all the laws of Ch'in. Let the officials and people remain undisturbed as before. I have come only to save you from further harm, not to exploit or tyrannize over you. Therefore do not be afraid! The reason I have returned to Pa-shang is simply to wait for the other leaders so that when they arrive we may settle the agreement."

He sent men to go with the Ch'in officials and publish this proclamation in the district towns and villages. The people of Ch'in were overjoyed and hastened with cattle, sheep, wine, and food to present to the soldiers. But the governor of P'ei declined all such gifts, saying, "There is plenty of grain in the granaries. I do not wish to be a burden to the people." With this the people were more joyful than ever and their only fear was that the governor of P'ei would not become king of Ch'in.

Someone advised the governor of P'ei, saying, "The area of Ch'in is ten times richer than the rest of the empire and the land is protected by strong natural barriers. Now word has come that Chang Han has surrendered to Hsiang Yü and that Hsiang Yü therefore has granted him the title of king of Yung, intending to make him ruler of the area within the Pass. If he arrives, I fear that you will not be able to maintain your present claim. It would be best to send soldiers at once to guard the Han-ku Pass and prevent any of the armies of the other leaders from entering. In the meantime you can little by little gather up soldiers from the area within the Pass and lead them yourself to reinforce those blocking the Pass." The governor of P'ei approved this plan and set about putting it into effect.

During the eleventh month Hsiang Yü led the troops of the various armies west, as the governor had expected, and attempted to enter the Pass. Finding the Pass blocked and hearing that the governor of P'ei had already conquered the land within the Pass, he was greatly enraged and sent Ch'ing Pu and others to attack and break through the Han-ku Pass. In the twelfth month he finally reached Hsi.

Ts'ao Wu-shang, marshal of the left to the governor of P'ei, hearing that Hsiang Yü was angry and wished to attack the governor of P'ei, sent a messenger to speak to Hsiang Yü, saying, "The governor of P'ei hopes to become king of the area within the Pass, employing Tzu-ying as his prime minister and keeping possession of all the precious articles and treasures of the capital." (He thought that by reporting thus he would be rewarded by Hsiang Yü with a fief.)

Fan Tseng strongly urged Hsiang Yü to attack the governor of P'ei. Accordingly Hsiang Yü feasted his soldiers and prepared to join in battle the following day. At this time Hsiang Yü claimed to have a force of 1,000,000 men, though the actual number was 400,000, while the governor of P'ei claimed a force of 200,000, which was actually only 100,000. Thus they were no match for each other in strength.

As it happened, Hsiang Po, hoping to save the life of his friend Chang Liang, had gone the night before to see Chang Liang and as a result was able to convince Hsiang Yü of the governor of P'ei's loyalty, so that Hsiang Yü abandoned his plan to attack. The governor of P'ei, accompanied by some hundred horsemen, hastened to Hung-men, where he met Hsiang Yü and apologized to him. Hsiang Yü replied, "It is your own marshal of the left, Ts'ao Wu-shang, who informed against you. If it were not for him, how would I ever have doubted you?" The governor of P'ei, through the efforts of Fan K'uai and Chang Liang, was at last able to escape and return to his own camp. Upon his return he immediately executed Ts'ao Wu-shang.

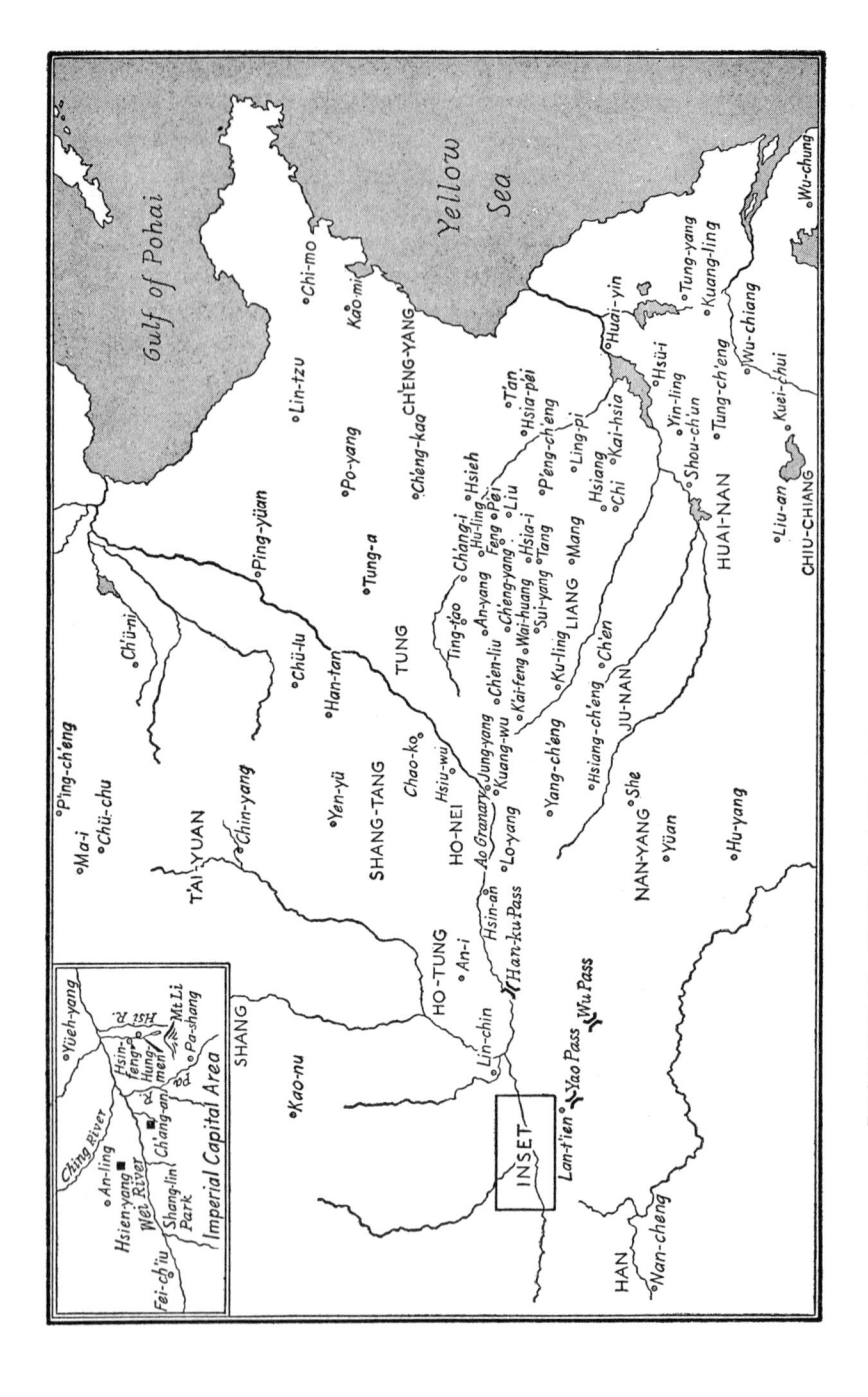

PRINCIPAL CITIES AND AREAS MENTIONED IN THE TEXT

Hsiang Yü then proceeded west and massacred the inhabitants of Hsien-yang, burning the city and the palaces of Ch'in, and leaving destruction everywhere he passed. The people of Ch'in were filled with despair, but they were so terrified they had no courage to resist. Hsiang Yü sent a messenger to return and report to King Huai. "Let all be done according to the agreement," King Huai replied. Hsiang Yü was angry that the king had not allowed him to march west with the governor of P'ei and enter the Pass, but instead had sent him north to rescue Chao, thus causing him to miss out on the agreement concerning the rulership of the area within the Pass. "King Huai," he said, "was set up solely through the efforts of my uncle Hsiang Liang. He has won no merit of his own. Why should he be made arbiter of the agreement? It is the other generals and I who actually conquered the empire!" Then he pretended to honor King Huai by giving him the title of "Righteous Emperor," but in fact paid no attention to his commands.

In the first month Hsiang Yü set himself up as "Dictator King of Western Ch'u," ruling nine provinces of Liang and Ch'u, with his capital at P'eng-ch'eng. In violation of the former agreement he made the governor of P'ei king of Han instead of Ch'in, giving him the lands of Pa, Shu, and Han to rule, with his capital at Nan-cheng. The area within the Pass he divided into three parts, setting up three former generals of Ch'in: Chang Han as king of Yung with his capital at Fei-ch'iu, Ssu-ma Hsin as king of Sai with his capital at Yüeh-yang, and Tung I as king of Ti with his capital at Kao-nu. The Ch'u general Shen Yang of Hsia-ch'iu was made king of Ho-nan with his capital at Lo-yang, while the Chao general Ssu-ma Ang was made king of Yin, his capital at Chao-ko. Hsieh, the king of Chao, was transferred to the position of king of Tai, while his prime minister, Chang Erh, was made king of Ch'ang-shan with his capital at Hsiang-kuo. The lord of T'ang-yang, Ch'ing Pu, was made king of Chiu-chiang, his capital at Liu; Kung Ao, chief minister to King Huai, was made king of Lin-chiang, his capital at Chiang-ling. The lord of P'o, Wu Jui, became king of Heng-shan, his capital at Chu. The Yen general Tsang Tu was made king of Yen, his capital at Chi, after the former king of Yen, Han Kuang, had been ordered to remove to the position of king of Liao-tung. When Han Kuang refused to obey, Tsang Tu attacked and killed him at Wu-chung. Ch'en Yü, the lord of Ch'eng-an, was enfeoffed with three districts in Ho-chien, at his residence at Nan-p'i, while Mei Hsüan was enfeoffed with a hundred thousand households.

In the fourth month the various armies left the command of Hsiang Yü and proceeded with the feudal leaders to their respective territories. When the king of Han departed for his kingdom, Hsiang Yü allowed him to take along thirty thousand soldiers. Gathering a force of twenty or thirty thousand of the soldiers of Ch'u and the other leaders, he accordingly proceeded from Tu-nan and entered the Li Gorge. As he proceeded, he burned and destroyed the wooden roadway [9] behind him in order to prevent bandit troops of the other feudal lords from attacking him and, at the same time, to demonstrate to Hsiang Yü that he had no intention of marching east again.

When he reached Nan-cheng he found that many of his officers and men had deserted along the way and returned home, while those who were left all sang the songs of their homeland and longed to go back east. Han Hsin advised the king of Han, saying, "Hsiang Yü has made kings of all his generals who achieved merit, but you alone he has sent to live in Nan-cheng as though you were being exiled for some crime. The officers and soldiers of your army are all men of the east, and day and night they gaze into the distance longing to return home. If you take up your lance now and use it, you can win great glory. But if you wait until the world is settled and all men are at peace, then you cannot hope to take it up again. You had best lay plans to return east and fight for mastery of the world!"

When Hsiang Yü returned east through the Pass he sent a messenger to transfer the residence of the Righteous Emperor, announcing that "the emperors of ancient times who ruled an area a thousand miles on each side invariably resided on the upper reaches of a river." The envoy accordingly moved the Righteous Emperor to the district of Ch'en in Ch'ang-sha, pressing him to hurry on his way. With this the emperor's ministers became increasingly disillusioned and turned their backs upon him. Hsiang Yü then secretly ordered the kings of

[9] Built out over the steep side of the gorge.

Heng-shan and Lin-chiang to attack and murder the Righteous Emperor at Chiang-nan.

Hsiang Yü, being angry with T'ien Jung, set up T'ien Tu, a general of Ch'i, as king of Ch'i, but T'ien Jung, enraged at this, declared himself king of Ch'i, murdered T'ien Tu, and revolted against Ch'u. Then he presented P'eng Yüeh with the seals of office of a general and sent him to lead a revolt in the region of Liang. Ch'u ordered Chüeh, lord of Hsiao, to attack P'eng Yüeh, but P'eng Yüeh inflicted a severe defeat on him.

Ch'en Yü, angry that Hsiang Yü had not made him a king, dispatched Hsia Yüeh to plead with T'ien Jung and persuade him to send troops to attack Chang Erh, the king of Ch'ang-shan. Ch'i in response sent a body of soldiers to aid Ch'en Yü in attacking Chang Erh. Chang Erh fled from his territory and went to join the king of Han. Ch'en Yü then proceeded to Tai to fetch Hsieh, the former king of Chao, and restore him to his throne in Chao. In return, the king of Chao set up Ch'en Yü as king of Tai. Hsiang Yü, greatly enraged at these moves, marched north to attack Ch'i.

In the eighth month the king of Han, having decided to follow the plan outlined by Han Hsin, marched back by the Old Road and returned east to attack Chang Han, the king of Yung. Chang Han proceeded west to meet the attack, clashing with the Han forces at Ch'en-ts'ang. The soldiers of Yung were defeated and fled back east but halted to fight at Hao-chih. Defeated again, they fled to Fei-ch'iu. Thus the king of Han was able eventually to win control of the region of Yung and proceed east to Hsien-yang. He led his troops and surrounded the king of Yung at Fei-ch'iu, at the same time dispatching his generals to seize control of the provinces of Lung-hsi, Pei-ti, and Shang. He also ordered his generals Hsieh Ou and Wang Hsi to proceed by the Wu Pass, join the forces of Wang Ling at Nan-yang, and go to fetch his father and mother from P'ei.

When Hsiang Yü heard of this, he dispatched troops to block their march at Yang-hsia and prevent them from advancing. At the same time he made the former district magistrate of Wu, Cheng Ch'ang, king of Hann so that he could aid in blocking the Han forces.

In the second year [205 B.C.] the king of Han proceeded east, seizing control of the land. Ssu-ma Hsin, the king of Sai; Tung I, the king of Ti; and Shen Yang, the king of Ho-nan, all surrendered to him, but Cheng Ch'ang, the king of Hann, refused to submit. Therefore he dispatched Han Hsin to attack and defeat him. Out of the land he had conquered he created the provinces of Lung-hsi, Pei-ti, Shang, Wei-nan, Ho-shang, and Chung-ti within the Pass and beyond the Pass the province of Ho-nan. He made his grand commandant Han Hsin the new king of Hann. Among his generals all those who had defeated a force of ten thousand men or captured a province were enfeoffed with ten thousand households. He then ordered the border defenses north of the Yellow River to be repaired and manned, and turned over all of Ch'in's former royal hunting parks, gardens, and lakes to the people to be converted into fields for farming. In the first month he took Chang P'ing, the younger brother of the king of Yung, prisoner. A general amnesty was declared, freeing criminals. The king of Han journeyed beyond the Pass as far as Hsia, looking after the wants of the people beyond the Pass. On his return, Chang Erh came to see him and the king of Han received him with kindness and generosity.

In the second month the king of Han gave orders for Ch'in's altars of the soil and grain to be abolished, and the altars of Han set up in their place.

In the third month the king of Han proceeded through Lin-chin and crossed the Yellow River, where Pao, the king of Wei, led his troops to join him. He conquered Ho-nei and took Ssu-ma Ang, the king of Yin, prisoner, making his territory into the province of Ho-nei. Proceeding south, he crossed the Yellow River at the P'ing-yin Ford and reached Lo-yang. Here Lord Tung, the elder of Hsin-ch'eng,[10] intercepted him and informed him of the death of the Righteous Emperor. When he heard this the king of Han bared his arms and lamented loudly. He then proclaimed a period of mourning for the sake of the emperor, with three days of lamentation, and dispatched envoys to report to the other nobles, saying, "The people of the world have joined together in setting up the Righteous Emperor and serving him as their sovereign. But now Hsiang Yü has banished him from

---

[10] The "elders" or *san-lao* were distinguished men over fifty chosen from among the common people to act as consultants to government officials.

his throne and murdered him at Chiang-nan. This is a most treasonable and heinous offense! I myself have proclaimed mourning on his behalf, and I trust the other lords will join me in donning the plain white garments of sorrow. Then I shall lead forth all the troops of the area within the Pass, gather together the forces of the three lands along the river, and in the south descend by the Han and Yangtze rivers, begging to join with the other lords and kings in attacking him of Ch'u who is the murderer of the Righteous Emperor!"

At this time Hsiang Yü had marched north to attack Ch'i, fighting with T'ien Jung at Ch'eng-yang. T'ien Jung was defeated and fled to P'ing-yüan, where the people of P'ing-yüan killed him, and with this all of Ch'i surrendered to the forces of Ch'u. But Hsiang Yü burned its cities and fortifications and enslaved its women and children until the men of Ch'i once more rose up in revolt. T'ien Jung's younger brother, T'ien Heng, set up T'ien Jung's son Kuang as king of Ch'i, holding the area of Ch'eng-yang in revolt against Ch'u.

Although Hsiang Yü had received word of the king of Han's march to the east, he was already engaged in a struggle with the forces of Ch'i and hoped to accomplish their defeat before proceeding to attack Han. For this reason the king of Han was able to commandeer the troops of five of the feudal lords and eventually enter the city of P'eng-ch'eng. When Hsiang Yü received news of this, he led his forces back from Ch'i, marching from Lu through Hu-ling as far as Hsiao, where he engaged the king of Han in a great battle at P'eng-ch'eng and east of Ling-pi on the Sui River, inflicting a severe defeat. So many of the Han officers and men were killed that the Sui River was blocked and ceased to flow. Then Hsiang Yü seized the parents, wife, and children of the king of Han at P'ei and placed them under guard in the midst of his army as hostages.

At this time, when the other nobles saw that the Ch'u forces were very strong and the Han forces were retreating in defeat, they all deserted Han and went over again to the side of Ch'u. Ssu-ma Hsin, the king of Sai, fled to Ch'u. The older brother of the king of Han's wife, Lü Tse, the marquis of Chou-lü, commanded a force of Han soldiers at Hsia-i, and the king of Han, joining him, gradually managed to gather together his soldiers and form an army at Tang. He then marched west through the territory of Liang as far as Yü. There he dispatched Sui Ho, his master of guests, as an envoy to go to the residence of Ch'ing Pu, the king of Chiu-chiang, telling him, "If you can persuade Ch'ing Pu to raise an army and revolt against Ch'u, Hsiang Yü will be bound to halt his advance and attack him. If I can get Hsiang Yü to delay for a few months, I will surely be able to seize control of the empire!" Sui Ho went and pleaded with Ch'ing Pu, who as a result revolted against Ch'u. With this, Hsiang Yü dispatched Lung Chü to go and attack him.

When the king of Han was marching west after his defeat at P'eng-ch'eng, he sent someone to look for the members of his family, but they had in the meantime all fled and he could not find them. After his defeat he was able to locate only his son (later Emperor Hui). In the sixth month he set up his son as heir apparent, proclaiming a general amnesty, and left him to guard the city of Yüeh-yang. All the relatives of the feudal lords in the area within the Pass gathered in Yüeh-yang to act as the heir apparent's bodyguards. Then the king of Han dug canals and flooded the city of Fei-ch'iu. Fei-ch'iu surrendered and its king, Chang Han, committed suicide. The king of Han changed the name of the city to Huai-li. At this time he ordered the officials in charge of religious ceremonies to perform sacrifices to heaven and earth, the four directions, the Lord on High, and the various mountains and rivers, all to be celebrated at the due seasons. He raised a force of soldiers from the area within the Pass to man the various fortifications.

At this time Ch'ing Pu, the king of Chiu-chiang, was fighting with Lung Chü but, failing to gain a victory, he proceeded with Sui Ho by a secret route and joined the forces of Han. The king of Han gradually recruited more soldiers and, with the other generals and the troops from within the Pass, little by little advanced. Thus he was able to muster a great force at Jung-yang and defeat the Ch'u army in the area of So in Ching.

In the third year [204 B.C.] Wei Pao, the king of Wei, begged leave to return to his home and look after his ailing parents but, when he had reached his destination, he cut off the ford across the Yellow River, revolted against Han, and declared himself in alliance with

Ch'u. The king of Han sent Master Li I-chi to persuade him to reconsider, but Wei Pao refused to listen. The king then dispatched his general Han Hsin, who inflicted a decisive defeat and took Wei Pao prisoner. Thus the king of Han managed to conquer the region of Wei, which he made into three provinces, Ho-tung, T'ai-yüan, and Shang-tang. He ordered Chang Erh and Han Hsin to proceed east down the Ching Gorge and attack Chao, where they executed Ch'en Yü and Hsieh, the king of Chao. The following year Chang Erh was made king of Chao.

The king of Han camped south of Jung-yang and constructed a walled supply road following along the banks of the Yellow River in order to transport grain from the Ao Granary. Here he and Hsiang Yü remained at an impasse for well over a year.

Hsiang Yü had several times attacked and cut off the Han supply road, and the Han army was growing very short of provisions. Finally Hsiang Yü succeeded in surrounding the king of Han, who made a bid for peace, suggesting that they divide the empire in two, he himself to retain all the land west of Jung-yang as part of Han. When Hsiang Yü refused to consent to this, the king of Han was much distressed but, following a plan suggested by Ch'en P'ing, he gave Ch'en P'ing a sum of forty thousand catties of gold to use as bribes in causing dissension between the leaders of Ch'u. As a result Hsiang Yü began to doubt his aide, Fan Tseng. Fan Tseng at the time was urging Hsiang Yü to carry through the assault on Jung-yang but, when he found that his loyalty was doubted, he grew angry and begged leave to retire, requesting that he be relieved of his duties and returned to the ranks of a common soldier. His request was granted and he departed, but died before he reached P'eng-ch'eng.

The Han army had by this time run completely out of food. The king of Han dressed some two thousand women in armor and sent them out at night from the eastern gate of Jung-yang. When the Ch'u forces flocked from all directions to attack them, the Han general Chi Hsin, in order to deceive Ch'u, rode forth in the royal chariot, pretending to be the king of Han. With shouts of victory, the men of Ch'u all rushed to the eastern side of the city walls to see him. In this way the king of Han, accompanied by twenty or thirty horsemen, was able to slip out by the western gate and flee, leaving the grand secretary Chou K'o, Wei Pao, the former king of Wei, and Lord Ts'ung to guard Jung-yang. The other generals and their men who had been unable to accompany the king all remained within the city. Chou K'o and Lord Ts'ung, agreeing with each other that it would be difficult to guard the city with the king of a country that had once revolted, proceeded to murder Wei Pao.

After the king of Han escaped from Jung-yang he retired within the Pass and gathered together more troops, hoping once more to march east. Master Yüan advised the king, saying, "While Han and Ch'u remained in stalemate at Jung-yang for several years, our men were in constant difficulty. I beg you this time to go out by the Wu Pass. Hsiang Yü will surely hasten south with his troops to meet you, and you may then take refuge behind heavy fortifications. In this way you can relieve the pressure on the men at Jung-yang and Ch'eng-kao, in the meantime sending Han Hsin and others to gather forces in Hopei and the region of Chao and to form an alliance with Yen and Ch'i. Then, if you should again march upon Jung-yang, it would still not be too late. Thus Ch'u will be obliged to guard a number of points and its strength will be divided, while the Han forces, having had time to rest before engaging in battle again, will certainly defeat Ch'u."

The king of Han, adopting this plan, proceeded with his army to the area between Yüan and She, he and Ch'ing Pu gathering troops as they went along. When Hsiang Yü heard that the king of Han was in Yüan, he led his forces south as had been expected, but the king of Han remained within his fortifications and would not engage in battle. At this time P'eng Yüeh crossed the Sui River and fought with the Ch'u general Hsiang Sheng and the lord of Hsieh at Hsia-p'ei, defeating their army. Hsiang Yü then led his troops east to attack P'eng Yüeh, while the king of Han in the meantime marched north and camped at Ch'eng-kao.

After Hsiang Yü had defeated P'eng Yüeh and put him to flight, he received news that the king of Han had moved his camp to Ch'eng-kao. He accordingly led his troops back west and seized Jung-yang, executing Chou K'o and Lord Ts'ung and taking Hsin, the king of Hann, prisoner, and then proceeded to surround Ch'eng-kao. The king of Han fled, accompanied only by Lord T'eng in a single carriage, escaping by the Jade Gate of the city of Ch'eng-kao.

Hastening north across the Yellow River, he stopped for a night at Little Hsiu-wu and at dawn the next day, pretending to be an envoy from the king of Han, hurriedly entered the fortifications of Chang Erh and Han Hsin and seized command of their armies. He at once dispatched Chang Erh to proceed north and gather more troops in the region of Chao and sent Han Hsin east to attack Ch'i.

Having gained command of Han Hsin's army and recovered his strength, the king of Han led his troops to the edge of the Yellow River and camped south of Little Hsiu-wu, facing south across the river. He intended to proceed once more to battle, but his attendant Cheng Chung advised him not to fight but instead to fortify his position with high walls and deep moats. The king followed this advice, sending Lu Wan and Liu Chia to lead a force of twenty thousand infantry and several hundred horsemen across the Yellow River at the White Horse Ford to invade Ch'u. They joined P'eng Yüeh in attacking and defeating the Ch'u army west of Yen-kuo, and then proceeded to seize control of ten or more cities in the region of Liang.

Han Hsin had already been ordered to march east but had not yet crossed the P'ing-yüan Ford when the king of Han dispatched Master Li I-chi to go to Ch'i and plead for him with T'ien Kuang, the king of Ch'i. As a result T'ien Kuang revolted against Ch'u and joined in alliance with Han, agreeing to participate in an attack on Hsiang Yü. But Han Hsin, following the advice of K'uai T'ung, proceeded to attack Ch'i in spite of this, inflicting a defeat. The king of Ch'i boiled Master Li I-chi alive for his supposed treachery and marched east to Kao-mi.

When Hsiang Yü heard that Han Hsin had already raised a force of troops north of the river, defeated Ch'i and Chao, and was about to attack Ch'u, he dispatched Lung Chü and Chou Lan to attack him. Han Hsin, aided in battle by the cavalry general Kuan Ying, attacked them and defeated the Ch'u army, killing Lung Chü. T'ien Kuang, the king of Ch'i, fled to join P'eng Yüeh. At this time P'eng Yüeh was in the region of Liang, leading his troops back and forth, harassing the Ch'u forces and cutting off their supplies of food.

In the fourth year [203 B.C.] Hsiang Yü said to the marquis of Hai-ch'un, the grand marshal Ts'ao Chiu, "Hold fast to the city of Ch'eng-kao. Even if the king of Han challenges you to a battle, take care and do not fight with him. By no means let him advance to the east. In fifteen days I will be able to bring the region of Liang under control, and then I will join you again." He then proceeded to attack and subdue Ch'en-liu, Wai-huang, and Sui-yang.

As Hsiang Yü had foreseen, the king of Han several times challenged the Ch'u armies to battle, but they refused to take up the challenge. Then the king of Han sent men to insult and revile them for five or six days, until the grand marshal in anger led his troops across the Ssu River. When the soldiers were halfway across the river the Han forces fell upon them, inflicting a crushing defeat on Ch'u and seizing all the gold, treasures, and wealth of the kingdom of Ch'u. The grand marshal Ts'ao Chiu and Ssu-ma Hsin, the king of Sai,[11] both committed suicide by cutting their throats on the banks of the Ssu.

When Hsiang Yü reached Sui-yang he received word of Ts'ao Chiu's defeat and led his forces back. The Han forces had at the time encircled Chung-li Mo at Jung-yang, but on Hsiang Yü's arrival they all fled to the safety of the mountains.

After Han Hsin had defeated Ch'i he sent someone to report to the king of Han, saying, "Ch'i lies directly upon the border of Ch'u and my grip upon it is still unsure. I fear that unless I am given the title of acting king I will not be able to hold the area."

The king of Han was in favor of attacking Han Hsin, but Chang Liang said, "It is better to comply with his request and make him a king so that he will guard the area in his own interest." The king of Han accordingly dispatched Chang Liang to present the seals and cords of authority, setting up Han Hsin as king of Ch'i. When Hsiang Yü heard that Han Hsin had defeated Lung Chü's army, he was very much afraid and sent Wu She, a man of Hsü-i, to attempt to bargain with Han Hsin, but Han Hsin would not listen to his arguments.

For a long while Ch'u and Han held their respective positions and

---

[11] Both here and in the corresponding passage in "The Annals of Hsiang Yü" there seems to be considerable confusion of names and titles. I have translated in accordance with suggested emendations.

made no decisive move, while their fighting men suffered the hardships of camp life and their old men and boys wore themselves out transporting provisions. The king of Han and Hsiang Yü faced each other across the ravine of Kuang-wu and talked back and forth. Hsiang Yü challenged the king of Han to meet him in single combat, but the king berated Hsiang Yü, saying, "When you and I bowed together before the command of King Huai, we agreed that whoever should enter the Pass first and conquer the land within should become its king. But you went back on this agreement, making me king of Shu and Han instead. This was your first crime. Feigning orders from King Huai, you murdered his lordship Sung I, the commander of the army, and elevated yourself to his position. This was your second crime. After you had gone to rescue Chao, it was proper that you should have returned and made your report to King Huai, but instead you wantonly seized the troops of the other leaders and entered the Pass. This was your third crime. King Huai had promised that whoever entered the Pass would commit no violence or theft. Yet you fired the palaces of Ch'in, desecrated the grave of the First Emperor, and appropriated the wealth and goods of Ch'in for your private use. This was your fourth crime. You inflicted violent death upon Tzu-ying, the king of Ch'in, who had already surrendered; this was your fifth crime. At Hsin-an you butchered two hundred thousand of the sons of Ch'in whom you had tricked into surrender and made their general, Chang Han, a king; this was your sixth crime. You enfeoffed all your generals as kings in the best lands and transferred or exiled the former kings, setting their subjects to strife and rebellion; this was your seventh crime. You drove the Righteous Emperor from P'eng-ch'eng and set up your own capital there, seized the territory of the king of Han and made yourself ruler of the combined areas of Liang and Ch'u, appropriating all for yourself. This was your eighth crime. You sent a man in secret to assassinate the Righteous Emperor at Chiang-nan, your ninth crime. As a subject you have assassinated your sovereign; you have murdered those who had already surrendered, administered your rule unjustly, and broken faith with the agreement that you made. You are guilty of such heinous treason as the world cannot forgive. This is your tenth crime. I and my soldiers of righteousness have joined with the other nobles to punish tyranny and rebellion. I have plenty of criminals and exconvicts that I can send to attack and kill you. Why should I go to the trouble of engaging in combat with you myself?"

Hsiang Yü was enraged and, with a crossbow that he had concealed, shot and hit the king of Han. The king was wounded in the breast, but he seized his foot and cried, "The scoundrel has hit me in the toe!" [12]

The king lay ill of his wound, but Chang Liang begged him to get up and walk about the camp in order to comfort and reassure his officers and men so that Ch'u would not be able to profit from its advantage. The king of Han went out and walked about his camp, but when the pain became too great he hurried into the city of Ch'eng-kao. After his wound had healed, he retired west through the Pass until he reached Yüeh-yang, where he held a feast for the elders of the city and set out wine for them. Then he had the head of the former king of Sai, Ssu-ma Hsin, exposed in the market place of his old capital, Yüeh-yang. After staying for four days the king returned to his army, which was still camped at Wu-kuang. A number of reinforcements of troops arrived from within the Pass.

At this time P'eng Yüeh was in the region of Liang, leading his troops back and forth, harassing the Ch'u forces and cutting off their supplies of food. T'ien Heng fled and joined him there. Hsiang Yü had several times attacked P'eng Yüeh and the others when Han Hsin, the new king of Ch'i, appeared and began to attack Ch'u as well. Hsiang Yü became fearful and made an agreement with the king of Han to divide the empire, all the territory west of the Hung Canal to belong to Han and all that east of the canal to belong to Ch'u. Hsiang Yü returned the king of Han's parents, wife, and children to him, amid cheers of welcome from the whole army of Han. Then the two leaders parted, and Hsiang Yü broke camp and started back east.

The king of Han was about to lead his forces west but, on the advice of Chang Liang and Ch'en P'ing, instead marched forward, sending his troops to pursue Hsiang Yü. When he reached the south of Yang-hsia, he stopped and made camp. He arranged with Han Hsin

[12] So that his men would not perceive the seriousness of his wound.

and P'eng Yüeh to meet on a certain date and join in an attack on Ch'u. But when he reached Ku-ling, they failed to appear for the meeting and Ch'u attacked Han, inflicting a grave defeat. The king of Han again withdrew behind his fortifications, deepened his moats, and guarded his position. Using a plan suggested by Chang Liang, he was finally able to induce Han Hsin and P'eng Yüeh to join him. Liu Chia also invaded Ch'u and surrounded Shou-ch'un. When the king of Han was defeated at Ku-ling, he sent an envoy to invite the grand marshal of Ch'u, Chou Yin, to revolt. Accordingly Chou Yin raised the forces of Chiu-chiang and marched to join Liu Chia and Ch'ing Pu, the king of Wu, in massacring the inhabitants of Ch'eng-fu. Following Liu Chia, he and the leaders of Ch'i and Liang all joined in a general meeting at Kai-hsia, at which Ch'ing Pu was made king of Huai-nan.

In the fifth year [202 B.C.] the king of Han with the forces of the other leaders joined in an attack on the army of Ch'u, fighting with Hsiang Yü for a decisive victory at Kai-hsia. Han Hsin led a force of three hundred thousand to attack in the center, with General K'ung leading the left flank and General Pi leading the right flank, while the king of Han followed behind. Chou P'o, the marquis of Chiang, and General Ch'ai followed behind the king. Hsiang Yü's troops numbered some one hundred thousand. Han Hsin advanced and joined in combat but, failing to gain the advantage, retired and allowed General K'ung and General Pi to close in from the sides. When the Ch'u forces began to falter, Han Hsin took advantage of their weakness to inflict a great defeat at Kai-hsia. The soldiers of Hsiang Yü, hearing the Han armies singing the songs of Ch'u, concluded that Han had already conquered the whole land of Ch'u. With this, Hsiang Yü fled in despair, leaving his soldiers to suffer total defeat. The king of Han dispatched his cavalry general Kuan Ying to pursue and kill Hsiang Yü at Tung-ch'eng. After cutting off the heads of eighty thousand of the enemy, he overran and conquered the land of Ch'u.

Lu held out on behalf of Hsiang Yü and refused to surrender but, when the king of Han led the forces of the various nobles north and displayed the head of Hsiang Yü before the elders of Lu, they finally capitulated. The king of Han buried Hsiang Yü at Ku-ch'eng with the title of "Duke of Lu." He then returned to Ting-t'ao, hastily entered the fortifications of Han Hsin, the king of Ch'i, and seized control of his army.

In the first month the various nobles and generals all joined in begging the king of Han to take the title of emperor, but he replied, "I have heard that the position of emperor may go only to a worthy man. It cannot be claimed by empty words and vain talk. I do not dare to accept the position of emperor."

His followers all replied, "Our great king has risen from the humblest beginnings to punish the wicked and violent and bring peace to all within the four seas. To those who have achieved merit he has accordingly parceled out land and enfeoffed them as kings and marquises. If our king does not assume the supreme title, then all our titles as well will be called into doubt. On pain of death we urge our request!"

The king of Han three times declined and then, seeing that he could do no more, said, "If you, my lords, consider it a good thing, then it must be to the good of the country." On the day *chia-wu* [13] [Feb. 28, 202 B.C.] he assumed the position of Supreme Emperor on the north banks of the Ssu River.

The Supreme Emperor declared, "The Righteous Emperor of Ch'u was without an heir, but Han Hsin, king of Ch'i, is well acquainted with the customs and ways of Ch'u." Accordingly he transferred Han Hsin to the position of king of Ch'u with his capital at Hsia-p'ei. Hsin, the former king of Hann, was confirmed in his title, with his capital at Yang-ti. P'eng Yüeh, the marquis of Chien-ch'eng, was made king of Liang, with his capital at Ting-t'ao; Wu Jui, the king of Heng-shan, was transferred to the position of king of Ch'ang-sha, his capital at Lin-hsiang. (Wu Jui's general, Mei Hsüan, had won merit in battle, while he himself had joined in the march through the Wu Pass, and therefore he was rewarded in this fashion.) Ch'ing Pu, the king of Huai-nan; Tsang Tu, the king of Yen; and Chang Ao,[14] the king of Chao, remained in their former positions. With the entire empire now

---

[13] To indicate days the Chinese employ a series of signs, the so-called ten stems and twelve branches, which combine to form sixty designations used to name the days (and in some cases the years) of a sixty-day or -year cycle.

[14] Chang Ao succeeded his father, Chang Erh, who had died this year.

at peace, Kao-tsu [15] made his capital at Lo-yang, where all the nobles acknowledged his sovereignty. Huan,[16] the former king of Lin-chiang, had in the name of Hsiang Yü revolted against Han, but Lu Wan and Liu Chia were sent to surround him and, though he held out for several months, he was eventually forced to surrender and was killed at Lo-yang.

In the fifth month the armies were disbanded and the soldiers returned to their homes. The relatives of the feudal lords who remained in the area within the Pass were exempted from all taxes and services for twelve years, while those who returned to their territories were exempted for six years and granted stipends of food for a year. Kao-tsu gave a banquet for the nobles in the Southern Palace of Lo-yang and announced, "My lords and generals, I ask you all to speak your minds quite frankly without daring to hide anything from me. Why is it that I won possession of the world and Hsiang Yü lost?"

Kao Ch'i and Wang Ling replied, "Your Majesty is arrogant and insulting to others, while Hsiang Yü was kind and loving. But when you send someone to attack a city or seize a region, you award him the spoils of the victory, sharing your gains with the whole world. Hsiang Yü was jealous of worth and ability, hating those who had achieved merit and suspecting anyone who displayed his wisdom. No matter what victories were achieved in battle, he gave his men no reward; no matter what lands they won, he never shared with them the spoils. This is why he lost possession of the world."

Kao-tsu said, "You have understood the first reason, but you do not know the second. When it comes to sitting within the tents of command and devising strategies that will assure us victory a thousand miles away, I am no match for Chang Liang. In ordering the state and caring for the people, in providing rations for the troops and seeing to it that the lines of supply are not cut off, I cannot compare to Hsiao Ho. In leading an army of a million men, achieving success with every battle and victory with every attack, I cannot come up to Han Hsin. These three are all men of extraordinary ability, and it

---

[15] From now on Liu Chi is called by his posthumous title, Kao-tsu, or "Exalted Ancestor."

[16] Probably a mistake for Kung Wei, who succeeded his father, Kung Ao, as king of Lin-chiang.

is because I was able to make use of them that I gained possession of the world. Hsiang Yü had his one Fan Tseng, but he did not know how to use him and thus he ended as my prisoner."

Kao-tsu wished to continue to make his capital at Lo-yang, but Liu Ching, a man of Ch'i, advised him against this and Chang Liang likewise urged him to establish his capital within the Pass. Accordingly on the same day Kao-tsu mounted his carriage and entered the Pass to take up residence there. In the sixth month he proclaimed a general amnesty for the empire.

In the seventh month Tsang Tu, the king of Yen, revolted, invading and seizing control of the land of Tai. Kao-tsu himself led a force to attack and capture him. He proceeded to set up the grand commandant Lu Wan as the new king of Yen, sending Fan K'uai with a force of troops to attack Tai.

In the autumn Li Chi revolted. Kao-tsu again led the troops in person to attack him, whereupon Li Chi fled. (Li Chi had originally been a general of the Hsiang family. When the Hsiangs were defeated, Li Chi, then the governor of the district of Ch'en, revoked his allegiance to the Hsiangs and fled and surrendered to Kao-tsu. Kao-tsu made him marquis of Ying-ch'uan. When Kao-tsu arrived in Lo-yang, he summoned to court all the marquises whose titles had thus far been registered, but Li Chi, misinterpreting the summons and fearing punishment for his former connection with the Hsiangs, revolted.)

The sixth year [201 B.C.]: Every five days Kao-tsu would go to visit his father, the "Venerable Sire," observing the etiquette proper for an ordinary son towards his father. The steward of his father's household spoke to the Venerable Sire, saying, "As heaven is without two suns, so the earth has not two lords. Now although the emperor is your son, he is the ruler of men, and although you are his father, you are his subject as well. How does it happen then that the ruler of men is doing obeisance to one of his subjects? If this is allowed to continue, the emperor's majesty will never prevail upon the world!"

The next time Kao-tsu came to visit, his father, bearing a broom in his hands as a sign of servitude, went to the gate to greet him and stood respectfully to one side. Kao-tsu in great astonishment descended from his carriage and hastened to his father's side. "The emperor is the ruler of men," his father said. "How should he on my account violate the laws of the empire?" With this Kao-tsu honored his father with the title of "Grand Supreme Emperor" and, because he was secretly pleased with the advice of his father's steward, he awarded the man five hundred catties of gold.

In the twelfth month someone reported a case of disaffection to the emperor, announcing that Han Hsin, the king of Ch'u, was plotting a revolt. When the emperor consulted his advisers, they all urged him to attack but, rejecting this advice, he instead employed a strategy suggested by Ch'en P'ing whereby, pretending to embark upon a pleasure visit to Yün-meng, he summoned the various feudal lords to a meeting at Ch'en. When Han Hsin appeared at the meeting, Kao-tsu immediately seized him. The same day he proclaimed a general amnesty to the empire.

T'ien K'en congratulated the emperor upon his success, saying, "Your Majesty has succeeded in seizing Han Hsin, and also fixed the capital in the area of Ch'in within the Pass. The land of Ch'in is of superlative configuration, surrounded by natural barriers of rivers and mountains and stretching a thousand miles. He who commands an army of a million lances commands a hundred times that number if he holds the land of Ch'in. From such an advantageous stronghold, sending forth troops to subdue the feudal lords is as easy as standing on a roof and pouring down water from a jug. But the land of Ch'i too has its rich fields of Lang-ya and Chi-mo in the east, the fastnesses of Mount T'ai to the south, in the west the banks of the muddy Yellow River, and in the north the resources of the Gulf of Pohai. Its land stretches for two thousand miles. He who commands an army of a million lances in this vast area commands ten times that number when he holds the land of Ch'i. Therefore there is a Ch'in in the east as well as in the west. Only one of the emperor's sons or brothers is fit to be made king of Ch'i."

Kao-tsu approved his words and rewarded him with five hundred catties of yellow gold. Ten or so days later he enfeoffed Han Hsin as marquis of Huai-yin. Han Hsin's original fief he divided into two kingdoms. Because General Liu Chia had several times achieved merit, he enfeoffed him as king of Ching ruling over one of them, the area of Huai-tung; he made his younger brother Liu Chiao king of Ch'u ruling over the other, the area of Huai-hsi. His own son Liu Fei he made king of Ch'i, ruling over more than seventy cities of Ch'i; all the people who spoke the dialect of Ch'i were to belong to the fief of Ch'i. The emperor held debates upon the merits of his followers and presented to the various feudal lords the split tallies, symbols of their formal enfeoffment. He transferred Hsin, the king of Hann, to the region of T'ai-yüan.

In the seventh year [200 B.C.] the Hsiung-nu [17] attacked Hsin, the king of Hann, at Ma-i. Hsin joined with them in plotting a revolt in T'ai-yüan. His generals, Man-ch'iu Ch'en of Po-t'u and Wang Huang, set up Chao Li, a descendant of the royal family of Chao,[18] as king of Chao in revolt against the emperor. Kao-tsu in person led a force to attack them, but he encountered such severe cold that two or three out of every ten of his soldiers lost their fingers from frostbite. At last he reached P'ing-ch'eng, where the Hsiung-nu surrounded him. After seven days of siege they finally withdrew. Kao-tsu ordered Fan K'uai to remain behind and subdue the region of Tai, and set up his older brother Liu Chung as king of Tai.

In the second month Kao-tsu passed through Chao and Lo-yang and returned to the capital at Ch'ang-an. With the completion of the Palace of Lasting Joy, the prime minister and subordinate officials all moved and took up residence in Ch'ang-an.

Eighth year [199 B.C.]: Kao-tsu marched east and attacked the remnants of the king of Hann's revolutionaries at Tung-yüan. The prime minister Hsiao Ho had been put in charge of the building of the Eternal Palace, constructing eastern and western gate towers, a front hall, an arsenal, and a great storehouse. When Kao-tsu returned from his expedition and saw the magnificence of the palace and its towers, he was extremely angry. "The empire is still in great turmoil," he said to Hsiao Ho, "and though we have toiled in battle these several years, we cannot tell yet whether we will achieve final success. What do you mean by constructing palaces like this on such an extravagant scale?"

---

[17] See note 11, "The Hereditary House of Ch'en She."
[18] Following the *Han shu* reading.

Hsiao Ho replied, "It is precisely because the fate of the empire is still uncertain that we must build such palaces and halls. A true Son of Heaven takes the whole world within the four seas to be his family. If he does not dwell in magnificence and beauty, he will have no way to manifest his authority, nor will he leave any foundation for his heirs to build upon." With these words, Kao-tsu's anger turned to delight.

When Kao-tsu was on his way to Tung-yüan he passed through a place called Po-jen. The prime minister of Chao, Kuan Kao, and others were at this time plotting to assassinate Kao-tsu, but when Kao-tsu heard the name of the place he grew uneasy in his heart and proceeded on without stopping.[19]

Liu Chung, the king of Tai, fled from his kingdom and returned to Lo-yang. Accordingly he was deprived of his title and made marquis of Ho-yang.

Ninth year [198 B.C.]: The plot of Kuan Kao and others to assassinate the emperor came to light, and they were executed along with their three sets of relatives.[20] Chang Ao, the king of Chao, was removed from his position and made marquis of Hsüan-p'ing. In this year the Chao, Ch'ü, Ching, and Huai families of Ch'u and the T'ien family of Ch'i, all powerful noble clans, were moved to the area within the Pass.[21]

When the Eternal Palace was completed, Kao-tsu summoned the nobles and officials to a great reception, setting forth wine for them in the front hall of the palace. Kao-tsu rose and, lifting his jade cup, proposed a toast to his father, the Grand Supreme Emperor. "You, my father, always used to consider me a worthless fellow who could never look after the family fortunes and had not half the industry of my older brother Chung," he said. "Now that my labors are com-

---

[19] Because the name "Po-jen" suggested to him the phrase "po yü jen" (to be pursued by someone).

[20] There is disagreement on the exact meaning of the term "three sets of relatives," but it is certain that, because of the principle of corporate responsibility recognized in Chinese law, the parents and the other members of a criminal's immediate family were executed along with him. One reason was to prevent the possibility of blood revenge.

[21] So that the emperor could keep a closer watch on them.

pleted, which of us has accomplished more, Chung or I?" All the officials in the hall shouted "Long life!" and roared with merriment.

In the tenth month of the tenth year [197 B.C.] Ch'ing Pu, the king of Huai-nan; P'eng Yüeh, the king of Liang; Lu Wan, the king of Yen; Liu Chia, the king of Ching; Liu Chiao, the king of Ch'u; Liu Fei, the king of Ch'i; and Wu Jui, the king of Ch'ang-sha, all came to pay homage at the Palace of Lasting Joy. The spring and summer passed without incident. In the seventh month [22] the Grand Supreme Emperor, father of Kao-tsu, passed away in the palace of Yüeh-yang. The kings of Ch'u and Liang came to attend the funeral. All prisoners in the district of Yüeh-yang were freed and the name of the city of Li-i was changed to "New Feng."

In the eighth month Ch'en Hsi, prime minister of the kingdom of Tai, started a revolt in the region of Tai.[23] "Ch'en Hsi," said the emperor, "formerly acted as my envoy, and I had the deepest faith in him. Tai is a region of crucial importance to me, and therefore I enfeoffed Ch'en Hsi as a marquis and made him prime minister of the kingdom so that he could guard Tai for me. But now he has joined with Wang Huang and the rest in plundering the land of Tai. The officials and people of Tai, however, are not to blame for this and therefore I absolve them of all guilt."

In the ninth month the emperor marched east to attack the rebels. When he reached Han-tan he announced with joy, "Since Ch'en Hsi has not come south to occupy Han-tan and guard the frontier of the Chang River, I am confident he will never be able to do me much harm." When he heard that all of Ch'en Hsi's generals had formerly been merchants he remarked, "I know how to take care of them." Then he offered large sums of money to tempt them to desert, so that most of Ch'en Hsi's generals surrendered to him.

Eleventh year [196 B.C.]: While Kao-tsu was still in Han-tan engaged in putting down the revolt of Ch'en Hsi and his followers, one of Ch'en's generals, Hou Ch'ang, with a band of some ten thousand men roamed from place to place, while Wang Huang camped at Ch'ü-ni

[22] See note 2, "The Hereditary House of Ch'en She."
[23] The text erroneously reads "prime minister of Chao."

and Chang Ch'un crossed the Yellow River and attacked Liao-ch'eng. Kao-tsu dispatched his general Kuo Meng to join with the general of Ch'i in attacking them, inflicting a decisive defeat. The grand commandant Chou P'o marched by way of T'ai-yüan into the region of Tai, conquering the area as far as Ma-i. When Ma-i refused to surrender, he attacked it and massacred its defenders. Kao-tsu attacked Tung-yüan, which was being held by Ch'en Hsi's general Chao Li. The city held out for over a month, while its men cursed the emperor. When the city finally capitulated, Kao-tsu had all those who had cursed him dragged forth and beheaded, while those who had not joined in cursing him he pardoned. With this, he took from Chao the land north of the Ch'ang Mountains and assigned it to Tai, setting up his son Liu Heng as king of Tai with his capital at Chin-yang.

In the spring Han Hsin, the marquis of Huai-yin, plotted a revolt in the area within the Pass. He was executed with his three sets of relatives.

In the summer P'eng Yüeh, the king of Liang, plotted a revolt. He was removed from his position and exiled to Shu but, when it was found that he was once more scheming to revolt, he was executed with his three sets of relatives. Kao-tsu set up his son Liu Hui as king of Liang and his son Liu Yu as king of Huai-yang.

In autumn, the seventh month, Ch'ing Pu, the king of Huai-nan, revolted, seized the land of Liu Chia, the king of Ching, to the east, and marched north across the Huai River. Liu Chiao, the king of Ch'u, fled to Hsieh. Kao-tsu in person led a force to attack Ch'ing Pu, setting up his son Liu Ch'ang as king of Huai-nan.

In the tenth month of the twelfth year [195 B.C.] Kao-tsu had already attacked Ch'ing Pu's army at Kuei-chui, and Ch'ing Pu was in flight. Kao-tsu dispatched a special general to pursue him, while he himself started back to the capital, passing through his old home of P'ei on his way. Here he stopped and held a feast at the palace of P'ei, summoning all his old friends and the elders and young men to drink to their hearts' content. He gathered together a group of some hundred and twenty children of P'ei and taught them to sing and, when the feast was at its height, Kao-tsu struck the lute and sang a song which he had composed:

> A great wind came forth;
> The clouds rose on high.
> Now that my might rules all within the seas,
> I have returned to my old village.
> Where shall I find brave men
> To guard the four corners of my land?

He made the children join in and repeat the song, while he rose and danced. Deeply moved with grief and nostalgia, and with tears streaming down his face, he said to the elders of P'ei, "The traveler sighs for his old home. Though I have made my capital within the Pass, after I have departed this life my spirit will still think with joy of P'ei. From the time when I was governor of P'ei, I went forth to punish the wicked and violent until at last the whole world is mine. It is my wish that P'ei become my bath-town.[24] I hereby exempt its people from all taxes. For generation after generation, nothing more shall be required of you." Then for over ten days the old men and women and Kao-tsu's former friends of P'ei spent each day drinking and rejoicing, reminiscing and joking about old times.

When Kao-tsu made ready to leave, the men of P'ei all begged him to stay a little longer. Kao-tsu replied, "My retinue is very large and I fear it would be too much for you to supply them with food any longer," and with this he departed. The entire district of P'ei became deserted as everyone flocked to the western edge of the city to present parting gifts. Kao-tsu again halted his progress, set up tents, and drank for three days more. The elders of P'ei all bowed their heads and said, "P'ei has been fortunate enough to have its taxes revoked, but the city of Feng has not been so blessed. We beg that Your Majesty will take pity upon it as well."

"Feng is the place where I was born and grew up," replied Kao-tsu. "It least of all could I ever forget. It is only that I remember how under Yung Ch'ih it turned against me and joined Wei." But the elders of P'ei continued to plead with him until he finally agreed to absolve

---

[24] A mark of special honor. Such estates were not required to pay taxes to the government, their revenues going instead to provide "bath-water," i.e., private funds for the holder. In later chapters we shall often find "bath-towns" being assigned to princesses.

Feng from its taxes in the same manner as P'ei. He then transferred the marquis of P'ei, Liu P'i, to the position of king of Wu.

The Han generals made separate attacks upon Ch'ing Pu's armies north and south of the T'ao River, defeating them all, and pursued and executed Ch'ing Pu at P'o-yang. Fan K'uai in the meantime led the troops under his command in pacifying the region of Tai and executed Ch'en Hsi at Tang-ch'eng. In the eleventh month Kao-tsu returned from his campaign against Ch'ing Pu to the capital at Ch'ang-an.

In the twelfth month Kao-tsu announced: "The First Emperor of Ch'in, King Yin of Ch'u [Ch'en She], King An-li of Wei, King Min of Ch'i, and King Tao-hsiang of Chao are all without surviving heirs. I hereby establish ten families for each to act as guardians of their graves, except that the First Emperor of Ch'in shall be granted twenty families. In addition the nobleman Wu-chi of Wei shall be granted five families."[25] He also granted pardon to the region of Tai and to all the people and officials who had been robbed and plundered by Ch'en Hsi and Chao Li.

One of Ch'en Hsi's generals who had surrendered reported to Kao-tsu that, at the time when Ch'en Hsi revolted, Lu Wan, the king of Yen, had sent an envoy to Ch'en Hsi to join in plotting with him. The emperor sent Shen I-chi, the marquis of Pi-yang, to fetch Lu Wan, but Lu Wan pleaded illness and declined to go with him. Shen I-chi returned and reported on his mission, declaring that there seemed to be some basis for the report of Lu Wan's disaffection.

In the second month the emperor dispatched Fan K'uai and Chou P'o to lead a force of soldiers and attack Lu Wan. He issued a proclamation freeing all the officials and people of Yen from responsibility for the revolt, and set up his son Liu Chien as the new king of Yen.

When Kao-tsu was fighting against Ch'ing Pu, he was wounded by a stray arrow and on the way back he fell ill. When his illness con-

[25] Since these men had no descendants of their own to look after their graves and perform sacrifices to them, the state undertook to provide families for this purpose, even in the case of the hated First Emperor of Ch'in. For one's grave to go entirely untended was in Chinese eyes the cruelest of fates.

tinued to grow worse, Empress Lü sent for a skilled doctor. The doctor examined Kao-tsu and, in answer to his question, replied, "This illness can be cured." With this, Kao-tsu began to berate and curse him, saying, "I began as a commoner and with my three-foot sword conquered the world. Was this not the will of Heaven? My fate lies with Heaven. Even P'ien Ch'üeh, the most famous doctor of antiquity, could do nothing for me!" In the end he would not let the doctor treat his illness, but gave him fifty catties of gold and sent him away.

When the doctor had gone, Empress Lü asked, "After my lord's allotted years have run out, if Prime Minister Hsiao Ho should die, who could be appointed to fill his place?"

"Ts'ao Ts'an will do," replied the emperor.

"And after him?" the empress asked.

"Wang Ling will do," he replied. "But Wang Ling is rather stupid. He will need Ch'en P'ing to help him. Ch'en P'ing has more than enough brains but he could hardly be entrusted with the position alone. Chou P'o has dignity and generosity, though he lacks learning. Yet it will be Chou P'o who will look out for the welfare of the Liu family. He deserves to be made grand commandant."

"And who after him?" the empress asked again.

"After all these men are gone," he replied, "you will no longer be here to know about it."

Lu Wan, with a force of several thousand cavalry, proceeded to a spot along the border, sending to inquire whether the emperor's condition had improved so that he might be allowed to come to the capital and apologize for his disaffection.

In the fourth month, the day *chia-ch'en* [June 1, 195 B.C.], Kao-tsu passed away in the Palace of Lasting Joy. Four days went by, but no mourning was announced. Empress Lü consulted with Shen I-chi, saying, "The other leaders, like the emperor himself, all made their way up from the ranks of the common people. At present they face north and acknowledge themselves his subjects, but in their hearts they nurse a constant discontent. Now they will be called upon to serve a young master. I fear that, if they and their families are not completely done away with, there will be no peace for the empire!"

Someone overheard these words and reported them to General Li Shang. The general went to visit Shen I-chi and said, "I have heard that the emperor passed away four days ago, but no mourning has yet been announced. I also understand that there are plans for executing all the present leaders. If this is actually carried out, I fear the empire will be in grave peril. Ch'en P'ing and Kuan Ying with a force of a hundred thousand are guarding Jung-yang, while Fan K'uai and Chou P'o with two hundred thousand men are engaged in pacifying Yen and Tai. If they hear that the emperor has passed away and that all the leaders in the capital have been executed, they will surely lead their troops back in this direction and attack the area within the Pass. With the major officials in the capital in revolt and the feudal lords beyond up in arms, we may look for total defeat in a matter of days."

Shen I-chi returned to the palace and reported these words to the empress. Accordingly, on the day *ting-wei* [June 4, 195 B.C.] mourning was proclaimed for the emperor and a general amnesty granted to the empire. When Lu Wan received word of the emperor's passing, he fled from the country and joined the Hsiung-nu.

On the day *ping-yin* [June 23] of the fifth month the emperor was buried at Ch'ang-ling.[26] On the day *chi-ssu* [June 26] the heir apparent was set up. He proceeded to the funerary temple of his grandfather, the Grand Supreme Emperor, where the assembled officials announced: "Kao-tsu rose from the humblest beginnings to correct a discordant age and turn it back to the right. He brought peace and order to the world and became the founder of the Han. His merit was of the most exalted order, and it is therefore appropriate that we should honor him with the title of 'Exalted Supreme Emperor.'" The heir apparent succeeded to the title of Supreme Emperor; he is known posthumously as Emperor Hui the Filial. He gave orders that the feudal lords in each province and kingdom should set up funerary temples to Kao-tsu and perform sacrifices in them at the appropriate seasons of the year. In the fifth year of his reign Emperor Hui, recalling how Kao-tsu had rejoiced and sorrowed on his last visit to P'ei, had the palace of

---

[26] The end of this sentence has been misplaced and appears in present texts at the very close of the chapter.

P'ei made into a funerary temple for Kao-tsu, ranking second only to the main temple in the capital. The hundred and twenty children whom Kao-tsu had taught to sing he ordered to perform the song to the accompaniment of wind instruments, and when any of the group later dropped out he had them immediately replaced.

Kao-tsu had eight sons. The oldest, a son by a concubine, was Fei, the king of Ch'i, posthumously titled King Tao-hui. The second, a son by Empress Lü, became Emperor Hui. The third, son of Lady Ch'i, was Ju-i, the king of Chao, posthumously titled King Yin. The fourth was Heng, the king of Tai, who later became Emperor Wen the Filial; he was a son of Empress Dowager Po. The fifth was Hui, the king of Liang, who in the reign of Empress Lü was transferred to the position of king of Chao; he was given the posthumous title of King Kung. The sixth was Yu, the king of Huai-yang, whom Empress Lü made the king of Chao; his posthumous title was King Yu. The seventh was Ch'ang, who became King Li of Huai-nan, and the eighth was Chien, the king of Yen.

The Grand Historian remarks: The government of the Hsia dynasty was marked by good faith, which in time deteriorated until mean men had turned it into rusticity. Therefore the men of Shang who succeeded to the Hsia reformed this defect through the virtue of piety. But piety degenerated until mean men had made it a superstitious concern for the spirits. Therefore the men of Chou who followed corrected this fault through refinement and order. But refinement again deteriorated until it became in the hands of the mean a mere hollow show. Therefore what was needed to reform this hollow show was a return to good faith, for the way of the Three Dynasties of old is like a cycle which, when it ends, must begin over again.

It is obvious that in late Chou and Ch'in times the earlier refinement and order had deteriorated. But the government of Ch'in failed to correct this fault, instead adding its own harsh punishments and laws. Was this not a grave error?

Thus when the Han rose to power it took over the faults of its predecessors and worked to change and reform them, causing men to be unflagging in their efforts and following the order properly ordained

Emperor Kao-tsu

by Heaven. It held its court in the tenth month,[27] and its vestments and carriage tops were yellow, with plumes on the left sides of the carriages.

[27] I.e., this was the time each year when the feudal lords were required to attend the court in person and pay their respects for the new year, which in the early Han began in this month.

Shih chi 16 (excerpt): Reflections on the Rise of Emperor Kao-tsu

[This introduction to the "Table by Months of the Times of Ch'in and Ch'u," *Shih chi* 16, is given with a title supplied by the translator.]

Against the tyranny and oppression of the Ch'in the men of Ch'u began their revolt, but Hsiang Yü in turn betrayed his ruler, until the king of Han came to the aid of right and conquered him. Thus in the course of eight years the rulership changed hands three times.[1] Since the period was so crowded with events and the shifts of power were so frequent, I have chosen to outline it in detail in this Table by Months of the Times of Ch'in and Ch'u.

On reading the accounts of the struggle between Ch'in and Ch'u, the Grand Historian remarks: It was Ch'en She who first began the uprising, the Hsiang family who with cruelty and treason destroyed the Ch'in, and the founder of the house of Han who dispersed the rebellion, punished the evildoers, brought peace to all within the seas, and in the end ascended the imperial throne. Within the space of eight years the command of the empire changed hands three times. Since the birth of mankind there have never before been such rapid changes of rulership!

In ancient times, when Shun and Yü became rulers, they had first to accumulate goodness and merit for twenty or thirty years, impress the people with their virtue, prove that they could in practice handle the affairs of government, and meet the approval of Heaven before they were able to ascend the throne. Again, when Kings T'ang and Wu founded the Shang and Chou dynasties, they had behind them over ten generations of ancestors, stretching back to Hsieh and Hou Chi respectively, who had been distinguished for their just and virtuous conduct. Yet, though eight hundred nobles appeared unsummoned to

[1] I.e., from the Ch'in to Hsiang Yü to Han Kao-tsu.

aid King Wu at the Meng Ford, he still did not venture to move; it was only later that he assassinated the tyrant Chou, and only after similar cautious delay that King T'ang banished the tyrant Chieh. Ch'in first rose to prominence under Duke Hsiang and achieved eminence under Dukes Wen and Mu. From the reigns of Dukes Hsieh and Hsiao on, it gradually swallowed up the Six States until, after a hundred years or so, the First Emperor was able to bring all the noblemen under his power. Thus, even with the virtue of Shun, Yü, T'ang, and Wu, or the might of the First Emperor, it is, as one can see, an extremely difficult task to unite the empire in one rule!

After the Ch'in ruler had assumed the title of emperor, he was fearful lest warfare should continue because of the presence of feudal lords. Therefore he refused to grant so much as a foot of land in fief, but instead destroyed the fortifications of the principal cities, melted down the lance and arrow points, and ruthlessly wiped out the brave men of the world, hoping thus to ensure the safety of his dynasty for countless generations to come. Yet from the lanes of the common people there arose a man with the deeds of a king whose alliances and campaigns of attack surpassed those of the three dynasties of Hsia, Shang, and Chou. Ch'in's earlier prohibitions against feudalism and the possession of arms, as it turned out, served only to aid worthy men and remove from their path obstacles they would otherwise have encountered. Therefore Kao-tsu had but to roar forth his indignation to become a leader of the world. Why should people say that one cannot become a king unless he possesses land? Was this man not what the old books term a "great sage"? Surely this was the work of Heaven! Who but a great sage would be worthy to receive the mandate of Heaven and become emperor?

Part IV
THE GREAT MINISTERS

Shih chi 53: The Hereditary House of Prime Minister Hsiao

When the armies of Ch'u surrounded us at Jung-yang and we were locked in stalemate for three years, Hsiao Ho governed the land west of the mountains, plotting our welfare, sending a constant stream of reinforcements, and supplying rations and provisions without end. He caused the people to rejoice in Han and hate the alliance of Ch'u. Thus I made The Hereditary House of Prime Minister Hsiao.

Prime Minister Hsiao Ho was a native of Feng in the district of P'ei. Because of his thorough understanding of law and letters he was made a director of officials in P'ei. While Kao-tsu was still a commoner, Hsiao Ho on numerous occasions took advantage of his official capacity to help Kao-tsu out. After Kao-tsu became a village head he in turn did all he could to assist Hsiao Ho. When Kao-tsu was sent with a band of *corvée* laborers to Hsien-yang, each of the other officials presented him with three hundred cash as a parting gift, but Hsiao Ho alone gave five hundred.

As an official of P'ei, Hsiao Ho worked with the secretary of Ch'in who was in charge of overseeing the province. Because he conducted his affairs with consistent discretion and understanding, he was given the position of a provincial secretary of Ssu River, where his record was also of the highest order. The secretary of Ch'in planned on his return to the capital to make a report of Hsiao Ho's good record and have him appointed to a position in the central government, but Hsiao Ho begged not to be transferred.

When Kao-tsu rose to the position of governor of P'ei, Hsiao Ho always served as his aide and looked after official business for him. At the time when Kao-tsu marched into the capital of Hsien-yang, all the generals rushed to the storehouses and fought with each other over Ch'in's goods and treasures. But Hsiao Ho entered ahead of them and gathered up all the maps and official records that had belonged to Ch'in's ministers and secretaries and stored them away. When Kao-tsu became king of Han, Hsiao Ho served as his prime minister. Hsiang Yü arrived later with the other nobles, massacred the inhabitants of Hsien-yang, burned the city, and then marched away. But because of the maps and registries of Ch'in which Hsiao Ho had in his possession, the king of Han was able to inform himself of all the strategic defense points of the empire, the population and relative strength of the various districts, and the ills and grievances of the people.

On the recommendation of Hsiao Ho, the king of Han took Han Hsin into his service and made him a major general. (A discussion of this will be found in the chapter on Han Hsin, the marquis of Huai-yin.)

When the king of Han led his forces east again to conquer the three kingdoms of Ch'in, he left Hsiao Ho behind as his prime minister to govern Pa and Shu, with instructions to ensure their well-being and loyalty, propagandize for his cause, and see that provisions were sent to feed his army.

In the second year of Han [205 B.C.], while the king of Han and the other feudal leaders were attacking Ch'u, Hsiao Ho remained behind to guard the area within the Pass and look after the heir apparent. Establishing the seat of government in Yüeh-yang, he worked to simplify the laws and statutes and set up dynastic temples and altars, palaces and district offices. All affairs he reported immediately to the king of Han, and acted only upon his permission and approval. If it was impossible to report to the king at the time, he disposed of the matter as he thought best and asked the king's opinion on his return. He had charge of all affairs within the Pass, drawing up registers of the population and sending supplies by land and water to provision the army. The king of Han several times lost large parts of his army and was forced to retreat in flight, but each time Hsiao Ho raised more troops from the area within the Pass and immediately brought the army back up to strength. For this reason the king entrusted sole charge of the land within the Pass to him.

In the third year of Han [204 B.C.], the king of Han and Hsiang Yü were locked in stalemate in the area So in Ching. The king several times sent envoys to reward and encourage Hsiao Ho for his labors. Master Po spoke to Hsiao Ho, saying, "While His Majesty is forced to camp in the fields and suffer the hardships of exposure, he sends envoys to reward and encourage you. It must be that he doubts your loyalty. I think it would be best for you to summon all your sons and brothers who are fit to take up arms and send them to join the army. Then the king will surely have greater confidence in you." Hsiao Ho followed his suggestion and the king was greatly pleased.

In the fifth year of Han [202 B.C.], after Hsiang Yü had been killed and the empire brought to peace, discussions were begun as to who had won merit and who should be enfeoffed but, because there was a great deal of contention among the officials over their respective achievements, the year passed before the matter could be settled.

The king of Han, now emperor, considered that Hsiao Ho had achieved the highest merit, and hence enfeoffed him as marquis of Tsuan with the revenue from a large number of towns. But the other distinguished officials objected, saying, "We have all buckled on armor and taken up our weapons, some of us fighting as many as a hundred or more engagements, the least of us fighting twenty or thirty. Each, to a greater or lesser degree, has engaged in attacks upon cities or seizures of territory. And yet Hsiao Ho, who has never campaigned on the sweaty steeds of battle, but only sat here with brush and ink deliberating on questions of state instead of fighting, is awarded a position above us. How can this be?"

"Gentlemen," the emperor asked, "do you know anything about hunting?"

"We do," they replied.

"And do you know anything about hunting dogs?"

"We do."

"Now in a hunt," the emperor said, "it is the dog who is sent to pursue and kill the beast. But the one who unleashes the dog and points out the place where the beast is hiding is the huntsman. You, gentlemen, have only succeeded in capturing the beast, and so your achievement is that of hunting dogs. But it is Hsiao Ho who unleashed you and pointed out the place, and his achievement is that of the huntsman. Also in your case only you yourselves, or at most two or three of your family, joined in following me. But Hsiao Ho dispatched his whole family numbering twenty or thirty members to accompany me. This is a service I can hardly forget."

None of the officials dared say anything further. The various marquises having been granted their fiefs, the question of what order of precedence they should take was brought before the emperor. "Ts'ao Ts'an, the marquis of P'ing-yang," the officials stated, "bears on his body the scars of seventy wounds. In attacking cities and seizing territory he has achieved the greatest merit. It is proper that he should be given first place."

The emperor had already contravened the will of his ministers by granting Hsiao Ho such a generous fief, and when it came to the question of precedence he did not feel that he could dispute their judgment a second time, though personally he wanted Hsiao Ho to be given first place. At this point Lord E, a marquis of the area within the Pass, came forward. "The opinion of the other ministers," he said, "is in my estimation a mistake. Although Ts'ao Ts'an has won merit by fighting in the field and seizing territory, this was an accomplishment of the moment. While the emperor was locked in battle with Hsiang Yü for five years, he several times lost the major part of his army, and was on occasion forced to flee for his life in retreat. But each time Hsiao Ho sent reinforcements from the area within the Pass to bring the army back to strength. The emperor sent no orders for men and yet, just when his forces were weakest and most in danger of annihilation, a new contingent of some ten thousand recruits would arrive. Again, when Han and Ch'u were stalemated for several years at Jung-yang, our army ran completely out of provisions, but Hsiao Ho sent supplies by land and water from the area within the Pass and saved our men from starvation. Though His Majesty several times lost control of the land east of the mountains, Hsiao Ho kept firm hold on the area within the Pass and awaited His Majesty's final return. His achievements were not a matter of a moment, but deserve everlasting honor. Han could have done without a hundred men like Ts'ao Ts'an and never felt the loss, nor would their presence have assured inevitable victory by any means. How then can one suggest that the achievements of a moment take precedence over those of all time? Hsiao Ho should clearly be granted first place, and Ts'ao Ts'an ranked second."

The emperor approved this suggestion; in addition he granted Hsiao Ho the privilege of wearing his sword and shoes when he ascended to the audience chamber, and absolved him from the duty of hurrying when he entered court.[1]

The emperor announced, "I have heard that he who works for the advancement of worthy men deserves the highest reward. Although Hsiao Ho achieved the most outstanding merit, it was Lord E who made this fact clear." With this he granted Lord E the title of marquis of P'ing-an, awarding him the cities from which he already received the revenue as a marquis within the Pass.[2] On the same day he enfeoffed all of Hsiao Ho's male relatives, some ten or more, with the revenue of various towns, and increased Hsiao Ho's original fief by two thousand households. This last, according to the emperor, was done because when he had once been sent on labor service to Hsien-yang Hsiao Ho had presented him with two hundred cash more than any of the other officials as a parting gift.

In the eleventh year of Han [196 B.C.] Ch'en Hsi revolted. Kao-tsu marched to Han-tan to attack him, but before the campaign was completed Han Hsin, the marquis of Huai-yin, began to plot a rebellion in the area within the Pass. Empress Lü followed Hsiao Ho's advice and executed Han Hsin. (A discussion will be found in the chapter on Han Hsin.) When the emperor received word of Han Hsin's execution, he sent a messenger to honor Hsiao Ho with the position of prime minister and increase his fief by five thousand households, granting him at the same time a private retinue of five hundred soldiers headed by a colonel to act as his bodyguard.

All the other ministers went to congratulate Hsiao Ho on his good fortune, but Shao P'ing alone presented condolences as though upon

---

[1] Chinese etiquette forbade ministers to wear their swords or shoes when they entered the emperor's presence. In addition they were required to scurry into court instead of walking at a normal pace. By excepting him from these requirements the emperor was conferring upon Hsiao Ho the marks of extreme honor.

[2] The "marquises within the Pass" ordinarily did not hold possession of any lands, but only received the revenues from the cities in their fiefs.

a death. (Shao P'ing had been the marquis of Tung-ling under Ch'in, but when Ch'in was defeated he was made a commoner. Being very poor, he used to raise melons east of the city of Ch'ang-an. His melons were known for their excellent flavor and everyone called them "Tung-ling melons" after the title that Shao P'ing had once held.) Shao P'ing said to him, "Some misfortune will come from this. The emperor is away in battle and has left you to guard the capital area, and yet, though you suffer none of the perils of war, he suddenly increases your fief and grants you a bodyguard. It must be that, because of the recent revolt of Han Hsin in the capital area, he doubts your loyalty. He has granted you a bodyguard not for your own protection but because he does not trust you. I beg you to decline the new enfeoffment and not accept it, but instead to make a contribution to the expenses of the campaign from your own private wealth. Then the emperor's mind will be set at ease." Hsiao Ho followed his advice, to the great pleasure of the emperor.

In the autumn of the twelfth year of Han [195 B.C.] Ch'ing Pu revolted. The emperor in person led a force to attack him, from time to time sending envoys back to the capital to ask what Hsiao Ho was doing. While the emperor was away in battle Hsiao Ho continued to look after the wants of the people and encourage them in their labors, sending all the assistance he could to the army as he had done at the time of Ch'en Hsi's revolt. But one of his retainers advised him, saying, "It will not be long before your family is wiped out. You have been made prime minister and given the highest rank in the empire. There is no further honor that can be added to this. Now it has been over ten years since you first entered the Pass and won the hearts of the people. They are all unswervingly loyal to you, for you have ceaselessly and with the greatest diligence worked for their peace and well-being. The reason the emperor keeps sending to ask what you are doing is that he is afraid you will betray him and start an uprising within the Pass. Why don't you buy up a lot of farm land on credit and start speculating in goods at a cheap price so that you will create a reputation for being corrupt? Then the emperor's mind will be set somewhat at ease."[3]

[3] This would seem an odd way to set the emperor's mind at ease, but all the

Prime Minister Hsiao

Hsiao Ho followed this suggestion and the emperor was very pleased. When his campaign against Ch'ing Pu was completed and he led his army back to the capital, the people crowded along the roadside presenting petitions to the emperor accusing the prime minister of forcing them to sell their land and houses at an unfair price and accumulating a fortune of twenty or thirty million cash. After the emperor reached the capital, Hsiao Ho appeared before him. "I see that you have been making a profit from the people," said the emperor laughing. He then handed over to Hsiao Ho the petitions that had been presented, adding, "You must do something to make amends to them!"

Hsiao Ho accordingly made this request on behalf of the people: "The region of Ch'ang-an is very narrow and constricted, and yet there is a great deal of idle land going to waste in the Shang-ling Park.[4] I beg that the people be allowed to use the park for farm land, leaving the straw and other remains of their crops as fodder for beasts."

The emperor flew into a rage. "You have succeeded in getting a lot of money and bribes from the merchants and now for their sake you want to take my park away from me!" He turned Hsiao Ho over to the law officials to be put into chains.

A few days later one of the palace guards named Wang who was in attendance advanced and inquired, "What terrible crime has the prime minister committed that Your Majesty has so suddenly thrown him into prison?"

"I have heard," replied the emperor, "that when Li Ssu was prime minister to the emperor of Ch'in if anything good came about he attributed it to his sovereign, but for anything bad he accepted responsibility himself. But now my prime minister has been accepting money from a lot of dirty merchants and in return asks for my park so that he can ingratiate himself with the people. Therefore I have had him put in chains and punished."

"But if in the course of his duties the prime minister becomes aware of something that will benefit the people," objected Wang, "it is his

---

suggestion means is that Hsiao Ho should do something to decrease his popularity, which had reached dangerous proportions.
[4] The emperor's private hunting park.

duty to request it. Why should Your Majesty suppose that he has been accepting money from the merchants? During the years when Your Majesty was battling Ch'u, and later, when Ch'en Hsi and Ch'ing Pu revolted, Your Majesty was away leading the armies, while the prime minister the whole time guarded the area within the Pass. At that time he had no more than to nod his head and Your Majesty would have lost possession of the whole area west of the Pass. But since he did not take that opportunity to scheme for his own profit, why should he now try to profit from the money of the merchants? As for the ruler of Ch'in, the reason he did not become aware of his own faults and eventually lost the empire was that Li Ssu kept accepting the blame for things himself. Ch'in can therefore hardly be taken as a model. Is it not very shortsighted of Your Majesty to suspect the prime minister in this fashion?"

The emperor was deeply perplexed, but before the day was over he dispatched a messenger bearing the imperial seals with orders to pardon Hsiao Ho and release him. Hsiao Ho was by this time well on in years and, being by nature extremely respectful and circumspect in his manner, came before the emperor barefooted and begged for forgiveness. "You may go!" said the emperor. "You asked for the park for the sake of the people. In denying your request I have acted no better than the tyrants Chieh and Chou of old, while you have shown yourself a worthy minister. The reason I had you bound was so that the people might all hear of my fault."

Hsiao Ho had never been on good terms with Ts'ao Ts'an. When Hsiao Ho fell ill Emperor Hui, who had succeeded his father, Kao-tsu, on the throne, came in person to inquire about his illness. "When your hundred years are ended," the emperor asked, "who can fill your place?"

"No one knows his ministers better than their lord," Hsiao Ho replied.

"What about Ts'ao Ts'an?"

Hsiao Ho bowed his head and answered, "As long as my lord has him, I may die without regret."

In selecting his lands and residence, Hsiao Ho always chose to live in an out-of-the-way place with no elaborate walls or roofs to his house.

"This way, if my descendants are worthy men," he used to say, "they will follow my example of frugal living. And if they turn out to be unworthy, they will at least have nothing that the more powerful families can take away from them."

In the second year of Emperor Hui [193 B.C.] Prime Minister Hsiao Ho died. He was granted the posthumous title of Wen-chung or "Civil Fulfillment Marquis." In the fourth generation his heirs, because of some offense, were deprived of the marquisate, but shortly afterwards the emperor sought out Hsiao Ho's descendant and enfeoffed him as marquis of Tsuan to carry on the line. None of the other distinguished ministers received such honor.

The Grand Historian remarks: Prime Minister Hsiao Ho in the time of Ch'in was a petty official, wielding his brush and scraper [5] and going about his business without distinction or honor. But when the Han, like a great sun or moon, rose in the sky, he caught a little of its brilliance. With the gravest care he guarded what was charged to him as though under lock and key and, because the people groaned under the laws of Ch'in, he gratified their wishes by making a new beginning for the empire. When Han Hsin, Ch'ing Pu, and the others had all been wiped out, his glory alone grew ever brighter. First among the ranks of officials, renowned in later ages, his fame rivals that of the ancient ministers Hung Yao and San I!

[5] Writing at this time was done on strips of wood. When the clerk made a mistake, he would scrape the surface of the wood clean and write on it again.

Shih chi 55: The Hereditary House of the Marquis of Liu (Chang Liang)

Plotted within the tents of command, shaping victory out of chaos, these were the schemes and strategies of Chang Liang. Though he lacked fame or the renown of valor, he foresaw the difficult while it was still easy and brought forth great things from small. Thus I made The Hereditary House of the Marquis of Liu.

The ancestors of Chang Liang,[1] the marquis of Liu, were men of the state of Hann. His grandfather Chang K'ai-ti served as prime minister to Marquis Chao and Kings Hsüan-hui and Hsiang-ai of Hann. His father, Chang P'ing, was prime minister to Kings Li and Tao-hui and died in the twenty-third year of King Tao-hui's reign. Twenty years after Chang P'ing's death Ch'in destroyed the state of Hann. Because of his youth, Chang Liang never had an opportunity to serve as a minister of Hann. When the state was destroyed, Chang Liang was left with a retinue of three hundred male servants. On his younger brother's death, he conducted no elaborate funeral but instead used all his family's wealth to search for someone who would undertake to assassinate the king of Ch'in for him, hoping thus to avenge the rulers of Hann, five generations of whom his father and grandfather had served.

Chang Liang once journeyed to Huai-yang to study ritual and there met the lord of Ts'ang-hai. Through him he obtained the services of a man renowned for his great strength. Chang Liang had an iron bludgeon made which weighed a hundred and twenty catties and, when the Ch'in emperor came east on a tour, he and the assassin lay in wait for him. When the emperor reached the area of Po-lang-sha they made their attack, but mistakenly struck the carriage of his attendants. The emperor was enraged and ordered an immediate search throughout the

[1] His polite name was Tzu-fang.

Marquis of Liu (Chang Liang) 135

empire for the rebels, hoping to seize Chang Liang. Chang Liang assumed a false name and fled into hiding in Hsia-p'ei.

Chang Liang was once strolling idly along an embankment in Hsia-p'ei when an old man wearing a coarse gown appeared. Reaching the place where Chang Liang was, he deliberately dropped his shoe down the embankment and, turning to Chang Liang, said, "Fetch me my shoe, young man!"

Chang Liang, completely taken aback, was about to hit him, but because the man was old he swallowed his resentment and climbed down and got the shoe. "Put it on for me!" ordered the old man, and Chang Liang, since he had already gone to the trouble of fetching it, knelt respectfully and prepared to put on the shoe. The old man held out his foot and, when the shoe was on, laughed and went on his way. Chang Liang, more startled than ever, stood looking after him. When the old man had gone some distance, he turned and came back. "You could be taught, young man," he said. "Meet me here at dawn five days from now!" Chang Liang, thinking this all very strange, knelt and replied, "I will do as you say."

At dawn five days later he went to the place, but found the man already there. "When you have an appointment with an old man, how is it that you come late?" he asked angrily. "Go away, and meet me at dawn five days from now, only come earlier!"

Five days later Chang Liang got up at the crow of the cock and went to the place, but once more the old man had gotten there before him. "Why are you late again?" the old man asked in anger. "Go away, and five days from now come earlier!"

Five days later Chang Liang went to the place before half the night was through. After a while the old man came along. "This is the way it should be!" he said. Then, producing a book, he said, "If you read this you may become the teacher of kings. Ten years from now your fortune will rise. Thirteen years from now you will see me again. A yellow stone at the foot of Mount Ku-ch'eng in northern Ch'i— that will be I." Without another word he left and Chang Liang never saw him again.

When dawn came Chang Liang examined the book which the old man had given him and found it to be *The Grand Duke's Art of*

War. He set great store by it and was to be found constantly poring over it.

Chang Liang lived the life of a wandering knight in Hsia-p'ei, where he was joined in hiding by Hsiang Po, who had killed a man. Ten years later Ch'en She and his men started their uprising. Chang Liang also gathered a band of some hundred young men and, when Ching Chü set himself up as acting king of Ch'u in Liu, started out to join him there. Along the way, however, he met the governor of P'ei, who was leading a force of a thousand soldiers and attempting to seize control of the region from Hsia-p'ei west. Chang Liang joined the governor of P'ei, who honored him with the position of cavalry general. From time to time Chang Liang expounded *The Grand Duke's Art of War* to the governor of P'ei. The latter greatly admired it and always followed the strategies which it outlined, but when Chang Liang discussed the book with other men they refused to pay him any heed. "The governor of P'ei will soon be chosen by Heaven," he said, and for this reason he followed him and did not go to join Ching Chü.

The governor of P'ei went to Hsieh to meet Hsiang Liang, who at this time set up King Huai of Ch'u. Chang Liang took this opportunity to speak to Hsiang Liang. "You have already set up the descendants of Ch'u," he said, "but Ch'eng, the lord of Heng-yang, who is a descendant of the royal house of Hann, is also a worthy man. If you were to set him up as a king you would greatly increase the strength of your party."

Hsiang Liang accordingly sent Chang Liang to seek out Hann Ch'eng and make him king of Hann, with Chang Liang as his minister of instruction. Chang Liang joined the king in leading a band of a thousand men west to seize the region of Hann but, though they captured several cities, the Ch'in forces immediately retook them. Chang Liang then roamed with his troops back and forth in the region of Ying-ch'uan.

When the governor of P'ei marched south from Lo-yang to Huan-yüan, Chang Liang led his men to join him; together they captured more than ten cities of Hann and defeated the Ch'in general, Yang Hsiung. The governor of P'ei ordered Ch'eng, the king of Hann, to stay behind and guard the city of Yang-ti while he and Chang Liang marched south, attacking and capturing Yüan. From there they marched west and entered the Wu Pass. The governor of P'ei wanted to take a force of twenty thousand men and attack the Ch'in army encamped at the foot of Mount Yao, but Chang Liang advised against this. "Ch'in's forces are still strong and cannot be lightly dismissed. I have heard that their general is the son of a butcher. Such paltry tradespeople are easily moved by the prospect of gain. I would advise you to remain here and build defense walls, sending someone ahead with a force of fifty thousand men and the necessary provisions, and set up pennants and flags on the surrounding hills so that they will think we have more soldiers than we do. Then you may dispatch Li I-chi with rich presents to tempt the Ch'in general."

As they had hoped, the Ch'in general succumbed to the temptation and turned traitor, asking to join the governor of P'ei in marching west to attack Hsien-yang. The governor of P'ei was about to grant his request, but Chang Liang once more intervened. "It is only the general who has expressed his willingness to revolt. I fear that his soldiers will not follow him. If his men do not follow his example, it will be most dangerous for us. It would be better to take advantage of their present laxity and attack."

The governor of P'ei accordingly led his troops in an attack on the Ch'in army, inflicting a great defeat. Pursuing them northward, he once more engaged them in battle at Lan-t'ien until the Ch'in army agreed to a final surrender. The governor of P'ei then marched to Hsien-yang where Tzu-ying, the king of Ch'in, surrendered to him.

When the governor of P'ei entered the palace of Ch'in, he found halls and pavilions, dogs, horses, treasures, and waiting women by the thousand. He wanted to remain in the palace, but Fan K'uai advised him to leave the capital and camp in the field. When the governor refused to listen, Chang Liang spoke up. "It is because of Ch'in's violent and unprincipled ways that you have come this far. Now that you have freed the world of these tyrannical bandits it is proper that you should don the plain white garments of mourning as a pledge of your sympathy for the sufferings of the people. Having just entered the capital of Ch'in, if you were now to indulge yourself in its pleasures, this would be 'helping the tyrant Chieh to work his violence.' Good advice is hard on the ears, but it profits the conduct just as good medicine, though bitter in the mouth, cures the sickness. I beg you to listen to Fan K'uai's counsel!"

The governor of P'ei accordingly returned and camped at Pa-shang. When Hsiang Yü reached Hung-men, he made preparations to attack the governor. Hsiang Po hastened in the night to the governor's camp and visited Chang Liang in secret, urging him to run away with him, but Chang Liang replied, "I have been sent by the king of Hann to follow the governor of P'ei. Now when he is in grave difficulty it would not be right for me to run away."

Chang Liang then went and reported to the governor all that Hsiang Po had told him. "What shall we do?" asked the governor in great astonishment.

"Do you really intend to defy Hsiang Yü?" Chang Liang asked in reply.

"Some fool advised me that if I blocked the Pass and did not allow the other leaders to enter, I could become king of the whole region of Ch'in," said the governor. "Therefore I followed his suggestion."

"And do you yourself actually believe that you can defeat Hsiang Yü?"

The governor of P'ei was silent for a long time and then said, "No, of course not. But what should we do now?"

Chang Liang went outside and urged Hsiang Po to come in and join them. When Hsiang Po had entered, the governor drank a toast with him and they swore to be friends. The governor requested Hsiang Po to explain to Hsiang Yü that he had no intention of betraying him, but had closed the Pass only to prevent bandits from getting in. On his return, Hsiang Po went to see Hsiang Yü and explained the situation so that the governor was cleared of suspicion. (A full account will be found in the chapter on Hsiang Yü.)

In the first month of the first year of Han [206 B.C.] the governor of P'ei became king of Han ruling the area of Pa and Shu. He presented Chang Liang with a gift of a hundred weights of gold and two pecks of pearls, which Chang Liang in turn presented to Hsiang Po. The king of Han also instructed Chang Liang to give Hsiang Po a generous farewell and request him on behalf of the king of Han to ask

Hsiang Yü for the territory of Han. Hsiang Yü granted the request, and as a result the region of Han was added to the territories of Pa and Shu as part of the king of Han's fief.

When the king of Han proceeded to his territory, Chang Liang accompanied him as far as Hsiu. The king then ordered Chang Liang to return to his own land of Hann. "Would it not be well," Chang Liang advised, "to burn and destroy the wooden roadway which you have passed over? This would prove to the world that you have no intention of marching east again and thus set Hsiang Yü's mind at ease." The king ordered Chang Liang to destroy the roadway on his way back.

When Chang Liang reached Hann, he discovered that Hsiang Yü had not allowed Ch'eng, the king of Hann, to proceed to his own territory, but instead had taken Ch'eng with him in his march to the east. This he had done because Ch'eng had sent Chang Liang to serve the governor of P'ei. Chang Liang reported to Hsiang Yü that the king of Han had destroyed the wooden roadway and had no intention of returning east; he also revealed to him that T'ien Jung, the king of Ch'i, was planning a revolt. Because of this Hsiang Yü considered that he had nothing to worry about from Han in the west and instead sent his troops north to attack Ch'i. But he would never allow the king of Hann to proceed to his kingdom; instead he changed his title to that of marquis and later murdered him at P'eng-ch'eng.

Chang Liang fled and secretly made his way to join the king of Han, who in the meantime had already marched back from his territory and conquered the three kingdoms of Ch'in. Chang Liang was made marquis of Ch'eng-hsin, and accompanied the king of Han east to attack Hsiang Yü at P'eng-ch'eng, but they were defeated and forced to retreat to Hsia-i. The king of Han dismounted, threw his saddle on the ground and, squatting on it, said, "I wish to give away the lands east of the Pass![2] But if I am in any case to abandon them, it would be best to assign them to someone who is likely to be of service to me. Who would be suitable?"

[2] The king's wish was rather premature, since he by no means possessed control of the area east of the Pass at this time. What he means is that he is willing to abandon any direct claim to the lands in an effort to win allies to his side.

Chang Liang came forward and said, "Ch'ing Pu, the king of Chiu-chiang, has fought courageously as a general for Ch'u but is now at odds with Hsiang Yü, while P'eng Yüeh has joined with T'ien Jung, the king of Ch'i, in raising a revolt in the region of Liang. It would be well to dispatch envoys to consult with these two men as soon as possible. Among your own generals Han Hsin alone could be entrusted with a fourth of our great undertaking. If you wish to give away your lands, you had best give them to these three. Then Hsiang Yü can surely be defeated."

The king of Han accordingly dispatched Sui Ho to bargain with Ch'ing Pu, and another envoy to conclude an agreement with P'eng Yüeh. When Pao, the king of Wei, revolted, he sent Han Hsin with a force to attack him. Thus he was able to win the lands of Yen, Tai, Ch'i, and Chao over to his side. It was due to the efforts of these three men—Ch'ing Pu, P'eng Yüeh, and Han Hsin—that he eventually destroyed Hsiang Yü. Chang Liang himself suffered from frequent illness and could not take part in any expeditions. Instead he plotted the course of the various campaigns for the king of Han and accompanied him from time to time.

In the third year of Han [204 B.C.] Hsiang Yü suddenly surrounded the king of Han at Jung-yang. Alarmed at the situation, the king consulted with Li I-chi to see if there were not some way to weaken Hsiang Yü's grip on the empire. "In ancient times," Li I-chi replied, "when T'ang overthrew Chieh, he enfeoffed Chieh's descendants in Chi, and later when King Wu attacked Chou, he enfeoffed Chou's heirs in Sung. Now Ch'in, abandoning virtue and disregarding righteousness, has overthrown the sacred altars of the feudal lords and wiped out the descendants of the Six States, leaving them not enough territory to stick the point of an awl into. If you could only reestablish the descendants of the former kingdoms and present them with the seals of enfeoffment, then they, their ministers, and their people, being every one indebted to your virtue, would one and all turn in longing toward your righteousness and beg to become your subjects. With virtue and righteousness made manifest, you might face south and name yourself a dictator, and Hsiang Yü, gathering his sleeves

Marquis of Liu (Chang Liang)

together in respectful salute, would most certainly come to pay you homage." [3]

"Excellent!" exclaimed the king. "I shall have the seals of enfeoffment carved at once and you, sir, shall bear them to the lords for me."

Li I-chi had not yet departed on his mission when Chang Liang entered the presence of the king, who was at his meal. "Come in," said the king. "One of my followers has just been explaining to me how I can break the power of Ch'u," and he repeated all that Li I-chi had said. "What do you think?" he asked.

"Who has thought up this plan for you?" said Chang Liang. "It will destroy you!"

"How so?" asked the king.

"Let me borrow this pair of chopsticks and I will explain my ideas to you," he said.[4] "Now in ancient times when T'ang attacked Chieh and enfeoffed his descendants in Chi he did so only because he knew that he had the power to put Chieh to death. But do you have the power to inflict death on Hsiang Yü?"

"No, not yet," said the king.

"That is the first reason this plan will not succeed. Again, when King Wu attacked Emperor Chou and enfeoffed his descendant in Sung, he knew that he could have Chou's head whenever he wanted it. But could you have Hsiang Yü's head?"

"Not yet."

"This is the second reason. When King Wu entered the capital of the Shang dynasty, he honored the village where Shang Yung lived, freed Chi Tzu from prison, and enlarged the grave of Pi Kan. Are you in a position to enlarge the graves of the sages, honor the villages of the virtuous, and bow before the gates of the wise?"

"No."

---

[3] The typical idealistic Confucian argument that virtue alone will conquer all obstacles.

[4] In the following discourse we must imagine Chang Liang marking off the points of his argument in some way with the chopsticks. He deliberately uses the same historical precedents which Li I-chi has used, but shows that they are not relevant to the present case.

"This is the third reason. In addition King Wu distributed grain from the Chü-ch'iao granary, and scattered among the poor and starving the riches of the Deer Terrace. Can you too open the storehouses and granaries to relieve the needy?"

"No," replied the king.

"The fourth reason," said Chang Liang. "When King Wu had completed the conquest of Shang, he converted his war chariots into carriages, cast aside his shields and spears, and covered them with tiger skins to show the world that he did not intend again to take up arms. But can you put away your weapons and apply yourself to the arts of peace, never again taking up arms?"

"No," replied the king.

"The fifth reason," said Chang Liang. "He loosed his war horses on the sunny side of Mount Hua to show he had no further use for them. Can you?"

"No."

"The sixth reason. He turned his oxen to pasture in the shade of the T'ao forest to show he would transport no more supplies. Can you do without oxen to haul supplies?"

Once more, "No."

"The seventh reason. At present all the brave men throughout the empire have taken leave of their families, left the graves of their ancestors, and flocked from their old homes to join in following you, only because day and night they dream of winning a bit of land for themselves. Now if you restore the Six States and set up the descendants of Hann, Wei, Yen, Chao, Ch'i and Ch'u, these followers of yours will go back to serve their own lords, return to their old homes and the graves of their ancestors, and look after their own families. And who will be left to fight with you? This is the eighth reason! As long as Hsiang Yü is as strong as he is, the descendants of the Six States will simply bow to his power and follow him. How could you possibly make him submit to you? Therefore I say that if you follow this plan, it will destroy you!"

The king of Han stopped eating, spat out a mouthful of food, and began to curse. "That idiot Confucianist came near to spoiling the whole business for his father!"[5] he cried, and sent orders at once to have the seals destroyed.

In the fourth year of Han [203 B.C.] Han Hsin conquered Ch'i and announced that he wished to set himself up as king of Ch'i. The king of Han was angry but, on the advice of Chang Liang, sent Chang to present Han Hsin with the seals making him king of Ch'i. (A full account will be found in the chapter on Han Hsin.)

In the autumn the king of Han pursued Hsiang Yü as far as the south of Yang-hsia but, failing to win a victory, fortified his position at Ku-ling. The other leaders did not appear for the meeting which had been arranged but Chang Liang suggested a plan for the king whereby they were induced to come. (Full account in the chapter on Hsiang Yü.)

In the first month of the sixth year [201 B.C.] the king of Han, now emperor, enfeoffed his followers who had won distinction. Though Chang Liang had achieved no glory on the field of battle, the emperor said to him, "Your merit was won by sitting within the tents of command and plotting strategies that assured us victories a thousand miles away. You must select for yourself thirty thousand households of Ch'i."

"When I first began an uprising at Hsia-p'ei," Chang Liang replied, "I met Your Majesty at Liu. It was as though Heaven had sent me to serve you. You listened to my suggestions, and fortunately they turned out to be apt for the times. I shall be content if I may be enfeoffed with Liu alone. I dare not accept thirty thousand households." The emperor made him marquis of Liu and enfeoffed him at the same time as Hsiao Ho and the others.

The sixth year: The emperor had already enfeoffed over twenty of his ministers who had achieved signal distinction, but the rest of his followers argued day and night over who had won greater merit so that no further enfeoffments could be carried out. When the emperor was residing at the Southern Palace in Lo-yang, he looked down one

---

[5] The use of the phrase "his father" or "your father" to denote one's self is highly insulting, implying as it does that one has made free with the mother of the person referred to or addressed.

day from a covered walk [6] and saw his followers walking restlessly about the courtyard and sitting on the ground talking together. "What are they talking about?" he asked Chang Liang.

"Your Majesty does not know?" said Chang Liang. "They are plotting a revolt."

"But peace and order have only just been restored to the empire. Why should they be planning a revolt?"

"When Your Majesty rose from among the common people, it was through these men that you seized control of the empire. You have become the Son of Heaven, but those whom you have enfeoffed have all been close friends from old days, such as Hsiao Ho and Ts'ao Ts'an, while all your enemies of former times you have had executed. Now these, the officers of your army, reckoning up the merits they have won, believe that there is not sufficient land in the whole empire to enfeoff them all. So some of them fear they will not receive a just allotment, while others tremble lest, falling under suspicion for some error of their past, they be condemned to execution. Therefore they gather together in this way and plot rebellion."

"What should I do?" asked the emperor in consternation.

"Among the men you dislike, and all your followers know you dislike, whom do you hate the most?"

"Yung Ch'ih and I are ancient enemies," replied the emperor. "Many times in the past he has brought me trouble and shame. I would like to have killed him, but because his merit is great I have not had the heart."

"You must hurry and enfeoff Yung Ch'ih before anyone else, and make known what you have done to your other followers. When they see that Yung Ch'ih has been enfeoffed, they will all feel assured of their own rewards," said Chang Liang.

The emperor thereupon held a feast and enfeoffed Yung Ch'ih as marquis of Shih-fang, ordering the prime minister and imperial secretary to settle the question of rewards and carry out the remainder of the enfeoffments with all dispatch. When the other ministers left

[6] These elevated walks were built to connect various buildings in the palace grounds and allowed the emperor to pass over the upper level undisturbed while lesser officials and lackeys went about their business in the courtyard below, thus saving time and bother for all concerned.

the banquet, they said to each other happily, "If even Yung Ch'ih can become a marquis, the rest of us have nothing to worry about!"

Liu Ching had advised the emperor to make his capital in the area within the Pass, but the emperor still hesitated. Since most of his followers came from east of the mountains, they urged him to establish the capital at Lo-yang, pointing out that it was protected by Ch'eng-kao on the east and Mount Yao and the Min Lake on the west, with its back to the Yellow River and the I and Lo rivers flowing before it, and could therefore be easily fortified and held. But Chang Liang objected, saying, "Although Lo-yang has these natural defenses, the area within is so small it does not exceed a few hundred *li*. The land is poor and open to attack from four sides, so that from a military point of view it is quite unsuitable. The area within the Pass, on the other hand, is protected by Mount Yao and the Han-ku Pass on the left and by Lung and Shu to the right,[7] comprising some thousand *li* of fertile plain, with the rich fields of Pa and Shu to the south and the advantages of the pasture lands of the barbarians to the north. With three sides protected by natural barriers, one has only to worry about controlling the feudal lords to the east. So long as the feudal lords are at peace, tribute can be transported up the Yellow and Wei Rivers to supply the capital area in the west, and if the lords should revolt one can descend these same rivers and attack them, assured of an adequate supply of provisions. The area within the Pass is in fact one vast fortress of iron, a veritable storehouse created by nature. Therefore Liu Ching's advice is correct."

The same day the emperor mounted his carriage and began the journey west to make his capital within the Pass, Chang Liang accompanying him through the Pass. Because he suffered from frequent illness, Chang Liang practiced various austerities, eating no grain and not venturing out of his house for a year or more.

The emperor wished to remove the heir apparent[8] and set up Ju-i, the king of Chao, his son by Lady Ch'i, in his place. Many of the high ministers had strongly advised him against this, but they could not get

---

[7] I.e., to the left and right of the emperor if he were imagined as seated in his capital within the Pass and facing south.

[8] The emperor's son by Empress Lü. He later became Emperor Hui.

him once and for all to give up the idea. Empress Lü, fearful for the position of her son, was at a loss what to do, when someone reminded her that Chang Liang was very skillful at devising schemes and enjoyed the confidence of the emperor. She therefore sent Lü Tse,[9] the marquis of Chien-ch'eng, to threaten Chang Liang, saying, "You have always advised the emperor on matters of policy. Now the emperor is planning to change the heir apparent. How can you sit calmly by and let this happen?"

"In the past," replied Chang Liang, "when the emperor on a number of occasions found himself in difficulty, he was good enough to follow certain plans which I suggested. Now, however, the world is at peace. If, because of his love for Lady Ch'i, the emperor wishes to change his choice of heir apparent, this is a family matter. Nothing I or all the other ministers might say could have any effect."

But Lü Tse persisted. "You must think of some plan for us!"

"In this sort of affair mere arguments and reproaches are of little use," Chang Liang replied. "I recall, however, that there are four men in the world whom the emperor has not succeeded in attracting to his court. These four men are very old and, because they believe that the emperor is haughty and rude to others, they have hidden themselves away in the mountains and refused on principle to acknowledge any allegiance to the house of Han. Yet I know that the emperor admires them greatly. Now if you are willing to spare no expense in gold and precious gifts, you might have the heir apparent write them a letter offering in the humblest possible terms to send carriages to fetch them, and at the same time dispatch some artful talker to press the invitation. In that case I think they would come. If they came, you could entertain them as your guests and from time to time take them with you to court. The emperor will be sure to wonder who they are and ask about them. When he discovers that they are worthy men, this will help somewhat to strengthen the position of the heir apparent."

Empress Lü, adopting this plan, had Lü Tse send someone to fetch the four old men, bearing a letter from the heir apparent couched in terms of humility and according them the highest respect and courtesy.

---

[9] Lü Tse's name is apparently used here in error for that of his younger brother, Lü Shih-chih.

When the four arrived, they were entertained as guests at the home of Lü Tse.

In the eleventh year [196 B.C.] Ch'ing Pu revolted. Since the emperor himself was ill, he planned to send the heir apparent to lead the attack against him. The four old men said to one another, "We have come all this way simply to help protect the heir apparent. But if he is sent to lead the troops, the whole plan will be imperiled." Accordingly they advised Lü Tse, saying, "We hear that the heir apparent is to be sent to lead the troops. But even if he is victorious he cannot be given any position higher than that which he already holds, while if he returns without merit he will henceforth face grave misfortune. The other generals who will go with him on the expedition are all veteran commanders who fought with the emperor in the past to win possession of the empire. To put the heir apparent in command of a group of men such as this is like sending a lamb to lead a pack of wolves. None of them will be willing to do his best for such a leader, and the failure of the expedition will be assured. The saying goes, 'If the mother is loved, the child will be embraced.' Now Lady Ch'i day and night attends the emperor, and her son Ju-i is always with him in his arms. The emperor himself, they say, has sworn that 'no unworthy son shall ever hold a place above this beloved child.' Is this not clear proof that he intends to replace the heir apparent? You must hasten to Empress Lü and beg her to take advantage of some moment of leisure to appear before the emperor and plead with him in tears. She must tell him that Ch'ing Pu is known throughout the world as a fierce fighter and a master at arms, while the other generals who will go to fight against him are all comrades of the emperor from former days. To send the heir apparent to lead such a group would be no different from setting a lamb to lead wolves. They would never consent to obey his orders, and Ch'ing Pu, learning of the situation, would march fearlessly west to attack us. Although the emperor is ill, he must make an effort to rise and accompany the expedition in a transport carriage. Even though he is bedridden, so long as he is directing them the other generals will not dare to shirk their duties. She must beg him, at whatever pain, to do this much for his wife and child."

Lü Tse went at night to see the empress, who did as he advised, appearing before the emperor in tears and repeating the words of the four old men. "It appears to me," the emperor replied, "that this worthless boy is not fit to be sent. Very well, then, I will go myself."

The emperor made preparations to lead the troops east himself; all the ministers who were to stay behind to guard the capital accompanied him as far as Pa-shang to see him off. Though Chang Liang was ill, he forced himself to get up and go to visit the emperor at Ch'ü-yu. "I should by right be accompanying you," he said, "but I am too sick. The men of Ch'u are very swift and nimble. I beg Your Majesty not to cross swords with them in person." Then before parting he advised the emperor, "It would be well to make the heir apparent a general of the army and put him in charge of the troops within the Pass."

"Although you are ill," replied the emperor, "I would like you to do as much as you can to instruct the heir apparent." Shu-sun T'ung was at this time grand tutor to the heir apparent, but because of the emperor's request Chang Liang undertook the duties of secondary tutor.

In the twelfth year of Han [195 B.C.] the emperor, having crushed Ch'ing Pu's army, returned to the capital. His illness had grown worse, and he was more than ever determined to change the heir apparent. Chang Liang counseled him against this, but he refused to listen and, because of his grave condition, ceased to attend to matters of state. Shu-sun T'ung also, as grand tutor, pleaded and argued, citing examples from ancient and recent history and begging that the present heir apparent be retained, though he knew that his stand might cost him his life. The emperor, although he had not altered his intention, finally pretended to give in.

It happened that a banquet was held and wine set out in the palace; the heir apparent waited upon the emperor and the four old men accompanied him. All of them were over eighty, with snow-white beards and eyebrows and arrayed in the most imposing caps and gowns. The emperor, struck with curiosity, asked who they were, whereupon each of them came forward and announced his name: "Master Tung-yüan," "Scholar Lu-li," "Ch'i Li-chi," "Master Hsia-huang."

"Gentlemen," the emperor replied in astonishment, "I have sought you for many years, but you have always hidden from me. How is it that you deign to come now and wait upon my son?"

"Your Majesty is contemptuous of others and given to cursing people," the four replied. "We did not consider it right to subject ourselves to insult, and therefore we were afraid and fled into hiding. But it came to our ears that the heir apparent was a man of kindness and reverence who loved others. The whole world, we heard, looked to him with yearning, and not a man but would give his life for him. Therefore we have come."

"If it is not too much trouble," said the emperor. "I hope you will be kind enough to look after the heir apparent and assist him."

The four men proposed a toast to the emperor's health and, when this was finished, rose and departed. The emperor stared after them and then, calling Lady Ch'i to his side, pointed to them and said, "I had hoped to change the heir apparent, but these four men have come to his aid. Like a pair of great wings they have borne him aloft where we cannot reach him. Empress Lü is your real master now!" Lady Ch'i wept.

"If you will do a dance of Ch'u for me," said the emperor, "I will make you a song of Ch'u," and he sang:

> The great swan soars aloft,
> In one swoop a thousand miles.
> He has spread his giant wings
> And spans the four seas.
> He who spans the four seas—
> Ah, what can we do?
> Though we bear stringed arrows to down him,
> Whereto should we aim them?

While Lady Ch'i sobbed and wept, the emperor sang the song through several times; then he rose and left the banquet. The fact that in the end the emperor did not change the heir apparent was due to the influence of these four men whom Chang Liang had originally summoned.

Chang Liang accompanied the emperor in his attack on Tai and devised the unusual plan by which the city of Ma-i was captured; later he was instrumental in having Hsiao Ho appointed prime minister. Chang Liang often freely discussed matters of state with the emperor, but since none of these were questions which vitally affected the existence of the empire I shall not go into them here.

"My family for generations served as ministers to the state of Hann," Chang Liang announced. "When Hann was destroyed, we spared no expense in rousing the world to revolt and avenging its fate upon the rapacious Ch'in. Now with the wagging of my meager tongue I have become teacher to an emperor, enfeoffed with ten thousand households and set among the ranks of the nobility. A common man can reach no greater heights; here I am content to rest. I wish now to lay aside the affairs of this world, and join the Master of the Red Pine [10] in immortal sport." He set about practicing dietary restrictions and breathing and stretching exercises to achieve levitation.

At the time of Kao-tsu's demise, Empress Lü, who was greatly indebted to Chang Liang, urged him to eat, saying, "Man's life in this world is as brief as the passing of a white colt glimpsed through a crack in the wall. Why should you punish yourself like this?" Chang Liang had no other recourse but to listen to her advice and begin eating again. Eight years later he died and was given the posthumous title of "Wen-ch'eng" or "Civil Accomplishment Marquis." His son Pu-i succeeded to the marquisate.

Thirteen years after Chang Liang had first met the old man on the embankment at Hsia-p'ei and had been given *The Book of the Grand Duke,* he was accompanying Kao-tsu through Chi-pei. There, at the foot of Mount Ku-ch'eng, just as the old man had said, he found a yellow stone, which he took away with him, treating it with the utmost reverence and worshiping it. When he died the stone was placed with him in the grave mound and in the sixth and twelfth months, when his descendants ascended the mound to pay their respects, they worshiped it. In the fifth year of Emperor Wen, Chang Liang's son Pu-i was accused of lese majesty and his territory taken away.

The Grand Historian remarks: Most scholars agree that there are no such things as ghosts and spirits, though they concede the existence of weird beings. What, I wonder, are we to make of the old man whom Chang Liang met and the book he gave him? Kao-tsu on a number of occasions found himself in grave difficulty, and yet Chang

---

[10] A legendary sage of ancient times who achieved immortality.

Liang always had a way out. Was this not the work of Heaven? The emperor himself admitted that "when it comes to sitting within the tents of command and devising strategies that will assure victory a thousand miles away, I am no match for Chang Liang." I had always imagined, therefore, that Chang Liang must have been a man of majestic stature and imposing appearance. And yet when I saw a picture of him, his face looked like that of a woman or a pretty young girl. Confucius once remarked, "If I had judged by looks alone I would have sadly mistaken Tzu-yü." The same might be said of Chang Liang.

Shih chi 56: The Hereditary House of Prime Minister Ch'en

With the six curious strategies of his devising, the other nobles were brought to submission and became followers of the Han, while in the overthrow of the Lü family he was the chief plotter, assuring in the end the safety of the dynasty's ancestral temples and the continuance of its altars of the soil and grain. Thus I made The Hereditary House of Prime Minister Ch'en.

Ch'en P'ing

Prime Minister Ch'en P'ing was a native of Hu-yu county in Yang-wu.[1] When he was young he loved to read books. His family was very poor and owned only thirty *mou*[2] of farm land. Ch'en P'ing lived alone with his older brother, who did all the work in the fields, leaving Ch'en P'ing free to pursue his studies as he wished. Ch'en P'ing was tall and very good-looking. Someone once remarked to him, "If your family is so poor, what in the world do you eat that you grow so big and plump?" Ch'en P'ing's older brother's wife, who was very put out that Ch'en P'ing did nothing to help the family finances, took it upon herself to answer. "And yet he eats nothing but husks and leavings like the rest of us!"[3] she exclaimed sarcastically. "Better to have no brother at all than one like this!" When Ch'en P'ing's older brother heard what his wife had said, he drove her out of the house and broke off the marriage.

After a while Ch'en P'ing reached the age for taking a wife himself. But since none of the wealthy families were willing to offer him their daughters, and since he was too proud to marry a girl from a poor family, time passed and he remained single. In Hu-yu there lived a rich old woman named Chang. This Dame Chang had a grand-

---

[1] In the region of Wei.
[2] The Han *mou* was equal to about 0.114 acre, so that the Ch'en family had less than 3½ acres.
[3] That is, he grows fat not by what he eats but because he does no work.

daughter who had married five times, but each time her husband had immediately died, so that no one dared to take her as a wife. Ch'en P'ing, however, decided that he wanted to marry her. It happened that there was a funeral in the city and Ch'en P'ing, being poor, acted as one of the hired attendants, helping out by arriving before the guests and leaving after the rest. Dame Chang noticed Ch'en P'ing at the funeral and was much impressed by his unusual good looks. Aware that he had attracted her attention, Ch'en P'ing purposely waited until the other guests had left before leaving, and when he did Dame Chang followed him to his house. His home was at the far end of a lane and backed against the city wall, with some old worn matting hung up for a gateway. Yet outside the gate were many tracks made by the sort of carriages ridden in by people of means.

When Dame Chang returned to her own home, she said to her son Chung, "I wish to marry my granddaughter to Ch'en P'ing."

"Ch'en P'ing is poor and does nothing to earn a living," objected her son. "Throughout the whole district people just laugh at his ways. Why should you want to marry this girl to him?"

"Anyone as good-looking as Ch'en P'ing will never stay poor and despised for long," said the old lady, and in the end she gave him the girl for a wife. Because Ch'en P'ing was so poor, she also lent him money to use for the betrothal gifts and sent him supplies of wine and meat for the wedding celebration. The old lady cautioned her granddaughter, saying, "You must never be inattentive in serving your husband just because he is poor! Treat his older brother as you would your father, and his brother's wife as you would your mother."

After Ch'en P'ing had married the daughter of the Chang family he found himself enjoying increasing prosperity and day by day broadened his circle of acquaintances. He was made steward of the local shrine and put in charge of the sacrifices, and he divided the sacrificial flesh among the worshipers with such fairness that the elders all remarked, "What an excellent steward young Ch'en is!" Ch'en P'ing sighed and said, "Ah, if I could only become steward of the empire I would divide it up in the same way as this flesh!"

When Ch'en She began his uprising and became king of Ch'en, he sent Chou Shih to seize and conquer the region at Wei and set up Wei

Chiu as king of Wei, encountering the Ch'in armies in an attack on Lin-chi. Ch'en P'ing had earlier taken leave of his older brother and gone with a group of young men to Lin-chi to serve the new king of Wei, who made Ch'en P'ing his master of carriage, but paid no attention to his suggestions. When someone slandered Ch'en P'ing to the king, he escaped and ran away. After some time, Hsiang Yü invaded the region and reached the Yellow River, whereupon Ch'en P'ing became a follower of his, accompanying him through the Pass to the destruction of Ch'in. He was awarded a noble rank for his services.

When Hsiang Yü returned east to rule from the city of P'eng-ch'eng and the king of Han marched back from his territory to conquer the three kingdoms of Ch'in, Ssu-ma Ang, the king of Yin, revolted against Hsiang Yü. Hsiang Yü gave Ch'en P'ing the title of lord of Hsin-wu and sent him to lead the followers of King Chiu of Wei who were in Ch'u in an attack on the king of Yin. The king of Yin surrendered and returned to the side of Hsiang Yü, whereupon Hsiang Yü sent Hsiang Han to make Ch'en P'ing a colonel and award him twenty pieces of gold. Before any time had passed, however, the king of Han attacked and won control of the region of Yin. Hsiang Yü was furious and set about to execute the generals and officers who were supposed to have conquered Yin for him. Ch'en P'ing, fearful that he would be among those executed, sealed up the gold which had been awarded him and sent it back by messenger to Hsiang Yü, while he himself, bearing only his sword, fled by a secret route into hiding.

As he was crossing the Yellow River, the boatman ferrying him began to wonder why such a fine, good-looking man should be traveling alone. Suspecting that he was a military leader in flight and would be likely to have gold or jewels or other precious goods concealed about his waist, he began to eye him with thoughts of murder. Ch'en P'ing, afraid of what the man might be thinking, stripped off his clothes until he was naked and began to help the boatman with his oar. The man realized then that Ch'en P'ing had nothing concealed on him, and gave up the idea of murder. Eventually Ch'en P'ing reached Hsiu-wu, where he surrendered to the king of Han.

Ch'en P'ing asked Wei Wu-chih to arrange an audience for him with the king of Han and as a result was summoned by the king. At this time Shih Fen (later known as "Lord Ten Thousand Piculs"), who was acting as page to the king of Han, took Ch'en P'ing's calling card and led him in to the interview. After Ch'en P'ing and six other guests at the interview had come forward and received gifts of food, the king announced, "You may return to your lodgings now."

"I have come on special business," said Ch'en P'ing, "and what I have to say cannot wait until another day." Accordingly the king began to converse with Ch'en P'ing and was much pleased with him. "What was your position under Hsiang Yü?" he asked. "I was a colonel," replied Ch'en P'ing. On the same day the king honored Ch'en P'ing with the rank of colonel, and made him one of his carriage attendants and a superintendent of the army. At this the other military leaders began to grumble vehemently. "The king gets hold of some runaway soldier from the army of Ch'u and, without knowing anything about his ability, he sets him by his side in the royal carriage and even makes him a supervisor over all of us who are his seniors!" But when the king heard what they were saying, he only continued to heap further honors on Ch'en P'ing.

Ch'en P'ing eventually accompanied him in the campaign against Hsiang Yü as far east as P'eng-ch'eng, where they were defeated by the Ch'u army and forced to retreat. The king gathered up his scattered forces and marched to Jung-yang, where he appointed Ch'en P'ing a lieutenant general under the command of Hsin, the king of Hann, and sent him to garrison Kuang-wu. Chou P'o, Kuan Ying, and others of the high officers all began to speak ill of Ch'en P'ing to the king of Han. "Ch'en P'ing is a handsome man," they said, "but good looks are like jeweled decorations on a hat—they do not necessarily indicate that there is anything inside! We have heard that while he was living at home he carried on in secret with his brother's wife. He went to serve the king of Wei but, when he could get nowhere there, he ran away and joined Hsiang Yü. And when he failed to make an impression on Hsiang Yü, he ran away again and came to join us. Today Your Majesty has honored him with a high position and put him in charge of the army. But we have heard that he is accepting money from the various generals—those who give a lot of money get good assignments, and those who give only a little get poor ones. As a subject, Ch'en P'ing is fickle and corrupt. We beg you to look into the matter!"

The king of Han, his suspicions aroused, summoned Wei Wu-chih, who had first recommended Ch'en P'ing, and began to berate him. "I recommended the man because of his ability," Wei Wu-chih replied, "but now Your Majesty questions me on his behavior! Even the most shining examples of chaste and loyal behavior would be of no help in deciding our fate in battle, so why should Your Majesty trouble about such questions? The armies of Ch'u and Han are locked in stalemate. When I recommended this man for his ability to devise ingenious strategies, I was only considering whether or not his schemes could be of actual benefit to the state. Why should the fact that he slept with his brother's wife or took bribes be grounds for doubting his ability?"

The king of Han then sent for Ch'en P'ing and upbraided him. "I understand, Master Ch'en, that you served Wei until you found you could not get your way, and then you joined Hsiang Yü, but left him too. Now you have decided to follow along with my party. Don't you think you have changed your allegiance rather often?"

"I served the king of Wei," replied Ch'en P'ing, "but he was unwilling to listen to my advice. Therefore I left him and went to serve Hsiang Yü. But Hsiang Yü is incapable of trusting others. The only men he employs or shows favor to are members of the Hsiang family or relatives of his wife. Although he has clever strategists, he is unwilling to use them. Hence I left him too. Then I heard that the king of Han knew how to use men, and so I joined Your Majesty. I came here naked and alone. Had I not accepted money from others, I would have had nothing to keep alive on. If among the schemes and plans which I have to suggest there are any that are worthy of attention, I hope that Your Majesty will use them. If there are none of use to you, I beg to be allowed to seal and hand over all the money in my possession, relinquish my position, and take my leave."

With this the king of Han pardoned Ch'en P'ing and rewarded him with generosity, making him colonel of the guard with supervision over all the other generals. After this the other generals dared say no more against him.

Later Hsiang Yü pressed his attack on the king of Han, cutting off the Han walled supply road and encircling the king in the city of Jung-yang. After some time had passed the king of Han, worried by the situation, offered to make peace on condition that he be allowed to retain possession of all the land west of Jung-yang, but Hsiang Yü refused to listen to such terms.

"When will this turmoil in the world ever come to an end?" the king of Han remarked to Ch'en P'ing.

Ch'en P'ing replied, "Hsiang Yü is by nature respectful and thoughtful of others. Hence the gentlemen of honor and integrity and the lovers of propriety all flock to his side. But when it comes to rewarding the achievements of others and conferring fiefs, he is too niggardly, and for this reason there are some men who will not stay with him. Your Majesty, on the other hand, is arrogant and unmindful of propriety, and therefore gentlemen of honor and integrity do not come to you. But because you are willing to enrich men with grants of territory, the dull and unscrupulous, the lovers of gain and the shameless all rush to your side. If only each of you could lay aside his shortcomings and build up his strong points, then the leadership of the world might be settled once for all. But because Your Majesty is so willful and insulting to others, it is impossible to win over men of honor and integrity!

"And yet there is a way to bring confusion to the Ch'u forces. Hsiang Yü has only a few honest and outspoken ministers such as Fan Tseng, Chung-li Mo, Lung Chü, and Chou Yin. Now if you were actually willing to part with thirty or forty thousand catties of gold, I could tempt them to revolt, bring about dissension between the leader and his men, and cast suspicion upon their loyalty. Hsiang Yü is by nature mistrustful and wary of others and quick to give credit to slanderous talk, so that he is sure to start executing the men within his own camp. Then you may raise the Han forces and attack from without and the defeat of the Ch'u army will be certain!"

The king of Han, considering the idea a reasonable one, gave Ch'en P'ing a sum of forty thousand catties of yellow gold to use as he wished, making no further inquiry about the matter. Ch'en P'ing used a large part of the money to create dissension within the Ch'u army, sending a message to Chung-li Mo and the various other generals pointing out that, though they had won great merit in the service of Hsiang Yü, they had in the end never been awarded grants of territory or become kings. He urged them to join forces with the Han to overthrow the Hsiang family and divide up its territory among themselves. As Ch'en P'ing had expected, Hsiang Yü became suspicious and began to mistrust Chung-li Mo and the others.

Hsiang Yü's suspicions had already been aroused when he happened to send an envoy to the Han camp. The king of Han had a meal of all sorts of fancy dishes prepared and brought in but, upon seeing the envoy, he pretended to be thoroughly startled and said, "I supposed you were the envoy from Fan Tseng, but I see that you have come from Hsiang Yü!" He then had the feast taken away and a meal of coarse food brought in and served to the envoy. The envoy returned and reported all that had happened to Hsiang Yü who, as Ch'en P'ing had hoped, grew deeply suspicious of Fan Tseng. Fan Tseng wished to make an immediate attack upon the city of Jung-yang but Hsiang Yü, because of his mistrust, refused to listen to this idea. When Fan Tseng heard that Hsiang Yü suspected his loyalty, he became very angry. "The affairs of the world have been largely settled," he said. "You must manage things for yourself, my lord. I beg to be relieved of my duties and allowed to go home!" His request was granted but, before he reached P'eng-ch'eng, an ulcerous sore broke out on his back and he died.

Later Ch'en P'ing sent some two thousand women of Jung-yang out of the east gate at night and, while the Ch'u forces were rushing to attack them, he and the king of Han slipped out by the west gate and made their escape. Eventually they reentered the Pass, gathered together more forces, and marched east again.

The following year Han Hsin conquered Ch'i and set himself up as king of Ch'i, sending an envoy to the king of Han to have his title confirmed. The king of Han was furious and began to curse the envoy, but Ch'en P'ing restrained him by stepping on his foot as a hint, and when the king realized the pointlessness of such behavior, he received the envoy with generosity and eventually dispatched Chang Liang to go and confirm Han Hsin in his title of king of Ch'i. Ch'en P'ing he enfeoffed with the district of Hu-yu and, by employing his ingenious schemes and strategies, was eventually able to destroy Hsiang Yü. Later, in his usual capacity of colonel of the guard, Ch'en P'ing accompanied the king of Han, now emperor, in his campaign to put down Tsang Tu, the king of Yen.

In the sixth year of Han someone reported to the emperor that Han Hsin, who had been transferred from the position of king of Ch'i to that of king of Ch'u, was planning revolt. Emperor Kao-tsu consulted his generals, who unanimously replied, "Send troops at once to butcher the villain!" The emperor was silent for a while and then summoned Ch'en P'ing and asked his opinion. Ch'en P'ing firmly declined to answer, but asked instead, "What do the generals say?" When the emperor had told him their opinion, he asked, "Is it known that someone has sent in a report accusing Han Hsin of revolt?"

"Not yet," replied the emperor.

"Does Han Hsin himself know?"

"No, he is unaware of it."

"Who has finer soldiers, Your Majesty or Han Hsin?" asked Ch'en P'ing.

"Mine are no better than his," said the emperor.

"And Your Majesty's generals—are they superior to Han Hsin in leading their men?"

"They are no match for him!"

"So our troops are not as well trained as his, and our generals are inferior. Yet if we were to call out our forces and attack him, this would be deliberately inciting him to battle. In my humble opinion, it would be a dangerous course for Your Majesty to take!" said Ch'en P'ing.

"Then what should we do?" asked the emperor.

"In ancient times the Son of Heaven used to go on royal tours and meet with his nobles. In the south there is a lake called Yün-meng. Your Majesty has only to pretend to set out on a pleasure trip to Yünmeng and arrange for the nobles to meet you at Ch'en. Ch'en is on the western border of Ch'u, so that when Han Hsin hears that the Son of Heaven is making a harmless pleasure trip, he will under the circumstances undoubtedly consider it quite safe to journey to the border to greet you. Then, when he comes to visit, you may take him prisoner. In this way you will have only one strong man to deal with instead of an army."

The emperor approved of the plan and proceeded to send envoys to the feudal lords instructing them to meet him at Ch'en, "since I shall be journeying south to Yün-meng." The emperor set out immediately afterward but, before he reached Ch'en, Han Hsin, as he had anticipated, came to meet him along the way. The emperor had prepared his guards beforehand and, when Han Hsin arrived, ordered them to seize and bind him and place him in the rear carriage. Han Hsin sighed and said, "Now that the world has been conquered, I suppose it is time that I be boiled alive!"

The emperor turned to look back at him. "Keep quiet, you!" he called. "It is clear you were plotting a revolt!" Then the guards tied Han Hsin's hands behind his back and the emperor proceeded to his meeting with the nobles at Ch'en and brought the region of Ch'u back to order again.

When he returned to Lo-yang he pardoned Han Hsin and made him marquis of Huai-yin. It was at this time that he awarded his meritorious ministers the split tallies of formal enfeoffment and settled their grants of territory. To Ch'en P'ing he awarded the split tallies to be passed on from generation to generation without end, making him marquis of Hu-yu, but Ch'en P'ing declined to accept, saying, "I have done nothing to merit this."

"By using your plans and strategies, Master Ch'en," said the emperor, "I won victory in battle and overcame my enemies. If this is not an achievement of merit, what is it?"

"But if it had not been for Wei Wu-chih," said Ch'en P'ing, "how would I ever have been recommended to Your Majesty?"

"You are the sort people mean when they say, 'He never forgets his old friends'!" said the emperor and proceeded to reward Wei Wu-chih as well.

The following year Ch'en P'ing in his capacity as colonel of the guard accompanied the emperor in an attack upon the rebellious King Hsin of Hann in Tai. When they finally reached P'ing-ch'eng they were surrounded by the Hsiung-nu and for seven days were unable to obtain food. Emperor Kao-tsu, following an ingenious plan suggested

Prime Minister Ch'en

by Ch'en P'ing, sent an envoy to the consort of the *Shan-yü*.[4] The siege was finally raised and Kao-tsu managed to escape. The exact plan used was secret so that nowadays no one knows just what it was.

When Kao-tsu was on his way south again he passed through Ch'ü-ni. Ascending the city walls and gazing out over the vast number of its houses, he exclaimed, "What a splendid district town this is! In all my travels about the empire I have seen nothing to compare with this outside of Lo-yang."

Then he turned to his secretary and asked, "What is the population of Ch'ü-ni?"

"Originally, during the time of Ch'in, it had over thirty thousand households," replied the secretary. "But since then, what with the frequent uprisings, many of the inhabitants have fled or gone into hiding so that now there are actually only five thousand households." With this the emperor ordered his secretary to transfer Ch'en P'ing to the position of marquis of Ch'ü-ni, receiving the revenue from the entire city, and to remove him from his former fief of Hu-yu.

Ch'en P'ing continued as before to serve as colonel of the guard, accompanying the emperor in his attacks against Ch'en Hsi and Ch'ing Pu. He is said to have devised in all six ingenious strategies, for each of which he was at once awarded additional grants of cities, so that his feudal holdings were six times enlarged. Some of the strategies were kept strictly secret, however, so that nowadays there is no way of determining what they were.

Kao-tsu, returning from his campaign to crush Ch'ing Pu, fell ill of a wound he had received and had to proceed to the capital at Ch'ang-an by slow stages. When word came that Lu Wan, the king of Yen, had revolted, he appointed Fan K'uai as prime minister of Yen and sent him to lead an army against the rebels. After Fan K'uai had departed, however, someone began to speak badly of him. The emperor, believing the slander, was in a rage. "Fan K'uai saw that I am ill, and now he is hoping I will die!" he declared. On the advice of Ch'en P'ing, he summoned Chou P'o, the marquis of Chiang, to his bedside and delivered these instructions: "Ch'en P'ing is to hasten at

---

[4] *Shan-yü* was the title of the Hsiung-nu chieftain. The word is said to mean "broad and great."

once by relay carriage with Chou P'o, who will replace Fan K'uai as commander. When Ch'en P'ing reaches the camp, he is to decapitate Fan K'uai on the spot!"

Ch'en P'ing and Chou P'o, having received the imperial command, set off in haste by relay carriage, but before they had reached the place where the army was camped, they began to discuss the matter between themselves as they went along. "Fan K'uai," they said, "is an old friend of the emperor and has won great merit. Moreover he is the husband of Empress Lü's younger sister Lü Hsü. He enjoys great intimacy with the imperial family as well as high position. It is only because the emperor is in a rage that he wants to cut off Fan K'uai's head, and in all probability he will regret it later. It would be better to make Fan K'uai a prisoner and bring him before the emperor. Then the emperor may carry out the punishment in person."

Accordingly, before they had reached the camp they halted and constructed an altar and, bearing the imperial credentials, summoned Fan K'uai. Fan K'uai appeared and accepted the emperor's command, whereupon his hands were bound behind his back and he was placed in a caged cart and sent by relay to Ch'ang-an. By the same order Chou P'o took his place as commander with instructions to lead the army in reconquering the districts of Yen which were in revolt.

While Ch'en P'ing was on his way back to the capital, he received word that Emperor Kao-tsu had passed away. Fearful that Empress Lü and her sister Lü Hsü, when they found out what had happened, would be angry and try to slander him, he hastened on ahead of Fan K'uai by relay carriage. Along the way he met an envoy bearing an imperial order for Ch'en P'ing and Kuan Ying to proceed to the garrison at Jung-yang. Ch'en P'ing accepted the order but at once resumed his journey until he reached the palace, where he wept with profound grief for the deceased emperor and then, from his place before the coffin, reported to Empress Lü what had taken place. Empress Lü felt sorry for him and said, "Very well. You may go now." But Ch'en P'ing was afraid that if he went away he would become the victim of slander and so he earnestly begged that he be given a position in the palace guards. Empress Lü accordingly made him a palace attendant and said, "You must act as tutor and instruct the new emperor." After this, although Lü Hsü attempted to defame him, she was able to accomplish nothing. When Fan K'uai arrived in the capital he was pardoned and restored to his former position and title.

In the sixth year of Emperor Hui, Prime Minister Ts'ao Ts'an died, and for this reason Wang Ling, the marquis of An-kuo, was made chancellor of the right and Ch'en P'ing chancellor of the left.

Wang Ling

Wang Ling was a native of P'ei and was originally one of the most powerful men in the district. When Kao-tsu was still a commoner he treated Wang Ling like an older brother. Wang Ling had little education but was high spirited and fond of speaking his mind.

Later, when Kao-tsu began his uprising in P'ei and made his way to the capital at Hsien-yang, Wang Ling gathered together his own band of several thousand men. He stayed in the region of Nan-yang, however, and was unwilling to become a follower of Kao-tsu. It was only later, after Kao-tsu had become king of Han and returned east to attack Hsiang Yü, that he took his forces and placed them under Kao-tsu's command.

Hsiang Yü seized Wang Ling's mother and held her captive in the midst of his camp. When an envoy arrived from Wang Ling, Hsiang Yü seated Wang Ling's mother in the place of honor facing east, hoping by such favorable treatment to induce Wang Ling to come over to his side. When the envoy was leaving, Wang Ling's mother, who had come to take her leave of him in private, wept and said, "There is something I want you to tell my son for me. Let him serve the king of Han with all diligence, for the king of Han is a worthy man. He must not be of two minds on my account! See, I send off his envoy with the gift of my death!" And with this she stabbed herself with a sword and died. Hsiang Yü was enraged and had her body boiled. In the end Wang Ling joined the king of Han in conquering the empire but, because he was good friends with Yung Ch'ih, who was an old enemy of Kao-tsu, and because he originally had not shown any inclination to join Kao-tsu, he was not enfeoffed until rather late, being made marquis of An-kuo.

Two years after Wang Ling took office as chancellor of the right, Emperor Hui passed away. Empress Lü, who wanted to set up the members of her own family as kings, asked Wang Ling's opinion, but he replied, "That cannot be done!" When she asked Ch'en P'ing's opinion, however, he said there was no objection. Irritated at Wang Ling, the empress pretended to promote him by making him grand tutor to the emperor,[5] but in fact she ceased to pay any more attention to him. Wang Ling angrily resigned from his position on grounds of illness, shut the gates of his house, and no longer appeared at court functions. He died in the seventh year of Empress Lü's reign.

Shen I-chi

After Wang Ling resigned as chancellor of the right, Empress Lü transferred Ch'en P'ing to the position of chancellor of the right and appointed Shen I-chi, the marquis of Pi-yang, to Ch'en P'ing's former position of chancellor of the left. The chancellor of the left, however, did not use the government offices, but conducted his affairs from the palace itself.

Shen I-chi was also a native of P'ei. When Kao-tsu was defeated at P'eng-ch'eng and forced to flee west, Hsiang Yü seized his father and Empress Lü and held them as hostages. Shen I-chi at this time acted as their attendant and waited on Empress Lü. Later he accompanied Kao-tsu in the final defeat of Hsiang Yü and was made a marquis. He enjoyed great favor with Empress Lü and, when he became chancellor and attended her in the palace, all the other officials were obliged to go through him before they could get anything done.

Lü Hsü, the empress's young sister, on a number of occasions spoke ill of Ch'en P'ing because he had once in the past plotted the arrest of her husband, Fan K'uai, for Emperor Kao-tsu. "Since Ch'en P'ing became chancellor, he pays no attention to his duties," she declared, "but spends his days drinking fine wines and dallying with women!"

---

[5] The child whom Empress Lü put on the throne after the death of her son, Emperor Hui. She herself continued as before to wield the actual power.

Ch'en P'ing, aware of what was being said of him, only indulged himself more openly each day. When Empress Lü heard of this she was secretly pleased,[6] but for the sake of appearances she questioned him about the things which Lü Hsü was saying. "The proverb has it that 'what comes from the mouths of women and children is not worth listening to'," she said. "All that matters is how you get along with me! You need have no fear of Lü Hsü's slander."

When Empress Lü proposed setting up members of her family as kings, Ch'en P'ing pretended to agree with the idea but, after the empress had passed away, he joined with the grand commandant Chou P'o in the plot whereby they eventually overthrew the Lü family and set up Emperor Wen the Filial. Ch'en P'ing was in fact the originator of the plot. Shen I-chi resigned from his position of chancellor of the left.

After Emperor Wen came to the throne Ch'en P'ing, considering that Chou P'o had won signal merit by personally leading the army in the overthrow of the Lü family, wished to yield the place of honor to him and so he pleaded illness and resigned. Emperor Wen, who had just ascended the throne, was suspicious of Ch'en P'ing's protestations of illness and questioned him. "While Kao-tsu was living," replied Ch'en P'ing, "Chou P'o did not win as much merit as I, but in the overthrow of the Lü family my merit is no match for his. Therefore I wish to yield the position of chancellor of the right to him." Emperor Wen accordingly made Chou P'o the chancellor of the right, ranking first among the officials, and transferred Ch'en P'ing to the secondary rank of chancellor of the left. He awarded Ch'en P'ing a thousand catties of gold and increased his fief by three thousand households.

A short while later, when Emperor Wen had grown somewhat accustomed to handling affairs of state, he one day at court asked Chou P'o, the chancellor of the right, "How many law cases are there in the empire in one year?"

"I do not know," replied Chou P'o apologetically.

"And what is the annual revenue and expenditure of the government in currency and grain?" asked the emperor.

---

[6] Because he was not attempting to exercise his authority but leaving everything to her favorite, Shen I-chi.

Again Chou P'o apologetically replied, "I do not know," and the sweat poured down and drenched his back, so chagrined was he at being unable to answer.

With this the emperor questioned the chancellor of the left, Ch'en P'ing. "There are men who handle such matters," replied Ch'en P'ing.

"And who are the men who handle them?" asked the emperor.

"If Your Majesty would know about law cases," said Ch'en P'ing, "you must ask the commandant of justice, and if you would know about matters of revenue and grain, you must inquire of the secretary in charge of grain."

"If each matter has someone in charge," said the emperor, "what sort of matters, may I ask, do you handle?"

"Forgive me if I speak too boldly," said Ch'en P'ing, apologizing. "Your Majesty, unaware of how stupid and inferior a person I am, has been pleased to honor me with the position of prime minister [7] in spite of my unworthiness. It is the duty of the prime minister to be an aid to the Son of Heaven above, to adjust the forces of the yin and yang, and to see that all proceeds in accordance with the four seasons. At the same time he must strive to nourish the best in all creatures, bring order to the feudal lords and barbarian tribes surrounding the country, and within the state to win over the common people and see to it that each of the other ministers and officials performs his proper duties."

Emperor Wen was pleased with the speech. Chou P'o, however, still greatly embarrassed by the incident, began to berate Ch'en P'ing when they got outside. "Why didn't you tell me before how to answer such questions?" he demanded.

Ch'en P'ing laughed and replied, "Since you hold the position, how is it you do not know what your duties are? I suppose if His Majesty had asked you how many thieves there are in the city of Ch'ang-an, you would have felt obliged to try to answer that too!" After this Chou P'o came to realize how vastly inferior he was in ability to Ch'en P'ing. Some time later Chou P'o pleaded illness and retired from the

---

[7] I.e., chancellor. At this time the old position of prime minister was called chancellor and divided between the two men, but the two titles prime minister and chancellor were used interchangeably.

position of chancellor, leaving Ch'en P'ing to occupy the post alone.

In the second year of Emperor Wen [178 B.C.] Ch'en P'ing died. He was awarded the posthumous title of "Hsien" or "Wise Marquis." His son Ch'en Mai, Marquis Kung, succeeded to the title but died two years later. Mai's son Ch'en Hui, Marquis Chieh, succeeded to the title and died twenty-three years later. Hui's son Ch'en Ho succeeded to the title, but twenty-three years later he was convicted of making off with another man's wife and condemned to execution in the marketplace and his fief was taken away.

Ch'en P'ing used to say, "I have engaged in many secret plottings, a thing forbidden by Taoist teachings. If my heirs should ever lose their position, that would be the end. They could never regain it again because of the many secret injuries which I have done!" As it happened, much later Ch'en P'ing's great-grandson Ch'en Chang, who was related by marriage to the powerful Wei family,[8] asked to have the fief restored to the Ch'en family, but his request was never granted.

The Grand Historian remarks: From the time Ch'en P'ing was a young man he was fond of the teachings of the Yellow Emperor and Lao Tzu, and while he was carving up the sacrificial meats on the altar of the neighborhood shrine his ambitions were already far away. He went from one camp to another, suffering hardship and danger, until at last he joined Kao-tsu. Under Kao-tsu he again and again devised ingenious plans, found a way out of the most perplexing crises, and solved the ills of the state. Later, during the reign of Empress Lü, although the situation at court was complex and delicate, he managed in the end not only to save himself from harm but to assure the safety of the dynasty's ancestral temples as well, so that he died surrounded by fame and praised as a wise and worthy statesman. Is this not what it means to be "good at starting things and good at finishing them"? Surely only a man who knows how to plan can accomplish such deeds as these!

[8] His wife was a younger sister of Lady Wei, a favorite concubine of Emperor Wu.

Part V
THE DISAFFECTED

Shih chi 89: The Biographies of Chang Erh and Ch'en Yü

They subjugated Chao, blocked Ch'ang-shan, and added to these the area of Ho-nei; they weakened the power of Ch'u and made manifest to the world the good faith of Han. Thus I made The Biographies of Chang Erh and Ch'en Yü.

Chang Erh was a man of Ta-liang in Wei. In his youth he became a follower of Wu-chi, prince of Wei, but later fled into hiding and journeyed to Wai-huang. In Wai-huang there lived a rich man who had a very beautiful daughter. He married her to a day laborer, but she deserted her husband and ran away to the home of one of her father's followers. This man had known Chang Erh for some time, and he said to the girl, "If you are determined to find a worthy husband, you should give yourself to Chang Erh!" The girl consenting, he asked her father on her behalf that the former marriage be dissolved and she be given to Chang Erh. Chang Erh at the time was traveling about in order to elude his pursuers, but the girl's family provided him with such a generous dowry and allowance that he was able to attract a band of followers from hundreds of miles around. Eventually he became an official of Wei, serving as magistrate of Wai-huang, and his worth became increasingly renowned.

Ch'en Yü was also a native of Ta-liang. He was fond of Confucian studies and from time to time traveled to K'u-hsing in Chao. There a wealthy man of the Kung-ch'eng family gave him his daughter for a wife because he recognized that Ch'en Yü was no ordinary man.

Ch'en Yü was younger than Chang Erh and looked up to him as a father. The two men were such fast friends that they would have died for each other.

At the time when Ch'in destroyed the city of Ta-liang, Chang Erh was making his home in Wai-huang. While Kao-tsu was still a commoner, he frequently journeyed to join Chang Erh, remaining as his guest for several months. In the years following the destruction of the state of Wei both Chang Erh and Ch'en Yü became famous as prominent gentlemen of Wei. The Ch'in government, hearing of their fame, sought their capture,[1] offering a reward of a thousand gold pieces for Chang Erh and five hundred for Ch'en Yü. The two men assumed false names and journeyed to the region of Ch'en where they became village gate keepers to make a living.

One day the two men were sitting on opposite sides of the gate when one of the village officials accused Ch'en Yü of some fault and began to beat him. Ch'en Yü was about to jump up and resist, but Chang Erh, stepping on his foot, signaled him to sit still and take the beating. When the official had gone on, Chang Erh pulled Ch'en Yü aside into a mulberry grove and began to berate him. "What about all the big things you and I have planned? Just because you have suffered some petty insult, are you going to throw away your life now on one little official?" Ch'en Yü admitted that Chang Erh was right. When Ch'in sent an edict offering a reward for the capture of the two men they calmly used their position as gate keepers to convey the order to the village.

When Ch'en She began his uprising in Chi, and reached Ch'en with a force of twenty or thirty thousand men, Chang Erh and Ch'en Yü presented their names and requested an audience. Ch'en She and his followers had in the past often heard of the worth of the two men but had never met them. When they appeared before Ch'en She he was delighted with them.

The elders and prominent men of Ch'en advised Ch'en She, saying, "You have buckled on your armor and taken up your sword to lead your army in punishing the violence of Ch'in and setting up once more Ch'u's altars of the soil and grain. You have preserved the perishing and restored that which was cut off, and your merit and virtue deserve the position of king. Moreover, if you hope to lead and direct the other generals of the empire it is imperative that you become a king. We beg you to declare youself king of Ch'u!"

[1] Part of Ch'in's policy of preventing the formation of possible centers of resistance.

Ch'en She questioned Chang Erh and Ch'en Yü about this, and they replied, "Ch'in has worked great evil, destroying states, overthrowing their sacred altars, wiping out their heirs, exhausting the strength of the common people, and using up their wealth. Now, your eyes fired with indignation and your heart steeled against all danger, you have fearlessly embarked upon a plan of incalculable risk in order to rid the world of this scourge. But, having only just reached Ch'en, should you at once make yourself a king, it would appear to the world that you were acting out of selfish interest. We beg you not to become king, but to lead your troops west and dispatch envoys to reestablish the heirs of the Six Kingdoms. Thus you will create allies for yourself and increase the number of Ch'in's foes. If Ch'in faces many foes, its power will be divided, while if you have many friends, your forces will be strengthened. This way you will meet no opposing armies in the field and no defenders in the cities, and you may punish the violence of Ch'in, occupy the capital of Hsien-yang, and give orders to the nobles. When the nobles who were once deposed find themselves set up again, they will bow before your will in gratitude. In this way you can make yourself emperor of a new dynasty. But now if you alone make yourself a king in Ch'en, we fear that the rest of the world will desert you!"

Ch'en She, however, did not listen to their advice but in the end set himself up as a king. Ch'en Yü again advised Ch'en She, saying, "You have raised the armies of Wei and Ch'u and sent them west, intent only upon penetrating the Pass, but you have not yet gained control of the area north of the Yellow River. I once spent some time in Chao and I am familiar with the prominent families and the configuration of the land there. I beg you to give me a force of surprise troops with which to march north and seize the region of Chao!"

With this Ch'en She made Wu Ch'en, a native of Ch'en whom he had known for a long time, a general, with Shao Sao as his lieutenant general and Chang Erh and Ch'en Yü as colonels of the left and right, and assigned them a force of three thousand men to march north and seize the region of Chao. Wu Ch'en and his group crossed the Yellow River at the White Horse Ford and marched from district to district, addressing the prominent men in each place in these words:

"For twenty or thirty years now, Ch'in with its turbulent rule and cruel laws has oppressed the world. In the north we have had the labor gangs on the Long Wall, in the south the garrisons of the Five Ranges, until all is unrest within and without the nation. The common people are exhausted, and yet the officials continue to count heads and demand from each his basketful of grain tax to supply the wants of the army. The wealth of the people is used up, their strength is gone, and they have no way to keep alive. And, on top of this, Ch'in adds its harsh laws and cruel punishments, setting the fathers and sons of the empire to strife. When King Ch'en raised his army and led the world in the song of revolt, he ruled only the land of Ch'u, but for two thousand miles on every side there were none who failed to echo his cry. Family by family they rose up in anger; man by man they fought. Each avenged his wrongs and attacked his foes, in the districts murdering the magistrates and their aides, in the provinces killing the governors and their guards. Now King Ch'en has made Ch'u great again and rules in Ch'en, and has sent Wu Kuang and Chou Wen with their forces of a million men west to attack Ch'in. Anyone who at such a time as this does not earn the right to a fief for himself is no true hero. Consult with each other, gentlemen, and see if you do not agree. The world has long suffered under Ch'in and is of one heart. Now you may rely upon the strength of the world, attack this unprincipled ruler, avenge the wrongs of your fathers and brothers, and earn for yourselves a grant of territory, a piece of land! Such a chance comes to a man only once!"

The men of prominence all approved his words and, gathering soldiers until they had a force of twenty or thirty thousand men, awarded Wu Ch'en the title of lord of Wu-hsin and conquered ten cities of Chao. But the other cities held fast and refused to surrender. Thereupon they led their troops to the northeast to attack Fan-yang.

K'uai T'ung, a man of Fan-yang, went to speak with the magistrate of Fan-yang. "The rumor reached me that you were about to die, and so I came to convey my condolences. On the other hand, since you now have me to save your life, I offer my congratulations."

"Why should you come with condolences?" asked the magistrate.

"Ch'in's laws are stern. You have been the magistrate of Fan-yang for ten years and the fathers you have killed, the orphans you have made, the feet you have chopped off, the heads you have branded are beyond counting. The only reason that all the loving fathers and filial sons have not dared to thrust their swords into your belly is that they fear the laws of Ch'in. But now the world is in such confusion that Ch'in's laws are no longer effective. And so the loving fathers and filial sons will now proceed to thrust their swords into your belly and make a name for themselves. This is why I have come to convey my condolences.

"The nobles are now revolting against Ch'in, and Wu Ch'en, the lord of Wu-hsin, and his army draw near. If you attempt to hold the city of Fan-yang, the young men will rise up and kill you and surrender to him. If, however, you will send me at once to visit him, you can turn misfortune into fortune. But the time to act is now!"

The magistrate of Fan-yang accordingly dispatched K'uai T'ung to visit Wu Ch'en. "In your view," said K'uai T'ung "you must win victory in battle before you can subjugate the region, and attack and seize the cities before you can make them surrender. In my opinion, however, this is a mistake. If you are willing to listen to my plan, you can capture cities without an attack, subjugate the land without a battle, and by mere proclamation win control of a thousand miles. How would that be?"

"And what is your plan?" asked Wu Ch'en.

"By right the magistrate of Fan-yang should dispose his soldiers and fight for the defense of the city. But he is such a coward and so fearful of death, so greedy for honor, that he would be the first man in the empire to surrender to you if he were not afraid that, because he served as an official under Ch'in, you would execute him as you did those in the other ten cities you captured. On the other hand the young men of Fan-yang are about to kill the magistrate themselves and defend the city against you. Why do you not give me the seals of enfeoffment for a marquis and let me take them to the magistrate? In that case he will surely surrender the city to you, and the young men will not dare to kill him. Then you can put him in a fine carriage with vermilion wheels and flowered hubs and send him parading in front of the cities of Yen and Chao. Everyone who sees him there will exclaim with delight, 'So this is the magistrate of Fan-yang who surrendered before anyone else!', and the lands of Yen and Chao will submit to you without a battle. This is what I mean by winning a thousand miles by mere proclamation."

Wu Ch'en followed K'uai T'ung's advice and sent him to present the magistrate of Fan-yang with the seals of a marquis. When news of this spread through the region of Chao, over thirty cities surrendered to him without a fight and he marched on to Han-tan.

There Chang Erh and Ch'en Yü received word that Chou Wen's army had entered the Pass and gotten as far as Hsi, but had been forced to retreat. They also heard that many of the generals who had been dispatched by Ch'en She to subjugate various regions had been slandered or unjustly accused of some crime and executed. Resenting the fact that Ch'en She had not listened to their advice and had made them colonels instead of generals, they counseled Wu Ch'en, saying, "Ch'en She began his uprising in Chi and when he got to Ch'en he became a king. It is not necessary that a man be a descendant of the rulers of the Six Kingdoms in order to sit on a throne. Now with an army of only three thousand you have conquered twenty or thirty cities of Chao and sit here all alone in the area north of the Yellow River. If you do not become a king, you cannot keep the region under control. Moreover, Ch'en She is apt to listen to all sorts of slander, and when you return to him and make your report, it is unlikely that you will escape misfortune. Anyway, if it were left to Ch'en She to select a king for Chao, he would certainly set up one of his own relatives, or if not, the heir of the former royal family, rather than you. You must not let this opportunity slip away! Time will not wait the drawing of a breath!"

Wu Ch'en followed their advice and set himself up as king of Chao, making Ch'en Yü his commanding general, Chang Erh minister of the right, and Shao Sao minister of the left, and sent an envoy to report what he had done to Ch'en She. Ch'en She was furious and was about to exterminate the families of Wu Ch'en and the others and send troops to attack Chao, but his chief minister, Ts'ai Tz'u, opposed him. "Ch'in has not yet been destroyed and still you wish to execute the families of Wu Ch'en and the others. This will only create a second Ch'in to plague us! It would be better to go along with what they have done, congratulate them on their new positions, and get them to lead their troops west to attack Ch'in."

Ch'en She, realizing the truth of what he said, followed his advice, but moved the families of Wu Ch'en and the others to his palace and kept them in bonds. He enfeoffed Chang Erh's son, Chang Ao, as lord of Ch'eng-tu, and sent an envoy to congratulate the king of Chao and give him an order urging him to send troops west to enter the Pass.

Chang Erh and Ch'en Yü advised Wu Ch'en, saying, "It was not Ch'en She's intention that you become king of Chao. He has only approved of the move for reasons of expediency and, when he has finished destroying Ch'in, he will certainly send troops against us. We beg you not to send your men west, but to march north and subjugate Yen and Tai, and in the south to gain control of Ho-nei, and thus broaden the area under your rule. If you occupy the Yellow River in the south and hold possession of Yen and Tai in the north, Ch'en She, even if he is victorious over Ch'in, will not dare try to impose his will upon Chao."

Wu Ch'en approved their suggestion and accordingly sent no troops west, but instead dispatched Han Kuang to seize Yen, Li Liang to seize Ch'ang-shan, and Chang Yen to seize Shang-tang.

When Han Kuang reached Yen the people of Yen made him their king. Wu Ch'en, accompanied by Chang Erh and Ch'en Yü, marched north to subjugate the region on the border of Yen, but Wu Ch'en, the king of Chao, attempting a secret excursion, was captured by the Yen army. The general of Yen imprisoned him and demanded half the territory of Chao as the price of his return. Envoys were sent from Chao, but Yen each time murdered them in order to force its demand for territory. Chang Erh and Ch'en Yü were deeply distressed. Then one of the menials in their camp took leave of his fellow soldiers and announced, "I will go talk to Yen for the gentlemen and come riding back with the king of Chao!"

"Already over ten envoys have been sent and they have all been killed. How could you possibly get the king back?" his comrades replied, laughing. But the man ran up to the city walls of Yen and, when he was brought before the general of Yen, he said, "Do you know why I have come?"

"Because you hope to get back the king of Chao," replied the Yen general.

"Do you know what sort of men Chang Erh and Ch'en Yü are?"

"Worthy men," said the general.

"And do you know what it is they hope to do?"

"Get back their king, that is all."

The soldier laughed and said, "Then you do not understand the ambitions of these two men. Wu Ch'en, Chang Erh, and Ch'en Yü brandished their horsewhips and conquered twenty or thirty cities of Chao and, when they were done, each hoped to face south and become a king. How could any of them be satisfied to remain a minister? There is a world of difference between being a minister and being a ruler. It is simply that, their power being only just established, they did not dare to divide the territory into three parts and all become kings. So for the time being they have made Wu Ch'en the king, because he is the oldest, in order to win the support of the people of Chao.

"But after the region of Chao had been completely conquered, these two men hoped to seize their share of Chao and become kings as well, only they had not yet found the opportunity. Now you have made the king of Chao your prisoner, and while these two men pretend to be seeking his release, they in fact hope that you will kill him so that they can divide up Chao and make themselves kings. If Chao with one king is contemptuous of Yen's power, how will it be when it has two wise kings, marching hand in hand to punish you for the crime of regicide! The destruction of Yen will be an easy matter then!"

The general of Yen, believing that he spoke the truth, released the king of Chao and the menial soldier drove with him back to the camp.

Li Liang, having subjugated Ch'ang-shan, returned to report to the king of Chao, who sent him out once more, this time to seize T'ai-yüan. He advanced as far as Shih-i but, since the Ch'in forces were blocking the Ching Gorge, he could go no farther. The general of the Ch'in army forged a letter in the name of the envoy of the Second Emperor and sent it to Li Liang, purposely leaving it unsealed. The letter read:

"You once served me in the past, and at that time enjoyed my favor and confidence. If you are willing to turn against Chao and work for Ch'in, your crimes will be forgiven and you will again obtain honor."

When Li Liang received the letter he was suspicious and did not believe it. He turned back and started for Han-tan to ask for more troops, but before he had reached the city he met the elder sister of the king of Chao coming along the road on her way from a drinking party, accompanied by over a hundred horsemen. When Li Liang saw them approaching in the distance, he supposed it to be the king's entourage and dismounted and bowed by the side of the road in obeisance. The king's sister when she passed by was too drunk to recognize the general and merely dispatched one of her horsemen to acknowledge his greeting. Li Liang, being a man of high position, rose to his feet in great embarrassment, believing that he had shamed himself in the sight of his officers. One of his men spoke up: "Now that the world is in revolt against Ch'in, those with the greatest ability should become kings first. The king of Chao was originally far inferior to you, general, and yet this bitch does not even get down from her carriage to greet you! Let me go after her and kill her!"

Li Liang had already received the letter from Ch'in and actually wanted to revolt against Chao, though he had not yet made up his mind. Now, however, he was so enraged that he sent his men to pursue and kill the king's sister on the road, and then led his forces to attack Han-tan. He took Han-tan completely by surprise and succeeded in killing Wu Ch'en and Shao Sao. A number of men of Chao who were acting as spies for Chang Erh and Ch'en Yü reported to them what was happening, so that they were able to escape.

Chang Erh and Ch'en Yü gathered together the scattered forces of Chao and had obtained an army of twenty or thirty thousand men when one of Chang Erh's retainers advised him, saying, "You two gentlemen have journeyed from another state and hope to win the loyalties of Chao, but this is very difficult. Only if you set up the heir of the royal family of Chao and support your cause with the claims of justice can you hope to succeed."

With this they sought out Chao Hsieh and made him king of Chao, with his residence in Hsin-tu. Li Liang advanced with his forces to attack Ch'en Yü but was defeated. He fled and joined the Ch'in general Chang Han, who led his army to Han-tan, moved the entire population to Ho-nei, and leveled the walls and fortifications of the city.

Chang Erh and King Hsieh of Chao fled to the city of Chü-lu, where they were surrounded by the Ch'in general Wang Li. Ch'en Yü marched north to levy troops from Ch'ang-shan, obtaining a force of twenty or thirty thousand, and camped north of Chü-lu. Chang Han stationed his army at Chi-yüan south of Chü-lu and built a walled road connecting it with the Yellow River in order to keep Wang Li supplied with provisions. Thus Wang Li's men had plenty of food and pressed their attack upon Chü-lu.

Within the city food was scarce and the number of defenders small. Chang Erh repeatedly sent messengers to Ch'en Yü asking him to advance, but Ch'en Yü considered that his forces were too small in number to face the Ch'in armies and for several months did not dare to advance.

Chang Erh was in a rage and, deeply angered at Ch'en Yü, sent Chang Yen and Ch'en Shih to rebuke him, saying, "Once you and I swore to be true to each other whatever might come. Now the king and I from dawn to dusk face imminent death, but you with your thousands of troops refuse to come to our rescue. Is this the way you die for your friend? If you care anything for honor, why do you not close with the Ch'in armies and die with us? There is still one chance in ten that we may come through!"

"Though I were to advance," replied Ch'en Yü, "I do not believe I could ever succeed in rescuing the men of Chao. I would only be throwing away my army for nothing. The reason I do not die with the others now is that I hope some day to make Ch'in pay for the fate of the king of Chao and my friend Chang Erh. To die with the others now would be but to throw one more morsel of meat to a starving tiger. What would it profit anyone?"

"The situation is very grave!" said Chang Yen and Ch'en Shih. "It is imperative that you die with the others for the sake of honor. Why think about what will happen later?"

"I can see no profit in my death. If you insist, however, I will give you five thousand of my men," and he ordered Chang Yen and Ch'en Shih to lead a force of five thousand in a trial attack upon the Ch'in army. The entire group was wiped out.

At this time Yen, Ch'i, and Ch'u, hearing of Chao's distress, all came with their forces to rescue it. In addition Chang Erh's son Chang Ao arrived with a force of over ten thousand men which he had gathered in Tai in the north. All made their fortifications alongside Ch'en Yü, but none dared to attack Ch'in.

Hsiang Yü several times cut Chang Han's supply road, so that Wang Li's army grew short of provisions. Hsiang Yü then led his whole force across the Yellow River and succeeded in defeating Chang Han. After Chang Han had retreated with his men, the other nobles at last ventured to attack and surround the Ch'in army at Chü-lu. Wang Li was taken prisoner and a second Ch'in general, She Chien, committed suicide. Thus it was the might of Hsiang Yü which eventually saved the city of Chü-lu.

King Hsieh of Chao and Chang Erh, finally able to leave Chü-lu, expressed their gratitude to the other nobles. When Chang Erh came face to face with Ch'en Yü, he berated him for failing to come to the rescue of Chao, and asked where Chang Yen and Ch'en Shih were.

"Chang Yen and Ch'en Shih," replied Ch'en Yü, "came rebuking me and telling me I must die. I sent them ahead with a force of five thousand men to test the power of the Ch'in army. They were all killed. No one escaped!"

Chang Erh, however, refused to believe him but, suspecting that he had murdered them, continued to question Ch'en Yü. "I did not think your hatred for me was so deep!" said Ch'en Yü in anger. "Do you suppose I care whether I keep the post of general or not?" With this he undid his general's seal-cords and offered the seals to Chang Erh, but Chang Erh was too startled to accept them.

When Ch'en Yü rose and left to go to the toilet, one of Chang Erh's retainers spoke to Chang Erh. "They say that if you do not accept something when Heaven offers it to you, you will incur misfortune instead. Now General Ch'en Yü has given you his seals. If you do not take them you will arouse the ill will of Heaven!"

Chang Erh thereupon hung the seals from his own girdle, thus assuming command of Ch'en Yü's troops. When Ch'en Yü returned, he found to his deep resentment that Chang Erh had not declined his offer, and he at once hurried from the place. Thus Chang Erh took over his troops and Ch'en Yü, left with only a few hundred of his former men who had been closest to him, went off to the swamps along the Yellow River to make his living by hunting and fishing. From this time on, Ch'en Yü and Chang Erh were enemies.

King Hsieh of Chao returned to his residence in Hsin-tu, and Chang Erh followed Hsiang Yü and the other nobles through the Pass. In the first year of Han, the second month, Hsiang Yü set up the various nobles as kings. Chang Erh had in the past traveled a good deal and had many friends who spoke on his behalf. Hsiang Yü himself had often heard reports of Chang Erh's worth, and so he divided the region of Chao and made Chang Erh the king of Ch'ang-shan, ruling from Hsin-tu, which he renamed Hsiang-kuo. Many of Ch'en Yü's former retainers pleaded with Hsiang Yü, claiming that Ch'en Yü and Chang Erh had won equal merit in Chao. Hsiang Yü could not forget that Ch'en Yü had failed to accompany him through the Pass, but when he heard that Ch'en Yü was in Nan-p'i, he enfeoffed him with the three surrounding districts. King Hsieh of Chao he transferred to the position of king of Tai.

When Chang Erh proceeded to his kingdom Ch'en Yü grew more and more resentful. "Chang Erh and I have won equal merit," he complained, "and yet Chang Erh is a king and I am only a marquis. Such is the injustice of Hsiang Yü!"

When T'ien Jung, king of Ch'i, revolted against Hsiang Yü, Ch'en Yü sent Hsia Yüeh as his envoy to speak with T'ien Jung. "Hsiang Yü's actions as ruler of the empire have been unjust. He has made all his own generals kings of the best lands, and moved the former kings to poorer territories. Now he has sent the king of Chao to live in Tai. I beg you to lend me troops so that I may make Nan-p'i a protecting barrier for you."

T'ien Jung hoped to create allies in Chao who would turn the state against Hsiang Yü and so he dispatched troops to serve under Ch'en Yü. Ch'en Yü then raised all the forces of the three districts in his possession and led his men in a surprise attack on Chang Erh, king of Ch'ang-shan. Chang Erh fled in defeat.

Chang Erh considered whether there were any of the nobles he could turn to. "The king of Han and I were friends in old times. Yet Hsiang Yü is also powerful and it was he who made me a king. Perhaps I should go to Hsiang Yü. . . ."

But Lord Kan said to him, "When the king of Han entered the Pass the five planets appeared in conjunction in the constellation of the Eastern Well. The Eastern Well is the portion of the heavens belonging to Ch'in, so that whoever reached Ch'in first must become its ruler. Although Hsiang Yü is powerful he came later and therefore he will undoubtedly bow before the king of Han!"

Because of this Chang Erh fled to join the king of Han. When the king returned to conquer the three kingdoms of Ch'in and was besieging Chang Han at Fei-ch'iu, Chang Erh went to visit him and was received with generosity.

After Ch'en Yü had defeated Chang Erh he gained control of all the region of Chao once more and sent to fetch the former king from Tai and make him king of Chao again. The king of Chao, much indebted to Ch'en Yü, made Ch'en Yü king of Tai in his place. Because the king of Chao was still in a weak position and his kingdom had only just been reconquered, Ch'en Yü did not proceed to his own kingdom but remained behind to advise the king, sending Hsia Yüeh to act as prime minister of Tai and guard his kingdom for him.

In the second year of Han, when the king of Han marched east to attack Hsiang Yü, he sent an envoy to ask Chao to join him. "If the king of Han will kill Chang Erh," Ch'en Yü replied, "we will join the attack."

The king of Han made a search for someone who resembled Chang Erh and, when a man was found, executed him and had his head sent to Ch'en Yü. Ch'en Yü then dispatched troops to aid the Han army. The Han forces, however, were defeated west of P'eng-ch'eng, and Ch'en Yü, discovering that Chang Erh was still alive, deserted from the side of Han.

In the third year of Han, after Han Hsin had conquered Wei, he was sent with Chang Erh through the Ching Gorge to attack Chao.

Han Hsin defeated Chao, executed Ch'en Yü on the banks of the Ch'ih River, and pursued and killed Hsieh, the king of Chao, at Hsiang-kuo. Chang Erh was made king of Chao in his place.

In the fifth year of Han, Chang Erh died and was given the posthumous title "Brilliant King." His son Chang Ao succeeded to the throne as king of Chao. Emperor Kao-tsu's oldest daughter, Princess Yüan of Lu, became his consort.

In the seventh year of Han, Kao-tsu visited Chao on his way from P'ing-ch'eng. Chang Ao, as king of Chao, morning and evening bared his shoulders, donned sleeve guards and apron, and served the emperor his meals in person, conducting himself with the deepest humility and waiting upon the emperor in the manner befitting a son-in-law. Kao-tsu for his part sprawled about and abused Chang Ao, treating him with the utmost contempt. Kuan Kao, the prime minister of Chao, Chao Wu, and others, men over sixty who had formerly been retainers of Chang Erh and were inclined to be strong willed, were infuriated. "Our king is a weakling!" they said and went to talk to Chang Ao.

"When the brave men of the world rose in arms," they said, "those with real ability became kings first. Now you wait upon the emperor with the utmost courtesy, but he shows no regard for etiquette. We beg to kill him for you!"

Chang Ao bit his finger until he drew blood and replied, "How can you speak in such error! When my father lost his kingdom, it was by the aid of the emperor that he recovered it. Now the goodness of the emperor has extended to me, his heir. Every particle I possess is due to the emperor's power. I beg you, speak no more of this!"

Kuan Kao, Chao Wu, and the other ten or more with them all replied, "We were at fault. Our king is a virtuous man and will not betray a debt of gratitude. But we believe that the just should suffer no insult. We were enraged that the emperor should insult our king, and therefore we thought to kill him. We surely had no thought of staining our sovereign's conduct. If the affair had succeeded, we would have attributed it to you, but if it had failed, we alone would have faced trial."

In the eighth year of Han the emperor passed through Chao on his way back from Tung-yüan. Kuan Kao and the others hid a man in the wall of the post station at Po-jen to attack him. The emperor was about to stop for the night but, suddenly growing uneasy, he asked, "What is the name of this district?"

"Po-jen," he was told.

"Po-jen—'pursue a man' [*po jen*]? Am I pursued by someone?" he exclaimed, and departed without spending the night.

In the ninth year of Han some family that bore a grudge against Kuan Kao learned that he was plotting against the emperor and reported his treason to the throne. The emperor had the king of Chao, Kuan Kao, and all the others seized. Each of the other ten or more men implicated was hurrying to be the first to cut his throat, but Kuan Kao, who alone made no move in that direction, cursed them all angrily. "Who was it that ordered you to revolt in the first place? The king had nothing to do with the plot! Yet now he has been arrested along with the rest of us. If all of you are dead, who is to testify that the king is innocent?"

They were put into caged carts and brought under lock to Ch'ang-an, along with the king, Chang Ao, where an investigation into the king's guilt was begun. Although the emperor issued an edict warning that any of the ministers or retainers of Chao who dared to accompany the king would be executed along with their families, Meng Shu and ten or more other retainers shaved their heads, put collars around their necks and, in the disguise of slaves of the king's household, accompanied him to the capital.

When Kuan Kao was brought before the inquisitors he told them, "I and my group alone are responsible. The king knew nothing about it!" The prison guards, hoping to force a confession, gave him several thousand lashes and stuck him with needles until there was no spot on his body left to pierce, but he would say nothing more.

Empress Lü several times told the emperor that since Chang Ao was the husband of her daughter, Princess Yüan of Lu, it was not right that he should be treated in such a way, but the emperor refused to listen and replied angrily, "If I were planning to give away the empire to Chang Ao, what difference would anyone like your daughter make anyway?"

The commandant of justice reported the results of the investigation and Kuan Kao's words. "He is a brave man!" said the emperor. "Is there someone who knows him? Have him go and question Kuan Kao as a friend."

Lord I, a palace counselor, replied, "He is a man of my township. I have known him a long time. Such a man is concerned only in guarding the name and honor of the state of Chao so that they shall suffer no insult. He is true to his word."

The emperor sent Lord I to bear the imperial credentials and question Kuan Kao. Kuan Kao, exhausted by his ordeal, was placed in a wicker cart and brought before Lord I. He looked up from the cart and asked, "My lord I, is it you?"

Lord I comforted him, talking freely with him as though nothing had happened, and asked whether Chang Ao had actually plotted against the emperor.

"Is it not human nature for each man to love his parents, his wife and children?" replied Kuan Kao. "My whole family to the third degree of kinship has now been sentenced to death. Would I sacrifice my own parents for the sake of the king? It is simply that the king is in fact not guilty of revolt. It was only I and my group who did it," and he described in detail how they had come to plot revolt and how the king knew nothing about it.

Lord I returned to the palace and reported all he had learned, and the emperor thereupon pardoned the king of Chao. The emperor greatly admired Kuan Kao for sticking by his word so faithfully and sent Lord I to inform him that Chang Ao had already been released and that Kuan Kao was pardoned as well.

"Has my king really been set free?" asked Kuan Kao joyfully.

"He has," replied Lord I. "And because the emperor admires you," he added, "he has pardoned you as well."

"The reason I did not choose death before, but suffered every torture that my body could endure, was so I could bear witness that King Chang was not disloyal. Now that the king has been released, my duty is fulfilled and I may die without regret. As a subject I have incurred the name of a would-be usurper and assassin. With what face could I appear again before the emperor? Though he might spare my life, would I not feel shame in my heart?"

Then he raised his head and, severing the artery in his neck, took his own life. His fame spread throughout the world of his day.

After Chang Ao had been released he was enfeoffed as marquis of Hsüan-p'ing, out of respect for his wife, Princess Yüan of Lu. The emperor highly admired Chang Ao's retainers who had put on the collars of slaves and accompanied him to Lo-yang, and he made all of them governors or ministers to the nobles. During the reigns of Emperor Hui, Empress Lü, Emperor Wen, and Emperor Ching the descendants of these retainers of Chang Ao all attained positions with a salary of two thousand piculs.[2]

Chang Ao died in the sixth year of Empress Lü's reign. His son Yen became King Yüan of Lu. (Yen's mother was the daughter of Empress Lü and therefore the empress enfeoffed him as King Yüan of Lu.) King Yüan was frail and had few brothers and so the empress also enfeoffed two of Chang Ao's sons by concubines, Shou, who became marquis of Lo-ch'ang, and Ch'ih, who became marquis of Hsin-tu. After Empress Lü passed away the Lü clan behaved lawlessly until the great ministers overthrew them and removed King Yüan of Lu and the marquises of Lo-ch'ang and Hsin-tu from their positions. When Emperor Wen came to the throne he enfeoffed King Yüan of Lu once more as marquis of Nan-kung in order to carry on the Chang family line.

The Grand Historian remarks: Chang Erh and Ch'en Yü are much talked of and praised in the world as worthy men. Their retainers, down to the lowest menial, were every one heroes of the empire; in whatever kingdom they lived they never failed to become high ministers.

In the beginning, when Chang Erh and Ch'en Yü were poor, they pledged their word to be true to death, nor would they have hesitated at anything for each other's sake. Yet when they came to possess kingdoms and contend for power, they ended by destroying each other. How sincerely they admired and trusted one another at first, and how

[2] Of grain annually, i.e., rather high posts in the bureaucracy.

cruelly they betrayed each other afterwards! Was this not because of self-interest? Though their fame is great, though their followers flourish, they walked a different way from that of T'ai-po and Yen-ling Chi-tzu of old! [3]

[3] Who unselfishly relinquished their claims to a kingdom.

Shih chi 90: The Biographies of Wei Pao and P'eng Yüeh

Wei Pao gathered up the soldiers of Shang-tang and the western reaches of the Yellow River, and fought his way to P'eng-ch'eng; P'eng Yüeh plundered the land of Liang and brought great grief to Hsiang Yü. Thus I made The Biographies of Wei Pao and P'eng Yüeh.

Wei Pao

Wei Pao was a member of the royal family of the state of Wei. In former times his elder cousin Wei Chiu had been enfeoffed as lord of Ning-ling but, when Ch'in destroyed Wei, Chiu was deprived of his title and made a commoner.

When Ch'en She raised his revolt and made himself a king Wei Chiu went to join him. Ch'en She had sent Chou Shih, a man of Wei, to subjugate the area of Wei and, after he had conquered it, the inhabitants wanted to join in making Chou Shih their king. But Chou Shih replied, "It is when the world is in chaos that the truly loyal minister is known. Now that the empire is united in revolt against Ch'in, the only just thing to do is to set up a descendant of the royal house of Wei."

Ch'i and Chao each sent gifts of fifty chariots, urging Chou Shih to become king of Wei, but he declined and refused to accept them. Instead he sent someone to fetch Wei Chiu from Ch'en. Five times envoys were exchanged, until Ch'en She at last made Chiu the king of Wei and sent him to his kingdom.

After the Ch'in general Chang Han had defeated Ch'en She he advanced with his troops to attack the king of Wei at Lin-chi. The king sent Chou Shih to go and beg help from Ch'i and Ch'u, who dispatched T'ien Pa and Hsiang T'o respectively to lead their armies and accompany Chou Shih to rescue Wei. Chang Han eventually attacked and destroyed the armies of Chou Shih and the others and surrounded Lin-chi. For the sake of his people Wei Chiu agreed to surrender to Chang Han but, when the agreement had been concluded, he burned himself to death. Wei Pao escaped and fled to Ch'u. King Huai of Ch'u gave Wei Pao a force of several thousand men and sent him to subjugate the region of Wei once more.

By the time Hsiang Yü had defeated the Ch'in army and captured Chang Han, Wei Pao had conquered more than twenty cities of Wei, for which Hsiang Yü made him king of Wei. Wei Pao then led his best troops and followed Hsiang Yü through the Pass.

In the first year of Han, when Hsiang Yü was enfeoffing the various nobles, he wanted to keep possession of the region of Liang [Wei] [1] himself, and so he moved Wei Pao, the king of Wei, to Ho-tung, making him king of Western Wei with his capital at P'ing-yang.

The king of Han returned from his territory and conquered the three kingdoms of Ch'in. When he crossed the Yellow River at Lin-chin, Wei Pao placed himself and his kingdom under his rule and joined the king of Han in attacking the Ch'u army at P'eng-ch'eng. The king of Han was defeated and retreated as far as Jung-yang. Wei Pao requested permission to go home in order to look after his ailing parents, but when he reached his kingdom he cut off the fords across the Yellow River and revolted against the king of Han. At the time when the king of Han received news of Wei Pao's defection, he was too concerned about the Ch'u forces to the east to go and attack him, but instead summoned Master Li I-chi and said, "You with the wagging jaws—go wag them at Wei Pao! If you can talk him into submitting, I will give you a fief of ten thousand households."

Master Li went and tried to persuade Wei Pao, but Wei Pao declined to listen to him. "Man's life in this world is as brief as the passing of a white colt glimpsed through a crack in the wall," he said. "The king of Han is arrogant and insulting to others, reviling the nobles and ministers as though he were cursing so many slaves. He has no sense of the proprieties to be observed between superiors and inferiors. I cannot endure to face him again!"

With this, the king of Han dispatched Han Hsin, who attacked

---

[1] Since the names Wei and Liang refer to the same general area, Ssu-ma Ch'ien often uses them interchangeably.

and captured Wei Pao at Ho-tung. Wei Pao was escorted back to Jung-yang and brought before the king, who made a province out of Wei Pao's kingdom. The king of Han ordered Wei Pao to guard the city of Jung-yang but, when the Ch'u forces surrounded it and the siege grew critical, he was murdered by Chou K'o.

P'eng Yüeh

P'eng Yüeh, whose polite name was Chung, was a native of Ch'ang-i. He was engaged in fishing in the marsh of Chü-yeh and had formed a band of robbers there when Ch'en She and Hsiang Liang began their uprisings. Some of the young men of the district said to him, "All the heroes and brave men are rising in revolt against Ch'in. When it comes to that, you could do the same yourself!"

"Now the two dragons are fighting it out," replied P'eng Yüeh. "I will wait a while."

By the time a year or so had passed the youths in the region of the swamp had gathered a band of over a hundred men and went to place themselves under P'eng Yüeh, saying, "We want you to be our leader."

"I have no desire to join up with you men," replied P'eng Yüeh, refusing them, but the youths pressed their demand until he finally consented. Then he agreed to meet with them at daybreak the following day, with the stipulation that anyone who arrived late should be beheaded.

When dawn came the next day over ten men arrived late for the meeting, some of them not appearing until noon. P'eng Yüeh thereupon apologized to the group, saying, "I am an old man. You gentlemen have forced me to become your leader, but now when I have set a time for meeting I find so many have come late that I am not capable of punishing them all. I will have to punish only the last man who arrived late." He gave the order to his subaltern to behead the last man.

"Surely you wouldn't go that far!" the men all exclaimed, laughing. "We promise we will never dare to be late again!"

But P'eng Yüeh proceeded to drag the man forward and behead him. Then he set up an altar, sacrificed upon it, and began to give the men orders as his followers. The whole group was astonished and terrified, and not a man dared to raise his eyes. P'eng Yüeh then set about overrunning the region and gathering together the scattered troops of the nobles until he had obtained a force of over a thousand men.

When the governor of P'ei marched north from Tang to attack Ch'ang-i, P'eng Yüeh aided him. Before the city capitulated the governor of P'ei led his troops west and P'eng Yüeh took his band back to the area of Chü-yeh, where he gathered up the scattered forces of Wei.

Hsiang Yü entered the Pass, made kings of the nobles, and sent them back to their territories, but P'eng Yüeh and his force of over ten thousand men were under no one's jurisdiction. In the autumn of the first year of Han, T'ien Jung, the king of Ch'i, revolted against Hsiang Yü. The king of Han sent a man to present P'eng Yüeh with the seals of a general and send him south through Chi-yin to attack Ch'u. Ch'u ordered Chüeh, lord of Hsiao, to lead his forces and attack P'eng Yüeh, but P'eng Yüeh inflicted a major defeat on the Ch'u army.

In the spring of the second year the king of Han, with Wei Pao and the other nobles, marched east to attack Ch'u. P'eng Yüeh led his force of over thirty thousand men and went to join the king of Han at Wai-huang.

"You have subjugated the land of Wei and conquered over ten cities," said the king of Han. "I am sure you are anxious as soon as possible to set up a descendant of the Wei family. Wei Pao, the king of Western Wei, is a younger cousin of Wei Chiu and therefore the rightful heir of Wei." He then made P'eng Yüeh prime minister of Wei and instructed him to use his troops as he saw fit to invade and subdue the region of Liang.

When the king of Han was defeated at P'eng-ch'eng and his forces were scattered and fled west, P'eng Yüeh, having lost all the cities which he had conquered, alone led his troops north and occupied Ho-shang. During the third year of Han, P'eng Yüeh constantly led the Han guerrilla forces back and forth through the area, striking at Ch'u and cutting off its supply lines in Liang. In the fourth year of Han, while Hsiang Yü and the king of Han were stalemated at Jung-yang, P'eng Yüeh attacked and captured seventeen cities of Sui-yang and Wai-huang. When Hsiang Yü received news of this, he left Ts'ao

Chiu to guard the city of Ch'eng-kao while he himself marched east, recapturing the cities which P'eng Yüeh had taken and restoring them all to Ch'u. P'eng Yüeh and his men fled north to Ku-ch'eng. In the autumn of the fifth year of Han, when Hsiang Yü fled south to Yang-hsia, P'eng Yüeh again seized twenty or more cities around Ch'ang-i and obtained over a hundred thousand bushels of grain which he sent as supplies to the king of Han. The king of Han several times dispatched envoys summoning P'eng Yüeh to join him in attacking Ch'u, but P'eng Yüeh replied, "The region of Wei has only just been subjugated and its people are still fearful of Ch'u. I cannot leave yet."

The king of Han pursued Hsiang Yü, but was defeated by him at Ku-ling. "The armies of the other generals do not come to join me. What should I do?" he asked Chang Liang.

"As for Han Hsin," replied Chang Liang, "since it was not your intention that he should become king of Ch'i, he himself does not feel secure in his position. P'eng Yüeh originally conquered the region of Liang and won great distinction, but because of the claims of Wei Pao to the throne of Wei, you made P'eng Yüeh only prime minister of Wei. Now Wei Pao is dead and has left no heir and so P'eng Yüeh naturally hopes to become king himself. And yet you have made no move to set him up. If you will give the kingdoms of Ch'i and Wei to these two men and make an alliance with them, then you can overcome Ch'u. The land from Sui-yang north to Ku-ch'eng should be given to P'eng Yüeh to rule, and that from Ch'en to the sea to Han Hsin as king of Ch'i. Since Han Hsin's home is in Ch'u, this would satisfy his desire to get control of his native city.[2] If you are willing to cede these territories to the two men, then they will come at once. But if you are not, then I cannot say how things will end."

The king of Han sent an envoy to P'eng Yüeh awarding him the territory which Chang Liang had suggested. When the envoy arrived P'eng Yüeh proceeded with his troops to the rendezvous at Kai-hsia, where Hsiang Yü was finally defeated.

In the spring of the fifth year of Han, after the death of Hsiang Yü,

[2] Han Hsin's birthplace was in Huai-yin, which would be included in the grant of land "from Ch'en to the sea."

P'eng Yüeh was made king of Liang with his capital at Ting-t'ao. In the sixth year he attended the emperor at court in Ch'en, and in the ninth and tenth years journeyed to attend court at Ch'ang-an.

In the autumn of the tenth year Ch'en Hsi raised a revolt in the region of Tai. Emperor Kao-tsu marched in person to attack him and, when he reached Han-tan, ordered P'eng Yüeh, the king of Liang, to raise his troops. P'eng Yüeh pleaded illness and sent his general to lead the troops to Han-tan. The emperor was angry and dispatched a man to reprimand him. P'eng Yüeh, growing fearful, was about to go in person to beg for pardon, but his general Wu Che said, "You did not go at first, but now that you have been reprimanded you are going. If you go now, you will be made a prisoner! It would be better to go on and dispatch your troops in revolt!"

P'eng Yüeh would not listen to his general, but pleaded illness once more. It happened that he was angry with his master of the carriage and was about to execute the man. The master of the carriage escaped and fled to the Han camp, where he reported that P'eng Yüeh and Wu Che were plotting revolt. The emperor sent men to take P'eng Yüeh by surprise. P'eng Yüeh, unaware of what was happening, was seized and imprisoned at Lo-yang. The officials, examining his case and finding full evidence for revolt, requested to pass sentence in accordance with the law, but the emperor pardoned him, made him a commoner, and ordered him transported under guard to Ch'ing-i in Shu.

P'eng Yüeh had gotten as far west as Cheng when Empress Lü, who was on her way from Ch'ang-an to Lo-yang, met him on the road. P'eng Yüeh wept before the empress and pleaded his innocence, begging that he be sent to his home in Ch'ang-i instead. Empress Lü granted his request and went with him back to Lo-yang. There she explained to the emperor what she had done. "P'eng Yüeh is a brave man," she said. "If now you exile him to Shu, you will only lay yourself open to trouble later on. It would be better to go ahead and execute him. That is why I took the liberty of bringing him with me."

Then she ordered one of her retainers to report that P'eng Yüeh was once again plotting revolt. The commandant of justice Wang T'ien-k'ai submitted a report asking that P'eng Yüeh and his family be executed, which the emperor approved. As a result P'eng Yüeh and his family were all exterminated and his kingdom abolished.

The Grand Historian remarks: Though Wei Pao and P'eng Yüeh both began in humble circumstances, they swept up a thousand miles in their grasp and faced south to call themselves rulers, trampling the blood of victory after victory while their fame grew with the passing days. In their breasts they nursed hopes of rebellion, yet when they had been defeated, they did not choose to die, but allowed themselves to be seized and imprisoned, their bodies bowed beneath the blows of the law. Why was this? A man of hardly more than mediocre character would be ashamed of such action, much less a king! There was but one reason: their schemes and ambitions far surpassed those of other men, and their only fear was that they might lose life itself. So long as they could wield an inch of power, their followers might mass again, their fortunes rise like dragons resurrected, and, so they hoped, they might still find a way to realize their dreams. This then was why they suffered the darkness of prison and did not take their leave![3]

[3] The reader should recall that Ssu-ma Ch'ien himself "suffered the darkness of prison and did not take his leave," i.e., commit suicide, for much the same reasons.

Shih chi 91: The Biography of Ch'ing Pu

With the region of Huai-nan he revolted against Ch'u and gave his allegiance to Han, and the king of Han was thus able to capture the grand marshal Chou Yin and defeat Hsiang Yü at Kai-hsia. Thus I made The Biography of Ch'ing Pu.

Ch'ing Pu was a native of Liu. His family, commoners in the time of Ch'in, was named Ying. When he was young someone once read his face for him and said, "You will suffer punishment and become a king." Later, after he grew up, he was implicated in some crime and was sentenced to be tattooed.[1] Ch'ing Pu was delighted. "The man who examined my face said I would suffer punishment and become a king," he said, laughing. "Now it is beginning to come true, is it not?" When others heard what he had said they all laughed and made fun of him.

Ch'ing Pu was sentenced to be transported to Mount Li, along with a group of laborers numbering several hundred thousand. He was on friendly terms with all of the leaders and powerful men in the group and eventually managed to escape with his friends to the region around the Yangtze, where they formed an outlaw band.

When Ch'en She began his uprising Ch'ing Pu went to see Wu Jui, the lord of P'o, and joined with his forces in rebellion against Ch'in, gathering a force of several thousand men. Wu Jui gave Ch'ing Pu his daughter for a wife.

After the Ch'in general Chang Han had wiped out Ch'en She and defeated Lü Ch'en's army Ch'ing Pu led his troops north to attack the Ch'in colonels of the left and right. He defeated them at Ch'ing-p'o and marched east. When word spread that Hsiang Liang had gained control of K'uai-chi and the land east of the Yangtze, Ch'en Ying, considering the fact that the Hsiang family had for generations been

[1] *Ch'ing.* From this time on it appears that he called himself, or was called by others, Ch'ing Pu or "Tattooed Pu," instead of his real name, Ying Pu.

generals of Ch'u, placed his troops under the command of Hsiang Liang, who had crossed into Huai-nan. Ch'ing Pu and General P'u also placed their troops under Hsiang Liang's command. When Hsiang Liang crossed the Huai River and marched west to attack Ching Chü, Ch'in Chia, and the others, Ch'ing Pu repeatedly distinguished himself as a leader of the army.

Hsiang Liang reached Hsieh where, having received definite news of Ch'en She's death, he set up King Huai of Ch'u. He himself took the title of lord of Wu-hsin, making Ch'ing Pu lord of Tang-yang. When Hsiang Liang was defeated and killed at Ting-t'ao, King Huai fled and made his capital at P'eng-ch'eng, Ch'ing Pu and the other generals all retiring to defend P'eng-ch'eng.

At this time the Ch'in armies had surrounded the king of Chao and were pressing the siege. Chao several times sent envoys begging for help. King Huai appointed Sung I supreme general, Hsiang Yü second general, Fan Tseng third general, and Ch'ing Pu and General P'u subordinate generals, and dispatched them all under the command of Sung I to march north and relieve Chao. Later, when Hsiang Yü murdered Sung I in the region of the Yellow River, King Huai appointed him supreme general, so that all the commanders were henceforth under Hsiang Yü.

Hsiang Yü ordered Ch'ing Pu to cross the Yellow River ahead of the rest and attack the Ch'in army. After Ch'ing Pu had won several victories Hsiang Yü led all the rest of his men across the river, defeated the Ch'in armies, and forced Chang Han and the other Ch'in commanders to surrender.

The Ch'u troops under Hsiang Yü had been continuously victorious and won greater glory than those of any of the other nobles. One of the reasons that the armies of the other nobles all submitted to Ch'u was that Ch'ing Pu had so often with his small force overcome armies of superior number.

Hsiang Yü led his men west to Hsin-an and sent Ch'ing Pu at night to attack and butcher the soldiers of the Ch'in general Chang Han who had already surrendered, a force of over two hundred thousand men. When Hsiang Yü reached the Pass and found he could not enter he again sent Ch'ing Pu ahead to march around by a different route and defeat the army guarding the Pass. Thus he was at last able to reach Hsien-yang, Ch'ing Pu constantly leading the vanguard for him.

When Hsiang Yü enfeoffed his generals he made Ch'ing Pu the king of Chiu-chiang with his capital at Liu. In the fourth month of the first year of Han the nobles all left the command of Hsiang Yü and proceeded to their respective kingdoms. Hsiang Yü set up King Huai with the title of "Righteous Emperor" and moved his capital to Ch'ang-sha, but he secretly ordered Ch'ing Pu and others to go and attack him. In the eighth month Ch'ing Pu dispatched his general to attack the Righteous Emperor, pursuing and murdering him in the district of Ch'en.

In the second year of Han, T'ien Jung, the king of Ch'i, revolted against Ch'u. Hsiang Yü set out to attack Ch'i, sending an order to Chiu-chiang for troops. Ch'ing Pu, king of Chiu-chiang, pleaded illness and did not go himself, but sent his general instead with several thousand men. When the king of Han defeated the Ch'u forces at P'eng-ch'eng, Ch'ing Pu again pleaded illness and refused to go to the aid of Ch'u. Because of this Hsiang Yü became angry with Ch'ing Pu and several times sent envoys to reprimand and summon him, but Ch'ing Pu grew increasingly fearful and did not dare to go. Hsiang Yü, on his part, beset by Ch'i and Chao in the north and harassed by the king of Han in the west, had only the troops of Ch'ing Pu to help him and, because he thought highly of Ch'ing Pu's abilities and hoped to secure his services again, he made no move to punish Ch'ing Pu.

In the third year the king of Han attacked Ch'u and fought a great battle at P'eng-ch'eng. Failing to win a victory, he retreated through Liang as far as Yü. Addressing his followers, he said, "Men like you are not worth planning great affairs of the world with!"

Sui Ho, his master of guests, came forward. "We do not understand Your Majesty's meaning," he said.

"Who can go as an envoy for me to Huai-nan [i.e., Chiu-chiang] and persuade Ch'ing Pu to dispatch his troops against Ch'u?" said the king. "If I can keep Hsiang Yü in Ch'i for a few months, there is no doubt that I can seize the whole empire!"

"I beg to undertake the mission," replied Sui Ho. He set out for

Chiu-chiang with twenty followers and, when he reached the court of the king of Chiu-chiang, stopped at the home of the chief steward.

When three days had passed, and he had not been granted an audience, he spoke to the chief steward. "The reason the king does not see me," he said, "must be that he considers Ch'u to be strong and Han weak. This is just what I have been sent to talk to him about. You must arrange to let me see him. If what I have to say is correct, the king will want to hear it. And if I speak nonsense, then he may chop off my head and those of my twenty attendants in the market place of Huai-nan to make clear that he has turned his back on Han and is an ally of Ch'u."

The chief steward accordingly spoke to the king, who granted Sui Ho an interview. "The king of Han has sent me to present a letter to Your Majesty's secretary," said Sui Ho. "But may I be so bold as to inquire what your relationship is with Hsiang Yü?"

"I face north and serve him as a subject," replied the king.

"You and Hsiang Yü are both lords of equal rank. If you face north and serve him as a subject, it must be because you believe that he is powerful and can insure the safety of your kingdom. When Hsiang Yü marched against Ch'i, he bore upon his own shoulders the boards and hammers for his fortifications, and led the way before all his men. It was only right that you should have raised the forces of your kingdom and led them in person to act as the vanguard of the Ch'u army. Yet now you send a mere four thousand men to aid Hsiang Yü. Can this be the way to serve him as a subject?

"When the king of Han fought at P'eng-ch'eng, Hsiang Yü could not leave Ch'i to oppose him. It was only right that you should have swept up every soldier in your kingdom, crossed the Huai River, and day and night joined in battle before the walls of P'eng-ch'eng. Yet you held your entire host of ten thousand in check, sending not a man across the Huai, folded your hands, and sat complacently watching to see who would be the victor. Is this the way to act toward one to whom you entrust the safety of your kingdom? You offer Hsiang Yü an empty allegiance, and expect him in turn to look after you generously. I fear for your sake that this will never do!

"Yet you do not turn against Hsiang Yü because you consider the king of Han too weak. The armies of Hsiang Yü are indeed powerful, but because their leader broke the agreement made among the nobles and murdered the Righteous Emperor, the world has branded them with the name of unrighteous. Hsiang Yü has relied upon victory in battle to make himself strong. But the king of Han has solicited the aid of the other nobles, returned from his kingdom to occupy Ch'eng-kao and Jung-yang, transported grain from Shu and Han, deepened his moats and walled his camp, and divided his soldiers to guard the outposts and man the passes. When the soldiers of Hsiang Yü return from Ch'i to attack him, they must cross the land of Liang and march hundreds of miles deep into enemy territory.[2] Though they long to fight, there will be no one to fight with; though they attack the cities, they will not have the strength to take them, while their men and boys transport supplies for them from a thousand miles away. And when they reach Jung-yang and Ch'eng-kao, if the king of Han guards the cities fast and refuses to make a move, they can neither advance and seize them, nor retire and retreat in safety. Therefore I say that the soldiers of Hsiang Yü cannot be relied upon.

"Even if Hsiang Yü should win a victory over the king of Han, the other nobles, fearful for their own safety, would come to the aid of Han. Thus the power of Hsiang Yü is fit only to bring down upon him the armies of the world. It is clear from the circumstances that Han would make a better ally than Ch'u. Yet now you do not join with Han, whose cause is certain, but entrust yourself to an endangered and forsaken Ch'u. In my humble opinion you are committing a grave error!

"I do not suggest that your armies alone are sufficient to destroy Ch'u. But if you were to dispatch your forces in revolt against Hsiang Yü, you could detain him and, if you can detain him for several months, it is absolutely certain that the king of Han can seize the empire. I ask you to take up your sword and join with the king of Han. He will be sure to divide his territory and enfeoff you, and of course you will keep possession of your present kingdom in Huai-nan. It is

---

[2] At this time P'eng Yüeh had turned against Hsiang Yü, and the region of Liang was full of guerrilla forces.

for this reason that the king of Han has sent me as his envoy to offer my humble advice. I beg you to give it grave consideration."

"I shall do as the king of Han wishes," replied Ch'ing Pu, and secretly agreed to revolt against Hsiang Yü and join Han, though he told no one of his decision. Just then an envoy from Ch'u arrived at Ch'ing Pu's residence and began urging him to send his troops to aid Ch'u.[3] Sui Ho walked without ceremony into the room where the interview was going on and, taking a seat above that of the envoy, said, "The king of Chiu-chiang has already gone over to the side of Han. You will never get him to send troops to Ch'u!"

Ch'ing Pu was greatly astonished, and the envoy of Ch'u got up and left the room. When he had gone Sui Ho turned to Ch'ing Pu and said, "Since the affair is all settled, it would be best now to kill the envoy of Ch'u instead of sending him back. Then you must hasten to join forces with the king of Han!"

"As you say, there is nothing to do but call up the army and attack Ch'u," replied Ch'ing Pu. He proceeded to murder the envoy of Ch'u and order his troops to attack Ch'u.

Hsiang Yü dispatched Hsiang Sheng and Lung Chü to attack Huai-nan, while he himself remained behind to attack Hsia-i. After several months Lung Chü attacked Huai-nan and defeated Ch'ing Pu's army. Ch'ing Pu hoped to lead his troops and flee to the king of Han but, as he was fearful of being attacked and killed by Hsiang Yü along the way, he escaped by a secret route and, accompanied only by Sui Ho, made his way to the king of Han. When he arrived the king of Han, at the moment sprawled upon a couch having his feet washed, summoned him to appear before him. Ch'ing Pu was outraged at such a reception and, regretting that he had ever come, was about to commit suicide. But when he left and went to the quarters which had been assigned to him he discovered that the furnishings, the food and drink, and the attendants were exactly like those of the king's quarters. This so far exceeded his expectations that he could not help but be greatly pleased.

Ch'ing Pu sent an envoy to return in secret to his kingdom of Chiu-

---

[3] Three characters have been omitted in translation, following the reading in *Han shu* 34.

chiang. Hsiang Yü had already dispatched Hsiang Po, who had led away the soldiers of the region and killed Ch'ing Pu's wife and children, but the envoy was able to gather together Ch'ing Pu's old friends and trusted ministers and lead a group of several thousand men back to the king of Han. The king of Han divided his troops with Ch'ing Pu and together they marched north, recruiting more forces, until they reached Ch'eng-kao.

In the seventh month of the fourth year of Han, Ch'ing Pu was made king of Huai-nan, and joined in attacking Hsiang Yü. In the fifth year he sent envoys in secret to Chiu-chiang and gained control of several districts. Ch'ing Pu and Liu Chia together entered the region of Chiu-chiang and invited Chou Yin, the grand marshal of Ch'u, to revolt.[4] Chou Yin revolted and, raising the soldiers of Chiu-chiang, joined with Han in attacking Hsiang Yü at Kai-hsia.

After Hsiang Yü was dead, and the empire at peace, the emperor held a banquet for his followers and began to belittle Sui Ho's achievements. "He is a rotten Confucianist! What use is a rotten Confucianist in ruling the world?"

Sui Ho knelt and said, "When Your Majesty led the armies in an attack upon P'eng-ch'eng and Hsiang Yü could not leave Ch'i to oppose you, you had a force of fifty thousand infantry and five thousand horsemen, but were you able to seize control of Huai-nan?"

"No, I was not," replied the emperor.

"But Your Majesty sent me with twenty men on a mission to Huai-nan and, after we got there, all proceeded according to your wishes. Hence my achievement is greater than that of fifty thousand infantry and five thousand cavalry. Yet you call me a rotten Confucianist and say I am no use in ruling the world. How can this be?"

"I shall reconsider your achievements," replied the emperor, and in the end he made Sui Ho a colonel of the guard. Ch'ing Pu finally received the split tallies signalizing his formal enfeoffment as king of Huai-nan. He made his capital at Liu, and the provinces of Chiu-

---

[4] The words "sixth year" which appear at the beginning of this sentence in the original are clearly an error. They belong somewhere farther along in the narrative, perhaps with the sentence in which Ch'ing Pu is formally enfeoffed as king of Huai-nan.

chiang, Lu-chiang, Heng-shan, and Yü-chang were all placed under his jurisdiction. In the seventh year he attended court at Ch'en, in the eighth year at Lo-yang, and in the ninth year at Ch'ang-an.

In the eleventh year, when Empress Lü had Han Hsin, the marquis of Huai-yin, executed, Ch'ing Pu began to grow fearful. In the summer of the same year P'eng Yüeh, the king of Liang, was executed and his flesh pickled, placed in vessels, and sent everywhere as a "gift" to the other nobles. When it arrived in Huai-nan, Ch'ing Pu was about to set out on a hunt but, seeing the pickled flesh, he was filled with terror. Secretly he ordered his men to call up the troops and he sent word to the nearby provinces to prepare for any emergency.

It happened that one of Ch'ing Pu's favorite concubines, falling ill, asked for permission to visit a doctor. The doctor's house was directly opposite that of the palace counselor Pi Ho. The concubine several times visited the doctor's house and Pi Ho, because he was a member of the palace staff, sent generous gifts of food to the house and joined the concubine in drinking there. When the concubine was waiting upon Ch'ing Pu and chatting of various things, she found occasion to mention what a fine man Pi Ho was.

"How do you happen to know him?" asked Ch'ing Pu angrily, whereupon she told him all that had happened. Ch'ing Pu began to suspect that there was something going on between them. Pi Ho, growing fearful, gave out that he was too ill to see anyone. Ch'ing Pu became angrier than ever and was about to have Pi Ho seized but Pi Ho, stating that he had to report a disaffection, got the government carriage officials to convey him by post relay to Ch'ang-an. Ch'ing Pu sent men to pursue him, but they were not able to overtake him in time. When Pi Ho reached the capital he made his report of disaffection, claiming that there was evidence that Ch'ing Pu was planning a revolt and suggesting that he be executed before he had time to dispatch troops.

The emperor read the report and discussed it with Hsiao Ho, the prime minister. "It is not like Ch'ing Pu to do this," Hsiao Ho said. "More likely someone who bears him a grudge has falsely invented the accusation. I would suggest that Pi Ho be put in chains and that someone be sent to observe Ch'ing Pu in secret."

Ch'ing Pu saw that Pi Ho had fled to avoid punishment, and made a report of disaffection to the emperor, and he also strongly suspected that Pi Ho had divulged state secrets. When, on top of this, an envoy arrived from the court and began a thorough investigation, he finally exterminated Pi Ho's family and dispatched his troops in revolt.

As soon as word of the revolt reached the emperor he pardoned Pi Ho and made him a general. Then he summoned his generals and said, "Ch'ing Pu has revolted. What are we to do?"

"Send troops to attack and butcher the villain!" they all replied. "What can he do against us?"

Lord T'eng, the marquis of Ju-yin, summoned Lord Hsieh, former prime minister of Ch'u, and asked him his opinion. Lord Hsieh replied, "It is only natural that Ch'ing Pu should revolt."

"But the emperor has divided his territory and made him a king and has honored him with a high rank," objected Lord T'eng. "Ch'ing Pu faces south as an independent ruler. He is master of a realm of ten thousand chariots. Why should he revolt?"

"Earlier this year," replied Lord Hsieh, "P'eng Yüeh was killed, and before that Han Hsin. Since P'eng Yüeh, Han Hsin, and Ch'ing Pu had won equal merit and were alike in all things, Ch'ing Pu fears that misfortune will strike him next. Therefore he has revolted."

Lord T'eng mentioned the matter to the emperor. "One of my guests, Lord Hsieh, a former prime minister of Ch'u, has good judgment in questions of strategy," he said. "It might be well to consult with him."

The emperor summoned Lord Hsieh and asked his opinion. "There is nothing surprising in the fact that Ch'ing Pu has revolted," said Lord Hsieh. "If Ch'ing Pu adopts a first-rate plan of action, Your Majesty will lose possession of all the land east of the mountains. If he adopts a second-rate course, it is hard to say who will end victorious. But if he takes a third-rate course, you may rest with an untroubled mind."

"What would a first-rate plan of action be?"

"He should seize Wu in the east, Ch'u in the west, add to them Ch'i and Lu, send a proclamation calling for the surrender of Yen and Chao, and guard fast his position. In such a case our forces could not keep possession of the region east of the mountains," said Lord Hsieh.

"And a second-rate plan?" asked the emperor.

"Seize Wu in the east, Ch'u in the west, add to them Hann and Wei, rely on the grain in the Ao Granary, and block the pass at Ch'eng-kao. In this case it would be hard to say which way victory would fall."

"And a third-rate plan?"

"Seize Wu in the east, Hsia-ts'ai in the west, send to Yüeh for supplies, and take up a position in Ch'ang-sha. In this case Your Majesty may rest with an easy mind, for the empire will be in no danger."

"And which of these plans do you think he will adopt?"

"The third-rate plan," replied Lord Hsieh.

"Why would he discard the first- and second-rate and adopt the third-rate one?"

"Ch'ing Pu was once a convict laborer at Mount Li. He rose to become the lord of a great kingdom, but in everything he has thought only of himself. He does not look ahead or take any thought for the future of his people. Therefore I say he will adopt the poorest plan of action."

The emperor was pleased and enfeoffed Lord Hsieh with a thousand households. He then set up his own son Liu Ch'ang as king of Huai-nan and, calling out the army, led the troops east in person to attack Ch'ing Pu.

When Ch'ing Pu first revolted he told his commander, "The emperor is old and tired of war. He will never come himself, but will send his generals. The only generals we had to fear were Han Hsin and P'eng Yüeh. Now that they are both dead, there is nothing more to worry about." So he revolted and adopted the plan of action which Lord Hsieh had predicted, marching east to attack Ching [i.e., Wu]. Liu Chia, the king of Ching, fled and was killed at Tang-ling. Ch'ing Pu put his whole army to rout and then crossed the Huai River and attacked Ch'u.

Ch'u sent troops to meet the attack between Hsü and T'ung, dividing its army into three groups that were intended to support each other and surprise the enemy. Someone advised the Ch'u general against this plan, saying, "Ch'ing Pu is an excellent fighter and the people are afraid of him. It is said in *The Art of War* that when a prince fights on his own land he fights on shaky ground.[5] Now that you have divided our army into three groups, if one of them is defeated the other two will run away. How do you expect them to support each other?"

But the general paid no attention and, as the man had predicted, one of the groups was defeated and the other two fled. Ch'ing Pu advanced west and eventually encountered the emperor's forces at Kueichui west of Ch'i. Finding that Ch'ing Pu's troops were spirited and well trained, the emperor fortified his position at Yung-ch'eng. As he looked out over Ch'ing Pu's army, he noted to his anger that it was drawn up in the same order which his old rival Hsiang Yü used to employ for his army. Spying Ch'ing Pu in the distance, the emperor shouted to him, "What is your grievance that you revolt against me?"

"I want to be emperor, that is all!" Ch'ing Pu shouted back, whereupon the emperor cursed him angrily.

A great battle followed and Ch'ing Pu's army fled in defeat across the Huai River, halting several times to fight, but always without success. Ch'ing Pu eventually fled with a hundred or more men to Chiang-nan.

Ch'ing Pu had once been married to the daughter of Wu Jui, the lord of P'o, and for this reason King Ch'eng[6] of Ch'ang-sha, Wu Jui's son, sent a messenger to deceive Ch'ing Pu, inviting him to flee with him to Yüeh. Ch'ing Pu believed the messenger and followed him to P'o-yang, where he was murdered by the men of the place in a field outhouse in Tzu County. Thus Ch'ing Pu was finally wiped out and the emperor's son Liu Ch'ang replaced him as king of Huai-nan. Pi Ho was made marquis of Ch'i-ssu, and a number of the generals who had distinguished themselves in the campaign were enfeoffed.

The Grand Historian remarks: Since Ch'ing Pu's family name was Ying, I wonder if he was related to the Yings of Liu, mentioned in the old annals as descendants of Emperor Shun's minister Kao Yao, who were overthrown by Ch'u? After being condemned as a criminal and suffering punishment, how spectacular was his rise to power! When

---

[5] Because men fighting near their homes are more apt to desert than those fighting in a strange land.

[6] The text erroneously reads "King Ai."

Hsiang Yü butchered his prisoners by the millions, it was always Ch'ing Pu who did the bloodiest work, and his distinction outshone that of all the other nobles. This was how he got to be a king. Yet in the end he himself could not escape the great slaughter of his time. Misfortune, born of the love for a concubine and bred in the fretfulness of a jealous mind, at last destroyed his kingdom.

Shih chi 92: The Biography of the Marquis of Huai-yin (Han Hsin)

The men of Ch'u harried us between Ching and So, but Han Hsin captured Wei and Chao, won over Yen and Ch'i, and made it possible for Han to control two thirds of the empire and thereby destroy Hsiang Yü. Thus I made The Biography of the Marquis of Huai-yin.

Han Hsin, the marquis of Huai-yin, was a native of Huai-yin. In his young days when he was still a commoner, being poor and without any noteworthy deeds, he was not able to get himself recommended for a position as an official. He was likewise unable to make a living as a merchant and so was constantly dependent upon others for his meals, which made many people dislike him. One of the persons whose hospitality he often imposed upon was the head of his village of Nan-ch'ang in Hsia County. After he had stayed for several months on end, the wife of the village head became much annoyed. One morning she got up very early, cooked her own breakfast, and ate it in bed. When breakfast time came, Han Hsin appeared as usual, but found that she had prepared nothing for him. Hsin perceived what she had in mind and was incensed and in the end he broke off the friendship and went away.

Han Hsin went fishing in the Huai River at the foot of the city wall, where some old women were washing coarse silk to bleach it. One of the old women noticed that Han Hsin was nearly starved and she fed him, and continued to do so for the twenty or thirty days until the bleaching was finished. Han Hsin was very grateful and said to the old woman, "Some day I will pay you back handsomely without fail!"

But the old woman was offended and replied, "I could tell you had no way of getting food for yourself, young gentleman, and so I felt sorry for you and gave you something to eat. What makes you think I was looking for any reward?"

Marquis of Huai-yin (Han Hsin)

Among the butchers of Huai-yin was a young man who jeered at Han Hsin and said, "You are big and tall and love to carry a sword, but at heart you're nothing but a coward!" In front of a crowd of people he insulted Han Hsin, and then said, "If you feel like dying, come on and attack me! If not, then crawl between my legs!"

Han Hsin looked him over carefully, and then bent down and crawled between the man's legs. The people in the market place all roared with laughter at Han Hsin's cowardice.

When Hsiang Liang crossed the Huai River, Han Hsin took up his sword and went to join the band under his command, but he did nothing to distinguish himself. After Hsiang Liang was defeated he joined Hsiang Yü, who made him one of his attendants. Han Hsin several times offered suggestions on strategy, but Hsiang Yü made no use of them.

After the king of Han had retired to his territory in Shu, Han Hsin fled from Ch'u and joined the forces of Han. Being still a man of no particular renown, he was given a minor position as attendant to guests.

Han Hsin became involved in an offense and was condemned to die. Thirteen other men in the group had already been beheaded and it was Han Hsin's turn next. He raised his head and looked about, when his eye fell upon Lord T'eng. "Has our sovereign no desire to win the world?" he asked. "Why does he deliberately cut off the head of a brave man?"

Lord T'eng was struck by his words and saw that he had a brave appearance, and so he did not execute him but set him free. After talking to Han Hsin, and finding him much to his liking, Lord T'eng mentioned him to the king of Han, who made him a commissary colonel, though the king saw nothing unusual in him. Han Hsin several times talked to Hsiao Ho, who regarded him with peculiar respect.

By the time the Han army reached Nan-cheng, it was found that twenty or thirty of the generals had deserted along the way. "Hsiao Ho and others have several times spoken about me to the king," Han Hsin considered to himself, "but the king has no use for me," and with this he too deserted. When Hsiao Ho heard that Han Hsin had run away, he did not wait to ask the king but started after him in person.

Someone reported to the king that Prime Minister Hsiao Ho had deserted. The king flew into a rage and was as distressed as if he had lost his right or left hand. After a day or so Hsiao Ho returned and appeared before the king. The king, half in anger and half in joy, began to curse him. "You deserted, didn't you!" he said. "Why?"

"How would I dare to desert?" replied Hsiao Ho. "I went after a deserter!"

"Who is it you went after?"

"Han Hsin."

The king cursed again. "When my generals were deserting me by the tens you did not pursue one of them. This going after Han Hsin is a lie!"

"Generals are easy enough to get," replied Hsiao Ho, "but men like Han Hsin are the best in the nation. If Your Majesty's ambition is to rule the area of Han for as long as possible, then you have no use for Han Hsin's services. But if you hope to contend for mastery of the world, then Han Hsin is the only man to lay plans with. It is entirely a matter of which course you choose to take."

"My whole ambition is to march east," the king replied. "How could I bear to stay pent up in a place like this forever?"

"Since your plans are aimed at moving east again, if you can make good use of Han Hsin, then he will stay with you. But if you cannot use him properly, then he will eventually desert!"

"For your sake I will make him a general," said the king.

"If you make him no more than a general, he will never stay."

"Then I will make him a major general!"

"That would be most gracious of you," Hsiao Ho replied. The king was about to summon Han Hsin and invest him with the position at once, but Hsiao Ho said, "Your Majesty is inclined to be rather brusque and lacking in ceremony. If you were to call him in and make him a general at once, it would be like ordering a little boy about. This is precisely the reason Han Hsin deserted. If you wish to confer a title on him, you must select an auspicious day, fast and purify yourself, erect an altar and go through the whole ceremony. This is the only way."

The king gave his consent to this. All of the generals were filled with joy, each considering that it was himself who was about to be made a major general. But when the title was conferred, to the astonishment of the entire army, it was upon Han Hsin. After the ceremony of investiture was concluded and Han Hsin had returned to his seat, the king said, "Prime Minister Hsiao Ho has often spoken to me about you, general. What sort of strategy is it that you would teach me?"

Han Hsin expressed his gratitude for the honor and took advantage of the king's inquiry to ask a question of his own. "Anyone who marched east to contend for the empire would have to face Hsiang Yü, would he not?"

"He would," replied the king.

"In Your Majesty's estimation, which of you, Hsiang Yü or yourself, excels in fierceness of courage and depth of kindness?"

The king of Han was silent for a while and then he said, "I am inferior to Hsiang Yü."

Han Hsin bowed once more and commended the king, saying, "Yes, I too believe that you are inferior. But I once served Hsiang Yü, and I would like to tell you what sort of person he is. When Hsiang Yü rages and bellows it is enough to make a thousand men fall down in terror. But since he is incapable of employing wise generals, all of it amounts to no more than the daring of an ordinary man.

"When Hsiang Yü meets people he is courteous and thoughtful, his manner of speaking is gentle and, if someone is ill or in distress, he will weep over him and give him his own food and drink. But when someone he has sent upon a mission has achieved merit and deserves to be honored and enfeoffed he will fiddle with the seal of investiture until it crumbles in his hand before he can bring himself to present it to the man. This sort of kindness deserves to be called merely womanish!

"Now although Hsiang Yü has made himself dictator of the world and subjugated the other nobles to his rule, he has not taken up residence in the area within the Pass, but has made his capital at P'eng-ch'eng. He has gone against the agreement made with the Righteous Emperor and instead given out kingdoms to the nobles on the basis of his own likes and preferences, which has resulted in much injustice. The nobles, seeing that Hsiang Yü has banished the Righteous Emperor and sent him to reside in Chiang-nan, when they return to their own territories in like manner drive out their sovereigns and make themselves rulers of the choicest lands. Hsiang Yü has left death and destruction everywhere he has passed. Much of the world hates him. The common people do not submit to him out of affection, but are awed by his might alone. In name he is a dictator, but in truth he has lost the hearts of the world. Therefore I say that his might can be easily weakened!

"Now if you could only pursue the opposite policy and make use of the brave men of the world, what enemy would not fall before you? If you were to enfeoff your worthy followers with the territories of the empire, who would not submit? If you were to take your soldiers of righteousness and lead them back east where they long to return, who would not flee from your path?

"The three kings of the region of Ch'in were formerly generals of Ch'in and led the sons of Ch'in for several years. The number of men who were killed under their command exceeds estimation. In addition they deceived their men into surrendering to the other nobles and, when they reached Hsin-an, Hsiang Yü treacherously butchered over two hundred thousand soldiers of the Ch'in army who had surrendered, sparing only the three generals Chang Han, Ssu-ma Hsin, and Tung I. Therefore the fathers of Ch'in loath these three men with a passion that eats into their very bones. Now Hsiang Yü has managed by sheer force to make kings of these men, but the people of Ch'in have no love for them. When you entered the Wu Pass, you inflicted not a particle of harm, but repealed the harsh laws of Ch'in and gave to the people a simple code of laws in three articles only, and there were none of the people of Ch'in who did not wish to make you their king. According to the agreement concluded among all the nobles, you ought to have been made king of the area within the Pass, and the people of the area all knew this. And when you were deprived of your rightful position and retired to the region of Han, the people of Ch'in were all filled with resentment. Now if you will raise your army and march east, you can win over the three kingdoms of Ch'in simply by proclamation!"

The king of Han was overjoyed and only regretted that he had been so long in discovering Han Hsin. He proceeded to follow the strategy

Han Hsin had outlined and assigned to his generals the areas which each was to attack. In the eighth month the king of Han raised his army, marched east out of Ch'en-ts'ang, and subjugated the three kingdoms of Ch'in.

In the second year of Han the king marched out of the Pass and seized control of Wei and Ho-nan. The kings of Hann and Yin both surrendered to him. Joining the forces of Ch'i and Chao, he attacked Ch'u. In the fourth month he reached P'eng-ch'eng, where his forces were defeated and compelled to retreat in disorder. Han Hsin gathered a second force of troops and joined the king of Han at Jung-yang and once more they attacked Ch'u in the region of Ching and So. As a result of this attack the armies of Ch'u were unable to proceed any further west.

When the Han army was defeated at P'eng-ch'eng and driven back, Ssu-ma Hsin, the king of Sai, and Tung I, the king of Ti, fled from Han and surrendered to Ch'u. Ch'i and Chao also revolted against Han and made peace with Ch'u.

In the sixth month Pao, king of Wei, asked to be allowed to go home and look after his ailing parents but, when he reached his kingdom, he cut off the fords over the Yellow River, revolted against Han, and concluded an alliance with Ch'u. The king of Han dispatched Master Li I-chi in an attempt to dissuade him, but he refused to listen. In the eighth month of this year Han Hsin was made prime minister of the left and sent to attack Wei. The king of Wei concentrated his forces at P'u-fan and blockaded Lin-chin. Han Hsin thereupon planted a dummy army and lined up a number of boats as though he were about to attempt to cross the river at Lin-chin. In the meantime he secretly led another force of men by way of Hsia-yang, where he ferried them across the river on floats and attacked An-i. Pao, the king of Wei, taken completely by surprise, led his troops to oppose Han Hsin but was taken prisoner. Han Hsin subjugated Wei and made it into the province of Ho-tung.

The king of Han dispatched Chang Erh to join Han Hsin and with him lead a force of troops to the northeast to attack Chao and Tai. In the intercalary ninth month they defeated the troops of Tai and took Hsia Yüeh prisoner at Yen-yü. As soon as Han Hsin had conquered

Wei and defeated Tai the king of Han hastily sent someone to take command of Han Hsin's best troops and bring them to Jung-yang to help in the blockade against Ch'u.

Han Hsin and Chang Erh with their force of twenty or thirty thousand men prepared to march east through the Ching Gorge to attack Chao. The king of Chao and Ch'en Yü, lord of Ch'eng-an, hearing that the Han forces were about to attack them, gathered an army, ostensibly numbering two hundred thousand, at the mouth of the gorge. Li Tso-ch'e, lord of Kuang-wu, advised Ch'en Yü, saying, "I have heard that the Han general Han Hsin has forded the Yellow River to the west, made the king of Wei and Hsia Yüeh his prisoners, and spilled blood anew at Yen-yü. Now with the help of Chang Erh he has laid his plans and intends to conquer Chao. An army such as his, riding the crest of victory and fighting far from its homeland, cannot be opposed.

"I have heard it said that, when provisions must be transported a thousand miles, the soldiers have a hungry look and, when fuel must be gathered before the mess is prepared, the army seldom sleeps with a full stomach. Now the road through the Ching Gorge is such that two carts cannot drive side by side, nor two horsemen ride abreast. On a march of several hundred miles under such circumstances, their provisions are sure to be in the rear. I beg you to lend me a force of thirty thousand surprise troops which I can lead by a secret route to cut off their supply wagons. In the meantime, if you deepen your moats, heighten your ramparts, strengthen your camp, and refuse to engage in battle, they will be unable either to advance and fight, or to retreat and go back home. With my surprise force I will cut off their rear and see to it that they get no plunder from the countryside, and before ten days are out I will bring the heads of their two commanders and lay them beneath your banners! I beg you to give heed to my plan for, if you do not, you will most certainly find yourself their prisoner!"

But Ch'en Yü was a Confucianist who always spoke of his "soldiers of righteousness" and had no use for tricky schemes or unusual strategies. "I have always heard that in the art of warfare," he said, "if you outnumber the enemy ten to one, you surround him, but if you outnumber him two to one, you engage him in battle. Now although Han Hsin's forces are reputed to be twenty or thirty thousand, they do not in fact exceed three or four thousand. Furthermore, he has marched a thousand miles to attack me, so he must already be thoroughly exhausted. If I were to flee and decline to fight under such circumstances, what would I do in the future when faced with a larger number? The other nobles would call me coward and think nothing of coming to attack me!"

Thus he refused to listen to the lord of Kuang-wu's plan, and the suggestion went unheeded. Han Hsin sent men to spy in secret and when they learned that the lord of Kuang-wu's plan was not being followed, they returned and reported to Han Hsin. He was overjoyed and proceeded without fear to lead his troops down the gorge. When they were still thirty *li* from the mouth of the gorge, he halted and made camp. During the night he sent an order through the camp to dispatch a force of two thousand light cavalry. Each man was to carry a red flag and, proceeding along a secret route, to conceal himself in the mountains and observe the Chao army. "When the Chao forces see me marching out, they are sure to abandon their fortifications and come in pursuit. Then you must enter their walls with all speed, tear down the Chao flags, and set up the red flags of Han in their place," he instructed them. Then he ordered his lieutenant generals to distribute a light meal to the army, saying, "This day we shall defeat Chao and feast together!" None of his generals believed that the plan would work, but they feigned agreement and answered "Very well."

Han Hsin addressed his officers, saying, "The Chao forces have already constructed their fortifications in an advantageous position. Moreover, until they see the flags and drums of our commanding general, they will be unwilling to attack our advance column for fear that I will see the difficulty of the position and retreat back up the gorge." Han Hsin therefore sent ten thousand men to march ahead out of the gorge and draw up in ranks with their backs to the river that ran through the gorge. The Chao army, observing this from afar, roared with laughter.[1]

At dawn Han Hsin raised the flags of the commanding general, set

---

[1] It was an axiom of Chinese military art that one should never fight with his back to a river.

his drums to sounding, and marched out of the mouth of the Ching Gorge. The Chao army opened their gates and poured out to attack, and for a long time the two armies fought together fiercely. At this point Han Hsin and Chang Erh deceptively abandoned their flags and drums and fled to the forces drawn up along the river. The columns along the river opened to receive them, and the battle continued to rage. As Han Hsin had anticipated, the Chao forces finally abandoned their fortifications completely in their eagerness to contend for the Han flags and pursue Han Hsin and Chang Erh. With Han Hsin and Chang Erh in their ranks, however, the army along the river determined to fight to the death and could not be defeated.

In the meantime the surprise force of two thousand cavalry which Han Hsin had sent out, waiting until the Chao forces had abandoned their camp in order to follow up their advantage, rushed into the Chao fortifications, tore down the Chao flags, and set up two thousand red flags of Han in their place. The Chao forces, unable to achieve a victory and capture Han Hsin and the others, were about to return to their fortifications when they discovered that the walls were lined with the red flags of Han. The soldiers were filled with alarm and, concluding that the Han army had already captured the generals of the king of Chao, fled in panic in all directions. Though the Chao generals cut them down on the spot, they could not stop the rout. With this the Han forces closed in from both sides, defeated and captured the Chao army, executed Ch'en Yü on the banks of the Ch'ih River, and took Hsieh, the king of Chao, prisoner.

Han Hsin issued orders to his army that the lord of Kuang-wu was not to be killed, and offered a reward of a thousand catties of gold to the man who could capture him alive. As a result the lord of Kuang-wu was bound by one of the men and led before the commanding general. Han Hsin loosed his bonds, placed him in the seat of honor facing east, and himself took a seat facing west, treating him with the respect due a teacher. The subordinate generals arrived to present their captives and the heads of their victims, and then rested from their labors and joined in congratulating Han Hsin on the victory.

Taking advantage of the opportunity, they began to question Han Hsin. "According to *The Art of War,* when one fights he should keep the hills to his right or rear, and bodies of water in front of him or to the left," they said. "Yet today you ordered us on the contrary to draw up ranks with our backs to the river, saying 'We shall defeat Chao and feast together!' We were opposed to the idea, and yet it has ended in victory. What sort of strategy is this?"

"This is in *The Art of War* too," replied Han Hsin. "It is just that you have failed to notice it! Does it not say in *The Art of War:* 'Drive them into a fatal position and they will come out alive; place them in a hopeless spot and they will survive'? Moreover, I did not have at my disposal troops that I had trained and led from past times, but was forced, as the saying goes, to round up men from the market place and use them to fight with. Under such circumstances, if I had not placed them in a desperate situation where each man was obliged to fight for his own life, but had allowed them to remain in a safe place, they would have all run away. Then what good would they have been to me?"

"Indeed!" his generals exclaimed in admiration. "We would never have thought of that."

Then Han Hsin questioned the lord of Kuang-wu. "I am planning to march north and attack Yen, and from there proceed east to strike at Ch'i. What would be the most effective way to go about it?"

The lord of Kuang-wu, however, declined to answer, saying, "The general of a defeated army, they say, is not qualified to talk of bravery, nor the minister of a lost nation to invent schemes for survival. Now that I am a prisoner taken in defeat, how could I be worthy to weigh such great undertakings?

Hans Hsin replied, "I have heard it said that when Po-li Hsi lived in Yü, Yü was destroyed, but when he lived in Ch'in, Ch'in became a great power. This was not because he was stupid when he was in Yü and wise when in Ch'in. It was only because in one he was employed and in the other he was not; in one he was listened to and in the other ignored. As a matter of fact, if Ch'en Yü had listened to your plan, even I would have become your prisoner. It is only because he did not make use of you that I have the honor of waiting upon you now." Han Hsin continued to press him for an answer, saying, "I shall set all of my ideas aside and do whatever you suggest. I beg you to decline no further!"

"They say," answered the lord of Kuang-wu, "that among the schemes of the wisest man one in a thousand will end in error, while among those of the greatest fool one in a thousand will succeed. Therefore it is said that a sage will find something to choose even from the words of a madman. I am doubtful whether any plan I might suggest would be worthy of consideration, but I beg to exercise the limits of my poor ability.

"Ch'en Yü had a plan which seemed to insure a hundred victories in as many battles, and yet in one morning it proved a failure, his army was defeated before the walls of Ho, and he himself met death on the banks of the Ch'ih. Now you have crossed the Yellow River to the west, made a prisoner of the king of Wei, captured Hsia Yüeh at Yen-yü, in one stroke descended the Ching Gorge and, before the morning was out, defeated Chao's great army of two hundred thousand and executed Ch'en Yü. Your fame resounds throughout the land and your might fills the world with awe. The farmers have left their plowing and cast aside their hoes and, anticipating that your armies will soon be upon them, have donned their finest clothes and are feasting while they may, inclining their ears in wait for your command. Such is the strength of your position.

"On the other hand, your troops are tired and worn out, and in point of fact are not of much use. Now you plan to lead this force of weary and exhausted men and further exhaust them before the stout walls of Yen. Yet, no matter how long you battle, your strength will not be sufficient to overcome them. The hopelessness of your situation will become apparent as your might declines, the days will pass fruitlessly while your supplies grow scarce, and still Yen, weak though it is, will not submit. Ch'i in the meantime will certainly man its frontiers and strengthen its defense and, with Yen and Ch'i supporting each other and refusing to capitulate, the king of Han and Hsiang Yü will continue at a stalemate and their fate will never be decided. This is the weak side of your position. In my humble opinion such a move would be a mistake, for one who is skilled in the use of arms never attacks strength with weakness, but only weakness with strength."

"Then what course should I follow?" asked Han Hsin.

"If I were to suggest a plan for you," replied the lord of Kuang-wu,

"I would say the best thing to do would be to halt your army and rest your soldiers. Patrol the land of Chao and comfort the orphans made in today's battle. From the surrounding area have oxen and wine brought each day to feast your officers and banquet your men, and face them north towards the roads of Yen. After that you may dispatch your rhetoricians bearing documents to prove how superior your strength is to that of Yen, and Yen will not dare to turn a deaf ear. When Yen has submitted, you may send your propagandists to the east to talk to Ch'i, and Ch'i too will be obliged by the trend of events to submit, for even her wisest councilors will be able to think of no alternative. In this way you can have your will with the whole empire. In warfare the important thing is to publicize yourself first, and act afterward. Therefore I have suggested this plan."

Han Hsin approved of his plan and set about putting it into action, dispatching an envoy to Yen. Yen bowed before the report of Han Hsin's power and submitted. Han Hsin sent an envoy to report this to the king of Han, at the same time requesting that Chang Erh be made king of Chao to bring peace and order to the land. The king of Han gave his permission and set up Chang Erh as king of Chao.

Ch'u from time to time sent surprise forces across the Yellow River to attack Chao, but Chang Erh and Han Hsin, by moving back and forth through the area, were able to save Chao, step by step gain control of its cities, and eventually dispatch a force of troops to aid the king of Han, who at this time was in Jung-yang surrounded and sorely pressed by the armies of Ch'u. The king of Han escaped south to the area of Yüan and She, where he obtained the aid of Ch'ing Pu, and then fled to safety in Ch'eng-kao. The Ch'u forces once more surrounded and pressed him. In the sixth month the king of Han fled from Ch'eng-kao, crossed to the east side of the Yellow River and, accompanied only by Lord T'eng, went to join the army of Chang Erh at Hsiu-wu. When he arrived he stopped for a night at the posthouse and at dawn the next day, representing himself as an envoy from the king of Han, hastened into the Chao camp. Chang Erh and Han Hsin being still in bed, he went to their chambers, seized their seals of command, and with these summoned all the subordinate generals and began assigning them to new posts. When Han Hsin and

Chang Erh woke up and found that the king of Han had arrived, they were astounded. Thus the king of Han seized the armies of both men, ordering Chang Erh to man and guard the region of Chao, and making Han Hsin his prime minister with orders to form an army from the men of Chao who had not yet been pressed into service and proceed to attack Ch'i.

Han Hsin led his troops east but, before he had crossed the Yellow River at the P'ing-yüan Ford, he received word that the king of Han had sent Li I-chi to bargain with Ch'i and that Ch'i had already submitted. Han Hsin wanted to halt his march, but K'uai T'ung, a rhetorician from Fan-yang, counseled him against this. "You have received a royal order to attack Ch'i. In the meantime the king of Han has independently dispatched a secret envoy to talk Ch'i into submission. But there has been no royal order instructing you to halt, has there? How can you fail to proceed on your mission? Furthermore, this one man, Master Li I-chi, by bowing graciously from his carriage and wagging his meager tongue, has conquered the seventy-odd cities of Ch'i, while you, with your army of thousands, needed a year and over before you could gain control of the fifty-odd cities of Chao. Could it be that what you have done in your several years as a general is not equal to the accomplishments of one wretched Confucianist?"

Persuaded by his arguments, Han Hsin followed his advice and proceeded to cross the Yellow River. Ch'i in the meantime, having heeded Master Li's persuasions, was detaining him with wine and feasts and had at the same time dispersed the defenses which it had prepared against the Han armies. Han Hsin was thus able to attack the Ch'i army at Li-hsia and proceed as far as Lin-tzu. T'ien Kuang, the king of Ch'i, concluding that Master Li had betrayed him, had Master Li boiled alive and then fled to Kao-mi, where he sent an envoy to Ch'u to beg for aid.

After conquering Lin-tzu, Han Hsin proceeded east in pursuit of T'ien Kuang as far as the west of Kao-mi. Ch'u also sent its general Lung Chü with a reputed force of two hundred thousand to aid Ch'i. The king of Ch'i and Lung Chü with their combined armies fought with Han Hsin but, before the armies had closed in battle, someone advised Lung Chü, saying, "The soldiers of Han, battling far from their homeland, will fight to the death. They cannot be opposed in combat. Ch'i and Ch'u, however, are fighting on their own ground and their soldiers may easily run away in defeat. It would be better to strengthen your fortifications and have the king of Ch'i send his trusted ministers to rally the lost cities of Ch'i. If the lost cities hear that their king is still alive and that aid has come from Ch'u, they will certainly revolt against the Han army. The Han soldiers have marched a thousand miles into a strange land. If the cities of Ch'i all turn against them, they will find themselves with no way to get food for their forces, and they can be overcome without a fight."

Lung Chü replied, "I have long known what sort of man Han Hsin is. He is easy enough to deal with. Furthermore, now that I have come to rescue Ch'i, if I were to overcome him without a battle, what merit would I gain from the expedition? But if I fight and beat him, half of Ch'i can be mine. Why should I stop now?"

In the end he engaged Han Hsin in battle, the two armies drawing up on opposite sides of the Wei River. In the night Han Hsin ordered his men to make more than ten thousand bags, fill them with sand, and block the flow of the river upstream. Then he led his army halfway across the river to attack Lung Chü but, pretending to be defeated, fled back to the shore. As Han Hsin had expected, Lung Chü announced delightedly, "I always knew that Han Hsin was a coward!" and forthwith pursued Han Hsin across the river. Han Hsin then ordered his men to break open the dam of sandbags. The water came rushing down so that the large part of Lung Chü's army could not get across the river. With all speed Han Hsin closed in and killed Lung Chü, while the men of Lung Chü's army who had crossed to the east side of the river fled in disorder. T'ien Kuang, the king of Ch'i, fled at the same time. Han Hsin pursued the defeated army as far as Ch'eng-yang, where he captured all the soldiers of Ch'u.

In the fourth year of Han, having completed the conquest and pacification of Ch'i, Han Hsin dispatched an envoy to report to the king of Han, saying, "Ch'i is full of deceit and shifty loyalties, a land fickle in its faith. Moreover, it borders Ch'u on the south. Unless I am made an acting king with power to bring it to order, the situation cannot be stabilized. For the sake of convenience I ask to be made an acting king."

Han Hsin's envoy arrived just at the time when the king of Han was being pressed in siege at Jung-yang. When Han Hsin's letter was handed to him the king began to curse. "Here I am in a critical position, hoping day and night that he will come to aid me, and now he wants to make himself a king!" Chang Liang and Ch'en P'ing stepped on the king's foot and, drawing close to his ear, whispered, "We are at a disadvantage at the moment. How can we stop Han Hsin from becoming a king? It would be better to go along with his request, make him a king, and treat him well so that he will guard Ch'i for his own sake. Otherwise he may desert us altogether!"

The king realized his error and began to curse again. "When one of my men overcomes a feudal lord I make him nothing less than a real king. Why should I make him only an 'acting' king?" Then he dispatched Chang Liang to go and install Han Hsin as king of Ch'i, and levy his troops to fight against Ch'u.

Ch'u had already lost Lung Chü, and Hsiang Yü, growing fearful, sent Wu She, a man of Hsü-i, to go and talk to the new king of Ch'i. "The world suffered a long time under the tyranny of Ch'in," he said, "until we joined our strength and attacked it. When Ch'in was defeated we calculated the merit each had won, divided up the land, gave each his portion to rule, and set our soldiers to rest. Now the king of Han has called up his army again and marched east, invading the territories of other men and seizing their lands. He has already destroyed the three kingdoms of Ch'in, led his men out of the Pass, drafted the soldiers of the other nobles, and marched east to attack Ch'u. It is his intention not to rest until he has swallowed up the whole empire, so insatiable are his desires!

"Moreover, the king of Han cannot be trusted. Several times Hsiang Yü, the king of Ch'u, has had him in his grasp, but always he has taken pity on him and let him live. And yet no sooner had the king of Han escaped than he went back on his agreement and once more attacked King Hsiang. This shows how untrustworthy he is. Now you consider yourself his fast friend and are doing your best to fight for him, but in the end you will find yourself his prisoner. The only reason you have been able to go your way so far is that King Hsiang is still alive.

"Today the fate of these two kings lies with you. If you throw your weight one way, the king of Han will win; if you throw it the other way, King Hsiang of Ch'u will win. But if King Hsiang should perish today, it would be your turn to be seized next. You and King Hsiang are old friends. Why do you not turn against Han, make your peace with Ch'u, and rule a third of the empire? Now you are going to throw this opportunity away, put your faith in Han, and attack Ch'u. Is this in truth the policy of a wise man?"

Han Hsin, however, declined his advice. "When I served under King Hsiang," he replied, "my office was no more than that of an attendant, and my position only that of spear bearer. He did not listen to my counsels nor make use of my plans. Therefore I turned my back on Ch'u and gave my allegiance to Han. The king of Han presented me with the seals of a commanding general and granted me a force of twenty or thirty thousand men. He doffed his own garments to clothe me, gave me food from his own plate, listened to my words, and used my counsels. Therefore I have been able to come this far. When a man has treated me with such deep kindness and faith, I could never be disloyal to him. I beg you to convey my regrets to King Hsiang."

When Wu She departed, K'uai T'ung, a man of Ch'i, realizing that Han Hsin held the balance of power in the empire, thought to sway his resolution by means of a curious scheme. Mentioning the art of physiognomy to Han Hsin, he said, "I once studied this art of reading people's faces."

"Just how do you go about reading faces?" asked Han Hsin.

"High or low position are revealed in the bone structure, sorrow or joy in the countenance, and success or failure in the power of decision. If one considers these three factors, he will make no mistake in a thousand cases!"

"Indeed! And what would you say of me?"

"May I speak to you a moment in private?" said K'uai T'ung.

"Let those about me retire!" Han Hsin ordered.

"Examining your face," K'uai T'ung continued, "I see that you will never be more than a feudal lord. And I see danger and unrest. But if you turn your back,[2] I see such honor as cannot be expressed in words!"

"How so?" asked Han Hsin.

"When revolt first broke out in the world the great warriors and brave heroes proclaimed their titles and shouted as with one voice, and the soldiers of all the world massed about them like thickening clouds, meshed their forces like the scales of a fish, flamed forth, and rose before the wind. At that time the thought of each was only to destroy Ch'in. But now Ch'u and Han rend the empire with their contention so that countless innocent men of the world spill their bowels upon the soaking earth and the bones of father and son are left to bleach in the open field. The men of Ch'u rose up from P'eng-ch'eng, and in battle after battle pursued the fleeing Han forces as far as Jung-yang, riding upon the crest of victory and rolling up the empire like a mat before them, until the whole world trembled at their might. But for three years now their soldiers have suffered reverses in the area between Ching and So, blocked by the western mountains and unable to advance. The king of Han with a host of two or three hundred thousand men has blocked their advance at Kung and Lo-yang, relying upon the defenses of mountains and rivers. But though he fights several engagements a day, he is powerless to win an inch of territory, nor can he break away and flee without perishing. He was defeated at Jung-yang, wounded at Ch'eng-kao, and finally forced to flee into the area of Yüan and She. This is a case in which both the wise and the brave are at a stalemate. The keen spirits of the one are dashed against impregnable barriers; the provisions of the other grow scarce in his storehouses, while the common people, exhausted and worn with hatred and resentment, reel and stagger without means of support. It is my judgment that under such conditions none but the wisest of men can ever bring surcease to the ills of the world!

"Now the fate of these two rulers lies with you. If you declare for Han, Han will win; if for Ch'u, then Ch'u will win. I would open my heart and mind to you, exhaust my poor energies, and devise for you a plan, but I fear that you will not heed it. If, however, you were truly

---

[2] A *double-entendre*, i.e., "if you turn against Han."

to give ear to my scheme, I would say that it would be best to take advantage of these two rivals and preserve them both. Divide the empire into three shares and let each of you stand like the legs of a tripod. Under such circumstances neither of the others will dare to make the first move.

"With your great wisdom and your host of soldiers, you could make your base in powerful Ch'i, command Yen and Chao and, moving out into the unoccupied lands, seize control of the areas to the rear of Han and Ch'u. Then you could gratify the desires of the people by facing the powers of the west and demanding that they spare the lives of the masses. The whole world will respond to your call and hasten to you as though upon the wind. Who would dare to turn a deaf ear? You could divide the great states, weaken the powerful, and set up feudal rulers and, when the lords were established, all the world would harken to your words and bow before the beneficence of Ch'i. You may base your power upon the old land of Ch'i, occupy the regions of Chiao and Ssu, win over the nobles through your favors, retire within your palace, fold your hands and bow in humble deprecation, and the rulers of the earth will lead each other on to pay homage to Ch'i. Yet I have heard that 'he who does not take when Heaven offers, receives misfortune instead; he who does not act when the time comes, suffers disaster instead.' I beg you to consider most carefully!"

Han Hsin replied, "The king of Han has treated me most generously, placing me in his own carriage, clothing me with his own garments, and giving me to eat from his own plate. I have heard it said that he who rides in another man's carriage must share his woes, he who puts on another man's clothes dons his sorrows as well, and he who eats another man's food must serve him to the death. How could I turn my back on what is right merely for the hope of gain?"

"You consider yourself a close friend of the king of Han," said K'uai T'ung, "and hope thereby to create a position for yourself and your family for all time to come. But if I may be so bold, I believe you are mistaken. When Chang Erh, the king of Ch'ang-shan, and Ch'en Yü, the lord of Ch'eng-an, were still commoners, they swore to be friends until death, and yet after they had quarreled over the affair of Chang Yen and Ch'en Shih, they grew to hate each other.

Chang Erh turned his back upon Hsiang Yü and, cowering with his head between his hands, crept off to join the king of Han. There he borrowed soldiers from the king of Han, marched east again, and, south of the Ch'ih River, slaughtered Ch'en Yü who, his head and feet torn asunder, ended as a laughingstock of the world. These two had been the fastest friends in the world. Why then did one end as the prisoner of the other? Because evil arises from excess of desires, and the heart of man is hard to fathom!

"Now though you hope to conduct your dealings with the king of Han in loyalty and good faith, you can never be closer to him than these two men, Chang Erh and Ch'en Yü, were to each other, while there are many things to stand between you more serious than the affair of Chang Yen and Ch'en Shih. Therefore I believe that you are mistaken in thinking that there is no danger in trusting the king of Han.

"Ta-fu Chung and Fan Li once saved the doomed state of Yüeh, made its ruler, Kou-chien, a dictator, and won fame and glory, and yet they themselves perished. 'When the wild beasts have all been captured,' says the old proverb, 'the hunting dog is put into the pot to boil.' You talk of friendship, but yours is nothing like that of Chang Erh and Ch'en Yü; you speak of loyalty, but you cannot do more than Ta-fu Chung and Fan Li did for Kou-chien. These two cases are well worth noting. I beg you to consider them deeply.

"They say that bravery and cunning which make even one's own ruler tremble only endanger one's self, while the merit which overshadows the world is never rewarded. Let me for a moment recount your own merit and cunning. You crossed the western reaches of the Yellow River, made a prisoner of the king of Wei, and captured Hsia Yüeh; you led your troops down the Ching Gorge, executed Ch'en Yü, subdued Chao, terrified Yen into submission, and subjugated Ch'i. In the south you crushed the Ch'u army of two hundred thousand men; in the east you killed Lung Chü, and now you have turned west to report your deeds to the king of Han. One may say that you have won merit unparalleled in the world, and shown a cunning unmatched in generations. Now that you wield power enough to make a sovereign tremble and have won more merit than can be rewarded, should you choose to follow Ch'u, the men of Ch'u would never trust you, and should you follow Han, the men of Han would quake with fear. With gifts such as these, whom should you follow? Your position is that of a subject, and yet you possess power enough to make a sovereign tremble and a name which resounds throughout the world. This is why I consider that you are in danger!"

Han Hsin thanked him and said, "Stop a while, I beg you. I will think over what you have said."

After several days K'uai T'ung began to lecture him again. "Listening to advice is the basis of an undertaking, and planning is the key to success. Where there is bad listening or faulty planning, the undertaking seldom prospers for long. But if one listens with a sense of logic, he will not be confused by mere words; if he plans with a sense of relative importance, he cannot be distracted by mere talk. One who contents himself with the labors of a menial will never wield the power of a great lord; one who clings to a post that pays only a bushel or two of grain will never occupy the position of prime minister.

"Therefore to be wise is to be resolute in decision, but to doubt is to destroy one's undertaking. The petty schemes which take account of every detail miss the greater destinies of the world. To be wise only in knowledge but lack the resoluteness to act is to meet disaster in every undertaking. Thus it is said, 'Better a wasp bent on stinging than a hesitant tiger; better an old nag plodding safely along than a hobbling thoroughbred; better a common man determined to act than the bravest hero vacillating! You may be as wise as Shun and Yü, but if you mumble and do not speak out, you are less use than a deaf mute making gestures!' These sayings prove the worth of being able to act. Merit is difficult to achieve and easy to lose. The right time is hard to find and easy to let slip. The time, my lord, the time! It will not come twice! I beg you to consider carefully!"

But Han Hsin hesitated and could not bear to turn against Han. Also he considered that he had won such merit that the king of Han would never take Ch'i away from him. So in the end he refused K'uai T'ung's advice. When K'uai T'ung realized that his advice would not be followed, he desisted and, feigning madness, became a shaman.

The king of Han was in considerable difficulty at Ku-ling but, employing a scheme suggested by Chang Liang, he summoned Han Hsin, the king of Ch'i, who led his army to join the Han forces at Kai-hsia. After Hsiang Yü had been defeated, the king of Han, now emperor, surprised Han Hsin and seized his army.

In the first month of the fifth year of Han the emperor moved Han Hsin from Ch'i to the position of king of Ch'u with his capital at Hsia-p'ei. When Han Hsin reached his state he summoned the old washerwoman who had given him food long ago and presented her with a thousand catties of gold. To the village head of Nan-ch'ang in Hsia he gave a hundred cash, remarking, "You are a small-minded man! When you do favors for people, you are not willing to see them through to the end!" Then he sent for the young man who had humiliated him and made him crawl between his legs, and made him a military commander. "He is a brave man," Han Hsin told his generals and ministers. "At the time when he humiliated me, I could of course have killed him. But killing him would have won me no fame. So I put up with it and got where I am today."

Chung-li Mo, a fugitive general of Hsiang Yü whose home was at Yin-lu, had long been a friend of Han Hsin and, after the death of Hsiang Yü, he fled to join Han Hsin. The king of Han hated Chung-li Mo and, hearing that he was in Ch'u, sent an order to Ch'u to have him seized. When Han Hsin first arrived in Ch'u, he made a tour of the various district towns, leading his soldiers in formation here and there about the state. In the sixth year of Han someone sent a report to the emperor stating that Han Hsin, king of Ch'u, was about to revolt. Kao-tsu, at the suggestion of Ch'en P'ing, decided to make an imperial tour and summon a meeting of the nobles. In the south there is a lake called Yün-meng, and so the emperor dispatched envoys to the nobles saying, "Meet me at Ch'en, since I am going to visit Yün-meng." His real intention was to make a surprise attack on Han Hsin, though Han Hsin was unaware of this.

With the emperor about to arrive in Ch'u, Han Hsin began to consider whether he should not dispatch his troops in revolt but, since he believed himself guilty of no crime, he decided to visit the emperor. He was afraid of being taken prisoner, however. Someone advised him, saying, "If you execute Chung-li Mo before you go to visit the

Marquis of Huai-yin (Han Hsin)

emperor, His Majesty is sure to be pleased and there will be no trouble." Han Hsin went to see Chung-li Mo to discuss what he ought to do. "The only reason the Han forces do not attack and take Ch'u away from you is that I am with you!" said Chung-li Mo. "Now if you wish to seize me in order to ingratiate yourself with the emperor, I am prepared to die today, but you yourself will follow close behind!" Then he cursed Han Hsin, saying, "You are no man of honor!" and in the end cut his own throat.

Han Hsin, bearing Chung-li Mo's head, went to visit Kao-tsu at Ch'en. The emperor ordered his guards to bind Han Hsin and place him in one of the rear carriages. "It is just as men say," sighed Han Hsin. "When the cunning hares are dead, the good dog is boiled; when the soaring birds are gone, men put away the good bow; when the enemy states have been defeated, the ministers who plotted their downfall are doomed. The world is now at peace, and so it is fitting that I be boiled!"

"Someone told me that you were about to revolt," said the emperor, and had Han Hsin put into fetters, but when they reached Lo-yang he absolved him of guilt and made him marquis of Huai-yin.

Han Hsin, knowing that the emperor feared and hated his ability, always pleaded illness and failed to attend court or join the imperial processions. He brooded day and night on his discontent and was ashamed to be ranked equal with Chou P'o and Kuan Ying. Once, when he visited General Fan K'uai, Fan K'uai knelt in deep respect to greet him and see him off and, employing terms of the greatest humility, said, "Your Highness has condescended to look upon his servant." "I am still alive," laughed Han Hsin as he went out the gate, "but I am now the same rank as you and the rest!"

The emperor was once casually discussing with Han Hsin the relative abilities of his generals and ranking them in order.

"About how many soldiers could a person like myself command?" asked the emperor.

"Your Majesty would not exceed the hundred thousand class," replied Han Hsin.

"And what about yourself?"

"As for me, the more the better!"

"If the more the better," laughed the emperor, "how is it that you became my prisoner?"

"Your Majesty cannot command soldiers," replied Han Hsin, "but you are good at commanding generals. That is why I became your prisoner. Moreover you are one of those who are 'chosen of Heaven.' Your power is not human!"

When Ch'en Hsi was appointed governor of Chü-lu, he went to take his leave of Han Hsin. Han Hsin grasped his hand and, dismissing his attendants, walked with him into the courtyard. Gazing up at the sky and sighing, he said, "I wonder if you are the sort I can talk with. . . . I have something I would like to say to you."

"You have only to mention it," replied Ch'en Hsi.

"The place where you live has the finest troops in the empire. And you, of course, are a trusted and favored minister of the emperor. If someone were to report that you were about to revolt, the emperor would certainly not believe it. If it were reported a second time, the emperor might begin to doubt, and if a third time he would surely become angry and lead an expedition in person. In that case I might contrive to raise an army for you and we could scheme for the empire!"

Ch'en Hsi had long known of Han Hsin's ability and trusted him. "I shall honor your instructions with the greatest care!" replied Ch'en Hsi.

In the tenth year of Han, Ch'en Hsi did in fact revolt. The emperor marched against him in person, but Han Hsin, ill as usual, did not join the expedition. He sent a man in secret to the place where Ch'en Hsi was, saying, "Just raise your troops! I will help you from here." Han Hsin then plotted with his ministers and in the middle of the night forged an edict pardoning all the convict laborers attached to the government offices, intending to dispatch them in an attack on Empress Lü and the heir apparent. After he had assigned them their various places he waited for a report from Ch'en Hsi. It happened that one of Han Hsin's retainers had committed some fault against Han Hsin, who had him imprisoned and was about to execute him. The retainer's younger brother reported Han Hsin's disaffection to the capital, sending a letter to inform Empress Lü that he was planning to revolt. The empress thought of summoning him, but she was afraid that he would not come, so together with Hsiao Ho, the prime minister, she devised a scheme whereby they had a man pretend to come from the emperor with news that Ch'en Hsi had already been captured and killed. When the nobles and ministers all appeared to offer their congratulations Hsiao Ho sent word to trick Han Hsin, saying, "Although you are ill, you must make an effort to come to the capital and present your congratulations." Han Hsin came.

Empress Lü ordered the guards to bind Han Hsin and execute him in the bell-room of the Palace of Lasting Joy. When he was about to be beheaded, he said, "To my regret I did not listen to K'uai T'ung's scheme. And now I have been tricked by this bitch and her lackey! Is it not fate?" Han Hsin's family, to the third degree of kinship, was exterminated.

Kao-tsu had completed his campaign against Ch'en Hsi's army and returned to the capital when he learned of Han Hsin's death. He was both pleased and saddened by the news, and asked whether Han Hsin had said anything before he died. "He said he regretted not having listened to the scheme of K'uai T'ung," said Empress Lü.

"He is a rhetorician of Ch'i," said Kao-tsu and sent an order to Ch'i to have K'uai T'ung arrested.

When K'uai T'ung was brought before him, the emperor asked, "Did you advise Han Hsin to revolt?"

"I did," he replied. "I advised him most strongly. But the idiot did not listen to my scheme and so brought destruction upon himself and his family. Idiot though he was, if he had used my plan, how would Your Majesty ever have been able to destroy him?"

"Boil him alive!" ordered the emperor in a rage.

"But, Your Majesty, how unjust! To have me boiled . . . !" cried K'uai T'ung.

"You advised Han Hsin to revolt! What do you mean, unjust?"

"The web of Ch'in's government had rotted away and the strands of its rule grew slack. East of the mountains all was in chaos, as men of the other clans raised their armies and brave men flocked about them. The empire slipped from the house of Ch'in like a fleeing deer and all the world joined in its pursuit. As it happened, he with the tallest stature and the swiftest feet seized it first. Now the bandit

Chih's dog would bark even at a sage like Yao, but that is not because Yao is evil, but because it is a dog's nature to bark at anyone who is not his master. At that time I knew only Han Hsin. I did not know Your Majesty. There are countless men in the empire who plucked up their spirits and seized their swords in hopes of doing what you did. It is only that their strength was not equal to the task. And do you think you can boil all of them alive as well?"

"Free him!" said the emperor, and he absolved K'uai T'ung of his guilt.

The Grand Historian remarks: When I visited Huai-yin one of the men of the place told me that even when Han Hsin was still a commoner his ambitions were different from those of ordinary men. At the time of his mother's death he was so poor that he could not give her a proper burial, and yet he had her buried on a high, broad expanse of earth with room enough around to set up ten thousand households,[3] this man said. I went to visit Han Hsin's mother's grave, and it was quite true.

If Han Hsin had given thought to the Way and been more humble instead of boasting of his achievements and priding himself on his own ability, how fine a man he might have been! For his services to the house of Han he might have ranked with the dukes of Chou and Shao and Grand Duke Wang of old, and for ages after have enjoyed the blood and flesh of sacrifices. Yet he did not strive for such things but, when the world was already gathered under one rule, plotted treason instead. Was it not right that he and his family should be wiped out?

[3] As grave tenders, in the manner of the most exalted ruler.

Shih chi 93: The Biographies of Hann Hsin and Lu Wan

When Ch'u and Han were locked in stalemate in the area of Kung and Lo, Hann Hsin seized control of Ying-ch'uan for the king of Han and Lu Wan cut off Hsiang Yü's lines of supply. Thus I made The Biographies of Hann Hsin and Lu Wan.

Hann Hsin

Hsin, the king of Hann, was a grandson of the former King Hsiang of Hann by a concubine. He was eight feet five inches tall.[1] When Hsiang Liang set up King Huai, descendant of the royal house of Ch'u, as king of Ch'u, the states of Yen, Ch'i, Chao, and Wei all had kings belonging to their former royal houses; only the state of Hann was without an heir. Hsiang Liang therefore selected Ch'eng, the lord of Heng-yang, from among the princes of Hann, to be king of Hann and bring order to the former region of Hann for him. After Hsiang Liang was defeated and killed at Ting-t'ao, Ch'eng fled to King Huai of Ch'u.

At the time when the governor of P'ei led his troops to attack Yang-ch'eng, he made Chang Liang the Hann minister of instruction and sent him to conquer the former region of Hann, where Chang Liang enlisted the aid of Hann Hsin, making him a general of Hann. Hann Hsin led his troops to follow the governor of P'ei through the Wu Pass. When the governor of P'ei was made king of Han, Hann Hsin accompanied him to the region of Han, where he advised the king,

---

[1] I.e., over six feet six inches. I have spelled this Hann Hsin's name with two n's to distinguish him from the Han Hsin who is the subject of the preceding chapter. In Chinese, however, the names are written alike and there is evidence that the two men were confused even in Ssu-ma Ch'ien's time. Thus he here attributes to Hann Hsin a speech which in The Annals of Kao-tsu is attributed to Han Hsin. I can only beg the reader's indulgence for the bewildering profusion of Hann's and Han's which the text forces upon me.

saying, "Hsiang Yü has made his generals kings of the regions near about him, but you alone he has sent to this faraway place, as though you were being exiled for some offense. Your officers and men are all from east of the mountains, and they gaze into the distance, longing to go home. If you would take up your lance and face eastward again, you could contend for control of the world!"

The king of Han returned east and conquered the three kingdoms of Ch'in. He gave Hann Hsin permission to become king of Hann, but first awarded him the title of grand commandant of Hann, and sent him with troops to seize the region of Hann.

All the kings whom Hsiang Yü had enfeoffed had already proceeded to their respective kingdoms except King Ch'eng of Hann who, because he had not accompanied Hsiang Yü through the Pass and had achieved no outstanding merit, was not sent to his kingdom but was demoted to the rank of marquis instead. When Hsiang Yü heard that the king of Han had sent Hann Hsin to seize the region of Hann he made Ch'eng Ch'ang, the magistrate of Wu whom he had known in former days when he was living in Wu, the king of Hann with orders to stop Hann Hsin's advance.

In the second year of Han, Hann Hsin invaded Hann and captured more than ten cities of the region. When the king of Han reached Honan, Hann Hsin made a sudden attack upon Ch'eng Ch'ang at Yang-ch'eng. Upon Ch'eng Ch'ang's surrender, Hann Hsin was made king of Hann and thereafter led his troops in the service of the king of Han.

In the third year the king of Han escaped from Jung-yang, leaving Hann Hsin, Chou K'o, and others to guard the city but, when Hsiang Yü finally took the city, Hann Hsin surrendered. Later he managed to escape and make his way back to the king of Han and was once more made king of Hann, joining in the final attack and the defeat of Hsiang Yü.

In the spring of the fifth year, after the empire was at peace, Hann Hsin at last received the split tallies officially making him the king of Hann ruling from Ying-ch'uan.

In the spring of the following year the emperor, considering that Hann Hsin was clever and brave and that the territory he ruled extended to Kung and Lo-yang in the north, Yüan and She in the south, and east to Huai-yang—regions possessing some of the finest troops in the empire—issued an edict transferring Hann Hsin to the rulership of the region of T'ai-yüan, with his capital at Chin-yang, so that he could guard the northern border against barbarian invasion. Hann Hsin submitted a letter to the throne, saying, "Since my kingdom lies along the northern frontier, it is often invaded by the Hsiung-nu. Chin-yang is too far away from the border. I request that the seat of government be moved to Ma-i." His request was granted and Hann Hsin's capital transferred to Ma-i.

In the autumn the Hsiung-nu chief Mo-tun surrounded Hann Hsin with a large force. Hann Hsin several times sent envoys to the barbarians seeking their peaceful withdrawal. The emperor dispatched troops to aid Hann Hsin but, suspecting him of disloyalty because of his frequent exchanges of secret envoys with the barbarians, he also sent a man to reprimand him. Hann Hsin, fearful of punishment, concluded an alliance with the Hsiung-nu to join in attacking Han, surrendering the city of Ma-i to them and attacking T'ai-yüan.

In the winter of the seventh year the emperor in person led an attack and defeated Hann Hsin's army at T'ung-ti, executing his general Wang Hsi. Hann Hsin escaped and fled to the Hsiung-nu, joining with his generals Man-ch'iu Ch'en of Po-t'u, Wang Huang, and others in setting up Chao Li, a descendant of the Chao royal family, as king of Chao. The generals gathered together Hann Hsin's defeated troops and with Hann Hsin and Mo-tun plotted to attack Han. The Hsiung-nu sent their Wise Kings of the Left and Right [2] with a force of ten thousand cavalry to join Wang Huang and the others in garrisoning Kuang-wu and, advancing as far south as Chin-yang, engaged the Han forces in battle. There they were severely defeated by the Han forces, pursued as far as Li-shih, and again defeated. The Hsiang-nu once more massed their forces in the northwest of Lou-fan. The emperor dispatched his general of carriage and cavalry to attack the Hsiung-nu. Because the Hsiung-nu constantly retreated in flight, the Han forces were able to follow up their advantage and pursue

[2] The "Wise Kings of the Left and Right" were the two highest ranking military leaders under the *Shan-yü*, hereditary commanders respectively of the eastern and western sections of the Hsiung-nu nation.

them north. Hearing that Mo-tun was in the Tai Valley, the emperor, who was staying in Chin-yang, sent scouts to spy on him. The scouts returned and reported that Mo-tun could be attacked, whereupon the emperor advanced as far as P'ing-ch'eng, taking up a position on the White Peak.

When the Hsiung-nu cavalry surrounded the emperor he sent generous gifts to Mo-tun's consort, who spoke to her husband, saying, "Even if you were now to get possession of the Han lands, you could not occupy them. It is better that the rulers of the two nations should not trouble one another."

After seven days the barbarian cavalry withdrew from their encirclement a little.[3] At this time there was a heavy fog, so that the Han army was able to send its men back and forth without the barbarians being aware of it. Ch'en P'ing, the colonel of the guard, said to the emperor, "The barbarians are anxious not to lose any of their men. I beg you to order the strong crossbows to be fitted with two arrows each and pointed towards the outside." When this had been done, they marched slowly out of the encirclement and entered the city of P'ing-ch'eng. At this time relief forces also arrived and the barbarian cavalry finally withdrew. The emperor likewise abandoned the expedition and withdrew. Hann Hsin, continuing to cooperate with the Hsiung-nu, led his troops back and forth in attacks on the frontier.

In the tenth year of Han, Hann Hsin sent Wang Huang and others to counsel Ch'en Hsi in the course which eventually proved to be his downfall. In the spring of the eleventh year Hann Hsin again joined with the barbarian cavalry in an invasion, taking up a position in the city of Ts'an-ho in order to block the Han army. The Han general Ch'ai, who was sent to attack him, dispatched a letter to Hann Hsin, saying, "His Majesty is lenient and kind. Even in the case of nobles who have revolted and fled, if they returned to him he has at once restored them to their former positions and titles without inflicting any penalty. This you know very well. Now because you were defeated

[3] According to *Shih-chi* 110, the chapter on the Hsiung-nu, the cavalry withdrew from one sector of the encirclement, the sector through which the Han forces later escaped.

and lost your army, you fled to the barbarians, but you are guilty of no grave offense. You should hurry back at once!"

To this Hann Hsin replied, "His Majesty raised me up from the lanes of the common people until I faced south and called myself a sovereign. Such was his goodness to me. Yet at the seige of Jung-yang I was not able to die for him, but fell prisoner to Hsiang Yü. This was my first offense. Again, when the barbarian bandits attacked Ma-i, I was not able to hold out against them but surrendered the city. This was my second offense. And now I have gone over to the barbarians and will lead their troops and engage with you in battle to settle our fate once for all. This will be my third offense. In former times Chung and Fan Li, the ministers of Yüeh, were guilty of no offense, and yet they were forced to flee or face death. With three offenses against the emperor, if I should return and seek to prolong my life in this world, I would only end like Wu Tzu-hsü of old who was stricken down upon the soil of Wu. Now I lurk hidden among the hills and valleys, day and night begging my sustenance from the barbarian tribes. As the cripple does not forget what it was to walk, nor the blind what it was to see, no more am I without thoughts of returning. Only, like them, I no longer have the power!"

In the end the two armies closed in battle. General Ch'ai massacred the inhabitants of Ts'an-ho and executed Hann Hsin.

When Hann Hsin fled to the Hsiung-nu he was accompanied by his son, the crown prince. After he reached the city of T'ui-tang a son was born to him whom he accordingly named T'ui-tang, and the crown prince also had a son named Ying. In the fourteenth year of Emperor Wen, T'ui-tang and Ying both led their followers and surrendered to the Han. The Han made T'ui-tang marquis of Kung-kao and Ying marquis of Hsiang-ch'eng. In the campaign against the revolt in Wu and Ch'u, T'ui-tang achieved outstanding distinction among the other generals. His fief passed in turn to his son and his grandson, but the last, being without an heir, lost the title. Ying's grandson was accused of disrespect and deprived of his title.

T'ui-tang's grandson by a concubine, Hann Yen, won great favor at court and was renowned for his fame and wealth in the world of his time. His younger brother Hann Yüeh was twice enfeoffed and several times appointed a general, the title he held at his death being marquis of An-tao. A year or so later, his son Tai was tried for an offense and died. After another year or so, Yüeh's grandson Tseng was made marquis of Lung-lo to carry on Yüeh's line.[4]

Lu Wan

Lu Wan, a native of Feng, was born in the same village as Kao-tsu. Lu Wan's father was a close friend of Kao-tsu's father, the Grand Supreme Emperor, and when sons were born to them, both births occurred on the same day. The people of the village came with gifts of lamb and wine to congratulate the families. When Kao-tsu and Lu Wan were young they studied writing together and were likewise close friends. The people of the village, seeing that the fathers of the two families were friends, that their sons had been born on the same day, and that the sons as well were fast friends, once more brought gifts of lamb and wine to congratulate the two families.

Once, while Kao-tsu was still a commoner, he got into trouble with the authorities and had to go into hiding. Lu Wan always went along with him wherever he fled and, when Kao-tsu began his uprising, Lu Wan became one of his followers. Accompanying Kao-tsu to his kingdom in Han, he became a general and constantly served in the palace. When Kao-tsu marched east to attack Hsiang Yü, Lu Wan served as grand commandant and had free access to Kao-tsu's sleeping quarters. Lu Wan received far more gifts of clothing and food from Kao-tsu than the other ministers even dared to hope for and, though men such as Hsiao Ho and Ts'ao Ts'an were treated with special courtesy because of their high offices, none could match the personal favoritism which Lu Wan enjoyed. Lu Wan was enfeoffed as marquis of Ch'ang-an, the former city of Hsien-yang.

In the winter of the fifth year of Han, after Kao-tsu had defeated Hsiang Yü, he dispatched Lu Wan as a special general to join Liu Chia in attacking Kung Wei, the king of Lin-chiang. After defeating him Lu Wan returned in the seventh month and joined in the attack on Tsang Tu, the king of Yen, who surrendered.

[4] These last two sentences are almost certainly a later interpolation.

Hann Hsin and Lu Wan

After Kao-tsu had gained control of the whole empire he made kings of seven of the nobles who did not belong to his own Liu family. He wanted to make Lu Wan a king as well, but he was afraid of arousing the envy of his other followers. When he took Tsang Tu prisoner he issued an edict to all his generals, ministers, and nobles asking them to select someone from among his followers who had achieved distinction to be made the new king of Yen. The officials, knowing that the emperor wished to make Lu Wan a king, all said, "The grand major Lu Wan, marquis of Ch'ang-an, has constantly aided in the pacification of the empire, and his distinction is the highest. He should be made king of Yen." The emperor issued an edict approving their suggestion and, in the eighth month of the fifth year of Han, Lu Wan was made king of Yen. Among the nobles and kings none enjoyed greater favor than Lu Wan.

In the autumn of the eleventh year of Han, Ch'en Hsi revolted in the region of Tai. Kao-tsu proceeded to Han-tan to attack Ch'en Hsi's troops, while Lu Wan attacked from the northeast. At this time Ch'en Hsi dispatched Wang Huang to seek aid from the Hsiung-nu, and Lu Wan also sent his minister Chang Sheng to go to the Hsiung-nu and report that the army of Ch'en Hsi and his associates had been defeated. When Chang Sheng reached the barbarian court, Tsang Yen, the son of Tsang Tu, the former king of Yen, who had fled to the barbarians, visited him. "The reason you enjoy importance in Yen," he said, "is that you are experienced in barbarian affairs. And the reason Yen has been able to continue this long without danger is that so many of the other nobles have one after another revolted and the warfare has gone on without reaching a settlement. Now you are anxious to help the king of Yen to wipe out Ch'en Hsi and his friends as soon as possible. But when Ch'en Hsi is finished with, it will be Yen's turn next, and you and the rest will end up as prisoners! Why do you not talk the king of Yen into easing his attack on Ch'en Hsi and making peace with the barbarians? If things continue to go well for the Han forces, your king can keep his throne in Yen that much longer, while if the Han forces should suffer some sudden upset, his kingdom will not be endangered."

Chang Sheng considered this sensible advice and secretly asked the

Hsiung-nu to aid Ch'en Hsi in attacking Yen. Lu Wan suspected that Chang Sheng had gone over to the side of the barbarians and sent a report to the emperor asking that Chang Sheng's family be exterminated. But when Chang Sheng returned from his mission and reported in full the reasons for his action, Lu Wan realized what he had been up to. Falsely condemning someone else in his place, he freed Chang Sheng's family and sent him to connive with the Hsiung-nu. He also secretly dispatched Fan Ch'i to go to the place where Ch'en Hsi was, hoping to prolong the revolt and delay any final settlement.

In the twelfth year of Han, when the emperor marched east to attack Ch'ing Pu, Ch'en Hsi continued to lead his troops in the region of Tai. Fan K'uai was dispatched to attack him, and succeeded in executing Ch'en Hsi. Ch'en Hsi's lieutenant general, who surrendered, reported that Lu Wan, the king of Yen, had sent Fan Ch'i to Ch'en Hsi's camp to join the plot with him. Kao-tsu dispatched an envoy to summon Lu Wan, but the latter pleaded illness. The emperor again sent Shen I-chi, the marquis of Pi-yang, and the grand secretary Chao Yao to go and fetch Lu Wan and make an investigation of his associates. Lu Wan, increasingly alarmed, retired into deep seclusion, saying to his trusted ministers, "Of the kings who are not of the Liu family, only I and the king of Ch'ang-sha are left. In the spring of last year Han Hsin and his family were wiped out, and in the summer P'eng Yüeh was executed. This is all Empress Lü's doing. The emperor these days is ill and entrusts everything to her. Since she is a woman she thinks only of finding some excuse or other to execute the kings of the other families and the great ministers." [5]

Lu Wan continued to plead illness, refusing to go to the capital, and his associates all fled into hiding. Eventually the words he had spoken to them leaked out and came to the ears of Shen I-chi, who returned and reported all he had learned to the emperor. The emperor was angrier than ever. In addition, one of the Hsiung-nu who had surrendered reported that Chang Sheng was hiding among the Hsiung-nu, having been sent by the king of Yen. "It appears that Lu Wan has really revolted," said the emperor and dispatched Fan K'uai to attack

[5] I.e., being only a woman, she is attempting by trickery to rid herself of all those who may be a threat to her and her family after the emperor's death.

Yen. Lu Wan took the members of his family and palace staff and a force of several thousand cavalry and went to stay by the Great Wall, sending to inquire whether the emperor's illness had improved so that he might come in person and beg pardon for his crime. In the fourth month Kao-tsu passed away and Lu Wan forthwith led his company in flight across the border to the Hsiung-nu. The Hsiung-nu gave him the title of "King Lu of the Eastern Barbarians," but the territory they assigned him was invaded and plundered by the barbarian tribes. He never ceased to think of returning home. After a year or so he died among the barbarians.

During the reign of Empress Lü, Lu Wan's wife and children fled from the Hsiung-nu and surrendered to the Han. At this time the empress was ill and could not see them. She had them quartered at the official residence of the state of Yen in the capital and planned to give a banquet and receive them, but she passed away before they were ever granted an audience. Lu Wan's wife also fell ill and died. In the sixth year of the middle period of Emperor Ching's reign [144 B.C.] Lu Wan's grandson T'o-chih, who held the title of "King of the Eastern Barbarians," surrendered and was enfeoffed as marquis of Ya-ku.

Ch'en Hsi

Ch'en Hsi was a native of Yüan-ch'ü. It is not known how he first got to be a follower of Kao-tsu. In the winter of the seventh year, when Hsin, the king of Hann, revolted and fled to the Hsiung-nu, Kao-tsu marched as far as P'ing-ch'eng and on his return enfeoffed Ch'en Hsi as a marquis, making him prime minister and general of Tai [6] with supervision over the troops guarding the border of Tai. All the border forces were placed under his command. Ch'en Hsi once requested leave from his position to return to his home for a visit, passing through Chao on his way. Chou Ch'ang, the prime minister of Chao, observed that Ch'en Hsi was accompanied by over a thousand carriages of retainers and followers, so many that they completely filled the official lodgings in the city of Han-tan. He also noted that Ch'en Hsi treated his retainers as though he and they were still no more than commoners, always putting himself last among them. After Ch'en

[6] The text erroneously reads "prime minister of Chao."

Hsi had returned to Tai, Chou Ch'ang requested an audience with the emperor and, when it was granted, reported on the extraordinary number of Ch'en Hsi's retainers, warning that, since Ch'en Hsi had had complete control of the troops on the border for several years, there was danger of his revolting. The emperor thereupon sent an envoy to conduct a special investigation into the private fortunes and illegal activities of Ch'en Hsi's followers in Tai, and it was found that in many cases Ch'en Hsi himself was implicated. Ch'en Hsi, growing fearful, secretly dispatched one of his retainers to communicate with Hann Hsin's generals Wang Huang and Man-ch'iu Ch'en.

In the seventh month of the tenth year, when the Grand Supreme Emperor passed away, Kao-tsu sent an envoy to summon Ch'en Hsi, but Ch'en Hsi declined to go on grounds of serious illness. In the ninth month he finally joined with Wang Huang and the others in revolt, setting himself up as king of Tai and plundering the regions of Chao and Tai.

When the emperor received word of this he issued a pardon, absolving the officials and people of Chao and Tai, who had been plundered and led astray by Ch'en Hsi, from all guilt. The emperor in person came as far as Han-tan, where he remarked with pleasure, "Since Ch'en Hsi has not come south to occupy the Chang River and guard Han-tan on its north side, I know he can do no harm."

Chou Chang, the prime minister of Chao, sent a request to the emperor that the governor and military commander of Ch'ang-shan Province be executed. "Because of Ch'en Hsi's revolt, twenty of the twenty-five cities of Ch'ang-shan have been lost," he said.

"Have the governor and military commander themselves revolted?" asked the emperor.

"No, they are not disloyal," replied Chou Ch'ang.

"Then it is simply that their strength was not sufficient to hold the cities," said the emperor and, pardoning them, he restored them to their positions in Ch'ang-shan. "Has Chao any brave men who could be made generals?" he asked Chou Ch'ang.

"We have four men," replied Chou Ch'ang. When the four appeared before the emperor, he abused them contemptuously. "Do you idiots think you can be generals?" he asked.

The four men prostrated themselves in great embarrassment. The emperor then enfeoffed each of them with a thousand households and made them generals. His ministers remonstrated with him, saying, "Among those who followed Your Majesty to Shu and Han and in the attacks on Ch'u, there are many who have not yet been rewarded for their merit. Now what merit have these men won that they should be enfeoffed?"

"This is not for you to understand," replied the emperor. "Ch'en Hsi has revolted and all the territory north of Han-tan is in his grip. I sent out an urgent proclamation summoning troops from all over the empire, but so far none of them have arrived. Now I have only the forces here in Han-tan. Why should I begrudge four thousand households and not enfeoff these four men so as to bring some comfort to the sons of Chao?"

"Yes, of course," they all replied. Then the emperor asked, "Who are Ch'en Hsi's generals?"

"Wang Huang and Man-ch'iu Ch'en, both of them formerly merchants," he was told.

"I know about them," replied the emperor, and offered rewards of a thousand pieces of gold for Wang Huang, Man-ch'iu Ch'en, and the rest.

In the winter of the eleventh year the Han forces attacked and killed Ch'en Hsi's general Hou Ch'ang [7] at Ch'ü-ni and defeated another of his generals, Chang Ch'ün, at Liao-ch'eng, killing over ten thousand of the enemy. The grand commandant Chou P'o marched into the areas of T'ai-yüan and Tai and brought them under control.

In the twelfth month the emperor in person led an attack on Tung-yüan, but the city refused to surrender, its soldiers cursing the emperor. When the city finally capitulated, the emperor had all those who had cursed him executed, and those who had not, tattooed, and changed the name of the city to Chen-ting. The subordinates of Wang Huang and Man-ch'iu Ch'en, taking advantage of the rewards which had been offered for their capture, handed them over to the emperor alive. Thus Ch'en Hsi's army was finally defeated.

The emperor made his way back to the capital and, when he reached

[7] The text reads "Hou Ch'ang and Wang Huang," which is clearly an error.

Lo-yang, announced, "Let Tai hold the area from the Ch'ang mountains north, and Chao the area from the mountains south. The region north of the mountains is too far away for Chao to administer." He then set up his son Liu Heng as king of Tai, ruling from Chung-tu. All of Tai and Yen-men both were put under the control of the king of Tai. In the winter of the twelfth year of Kao-tsu, Fan K'uai's army pursued Ch'en Hsi to Ling-ch'iu and killed him.

The Grand Historian remarks: Hann Hsin and Lu Wan had no past of accumulated merit, no family history marked by repeated goodness behind them but, benefiting by a sudden shift of political power, by craft and force won distinction. They happened upon the time when Han first took control of the empire, and thus were able to gain a share of land, face south, and call themselves sovereigns. But within the empire they aroused suspicion by their great strength, while beyond its borders they sought aid from the barbarians, so that with each day they became further alienated from the emperor and moved deeper into danger. At last, when their position became impossible and their wisdom failed, they went over to the Hsiung-nu. Are they not a pitiful sight?

Ch'en Hsi was a native of Liang, the old state of Wei. In his young days he greatly admired Wu-chi, the former prince of Wei,[8] and often praised him. When he became a general and was sent to guard the frontier, he invited guests and retainers to his household, humbling himself before them in the manner of Wu-chi, so that his fame surpassed the actual facts. After Chou Ch'ang grew suspicious of him, his faults all came to light and, fearing that disaster would overtake him, he allowed himself to be misled by the advice of evil men and trapped at the last into the gravest treason. Alas, how tragic! The ripeness or unripeness of a man's schemes, their success or failure—how vitally these things affect him!

[8] His biography is the subject of *Shih chi* 77. He was famous for the respectful and generous treatment he accorded his followers.

Shih chi 94: The Biography of T'ien Tan

When the other nobles revolted against Hsiang Yü, it was only because the armies of Ch'i joined to attack him at Ch'eng-yang that the king of Han was able in the meantime to enter P'eng-ch'eng. Thus I made The Biography of T'ien Tan.

T'ien Tan was a native of Ti and a member of the same T'ien family who had been kings of Ch'i in former times. His younger cousin T'ien Jung and T'ien Jung's younger brother T'ien Heng were both outstanding men who headed powerful families and were good at attracting followers.

When Ch'en She began his rebellion and made himself king of Ch'u he sent Chou Shih to invade and conquer the region of Wei. Chou Shih advanced as far north as Ti, but the city of Ti held fast and refused to surrender.

Planning a trick, T'ien Tan had one of his slaves bound like a criminal and, accompanied by a group of his young followers, went to the district magistrate's office and requested an interview, pretending that he wished to execute the slave. When he was granted an audience, he used the opportunity to attack and murder the magistrate. He then summoned the high officials and their staffs and announced, "The other nobles have all revolted against Ch'in and set up their own rulers. Ch'i was one of the kingdoms established in ancient times and, since I belong to the T'ien family who were its rulers, it is right that I should be king!" He accordingly set himself up as king of Ch'i and dispatched troops to attack Chou Shih. When Chou Shih's army retreated, T'ien Tan led his forces east to invade and gain control of the region of Ch'i.

King Chiu of Wei, surrounded at Lin-chi and hard pressed by the Ch'in general Chang Han, sent to Ch'i begging for assistance. T'ien Tan led his troops to the rescue of Wei, but Chang Han, putting gags in the mouths of his men to prevent any noise, made a night attack and inflicted a crushing defeat on the armies of Ch'i and Wei. T'ien Tan was killed before the walls of Lin-chi, and T'ien Tan's younger cousin T'ien Jung gathered up the remnants of his army and fled east to Tung-a.

When the people of Ch'i heard that T'ien Tan had been killed they set up T'ien Chia, the younger brother of the former King Chien of Ch'i, as their new king, with T'ien Chüeh as his prime minister and T'ien Chien as his general, in order to block the advance of the other nobles.

When T'ien Jung fled to Tung-a, Chang Han pursued and surrounded him. Hsiang Liang, hearing that T'ien Jung was in difficulty, led his troops and attacked and defeated Chang Han's army before Tung-a. Chang Han fled west with Hsiang Liang in pursuit. T'ien Jung, angry that the people of Ch'i had set up T'ien Chia as their king, led his troops back and attacked and drove T'ien Chia from the throne. T'ien Chia escaped and fled to Ch'u, while his prime minister T'ien Chüeh fled to Chao. T'ien Chüeh's younger brother T'ien Chien was already in Chao, having gone there earlier to seek aid, and remained there, afraid to return to his home.

T'ien Jung then set up T'ien Tan's son Shih as king of Ch'i, making himself prime minister and T'ien Heng his general, and set about pacifying Ch'i.

Hsiang Liang had gone in pursuit of Chang Han but, when Chang Han's forces grew increasingly powerful, he sent an envoy to Chao and Ch'i asking them to send forces to join him in the attack on Chang Han. T'ien Jung replied, "If Ch'u will kill T'ien Chia and Chao will kill T'ien Chüeh and T'ien Chien, then I am willing to send out my troops."

King Huai of Ch'u sent a reply saying, "T'ien Chia is the king of an allied state. He has come in distress and given me his loyalty. It would not be just to kill him." Chao also refused to kill T'ien Chüeh and T'ien Chien for the sake of buying favor with Ch'i.

"When a viper stings you in the hand, you cut off the hand," warned T'ien Jung, "and when one stings you in the foot you cut off the foot. Why? Because if you do not, the harm will spread through your whole body. Now T'ien Chia, T'ien Chüeh, and T'ien Chien are a graver peril to Ch'u and Chao than a poisoned hand or foot. Why will you not kill them? If Ch'in is allowed to have its way with the world again, it will devour all those who have risen against it, even to the graves of their ancestors!"

But Ch'u and Chao would not listen to him, and in the end T'ien Jung angrily refused to send his troops. As he had foreseen, Hsiang Liang was defeated and killed by Chang Han, and the Ch'u forces fled east in retreat. Chang Han then crossed the Yellow River and besieged the king of Chao at Chü-lu, where Hsiang Yü marched to his rescue. Because of this incident Hsiang Yü grew to hate T'ien Jung.

After Hsiang Yü had saved Chao, and Chang Han and the other Ch'in generals had surrendered, he marched west, massacred the inhabitants of Hsien-yang, and destroyed the Ch'in dynasty, setting up new rulers in its place. T'ien Shih, the king of Ch'i, he transferred to the position of king of Chiao-tung, ruling from Chi-mo. Because the Ch'i general T'ien Tu had joined him in saving Chao and followed him within the Pass, he made T'ien Tu the king of Ch'i, ruling from Lin-tzu. T'ien An was the grandson of King Chien, the king of Ch'i in former times. When Hsiang Yü crossed the Yellow River on his way to rescue Chao, T'ien An captured several cities of Chi-pei and led his troops and surrendered to Hsiang Yü. Hsiang Yü therefore made him king of Chi-pei, with his capital at Po-yang. Because T'ien Jung had betrayed Hsiang Liang and been unwilling to send troops to aid Ch'u and Chao in attacking Ch'in, he was not made a king.

Ch'en Yü, general of Chao, had been removed from his position and likewise was not made a king. Both he and T'ien Jung therefore hated Hsiang Yü and, when Hsiang Yü had gone back to Ch'u and the other nobles had proceeded to their territories, T'ien Jung sent one of his men with troops to aid Ch'en Yü in raising a revolt in the region of Chao. T'ien Jung also dispatched troops to attack T'ien Tu, who escaped and fled to Ch'u. T'ien Jung detained T'ien Shih and would not let him go to his kingdom in Chiao-tung, whereupon T'ien Shih's followers warned him, saying, "Hsiang Yü is powerful and ruthless. He has ordered you to go to Chiao-tung, and if you do not proceed to your kingdom, you will face peril!" T'ien Shih was frightened and fled in secret to his kingdom, but T'ien Jung, enraged, pursued him and attacked and killed him at Chi-mo. Then he marched back and attacked and killed T'ien An, the king of Chi-pei, and set himself up as king of Ch'i, ruling all of the three kingdoms into which Ch'i had been divided.

When Hsiang Yü received word of this he was very angry and proceeded north to attack Ch'i. T'ien Jung's army was defeated and he himself fled to P'ing-yüan, where he was killed by natives of the place.

Hsiang Yü set about burning and destroying the walls and fortifications of Ch'i and massacring the people wherever he passed until the men of Ch'i, gathering their forces, turned upon him in revolt. T'ien Jung's younger brother T'ien Heng collected the scattered forces of Ch'i, obtaining twenty or thirty thousand men, and revolted and attacked Hsiang Yü at Ch'eng-yang.

Meanwhile the king of Han, leading the other nobles, defeated the Ch'u army and entered P'eng-ch'eng. When Hsiang Yü received word of this he abandoned Ch'i and returned to Ch'u, attacking the Han forces at P'eng-ch'eng. The two leaders continued in battle for some time, being locked in stalemate at Jung-yang, and thus T'ien Heng was able to regain control of the cities of Ch'i. He set up T'ien Jung's son T'ien Kuang as king of Ch'i and he himself acted as prime minister. He had sole power in the government and all affairs of state, great or small, were decided by him.

Three years after T'ien Heng gained control of Ch'i the king of Han dispatched Master Li I-chi to go to Ch'i and attempt to persuade T'ien Kuang and his prime minister T'ien Heng to acknowledge allegiance to Han. T'ien Heng considered his arguments reasonable and disbanded the army which was stationed at Li-hsia. The Han general Han Hsin then led his troops east and made ready to attack Ch'i.

Earlier Ch'i had sent Hua Wu-shang and T'ien Hsieh with an army to Li-hsia to block the Han troops. But when the Han envoy, Master Li, arrived, Ch'i dismissed its forces and relaxed its military preparations, indulging instead in feasting and drinking, in the meantime sending an envoy to conclude peace with the king of Han. The Han general Han Hsin, having already conquered Chao and Yen, was persuaded by the advice of K'uai T'ung to cross the Yellow River at P'ing-yüan, where he attacked and defeated the Ch'i army at Li-hsia and eventually entered Lin-tzu. The king of Ch'i and his prime minister, enraged at the thought that they had been betrayed by Master Li, had him boiled alive.

T'ien Kuang, the king of Ch'i, fled east to Kao-mi, his prime minister T'ien Heng to Po-yang, and the deputy prime minister T'ien Kuangg [1] to Ch'eng-yang. The general of Ch'i, T'ien Chi, stationed his army in Chiao-tung. Hsiang Yü dispatched Lung Chü to go to the rescue of Ch'i, his army joining that of the king of Ch'i at Kao-mi. There the Han generals Han Hsin and Ts'ao Ts'an defeated and killed Lung Chü and took T'ien Kuang prisoner. The Han general Kuan Ying pursued and captured the deputy prime minister T'ien Kuangg, and then advanced to Po-yang.

When T'ien Heng heard rumors that the king of Ch'i was dead he set himself up as king and returned to attack Kuan Ying. His army was defeated by Kuan Ying at Ying-hsia but he himself escaped and fled to Liang, where he joined P'eng Yüeh. P'eng Yüeh was at this time occupying the region of Liang and had adopted a middle position between the two factions, sometimes fighting on the side of Han and sometimes on the side of Ch'u.

After Han Hsin had killed Lung Chü he ordered Ts'ao Ts'an to lead his troops to Chiao-tung, where he defeated and killed T'ien Chi. He also sent Kuan Ying to defeat and kill the Ch'i general T'ien Hsi at Ch'ien-ch'eng. Having thus brought all of Ch'i under control, Han Hsin requested to be made an acting king of Ch'i. The king of Han accordingly made him king.

A year or so later, when the king of Han wiped out Hsiang Yü and became Supreme Emperor, he made P'eng Yüeh king of Liang. T'ien Heng, fearful of punishment, journeyed with five hundred or so of his followers to the seacoast and took refuge among the islands there. When the emperor received word of this he considered that, since T'ien Heng and his brother had originally controlled Ch'i, he must have

[1] To distinguish this man from the king of Ch'i, whose name is pronounced the same way, I have spelled "Kuangg" with two g's.

many worthy men of Ch'i among his followers and that if they were left to themselves in the islands there would be danger of their revolting later. Therefore he sent an envoy to pardon T'ien Heng for his offenses and summon him to court. T'ien Heng, however, declined. "I boiled alive His Majesty's envoy Master Li I-chi," he replied. "Now I have word that his younger brother Li Shang is a general of Han and a worthy man. I am filled with fear and dare not obey the imperial command. I beg to be made a commoner and left to guard the islands of the sea."

When the envoy returned and reported this to the emperor, he issued an order to Li Shang, his colonel of the guard, saying, "When T'ien Heng, the king of Ch'i, arrives, if any of your soldiers or followers dare to cause him trouble, the offenders and their families will be wiped out!" He then sent the envoy once again bearing the imperial credentials to report in detail the order which had been issued to Li Shang and say, "If T'ien Heng answers the summons, he may be made a king; at the least he will become a marquis. If he does not come, troops will be sent out to punish him!"

T'ien Heng, accompanied by two followers, set off by relay carriage to appear before the emperor at Lo-yang. When they reached the carriage station at Shih-hsiang, some thirty *li* away from Lo-yang, T'ien Heng greeted the official in charge and, explaining that "when a subject is to appear before the Son of Heaven, it is proper for him to bathe and wash his hair," he stopped at the station. Then he said to his two followers, "Once the king of Han and I both faced south and called ourselves sovereigns. Now the king of Han has become the Son of Heaven, and I have become a captive fugitive. How great would be my shame were I to face north and acknowledge him as my ruler! Moreover, I would be serving him side by side with Li Shang, a man whose elder brother I boiled to death. Even though Li Shang does not dare to harm me out of fear for the emperor's orders, could I help but feel shame in my heart? The only reason His Majesty wishes to see me is so that he may for once have a look at my face, that is all. Since he is now in Lo-yang, if you cut off my head and hasten with it the thirty *li* from here to there, my features will not have decayed and he may still observe them." Then, ordering his followers to bear his head and hurry with the envoy to present it to the emperor, he cut his throat.

"Ah!" exclaimed the emperor, "it was no accident that this man rose from the rank of commoner and that he and his brothers all three in turn became kings! Was he not a worthy man?" And he wept for him. He honored T'ien Heng's two followers with the rank of colonel and ordered out two thousand soldiers to give T'ien Heng a burial befitting a king.

When the burial was completed the two followers of T'ien Heng both scooped holes in the side of the grave mound and, cutting their throats, followed him to the world below. When the emperor heard of this he was astonished and concluded that all of T'ien Heng's followers must be worthy men as well. "I have heard that the rest of the five hundred men are still in the islands," he said, and sent an envoy to summon them. When the envoy arrived and the men heard that T'ien Heng was dead they all committed suicide. From this one may see what fine men T'ien Heng and his brothers were able to attract.

The Grand Historian remarks: How terrible were the plottings of K'uai T'ung! They brought confusion to Ch'i, filled Han Hsin with overbearing ambition, and in the end destroyed both him and T'ien Heng. K'uai T'ung was skilled at persuading people of the advantages and disadvantages of various courses of action and at discoursing on the shifts of power that occurred in the Warring States period, writing a work in eighty-one sections on the subject. He was a friend of An Ch'i-sheng, a native of Ch'i. An Ch'i-sheng once attempted to advise Hsiang Yü, but Hsiang Yü did not listen to his suggestions. Later Hsiang Yü wished to enfeoff the two men, but they were unwilling to accept and instead ran away.

T'ien Heng was a man of such high honor that his retainers, moved by his integrity, followed him in death. All were manifestly men of the highest worth and I have therefore taken this opportunity to recount their story. Yet since they were all supposedly good at laying plans, why, I wonder, was there none who could think of a way to save the situation?

Part VI
THE LOYAL FOLLOWERS

Shih chi 95: The Biographies of Fan K'uai, Li Shang, Lord T'eng, and Kuan Ying: Concluding Remarks

[This chapter records the biographies of four men who fought under Kao-tsu from the early days of his uprising and were rewarded with marquisates after the dynasty was established. All were notable for their humble beginnings, Fan K'uai making his living as a dog butcher in P'ei (dogs were raised for food at this time), Hsia-hou Ying, better known as Lord T'eng, as a carriage driver for the officials of P'ei, and Kuan Ying as a silk dealer. Li Shang was the younger brother of Li I-chi, whose biography appears in Chapter 97 translated below. The biographies consist almost entirely of lists of the military campaigns in which these men participated, the number of enemy dead and prisoners taken, and the promotions they received, interspersed by a few anecdotes, nearly all of which have already appeared in earlier chapters. For this reason it has not seemed worth while to translate the chapter in full. Ssu-ma Ch'ien's closing remarks indicate why he did not feel he could record the more colorful accounts of these men which circulated in his time, and how he came by the information he does record.—*Trans.*]

In attacking cities and fighting on the plains, in winning merit and returning to report their deeds, Fan K'uai and Li Shang showed great ability. They not only lashed forward their own steeds, but helped their leader to escape from peril as well. Thus I made The Biographies of Fan K'uai and Li Shang.

The Grand Historian remarks: When I had occasion to pass through Feng and P'ei I questioned the elderly people who were about the place, visited the old homes[1] of Hsiao Ho, Ts'ao Ts'an, Fan K'uai, and Hsia-hou Ying, and learned much about their early days. How different it all was from the stories one hears! At the time these men were wielding brush and scraper as petty officials, butchering dogs, or peddling silk, I wonder if they ever imagined that, by clinging to the

[1] Some texts read "graves," which does not make very good sense.

tail of a swift stallion,[2] they would leave their names behind in the annals of the Han court and pass on blessings to their sons and grandsons? Fan K'uai's grandson Fan T'o-kuang, with whom I have had some association, has recounted to me the rise of these meritorious ministers of Kao-tsu as I have recorded it here.

[2] I.e., Kao-tsu.

Shih chi 96: The Biography of Chancellor Chang

When the Han was first set up, its civil affairs were not yet in order. Chang Ts'ang as master of calculations adjusted the weights and measures and arranged the pitch pipes and calendar.[1] Thus I made The Biography of Chancellor Chang.

Chang Ts'ang

Chancellor Chang Ts'ang was a native of Yang-wu. He was fond of books and matters concerning the pitch pipes and the calendar. During the Ch'in dynasty he became an imperial secretary and handled the records on slips of wood "at the foot of the pillar."[2] Because of some fault, however, he was forced to flee to his native village. When the governor of P'ei seized control of the region of Yang-wu on a plundering expedition Chang Ts'ang became one of his followers and joined in the attack on Nan-yang. Later, however, Chang Ts'ang became involved in some offense and was condemned to be beheaded. He had already removed his robe and bowed his head upon the executioner's block when Wang Ling, noticing his great size and his body, which was as plump and white as a gourd, was struck by his handsomeness and went and spoke to the governor of P'ei. The governor pardoned him and called off the execution, so that he was able to join in the march west through the Pass to Hsien-yang.

Later, when the governor of P'ei had become king of Han, retired to his territory in Han, and returned again to conquer the three kingdoms of Ch'in, Ch'en Yü attacked Chang Erh, the king of Ch'ang-shan, and forced him to flee. Chang Erh joined the king of Han, who thereupon made Chang Ts'ang the governor of Ch'ang-shan and sent

---

[1] There were twelve pitch pipes, made of bamboo or metal and said to have been in use since very ancient times. A large body of astrological and numerological lore surrounded them, hence their connection with the calendar and matters of weights and measures.

[2] That is, in carrying out his duties he stood or sat at the foot of a pillar of the palace hall.

him to join Han Hsin in attacking Ch'en Yü in Chao. After Chang Ts'ang had helped to take Ch'en Yü prisoner and conquer the region of Chao the king of Han made him prime minister of Tai so that he could guard the frontier against the barbarians. Later he was transferred to the position of prime minister of Chao, serving Chang Erh, the king of Chao. After Chang Erh's death he continued to serve Chang Erh's son Chang Ao. He was again transferred, this time to the position of prime minister to the king of Tai. When Tsang Tu, the king of Yen, revolted, Kao-tsu marched in person to attack him. As prime minister of Tai, Chang Ts'ang joined in the attack and achieved distinction. During the sixth year of Han he was enfeoffed as marquis of Pei-p'ing with the revenue from an estate of one thousand two hundred households. He was transferred to the position of calculation minister, which he held for four years. A month later, because he was a marquis, the title of the position was changed to master of calculations. At this time Hsiao Ho was prime minister. Since he had been a "foot of the pillar" secretary under the Ch'in, Chang Ts'ang knew a great deal about the various documents and registers of the empire, and was also skilled at matters of calculation, the pitch pipes, and the calendar. For this reason he was made a resident marquis in the prime minister's office and put in charge of the reports which were submitted from the various provinces and kingdoms. After Ch'ing Pu revolted and was killed the emperor set up his own son, Prince Ch'ang, as king of Huai-nan and made Chang Ts'ang his prime minister. In the fourteenth year of Han, Chang Ts'ang was transferred to the position of imperial secretary.

Chou Ch'ang

Chou Ch'ang was a native of P'ei. He had an older cousin named Chou K'o. During the Ch'in they were both provincial secretaries in the government office of Ssu River. When Kao-tsu began his uprising in P'ei, and attacked and defeated the magistrate and overseer of Ssu River, Chou Ch'ang and Chou K'o, because of their jobs as provincial secretaries, joined Kao-tsu, at this time the governor of P'ei. Kao-tsu made Chou Ch'ang his banner master and Chou K'o a follower, and they accompanied him through the Pass in the defeat of Ch'in.

Chancellor Chang

After the governor of P'ei had become king of Han he made Chou K'o his royal secretary and Chou Ch'ang a military commander.

In the fourth year of Han, when Hsiang Yü and the forces of Ch'u had surrounded the king of Han at Jung-yang and had him in a difficult position, he managed to escape and flee, leaving Chou K'o to guard the city of Jung-yang. After Hsiang Yü captured the city he offered to make Chou K'o a general, but Chou K'o cursed him and replied, "You had better hurry and surrender to the king of Han! If you do not, you will find yourself his prisoner!" Hsiang Yü, enfuriated, had Chou K'o boiled alive.

After this Chou Ch'ang was given the position of royal secretary vacated by Chou K'o and constantly accompanied the king in the attack and defeat of Hsiang Yü. In the course of the sixth year he was enfeoffed along with Hsiao Ho, Ts'ao Ts'an, and others, receiving the title of marquis of Fen-yin. Because Chou K'o had given his life for the Han cause his son Chou Ch'eng was enfeoffed as marquis of Kao-ching.

Chou Ch'ang had great physical strength and was the sort of person who never hesitated to speak his mind. From Hsiao Ho and Ts'ao Ts'an on down, the other officials all treated him with extreme deference. Once Chou Ch'ang entered the palace at a time when the court was not in session, intending to report some affair, when he came upon Emperor Kao-tsu in the midst of embracing his concubine Lady Ch'i. Chou Ch'ang turned around and hurried out, but the emperor ran after him, caught him and, throwing him down and sitting on his neck, asked, "What sort of a ruler do you think I am?"

Chou Ch'ang twisted his head around to look up at the emperor and replied, "A rowdy tyrant no better than Chieh and Chou of ancient times, Your Majesty!" The emperor laughed at his reply, but as a matter of fact there was no one whom he regarded with such awe as Chou Ch'ang.

When the emperor decided to remove the heir apparent and make Ju-i, his son by Lady Ch'i, the new heir apparent in his place, all the great officials argued vehemently against the move, but none could get him to listen. (The emperor did, however, eventually abandon the idea as a result of a plan devised by Chang Liang.) Since Chou Ch'ang was among the most vehement opponents of the move, the emperor asked him to explain his reasons. Chou Ch'ang stuttered by nature, and on top of this he was at the time overwhelmed with anger. "I cannot get the words out of my mouth," he replied. "But all the same I know it will n-n-never do! Although Your Majesty wishes to remove the heir apparent, I shall n-n-never obey such an order!"

The emperor laughed with delight. When the court was dismissed Empress Lü, who had been listening to the proceedings from the eastern wing of the throne room, appeared before Chou Ch'ang and fell on her knees to thank him. "If it had not been for you," she said, "the heir apparent would almost certainly have been dismissed!"

Shortly after this Lady Ch'i's son Ju-i was made king of Chao. He was only ten years old and Kao-tsu was worried that when he himself passed away, the boy would be unable to escape harm.

There was a young man named Chao Yao who was made keeper of the seals for the royal or imperial secretary, Chou Ch'ang. The district magistrate of Fang-yü, a man of Chao, spoke to Chou Ch'ang about him, saying, "Your secretary Chao Yao is still very young, but he has extraordinary ability. You had best treat him with special care, for he will most likely take over your position some day!"

Chou Ch'ang laughed and replied, "Chao Yao is a youth. He is no more than a scraper-and-brush-wielding clerk! How could he fill my position?"

Some time had passed when Chao Yao was one day waiting upon the emperor, who could find nothing to amuse himself with, but only sang sad songs. The rest of the officials did not know what was troubling him, but Chao Yao advanced and said, "The reason Your Majesty is without joy—is it not that, the king of Chao being still young and Lady Ch'i and Empress Lü enemies, you fear that after your days are ended, the king of Chao will not be able to save himself from harm?"

"That is indeed the reason," replied Kao-tsu. "I keep thinking anxiously to myself about it, but I know of no way out."

"If Your Majesty will appoint as prime minister for the king of Chao someone who is highly placed and powerful and whom Empress Lü and the heir apparent and the high officials are accustomed to respect and defer to, then I think it may be all right," said Chao Yao.

"Yes," replied Kao-tsu. "I have thought of doing just that. But who among the various officials would be suitable?"

"The imperial secretary Chou Ch'ang," said Chao Yao, "is a man of integrity, patience, simplicity, and forthrightness. Empress Lü and the heir apparent, as well as the great ministers, have always treated him with respect and deference. Only Chou Ch'ang will do!"

"Good!" replied the emperor, and sent for Chou Ch'ang. "I have something I want you to do for me," the emperor said. "Much as you may dislike it, you must act as prime minister to the king of Chao for me."

Chou Ch'ang wept and replied, "I have served Your Majesty ever since the beginning of the uprising. Why should you suddenly discard me along the way and send me off among the feudal lords?"

"I am deeply aware that this will amount to a demotion for you. But I keep worrying to myself about the king of Chao and I feel that no one but you will do for the post. You must resign yourself and go at all cost!"

Thus the grand secretary Chou Ch'ang became prime minister of Chao. He had already gone to his new post and some time had passed when Kao-tsu one day took the seals of the imperial secretary and, twirling them in his hand, said, "Who will do to be the next imperial secretary?" After staring intently at Chao Yao he said, "No one could do better than Chao Yao," and in the end he honored him with the post of imperial secretary. Chao Yao already enjoyed the revenue from a town because of the military distinction he had previously won. When he became imperial secretary he accompanied the emperor in the attack on Ch'en Hsi, achieving further merit, and was enfeoffed as marquis of Chiang-i.

After Kao-tsu passed away Empress Lü sent an envoy to summon the king of Chao, but his prime minister, Chou Ch'ang, instructed the king to say that he was ill and not to go. Envoys went back and forth three times, but Chou Ch'ang adamantly refused to listen to their request and send the king of Chao. At this Empress Lü grew alarmed and sent an envoy summoning Chou Ch'ang himself. When he arrived and proceeded to an audience with her the empress cursed him angrily. "Surely you know my hatred for the king of Chao and his mother, do you not?" she said. "Why then would you not send him to me?"

After she had called Chou Ch'ang to the capital the empress again sent an envoy to summon the king of Chao, and this time he came. A month or so after his arrival in Ch'ang-an he was given poison to drink and died. Chou Ch'ang thereupon pleaded illness and no longer appeared at court. Three years later he died.

Five years afterwards Empress Lü discovered that the imperial secretary Chao Yao, marquis of Chiang-i, had helped lay plans while Kao-tsu was still alive to protect Ju-i, the king of Chao. She therefore had him accused of some crime and made Jen Ao, the marquis of Kuang-a, imperial secretary in his place.

Jen Ao

Jen Ao had originally been a police official of P'ei. Kao-tsu was once in his young days obliged to hide from the law officers, but the officers bound Empress Lü instead and took her to jail, treating her very roughly. Jen Ao, who had long been a friend of Kao-tsu, was incensed by this and struck and wounded the law officer who was in charge of Empress Lü. When Kao-tsu began his uprising Jen Ao became one of his followers. He was made a secretary and left to guard Feng. Two years later, after Kao-tsu had become king of Han and marched east to attack Hsiang Yü, Jen Ao was transferred to the position of governor of Shang-tang. At the time of Ch'en Hsi's revolt he remained loyally by his post and as a result was enfeoffed as marquis of Kuang-a with the revenue from one thousand eight hundred households. In the time of Empress Lü he was made imperial secretary but three years later was removed from office. Ts'ao Chü, the marquis of P'ing-yang, became imperial secretary. After Empress Lü passed away he plotted with the other high ministers to exterminate Lü Lu and the rest of the Lü clan.[3] He was later removed from office, and Chang Ts'ang, the marquis of Huai-nan, made imperial secretary.

Chang Ts'ang joined with Chou P'o and others in setting up the king of Tai as emperor, posthumously entitled Wen the Filial. In the

---

[3] Following the *Han shu* reading, which omits the negative.

fourth year of Emperor Wen's reign the chancellor Kuan Ying died and Chang Ts'ang became chancellor.

During the twenty-odd years from the rise of the Han to the time of Emperor Wen, while peace was at last being brought to the world, all the great generals, ministers, and high officials were professional military men. When Chang Ts'ang became minister of calculations, however, he set to work arranging and rectifying the calendar and the pitch pipes, which had been neglected up to this time. Since Kao-tsu had first reached Pa-shang in the tenth month, he continued the old Ch'in practice of beginning the new year with the tenth month and made no change. Calculating the cycle of the Five Elements, Chang Ts'ang decided that the Han corresponded to a period dominated by the element water, and should therefore honor black, the color of water, as before. He sounded the pitch pipes and adjusted their tones; then he matched them with the notes of the scale, used them as a standard in establishing rules and statutes, and thus made weights and measurements for all the various crafts. When Chang Ts'ang became chancellor he brought his labors to completion, and for this reason all who expound the pitch pipes and the calendar for the house of Han base themselves upon Chang Ts'ang's work. Chang Ts'ang always loved books. There were none he did not examine, and none he did not understand, but what he loved most were matters pertaining to the pitch pipes and the calendar.

Chang Ts'ang was deeply indebted to Wang Ling, the marquis of An-kuo, who had saved him from execution and, even after he rose to high position, he always treated Wang Ling as a father. After Wang Ling died and Chang Ts'ang became chancellor, whenever his "bath and hair washing" day came around,[4] he would always go first to call on Wang Ling's widow and take her gifts of food, and only after this was done would he return to his own home.

Chang Ts'ang was chancellor for something over ten years. A man of Lu named Kung-sun Ch'en sent a report to the throne arguing that the Han corresponded to a period dominated by the element

---

[4] Every five days Han officials, who ordinarily lived in dormitories near the palace, were allowed to leave court and return to their homes for a day. The holiday was known as the "bath and hair washing" day.

earth. As proof of this fact, he said, a yellow dragon would appear. The emperor referred the matter to Chang Ts'ang for deliberation but, because Chang Ts'ang considered the opinion erroneous, the affair was dropped. Some time later, however, a yellow dragon did appear at Ch'eng-chi, whereupon Emperor Wen summoned Kung-sun Ch'en to court, made him an erudit,[5] and set him to drafting a new calendar and set of regulations based upon the theory of the dominance of the element earth, and to working on plans for changing the beginning of the year. From this time on Chang Ts'ang began to bow his way out of affairs, pleading illness and saying he was too old. Chang Ts'ang had recommended someone for the position of master of guests, but the man used the post for all manner of illicit gain. The emperor blamed Chang Ts'ang, who finally left his position on grounds of illness. He held the position of chancellor for fifteen years before he retired. He died in the fifth year of the former part of Emperor Ching's reign [152 B.C.] and was given the posthumous title of "Wen" or "Civil Marquis."

His son Chang K'ang succeeded to the marquisate but died eight years afterwards. K'ang's son Chang Lei in turn became marquis but eight years later was accused of disrespect for having proceeded to his place at court after having taken part in the funeral mourning for one of the nobles, and his fief was taken away.[6]

Chang Ts'ang's father, who founded the family, was not a full five feet in height. Chang Ts'ang, who became a marquis and chancellor, grew up to be over eight feet tall, and his son was of the same height. But when it came down to his grandson Lei, who was tried for an offense and lost the marquisate, he was only something over six feet.

After Chang Ts'eng retired from the chancellorship he was so old that he had not a single tooth in his mouth, but lived on milk, employing a young woman as a wet nurse. He numbered his wives and concubines by the hundreds but after one of them had once become pregnant he never slept with her again. He was over a hundred years old when he died.

[5] The erudits were professional scholars who acted as advisers to the court.
[6] Commentators have offered no explanation as to why this was considered disrespectful.

Shen-t'u Chia

Chancellor Shen-t'u Chia was a native of Liang. He accompanied Kao-tsu in his attacks on Hsiang Yü, holding the position of "foot-stretcher crossbowman."[7] Later he was made head of a battalion. He accompanied the emperor in his attack on Ch'ing Pu's army and was made a colonel. During the reign of Emperor Hui he was made governor of Huai-yang. In the first year of Emperor Wen's reign, when all the former officials who held posts paying two thousand piculs and who had been followers of Emperor Kao-tsu were given the title of marquises within the Pass, twenty-four men received grants of revenue, among them Shen-t'u Chia, who was granted the revenue from five hundred households. After Chang Ts'ang was made chancellor, Shen-t'u Chia was transferred to Chang Ts'ang's old post of imperial secretary.

When Chang Ts'ang retired Emperor Wen wanted to appoint Tou Kuang-kuo, the younger brother of his empress, as the new chancellor. Tou Kuang-kuo was a worthy man who had distinguished himself in action, and for this reason the emperor hoped to make him chancellor, but he said to himself, "People will perhaps suppose that I am honoring him only for personal reasons," and, after considering it for a long time, gave up the idea. Yet nearly all the great ministers from the time of Emperor Kao-tsu had by this time died and, of those who were still alive, there was none suitable for the position. Therefore the emperor made the imperial secretary Shen-t'u Chia the new chancellor, enfeoffing him with the territory the revenue of which he had up to now received, and the title of marquis of Ku-an.

Shen-t'u Chia was very honest and direct, and refused to receive people who came to his house with private requests. At this time the palace counselor Teng T'ung was enjoying the height of the emperor's favor and attention and had received a countless amount of wealth in gifts and presents. Emperor Wen even used to go to Teng T'ung's

[7] There were two types of crossbowmen, the "foot-stretchers" who cocked their bows with their feet, and the "strong-pullers" who stretched them with their arms. The bowmen were members of a local militia which was called up in times of emergency.

house for banquets and drinking parties, so great was the favor he bestowed on him.

It was at this time that Chancellor Shen-t'u Chia one day entered the court and found Teng T'ung seated by the emperor's side, behaving himself in a rude and slovenly manner. After Shen-t'u Chia had finished reporting his business, he took advantage of the occasion to add, "When Your Majesty bestows love and favor upon one of your subjects, it is well that he should be made rich and honorable. But when it comes to the etiquette of the court, one cannot be too strict!"

"Say no more," replied the emperor. "I will attend to the boy in private."

After court was over Shen-t'u Chia retired to his office, sat down, and wrote out an order summoning Teng T'ung to appear at the chancellor's office and stating that, if he did not come, he would be beheaded. Teng T'ung was frightened and went to speak to Emperor Wen about it. "Just go on," said the emperor, "and I will send someone in a little while to call you back."

When Teng T'ung reached the chancellor's office, he removed his cap and shoes and struck his head upon the ground, apologizing for his offense, but Shen-t'u Chia sat completely unmoved, deliberately refusing to acknowledge the apology. Then he began to berate Teng T'ung, saying, "This court is the court of the Founding Ancestor, Emperor Kao-tsu. For a petty official like you to be disporting yourself in the throne room is the height of disrespect! You deserve to be beheaded. Officer, prepare to behead this man!"

Teng T'ung beat his head upon the ground until it was covered with blood, but Shen-t'u Chia would not relent. In the meantime Emperor Wen, calculating that the chancellor would by this time have finished reprimanding Teng T'ung, sent a messenger bearing the imperial seal to summon him and apologize to the chancellor, saying, "This fellow is my playmate. You must forgive him!" When Teng T'ung returned to the palace, he went weeping to Emperor Wen and cried, "The chancellor came close to killing me!"

Shen-t'u Chia was chancellor for five years, during which Emperor Wen passed away and Emperor Ching came to the throne. In the second year of Emperor Ching's reign Ch'ao Ts'o was made prefect of the capital, enjoying great honor and favor in the execution of his duties. At his request, many laws and regulations were changed and inquiries held at which the feudal lords were accused of some crime, fined, and deprived of territory. Since his own words were ignored, Shen-t'u Chia retired modestly into the background, deeply resentful of Ch'ao Ts'o.

After Ch'ao Ts'o became prefect of the capital he decided that the gate of his office, which opened east, was too inconvenient and so he had another gate cut through to the south. This southern exit passed through the compound and pierced the outer wall of the mortuary temple of the Grand Supreme Emperor, Kao-tsu's father.

When Shen-t'u Chia heard of this he thought he could use it to bring Ch'ao Ts'o before the law by accusing him of "wantonly piercing the wall of a mortuary temple of the imperial family for the purpose of making a gate," and requesting that he be executed. One of Ch'ao T'so's retainers reported to him what Shen-t'u Chia was planning and Ch'ao Ts'o, alarmed, went at night to the palace to see the emperor, throwing himself upon Emperor Ching's mercy. When morning came the chancellor submitted his petition asking for Ch'ao Ts'o's execution, but Emperor Ching replied, "The wall which Ch'ao Ts'o pierced was not the actual wall of the mortuary temple, but an outer wall separated from it by an open space. The area between was formerly used to house extra officials. Moreover, I was the one who ordered the work done. Ch'ao Ts'o is guilty of no crime!"

When court was over Shen-t'u Chia remarked to the chief secretary, "I am sorry I did not behead him straightaway. Instead I first submitted a request, and gave Ch'ao Ts'o a chance to trick me!" When he returned to his quarters he spat blood and died. He was given the posthumous title of "Chieh," or "Virtuous Marquis."

His son Shen-t'u Mieh, Marquis Kung, succeeded to the marquisate but died three years later. Mieh's son Shen-t'u Ch'ü-ping succeeded to the title and died thirty-one years later. Ch'ü-ping's son Shen-t'u Yü in turn became marquis, but six years later, when he was governor of Chiu-chiang Province, he was accused of having accepted parting gifts from his predecessors in office. He was found guilty and his fief taken away.

After the death of Shen-t'u Chia, T'ao Ch'ing, marquis of K'ai-feng, and Liu Han, marquis of T'ao, served in turn as chancellor during the reign of Emperor Ching, while in the reign of our present emperor, Hsü Ch'ang, marquis of Po-chih; Hsieh Tse, marquis of P'ing-chi; Chuang Ch'ing-ti, marquis of Wu-ch'iang; Chao Chou, marquis of Kao-ling, and others have been chancellor. All were men who succeeded to their noble titles by birth, being of impeccable demeanor and sterling integrity, fully qualified to fill the office of chancellor, but that was all. None of them proved capable of making any brilliant contributions to the government or doing anything to distinguish his name in the eyes of his contemporaries.

The Grand Historian remarks: Chang Ts'ang was learned in literature and in matters of the pitch pipes and the calendar and was one of the most eminent ministers of the Han. And yet he disparaged the proposals of Chia I, Kung-sun Ch'en, and others to change the beginning of the year and the color of the vestments. He refused to go by what was obviously correct, but instead continued the so-called Calendar of Emperor Chuan Hsü which had been used by the Ch'in. Why was this? [8]

Chou Ch'ang was as stalwart and upright as a tree. Jen Ao obtained his position because of a favor he had done the emperor in former times, and Shen-t'u Chia can be called a man of the strictest honesty and integrity. Yet none of these men possessed any art or learning, so that they can scarcely compare with Hsiao Ho, Ts'ao Ts'an, or Ch'en P'ing.[9]

---

[8] Ssu-ma Ch'ien himself was largely responsible for carrying out the calendrical reform which was first advocated by Chia I and Kung-sun Ch'en, and so he had a personal interest in the question.

[9] The remainder of this chapter is not by Ssu-ma Ch'ien but has been added by a later hand, and hence I have omitted it here.

Shih chi 97: The Biographies of Li I-chi and Lu Chia

With artful words they carried out their missions, and won over the nobles so that, united in goodwill, the nobles gave their allegiance to the Han and became its protectors and guardians. Thus I made The Biographies of Li I-chi and Lu Chia.

Li I-chi

Li I-chi was a native of Kao-yang in Ch'en-liu. He loved to read books. His family was poor and had fallen on such hard times that they had no means of procuring food and clothing, so Li I-chi became keeper of the village gate, but the worthy and influential people of the district would not venture to employ him at anything else. Throughout the district everyone called him "the Mad Scholar."

After Ch'en She, Hsiang Liang, and others had begun their uprisings several dozen of their generals, sent to subdue various regions, passed through Kao-yang. Li I-chi made inquiries about each of these generals, but found them all to be petty-minded and given to empty ceremony, vain men quite incapable of listening to plans for greater and nobler deeds. Therefore Li I-chi withdrew deep within himself.

Later, word came that the governor of P'ei was leading his troops to seize the region about the outskirts of Ch'en-liu. It happened that one of the cavalrymen under the governor's command was from the same village as Li I-chi, and the governor several times inquired of this man who were the wise and important people of the city. When the cavalryman paid a visit to his old home Li I-chi went to see him and said, "I have heard that the governor of P'ei is arrogant and treats others with contempt, but that he has many great plans. This is truly the sort of man I would like to follow after, but I have no one to recommend me. If you should see him, you must tell him, 'In my village there is a man named Master Li who is over sixty years old and eight feet tall. People all call him the Mad Scholar, but he himself insists that he is not mad.'"

"The governor of P'ei does not care for Confucian scholars," replied the cavalryman. "Whenever a visitor wearing a Confucian hat comes to see him, he immediately snatches the hat from the visitor's head and pisses in it, and when he talks to other people he always curses them up and down. He will never consent to be lectured to by a Confucian scholar!"

"Just tell him what I said, anyway," answered Li I-chi. The cavalryman took advantage of a propitious moment to speak to the governor as Li I-chi had instructed him and, when the governor reached the official lodge in Kao-yang, he sent for Li I-chi. Li I-chi arrived and went in for the interview. It happened that the governor was sprawled upon a couch with two servant girls washing his feet when he received Li I-chi. On entering, Li I-chi did not make the customary prostration, but instead gave a deep bow and said, "Do you intend to assist Ch'in in attacking the nobles, or do you intend to lead the nobles in overthrowing Ch'in?"

"Stupid pedant!" cursed the governor. "It is because the whole world has suffered so long together under the Ch'in that the nobles have joined in leading forth their troops to attack it! What do you mean by asking if I intend to 'assist Ch'in in attacking the nobles'?"

"If you really mean to gather a band of followers and create a righteous army to punish the unprincipled Ch'in, it is hardly proper for you to receive your elder sprawled about in this fashion!"

With this the governor stopped the foot washing, rose, straightened his clothes and, apologizing, led Li I-chi to a seat of honor. Li I-chi proceeded to talk to him about the horizontal and vertical alliances of the period of the Six States. The governor was pleased and ordered a meal brought for him, asking, "What strategy do you consider best for me to adopt?"

"You have taken up arms with this motley band, gathered together this disordered army, which does not number a full ten thousand men, and with this you plan to march straight into the powerful Ch'in. Such action is what men call 'seeking out the tiger's jaws.' Now the city of Ch'en-liu is a thoroughfare of the world. From its suburbs roads lead in every direction, while within its walls are many stores of grain. Since I am friendly with its magistrate, I beg to be sent as your emissary so that I can bring the city over to your side. If it should happen that the magistrate will not listen to me, then you may raise your troops and attack, and I will aid you from within the city."

Accordingly the governor of P'ei sent Master Li ahead, while he led his troops after him, and eventually they seized control of Ch'en-liu. He awarded Li I-chi the title of lord of Kuang-yeh. Master Li mentioned his younger brother Li Shang to the governor and managed to have him put in command of several thousand men and sent with the governor to seize the land to the southwest. Li I-chi himself constantly acted as spokesman for the governor's cause, hastening on diplomatic missions from one feudal lord to another.

In the autumn of the third year of Han, Hsiang Yü attacked the Han forces and captured the city of Jung-yang. The Han troops fled and took up a defensive position in the area of Kung and Lo-yang. In the meantime Hsiang Yü, receiving word that Han Hsin had defeated Chao and that P'eng Yüeh was inciting frequent rebellions in the region of Liang, divided his forces and sent troops to the aid of these two areas. Han Hsin was at the time marching east to attack Ch'i.

The king of Han had several times found himself sorely pressed in the area of Jung-yang and Ch'eng-kao and had decided that the best plan would be to abandon any attempt to hold the territory east of Ch'eng-kao, garrisoning Kung and Lo-yang instead, in order to block the advance of the Ch'u forces. It was at this point that Master Li said to the king, "There is a saying that 'he who knows the "heaven" of Heaven may make himself a king, but he who has not this knowledge may not. To a king the people are "heaven," and to the people food is "heaven".'[1] For a long time now grain from all over the empire has been transported to the Ao Granary and I have heard that huge quantities are stored in its vaults. After Hsiang Yü captured Jung-yang, however, he did not remain to guard the Ao Granary, but instead led his men east, leaving only a party of convict soldiers to hold

---

[1] In this rather curious expression the word "heaven" is being used in the sense of a *sine qua non*.

Ch'eng-kao. Heaven, it seems, has come to the aid of the Han! Now when the Ch'u forces can most easily be overcome, if we were on the contrary to retreat and allow this advantage to be snatched from our hands, I cannot help feeling it would be a grave error indeed!

"Two great heroes cannot stand forever side by side. Ch'u and Han have long faced each other without reaching a final decision, while the common people have been driven to confusion and all within the four seas are swayed and tossed in the struggle. The farmer abandons his plough and the weaving girl steps down from her loom, for the hearts of the world find no security or rest. I beg you therefore to advance your troops with all speed and retake Jung-yang. With the grain of the Ao Granary as a basis, you may blockade the strategic points of Ch'eng-kao, close the road along Mount T'ai-hsing, block the pass at Flying Fox, and hold the White Horse Ford across the Yellow River. In this way you will demonstrate to the other nobles that you are holding the most strategic points and taking advantage of the circumstances, and the whole world will thenceforth turn to you.

"At the present time both Yen and Chao are already in your control, and only Ch'i remains to be won over. Now T'ien Kuang is ruling over the thousand square miles of Ch'i, while T'ien Hsien has led a force of two hundred thousand and made camp at the city of Li-hsia. The T'ien family are very powerful and are protected in their position by the sea at their backs and the Yellow River before them. The state of Ch'i borders Ch'u on the south and its people are deceitful and shifty in their loyalties. Though you were to send a force of two or three hundred thousand men, you would be unable to defeat it in a matter of months or even years. I beg to be honored with the mission of envoy to the king of Ch'i, so that I may persuade him to declare himself on the side of Han and act as our protector in the east."

The king of Han approved his suggestion and set about putting the plan into action, seizing the Ao Granary and sending Master Li to plead with the king of Ch'i.

"Do you know which side the empire will turn to?" Master Li asked the king of Ch'i.

"I do not," the king replied.

"If you only knew which side the world would turn to, you could keep possession of the kingdom of Ch'i. But if not, you cannot keep hold of it."

"Which side *will* the world go over to?"

"The side of Han!"

"And why do you say that?"

"When the king of Han and Hsiang Yü joined their strength and faced west to attack Ch'in, they agreed that whoever entered Hsien-yang first should become its king. The king of Han was the first to enter, yet Hsiang Yü went back on the agreement and would not grant him the area of Hsien-yang, but made him king of Han instead. Later Hsiang Yü moved the Righteous Emperor from his residence and murdered him. When the king of Han heard of this he raised the troops of Shu and Han and attacked the three kingdoms of Ch'in, marched out of the Pass, and demanded to know what had happened to the Righteous Emperor. He gathered together the soldiers of the empire and set up the heirs of the former nobility. Whenever a city was captured he made the commanding general a marquis; whenever any spoils were seized he divided them with his men, so that the whole world shared the gains, and brave and distinguished men all delighted in serving him. Thus the troops of the other nobles flocked to him from every direction, while the grain of Shu and Han poured down the rivers in fleets of boats sailing abreast.

"Hsiang Yü, however, bears the name of a promise-breaker and the stain of the Righteous Emperor's murder is upon him. Never does he remember the achievements of others, nor does he ever forget their errors. A battle won for him receives no reward; a city taken wins no fief. No one but a member of the Hsiang family is allowed to handle important affairs. Though he has seals of enfeoffment carved to award to others, he will fiddle with them in his hands until they are worn smooth before he can bear to present them to anyone. When he attacks a city and seizes the spoils he lays it all aside, unwilling to give any away as a reward. The world turns against him, men of intelligence and ability have grown to hate him, and there is no one left who will do his business for him. Hence it is the easiest thing possible to predict that the men of the world will all go over to the side of the king of Han!

"Now the king of Han has led his men forth from Shu and Han, and recaptured the three kingdoms of Ch'in. His forces have crossed the western reaches of the Yellow River to the northern side, gathered up the troops of Shang-tang, descended the Ching Gorge, overthrown Ch'en Yü, the lord of Ch'eng-an, defeated the Northern Wei, and captured thirty-two cities. Such an army is like that of the great Ch'ih Yu of ancient times, winning its victories not by human strength but by the blessing of Heaven. Now the king of Han has acquired the grain supplies of the Ao Granary, blockaded the strategic points of Ch'eng-kao, guarded the White Horse Ford, blocked the slopes of Mount T'ai-hsing, and closed the pass at Flying Fox. Therefore those who are slow to submit to him will be the first to perish. If you will hasten to bow before the king of Han, then you may keep possession of Ch'i's altars of the soil and grain. But if you do not bow to him, you may expect danger and destruction in a matter of days!"

T'ien Kuang, the king of Ch'i, considered that Master Li spoke the truth. He therefore heeded his advice, dispersed the troops which he had sent to defend Li-hsia, and spent the days drinking to his heart's content with Master Li.

When Han Hsin got word that Master Li, by no more than nodding a diplomatic greeting from his carriage, had won over Ch'i with its seventy-odd cities, he led his troops across the Yellow River at P'ing-yüan and made a surprise attack on Ch'i. T'ien Kuang, hearing that the Han soldiers had arrived, supposed that Master Li had betrayed him. "If you can halt the Han armies," he told Li I-chi, "I will let you live. But if not, I will boil you alive!"

"Great deeds do not wait upon petty caution," replied Master Li, "nor shining virtue upon niceties of etiquette. Your father[2] has no intention of going back on what he has said for the sake of the likes of you!"

With this the king of Ch'i boiled Master Li alive and fled east with his army.

In the twelfth year of Han, Li I-chi's brother Li Shang, the marquis of Ch'ü-chou, acting as chancellor of the right, led a force of troops

---

[2] For the use of this insulting phrase, see note 5, "The Hereditary House of the Marquis of Liu."

in an attack on Ch'ing Pu, winning distinction in battle. When Kao-tsu was rewarding the various nobles and great ministers he remembered Li I-chi, whose son Chieh had from time to time led bands of troops, though his achievements had not qualified him for the rank of marquis. For his father's sake the emperor enfeoffed Li Chieh as marquis of Kao-liang, and later changed the territory which he was awarded to Wu-sui. The marquisate was handed down for three generations. During the first year of the era *yüan-shou* [122 B.C.] Li P'ing, then the marquis of Wu-sui, was tried on charges of forging an imperial edict and extorting from the king of Heng-shan a sum of a hundred catties of gold. He was condemned to be executed in the public market, but before the sentence could be carried out he died of illness and his territory was abolished.

Lu Chia

Lu Chia was a native of Ch'u who became a follower of Kao-tsu and joined him in conquering the world. He was renowned as a skillful speaker and rhetorician and was one of Kao-tsu's trusted advisers, serving time and again as envoy to the various nobles.

When Kao-tsu became emperor, and peace was first restored to China, the military commander Chao T'o conquered the region of Southern Yüeh and proceeded to make himself its ruler. Kao-tsu dispatched Lu Chia to present Chao T'o with the imperial seal making him king of Southern Yüeh. When Master Lu[3] arrived Chao T'o received him in audience with his hair done up in the mallet-shaped fashion of the natives of Southern Yüeh, and sprawled on his mat. Master Lu advanced and addressed Chao T'o. "You are a Chinese, and your forefathers and kin lie buried in Chen-ting in the land of Chao. Yet now you turn against that nature which Heaven has given you at birth, cast aside the dress of your native land and, with this tiny, far-off land of Yüeh, think to set yourself up as a rival of the Son of Heaven and an enemy state. Disaster will surely fall upon you!

"When Ch'in lost control of the empire the nobles and heroes rose on all sides, yet it was the king of Han alone who entered the Pass

---

[3] Because he was a scholar and a writer, Ssu-ma Ch'ien refers to him as "Master," as in the case of Li I-chi above.

ahead of the others and took possession of Hsien-yang. Hsiang Yü broke the promise which he had made to the nobles and set himself up as 'Dictator King of Western Ch'u,' and all the other nobles became subject to his command, for his strength was the greatest. Yet the king of Han rose up from Pa and Shu, chastised the world as with a great whip, drove the nobles before him, and in the end punished and destroyed Hsiang Yü until, in the space of five years, he had brought all within the four seas to peace and unity. Such deeds were not done by human strength, but were ordained by Heaven!

"Now it has come to the ears of the Son of Heaven that, although you lent no aid in punishing the traitors who plagued the world, you have made yourself ruler of Southern Yüeh. The generals and high ministers wish to send out an army to punish you. But because the Son of Heaven is unwilling in his compassion to inflict new suffering and hardship upon the common people, he has set aside their proposals and sent me instead to confer upon you the seals of a king, splitting the tallies of enfeoffment and opening diplomatic intercourse. It is proper under such circumstances that you should advance as far as the suburbs to greet me and bow to the north and refer to yourself as a 'subject.' Yet with this newly created state of Yüeh, which is not even firmly established, you behave with such effrontery! If the Han emperor should actually hear of this, he would dig up and desecrate the graves of your ancestors, wipe out your family, and dispatch one of his subordinate generals with a force of a hundred thousand men to march to the borders of Yüeh. At that point the people of Yüeh would murder you and surrender to the Han forces faster than I can turn my hand!"

With this, Chao T'o scrambled up off his mat in the greatest alarm and apologized to Master Lu, saying, "I have lived among these barbarians for so long that I have lost all sense of manners and propriety!"

In the course of their conversations Chao T'o asked Master Lu, "Who is worthier, I or the great ministers Hsiao Ho, Ts'ao Ts'an, and Han Hsin?"

"You would appear to be the worthier man," replied Master Lu.

"And of the emperor and myself, who is worthier?" he asked again.

"The emperor rose up from the city of Feng in P'ei, overthrew the violent Ch'in, and punished the powerful leaders of Ch'u, driving out harm and bringing benefit to the whole world. He succeeded to the labors of the Five Emperors and the Three Dynasties of the past, uniting all China under a single rule. The population of China numbers in the millions, while its land area measures thousands of square miles. It occupies the richest and most fertile region of the world, with an abundance of people, carriages, and every other thing imaginable. And yet its government proceeds from a single family. Since the creation of heaven and earth there has never before been such a thing!

"Now Your Majesty's people do not number over a few hundred thousand, and all of them are barbarians, crowded awkwardly between the mountains and the sea. Such a kingdom would amount to no more than a single province of the Han empire! How can you compare yourself with the emperor of Han?"

Chao T'o laughed loudly and replied, "It is only because I did not begin my uprising in China that I have become king of this region. If I had been in China, would I not have done just as well as the Han emperor?"

Chao T'o took great delight in Master Lu and detained him with feasts and drinking parties for several months. "There is no one in all of Yüeh worth talking to," he said. "Now that you have come, every day I hear something I have never heard before!" He presented Master Lu with a bag of precious objects worth a thousand pieces of gold and in addition gave him a thousand pieces of gold as a going away present. In the end Master Lu awarded him the title of king of Yüeh and persuaded him to acknowledge his allegiance to the Han and enter into relations with it.

When Lu Chia returned and reported on his mission, Kao-tsu was greatly pleased and honored him with the rank of palace counselor.

In his audiences with the emperor, Master Lu on numerous occasions expounded and praised the *Book of Odes* and the *Book of Documents*, until one day Kao-tsu began to rail at him. "All I possess I have won on horseback!" said the emperor. "Why should I bother with the *Odes* and *Documents*?"

"Your Majesty may have won it on horseback, but can you rule it on horseback?" asked Master Lu. "Kings T'ang and Wu in ancient times won possession of the empire through the principle of revolt, but it was by the principle of obedience that they assured the continuance of their dynasties. To pay due attention to both civil and military affairs is the way for a dynasty to achieve long life. In the past King Fu-ch'a of Wu and Chih Po, minister of Chin, both perished because they paid too much attention to military affairs. Ch'in entrusted its future solely to punishments and laws, without changing with the times, and thus eventually brought about the destruction of its ruling family. If, after it had united the world under its rule, Ch'in had practiced benevolence and righteousness and modeled its ways upon the sages of antiquity, how would Your Majesty ever have been able to win possession of the empire?"

The emperor grew embarrassed and uneasy and finally said to Master Lu, "Try writing something for me on the reasons why Ch'in lost the empire and I won it, and of the successes and failures of the states of ancient times."

Master Lu accordingly set out to describe in brief the keys to political survival and defeat in a work running to twelve sections in all. As each section was presented to the throne, the emperor never failed to express his delight and approval and all those about him cried, "Bravo!" The book was given the title *New Discourses*.

During the time of Emperor Hui, Empress Lü, who managed all affairs of state, wished to make kings of the members of the Lü family, but she was afraid of the opposition of the great ministers and clever speakers at court. Master Lu judged that he could not persuade her to desist and so he pleaded illness and retired from court to reside at home. He decided to make his home in Hao-chih because the land there was good for farming. He took the bag of precious objects which he had received when he was an envoy to Yüeh, sold the contents for a thousand pieces of gold, and divided the money among his five sons, giving two hundred to each, so that they could make a livelihood for themselves.

Master Lu always traveled in a comfortable carriage drawn by a team of four, accompanied by ten attendants who sang songs, danced, and played the drums and a variety of lutes. He carried with him a precious sword worth a hundred pieces of gold. Master Lu said to his five sons, "I will make an agreement with you. Whenever I visit any of you, you must provide wine and food for my people and my horses. After I have enjoyed myself to the full for ten days, I shall be on my way. He at whose house I die shall inherit my precious sword, my carriage, and my riders and attendants. In the course of a year, what with the time spent in traveling back and forth and visits elsewhere, I shall not have visited any one of you more than two or three times. If we were to see each other too often, our meetings would lose their freshness, and I would not like to burden you with a prolonged stay."

Empress Lü at this time made kings of the various members of the Lü family, so that the Lü family wielded unlimited power. They were plotting to do away with the young ruler,[4] and threatened the existence of the whole Liu family. Ch'en P'ing, the chancellor of the right, was deeply distressed, but he was powerless to oppose them and, being fearful that disaster would fall upon himself, sat quietly by and constantly pondered the problem. Master Lu once went to visit Ch'en P'ing to inquire how he was. He walked directly into the room and took a seat without ado, but Ch'en P'ing, lost in thought, did not even notice his arrival. "What are you thinking so hard about?" asked Master Lu.

"What do you suppose I am thinking about, Master Lu?" asked Ch'en P'ing in reply.

"Your position is the highest in the government and you enjoy a marquisate with the revenue from thirty thousand households. Surely you must admit that one could desire nothing further in the way of wealth and honor. If you still have anxious thoughts, it can only be that you are worried about the Lü clan and our young ruler."

"You are quite right," said Ch'en P'ing. "And what is to be done?"

"When the world is at peace all eyes are upon the prime minister, but when the world is in danger attention turns to the commanding general. If the general and the prime minister are in agreement with one another, then the rest of the officers and officials will gladly follow them and, with all the rest behind them, though trouble and disaffection

[4] The child ruler whom Empress Lü had set on the throne after the death of Emperor Hui, 188 B.C.

occur in the empire, there will be no danger of authority slipping from their grasp. Hence the security of the altars of the state lies solely in the hands of these two men. I have always wanted to speak to the grand commandant Chou P'o, the marquis of Chiang, but he and I are only on joking terms and I am afraid he would dismiss my words too lightly. Why do you not establish more friendly relations with him so that you two can cooperate to the fullest in this matter?"

This and several other plans he suggested to Ch'en P'ing concerning the matter of the Lü family. Ch'en P'ing followed his advice and proceeded to spend five hundred pieces of gold on a birthday celebration for Chou P'o at which, amid a lavish array of dishes, they drank and feasted merrily. Chou P'o in turn responded with similar generosity, so that the two men became close friends and the plottings of the Lü clan accordingly met with less and less success.

Ch'en P'ing sent Master Lu a hundred female slaves, fifty carriages and horses, and a sum of five million cash to be used to cover drinking and eating expenses. With this Master Lu began to mingle freely with the highest officials of the Han court, and his fame spread in all directions.

When the Lü family was overthrown and Emperor Wen set up, Master Lu acquired unprecedented power. After Emperor Wen had come to the throne he wished to send an envoy to Southern Yüeh, and Prime Minister Ch'en P'ing and others immediately suggested Master Lu. Master Lu was accordingly made a palace counselor and sent as an envoy to Chao T'o, where he succeeded in persuading Chao T'o to stop riding in a yellow-covered carriage and calling his orders "edicts" in imitation of the Han emperors, and to conduct himself in the same way as the feudal lords of China proper. Chao T'o agreed to do just as the Han court suggested. (A more detailed discussion will be found in the chapter on Southern Yüeh.) Master Lu finally died of old age.

Chu Chien

Chu Chien, lord of P'ing-yüan, was a native of Ch'u. Originally he served as prime minister to Ch'ing Pu, the king of Huai-nan, but because of some offense he was removed from his post. Later he returned to the service of Ch'ing Pu. When Ch'ing Pu was planning to revolt he asked Chu Chien's advice. Chu Chien counseled him to desist. Ch'ing Pu, however, refused to heed him but instead listened to the marquis of Liang-fu and eventually revolted. After the Han forces had executed Ch'ing Pu it was learned that Chu Chien had remonstrated with Ch'ing Pu and refused to take part in the plot, and he was thus allowed to go free without punishment.

Chu Chien was a very eloquent speaker and a man of strict honesty and integrity. In his actions he refused to compromise with expediency, nor would he modify his principles for the sake of appearances. He made his home in Ch'ang-an.

Shen I-chi, the marquis of Pi-yang, who at the time had managed by dubious ways to win great favor with Empress Lü, was desirous of becoming friends with Chu Chien, but the latter refused to receive him. It happened that Chu Chien's mother died and Master Lu, who from early days had been a friend of Chu Chien, went to visit him. Chu Chien's family, he found, was so poor that Chu Chien was forced to delay announcement of the funeral while he looked about for some place to borrow the necessary clothes and accessories. Master Lu instructed Chu Chien to go ahead and announce the funeral, while he himself went to call on Shen I-chi and congratulated him, saying, "The mother of Chu Chien, lord of P'ing-yüan, has died!"

"Why in the world should you congratulate *me* on the death of Chu Chien's mother?" asked Shen I-chi.

"Some time ago," said Master Lu, "you expressed a desire to get to know Chu Chien. At that time, however, he did not consider it proper to become friends with you because his mother was still alive.[5] Now that she is dead, if you are willing to arrange a generous funeral for her, Chu Chien will do anything for you."

Shen I-chi accordingly went to Chu Chien's house and presented a hundred pieces of gold as a funeral gift, and the other nobles and high officials, because Shen I-chi had brought a gift, followed his

---

[5] The reader should recall that, under the system of corporate responsibility before the law, if Chu Chien's association with Shen I-chi had led to his being implicated in any offense of Shen I-chi's, his mother would be held as guilty and punished as severely as Chu Chien himself. Because Shen I-chi's power was based not on ability but on the personal favoritism of Empress Lü, his position at court was naturally precarious.

example until Chu Chien had received a sum of five hundred pieces of gold in all.

Shen I-chi enjoyed unusual favor with Empress Lü. It happened that someone slandered him to Emperor Hui, who was enraged and had Shen I-chi seized by the law officers in preparation for executing him. Empress Lü was chagrined and could say nothing in his defense, while many of the high officials joined in criticizing his activities and pressing for his execution. Shen I-chi, in a most difficult position, sent someone to ask Chu Chien to come to see him, but Chu Chien declined to go, saying, "Your trial is about to take place. I dare not see you!" Meanwhile, however, he requested an interview with Emperor Hui's favorite, the catamite Hung, and attempted to persuade him to act. "There is no one in the empire who does not know why you enjoy such favor with the emperor," he said. "And yet now Shen I-chi, who enjoys similar favor with Empress Lü, is seized by the law officers. People about town all say that you have slandered him and are trying to have him killed. But if Shen I-chi is executed today, you may be sure that by tomorrow morning Empress Lü in her rage will have you executed, too! Would it not be better to bare your shoulders like a suppliant and plead for Shen I-chi with the emperor? If the emperor listens to you and frees Shen I-chi, Empress Lü will be overjoyed. Then you will enjoy the favor of both sovereigns, and your honor and wealth will be doubled!"

The catamite Hung, thoroughly alarmed, followed his suggestion and spoke to the emperor, who as a result released Shen I-chi. Earlier, when Shen I-chi sent for Chu Chien to come to see him in prison and Chu Chien refused to appear, he had been enraged, believing that Chu Chien had betrayed him, but his rage turned to complete astonishment when Chu Chien's plan succeeded and he was released.

After Empress Lü passed away, the high officials executed the members of the Lü family, but Shen I-chi, who had had the most intimate connections with the family, managed in the end to escape. In all cases the schemes which saved his life were due to the efforts of Master Lu and Chu Chien.

During the reign of Emperor Wen, King Li of Huai-nan killed Shen I-chi on the grounds that he had been an associate of the Lü family. When Emperor Wen heard that one of Shen I-chi's friends, Chu Chien, had planned his affairs for him, he sent a law officer to arrest Chu Chien and bring him to trial. Word being brought to him that the law officer was at his gate, Chu Chien prepared to commit suicide, but his son and the officer both said, "No one knows yet how the affair will end! Why should you make such haste to commit suicide?"

"If I am dead the trouble will come to an end," he replied, "and no harm will fall upon you, my son!" and with this he cut his throat.

When Emperor Wen received the news he was filled with regret. "I had no intention of killing him," he said, and summoned Chu Chien's son and made him a palace counselor. He was sent as an envoy to the Huns. When the *Shan-yü* behaved rudely to him, he proceeded to curse the *Shan-yü*, and eventually died among the Hsiung-nu.[6]

The Grand Historian remarks: Many of the books circulating these days which record the story of Master Li state that it was after the king of Han had captured the three kingdoms of Ch'in, marched east to attack Hsiang Yü, and was encamped with his army in the area between Kung and Lo-yang that Master Li, dressed in the robes of a Confucian, went to advise him. But this is an error. It was actually while the emperor was still governor of P'ei and before he had entered the Pass that, parting from Hsiang Yü and marching to Kao-yang, he obtained the services of Master Li and his brother.

I have read Master Lu's *New Discourses* in twelve sections. He was surely one of the outstanding rhetoricians of his day. In the case of Chu Chien, lord of P'ing-yüan, I was a friend of his son and so have been able to obtain a full account of his life.

---

[6] At this point in the text there appears a variant account of the meeting of Master Li I-chi and the governor of P'ei. Scholars have long regarded it with suspicion and considered it to be a later interpolation. I have omitted the entire section.

Shih chi 98: The Biographies of Fu K'uan, Chin Hsi, and the Marquis of K'uai-ch'eng: Concluding Remarks

[This chapter records the biographies of three men, Fu K'uan, Chin Hsi, and Chou Hsieh (the marquis of K'uai-ch'eng), who fought under Kao-tsu in his rise to power and were rewarded with noble titles. Like the biographies in *Shih chi* 95 above, it is made up almost entirely of brief, bare statistics on military achievements and promotions in rank. The lives of such men, marked by continuous but scarcely memorable success, obviously had little appeal for Ssu-ma Ch'ien, and this seems to be the best he could do. His closing words reveal a trace of envy at their good luck.—*Trans.*]

If one would know the details of the struggle against Ch'in and Ch'u, he would have to be acquainted with Chou Hsieh, for he alone constantly accompanied Kao-tsu in gaining control over the feudal lords. Thus I made The Biographies of Fu K'uan, Chin Hsi, and the Marquis of K'uai-ch'eng.

The Grand Historian remarks: Fu K'uan, the marquis of Yang-ling, and Chin Hsi, the marquis of Hsin-wu, both achieved noble titles. They followed Kao-tsu when he rose east of the mountains, and in his attacks on Hsiang Yü, killing renowned generals, defeating armies, and capturing cities by the tens, and yet they never encountered difficulty or disgrace. Such good fortune must indeed have been bestowed by Heaven!

Chou Hsieh, the marquis of K'uai-ch'eng, was a man of such prudence and integrity that suspicion never touched his person. Whenever the emperor was about to undertake a military expedition in person Chou Hsieh would always attempt to dissuade him with tears, like a man who is distressed at heart. He is worthy to be called a gentleman of deep sincerity.

Shih chi 99: The Biographies of Liu Ching and Shu-sun T'ung

They moved the powerful clans, established the capital within the Pass, made a treaty of peace with the Hsiung-nu, and clarified the ritual of the court and the ceremonial laws concerning the ancestral temples. Thus I made The Biographies of Liu Ching and Shu-sun T'ung.

Liu Ching

Liu Ching, whose family name was originally Lou, was a native of Ch'i. In the fifth year of Han, while he was on his way to garrison duty in Lung-hsi, he passed through Lo-yang, where Emperor Kao-tsu was at the time residing. He climbed out of the little, man-drawn cart in which he was riding and, still wearing his lambskin traveling clothes, went to see General Yü, who was also a native of Ch'i, and said, "I wish to see the emperor and talk to him about a matter which will be to his advantage."

General Yü wanted to give him some fresh clothes to wear, but Liu Ching replied, "If I were wearing silk, I would see him wearing silk, and if I were wearing the coarsest haircloth, I would see him in that!" He refused to change his clothes.

General Yü accordingly went in and spoke to the emperor, who summoned Liu Ching to an audience and had a meal brought for him. This done, he asked Liu Ching his business and the latter began his discourse: "Your Majesty, in establishing the capital at Lo-yang, is, I should say, attempting to imitate the glory of the house of Chou."

"That is correct," replied the emperor.

"And yet the way Your Majesty acquired the empire was quite different from the way the house of Chou acquired it. The Chou ancestral line began with Hou Chi, who was enfeoffed in T'ai by Emperor Yao. The family continued to accumulate virtue and goodness for over ten generations until Kung Liu fled from the tyrant Chieh and went to live in Pin. Later, because of the attacks of the Ti barbarians, he left Pin, with only his horsewhip in his hand, and went to live in Ch'i, but the people of his former kingdom hastened to follow after him. When King Wen became chief of the west and settled the dispute between the states of Yü and Jui, he first received the mandate of Heaven, and Lü Wang and Po-i journeyed from the distant borders of the sea to be his followers. Then King Wu set out to attack the Shang tyrant Chou and, at the Meng Ford, though he had not summoned them, eight hundred of the other nobles gathered to join him. All of them cried, 'Let us attack the tyrant Chou!' And in the end they overthrew the Shang dynasty. After King Ch'eng came to the throne he had as his aides and ministers the duke of Chou and others, who at this time established a capital called Ch'eng-chou at the city of Lo because it is the center of the world.[1] The feudal lords were able to present their tribute and journey to the capital for *corvée* services from all four sides, and the distance was equal for all.

"From such a capital it is easy for a king who is virtuous to rule, but it is also easy for a king who is not virtuous to be overthrown. In establishing the capital here, it was the hope of the founders that their descendants would devote themselves wholly to virtue and thereby attract the people to their rule, rather than, by placing the capital in a strong position militarily, to encourage later rulers to become arrogant and wasteful and tyrannize over the people. At the height of the Chou dynasty the whole world was at peace and the barbarians of the four quarters turned in longing and admiration toward its virtuous ways, submitted to its rule, and paid homage to the Son of Heaven. Not one soldier was sent off to garrison duty, not one man marched into battle, and yet the eight barbarian tribes and the people of the other great states all without exception came of their own accord in submission to the Chou to bear tribute and undertake its duties.

"But, when the Chou declined, it split into two parts. The world ceased to attend its court, and the house of Chou could no longer enforce its will. This was not because its virtue had grown ineffective, but rather because its geographical position was too weak.

[1] Lo-yang was reputed to be the geographical center of the world.

"Now Your Majesty, rising up from Feng in P'ei, gathered together a band of three thousand men and proceeded at once to roll up the areas of Shu and Han and conquer the three kingdoms of Ch'in. You fought with Hsiang Yü at Jung-yang, and contended for the pass at Ch'eng-kao, engaging in seventy major battles and forty skirmishes. You have caused the men of the world to spill their blood and bowels upon the earth, and the fathers and sons to bleach their bones in the open fields, in numbers too great to reckon. The sound of weeping has not yet ceased, the wounded have not yet risen from their beds, and still you would attempt to imitate the glorious reigns of Kings Ch'eng and K'ang of the Chou. Yet, if I may be so bold as to say so, there is no resemblance.

"The area of Ch'in, surrounded by mountains and girdled by the Yellow River, is strongly protected on all four sides. In the case of sudden need it is capable of supplying a force of a million soldiers. He who holds the old area of Ch'in and enjoys the advantages of its vast and fertile fields possesses a veritable storehouse created by nature. If Your Majesty will enter the Pass and make your capital there, then, although there should be an uprising east of the mountains, you can still keep complete control of the old land of Ch'in. Now when you fight with a man, you have to grip his throat and strike him in the back before you can be sure of your victory. In the same way, if you will now enter the Pass and make your capital there, basing yourself upon the old land of Ch'in, you will in effect be gripping the throat and striking the back of the empire!"

Emperor Kao-tsu consulted his various officials, but the officials, all being men from east of the mountains, hastened to point out that the house of Chou had lasted several hundred years, while the Ch'in perished with the Second Emperor, and that it was therefore wiser to establish the capital at the site of the Chou capital in Lo yang. The emperor was in doubt and had not yet made up his mind when Chang Liang, the marquis of Liu, made clear to him the advantages of locating the capital within the Pass, and on the same day he mounted his carriage and began the journey west, determined to establish the capital within the Pass.

"Since it was Lou Ching who first advised me to make my capital in the land of Ch'in," the emperor announced, "let Lou from now on become Liu," and he awarded Lou Ching the imperial surname Liu, made him a palace attendant, and gave him the title of lord of Feng-ch'un.

In the seventh year Hsin, the king of Hann, revolted and Kao-tsu went in person to attack him. When the emperor reached Chin-yang he received word that Hsin was about to join the Hsiung-nu in a joint attack on the Han. In a rage, the emperor dispatched envoys to the Hsiung-nu. The Hsiung-nu took care to conceal all of their fine young men and fat cattle and horses, and let the envoys see only the old men and boys and the leanest of their livestock. As many as ten envoys made the trip but all, when they returned, announced that the Hsiung-nu could be attacked. The emperor then sent Liu Ching to go as his envoy. On his return, Liu Ching reported on his mission. "When two states are about to attack each other, it is customary for each to exaggerate and make a show of its superiority. Now when I journeyed to the Hsiung-nu, I saw only emaciated animals, old men, and boys. It can only be that they deliberately wish to appear inferior and are counting on surprising us with an ambush attack and winning victory. In my opinion the Hsiung-nu cannot be attacked!"

At this time the Han force of two hundred thousand or more had already crossed Chü-chu Mountain and arrived for the assault. The emperor began to curse Liu Ching angrily. "This scoundrel from Ch'i has managed to win himself a position with his wagging tongue, and now he comes with his foolish lies and tries to halt my army!" He had Liu Ching fettered and bound at Kuang-wu, and proceeded on his way as far as P'ing-ch'eng.

As Liu Ching had foreseen, the Hsiung-nu sent out a surprise force and surrounded the emperor on the White Peak for seven days, until they at last withdrew. When the emperor returned to Kuang-wu he pardoned Liu Ching, saying, "Because I did not listen to your advice I encountered great difficulty at P'ing-ch'eng. I have already executed the ten earlier envoys who advised me that the Hsiung-nu could be attacked!" He proceeded to enfeoff Liu Ching as a marquis in the area within the Pass, awarding him two thousand households and the title of marquis of Chien-hsin.

Kao-tsu abandoned the P'ing-ch'eng campaign and returned to the capital, while Hsin, the king of Hann, fled to the Hsiung-nu. Mo-tun, who at this time had just become *Shan-yü*, had a powerful force of troops, including three hundred thousand crossbow-stretchers, and several times attacked the northern frontier. The emperor, troubled about the situation, consulted Liu Ching, who replied, "The empire has only just been brought to peace and the officers and men are worn out by fighting. It is not possible at this time to make the Hsiung-nu submit by force of arms. Moreover, Mo-tun acquired the position of *Shan-yü* by murdering his father. He has taken his father's concubines as wives and relies solely on force to maintain his rule. Such a man can never be swayed by appeals to benevolence and righteousness. Therefore I can only suggest a plan whereby in time Mo-tun's descendants can be made subjects of the Han. But I fear Your Majesty will not be able to carry it out. . . ."

"If it will actually work, why should I not be able to carry it out?" asked the emperor. "Only tell me what I must do!"

"If you could see your way clear to send your eldest daughter by the empress to be the consort of Mo-tun, accompanied by a generous dowry and presents, then Mo-tun, knowing that a daughter of the emperor and empress of the Han must be generously provided for, would with barbarian cunning receive her well and make her his legitimate consort and, if she had a son, he would make him heir apparent. Why would he do this? Because of his greed for Han valuables and gifts. Your Majesty might at various times during the year inquire of his health and send presents of whatever Han has a surplus of, and the Hsiung-nu lack. At the same time you could dispatch rhetoricians to begin expounding to the barbarians in a tactful way the principles of etiquette and moral behavior. As long as Mo-tun is alive he will always be your son-in-law, and when he dies your grandson by your daughter will succeed him as *Shan-yü*. And who ever heard of a grandson trying to treat his grandfather as an equal? Thus your soldiers need fight no battles, and yet the Hsiung-nu will gradually become your subjects. If, however, Your Majesty cannot send the eldest princess, but should attempt to deceive Mo-tun by sending someone else and having the princesses and their ladies in waiting address her as 'Princess,' I fear he would discover the deception and be unwilling to pay her any honor, so that no advantage would be gained."

"Excellent!" agreed the emperor, and prepared to send the eldest princess, but Empress Lü day and night wept and pleaded, saying, "The only children I have are the heir apparent and this one girl! How can you bear to cast her away to the Hsiung-nu?"

In the end the emperor could not bring himself to send the princess, but instead selected the daughter of another family and, calling her the eldest princess, sent her to marry Mo-tun, dispatching Liu Ching to go along at the same time and conclude a peace treaty.

When he returned from his mission to the Hsiung-nu, Liu Ching spoke to the emperor, saying, "The Hsiung-nu in the Ordos region south of the Yellow River who are under the Po-yang and Lou-fan kings are situated no more than seven hundred *li* from Ch'ang-an. With a day and a night of riding their light cavalry can reach the old land of Ch'in within the Pass. This region has only recently suffered conquest, so that its people are rather few in number, but the land is rich and fertile and can support many more. Furthermore, at the time when the nobles began their uprisings against Ch'in, it was said that no one but a member of the T'ien clan of Ch'i or the Chao, Ch'ü, or Ching clans of Ch'u could ever succeed. Now although Your Majesty has established the capital within the Pass, there are in fact few people in the area. Close to the north are the barbarian bandits, while in the east live these powerful clans of the Six States of former times, so that if some day trouble should arise somewhere, I fear you could never rest with an easy mind. I beg therefore that you move the various members of the T'ien clan of Ch'i, the Chao, Ch'ü, and Ching clans of Ch'u, the descendants of the former royal families of Yen, Chao, Hann, and Wei, and the other powerful and renowned families to the area within the Pass. As long as things are going well, they can defend the area against the barbarians, and if there should be disaffection among the feudal lords, they would form an army which could be led east and used in putting down the trouble. This is the type of strategy known as 'strengthening the root and weakening the branches' of the empire."

The emperor approved the plan and sent Liu Ching to see to the moving of the said clans to the area within the Pass, over a hundred thousand persons in all.

Shu-sun T'ung

Shu-sun T'ung was a native of Hsieh. During the Ch'in dynasty he was summoned to court because of his literary ability and served along with the erudits for several years. When Ch'en She began his uprising east of the mountains, messengers came to report the fact to the throne. The Second Emperor summoned the erudits and various Confucian scholars and questioned them. "Some soldiers from a garrison in Ch'u have attacked Chi and made their way into Ch'en," he announced. "What do you make of this, gentlemen?"

One after another some thirty or more erudits and scholars came forward and gave their opinion: "A subject must not harbor so much as the thought of disaffection. If he has even the thought, he is already guilty of rebellion, an unpardonable crime which deserves only death. We beg Your Majesty to dispatch troops at once to attack this fellow!"

At this the emperor's face flushed with rage. Then Shu-sun T'ung advanced and began to speak. "The other scholars are all mistaken," he announced. "The whole world is now united as one family. The walls of the provincial and district cities have been razed and their weapons melted down to make clear to the world that these things of war will never again be used. Moreover, an enlightened lord now reigns above, while laws and ordinances order all below, so that all men attend to their own duties and on every side acknowledge allegiance to the central authority. Under such circumstances who would dare to rebel? These men are clearly no more than a band of petty outlaws—rat thieves, dog bandits, no more! They are not worth wasting breath on. Even now the provincial governor is arresting and sentencing them. What is there to worry about?"

"Why of course!" cried the Second Emperor with delight. Then he questioned the rest of the scholars, and some of them said the uprising was a rebellion and others said it was only the work of bandits. The emperor then ordered the imperial secretary to make a note of all the scholars who had called it a rebellion and have them sent to jail on charges of speaking improperly, while those who had called it the work of bandits were all dismissed without further incident. To Shu-sun T'ung he awarded twenty rolls of silk and a suit of clothes and honored him with the position of erudit.

After Shu-sun T'ung had left the palace and returned to the officials' lodge the other scholars said to him, "Master Shu-sun, what made you speak such flattery?"

"You would not understand," he replied, "but if I had not, I could hardly have escaped from the tiger's jaws!"

After this Shu-sun T'ung ran away from the capital and fled to his old home in Hsieh. When Hsieh surrendered to the Ch'u forces and Hsiang Liang reached there, Shu-sun T'ung became a follower of his but, after Hsiang Liang was defeated at Ting-t'ao, he joined the followers of King Huai of Ch'u in P'eng-ch'eng. Later King Huai was given the title of Righteous Emperor and transferred to Ch'ang-sha, but Shu-sun T'ung remained behind in P'eng-ch'eng to serve Hsiang Yü.

In the second year of Han the king of Han, accompanied by five of the other nobles, entered P'eng-ch'eng, at which time Shu-sun T'ung surrendered to him. When the king of Han was defeated and fled west, Shu-sun T'ung accordingly followed along. Shu-sun T'ung customarily wore the robes of a Confucian scholar but, because the king of Han had such a great dislike for this costume, he changed to a short robe cut in the fashion of Ch'u, which pleased the king.

When Shu-sun T'ung surrendered to the king of Han, he was accompanied by over a hundred Confucian scholars who had been studying under him. However, he did not recommend any of them to the king, but instead spent his time recommending all sorts of men who had originally been outlaws or roughnecks. His disciples began to curse him behind his back, saying, "Here we have served the master for a number of years until at last we are lucky enough to surrender and join the forces of the king of Han. But now, instead of recommending us for positions, he spends all his time recommending a bunch of gangsters! What sort of behavior is this?"

Shu-sun T'ung got word of what they were saying, and told them, "The king of Han is at the moment busy dodging arrows and missiles in a struggle for control of the world. What could a lot of scholars like you do in such a fight? Therefore I have first recommended the sort of men who can cut off the heads of enemy generals and seize their pennants. Wait a while! I won't forget you!"

The king of Han made Shu-sun T'ung an erudit and awarded him the title of lord of Chi-ssu. In the fifth year of Han, after the entire empire had been conquered, the nobles joined in conferring upon the king of Han the title of Supreme Emperor at Ting-t'ao, and Shu-sun T'ung arranged the ceremony and titles to be used. The emperor completely did away with the elaborate and irksome ritual which the Ch'in had followed and greatly simplified the rules of the court. His followers and ministers, however, were given to drinking and wrangling over their respective achievements, some shouting wildly in their drunkenness, others drawing their swords and hacking at the pillars of the palace, so that Emperor Kao-tsu worried about their behavior. Shu-sun T'ung knew that the emperor was becoming increasingly disgusted by the situation, and so he spoke to him about it. "Confucian scholars," he said, "are not much use when one is marching to conquest, but they can be of help in keeping what has already been won. I beg to summon some of the scholars of Lu who can join with my disciples in drawing up a ritual for the court."

"Can you make one that is not too difficult?" asked the emperor.

"The Five Emperors of antiquity all had different types of court music and dance; the kings of the Three Dynasties by no means followed the same ritual. Rites should be simplified or made more elaborate according to the state of the times and the people's feelings. Therefore, as Confucius has said, the way in which the Hsia, Shang, and Chou dynasties took from or added to the rites of their predecessors may be known. He meant by this that they did not merely copy their predecessors. It is my desire to select from a number of ancient codes of ritual, as well as from the ceremonies of Ch'in, and make a combination of these."

"You may try and see what you can do," replied the emperor. "But make it easy to learn! Keep in mind that it must be the sort of thing I can perform!"

Shu-sun T'ung accordingly went as an envoy to summon some thirty or more scholars of Lu. Two of the Lu scholars, however, refused to come. "You have served close to ten different masters," they replied, "and with each of them you have gained trust and honor simply by flattering them to their faces. Now the world has just been set at peace, the dead have not been properly buried, and the wounded have not risen from their beds, and yet you wish to set up rites and music for the new dynasty. But rites and music can only be set up after a dynasty has accumulated virtue for a period of a hundred years. We could never bring ourselves to take part in what you are doing, for what you are doing is not in accord with the ways of antiquity. We will never go! Now go away and do not defile us any longer!"

"True pig-headed Confucianists you are, indeed!" said Shu-sun T'ung, laughing. "You do not know that the times have changed!"

Shu-sun T'ung eventually returned west to the capital, accompanied by the thirty or so scholars he had summoned. There, with the learned men who acted as the emperor's advisers and his own disciples, making up a group of over a hundred, he stretched ropes and constructed a pavilion out in the open where for over a month he and the others worked out the ritual. Then he asked the emperor to come and see what he thought of it. "I can do that all right!" said the emperor when he had seen it, and ordered it to be put into effect, instructing all the officials to practice it so that it could be used in the tenth month at the beginning of the year.

In the seventh year, with the completion of the Palace of Lasting Joy, all the nobles and officials came to court to attend the ceremony in the tenth month. Before dawn the master of guests, who was in charge of the ritual, led the participants in order of rank through the gate leading to the hall. Within the courtyard the chariots and cavalry were drawn up. The foot soldiers and palace guards stood with their weapons at attention and their banners and pennants unfurled, passing the order along to the participants to hurry on their way. At the foot of the hall stood the palace attendants, lined up on either side of the stairway, several hundred on each step. The distinguished officials, nobles, generals, and other army officers took their places on the west side of the hall facing east, while the civil officials from the chancellor on down proceeded to the east side of the hall facing west. The master of ceremonies then appointed men to relay instructions to the nine degrees of guests.

At this point the emperor, borne on a litter, appeared from the inner rooms, the hundred officials holding banners and announcing his arrival. Then each of the guests, from the nobles and kings down to the officials of six hundred piculs' salary, was summoned in turn to come forward and present his congratulations, and from the nobles down every one trembled with awe and reverence.

When the ceremony was finished ritual wine was brought out. All those seated in attendance in the hall bowed their heads to the floor and then, in the order of their rank, each rose and drank a toast to the emperor. The grand secretary was charged with seeing that the regulations were followed, and anyone who did not perform the ceremony correctly was promptly pulled out of line and expelled from the hall. During the drinking which followed the formal audience there was no one who dared to quarrel or misbehave in the least. With this, Emperor Kao-tsu announced, "Today for the first time I realize how exalted a thing it is to be an emperor!" He appointed Shu-sun T'ung his master of ritual and awarded him five hundred catties of gold.

Shu-sun T'ung took advantage of the opportunity to speak to the emperor. "My disciples, students of Confucianism, have been with me a long time and worked with me in drawing up the new ceremonial. I beg Your Majesty to make them officials." The emperor accordingly made all of them palace attendants. When Shu-sun T'ung emerged from his audience with the emperor he proceeded to give away the entire five hundred catties of gold to the scholars who had worked with him. "Master Shu-sun is a true sage!" they all exclaimed with delight. "He knows just what is important and appropriate for the times."

In the ninth year of Han, Emperor Kao-tsu transferred Shu-sun T'ung to the position of grand tutor to the heir apparent. Later, in the twelfth year, when Kao-tsu was considering removing the heir apparent and putting Ju-i, the king of Chao, in his place, Shu-sun T'ung remonstrated with him. "In ancient times," he said, "Duke Hsien of Chin, because of his love for Princess Li, removed the heir apparent and set up her son Hsi-ch'i in his place, and as a result the state of Chin was thrown into chaos for several decades and became a laughing-stock before the world. Because the First Emperor of Ch'in did not decide in time to designate Prince Fu-su as his heir, he made it possible for the eunuch Chao Kao, after his death, to set up Hu-hai by trickery and thus bring about the destruction of the dynastic altars. This last is a case Your Majesty witnessed in person. Now the present heir apparent is kind and filial, and all the world has heard of his fame. It was his mother, Empress Lü, who shared your struggles to power and ate with you the insipid fare of poverty! How can you turn your back upon them now? If Your Majesty persists in this desire to cast aside the legitimate heir and set up a junior in his place, I beg that before the deed is done I be granted the executioner's axe, and let the blood from my severed neck drench this ground!"

"That is enough!" said the emperor. "I was only joking, anyway."

"The heir apparent is the foundation of the empire," protested Shu-sun T'ung. "If the foundation once should rock, the whole empire would rock! How can Your Majesty jest about such a matter?"

"I shall do as you say," said the emperor. Later the emperor gave a banquet and, when he saw the venerable guests whom Chang Liang had invited attending the heir apparent and appearing in court, he abandoned once for all his intention of changing the heir.

After Kao-tsu had passed away, and Emperor Hui had come to the throne, he sent for Shu-sun T'ung. "None of the officials know what sort of ceremonies should be performed at the funerary park and temple of the former emperor," he complained, and transferred Shu-sun T'ung back to the position of master of ritual. Shu-sun T'ung established the ceremonial rules for the ancestral temples of the dynasty, and settled the various ceremonial procedures for the Han as a whole, all set down in works which he wrote during his time as master of ritual.

When Emperor Hui went to the eastern side of the palace grounds to pay his formal respects to his mother, Empress Dowager Lü, in the Palace of Lasting Joy, or visited her informally at other times, it was often necessary to stop the passers-by and clear the path for him. For this reason the emperor had an elevated walk built above the path from the main palace to the Palace of Lasting Joy and extending along the south side of the arsenal.

After reporting some other affairs to the throne one day, Shu-sun T'ung asked for a moment of leisure to speak to the emperor in private. "Why has Your Majesty had this elevated walk built?" he asked. "The robes and caps of Emperor Kao-tsu, when they are taken out of his tomb and brought to his funerary temple once a month, must pass beneath this walk. The temple of Kao-tsu is dedicated to the Founding Father of the Han! Surely Your Majesty will not make it necessary for your descendants in later ages to walk *above* the path leading to the temple of the Founder!"

Emperor Hui was horrified and said, "Let the walk be torn down at once!" But Shu-sun T'ung replied, "The ruler of men never makes a mistake! The walk is already built, and the common people all know about it. Now if Your Majesty were to tear it down, it would be admitting that you had made a mistake in the first place. I beg you instead to set up a second funerary temple north of the Wei River to which the late emperor's robes and caps may be taken each month. To enlarge or increase the number of ancestral temples is after all the beginning of true filial piety!"

The emperor accordingly issued an edict to the authorities to set up a second funerary temple to Kao-tsu, the establishment of which was due in fact to this elevated walk.

Emperor Hui one spring was setting out on an excursion to one of the detached palaces to enjoy himself when Shu-sun T'ung said, "In ancient times in spring they used to have something called the 'Presentation of Fruits.' Right now the cherries are ripe and might be used as an offering. While Your Majesty is in the country, I beg you to gather some cherries and offer them in the ancestral temple." The emperor approved the suggestion, and from this arose the custom of making offerings of various kinds of fruit.

The Grand Historian remarks: There is a saying that the pelt of one fox will not make a costly robe of fur, one limb of a tree will not do for the rafters of a tall pavilion, and the wisdom of one man alone cannot bring about the great ages of the Three Dynasties of old. How true! Kao-tsu, who rose from humble beginnings to conquer all within the seas, knew all there was to know, one may say, about strategies and the use of arms. And yet Liu Ching stepped down from his little cart and made a single suggestion which assured the security of the dynasty for countless years to come. Truly, no one has a monopoly on wisdom!

Shu-sun T'ung placed his hopes in the world and calculated what was needed; in planning rites and in all his other actions, he changed with the times, until in the end he became the father of Confucian scholars for the house of Han. The greatest directness seems roundabout, people say. Even the Way itself twists and turns. Is this perhaps what they mean?

Shih chi 100: The Biographies of Chi Pu and Lüan Pu

Because he was able to swallow his pride and make himself subservient, Chi Pu at last became an important official. Lüan Pu refused to be intimidated by might or betray his duty to the dead. Thus I made The Biographies of Chi Pu and Lüan Pu.

Chi Pu

Chi Pu was a native of Ch'u, where he enjoyed a reputation for his spirited and cavalier behavior.[1] Hsiang Yü put him in charge of a body of troops, and he several times made serious trouble for Kao-tsu. After Hsiang Yü was destroyed Kao-tsu ordered a search made for Chi Pu, offering a reward of a thousand pieces of gold for his capture and threatening extermination of the entire family to the third degree of anyone who dared to quarter or hide him.

Chi Pu hid at the home of a Mr. Chou of P'u-yang. "The emperor is making a frantic search for you, general," said Mr. Chou. "Your trail, I am afraid, will eventually lead the searchers to my house. If you are willing to do as I say, I will venture to suggest a plan for you. But if you are not willing, then I must ask you to cut your throat before anything happens."

Chi Pu agreed to do anything he said. Mr. Chou thereupon shaved Chi Pu's head, put a collar around his neck, dressed him in coarse clothes of hair and, placing him in a covered cart along with twenty or thirty of the slaves from his household, took him to the home of

---

[1] It is difficult to pin down the exact meaning of *jen-hsia* and other terms with the element *hsia*, and even more difficult to find English equivalents. The men designated by these terms were at best a sort of chivalrous "redressors of wrongs" who maintained their own bands of retainers, undertook private vendettas or similar favors for others, and took great pride in their reputations for recklessness, honor, and faithfulness to their word. At worst they were no more than swaggering gangster bosses who took the law completely into their own hands. *Shih chi* 124 deals with the lives of the more famous of these "wandering knights."

Chu Chia in Lu to sell. Chu Chia, guessing that it was Chi Pu, bought him and set him to work in the fields. He admonished his son, saying, "When it comes to the work in the fields, do as this slave says, and see that you eat all your meals with him!" Chu Chia himself mounted a one-horse carriage and journeyed to Lo-yang to visit Lord T'eng, the marquis of Ju-yin.

Lord T'eng put Chu Chia up at his home and for several days they drank together, during which time Chu Chia took the opportunity to speak about Chi Pu. "What great crime is Chi Pu guilty of," he asked, "that the emperor should seek for him so ruthlessly?"

"When Chi Pu was fighting for Hsiang Yü he several times caused the emperor serious trouble. The emperor is deeply resentful over this and is therefore determined to seize him," said Lord T'eng.

"In your estimation, what sort of man is Chi Pu?" asked Chu Chia.

"A worthy man," Lord T'eng replied.

"Every subject serves his own lord," Chou Chia continued. "When Chi Pu served Hsiang Yü, he was merely doing his duty. Does the emperor think he can wipe out all of Hsiang Yü's former followers? The emperor has only just won control of the world. Now if he is to search all over for one man simply because of some private resentment he bears, what an example of pettiness he will be showing to the world!

"Furthermore, if Chi Pu is a worthy man as you say, and if the emperor continues to search for him with such diligence, he is sure to flee either to the barbarians in the north or the people of Yüeh in the south. This driving fine men to the aid of enemy states because of resentment is the sort of thing that led to Wu Tzu-hsü's thrashing the corpse of King P'ing of Ch'u.[2] Why do you not at some propitious moment speak to the emperor on his behalf?"

Lord T'eng was aware that Chu Chia was renowned as a chivalrous gentleman and he guessed that Chi Pu was hiding at his home. So he consented to Chu Chia's request and, when he found the emperor at leisure, spoke to him as Chu Chia had suggested. The emperor

[2] Because of the cruel treatment which King P'ing of Ch'u inflicted upon his father and older brother, Wu Tzu-hsü fled from Ch'u and went to the aid of Ch'u's enemy, the state of Wu. When the army of Wu eventually conquered Ch'u, Wu Tzu-hsü exhumed the corpse of King P'ing from its grave and thrashed it to avenge the wrong. His biography is the subject of *Shih chi* 66.

accordingly pardoned Chi Pu. Gentlemen of the day all admired Chi Pu for being able to swallow his pride and assume a subservient role, while Chu Chia also became famous in his time because of the incident. Chi Pu was summoned to appear before the emperor, and begged forgiveness for his offense. The emperor honored him with the post of palace attendant.

During the reign of Emperor Hui he was made general of palace attendants. The *Shan-yü* once sent an insulting and immodest letter to Empress Lü.[3] Empress Lü was furious and summoned all the generals to discuss what should be done. Fan K'uai, the supreme general, said, "I beg to be given a force of a hundred thousand men, and I shall trample the Hsiung-nu underfoot!"

All the other generals, toadying to the empress's will, seconded the request, but Chi Pu announced, "Fan K'uai deserves to be beheaded! Emperor Kao-tsu in command of a force of over three hundred thousand[4] met serious difficulty from the Hsiung-nu at P'ing-ch'eng. How does Fan K'uai think he is going to take a hundred thousand men and 'trample the Hsiung-nu underfoot'? He is lying to Her Majesty's face! Furthermore, it was because the Ch'in government was so occupied with barbarian affairs that Ch'en She and the rest were able to start a rebellion. The wounds of that strife have still not healed, yet Fan K'uai speaks flattery to Her Majesty's face and would bring new unrest to the empire!"

At these words the entire throne room was filled with fear. Empress Lü dismissed the court and did not again bring up the question of a campaign against the Hsiung-nu.

Chi Pu became governor of Ho-tung Province. In the time of Emperor Wen someone praised him as a worthy man, whereupon Emperor Wen summoned him to the capital, expecting to make him grand secretary. Someone else, however, reported that Chi Pu was reckless, difficult when in his cups, and hard to get to know. When Chi Pu arrived the emperor kept him at the governor's lodge for a month and then dismissed him and sent him back to Ho-tung. On the occa-

[3] The Hsiung-nu ruler wrote Empress Lü suggesting that, since both were old and alone, they should marry. The empress was in favor of launching an immediate military expedition to avenge the insult.
[4] The text erroneously reads "four hundred thousand."

sion of his departure Chi Pu appeared before the emperor and said, "Although I was without distinction, I received undeserved favor, and humbly and diligently went to pursue my duties in Ho-tung. Then for no apparent reason Your Majesty summoned me to the capital. It must have been that someone gave an exaggerated report of my worth. Yet, now that I have arrived, I am assigned no new task, but instead am dismissed and sent back again. I suppose this is because this time some person has spoken ill of me. In other words, because of one man's recommendation Your Majesty summoned me, and because of one man's slander I am now being dismissed. I fear that if such an affair should come to the ears of knowledgeable men of the world, they might draw conclusions concerning Your Majesty's judgment."

The emperor sat for a long while in embarrassed silence and at last said, "Ho-tung is a province of vital importance to me. Therefore I wished to make a special point of summoning you for the position, that is all." Chi Pu took his leave and went back to his post.

There was a rhetorician named Master Ts'ao Ch'iu, a native of Ch'u, who from time to time made up to influential people with an eye to receiving money. He performed services for the eunuch Chao T'an and other famous people, and was a friend of Tou Ch'ang-chün, Emperor Ching's uncle.

Chi Pu, hearing of this, sent a letter reprimanding Tou Ch'ang-chün. "From what I have heard, Ts'ao Ch'iu is not a good man," he wrote. "I would not have anything to do with him if I were you!"

It happened that Ts'ao Ch'iu was making a visit to his native place and he asked Tou Ch'ang-chün to give him a letter of introduction to Chi Pu. "General Chi does not care for you," replied Tou Ch'ang-chün. "I advise you not to go see him."

But Ts'ao Ch'iu pressed his request until he got the letter and, when he started on his way, he sent a man ahead to deliver it. As might be expected, Chi Pu awaited Ts'ao Ch'iu's visit with great anger. When Ts'ao Ch'iu appeared he gave only a slight bow and said to Chi Pu, "People in Ch'u have a saying that 'a hundred catties of pure gold are not as good as one of Chi Pu's promises.' I wonder how you have managed to get such a reputation in this region of Liang and Ch'u?

Now I am a man of Ch'u and you are a man of Ch'u as well. In the course of my travels I could spread your fame all over the world. Would that not be even better than being famous in Liang and Ch'u? Why do you object to me so?"

With this Chi Pu took a great liking to Ts'ao Ch'iu and insisted upon keeping him at his home for several months, treating him as an honored guest and giving him a generous farewell party. As a result of Ts'ao Ch'iu's efforts to spread his fame, Chi Pu's renown grew even greater than before.

Chi Pu's younger brother Chi Hsin wielded great influence in the area within the Pass. He treated others respectfully and was fond of performing chivalrous actions, so that for a thousand miles around men vied with one another for the honor of serving him to the death. He once murdered a man and fled to Wu, getting Yüan Ang to hide him. He looked up to Yüan Ang as a superior and treated Kuan Fu, Chi Fu, and others like younger brothers. He once acted as marshal for the military commander, Chih Tu, who did not dare to treat him disrespectfully. Many of the young men of the time, when they carried out some deed or other, would often claim that they were secretly acting in Chi Hsin's name. In their day Chi Hsin and Chi Pu were both renowned throughout the area within the Pass, the former for his bravery and the latter for the way he stuck by his word.

Chi Pu's mother's younger brother, Lord Ting, was a general of Ch'u. While serving under Hsiang Yü he once pursued Kao-tsu and his men west of P'eng-ch'eng. Lord Ting's forces bore down upon them and the men had closed swords when Kao-tsu, sorely pressed, turned about and said to Lord Ting, "Why should two worthy men like us vex one another in this way?" With this, Lord Ting called off his troops and withdrew, allowing Kao-tsu to escape unharmed.

After Hsiang Yü had been destroyed Lord Ting came to visit Kao-tsu. Kao-tsu had him seized and paraded before his army, announcing, "Lord Ting was disloyal in his service to Hsiang Yu. It was none other than he who caused Hsiang Yü to lose the empire!" Then he ordered Lord Ting beheaded. "I want to make sure," he said, "that no subject hereafter shall imitate Lord Ting's example!"

Lüan Pu

Lüan Pu was a native of Liang. When P'eng Yüeh, the king of Liang, was still a commoner he and Lüan Pu were friends. Finding themselves impoverished, they traveled together to Ch'i to seek employment as wage laborers, becoming bond servants to a wine maker. After several years P'eng Yüeh went off to the marsh of Chü-yeh and became a bandit, but Lüan Pu was seized and sold as a slave in Yen. There he carried out a vendetta for his master, and the Yen general Tsang Tu, hearing of this, raised him to the position of colonel. Later, after Tsang Tu became king of Yen, he made Lüan Pu a general.

When Tsang Tu revolted, the Han forces attacked Yen and took Lüan Pu prisoner. P'eng Yüeh, the king of Liang, hearing of this, sent word to the emperor asking that he be allowed to ransom Lüan Pu and make him a courtier of Liang. The request was granted and Lüan Pu was sent on a mission to Ch'i but, before he had returned, Kao-tsu summoned P'eng Yüeh to the capital, accused him of plotting revolt, and executed him along with the members of his family to the third degree. This done, he had the head of P'eng Yüeh exposed in the city of Lo-yang with an edict posted below it reading, "Whoever shall dare to dispose of or look after this head shall be immediately arrested."

When Lüan Pu passed by on his way back from Ch'i, he reported on his mission before the head of P'eng Yüeh, sacrificed to it, and lamented. The officials arrested Lüan Pu and submitted an account of what had happened. The emperor had Lüan Pu brought before him and cursed him, saying, "Were you plotting rebellion along with P'eng Yüeh? I forbade any man to tend to his head, yet you ventured to sacrifice and weep for it. It is clear that you are as disloyal as P'eng Yüeh. Boil this man alive at once!"

After the necessary preparations, Lüan Pu was dragged forward and was about to be thrown into the boiling water when he turned to the emperor and said, "I beg to speak one word before I die."

"What is it you would say?" asked the emperor.

"When Your Majesty was in trouble at P'eng-ch'eng and suffered defeat in the area of Jung-yang and Ch'eng-kao it was only because

P'eng Yüeh occupied the region of Liang and cooperated with the Han forces in harassing the Ch'u armies that Hsiang Yü was in the end unable to advance farther west. At that time all depended upon a nod from P'eng Yüeh. If he joined with Ch'u, then Han would be lost; if he joined with Han, then Ch'u would be defeated. Again, when the armies came together at Kai-hsia, if P'eng Yüeh had not appeared, Hsiang Yü would never have been destroyed.

"After the world was at peace P'eng Yüeh received the split tallies and the rites of enfeoffment as a king, and his hope was that he might hand them down to his heirs for ten thousand generations. Yet recently Your Majesty sent out a single call for troops from Liang and, because King P'eng was ill and did not respond, you suspected him of disaffection. And then, before evidence of revolt had even been found, he was subjected to a cruel inquisition and he and his family wiped out. Such treatment must surely fill every other worthy minister with terror and doubt. Now that King P'eng is dead I too will be better off dead than alive. I beg you to proceed with the boiling!"

Hearing these words, the emperor pardoned his offense, set him free, and made him a colonel.

During the reign of Emperor Wen, Lüan Pu became prime minister of Yen and later a general. He used to say, "If, when things are going poorly, a man cannot endure some shame and modify his ambitions, he is no man. And if, when he has became rich and honored, he cannot fulfill his heart's desires, he is no sage!" Accordingly he repaid with great generosity all those who in the past had done him favors and, in the case of those he bore grudges against, he used the law to wipe them out.

When the army of Wu revolted he won military merit and was enfeoffed as marquis of Yü, and once more became prime minister of Yen. Throughout Yen and Ch'i altars were set up to him, called "Altars of Lord Lüan." He died in the fifth year of the middle era of the reign of Emperor Ching [145 B.C]. His son Lüan Fen succeeded to the marquisate and was made master of ritual, but he was condemned for performing sacrifices in a manner at variance with the law and his territory taken away.

The Grand Historian remarks: With a spirit like that of Hsiang Yü, Chi Pu made a name for daring in Ch'u. From time to time he commanded armies and several times seized the enemy pennants. He deserves to be called a brave man. Yet he suffered punishment and disgrace and became a slave and did not commit suicide. Why did he stoop to this? Because he chose to rely upon his abilities. Therefore he suffered disgrace without shame, for there were things he hoped to accomplish and he was not yet satisfied. Thus in the end he became a renowned general of Han. Truly the wise man regards death as a grave thing. When slaves and scullion maids and such mean people in their despair commit suicide it is not because they are brave; it is because they know that their plans and hopes will never again have a chance of coming true!

Lüan Pu wept for P'eng Yüeh and hastened to the boiling water as though it were his true destination. This is indeed what it means to know the right place to die, not counting death as important in itself. The most determined men of ancient times could do no better than these two!

The Second Era of Han History
(PARTS VII–XI)

The second stage of Han history embraces the reigns of Emperor Hui, Empress Lü, Emperor Wen, and Emperor Ching, or the period from the death of Emperor Kao-tsu in 195 B.C. to the accession of Emperor Wu in 141 B.C. For the empire as a whole these were relatively uneventful years. The common people, recovering from the wars and confusion which had accompanied the establishment of the dynasty, appear to have enjoyed a considerable measure of contentment and well-being, though Ssu-ma Ch'ien makes little more than passing reference to their condition. Chinese historians tend to take note of the common people only when they are starving or restless—that is, when they pose a threat to their rulers. When they disappear from the pages of history, as they do in these early years of the Han, we may suppose that their lot was on the whole a happy one.

A similar contentment, however, did not prevail within the ruling house, and much of what follows centers around two political crises that threatened the very life of the dynasty: the usurpation of power by the members of the Lü family, and the Revolt of the Seven Kingdoms.

With the death of Kao-tsu, the throne passed to his young son, who became Emperor Hui, but the real power was in the hands of the new ruler's strong-willed mother Empress Dowager Lü, the widow of Kao-tsu. When Emperor Hui died in 188 B.C. the empress dowager placed on the throne two boy rulers in succession, children of other men whom she attempted to pass off as sons of the emperor, while she herself continued to rule as before. Up until her death in 180 B.C. she did everything in her power to consolidate the position of her own clan, having her male relatives appointed to high posts at court, marrying their daughters to members of the imperial family, and even contriving to enfeoff them as marquises and kings. In doing so, she aroused bitter animosity among the peers of the Liu family and the high ministers who remained loyal to them, and it was only her remarkable stubbornness and audacity, coupled with an astute political intelligence, that enabled her to achieve the success she did. She hoped to maneuver her relatives into a position of sufficient strength to enable them to survive the opposition they would surely face after her death. But her hopes were in vain. Within a few months of her demise the members of her clan, who seemed to share none of her craft or strength of character, allowed themselves to be outwitted and toppled from power by the Liu peers and the high officials. The entire Lü clan was massacred and Kao-tsu's son Liu Heng, the king of Tai, posthumously known as Emperor Wen, was summoned to take the throne.

The second crisis occurred in 154 B.C., the third year of the reign of Emperor Wen's successor, Emperor Ching. The founder of the Han, hoping to insure greater stability to his regime, had granted fiefs both to his followers and to the male members of his family. The first group—those who did not belong to the imperial family—fared badly from the beginning. One by one, as they were tempted into futile revolt or incurred the suspicion of revolt, they were cut down in battle, executed, or forced to flee from China. By the end of Kao-tsu's reign all but one of the feudal kingdoms were in the hands of members of the imperial family.

The central court appointed "tutors" to the feudal kings to guide their footsteps in the Way, and prime ministers to see that they administered their domains properly, but with these exceptions the kings were free to select their own officials and rule as they pleased. During the long years of peace and prosperity under Emperor Wen a number of these vassal kings, by exploiting the natural resources of their lands, inviting fugitives from other regions to swell their populations, and building up large armies, succeeded in acquiring such wealth and power that they rivaled the supreme ruler himself. Emperor Wen was aware of the danger inherent in such a situation, but preferred whenever possible to take a conciliatory attitude, hoping that the kings would be deterred by moral considerations from open insubordination. His son and successor Emperor Ching, however, egged on by his trusted adviser Ch'ao Ts'o, adopted sterner measures, accusing the kings of various offenses, depriving them of territory, and taking steps to curb their powers. Angered by the unprecedented severity of such treatment and unwilling to sit by while their domains were dismembered, seven of the most powerful of them, led by the kings of Wu and Ch'u, called out their troops in revolt and began a march on the capital. It would appear, however, that they had badly underestimated the power and prestige of the dynasty. After a brief period of panic, during which the emperor reluctantly ordered the execution of Ch'ao Ts'o in an effort at appeasement, the central court rallied its forces and quickly put an end to the rebellion. By their rashness the kings had succeeded only in alerting the Han court to the gravity of the situation and speeding the process of their own debilitation. To prevent a recurrence of revolt, Emperor Ching and his successor, Emperor Wu, little by little deprived the vassal kings of all rights to the actual administration of their domains and continued to divide up and whittle away their lands until, as Ssu-ma Ch'ien says, they "grew so poor that they were obliged to ride about in oxcarts" in the manner of commoners.

Philosophies of Government

China in late Chou times saw the rise of a number of schools of philosophy which competed for the attention of the rulers of the period. Although some of these schools took an interest in questions of metaphysics, epistemology, and the moral life of the individual, their principal concern was invariably politics—the "way of the ruler." Of these so-called hundred schools of earlier times only three continued to be of any real importance in the Han period: the Confucian, the Legalist, and the Taoist, the last often referred to as "the teachings of the Yellow Emperor and Lao Tzu." Although Confucianism later succeeded in securing state support and having itself declared the orthodox philosophy of the government, during the period covered in this volume we find exponents of all three doctrines holding high positions at court. As early as pre-Ch'in times there had been considerable exchanging of ideas and terms among the three schools, and this process continued in the Han, so that it is often difficult to decide which school a particular scholar or official belonged to; most educated men of the period studied all three doctrines and chose their ideas at random to fit practical exigencies. Behind the words and actions of the rulers and their ministers at various times, however, we may still distinguish the basic political attitudes of each of the three schools of antiquity.

TAOISM. First was the attitude of Taoist quietism, with its philosophy of "nonaction." For the empire as a whole Taoism advocated a policy of laissez-faire, allowing the people to follow their desires and instincts without interference from the government. This, it was believed, would lead to an era of peace, stability, and rustic content. Those officials who followed Taoist teachings, the most famous among them being the prime minister Ts'ao Ts'an, therefore aimed at self-effacement and anonymity, avoiding wherever possible any positive exercise of authority. During the reigns of Empress Lü and Emperor Wen, as has often been pointed out, the government as a whole pursued just such a laissez-faire policy, which allowed the nation to recover from the effects of the previous civil strife and attain a high level of prosperity. But whether this was actually done at the instigation of Taoist-minded officials, or whether the rulers were even conscious that they were following Taoist theories, is a matter of conjecture. At any rate, this so-called Taoist period was only a temporary phase. By the end of Emperor Wen's reign it had come to be recognized that such a course of action created as many problems as it solved. If the empire was ever to be freed from the threat of periodic invasion by the Hsiung-nu tribes to the north, if the growing power of the feudal lords was to be curbed, if law and order were to be enforced and the powerful families and local "bosses" that had appeared in the countryside were to be kept in check, it was obvious that the central court would have to adopt a more positive approach. Emperor Ching set out to do just this, and from his reign on, though Taoism continued to flourish as a semireligious cult among the people, it dropped almost out of sight in discussions of the philosophy of rule.

LEGALISM. As a matter of fact, this early Han period of laissez-faire government can just as well be explained as a natural reaction against the practices of Legalism, the state philosophy of the preceding Ch'in dynasty. The fathers of the Legalist school in Chou times—Lord Shang, Shen Pu-hai, and Han Fei Tzu—had advocated the establishment of a strong central government, the suppression of feudalism, and the regimentation of the people by stern and inflexible laws; and these measures the First Emperor of the Ch'in had proceeded to carry out with great energy and ruthlessness. It was understandable, therefore, that the founders of the Han, who had been commoners under the First Emperor, should desire, when they came to power, to avoid the same errors that had brought the Ch'in to such an expeditious end. Thus we find Kao-tsu drastically simplifying the legal code, lightening the burden of taxation on the people, and parceling out fiefs to his followers and kin. But the Han rulers soon discovered that this type of limited government, though ingratiating enough to the people as a whole, would hardly suffice for a vast, unified empire the size of China. Before long ministers appeared at court who, though they sometimes took pains to disguise the source of their ideas, advocated a return to characteristically Legalist policies. Ch'ao Ts'o, the ill-fated adviser to Emperor Ching, who attempted to weaken the power of the vassal kings, is perhaps the best example. Unlike Taoism, the philosophy of "no-government," Legalism, far from dropping out of sight, continued to grow in influence until it was able to come completely out in the open in the reign of Emperor Wu and challenge its only remaining rival, Confucianism. Most of the history of the following two thousand years of Chinese political philosophy is concerned with the struggle between the exponents of these two rival theories of rule, the Legalist-minded advocates of government by force, and the Confucian-minded advocates of government by virtue.

CONFUCIANISM. There is, of course, a great deal more to Confucianism than the theory of government by virtue, but it is this aspect that is most in evidence in the pronouncements of the early Han rulers and their advisers. As pointed out by Arthur Waley in the introduction to his *Analects of Confucius,* the word *te,* which I have for the sake of expedience translated as "virtue," actually denotes a kind of moral force which emanates from the truly good ruler and enables him to convert his people, and even the inhabitants of foreign lands, to the practice of goodness. Indeed, so great is the power of this force that its influence extends to the world of nature and the supernatural, calling forth in the reign of its possessor the tokens of cosmic approval: formations of many-colored clouds, rains of sweet dew, and the appearance of fabulous beasts and birds such as the unicorn and the phoenix. But if it is the personal moral power or virtue of the ruler, and not the threat of physical force, which insures the effectiveness of his rule, then failures in government must conversely be due to a lack of virtue in the sovereign himself. Hence the Confucian ruler must ultimately hold himself morally responsible for disorders within his realm, for defiance among the barbarian tribes surrounding China, and for signs of cosmic confusion and displeasure such as droughts, earthquakes, locusts, eclipses, and similar prodigious occurrences in nature.

The reign of Emperor Wen represents an interesting combination of the Taoist ideal of "nonaction" and the Confucian theory of government by virtue, a combination characteristic of early Han times. In his personal life, we are told, Emperor Wen set an example for his people in simplicity and frugal living. In his relations with the Hsiung-nu tribes, as well as with the recalcitrant kings of his own family, he declined the use of force wherever possible, preferring to buy peace from the Hsiung-nu with tribute and to attempt to reform his kinsmen by leniency and gentle reprimand. And when some unfavorable portent appeared in the form of an eclipse or a comet, he publicly proclaimed his concern and sought to discover what error of his had brought it about.

His edicts are model expressions of the Confucian ideal of the good ruler: full of humble protestations of his own lack of virtue and pleas for guidance from his ministers and his people. They were written, I believe, in all sincerity, and should be read in that spirit, though I admit that this may be difficult for anyone familiar with the endless vain and hypocritical imitations of them which fill the annals of later Chinese rulers. That Emperor Wen did not always succeed in living up to the sentiments proclaimed in his edicts is obvious from the anecdotes related about him in the chapters dealing with his ministers. But this is hardly reason for doubting the sincerity of his purpose.

The Position of Women

One more aspect of the narrative, not necessarily related to any particular school of philosophy but having its roots far deeper in the structure of Chinese society, requires comment here, and this is the extraordinary power of older women. The Chinese family system demanded that children accord old people in general and their parents in particular the utmost respect and obedience, and we often find high officials retiring from their posts or declining to undertake some dangerous task because of their obligations to their parents. But because wives have a way of outliving their husbands, and because in most cases a ruler or a noble cannot become such until the death of his father, it is generally the mothers rather than the fathers of eminent men who figure most prominently in the *Shih chi* narrative. Thus Ssu-ma Chi'en devotes one chapter among his annals of rulers to an empress dowager, and another among the histories of eminent families to the consorts of the emperors. It is true that, with the exception of Empress Lü, whom I shall discuss below, we do not find the women in the *Shih chi* meddling as openly in politics as they do in earlier historical works, such as the *Tso chuan*. And yet time and again we discover them maneuvering behind the scenes to bring pressure upon their lovers and sons; in scene after scene we see concubines dissolving into persuasive tears before their lords, or testy old women carrying on like spoiled children until they get their way with their sons. At no point do the histories of imperial Rome and of China diverge more sharply than in this question of the respect and awe accorded the mothers of rulers. Not only do we find no Neros in the Han annals; the mere suggestion that a king or an emperor had failed to treat his mother with the proper deference would be sufficient to cast a shadow of guilt over his whole regime. The figure of the determined matriarch contriving to dictate the lives of her offspring is familiar enough to the Western reader that he will have no trouble recognizing her Chinese counterpart. I mention the subject here only because he may not be quite prepared for the degree to which the Chinese *grande dame* was honored and heeded in this role. Therefore, when the reader finds a Han emperor replying to the advice of his counselors with words to the effect that "I will have to ask my mother," I would caution him that, whatever his own reaction may be, he is expected from the traditional Chinese point of view not to snicker but to be filled with a warm glow of admiration.

I have said that the case of Empress Lü was an exception in Han times, and happily this is true for later Chinese history as well. She had actively aided her husband in his long and bitter struggle to gain control of the empire, and it was not surprising that, after his death, she should dominate her son, Emperor Hui, and the two child rulers whom she set up, one after the other, to succeed him. But her cruel and vindictive temperament and the irregular steps she took to strengthen the position of her own clan at court eventually imperiled the future of the dynasty. After her death and the overthrow of the Lü clan the Han ministers were concerned in selecting a new emperor to find one whose mother would not turn into another Empress Lü, and later Chinese statesmen have been equally mindful of the threat posed by overambitious empress dowagers and their male kin. Ssu-ma Ch'ien, when he wrote his account of the period, realistically treated the reigns of Emperor Hui and Empress Lü as one unit, since she had exercised the real power throughout, entitling his chapter "The Basic Annals of Empress Lü." But when Pan Ku came to rework the *Shih chi* material for his *Han shu* or "History of the Former Han," he found it unseemly that Emperor Hui should be lumped together with his mother, and he accordingly removed the account of the young ruler's brief reign and created a separate "Annals of Emperor Hui." Some six centuries later, in the early years of the T'ang dynasty, an empress dowager came to power who, not content merely to rule in the name of a puppet, as Empress Lü had done, went so far as to declare herself the foundress of a new dynasty before death brought an end to her usurpations. With this frightening example in mind, Chinese historiographers concluded that even Pan Ku's arrangement was unsatisfactory and declared that it was improper for a woman to be represented in the "annals" section of a history at all, since a woman attempting to exercise the functions of a "Son of Heaven" was a contradiction in terms. Thus, although the mothers of rulers continued as before to exert great influence in court politics, they never received in later Chinese histories such open and realistic recognition of their power as Ssu-ma Ch'ien had accorded them.

The Character of the Period

The chapters of the *Shih chi* dealing with the overthrow of the hated Ch'in and the founding of the Han are characterized by an air

The Second Era of Han History

of heroic vigor and optimism. The leaders of the era—the military adventurer Hsiang Yü; the famous aides to Kao-tsu, Chang Liang, Hsiao Ho, and Han Hsin; the founder of the dynasty himself, who fought his way up from the post of a petty clerk to become supreme ruler of the empire—have won an immortal place in the memory of the Chinese people. Time and again, when the poets and philosophers of later ages seek for symbols of tragic downfall or stubborn perseverance, political astuteness or craft in battle, it is to the history of this period that they turn. Indeed, when Ssu-ma Ch'ien came to compile his account of the establishment of the dynasty, less than a hundred years later, the men and events of the period had already taken on a legendary and larger-than-life quality.

To these the events of the succeeding era form a striking contrast. "All within the seas"—the world of ancient China—is finally at peace; there are no more military upstarts to threaten the nation with civil strife, and only the occasional annoyance of plundering raids by the Hsiung-nu tribes to the north. Revolution and conquest are temporarily a thing of the past, and the rulers must settle down to work out the problems of administering their new domains, consolidating their power, and insuring the continuance of the dynasty. In comparison with their fathers and predecessors, the men of this period seem to have dwindled in stature; neither the crises they face nor the actions they take are on the former grand scale. Whereas Ssu-ma Ch'ien characterized the earlier leaders as courageous and far-sighted, his highest praise in these chapters goes to those who are circumspect, for circumspection is the quality most appropriate to this new era in Han history. The scope of the historian's narrative has shrunk to fit his subject, and we find him more and more involved in accounts of elaborate plots at court, grubby family squabbles, and that dullest of the departments of history, genealogy. Instead of the glorious deeds and battles of the previous age, we read of a high official who utilized his spare time to wash his father's dirty underwear, of a king who slammed a door on his grandmother's fingers, and of two princes who fell into a fatal quarrel over a game of chess. Slowly, imperceptibly, as the narrative draws nearer to the historian's own time, it takes on a mood of sordidness and disillusion, a mood which will deepen to despair in the translations of the second volume. The dynasty is still young, but already it is showing the signs of moral decay.

The reader is not likely to find here much to excite admiration or a feeling of moral uplift, except perhaps the poetry of Ch'ü Yüan and Chia I or the edicts of Emperor Wen. But, as Ssu-ma Ch'ien no doubt believed when he wrote it, the account of the origins of decay, though scarcely uplifting, conveys its own apt and bitter wisdom. The protagonists of his tale are no longer legendary heroes but men of flesh and blood, timorous, cruel, spiteful, and petty—men as we know them in real life—and his subject is the oldest axiom of the moralists, the corrosive effects of power.

Part VII
THE RULERS

Shih chi 9: The Basic Annals of Empress Lü

Emperor Hui passed away at an early age and the Lü family were filled with uneasiness. When they heaped honor and position on Lü Ch'an and Lü Lu the feudal lords began to plot against them, and when they murdered Liu Ju-i and Liu Yu, the kings of Chao, the high ministers were filled with fear and mistrust. In the end disaster fell on the house of Lü. Thus I made The Basic Annals of Empress Dowager Lü.

Empress Dowager Lü was the consort of Kao-tsu from the time when he was still a commoner. She bore him Emperor Hui the Filial and the queen mother, Princess Yüan of Lu. When Kao-tsu became king of Han he took into his service Lady Ch'i of Ting-t'ao, whom he loved dearly, and she bore him a son, Liu Ju-i, king of Chao, posthumously known as Yin, the "Melancholy King."

Emperor Hui was by nature weak and soft-hearted. Kao-tsu, convinced that the boy was of a wholly different temperament from himself, wanted to remove him from the position of heir apparent and set up his son by Lady Ch'i, Ju-i, instead, "for Ju-i is just like me," he would say. Lady Ch'i always accompanied Kao-tsu on his trips east of the Pass, and day and night wept and begged that her son be set up in place of the heir apparent. Empress Lü, being well along in years, invariably stayed behind in the capital, so that she rarely saw the emperor and they became more and more estranged. Ju-i was made king of Chao and later several times came very near to replacing the future Emperor Hui as heir apparent. But, because of the objections of the high officials and the strategy devised by Chang Liang, the heir apparent was able to keep his position.

Empress Lü was a woman of very strong will. She aided Kao-tsu in the conquest of the empire, and many of the great ministers who were executed were the victims of her power. She had two older brothers, both of whom were generals. Her oldest brother, Lü Tse, marquis of Chou-lü, died in the service of the dynasty. His son Lü

T'ai was enfeoffed as marquis of Li, and his son Lü Ch'an as marquis of Chiao. Her other brother, Lü Shih-chih, was made marquis of Chien-ch'eng.

In the fourth month, the day *chia-ch'en,* of the twelfth year of his reign [June 1, 195 B.C.], Emperor Kao-tsu passed away in the Palace of Lasting Joy and the heir apparent, Emperor Hui, succeeded to the throne. At this time Kao-tsu's eight sons occupied the following positions. The oldest, Liu Fei, was king of Ch'i; he was an elder brother of Emperor Hui by a different mother; all the rest were younger than Emperor Hui. Lady Ch'i's son Liu Ju-i was king of Chao and Lady Po's son Liu Heng was king of Tai. The rest, sons of Kao-tsu by other ladies of the court, were Liu Hui, king of Liang; Liu Yu, king of Huai-yang; Liu Ch'ang, king of Huai-nan; and Liu Chien, king of Yen. Kao-tsu's younger brother Liu Chiao was king of Ch'u, and Liu P'i, the son of Kao-tsu's older brother, was king of Wu. There was one king who was not of the Liu family, Wu Ch'en, king of Ch'ang-sha, the son of Wu Jui, the lord of P'o, who had achieved merit as a minister of the Han.

Empress Lü bore the greatest hatred for Lady Ch'i and her son, the king of Chao. She gave orders for Lady Ch'i to be imprisoned in the Long Halls [1] and summoned the king of Chao to court. Three times envoys were sent back and forth, but the prime minister of Chao, Chou Ch'ang, the marquis of Chien-p'ing, told them, "Emperor Kao-tsu entrusted the king of Chao to my care, and he is still very young. Rumors have reached me that the empress dowager hates Lady Ch'i and wishes to summon her son, the king of Chao, so that she may do away with both of them. I do not dare send the king! Moreover, he is ill and cannot obey the summons."

Empress Lü was furious and proceeded to send an envoy to summon Chou Ch'ang himself. When Chou Ch'ang obeyed her order and arrived in Ch'ang-an, she dispatched someone to summon the king of Chao once more. The king set out, but before he reached the capital, Emperor Hui, compassionate by nature and aware of his mother's hatred for the king of Chao, went in person to meet him at the Pa River and accompanied him back to the palace. The emperor

[1] A designation for the women's apartments at the back of the palace.

looked out for the boy and kept him by his side, eating and sleeping with him, so that, although the empress dowager wished to kill him, she could find no opportunity.

In the first year of Emperor Hui's reign, the twelfth month, the emperor one morning rose at dawn and went out hunting, but the king of Chao, being very young, could not get up so early. When the empress dowager heard that he was in the room alone, she sent someone to bear poison and give it to him to drink. By the time Emperor Hui returned, the king of Chao was already dead. After this Liu Yu, the king of Huai-yang, was transferred to the position of king of Chao.

In the summer an edict was issued awarding Lü T'ai's father Lü Tse the posthumous title of Ling-wu or "Outstanding Warrior Marquis."

Empress Lü later cut off Lady Ch'i's hands and feet, plucked out her eyes, burned her ears, gave her a potion to drink which made her dumb, and had her thrown into the privy, calling her the "human pig."[2] After a few days, she sent for Emperor Hui and showed him the "human pig." Staring at her, he asked who the person was, and only then did he realize that it was Lady Ch'i. Thereupon he wept so bitterly that he grew ill and for over a year could not leave his bed. He sent a messenger to report to his mother, "No human being could have done such a deed as this! Since I am your son, I will never be fit to rule the empire." From this time on Emperor Hui gave himself up each day to drink and no longer took part in affairs of state, so that his illness grew worse.

In the second year of Emperor Hui's reign Liu Chiao, king of Ch'u, and Liu Fei, king of Ch'i, came to court. In the tenth month Emperor Hui held a banquet for the king of Ch'i which the empress dowager attended. Because the king of Ch'i was his elder brother, Emperor Hui seated him in the place of honor and treated him with the courtesy customary among members of the same family. Empress Lü was furious at this and ordered two goblets to be prepared with poison and placed before the king of Ch'i. Then she instructed the king

---

[2] Early Chinese privies consisted of two parts, an upper room for the user and a pit below in which swine were kept. Apparently Lady Ch'i was thrown into the lower part, hence the epithet.

to rise and propose a toast. When he did so, however, Emperor Hui also rose and picked up the other goblet, intending to join in the toast. Empress Lü, terrified, rose from her own place and overturned Emperor Hui's goblet. The king of Ch'i grew suspicious and did not dare to drink any more, but instead feigned drunkenness and left the banquet.

Later, when he learned that the goblet had indeed contained poison, he began to fear that he would not be able to escape from Ch'ang-an. Shih, the internal secretary of Ch'i, spoke to the king, saying, "The empress dowager has only two children, the emperor and Princess Yüan of Lu. Now Your Majesty possesses over seventy cities, while the princess receives the revenue from only a very few. If you were willing to donate one province to the empress dowager which could be assigned to the princess as her 'bath-town' revenue, then the empress dowager would surely be pleased and you would have nothing more to fear."

The king of Ch'i accordingly donated the province of Ch'eng-yang and honored the princess with the title of "Queen Mother of Lu." Empress Lü accepted these honors with delight and held a banquet at the Ch'i state residence. When the drinking and rejoicing were over she sent the king of Ch'i back to his kingdom.

In the third year work on the walls of Ch'ang-an was begun. By the fourth year half the work was done and in the fifth and sixth years the walls were completed. In the tenth month the various feudal lords journeyed to court to present their congratulations on the beginning of the new year.

In the seventh year, the day *mou-yin* of the eighth month [Sept. 26, 188 B.C.], Emperor Hui the Filial passed away.[3] Mourning was announced and Empress Dowager Lü lamented, but no tears fell from her eyes.

Chang Pi-ch'iang, the son of Chang Liang, was a page in the palace and, though he was only fifteen, he said to the prime minister Ch'en P'ing, "The empress dowager had only this one son, Emperor Hui. Yet now that he has passed away, her lamentations are without real grief. Can you solve this riddle, my lord?"

[3] He was twenty-three years old.

"How would you explain it?" asked Ch'en P'ing.

"Emperor Hui left no grown sons, and so the empress dowager is afraid of you and the others. I would suggest now that you honor Lü T'ai, Lü Ch'an, and Lü Lu with the rank of general and put them in charge of the soldiers in the northern and southern garrisons,[4] and allow the various members of the Lü family to enter the palace and take part in the government. If this is done, the empress dowager will feel more at ease and you and the other ministers may be fortunate enough to escape disaster."

Ch'en P'ing did as the boy suggested. Empress Lü was pleased and her lamentations took on an air of genuine sorrow. This was the start of the Lü family's rise to power.

A general amnesty was proclaimed to the empire and in the ninth month, on the day *hsin-ch'ou* [Oct. 19, 188 B.C.], Emperor Hui was interred. The heir apparent succeeded to the throne and became emperor, paying his respects at the funerary temple of Emperor Kao-tsu.[5]

The first year: All orders issued from the empress dowager and she called them "decrees" after the manner of an emperor. She began deliberations with the idea of making kings of the members of her own Lü family, asking Wang Ling, the chancellor of the right, what he thought of such a step. "Emperor Kao-tsu killed a white horse and made an oath with us that 'if anyone not of the Liu family becomes a king, the empire shall unite in attacking him,'" Wang Ling replied. "Now if members of the Lü family were to be made kings, it would be a violation of this agreement!"

Empress Lü was displeased and consulted Ch'en P'ing, the chancellor of the left, and Chou P'o, the marquis of Chiang. Chou P'o and the others replied, "When Emperor Kao-tsu conquered the world he made kings of his sons and younger brothers. Now that the empress dowager is issuing decrees in the manner of an emperor, if she wishes to make kings of her brothers, we cannot see that there is any objection."

The empress dowager was pleased and dismissed the court. When the proceedings were over Wang Ling began to berate Ch'en P'ing

[4] Which guarded the capital.
[5] The identity of the new emperor is explained below on pp. 327-28.

and Chou P'o. "Were you not present when Emperor Kao-tsu and the rest of us smeared our lips with the blood of the white horse and took the oath?" he said. "Now that Emperor Kao-tsu has passed away, the empress dowager has made herself ruler and wants to elevate the members of her family to the position of kings. All of you think perhaps that you can ignore your oath and flatter the will of the empress. But how will you dare to face Emperor Kao-tsu in the world below?"

"When it comes to opposing the ruler and speaking out in court," replied Ch'en P'ing and Chou P'o, "we are no match for you. But in preserving the altars of the dynasty and assuring the continuance of the Liu family, it is possible that you are no match for us." Wang Ling had no answer to this.

In the eleventh month the empress dowager, anxious to remove Wang Ling from his position, appointed him grand tutor to the emperor and deprived him of his authority as chancellor. Wang Ling eventually left his post on grounds of illness and retired to his home. Ch'en P'ing was moved from the position of chancellor of the left to Wang Ling's former position of chancellor of the right, and Shen I-chi, the marquis of Pi-yang, was appointed as the new chancellor of the left. Shen I-chi did not use the government offices but conducted his affairs from the palace itself like a palace secretary. Because of the great favor which Shen I-chi enjoyed with the empress dowager, he constantly handled the affairs of government, and the lords and ministers were all obliged to go through him before they could get anything done. As a first step toward making kings of the members of the Lü family the empress dowager awarded Lü T'ai's deceased father Lü Tse the posthumous title of Tao-wu, "The Slain Warrior King."

In the fourth month the empress dowager, with a view to making marquises of the members of her own family, first enfeoffed the palace secretary Feng Wu-tse, who had been a faithful follower of Kao-tsu, with the title of marquis of Po-ch'eng.

Princess Yüan of Lu died and was given the posthumous title of "Queen Mother Yüan of Lu." Her son Chang Yen was made king of Lu. (His father was Chang Ao, the marquis of Hsüan-p'ing.) Liu Chang, the son of Liu Fei, king of Ch'i, was enfeoffed as marquis of

Chu-hsü, and Lü Lu's daughter given to him as a wife. Ch'i Shou, the prime minister of Ch'i, was made marquis of P'ing-ting, and Yang-ch'eng Yen, the minister of the privy treasury, became marquis of Wu. Following this Lü Chung was made marquis of P'ei and Lü P'ing marquis of Fu-liu. Chang Mai was made marquis of Nan-kung.

Still with an eye to making kings of the members of her own family, the empress dowager granted positions to the sons of Emperor Hui by his ladies in waiting.[6] His son Ch'iang she made king of Huai-yang, his son Pu-i king of Ch'ang-shan; his son Shan she enfeoffed as marquis of Hsiang-ch'eng, his son Ch'ao as marquis of Chih, and his son Wu as marquis of Hu-kuan. Because the empress dowager let it be known to the high ministers that she would welcome such a move, they requested that Lü T'ai, the marquis of Li, be given the title of king of Lü. The empress dowager approved their suggestion.

Lü Shih-chih, Marquis K'ang of Chien-ch'eng, died. His rightful heir was found guilty of some crime and removed from his position; instead his younger son Lü Lu was made marquis of Hu-ling in order to carry on the line.

In the second year the king of Ch'ang-shan died. His younger brother Shan, the marquis of Hsiang-ch'eng, was made king of Ch'ang-shan and his name changed to I.

In the twelfth month Lü T'ai, the king of Lü, died, and was awarded the posthumous title of Su or "Majestic King." His heir Lü Chia succeeded him as king of Lü. The third year passed without incident.

In the fourth year the empress dowager enfeoffed her younger sister Lü Hsü as marchioness of Lin-kuang, Lü T'o as marquis of Yü, Lü Keng-shih as marquis of Chui, and Lü Fen as marquis of Lü-ch'eng. She also enfeoffed five of the prime ministers of the various feudal lords as marquises.

The daughter of Chang Ao, the marquis of Hsüan-p'ing, had been made the empress of Emperor Hui. When she failed to give birth to a son, she pretended to be pregnant and, substituting a child born to

[6] We are told later that these were not really sons of Emperor Hui but the children of other men whom the empress dowager attempted to pass off as the emperor's sons. I have therefore given only their personal names and omitted the surname Liu; no surname is given in the original.

one of the emperor's ladies in waiting, called it her own. Then she murdered the mother and set the child up as heir apparent. When Emperor Hui passed away it was he who became emperor.

As the emperor grew a little older, he began to hear rumors that his mother had been killed and that he was not the real son of the empress. "What right had the empress to kill my mother and call me her son?" he declared. "I am not old enough now, but when I grow up I will make trouble for her!"

Empress Dowager Lü, hearing of this, became worried and feared that he might start a revolt, so she kept him shut up in the Long Halls and gave it out that the emperor was gravely ill. None of the officials were allowed to see him.

The empress dowager announced: "He who holds possession of the empire and rules the destinies of the multitude must shelter them like the heavens and support them like the earth. The ruler must with a joyous heart bring peace to the people, and the people in gladness serve their ruler, and when this joy and gladness mingle together, then the empire will be well governed. Now the emperor's illness has continued for a long time without abating until his wits have gone astray and he has become demented. He is not fit to carry on the imperial line and perform the sacrifices in the ancestral temples, nor can he be entrusted with the care of the empire. Let him be replaced!"

The host of officials all bowed their heads and replied, "The empress dowager has taken deep thought for the multitudes of the empire and considered how best to preserve the ancestral temples and sacred altars of the dynasty. With bowed heads we shall obey her edict." The emperor was removed from his position and the empress dowager had him murdered in his place of confinement.

In the fifth month, on the day *ping-ch'en* [June 15, 184 B.C.], I, the king of Ch'ang-shan, was made emperor and his name changed to Hung. (The reason the year is not designated as the first year of a new reign is that the empress dowager directed the government of the empire.) Ch'ao, the marquis of Chih, was made king of Ch'ang-shan. The office of grand commandant was established and Chou P'o, the marquis of Chiang, appointed to fill it.

In the fifth year, the eighth month, Ch'iang, the king of Huai-yang, died. His younger brother Wu, the marquis of Hu-kuan, was made king of Huai-yang.

In the sixth year, the tenth month, the empress dowager, announcing that "Lü Chia, the king of Lü, has consistently behaved in an arrogant and imperious fashion," removed him from his position and made his father's younger brother, Lü Ch'an, the new king of Lü.

In the summer a general amnesty was granted to the empire and Liu Hsing-chü, the son of Liu Fei, the king of Ch'i, was enfeoffed as marquis of Tung-mou.

In the first month of the seventh year the empress dowager summoned Liu Yu, the king of Chao, to the capital. Liu Yu had taken a daughter of the Lü family as his queen, but he had no love for her and favored a concubine instead. The daughter of the Lü family, consumed with jealousy, left him and began to slander him to the empress dowager. She accused him of sedition and reported that he had said, "What right have the Lü family to become kings? When the empress dowager's days are over, I will certainly attack them!" The empress dowager was furious and for this reason summoned the king of Chao to the capital. When he arrived, she kept him at the state residence of Chao and would not see him. She ordered the place surrounded by guards and refused to give him anything to eat. When some of the officials secretly sent him provisions she had them summarily arrested and condemned to punishment. When the king of Chao was starving he composed this song:

> The Lüs order all affairs;
> The Liu clan is in peril.
> They have oppressed the nobles,
> And forced upon me this wife:
> A wife who in her jealousy
> Speaks wanton evil of me.
> A slandering woman will undo the state,
> For those in power are blind.
> Though I lack loyal ministers,
> Why should I cast away my kingdom?
> Were I to slay myself in the open fields
> Azure Heaven would speak the justice of my cause.
> Alas, it is too late for regretting;

> Better had I made an end at once.
> A king and yet to starve to death—
> Who will pity such as I?
> The Lü clan have overthrown right:
> I charge Heaven with my revenge!

On the day *ting-ch'ou* [Feb. 21, 181 B.C.] the king of Chao died in confinement. He was mourned with the rites of a commoner and interred in the graveyard of the common people of Ch'ang-an. On the day *chi-ch'ou* [March 4] there was an eclipse of the sun and the day grew dark. The empress dowager was filled with loathing and her heart grew uneasy. Turning to those about her, she said, "This has happened because of me!"

In the second month Liu Hui, the king of Liang, was transferred to the position of king of Chao, and Lü Ch'an, the king of Lü, was made king of Liang. Lü Ch'an did not proceed to his new kingdom, however, but became grand tutor to the emperor. Prince T'ai, the marquis of P'ing-ch'ang, was made king of Lü. The kingdom of Liang was renamed Lü and the former kingdom of Lü called Chi-ch'uan.

The daughter of Lü Hsü, the empress dowager's younger sister, was married to Liu Tse, who was a general of the army. Because she had made kings of the members of her family, the empress dowager was afraid that after she passed away Liu Tse might use his troops to do them some harm, and so she made him king of Lang-ya in order to assuage his feelings.

Liu Hui, the king of Liang, was deeply disturbed at being transferred to the position of king of Chao.[7] The empress dowager had given him the daughter of Lü Ch'an to be his queen, and all of her attendants and ministers were members of the Lü family. They exercised authority in a completely arbitrary fashion and secretly spied on the king so that he could do nothing as he wished. The king had a concubine whom he loved dearly, but the queen sent someone to poison her. The king, deeply grieved, composed a song in her memory in four stanzas and ordered his musicians to sing it. In the sixth

---

[7] As well he might be, since the two previous kings of Chao had both been murdered by the empress dowager.

month he committed suicide. When the empress dowager received the news she declared that he had been guilty of abandoning his duties to his ancestral temples by committing suicide for the sake of a woman, and deprived his heir of the title.

Chang Ao, the marquis of Hsüan-p'ing, died, and his son Chang Yen became king of Lu. Chang Ao was given the posthumous title of Yüan, "First King of Lu."

In the autumn the empress dowager sent an envoy to announce to Liu Heng, the king of Tai, that she wished to transfer him to the position of king of Chao. The king of Tai declined the move, begging to be allowed to remain in Tai to guard the frontier. The grand tutor Lü Ch'an, Prime Minister Ch'en P'ing, and others asserted that, since Lü Lu, the marquis of Wu-hsin, held the highest position among those of the rank of marquis, he should be made king of Chao. The empress dowager consented to this suggestion and awarded Lü Lu's father, Marquis K'ang, the posthumous title of Chao, "Bright King of Chao."

In the ninth month Liu Chien, the king of Yen, died. He had a son by a concubine, but the empress dowager sent someone to murder the boy and, on the grounds that there was no heir, deprived the family of the kingdom. In the eighth year, the tenth month, she set up Lü T'ai's son Lü T'ung, the marquis of Tung-p'ing, as king of Yen, and enfeoffed Lü T'ung's younger brother Lü Chuang as marquis of Tung-p'ing in his place.

During the third month the empress dowager was passing Chih Road on her way back from a sacrifice when something that looked like a blue dog appeared and bit her under the arm, and then suddenly disappeared. A diviner called in to interpret the happening announced that it was Liu Ju-i, the king of Chao, who had turned into an evil spirit. The empress dowager soon grew ill of the wound under her arm.

Because Chang Yen, the king of Lu and the empress dowager's grandson by her daughter, Princess Yüan of Lu, was very young and was an orphan, having lost both his father and mother at an early age, the empress dowager enfeoffed two of his half brothers, sons of Chang Ao by former concubines, so that they could assist him in his rule, making Chang Ch'ih the marquis of Hsin-tu and Chang Shou the marquis of Lo-ch'ang. She also enfeoffed the palace master of guests, Chang Ch'ing, as marquis of Chien-ling and Lü Jung as marquis of Chu-tzu. All of the palace eunuchs and their secretaries and assistants she made marquises of the area within the Pass with the revenue from five hundred households each.

During the seventh month the empress dowager's illness grew worse. She appointed Lü Lu, the king of Chao, as supreme commander of the army and ordered him to the northern garrison, and ordered Lü Ch'an, the king of Lü, to take over the southern garrison. "When Emperor Kao-tsu conquered the empire," she warned them, "he made a compact with his followers that if anyone not of the Liu family became a king, the empire should join together in attacking him. Now the members of the Lü family have become kings and the great ministers are displeased. The emperor is very young and I fear that when I have passed away the ministers will make trouble for you. You must bring your soldiers to guard the palace. Take care and do not accompany the funeral procession. Do not allow yourselves to be coerced by others!"

On the day *hsin-ssu* [Aug. 18, 180 B.C.] the empress dowager passed away. In her testamentary edict she left a thousand catties of gold to each of the kings who had been advanced from the rank of marquis, as well as grants of gold to the generals, ministers, marquises, and palace officials according to their ranks, and proclaimed a general amnesty to the empire. She appointed Lü Ch'an, the king of Lü, as prime minister, and the daughter of Lü Lu as empress to the boy ruler. After the burial of the empress dowager, Shen I-chi, the chancellor of the left, was made grand tutor to the emperor.

Liu Chang, the marquis of Chu-hsü and younger brother of Liu Hsiang, King Ai of Ch'i, was a man of great spirit and strength. He and his younger brother Liu Hsing-chü, the marquis of Tung-mou, both resided in Ch'ang-an. At this time the various members of the Lü family wielded authority with complete freedom and were hoping to overthrow the government but, because they were afraid of Chou P'o, Kuan Ying, and the others who had been followers of Kao-tsu in the old days, they did not dare to make a decisive move. Liu Chang's wife, being a daughter of Lü Lu, secretly learned of the plottings of the Lü family. Fearful that she herself might become involved in their downfall, she had her husband, Liu Chang, send a man to report to his older brother, the king of Ch'i, asking him to send his troops west to wipe out the Lü family and make himself ruler. Liu Chang would in that case join with the high officials in aiding his cause from within the capital.

The king of Ch'i was in favor of dispatching troops, but his prime minister Chao P'ing refused to consent. On the day *ping-wu* of the eighth month [Sept. 12] the king of Ch'i was about to send someone to execute his prime minister when the latter revolted, called out the troops, and made ready to surround the king. The king succeeded in killing the prime minister and eventually dispatched his troops east. By means of deception he seized the troops of the king of Lang-ya and, joining them to his own, led the whole force west. (A fuller description will be found in the chapter on the king of Ch'i.) The king of Ch'i then sent the following letter to the various kings and marquises:

When Emperor Kao-tsu conquered the empire he made kings of his sons and younger brothers. Among these was King Tao-hui, who was made king of Ch'i. After King Tao-hui died Emperor Hui sent Chang Liang to establish me as king of Ch'i. When Emperor Hui passed away the empress dowager took over the management of the government. But she was far along in years and, heeding the advice of the members of the Lü family, she arbitrarily deposed the emperor who had been set up and put another on the throne. On top of this she killed three kings of Chao in succession, wiped out the royal families of Liang, Chao, and Yen, made kings of the members of the Lü clan, and divided the territory of Ch'i into four kingdoms. Although the loyal ministers advised her against these moves, she refused in her delusion to heed them. Now the empress dowager has passed away and the emperor, being young in years, is incapable of governing the empire, but must rely solely upon the aid of the officials and lords. The members of the Lü family have therefore proceeded to help themselves to official posts, have massed soldiers to consolidate their power, have terrorized the marquises and loyal officials, and are forging imperial decrees and issuing orders to the empire. Such actions imperil the ancestral temples of the dynasty. I have therefore led forth my troops and shall enter the capital to punish all those who have unrightfully become kings!"

When news of this reached the Han court the prime minister Lü Ch'an and the others dispatched Kuan Ying, the marquis of Ying-yin, to lead troops to attack the king of Ch'i. After Kuan Ying reached Jung-yang, he began to consider what to do. "The Lü family have seized control of the troops in the area within the Pass and are imperiling the Liu clan, intending to make themselves rulers," he said to himself. "Now if I defeat the forces of Ch'i and return to court to report my victory, this will only increase the power of the Lü clan." He therefore halted and made camp at Jung-yang, sending envoys to the king of Ch'i and the other nobles asking them to join with him in peaceful alliance and wait and, if the Lü clan should attempt to overthrow the government, to unite in wiping them out. When the king of Ch'i received word of this he led his troops back to the western border of his kingdom to await further developments in accordance with the agreement.

Lü Lu and Lü Ch'an wanted to start an open revolt against the dynasty in the area within the Pass, but they were afraid of men like Chou P'o and Liu Chang in the capital and of the troops of Ch'i and Ch'u beyond the Pass. They were also fearful that Kuan Ying might turn against them, and so they wanted to wait until Kuan Ying's troops had joined in battle with those of the king of Ch'i before beginning a revolt. Thus they hesitated and made no decisive move.

At this time T'ai, the king of Chi-ch'uan; Wu, the king of Huai-yang; and Ch'ao, the king of Ch'ang-shan, who were supposed to be younger brothers of the boy emperor, and King Yüan of Lu, the grandson of Empress Dowager Lü by her daughter, were all very young and had not proceeded to their respective kingdoms but lived in the capital. Lü Lu, the king of Chao, and Lü Ch'an, the king of Lu, were in charge of the troops and resided in the southern and northern garrisons respectively. All were members of the Lü party. Under such circumstances none of the lords or officials of the court could make a move without fear of them, and Chou P'o, the marquis of Chiang, though officially the grand commandant, was unable to enter the garrisons and take command of the troops.

Li Shang, the marquis of Ch'ü-chou, was at this time old and infirm, and his son Li Chi was on good terms with Lü Lu. Chou P'o accordingly plotted with the prime minister Ch'en P'ing and together they sent someone to threaten Li Shang and force him to send his son Li Chi to talk with Lü Lu. Li Chi was to deceive Lü Lu by saying to him, "After Emperor Kao-tsu and Empress Lü together conquered the world, nine kings of the Liu family were set up and three of the Lü family. All of this was done after deliberation with the high officials, the decisions were announced to the various feudal lords, and they in turn expressed their approval. Now the empress dowager has passed away and the emperor is still very young. And yet although you wear at your girdle the seals of the king of Chao, you have not hastened to your new kingdom to guard it as a feudal lord should, but have become supreme commander and remain here in charge of the troops. This has aroused the suspicions of the great ministers and nobles. Would it not be better to return your general's seals and transfer your troops to the grand commandant Chou P'o? If you can persuade Lü Ch'an, the king of Lü, to relinquish his seals of prime minister as well and if both of you take an oath with the high officials that you will proceed to your kingdoms, then the armies of Ch'i will surely disband, the officials will rest easy again, and you may rule your vast kingdom with a tranquil mind. In this way you will assure the safety of your heirs for countless generations to come!"

Lü Lu trusted Li Chi and approved his suggestion. He was about to return his general's seals and transfer his troops to the grand commandant but, when he sent men to inform Lü Ch'an and the elders of the Lü clan, some of them were in favor of the move and some were opposed, so that he hesitated over what to do and could come to no decision. Lü Lu, however, continued to trust Li Chi as before.

One time he was out hunting with Li Chi when he stopped to visit his aunt, Lü Hsü, the younger sister of the empress dowager. Lü Hsü was furious with him. "You a general and you go and throw away your army!" she cried. "Now the Lüs will not be safe anywhere!"

Then she dragged out all her jewels and precious vessels and threw them on the ground outside the hall. "I won't keep them around for somebody else to enjoy!" she declared.

At dawn on the day *keng-shen* of the ninth month [Sept. 26, 180 B.C.] [8] Ts'ao Cho, the marquis of P'ing-yang, who was performing the duties of imperial secretary, went to see the prime minister Lü Ch'an to settle some government business. The palace attendant Chia Shou had at the time just returned from a mission to the king of Ch'i and was berating Lü Ch'an. "Though you are a king, you would not go to your kingdom earlier. Now, even if you wanted to, do you think you could?" Then he reported in detail to Lü Ch'an how Kuan Ying had joined with the forces of Ch'i and Ch'u and was planning to overthrow the Lü family, urging him to flee to the palace for protection at once. Ts'ao Cho overheard all that was said and rushed off to report it to Ch'en P'ing and Chou P'o.

Chou P'o wished to enter the northern garrison, but he was not able to do so until Chi T'ung, the marquis of Hsiang-p'ing, who was in charge of the imperial credentials, sent someone to bear the credentials and, under pretended orders from the emperor, had Chou P'o admitted to the garrison. Chou P'o in the meantime ordered Li Chi and the director of guests Liu Chieh to report to Lü Lu: "The emperor has put the grand commandant Chou P'o in charge of the northern garrison and wishes you to proceed to your kingdom. You must surrender your general's seals and take your leave at once. If you do not, disaster will befall you!"

Lü Lu was convinced that Li Chi would not deceive him, and so he took off his general's seals and handed them over to the director of guests, thus transferring his soldiers to Chou P'o. Chou P'o went to take command of the troops and, as he entered the gate of the garrison, circulated an order to the army saying, "Those who are for the Lü family bare their right arms, those for the Liu family bare their left arms!" Throughout the garrison the men all bared their left arms, showing that they were loyal to the Liu family. Thus Chou P'o eventually gained admission to the northern garrison and became its commander, General Lü having surrendered his seals as supreme com-

---

[8] The text erroneously reads "eighth month."

mander and relinquished his post. But there was still the southern garrison.

Ch'en P'ing summoned Liu Chang and sent him to assist Chou P'o,[9] who ordered him to guard the gate of the garrison. He also sent Ts'ao Cho to tell the colonel of the palace guards not to let the prime minister Lü Ch'an through the gate of the imperial apartments. Lü Ch'an, completely unaware that Lü Lu had already surrendered command of the northern garrison, entered the Eternal Palace, intending to start a revolt, but when he found he could not gain admittance to the imperial apartments, he paced back and forth indecisively. Ts'ao Cho in the meantime galloped back to report what had happened to Chou P'o.[10]

Chou P'o was still afraid that he would not be strong enough to overpower all of the Lü family, and so he did not dare to issue a public order for their execution. Instead he dispatched Liu Chang again, with instructions to enter the palace with all speed and guard the emperor. When Liu Chang asked for a body of troops he gave him a force of over a thousand men to accompany him.

By the time Liu Chang and his men entered the gate of the Eternal Palace and spotted Lü Ch'an in the courtyard it was already late afternoon. He fell upon Lü Ch'an, who fled, while a great wind rose from heaven and threw Lü Ch'an's attendants into such confusion that none of them dared to fight in his defense. Liu Chang pursued Lü Ch'an and killed him in the privy of the palace attendants' office.

After Liu Chang had killed Lü Ch'an, the emperor sent his master of guests bearing the imperial credentials to thank him for his trouble. Liu Chang tried to seize the credentials but, since the man refused to give them up, he brought him along in the same carriage and, using the credentials to gain admittance, raced to the Palace of Lasting Joy and beheaded the colonel of the guard of the palace, Lü Keng-shih. Then he galloped back to the northern garrison to report to Chou P'o.

Chou P'o rose from his seat, bowed, and congratulated Liu Chang on his work. "The only one we had to worry about was Lü Ch'an," he

---

[9] The sentence which precedes this in the original is an interpolation which does not appear to belong here and has accordingly been omitted in translation.

[10] In the original the words "afraid they would not win" have been erroneously interpolated from the sentence below.

said. "Now that he has been killed, the empire is safe." Then he divided his men into groups and sent them out to arrest the men and women of the Lü family and, without distinction of age or youth, to behead them all. On the following day, *hsin-yu* [Sept. 27], he arrested and beheaded Lü Lu and had the empress dowager's sister, Lü Hsü, beaten to death. He also dispatched men to execute Lü T'ung, the king of Yen, and remove Chang Yen, the king of Lu, from his position. On the day *jen-hsü* [Sept. 28] he appointed the emperor's grand tutor, Shen I-chi, to the position of chancellor of the left, and on the day *mou-ch'en* [Oct. 4] moved the king of Chi-ch'uan to the position of king of Liang and set up Liu Sui, the son of Liu Yu, King Yu of Chao, as the new king of Chao. He also dispatched Liu Chang to go and report the overthrow of the Lü family to the king of Ch'i and order him to disband his army. Kuan Ying's army was also disbanded at Jung-yang and returned to the capital.

The high officials plotted together in secret, saying, "The young emperor and the kings of Liang, Huai-yang, and Ch'ang-shan are not true sons of Emperor Hui. As part of her plans Empress Lü took the children of other men, murdered their mothers, and had them brought up in the women's quarters, pretending that they were the children of Emperor Hui. Then she had him recognize them as his sons and set them up as heir apparent or as kings in order to strengthen the power of the Lü family. Now that the Lü clan has been annihilated, if we leave them in their positions, then when they grow up and begin to take a part in government affairs we ourselves will suffer! It would be better to look over the other kings and pick out the one who is wisest to set up as the new ruler."

Someone pointed out that Liu Fei, King Tao-hui of Ch'i, was the oldest son of Emperor Kao-tsu, and that his legitimate heir had succeeded him as king of Ch'i, so that from the point of view of genealogy the king of Ch'i was the oldest grandson of Emperor Kao-tsu in the legitimate line of descent and therefore the proper successor to the throne. But the high officials all objected. "It was the Lü family who, as maternal relatives of the ruler, made all the trouble and almost brought disaster to the ancestral temples of the dynasty and ruin to the worthy officials," they said. "Now the king of Ch'i's mother belongs to the same family as Ssu Chün, and Ssu Chün is an evil man. If we set up the king of Ch'i, we will have the Lü family all over again." Others suggested setting up the king of Huai-nan, but it was objected that he was too young and that his mother's family likewise had a bad reputation. Finally they said, "Liu Heng, the king of Tai, is the oldest of Kao-tsu's sons who are still living and a kind and generous man, and his mother's family, the Po clan, are respectable and upright people. As the eldest in line he is the obvious successor, and his reputation for kindness and filial obedience, which is known throughout the empire, will be of great advantage."

Having thus agreed among themselves, they secretly sent a messenger to summon the king of Tai. The king sent back word declining the offer but, when they sent a request once more, he started on his way with his attendants in six relay carriages. On the last day of the ninth month, the day *chi-yu* [Nov. 14, 180 B.C.], he reached Ch'ang-an and proceeded to the state residence of Tai to spend the night. The high officials all went to visit him there and, bearing the imperial seals, presented them to the king and honored him as the new Son of Heaven. The king of Tai declined several times but, at the urgent request of the various officials, he finally acceded to their demands.

Liu Hsing-chü, the marquis of Tung-mou, said to the king, "I played no part in the overthrow of the Lü clan, but I beg to be allowed to prepare the palace for your coming."[11] Then he and the master of carriage, Lord T'eng, the marquis of Ju-yin, entered the palace and appeared before the young emperor. "You are not of the Liu family," they announced, "and so you have no right to the throne." Then they waved to the spear bearers who were ranged on either side of the emperor to lay down their weapons and depart. Several of them were unwilling to give up their arms until the chief eunuch Chang Tse explained to them what had happened, after which they too abandoned their weapons. Lord T'eng summoned a carriage and, placing the young emperor in it, drove out of the palace. "Where are you taking me?" asked the boy. "You are going to leave the palace and stay in one of the lodges," replied Lord T'eng, and took

[11] Literally "to clean the palace," where the boy emperor Hung was still theoretically enthroned.

him to the apartments of the privy treasury. After this he prepared the imperial carriage of state and went to the state residence of Tai to meet the king of Tai. "The palace has been duly prepared," he reported.

At sundown the king of Tai entered the Eternal Palace. Ten palace attendants bearing spears were guarding the main gate of the palace. "The Son of Heaven is in residence," they said. "What business have you that you wish to enter?"

The king of Tai spoke to Chou P'o, who went and explained to them what had happened, after which they laid down their weapons and left. So the king of Tai finally entered and took over the business of government. That night the authorities were dispatched in groups to do away with the kings of Liang, Huai-yang, and Ch'ang-shan, and the young emperor at their various residences.

The king of Tai became Son of Heaven and passed away after twenty-three years on the throne. He was given the posthumous title of "Supreme Emperor Wen the Filial."

The Grand Historian remarks: In the reign of Emperor Hui and Empress Lü, the common people succeeded in putting behind them the sufferings of the age of the Warring States and ruler and subject alike sought rest in surcease of action.[12] Therefore Emperor Hui sat with folded hands and unruffled garments and Empress Lü, though a woman ruling in the manner of an emperor, conducted the business of government without ever leaving her private chambers, and the world was at peace. Punishments were seldom meted out and evildoers grew rare, while the people applied themselves to the tasks of farming, and food and clothing became abundant.

[12] The political ideal of "nonaction" or laissez-faire in which the government exercises a minimum of control. Ssu-ma Ch'ien is implying a contrast with the vast government projects and strict regimentation of the people which characterized the Ch'in dynasty.

Shih chi 10: The Basic Annals of Emperor Wen the Filial

After the Han had risen to power and the line of succession became unclear, the king of Tai was brought to the capital to ascend the imperial throne, and the whole world gave him its allegiance. He abolished the mutilating punishments and opened up the barriers and bridges; his goodness and charity spread far and wide, and he came to be called the Great Patriarch. Thus I made The Basic Annals of Emperor Wen the Filial.

Emperor Wen the Filial was the fourth of Kao-tsu's eight sons. In the eleventh year of Kao-tsu's reign, after the army of Ch'en Hsi had been defeated and peace had been restored to the region of Tai, he was set up as king of Tai with his capital at Chung-tu. His mother was Empress Dowager Po.

Seventeen years after he became king of Tai, Empress Lü passed away in the seventh month of the eighth year of her reign. In the ninth month, because Lü Ch'an and the other members of the Lü clan were threatening to endanger the position of the Liu family by starting a revolt, the great ministers joined in overthrowing them and laid plans to summon the king of Tai to take the throne. (An account of the affair will be found in the chapter on Empress Lü.)

The chancellor Ch'en P'ing, the grand commandant Chou P'o, and the others sent an envoy to fetch the king of Tai. The king consulted Chang Wu, his chief of palace attendants, and others of his court, and in the course of the debate they expressed their opinion as follows: "The great ministers of the Han were all originally generals in the time of Emperor Kao-tsu. They are experienced in warfare and given to plots and deceits. There is more behind their proposal than simply this. In the past they have been restrained only by their awe of Emperor Kao-tsu and Empress Lü, but now they have succeeded in wiping out the Lü clan and have newly tasted blood in the capital. They say that they have come to fetch Your Majesty, but in truth they cannot be trusted. We beg you not to go, but to put them off with an excuse of illness and wait to see how the situation develops."

The military commander Sung Ch'ang then came forward and spoke: "The opinion of the courtiers is utterly wrong! When the Ch'in lost control of the government, the feudal lords and local heroes sprang up on all sides in inestimable numbers, each one believing that he could become ruler. But it was a member of the Liu family who in the end succeeded in stepping into the position of Son of Heaven, and with that the hopes of the rest of the world came to an end. This is the first point to be noted.

"Emperor Kao-tsu made kings of his sons and brothers and laid out their territories so that they interlocked like the teeth of a dog. His may be called a house set on a firm rock, and the world has bowed before its might. This is the second point.

"When the Han arose it abolished the harsh administration of the Ch'in, simplified the laws and ordinances, and ruled with virtue and kindness so that all men are now at peace and cannot easily be roused to action. This is the third point.

"Because of the authority she wielded, Empress Lü was able to make kings of three of her family, exercising power as she pleased and dominating the government. And yet with a single set of credentials Chou P'o entered the northern garrison, and he had only to give a single cry when the soldiers all bared their left arms and declared themselves loyal to the Liu family, so that he turned upon the Lü clan and in the end annihilated it. Thus it is that the throne is bestowed by Heaven and cannot be won by human strength alone!

"Now, although the great ministers might hope to revolt against the Liu family, the common people would never support them, and indeed it is doubtful that they could even reach agreement within their own party. They are restrained by your own kinsmen Liu Chang and Liu Hsing-chü who reside in the capital, and they fear the power of the kings of Wu, Ch'u, Huai-nan, Lang-ya, Ch'i, and Tai in the provinces beyond.

"Of the sons of Emperor Kao-tsu there remain today only the king of Huai-nan and Your Majesty. Moreover, you are the elder, and your wisdom and goodness are known throughout the empire. It is for this reason that the great ministers, according with the wishes of the world, have come to fetch you and desire you to take the throne. You need not doubt their intentions!"

The king of Tai informed his mother of the matter and they discussed what to do, but hesitated and came to no decision. Then the king divined by the tortoise shell and the lines obtained indicated the "Great Transversal," the interpretation of which reads:

> Crosswise the lines of the Great Transversal!
> I shall become a heavenly king
> Like Ch'i of the Hsia who brought glory! [1]

"But surely I am a king already," exclaimed the king of Tai. "How should I become a king again?"

"The words 'heavenly king,'" replied the diviner, "refer to the Son of Heaven!"

With this the king of Tai dispatched Po Chao, his mother's younger brother, to go to the capital to see Chou P'o. Chou P'o and the others explained to him their reasons for wishing to fetch the king of Tai and make him ruler. Po Chao returned and reported on the interview. "They speak in good faith. There is no need to mistrust them!"

The king turned to Sung Ch'ang with a laugh and said, "It was indeed just as you said!" Then he ordered Sung Ch'ang to join him in his carriage and, accompanied by Chang Wu and the others, six men in all, he journeyed by relay carriage to Ch'ang-an. When he reached Kao-ling he stopped to rest, sending Sung Ch'ang ahead to observe the situation in the capital.

When Sung Ch'ang reached the bridge over the Wei River he found that the chancellor and the lesser officials had all come out to welcome the king. Sung Ch'ang returned to report the situation to the king, who hastened as far as the Wei Bridge, where the host of officials bowed in greeting, acknowledging themselves his subjects. The king descended from his carriage and bowed in return. The grand commandant Chou P'o then came forward. "I beg to have a word in private," he said.

[1] Ch'i was the son of Emperor Yü, the founder of the Hsia dynasty in the legendary period. The sense of the first line is obscure and there may be a meaning of "to change over" in the word "crosswise." In the original the three lines are rhymed.

"If you would speak of public affairs, speak of them in public!" said Sung Ch'ang. "And if you would speak of private affairs, you should know that a king gives no ear to such!"

Chou P'o thereupon knelt and presented the seals and credentials of the Son of Heaven, but the king declined to accept them, saying, "Let us go to the state residence of Tai and discuss the matter."

The king hastened to the state residence of Tai, with the various officials accompanying him. The chancellor Ch'en P'ing, the grand commandant Chou P'o, the commander in chief Ch'en Wu,[2] the imperial secretary Chang Ts'ang, the director of the imperial clan Liu Ying-k'o, the marquis of Chu-hsü, Liu Chang, the marquis of Tung-mou, Liu Hsing-chü, and the director of guests Liu Chieh all bowed twice and said, "The boy named Hung and the others are none of them true sons of Emperor Hui and hence have no right to serve the ancestral temples of the dynasty. We have respectfully consulted the marchioness of Yin-an, queen of the late King Ch'ing of Tai, the king of Lang-ya, and the other high ministers of the imperial family, as well as the marquises and officials of the rank of two thousand piculs, and it is our opinion that Your Majesty, as the eldest surviving son of Emperor Kao-tsu, is the proper person to succeed to the line established by Emperor Kao-tsu. We beg Your Majesty to take the throne of the Son of Heaven."

The king of Tai replied, "It is a grave task to undertake the service of the ancestral temple of Emperor Kao-tsu. I am a man of no ability and am not worthy to be appointed to such a charge. I beg you to consult with the king of Ch'u[3] and select someone who is suitable. I dare not undertake the task."

The officials prostrated themselves and pressed their request while the king of Tai, facing west, declined three times and then, facing toward the south, declined twice.[4]

[2] Some commentators would correct the name to read Kuan Ying, which seems more likely in view of the important part Kuan Ying is reported in other chapters to have played in the enthronement of Emperor Wen.

[3] Liu Chiao, younger brother of Kao-tsu and the eldest male member of the founder's immediate family.

[4] A host when receiving guests faces west, but a sovereign faces south. Some commentators believe that the king deliberately changed the direction in which

The chancellor Ch'en P'ing and the others all said, "We have humbly deliberated upon the matter, and we believe that Your Majesty should properly be named to attend the ancestral temple of Emperor Kao-tsu. Though the nobles and common people of the empire consider this opinion just, we have not come to our decision lightly, but have deliberated for the sake of the ancestral temples and the sacred altars of the dynasty. We beg Your Majesty to give ear to us. In due respect we present the seals and credentials of the Son of Heaven, offering them with repeated bows."

The king of Tai replied, "If the imperial household, the generals and ministers, and the kings and nobles all believe that there is no one more suitable than I, I dare not decline."

Thereupon he ascended the throne of the Son of Heaven, and the officials ranged themselves in attendance according to the dictates of ritual. Then he sent the master of carriage Lord T'eng and the marquis of Tung-mou, Liu Hsing-chü, to prepare the palace for his entry. The imperial carriage of state was brought to the residence of Tai to fetch the emperor, and at sundown of the same day he entered the Eternal Palace.

That evening he appointed Sung Ch'ang as general of the guards to bring order to the northern and southern garrisons, and made Chang Wu his chief of palace attendants. After inspecting the various halls of the palace he returned and took his seat in the front hall where, on the same evening, he issued an edict saying:

Recently the members of the Lü clan, seizing control of the government and arbitrarily exercising power, plotted an act of major treason and sought to endanger the ancestral temples of the Liu family. But, through the efforts of the generals and ministers, the nobles, the members of the imperial family, and the high officials, they have been overthrown and the guilty have been brought to punishment. I, your ruler,[5] have newly ascended the throne.

---

he faced to indicate his willingness to take the throne, while others believe that the officials picked up the reluctant king bodily and forced him to face south in the manner of an emperor.

[5] Here for the first time the emperor uses the pronoun *ch'en*, the imperial "we." But his use of it in later edicts is by no means consistent; he often refers to himself by the ordinary pronoun *wu*, and I have therefore used "I" throughout.

Let there be a general amnesty throughout the empire and let there be granted to the people one step in rank and to women of a hundred households oxen and wine.[6] Let there be five days of drinking and feasting.

In the first year of his reign, the day *keng-hsü* of the tenth month [Nov. 15, 180 B.C.], Emperor Wen transferred Liu Tse, the former king of Lang-ya, to the position of king of Yen.

On the following day, the day *hsin-hai,* the emperor officially ascended the throne and paid his respects at the ancestral temple of Emperor Kao-tsu. The chancellor of the right Ch'en P'ing was transferred to the position of chancellor of the left and the grand commandant Chou P'o appointed as chancellor of the right. The commander in chief Kuan Ying was made grand commandant. All the lands which the members of the Lü clan had seized from the territories of Ch'i and Ch'u were restored to their original jurisdiction.

On the following day, *jen-tzu,* the emperor dispatched the general of carriage and cavalry Po Chao to Tai to escort his mother, Empress Dowager Po, to the capital.

The emperor announced:

Lü Ch'an set himself up as prime minister. Lü Lu became supreme commander of the army and, pretending to be acting on imperial orders, they arbitrarily dispatched General Kuan Ying to lead his troops in an attack on the state of Ch'i, for it was their intention to replace the Liu family as rulers. But Kuan Ying halted his march at Jung-yang and, instead of attacking, joined with the feudal lords in plotting the overthrow of the Lü clan. Lü Ch'an sought to do evil, but the chancellor Ch'en P'ing and the grand commandant Chou P'o laid plans against him and seized the troops of Lü Ch'an and the others. Liu Chang led the way by capturing Lü Ch'an and his party; Chou P'o directed Chi T'ung to hand over to him the credentials and give him official permission to enter the northern garrison, while the director of guests Liu Chieh personally seized the general's seals from the king of Chao, Lü Lu. The fief of the grand commandant Chou P'o shall therefore be increased by ten thousand households and he shall be granted five thousand catties of gold. The chancellor Ch'en P'ing and General Kuan Ying shall be granted an addition of three thousand households and two thousand catties of gold each. The marquis of Chu-hsü, Liu Chang, the

---

[6] There is unfortunately no agreement among commentators as to exactly what "one step in rank" or "women of a hundred households" means.

marquis of Hsiang-p'ing, Chi T'ung, and the marquis of Tung-mou, Liu Hsing-chü, shall be granted an addition of two thousand households and a thousand catties of gold each. The director of guests Liu Chieh shall be enfeoffed as marquis of Yang-hsin and granted a thousand catties of gold.

In the twelfth month the emperor announced:

Laws serve to insure the justness of rule, for they restrain violence and guide men of good intention. But at present when a man has been found guilty of violating the law, his parents, his wife and children, and the other members of his family, though they are guilty of no offense, are brought under accusation as well and even forced to become slave laborers. I find this practice utterly unacceptable. Let the matter be brought to discussion.

The officials concerned with such affairs all replied, "The people are incapable of governing themselves, and therefore we must have laws to restrain them. The practice of joint accusation and joint punishment is intended to trouble the hearts of the people so that they will regard violations of the law with proper gravity. The system has been in use for a long time and it is expedient that it be continued as before."

The emperor said, "It is my understanding that if the laws are just, the people will be obedient, and if the punishments are meet, the people will comply. Moreover, it is the duty of the officials to shepherd the people and lead them into good. If the officials, having proved themselves incapable of such leadership, should in addition punish the people in the name of laws which are unjust, they would become on the contrary the injurers of the people and the doers of violence themselves. How then could violence be restrained? I cannot see anything expedient in such a system! Let the matter be examined with greater care!"

The officials all replied, "Your Majesty would bestow great mercy upon the empire and manifest such virtue as we could never hope to attain. We beg to draw up an edict abolishing the statutes pertaining to the system of joint accusation and enslavement of relatives."

In the first month the officials said to the emperor, "Setting up the heir apparent as soon as possible is a sign of respect for the ancestral temples. We beg Your Majesty to appoint an heir apparent!" But the emperor replied, "I am without virtue. The Lord on High and the other spirits do not accept my sacrifices and the people of the empire have not yet found satisfaction for their desires. Now though I may never be able, like the most ancient rulers, to search far and wide throughout the empire for a man of true wisdom and virtue to whom I may cede my throne, yet to announce at this early date that I am setting up an heir apparent would only be to emphasize my lack of virtue. What would I say to the world? Let us let the matter rest a while."

"To set up the heir apparent beforehand," said the officials, "is to show concern for the ancestral temples and sacred altars of the dynasty and to indicate that one has not forgotten the fate of the empire!"

The emperor replied, "Liu Chiao, the king of Ch'u, is my father's younger brother. He is rich in years and has great insight into the moral order of the world and a clear understanding of the structure of the nation. Liu P'i, the king of Wu, is an elder brother to me, a kind man and a lover of virtue.[7] Liu Ch'ang, the king of Huai-nan, my younger brother, aids me with his virtue. How can you say that I have taken no thought beforehand for the fate of the empire? Among the nobles, my kinsmen of the imperial house, and the worthy officials there are many men of wisdom and virtue. If you would select one of these virtuous men to aid my shortcomings, this would truly be a blessing to the sacred altars and a benefit to the empire. Yet you do not select from among these, but tell me I must appoint my son, so that others will think I have forgotten the wise and virtuous and dote only upon my own children. This is no way to care for the empire! I cannot accept such a suggestion!"

But the officials continued to press their request: "In ancient times, when the dynasties of Yin and Chou headed the nation, they managed to maintain their rules for over a thousand years, longer than any of the dynasties of antiquity, because they followed the practice which we recommend. The custom of limiting the succession to the son of the ruler has been in use for a long time.

"When Emperor Kao-tsu in person first led his followers and min-

[7] Actually Liu P'i was a cousin, the son of Kao-tsu's older brother Liu Chung. The *Han shu* at this point (ch. 4) omits the phrase "a kind man and a lover of virtue," probably because, in the reign of Emperor Ching, Liu P'i led a revolt against the Han government. The presence of the phrase here speaks strongly for the authenticity of the speech.

isters in bringing peace to the world, he set up the feudal lords and himself became the Great Founder of the imperial line, while the kings and marquises who first received grants of territory in turn all became the founders of their respective lines. That their sons and grandsons should succeed them generation after generation without end is a fundamental principle of the empire. Therefore Emperor Kao-tsu established this practice in order to bring order to the entire area within the seas. Now to pass over the rightful successor and instead choose someone from among the feudal lords or the other members of the imperial house would not be in accordance with the will of Emperor Kao-tsu. We do not consider it right to deliberate further on the question! Liu Ch'i is the eldest of Your Majesty's sons and a man of sincerity and kindness. We beg that he be appointed heir apparent."

With this the emperor gave his consent and, in commemoration of the occasion, granted one step in rank to all those among the common people who were entitled to succeed their fathers. He enfeoffed his uncle, General Po Chao, as marquis of Chih.

In the third month the officials requested that an empress be appointed.[8] The emperor's mother, Empress Dowager Po, said, "Since the feudal lords all bear the same surname as the imperial family, any daughter of theirs is out of the question.[9] Let the mother of the heir apparent be appointed as empress." The mother of the heir apparent was a member of the Tou family. When the emperor made her his empress, he ordered that linen and silk cloth, grain and meat be granted to all the widowers and widows and homeless and impoverished people of the empire, as well as to all those over eighty years of age and orphans under nine, in quantities appropriate to their respective needs.

When the emperor first arrived from Tai and took the throne he administered his rule with kindness and brought order to the feudal lords, and the barbarians on all sides were pleased. He set about

---

[8] The emperor's former consort had died earlier, along with her three sons. Lady Tou, the mother of the heir apparent, had been a concubine of the emperor from the time he was king of Tai.

[9] Marriage between persons of the same surname, no matter how distantly related, was taboo.

making provisions for the able ministers who had accompanied him from Tai and announced:

At the time when the high officials overthrew the Lü family and invited me to come to the capital, I was doubtful and hesitated, for all my courtiers attempted to stop me. Only my military commander Sung Ch'ang urged me to come, and thus I have been able to guard and serve the ancestral temples. I have already honored Sung Ch'ang with the post of general of the guards. Let him now be enfeoffed as marquis of Chuang-wu. As for the other six men who accompanied me to the capital, they may be given offices ranging as high as the nine highest ministers.

The emperor announced:

Among the marquises are sixty-eight persons who accompanied Emperor Kao-tsu to his territory in Shu and Han; let all of their fiefs be increased by three hundred households each. Among those who were originally officials of two thousand picul rank and who accompanied Emperor Kao-tsu, let the governor of Ying-ch'uan, Tsun, and others, ten in all, be granted the revenue from six hundred households; the governor of Huai-yang, Shen-t'u Chia, and others, ten in all, be granted that of five hundred households; and the colonel of the guard, Ting, and others, ten in all, be granted that of four hundred households.

He enfeoffed Chao Chien, the maternal uncle of the king of Huai-nan, as marquis of Chou-yang, and Ssu Chün, the maternal uncle of the king of Ch'i, as marquis of Ch'ing-kuo. In the autumn he enfeoffed Ts'ai Chien, the former prime minister of Ch'ang-shan, as marquis of Fan.

Someone advised Chou P'o, the chancellor of the right, saying, "Originally you played a part in overthrowing the Lü family and inviting the king of Tai to take the throne, and now you are very proud of your accomplishments. You have received the highest rewards and enjoy a position of great honor. Is it not possible that after all this some misfortune may befall you?" [10] Because of this Chou P'o pleaded illness and resigned his position as chancellor of the right, leaving the chancellor of the left Ch'en P'ing to manage affairs by himself. In the tenth month of the second year of Emperor Wen's

---

[10] Because of the Chinese conviction that too much of a good thing is likely to summon its opposite.

reign, when Ch'en P'ing died, Chou P'o was recalled to the post of chancellor.

The emperor announced:

I have heard that in ancient times, when the feudal lords were set up to rule over a thousand or more domains,[11] each one guarded his own fief, sending tribute to the central court at the appropriate seasons. Thus the common people were put to no excessive labor, superior and inferior worked together in happy accord, and there was no virtue which was neglected. But these days a great many of the marquises reside in Ch'ang-an, far from their own cities. As a result the officials are put to great labor and expense transporting provisions for them, while the marquises themselves are cut off from any means of instructing their own people. Let the marquises therefore proceed to their territories. In the case of those who are acting as officials or who have been specifically instructed by edict to remain in the capital, let their heirs be sent instead.

On the last day of the eleventh month [Jan. 2, 178 B.C.] there was an eclipse of the sun. In the twelfth month, on the night of the full moon, there was also an eclipse of the moon.[12]

The emperor announced:

I have heard it said that when Heaven gave birth to the multitude of people, it set up for them a ruler so that he might look after them and order them. If the lord of men is without virtue, and if his administration is not conducted with equity, then Heaven will bear witness of this fact by some portentous happening in order to warn him of his misrule. Thus on the last day of the eleventh month there occurred an eclipse of the sun, a reproach appearing in the heavens. Could there be any greater portent?

I have been entrusted with the protection of the ancestral temples and, with my frail person, placed in a position above the common people, the nobles, and the kings. The order or disorder of the entire empire rests upon me, a single man, and upon the two or three administrators who, like arms and legs, assist me. I have not succeeded in bringing order and aid to the living creatures under me, while in the realms above I have brought affliction

---

[11] The text reads "to rule states which lasted over a thousand years," but this appears to be a contamination from the passage above describing the rules of the Yin and Chou dynasties which lasted "over a thousand years."

[12] The text calls this an "eclipse of the sun," but astronomical calculations show that the word "sun" must be an error for "moon."

even to the three luminaries of heaven, the sun, the moon, and the starry host. So great is my lack of virtue!

Wherever this order shall reach, let all give thought to my errors and consider in what way I have fallen short in understanding, vision, and thought. I beg you to inform me, and to select for me wise and upright men who will speak frankly and reprimand me, that I may repair my shortcomings.

On this occasion I urge all in official positions to attend to their duties and to strive to reduce their demands in labor and expenses in order that the people may be benefited. I have been unable to extend the practice of virtue to distant regions, and I brood with anxiety upon the misconduct of foreign peoples. Therefore I am not yet able to dispense with defense measures. But, though I cannot at this time abolish the garrisons which guard our borders, there is no reason to train further troops or to increase my personal guards. Therefore let the army of the general of the guards be abolished and, of the horses now in the possession of the master of carriage, let him retain only enough for actual use, and let the rest be allotted to the relay stations.

In the first month the emperor announced:

Agriculture is the basis of the empire. Let the Field of Tribute be laid out and I in person shall lead the plowing in order to provide offerings of millet for the ancestral temples.[13]

In the third month the officials requested the emperor to set up his sons as marquises or kings. The emperor replied, "When Liu Yu, King Yu of Chao, died in confinement, I was deeply grieved. I have already set up his oldest son Liu Sui as king of Chao. Liu Sui's younger brother Liu Pi-ch'iang, as well as the sons of King Tao-hui of Ch'i, the marquis of Shu-hsü, Liu Chang, and the marquis of Tung-mou, Liu Hsing-chü, are all men of merit and deserve to be kings." Accordingly he set up Liu Pi-ch'iang, the younger son of King Yu of Chao, as king of Ho-chien ruling over the province of Chi in Ch'i, and set up Liu Chang as king of Ch'ang-yang and Liu Hsing-chü as king of Chi-pei. Of his own sons he set up Liu Wu as king of Tai, Liu Ts'an as king of T'ai-yüan, and Liu I as king of Liang.

The emperor announced:

---

[13] The emperor in person led his ministers in beginning the plowing of the Field of Tribute or Sacred Field, the produce of which was used for offerings in the ancestral temples of the dynasty. Emperor Wen is here reviving what was said to be a practice of the rulers of antiquity.

When the dynasties of ancient times ruled the empire, they set up in their courts the "flags for advancing good" and the "boards for recording criticisms." [14] In this way they were able to carry out their rule successfully and to invite criticisms of their policies. The present laws, however, recognize a category of offenses known as "criticism and evil talk," and because the officials are afraid of being accused of these they do not dare to express their feelings in full. The emperor accordingly has no way to learn of his errors. Under such circumstances, how can I expect to attract worthy men from distant regions? Let the laws pertaining to these offenses be abolished.

There are cases among the common people in which men have banded together under oath to put a curse on the emperor; later, one of the members having broken his oath and reported the matter, the law officials accuse them of high treason. Sometimes people may be speaking of quite different matters, but again the officials believe they are criticizing the government. Such acts represent only the foolishness of insignificant people who are unaware that they are thereby inviting death. I cannot under any circumstances sanction action against such men. In the future no one accused of such violations shall be brought to trial.

In the ninth month the bronze tiger credentials and bamboo envoys' credentials were first distributed to the governors of provinces and prime ministers of kingdoms.[15]

In the third year, on the last day of the tenth month, the day *ting-yu* [Dec. 22, 178 B.C.], there was an eclipse of the sun.

In the eleventh month the emperor announced:

Some time ago arrangements were made to send the marquises to their territories, but some of them have made excuses and have not yet left the capital. The chancellor is one of my most trusted officials, and therefore I have asked him to lead the other marquises in proceeding to their territories.

The chancellor Chou P'o, marquis of Chiang, left his post and proceeded to his domain. The grand commandant Kuan Ying, the marquis of Ying-yin, was made chancellor in his place and the post

[14] Anyone who had suggestions to make to the government stood under the flags and made his announcement; anyone with criticisms wrote them on the boards. According to legend they were set up at the courts of the ancient emperors Yao and Shun.

[15] Credentials of this type, of which one half was given to the local administrator and the other half retained by the central government, had long been in use. These were probably of a new or standardized design.

of grand commandant abolished, its duties being assumed by the chancellor.

In the fourth month Liu Chang, the king of Ch'eng-yang, died. The king of Huai-nan, Liu Ch'ang, and his follower Wei Ching killed Shen I-chi, the marquis of Pi-yang.

In the fifth month the Hsiung-nu invaded Pei-ti, advancing through the region south of the great bend of the Yellow River and marauding. The emperor paid his first visit to the Palace of Sweet Springs.

In the sixth month the emperor announced:

The Han has entered into an alliance of brotherhood with the Hsiung-nu so that they will bring no harm to our borders, and for this reason we have sent them generous gifts. Yet now the Hsiung-nu Wise King of the Right has left his territory and led his hordes into the regions south of the Yellow River which were formerly surrendered to us. It is evident that he has some underhanded scheme in mind, for he has been marching back and forth in the vicinity of our border stations, seizing and killing our officials, and driving away the foreign peoples who defend our borders so that they can no longer occupy their former lands. He has trampled down our border guards and invaded and plundered with arrogance, committing acts of lawlessness, and violating the alliance. Let a force of eighty-five thousand cavalry be sent to Kao-nu to defend the borders.

The emperor dispatched the chancellor Kuan Ying to attack the Hsiung-nu, who thereupon withdrew. He also called out the skilled soldiers of the military commanders and, placing them under the general of the guards, stationed them in Ch'ang-an.

On the day *hsin-mao* [Aug. 12, 177 B.C.] the emperor proceeded from the Palace of Sweet Springs to Kao-nu, visiting the kingdom of T'ai-yüan on his way, where he saw many of the officials who had formerly served under him in Tai.[16] He presented them with gifts, promoted those who had won merit, and rewarded the deserving. To the common people he granted oxen and wine for each neighborhood, and he exempted the people of Chin-yang and Chung-tu from land taxes for three years. He remained in T'ai-yüan for over ten days, taking his ease.

[16] T'ai-yüan was in the area of the former kingdom of Tai, and the cities of Chin-yang and Chung-tu had been the capitals when Emperor Wen was king of Tai.

When Liu Hsing-chü, the king of Chi-pei, heard that the emperor had gone to the region of Tai and was about to launch an attack on the Hsiung-nu, he started a revolt, sending out his troops to make a surprise attack on Jung-yang. With this the emperor issued an edict releasing the troops that had been sent under the chancellor Kuan Ying to attack the Hsiung-nu, and dispatched Ch'en Wu, the marquis of Chi-p'u, as general in chief in command of a hundred thousand men to go and attack him. Tseng Ho, the marquis of Ch'i, was made a general and sent to camp at Jung-yang.

On the day *hsin-hai* [Sept. 1] of the seventh month the emperor returned to the capital from T'ai-yüan and at once issued an edict to the authorities stating:

The king of Chi-pei has turned his back upon virtue and rebelled against his sovereign. He has led his officials and people into error and is guilty of high treason. Any of the officials and people of Chi-pei who had already by their own efforts restored order before our troops arrived, or who surrendered with their armies and lands, shall be pardoned and restored to their former posts and ranks. Any persons now with the king who shall desert him and come over to the side of the Han shall likewise be pardoned.

In the eighth month the army of the king of Chi-pei was defeated and the king was taken prisoner.[17] The emperor pardoned all the officials and people of Chi-pei who had joined with the king in revolt.

In the sixth year the officials concerned reported that Liu Ch'ang, the king of Huai-nan, was disregarding the laws of the previous emperors and failing to obey the edicts of the Son of Heaven. His dwellings exceeded what was proper for his position, they asserted, while in his manner of coming and going he imitated the Son of Heaven. He arbitrarily issued laws and commands, was secretly plotting with Ch'en Wu's heir, Ch'en Ch'i, the marquis of Chi-p'u, and had dispatched men to the Min-yüeh people of the south and the Hsiung-nu to encourage them to send out their troops, intending to threaten the ancestral temples and sacred altars of the dynasty. The various officials debated the matter and announced that "Liu Ch'ang deserves to be executed and his corpse exposed in the market place!" The emperor, however, could not bear to apply the law to the king, who was his

[17] He committed suicide.

younger brother. Instead he pardoned his offenses but removed him from his position as king of Huai-nan. The officials requested that the deposed king be exiled to Ch'iung-tu in Yen-tao in the province of Shu. The emperor sanctioned the move, but before Liu Ch'ang reached his place of exile he fell ill and died along the way. The emperor was grieved by his death and later, in the sixteenth year of his reign, honored him with the posthumous title of Li, the "Cruel King," [18] and set up his three sons as the kings of Huai-nan, Heng-shan, and Lu-chiang respectively.

In the summer of the thirteenth year the emperor announced:

I have heard that disaster arises naturally in response to the hatreds of the ruler, while good fortune is brought about by his virtue; it is thus that the way of Heaven operates. Therefore all the faults of my officials must have their origin in me. Now the post of private invocator [19] is intended to transfer the ruler's errors to his subordinates, which is only to make my lack of virtue clearer than ever. I find such a practice wholly unacceptable. Let the post be abolished.

In the fifth month Lord Ch'un-yü, the chief of the treasury in the state of Ch'i, was accused of some crime and sentenced to punishment. Orders were issued to have him bound and escorted under guard to the capital for imprisonment. Lord Ch'un-yü had no sons, but only five daughters, and when he was about to be taken away under guard, he railed at them, saying, "I had the bad luck to sire you instead of sons, and now when trouble is upon me you are no use at all!"

His youngest daughter T'i-jung was deeply grieved and, weeping bitterly, followed her father to Ch'ang-an, where she sent a letter to the officials saying:

When my father was an official everyone in Ch'i praised him for his integrity and fairness, but now he has been brought before the law and condemned to punishment. I grieve to think that those who are dead can never return

---

[18] Posthumous titles were by no means always complimentary, and the title Li—"Cruel" or "Stern"—was often given to kings or feudal lords who were judged to have been guilty of misrule.

[19] An official who offered prayers in the palace and begged that he, the other officials, and the people might receive divine punishment for any faults committed by the emperor.

to life again, and those who have suffered mutilating punishments can never again be like other men. Thus, though they might hope to mend their errors and make a new beginning, the way is forever cut off. I beg that I may give myself up and become a government slave to atone for my father's offense so that he himself may have a chance to begin anew!

The letter was brought to the attention of the emperor who, moved to pity by her request, forthwith issued an edict saying:

I have heard that in the time of the sage emperor Shun only painted robes, caps, or different kinds of uniforms were prescribed as punishments, and yet none of the people violated the laws. Such was the excellence of his rule! Today the laws impose three types of mutilating punishments, and still evil-doers do not desist.[20] Where does the fault lie? Is it not that my virtue is insufficient and my teachings lacking in enlightenment? I am filled with the deepest shame! Thus it is that if the leadership and guidance of the ruler are not sincere the people in their ignorance will fall into crime. The *Book of Odes* says:

> Just and gentle is the true prince,
> Father and mother to his people.[21]

Now, when men have some fault, punishments are imposed upon them before they have even been taught what is right, so that although they may wish to mend their actions and do good, there is no way open for them. I am deeply grieved at this. Punishments which extend to the cutting off of limbs or the piercing of flesh, leaving the victim maimed for life, are unspeakably cruel and unjust. How can a ruler who countenances such things be called a "father and a mother to his people"? Let the mutilating punishments be abolished![22]

The emperor announced:

Agriculture is the basis of the empire. Among the endeavors of man, none is more important. Yet at present those who labor at agricultural pursuits still have to pay both the land tax and the produce tax. In this respect there is no difference made between the fundamental pursuits of agriculture and the

---

[20] Commentators disagree, but it is probable that the three punishments were tattooing, cutting off the nose, and cutting off the heel. Castration may perhaps be included.

[21] *Ta-ya* section, decade of "Sheng-min," "Chiung-cho."

[22] Other types of punishment, such as flogging or binding with manacles, were substituted.

secondary pursuits of trade. This is surely not the proper way to encourage agriculture. Let the land and produce taxes on cultivated fields be abolished.

In the winter of the fourteenth year the Hsiung-nu, having laid plans to invade our borders for the purpose of plunder, attacked the bastion at Ch'ao-na and killed Sun Ang, the chief commandant of the province of Pei-ti. The emperor accordingly dispatched three generals to garrison the provinces of Lung-hsi, Pei-ti, and Shang. The palace military commander Chou She was made general of the guards and the chief of palace attendants Chang Wu was made general of carriage and cavalry and sent to camp north of the Wei River with a force of a thousand carriages and a hundred thousand cavalry and foot soldiers. The emperor went himself to comfort and exhort the troops, announcing to them their orders and presenting gifts to the officers and men. It was the emperor's desire to lead them in person against the Hsiung-nu and, although his officials remonstrated with him, he refused to heed them. It was not until his mother, Empress Dowager Po, pleaded with him that he abandoned the idea. Instead he appointed Chang Hsiang-ju, the marquis of Tung-yang, as general in chief; Tung Ch'ih, the marquis of Ch'eng, as prefect of the capital; and Lüan Pu as a general and sent them to attack the Hsiung-nu. The Hsiung-nu fled from the land.

In the spring the emperor announced:

For fourteen years now I have been allowed to present the sacrificial victims, the jade tablets, and offerings of silk in the service of the Lord on High and the ancestral temples. The days are long in which, with neither wisdom nor understanding, I have watched over the empire, and I am filled with shame. Let the altars and altar grounds be broadened and the jade tablets and silks for the various sacrifices be increased.

Though the kings of ancient times spread their goodness abroad, they did not seek for any reward. Though they sacrificed to the mountains and rivers, they did not pray for their own good fortune. They honored the wise above all and considered their own kin second; they put the people first and themselves last. Theirs was the highest order of wisdom.

Now I have heard that, when the sacrificial officials pray for blessings, they ask that all the good fortune may come to me in person, and say nothing of the common people. I am deeply shamed by this. Am I, who am without virtue, alone to enjoy good fortune and receive blessings, and are my people to have no part in them? This is only to double my lack of virtue! Let the sacrificial officials conduct their duties with all due reverence, but let them not pray for such blessings!

Chang Ts'ang, the marquis of Pei-p'ing, who at this time was acting as chancellor, was very learned in matters of the pitch pipes and the calendar. It happened that a man of Lu named Kung-sun Ch'en submitted a letter to the authorities expounding the manner in which the five elements succeed each other in a continuous cycle, and stating that the present age was under the dominance of the element earth. As proof of this, he asserted, a yellow dragon would appear, yellow being the color of the element earth. He therefore believed it appropriate for the dynasty to change the month on which the year began, to alter the color of the vestments, and to change other regulations of the government to accord with this fact.

The emperor referred the matter to his ministers and deliberated on it with the chancellor Chang Ts'ang. But Chang Ts'ang, insisting that the element water was clearly in the ascendancy, asserted that the dynasty should honor black, the color of the element water, and continue to begin the year with the tenth month. He regarded Kung-sun Ch'en's assertions as completely false and requested that they be disregarded.

In the fifteenth year a yellow dragon appeared at Ch'eng-chi, and the emperor reopened the matter, summoning Kung-sun Ch'en to court and making him an erudit, with instructions to explain in full his theory of the ascendance of the element earth. The emperor then issued an edict saying:

A supernatural being in the form of a strange creature has appeared at Ch'eng-chi, but no harm will come to the people, and the year will be a plentiful one. I wish in person to perform the suburban sacrifice to the Lord on High and to the other spirits. Let the officials in charge of rites deliberate on the matter. Let them not hesitate in their recommendations for fear of putting me to too much trouble.

The officials in charge of rites all replied, "It was customary for the Son of Heaven in ancient times to proceed to the suburbs in the summer to sacrifice in person to the Lord on High. Hence this was called the 'suburban sacrifice.'" In accordance with their instructions the emperor for the first time paid a visit to Yung and performed the suburban sacrifice to the Emperors of the Five Directions. The ceremony was performed in the fourth month, the first month of summer.

A man of Chao named Hsin-yüan P'ing, appearing before the emperor to report an unusual cloud formation he had seen, advised the emperor to set up temples to the Five Emperors north of the Wei River. He requested that a search be made for the cauldrons of Chou and predicted that a jade of extraordinary beauty would appear.[23]

In the sixteenth year the emperor in person performed the suburban sacrifice at the temples of the Five Emperors. Because, like the previous ceremony, this one was also performed in the summer, the highest honor was paid to red, the color of the summer season.

In the seventeenth year a jade cup was found bearing the inscription "Long Life to the Lord of Men." Because of this the emperor began to number the years of his reign over again, calling this year the "first year." He ordered that there be great feasting and drinking throughout the empire. In the same year it was discovered that the jade cup and the other signs and wonders reported by Hsin-yüan P'ing were all frauds, and he was executed along with his three sets of relatives.

In the second year of the latter part of his reign the emperor announced:

I am without understanding and have been unable to spread virtue abroad, and so I have not brought order and quiet to the lands beyond our borders. Thus the people who dwell in the wastelands that surround China are not at peace in their way of life, while those within our realm labor and find no rest. Both of these faults have come about because my virtue is insufficient and has failed to penetrate to distant regions.

For several years past the Hsiung-nu have repeatedly violated our borders and killed many of our officials and people, while the ministers and troops stationed on the border have been unable to convince them of my good will. Thus the evidence of my lack of virtue has been doubled. Yet, if we were

---

[23] The Five Emperors are the deities of the four directions and the center. The "cauldrons of Chou," sacred vessels used by the royal house of Chou, were supposedly lost when the Ch'in overthrew the dynasty. A much fuller account of this incident is given in the "Treatise on the Feng and Shan Sacrifices," *Shih chi* 28, translated in Volume II. To make the narrative clearer here I have supplemented it slightly with material from that account.

to continue to face them as enemies and join our troops in battle, how would peace ever be brought to our country and theirs?

I have risen early and retired late, laboring for the sake of the empire and taking thought for the people: for them I have been filled with concern and unrest, and their troubles have not left my mind for a single day. Therefore I have dispatched envoys in such profusion that their caps and cart covers are within sight of each other on the road, and their wheel tracks are joined, in order to explain my intentions to the *Shan-yü,* the ruler of the Hsiung-nu. At last the *Shan-yü* has returned to the wise ways of earlier times and, to insure the safety of the sacred altars of the soil and grain and to bring benefit to the common people, has joined with me anew. Together we have cast aside our petty faults and together we will walk the higher road of virtue. We have united ourselves in bonds of brotherhood in order to preserve the multitudes of the world. Our peace has been concluded; let it begin from this year!

In the sixth year of the latter part of the emperor's reign, in the winter, the Hsiung-nu invaded the province of Shang with a force of thirty thousand men, and the Yün-chung province with the same number. In order to defend the empire against the barbarians the emperor appointed the palace counselor Ling Mien as general of carriage and cavalry and sent him to guard the pass at Flying Fox; the former prime minister of Ch'u, Su I, he made a general and sent to guard the Chü-chu Pass; General Ch'ang Wu was ordered to garrison Pei-ti; the governor of Ho-nei, Chou Ya-fu, was made a general and ordered to Hsi-liu; the director of the imperial clan Liu Li was made a general and sent to the Pa River; and the marquis of Chu-tzu, Hsü Li, was made a general and sent to garrison Chi-men. After a few months the barbarians withdrew and the armies were recalled.

The empire was afflicted by drought and locusts. The emperor showed his mercy by ordering the feudal lords not to send their usual offerings of tribute, relaxing the laws which prohibited the use of the natural resources of mountains and lakes, economizing on the imperial robes, carriages, dogs, and horses, reducing the number of palace attendants and officials, and opening the storehouses and granaries in order to relieve the sufferings of the poor. He also allowed the people to buy and sell noble ranks.

It had now been twenty-three years since Emperor Wen the Filial first arrived from Tai to take the throne. In that time he had made no move to increase the size of the palaces or halls, the parks or enclosures, or the number of dogs and horses, vestments and carriages. Whenever some practice proved harmful, he immediately abandoned it in order to insure benefit to the people. Once the emperor thought of constructing an open terrace and summoned artisans to discuss the matter. When they informed him that it would cost a hundred catties of gold, he replied, "A hundred catties of gold is as much as the wealth of ten families of moderate means! Since I inherited the palaces of the former emperors I have constantly been afraid that I might dishonor them. What business would I have in building such a terrace?"

The emperor always dressed in robes of thick, coarse silk. He would not allow his favorite, Lady Shen, to wear gowns that trailed on the ground, nor would he have curtains or hangings with embroidered patterns on them. Thus he set an example for the empire in the simplicity of his way of life. In constructing his tomb at Pa-ling he had pottery vessels used throughout, not permitting gold, silver, copper, or tin to be employed for ornamentation, and he did not have a mound constructed. All this he did to save expense and because he did not wish to put the people to great labor.

When Chao T'o, the king of Southern Yüeh, declared himself an emperor with the title "Emperor Wu," Emperor Wen summoned Chao T'o's brothers to court and treated them with great honor, requiting all of Chao T'o's deeds with virtue, so that Chao T'o eventually renounced the title of emperor and acknowledged himself a subject of the Han. The emperor made peace with the Hsiung-nu and, when they violated their agreement and invaded and plundered the borders, he ordered the border guards to stick to their posts but would not send troops deep into barbarian territory. This was because he hated to bring hardship and suffering to the common people. When Liu P'i, the king of Wu, feigned illness and would not come to court, the emperor granted him a stool and cane.[24]

Although among his officials there were men like Yüan Ang who

[24] Gifts made to aged officials, indicating that the emperor was willing to excuse his absence because of old age.

advised him in a very outspoken manner, he forgave their sharpness and listened to their advice; when he discovered that others of his officials, like Ch'ang Wu, were accepting bribes of gold or cash, he would not have them hauled before the law officials but would open his own private coffers and present them with further gifts of gold and cash so as to make them ashamed of their conduct. His whole concern was to transform the people by means of virtue. Thus the entire region within the four seas enjoyed wealth and plenty and devoted itself to the observance of propriety and duty.

In the seventh year of the latter part of his reign, on the day *chi-hai* of the sixth month [July 6, 157 B.C.], the emperor passed away in the Eternal Palace. His testamentary edict read:

> I have heard that of all the countless beings beneath heaven which sprout or are brought to life, there is none which does not have its time of death, for death is a part of the abiding order of heaven and earth and the natural end of all creatures. How then can it be such a sorrowful thing? Yet in the world today, because all men rejoice in life and hate death, they exhaust their wealth in providing lavish burials for the departed, and endanger their health by prolonged mourning. I can in no way approve of such practices.
>
> I, who am without virtue, have had no means to bring succor to the people. Now that I have passed away, if I were to inflict upon them deep mourning and prolonged lamentation, exposing them to the cold and heat of successive seasons, grieving the fathers and sons of the people and blighting the desires of old and young, causing them to diminish their food and drink and to interrupt the sacrifices to the ancestors and spirits, I would only deepen my lack of virtue. What then could I say to the world?
>
> For over twenty years now I have been allowed to guard the ancestral temples of the dynasty, and with my poor person have been entrusted with a position above the lords and kings of the empire. With the aid of the spirits of heaven and earth and the blessings of our sacred altars, peace has been brought to the region within the seas, and the empire is without armed strife. I, who am without wisdom, have been in constant fear that I might commit some fault to bring dishonor upon the virtue handed down to me by those rulers who went before me. As my years of rule grew longer, I trembled lest they should not reach a just conclusion. Yet now I have been permitted to live out the years which heaven granted to me, and graciously allowed to serve the ancestral temple of Emperor Kao-tsu. For one so un-

enlightened as I, is this not a cause for rejoicing? Why should there be any sadness or sorrow?

Let the officials and people of the empire be instructed that, whenever this order shall reach them, they shall take part in lamentations for three days, after which all shall remove their mourning garments. There shall be no prohibitions against taking a wife or giving a daughter in marriage, or against performing sacrifices or partaking of wine and meat.

As for those who shall take part in the actual funeral proceedings and lamentations, they need not wear the customary unhemmed robes, and their headbands and sashes should not exceed three inches in width. There shall be no display of chariots or weapons, nor shall men and women be summoned from among the people to wail and lament in the palace. Those whose duty it is to lament in the palace shall do so only in the morning and evening, raising their voices fifteen times on each occasion, and, when the funeral rites have come to an end, this practice shall cease. There shall be no indiscriminate wailing other than at these prescribed times. After the coffin has been lowered into the grave, deep mourning shall be worn for fifteen days, light mourning for fourteen days, and thin garments for seven days, and then all mourning clothes shall be removed. Matters which are not specifically covered herein shall be disposed of in accordance with the spirit of this order. All of this shall be announced to the people of the empire so that they may understand my will. The hills and rivers around my tomb at Pa-ling may be left in their natural state and need not be altered in any way. The ladies of the palace, from those of the highest rank down to the junior maids, shall be sent back to their homes.

By the same edict the military commander Chou Ya-fu was appointed general of carriage and cavalry; the director of dependent states Hsü Tao was made general of encampments; and the chief of palace attendants Chang Wu was made general in charge of replacing the grave earth. Sixteen thousand soldiers from the nearby districts and fifteen thousand who were under the prefect of the capital were called out to attend the funeral. The interment of the coffin and the digging out and replacing of the earth were under the supervision of General Chang Wu.

On the day *i-ssu* [July 12, 157 B.C.] the emperor was interred.[25] All the officials bowed their heads and honored him with the title of

---

[25] The end of the sentence has dropped out of the present text but is found in the parallel passage in *Han shu* 4.

Emperor Wen the Filial

Supreme Emperor Wen the Filial. The heir apparent succeeded to the throne in the funerary temple of Emperor Kao-tsu. On the day *ting-wei* [July 14] he inherited the title of "Supreme Emperor."

In the first year, the tenth month of his new reign, the new emperor, whose posthumous title is Supreme Emperor Ching the Filial, issued an edict to the imperial secretary which read:

It is said that the ancients named as founder of a dynasty him who had achieved great deeds, and as its patriarch him who possessed true virtue, and that each was honored with the appropriate types of rites and music. Songs, they say, give expression to virtue, while dances show forth great deeds. At present, when the sacrificial wine is presented in the ancestral temple of Emperor Kao-tsu, the dances of Military Virtue, the Peaceful Beginning, and the Five Elements are performed, and at the presentation of the wine in the temple of Emperor Hui, the dances of the Peaceful Beginning and the Five Elements.

When Emperor Wen the Filial ruled over the empire he opened up the passes and bridges so that it was as easy to travel to distant regions as to those nearby; he abolished the laws against treasonable talk, did away with mutilating punishments, bestowed gifts upon the aged, and in his mercy took care of the homeless and orphaned, so that all living creatures might find succor. He restrained his own tastes and desires and would not accept the gifts presented to him; in no way would he seek for personal gain. He abolished the laws which enslaved the families of criminals and refrained from punishing the innocent; he did away with the punishment of castration,[26] and sent the women of the palace back to their homes, for he held it a grave matter that families should be left without heirs.

I am without wisdom and can scarcely understand such matters, and yet it seems to me that these deeds which Emperor Wen himself carried out are such as even the rulers of ancient times could not rival. The wealth of his virtue matched that of heaven and earth, his blessings flowed to all within the seas, and there were none who did not enjoy good fortune therein. His enlightenment shone like the very sun and moon themselves, and yet I am deeply fearful that the music of his ancestral temple will be inadequate to express it. Therefore let the dance of Glorious Virtue be prepared for performance in his ancestral temple, in order to make clear to all the beauty of his virtue. Then if the great deeds and virtue of the Founder and the Patriarch may be recorded upon bamboo and silk and handed down to

---

[26] Following the reading in *Han shu* 5.

countless generations so that they are known forever, I may indeed rejoice. Let the chancellor, the marquises, the high officials, and the officers in charge of rites draw up the full details of the ceremony and present them to me.

The chancellor Shen-t'u Chia and the other officials replied, "Your Majesty, thinking always of the fulfillment of filial duty, has ordered the performance of the dance of Glorious Virtue in order to manifest the abundant virtue of Emperor Wen. Though we, your subjects, were incapable in our ignorance of envisioning such a move, we have respectfully deliberated the question and wish to announce that, since no one achieved greater deeds than Emperor Kao-tsu and no one possessed such abundant virtue as Emperor Wen, the funerary temple of Emperor Kao-tsu should be designated the Temple of the Great Founder, and that of Emperor Wen the Temple of the Great Patriarch. The Sons of Heaven in generations to come shall present their offerings in these temples. The provinces and feudal territories should each be instructed to set up a temple to Emperor Wen, the Great Patriarch, and delegates from the kings and marquises should be sent to the capital to attend the sacrifices which the Son of Heaven offers yearly in the temples of the Founder and the Patriarch. If these proposals are acceptable, we beg that they be recorded on bamboo and silk and published throughout the empire." The emperor gave his approval.

The Grand Historian remarks: Confucius said that when a dynasty is founded, "a generation must pass before there can be truly benevolent government," and that "if good men rule the state, they may in the course of a hundred years succeed in wiping out violence and do away with capital punishment." [27] How true are his words!

Emperor Wen reigned some forty years after the founding of the Han, and his virtue was of the highest order. The time had drawn near when he might appropriately have changed the beginning of the year, altered the court vestments, and performed the Feng and Shan sacrifices. But the emperor modestly declined within his reign to take such steps. Ah, was he not benevolent indeed? [28]

[27] *Analects* XIII, 12 & 11.
[28] This last appears to be a veiled attack on Emperor Wu who, in Ssu-ma Ch'ien's estimation, was far less "virtuous" and "benevolent" than Emperor Wen, but who nevertheless did not hesitate to take the steps mentioned.

Shih chi 11: The Basic Annals of Emperor Ching the Filial

The feudal lords grew arrogant and the king of Wu led them in revolt, until the armies of the capital marched to punish them and the seven kingdoms suffered for their crimes. The empire was restored to harmony, and peace and prosperity reigned. Thus I made The Basic Annals of Emperor Ching the Filial.[1]

Emperor Ching the Filial was one of the younger sons of Emperor Wen. His mother was Empress Dowager Tou. While Emperor Wen was still king of Tai he had three sons by his first consort, but after Lady Tou obtained favor with the king this earlier consort died, and was soon followed in death by each of her three sons in turn. Therefore it was Lady Tou's son Emperor Ching who succeeded to the throne.

In the fourth month of the first year of his reign, on the day *i-mao* [May 18, 156 B.C.], a general amnesty was granted to the empire and the common people were given one step in rank.[2]

In the fifth month the tax on cultivated fields was reduced to half the former amount. The Temple of the Great Patriarch was set up

---

[1] The reader is almost certain to find this chapter exasperatingly dull. It is made up neither of lively anecdotes such as fill the annals of Kao-tsu or Empress Lü, nor of stately edicts like the preceding chapter: it is in fact no more than a dry outline of administrative acts, changes in government personnel, and natural phenomena during the reign of Emperor Ching, in many places confused and of doubtful accuracy. This fact has led some commentators to surmise that it was not composed by Ssu-ma Ch'ien at all, but there is no evidence for this view. It is more likely that Ssu-ma Ch'ien wrote the summary and closing remarks of the chapter as he wished them to appear, and left the rest in the form of notes on the material he intended to include. Ssu-ma Ch'ien, one may recall, lived during the reign of Emperor Wu, Emperor Ching's son and successor. Perhaps he put off completing the chapter in hopes of gathering more material on so recent a period. Or perhaps he despaired of ever being able to write frankly about the father so long as he served at the court of the son. Whatever the case, this is the chapter as it has come down to us.

[2] The second date *i-ssu*, which appears in the original at this point, is an error.

for Emperor Wen, but the various officials were not required to come to court to present their congratulations. The Hsiung-nu invaded Tai, but an alliance of peace was made with them.

In the spring of the second year Hsiao Hsi, the grandson of the former prime minister Hsiao Ho, was enfeoffed as marquis of Wu-ling. Young men were ordered to register for military service at the age of twenty.[3]

In the fourth month, on the day *jen-wu* [June 9, 155 B.C.], Empress Dowager Po, the mother of Emperor Wen, passed away. The kings of Kuang-ch'uan and Ch'ang-sha both proceeded to their kingdoms. The chancellor Shen-t'u Chia died.

In the eighth month the imperial secretary T'ao Ch'ing, the marquis of K'ai-feng, was appointed chancellor. A comet appeared in the northeastern sky.

In the autumn hail fell in Heng-shan; the hailstones measured as much as five inches and penetrated two feet into the ground. Mars reversed its course and took up a position near the North Star, the moon appeared in the sector of the North Star, and Jupiter moved backwards and passed through the constellation of the Heavenly Court.[4] Nan-ling and Tui-yü, in the capital area, were made into districts.

In the first month of the third year, the day *i-ssu* [Feb. 27, 154 B.C.], a general amnesty was granted to the empire. A long-tailed star was seen in the east. Fire appeared in the sky, and the main hall and other buildings of the Eastern Palace at Lo-yang burned down.

The king of Wu, Liu P'i; the king of Ch'u, Liu Mou; the king of Chao, Liu Sui; the king of Chiao-hsi, Liu Ang; the king of Chi-nan, Liu Pi-kuang; the king of Tzu-ch'uan, Liu Hsien; and the king of Chiao-tung, Liu Hsiung-ch'ü, revolted and sent their troops west toward the capital. To appease them the emperor executed Ch'ao Ts'o and dispatched Yüan Ang to report what he had done and persuade them to desist, but they refused to halt their troops. Eventually they marched west and surrounded the king of Liang. The emperor there-

[3] The military age before this, and again later, was twenty-three.

[4] Various emendations have been suggested to try to make the text conform with astronomical common sense. Unusual movements of Mars were regarded as portents of war.

upon dispatched the general in chief Tou Ying and the grand commandant Chou Ya-fu to lead their troops and put down the revolt.

In the sixth month, the day *i-hai* [July 27, 154 B.C.], pardon was granted to those who had deserted the army of rebellion and to Liu I, the son of King Yüan of Ch'u, and others who had taken part in the plot. The general in chief Tou Ying was enfeoffed as marquis of Wei-ch'i. The marquis of P'ing-lu, Liu Li, the son of King Yüan of Ch'u, was set up as the new king of Ch'u. The emperor also set up his own son Liu Tuan as king of Chiao-hsi and his son Liu Sheng as king of Chung-shan; Liu Chih, the king of Chi-pei, he transferred to the position of king of Tzu-ch'uan; Liu Yü, the king of Huai-yang, he made king of Lu, and Liu Fei, the king of Ju-nan, he made king of Chiang-tu. Liu Chiang-lü, the king of Ch'i, and Liu Chia, the king of Yen, both died.

In the summer of the fourth year the emperor named his son Liu Jung as heir apparent and set up his son Liu Ch'e as king of Chiao-tung. In the sixth month, on the day *chia-hsü* [July 20, 153 B.C.], a general amnesty was granted to the empire.

In the intercalary ninth month the place called I-yang was renamed Yang-ling.[5] The emperor reestablished the barriers at the fords and passes and ordered the use of passports for persons traveling through them.

In the winter the kingdom of Chao was made into the province of Han-tan.

In the third month of the fifth year a bridge over the Wei River was built at Yang-ling. In the fifth month the emperor invited people to move to Yang-ling, granting them two hundred thousand cash. At Chiang-tu a violent wind blew up from the west and destroyed the city wall for a length of twelve spans. On the day *ting-mao* [July 8, 152 B.C.] the emperor enfeoffed Liu Chiao, the son of his daughter, Princess Ch'ang, as marquis of Lung-lü and transferred the king of Kuang-ch'uan to the position of king of Chao.

In the spring of the sixth year the emperor enfeoffed the military commander of the capital, Chao Wan, as marquis of Chien-ling; the

[5] Or "Yang Tomb," the place where Emperor Ching was planning to build his mausoleum.

chancellor of Chiang-tu, Ch'eng Chia, as marquis of Chien-p'ing; the governor of Lung-hsi, Hun Hsieh, as marquis of P'ing-chü; the chancellor of Chao, Su Chia, as marquis of Chiang-ling; and the former general Pu as marquis of Yü. The kings of Liang and Ch'u both died. In the intercalary ninth month the trees along the imperial highway were cut down and used to fill in the Orchid Lake.

In the winter of the seventh year the emperor removed Liu Jung, his son by Lady Li, from the position of heir apparent and made him king of Lin-chiang. On the last day of the twelfth month there was an eclipse of the sun.

In the spring the emperor dismissed the convict laborers who had been brought to construct his tomb at Yang-ling. T'ao Ch'ing resigned from the post of chancellor and, in the second month, on the day *i-ssu* [April 7, 150 B.C.], the grand commandant Chou Ya-fu, the marquis of T'iao, was appointed chancellor.

In the fourth month, on the day *i-ssu* [June 6], the emperor set up Lady Wang (later Empress Dowager Wang), as his empress, and on the day *ting-ssu* [June 18] designated her son, the king of Chiao-tung, as heir apparent. (His name was Liu Ch'e.) [6]

In the first year of the middle period of his reign [7] the emperor enfeoffed Chou P'ing, the grandson of the former imperial secretary Chou Ho, as marquis of Sheng, and Chou Tso-ch'e, the son of the former imperial secretary Chou Ch'ang, as marquis of An-yang.

On the day *i-ssu* of the fourth month [May 31, 149 B.C.] a general amnesty was proclaimed to the empire and the common people were awarded one step in rank. The practice of holding offending officials in custody and debarring them from further office was abolished. There was an earthquake, and at Yüan-tu in Heng-shan hail fell, the stones reaching a size of a foot and eight inches.

[6] This and the earlier mention of Liu Ch'e's given name above are probably later interpolations, since Ssu-ma Ch'ien was writing during the lifetime of Liu Ch'e, i.e., Emperor Wu, and would have been forbidden by taboo to mention the emperor's personal name.

[7] In imitation of his father's practice, Emperor Ching began at this date to number the years of his reign from one again. Under Emperor Wu this practice was elaborated by the selection of "era names" each time the numbering began anew.

In the second year of the middle period, the second month, the Hsiung-nu invaded Yen, and peaceful relations with them came to an end.

In the third month Liu Jung, the king of Lin-chiang, was summoned to the capital and died in the offices of the military commander of the capital.

In the summer the emperor set up his son Liu Yüeh as king of Kuang-ch'uan and his son Liu Chi as king of Chiao-tung. He enfeoffed four men as marquises.

In the ninth month, on the day *chia-hsü* [Oct. 22, 148 B.C.], there was an eclipse of the sun.

In the winter of the third year of the middle period the office of grand secretary at the courts of the various feudal lords was abolished.

In the spring two kings of the Hsiung-nu appeared with their followers and surrendered to the Han. Both were enfeoffed as marquises. The emperor set up his son Liu Fang-sheng as king of Ch'ing-ho.

In the third month a comet appeared in the northwest. The chancellor Chou Ya-fu died, and the imperial secretary Liu She, the marquis of T'ao, was made chancellor. In the fourth month an earthquake occurred.

On the last day of the ninth month, the day *mou-hsü* [Nov. 10, 147 B.C.], there was an eclipse of the sun. A garrison was established outside the Gate of the Eastern Capital.[8]

In the fourth year of the middle period, the third month, the Palace of Virtue Ascendant was established. There was a great plague of locusts. In the autumn the convict laborers from Yang-ling were pardoned.

In the summer of the fifth year of the middle period the emperor set up his son Liu Shun as king of Ch'ang-shan and enfeoffed ten men as marquises. On the day *ting-ssu* of the sixth month [July 21, 145 B.C.] a general amnesty was proclaimed to the empire and the common people were granted one step in rank. Torrential rains fell throughout

[8] Gates of Chinese cities were often named after the places to which people who went out of them were traveling, so that this would seem to be the gate one left from when going to Lo-yang, the "Eastern Capital." But Lo-yang was not known by this title, at least officially, until some time later, so the name may mean the "Gate of the Eastern Wall of the Capital."

the empire. The office of chancellor to the feudal lords was renamed prime minister. In the autumn there was an earthquake.

In the second month of the sixth year of the middle period, on the day *chi-mao* [April 7, 144 B.C.], the emperor paid a visit to Yung and performed the suburban sacrifice to the Five Emperors. In the third month there was a hail storm. In the fourth month King Hsiao of Liang, King Kung of Ch'eng-yang, and the king of Ju-nan all died. The emperor set up King Hsiao's son Liu Ming as king of Chi-ch'uan, his son Liu P'eng-li as king of Chi-tung, his son Liu Ting as king of Shan-yang, and his son Liu Pu-shih as king of Chi-yin. He divided the territory of Liang into five parts and enfeoffed four men as marquises.[9]

The office of commandant of justice was renamed grand examiner; that of master of the privy treasury was renamed master of public works; the master of titles military commander was renamed master of titles chief commandant; the purveyor of the Palace of Lasting Trust, where the empress and heir apparent lived, was renamed privy treasurer of the Palace of Lasting Trust; the general messenger of the empress was renamed messenger of the long autumn; the grand messenger was renamed messenger; the director of ritual was renamed master of ritual; the director of guests was renamed grand messenger; the secretary in charge of grain was renamed master of agriculture; the inner treasury was put under the charge of an official of the two thousand picul rank, and officers of the left and right inner treasury were established under him.

In the seventh month, on the day *hsin-hsi* [Sept. 8, 144 B.C.], there was an eclipse of the sun. In the eighth month the Hsiung-nu invaded Shang Province.

In the winter of the first year of the latter part of Emperor Ching's reign[10] the office of head of palace counselors was renamed colonel of the guard.

In the third month, on the day *ting-yu* [April 22, 143 B.C.], a general amnesty was proclaimed to the empire and the people were granted

---

[9] Almost every statement in this paragraph is contradicted or called into doubt in some fashion by the material in the *Han shu*.

[10] Emperor Ching began the numbering of the years of his reign again.

one step in rank. Officials with salaries of two thousand piculs of grain and prime ministers of feudal lords were granted the rank of senior chiefs of the multitude. In the fourth month there was universal feasting.

In the fifth month, on the day *ping-hsü* [June 10, 143 B.C.], there was an earthquake. At the time of the morning meal the earth shook again. In Shang-yung the earthquakes lasted for twenty-two days and destroyed the wall around the city.

In the seventh month, on the day *i-ssu* [Aug. 28, 143 B.C.], there was a solar eclipse. The chancellor Liu She resigned from his post.

On the day *jen-ch'en* of the eighth month [11] the imperial secretary Wei Wan was made chancellor and enfeoffed as marquis of Chien-ling.

In the second year of the latter period, the first month, earthquakes occurred three times in one day. General Chih attacked the Hsiung-nu. There was general feasting for five days. An order was given to the prefects of the capital area not to feed grain to horses, but to turn it in to the district officials. Convict laborers were to be dressed in seventh-grade coarse cloth; horses were no longer to be used to grind grain. Because the harvest was poor, the people of the empire were forbidden to eat in such quantity or fashion that the supplies would not last through the year. The number of marquises residing in the capital was reduced and the remainder were ordered to their territories.

In the third month the Hsiung-nu invaded Yen-men. In the tenth month taxes were levied on the cultivated fields at Ch'ang-ling.[12] There was severe drought, and in the kingdom of Heng-shan and the provinces of Ho-tung and Yün-chung the people suffered from disease.

In the third year of the latter period, the tenth month, both the sun and the moon were eclipsed and appeared red for five days. On the last day of the twelfth month it thundered. The sun turned purple; the five planets turned back in their courses and remained in the constellation of the Great Secret; the moon passed through the constellation of the Heavenly Court.

In the first month, the day *chia-yin* [Feb. 28, 141 B.C.], the heir ap-

[11] Something is wrong with the text, since no such day is possible in the eighth month.

[12] Which had previously been exempted because it was the site of Emperor Kao-tsu's tomb.

parent was awarded the cap of manhood. On the day *chia-tzu* [March 9] Emperor Ching the Filial passed away.

In his testamentary edict he directed that, from the feudal kings and marquises down to the sons of the common people who would succeed their fathers as heirs, all should be granted one step in rank; to each household of the empire he presented a hundred cash. He ordered his ladies of the palace to be sent back to their homes and exempted from taxes for life.

The heir apparent ascended the throne. (This was Emperor Wu the Filial.) [13]

In the third month the younger brothers of the empress dowager were enfeoffed, T'ien Fen as marquis of Wu-an and T'ien Sheng as marquis of Chou-yang. The emperor was interred at Yang-ling.

The Grand Historian remarks: After the Han arose, Emperor Wen conducted his rule with the utmost virtue so that the whole empire was brought to peace, and by the time of Emperor Ching the nobles who were not of the imperial family were no longer a source of anxiety. But Ch'ao Ts'o whittled away at the fiefs of the other nobles until he had caused the seven kingdoms to rise up, join together in alliance, and defy the capital. This came about because the nobles were too powerful, and because Ch'ao Ts'o's measures to suppress them were not gradual enough. Later, when the suggestions of Chu-fu Yen were put into effect, the nobles were weakened and eventually pacified. Truly, whether one achieves order or unrest in government depends in the end upon how well one plans!

[13] Since Ssu-ma Ch'ien wrote during Emperor Wu's reign, he always refers to him as "the present emperor." The use of the posthumous name "Wu" here and elsewhere in the *Shih chi* must be a later emendation of the text.

Shih chi 12: The Basic Annals of Emperor Wu (fragment)

When the fifth ruler came to the throne and began his reign in the era *chien-yüan* the Han dynasty reached its height of glory. He drove back the barbarian tribes beyond the borders, and within the country put the laws and regulations into order. He carried out the Feng and Shan sacrifices, changed the month on which the year began, and altered the color of the vestments. Thus I made The Basic Annals of the Present Emperor.

Emperor Wu the Filial was the ninth son of Emperor Ching. His mother was Empress Dowager Wang. In the fourth year of his reign Emperor Ching appointed this son as king of Chiao-tung. In the seventh year the heir apparent Liu Jung, the emperor's son by Lady Li, was removed from his position and appointed king of Lin-chiang. The king of Chiao-tung was designated as heir apparent in his place.

In the sixteenth year of his reign [141 B.C.] Emperor Ching passed away and the heir apparent succeeded to the throne. He is posthumously known as Emperor Wu the Filial.[1]

---

[1] From this point on the text is a duplication of *Shih chi* 28, the Treatise on the Feng and Shan Sacrifices, which someone has copied in to replace the missing chapter. Even the short passage with which the chapter opens is suspect, since it uses the emperor's posthumous title, Emperor Wu, which Ssu-ma Ch'ien presumably would never do. Only the résumé, which uses instead the phrase "the present emperor," seems to be indisputably the work of Ssu-ma Ch'ien. Whether Ssu-ma Ch'ien never got around to writing his chapter on "The Basic Annals of the Present Emperor," or whether he wrote it and it was later lost or suppressed, we do not know.

Part VIII
THE EMPRESSES

Shih chi 49: *The Hereditary Houses of the Families Related to the Emperors by Marriage*

It was on the Terrace of Perfect Blessing that Lady Po first attracted favor. Much against her will Lady Tou went to Tai and as a result her whole family won honor. Lady Li presumed upon her high position, and Lady Wang finally replaced her. Empress Ch'en was too proud, and Wei Tzu-fu in the end enjoyed higher honor. In recognition of the virtue which the succeeding empresses displayed, I made The Hereditary Houses of the Families Related to the Emperor by Marriage.

From antiquity the emperors and kings who were chosen by destiny to found new dynasties, as well as those who by birth succeeded to the throne and carried on the institutions of their predecessors, have won glory not only through the virtue of their own families, but have been aided also by the families related to them by marriage. Thus the Hsia dynasty arose from Emperor Yü's marriage to the Tu-shan family, while the banishment of the last Hsia ruler, Chieh, was brought about by his empress, Mo-hsi. The Yin dynasty had its beginning in the ancestress Yu-sung, but the death of its last emperor, Chou, was caused by his favorite, Ta-chi. The Chou dynasty began auspiciously with the ladies Chiang Yüan and Ta-jen, but it was King Yu's infatuation for Pao-ssu which led to his being seized by the invading barbarians. Therefore the *Book of Changes* takes as its basis *ch'ien* and *k'un*, the trigrams of the male and female; the *Book of Odes* opens with "The Crying Ospreys," a song in praise of the royal consort; the *Book of Documents* celebrates the marriage of Emperor Yao's daughters; and the *Spring and Autumn Annals* censures laxity in the wedding ceremonies. The bond between husband and wife is among the most solemn of human relationships. Of the prescriptions of ritual, none demand more strict observance than those of marriage. As the harmony of music brings order to the four seasons, so the interactions of the yin and yang, the male and female principles, are the origin of all creatures. How then can one fail to approach matters of marriage with the utmost circumspection? "Man may make great the Way," as Confucius says,[1] but over destiny he has no control. How profound a thing is the love between a lord and his consort! A love such as no ruler can win from his subjects, no father enjoy from his sons—how could such a love be mean and worthless?

Yet even the happiest unions are not always blessed with sons, and even when sons are given they do not always fulfill their promised ends. Is this not destiny? But destiny even Confucius seldom spoke of,[2] so difficult a subject is it to discuss. Unless one could penetrate all the interactions of universal light and darkness, how could he hope to understand the destinies of birth?

Empress Dowager Lü, Mother of Emperor Hui

The Grand Historian remarks: The ages before the Ch'in dynasty are too far away and the material on them too scanty to permit a detailed account of them here. When the Han was founded Lü E-hsü was made the official empress of Kao-tsu and her son became heir apparent. But as she grew older and her beauty faded, the emperor's affection for her waned; Lady Ch'i enjoyed all his attentions and her son Liu Ju-i several times came near to replacing the empress's son as heir apparent. After Kao-tsu passed away Empress Lü murdered Lady Ch'i and executed her son Ju-i, the king of Chao. Of the women of the inner palace, only those who had been left unnoticed and never enjoyed Kao-tsu's favor managed to escape harm.

Empress Lü's daughter was married to Chang Ao, the marquis of Hsüan-p'ing, and their daughter became the empress of Emperor Hui. Empress Lü, now known as the empress dowager, anxious to increase her ties with the imperial family, hoped that this girl would have a son but, though she resorted to every possible device, the young empress remained childless. Empress Dowager Lü then secretly took the

---

[1] *Analects* XV, 28. Throughout the chapter Ssu-ma Ch'ien keeps returning to the word *ming*—"destiny" or "fate"—by which he means specifically the fate that decrees whether an empress shall remain barren or bear a son to succeed to the throne.

[2] A reference to *Analects* IX, 1.

child of one of Emperor Hui's concubines and pretended that he was the son of the empress. When Emperor Hui passed away it was still only a short while since the dynasty had been founded and the question of who might succeed to the throne was unclear. Empress Dowager Lü accorded great honor to the members of her own clan, making kings of some of the men of the Lü family so that they might act as aides to the ruler. She also appointed the daughter of Lü Lu as empress to the child emperor whom she had selected to succeed Emperor Hui. Thus she hoped to establish firm ties that would bind her family more securely to the source of power. But it was to no avail.

When Empress Dowager Lü passed away she was buried with her husband, Emperor Kao-tsu, at Ch'ang-ling. Lü Lu, Lü Ch'an, and others of the Lü family, fearing punishment for their usurpations of power, plotted a revolt, but the great ministers overthrew them. Thus did Heaven guide the imperial line and in the end wipe out the Lü clan. Only the empress of Emperor Hui was spared, being sent to live in the Northern Palace. The king of Tai was invited to come and take the throne, and it was he, Emperor Wen, who with due reverence carried on the service of the ancestral temples of the Han. Was this not the work of Heaven? Who but one destined by Heaven for rule could assume such a charge?

Empress Dowager Po, Mother of Emperor Wen

The father of Empress Dowager Po was a man of Wu whose family name was Po. In the time of the Ch'in dynasty he had once had relations with Dame Wei, a daughter of the former royal family of the state of Wei, and from this union was born Lady Po. When Lady Po's father died he was buried at Shan-yin. After the feudal lords revolted against the Ch'in dynasty Wei Pao was set up as king of Wei, and Dame Wei summoned her daughter to live in the palace of Wei. Dame Wei once took her daughter to be physiognomized by a certain Hsü Fu. When he had examined Lady Po's face he said, "She shall give birth to a Son of Heaven." At this time Hsiang Yü and Kao-tsu, the king of Han, were locked in combat at Jung-yang, and the fate of the empire was uncertain. Wei Pao at first had joined with Kao-tsu's forces in attacking Hsiang Yü but, when he heard of Hsü

Fu's prediction, he was secretly pleased and, deserting Kao-tsu, took up a neutral position, at the same time concluding an alliance of peace with Hsiang Yü. Kao-tsu dispatched Ts'ao Ts'an and others to attack Wei Pao, who was taken prisoner. His kingdom was made into a province and Lady Po was sent to work in the Weaving Rooms.[3] After Wei Pao died Kao-tsu happened to visit the Weaving Rooms and, noticing the beauty of Lady Po, summoned her to his palace. Over a year passed, however, and she still had not enjoyed his favor.

When Lady Po was a little girl she was close friends with Madam Kuan and Chao Tzu-erh, and the three of them had once made a promise that "whichever wins honor first shall not forget her friends." Now Madam Kuan and Chao Tzu-erh were ladies in waiting in Kao-tsu's palace and had already enjoyed his favor. One day, when Kao-tsu was seated on the Terrace of Perfect Blessing of the Ho-nan Palace, these two ladies were laughing together over the promise they had made long ago with Lady Po. Kao-tsu, hearing their laughter, asked the cause, and they told him the whole story. The emperor was deeply moved and, out of pity for Lady Po, summoned her that very day and favored her. "Last night," said Lady Po, "I dreamed that an azure dragon lay upon my belly." "This is a wonderful sign," replied the emperor, "and for your sake I will make it come true!" From her one moment of favor a son was born who became the king of Tai. After this Lady Po seldom saw Kao-tsu.

After Kao-tsu passed away Lady Ch'i and all of the other concubines who had enjoyed the emperor's attentions were shut up in the palace by Empress Dowager Lü, because of the hatred she bore them, and were not allowed to leave. Only Lady Po, because she had rarely seen the emperor, was permitted to depart and accompany her son to Tai, where she was known as queen dowager of the king of Tai. Her younger brother Po Chao also went to Tai. After the king of Tai had held his position for seventeen years Empress Dowager Lü passed away and the great ministers began to discuss who should be set up as emperor. They resented the power which the Lü clan, as relatives through marriage of the imperial family, had managed to acquire, but

---

[3] Government-operated silk-weaving factories where women condemned for some offense were sent to work.

were unanimous in praising the members of the Po family for their humane and upright conduct. They therefore invited the king of Tai to come to the capital, where he was set up as Emperor Wen. Lady Po's title was changed from "Queen Dowager" to "Empress Dowager," and her brother Po Chao was enfeoffed as marquis of Chih.

The mother of Empress Dowager Po had died long before and was buried north of Li-yang. The father of Empress Dowager Po was honored with the posthumous title of Ling-wen or "Divine Order Marquis," and in the prefecture of K'uai-chi a park and village of three hundred families was set up, with a superintendent, assistants, and subordinate officials, to tend his grave, offer food before his sanctuary and temple, and perform sacrifices according to the law; north of Li-yang there was also set up the Park of the Lady of Marquis Ling-wen, modeled on that of the marquis. Empress Dowager Po considered that, since her mother's family had been descendants of the kings of Wei, and since she had lost her father and mother very early, her high position as empress dowager was due in reality to the efforts of the Wei family. Therefore she ordered that the Wei family be exempted from labor services, and further honored them with gifts, seeing to it that each person received something according to his degree of kinship. Of the Po family only one man, Po Chao, was made a marquis. Empress Dowager Po outlived her son Emperor Wen by two years, passing away in the second year of Emperor Ching's reign [155 B.C.]. She was buried at Nan-ling. This was because, Empress Lü having been buried with Emperor Kao-tsu at Ch'ang-ling, it was necessary to raise a separate grave mound for Empress Dowager Po, near to that of her son, Emperor Wen, at Pa-ling.

Empress Dowager Tou, Mother of Emperor Ching

Empress Dowager Tou was a native of Kuan-chin in Ch'ing-ho in the region of Chao. In the time of Empress Dowager Lü, Lady Tou, having been born of a good family, was sent to the palace to wait upon the empress dowager. Later Empress Dowager Lü selected a number of palace ladies to be presented to the various kings, bestowing five women upon each king, and Lady Tou was among those chosen to be sent. Since Lady Tou's family lived in Ch'ing-ho, she hoped to be sent to Chao so that she could be near them, and she asked the eunuch official in charge of making up the parties to put her name down on the list of those to be sent to the court of Chao. But the eunuch forgot and by mistake entered her name on the list for the court of Tai. The lists were then presented to the throne and received imperial approval. When the time came to depart Lady Tou was furious with the eunuch and, weeping bitterly, refused to go. Only after considerable urging was she persuaded to start on her way.

When she reached Tai the king of Tai gave all his attention to Lady Tou. She bore him a daughter named P'iao and later two sons. The queen of Tai also bore the king four sons, but she died before he was made emperor, and after he came to the throne his four sons by the queen one by one sickened and died.

Several months after the king of Tai became emperor the high officials requested that he appoint an heir apparent. Since Lady Tou's elder son was the oldest male heir, the emperor appointed him heir apparent and made Lady Tou his empress. Her daughter Liu P'iao was given the title of Princess Ch'ang. The following year her younger son Liu Wu became king of Tai. He was later removed from this position and transferred to that of king of Liang. He is posthumously known as King Hsiao of Liang.

Empress Tou's parents had died very early and were buried at Kuan-chin. Empress Tou therefore sent instructions to the officials that her father should be honored with the title of Wen-ch'eng or "Peaceful Accomplishment Marquis," and her mother with that of Lady Wen-ch'eng. A park and village of two hundred families was set up in Ch'ing-ho with a superintendent and assistants to tend the grave and offer sacrifices in the same way as was done at the Ling-wen Park, the grave of Empress Dowager Po's parents.

Empress Tou's elder brother was named Tou Ch'ang-chün, and her younger brother Tou Kuang-kuo or Shao-chün. When Shao-chün was four or five years old, and his family still very poor, he was carried off by kidnapers and sold as a servant. His family knew nothing of what had become of him. After being passed from one household to another some ten times or more he at last came to I-yang, where he was sent by his master into the mountains to make charcoal. When evening came [4] he lay down with a hundred or so other workmen beneath an embankment to sleep, but the embankment caved in and crushed the sleeping men to death. Only Shao-chün managed to escape alive. Consulting the arts of divination on what fate had in store for him after such a miraculous escape, he was informed that he would one day become a marquis.

Accompanying the family he was working for to Ch'ang-an, he heard that Empress Tou had just been named imperial consort, that her home was in Kuan-chin, and that her family name was Tou. At the time Shao-chün was stolen from his family he was still very young, but he had managed to remember the name of the district where he was born and his surname. He also remembered that once, when he was picking mulberry leaves with his sister, he fell out of the tree. Using these facts as proof of his identity, he sent a letter to the palace explaining his case. Empress Tou mentioned the matter to Emperor Wen, who summoned him to an audience and questioned him. Everything he said about his past did, indeed, seem to tally with the facts. The emperor then asked him if he had no further proof of his identity.

"When my sister left us and went off to the capital," he replied, "she said good-by to me at the post station. She called for rice water and washed my hair,[5] and then she ordered a meal and fed me—after that she went away." With this, Empress Tou embraced him and wept and the tears streamed down her cheeks. Her ladies in waiting all sank to the ground and wept, adding their sighs of pity to those of the empress. The empress rewarded him with generous gifts of land, houses, and money, and arranged for him and his older brother to reside in Ch'ang-an.

Chou P'o, Kuan Ying, and other important officials in the government consulted together, saying, "Even if men like ourselves manage to escape death, our lives will always be at the mercy of these two brothers. Since both of them are of humble origin, it is imperative that we select proper tutors and retainers for them. Otherwise they may try to imitate the fearful ways of the Lü family!" Accordingly they

[4] Following the reading in *Han shu* 97A.
[5] In place of soap, which was unknown, water in which rice or millet had been washed was used for washing the body or hair.

selected a number of worthy men and gentlemen known for virtuous conduct and sent them to live with the brothers. From this time Tou Ch'ang-chün and Tou Shao-chün conducted themselves as modest and retiring gentlemen and never ventured to make use of their position or influence to intimidate others.

Later, when Empress Tou fell ill and lost her sight, Emperor Wen favored Lady Shen of Han-tan and Lady Yin, but both were childless. After Emperor Wen passed away, when Emperor Ching came to the throne, he enfeoffed Tou Shao-chün as marquis of Chang-wu. Tou Ch'ang-chün had died sometime earlier, but the emperor enfeoffed his son Tou P'eng-tsu as marquis of Nan-p'i. At the time of the revolt of the kingdoms of Wu and Ch'u, Tou Ying, the son of Empress Dowager Tou's cousin, who delighted in adventurous exploits, was put in charge of a body of troops. As a result of his military achievements he was made marquis of Wei-ch'i. Thus three men of the Tou family became marquises.

Empress Dowager Tou was very fond of the doctrines of the Taoist school and as a result Emperor Wen, the heir apparent, and all the members of the Tou family were obliged to read the works of the Yellow Emperor and Lao Tzu and to honor their teachings. The empress dowager outlived her son Emperor Ching by six years, passing away in the sixth year of the *chien-yüan* era [135 B.C.]. She was buried with her husband Emperor Wen at Pa-ling. In her will she left her residence, the Eastern Palace, along with all her money and other possessions, to her daughter Liu P'iao, Princess Ch'ang.

Empress Dowager Wang, Mother of Emperor Wu

Empress Dowager Wang was a native of Huai-li. Her mother, whose name was Tsang Erh, was a granddaughter of Tsang Tu, at one time the king of Yen. Tsang Erh was married to a man of Huai-li named Wang Chung, to whom she bore a son, Wang Hsin, and two daughters. When her husband died she remarried into the T'ien family of Ch'ang-ling and bore two sons, T'ien Fen and T'ien Sheng. In time her older daughter married a man named Chin Wang-sun and bore a daughter. When Tsang Erh divined with the milfoil stalks, however, she was told that both of her daughters would become highly honored. She therefore decided to take greater pains with their futures and tried to get the older daughter away from the Chin family. The Chin family angrily refused to give up the girl, but Tsang Erh forced a separation and entered her in the palace of the heir apparent, the future Emperor Ching. The heir apparent took a great liking to the girl, who was known as Madam Wang, and she bore him three daughters and a son. While her son was still in the womb Madam Wang dreamed that the sun entered her breast.[6] She reported her dream to the heir apparent, who replied, "This is a sign of great honor!" Before the boy was born Emperor Wen passed away and the heir apparent ascended the throne to become Emperor Ching. It was after this that Madam Wang bore her son. Previously, Tsang Erh had also entered her younger daughter Wang Erh-hsü in the service of Emperor Ching. She bore the emperor four sons.

While Emperor Ching was still heir apparent his grandmother, Empress Dowager Po, had arranged for him to marry a girl of her own family, and when he became emperor this wife was given the title of Empress Po. But Empress Po had no sons and did not enjoy the affections of the emperor, so when Empress Dowager Po passed away the emperor removed her from the position of empress.

Emperor Ching's oldest son was Liu Jung, whose mother was Lady Li, a native of Ch'i. It was he whom Emperor Ching first designated as heir apparent. Princess Ch'ang had a daughter whom she wished to give to the heir apparent as a wife, but Lady Li was by nature jealous and, because all of Emperor Ching's other concubines, who far surpassed her in favor and honor, had obtained their positions in the palace through the introduction of Princess Ch'ang, she grew more resentful each day and declined Princess Ch'ang's offer of a bride for her son. Princess Ch'ang then offered her daughter to Madam Wang as a bride for *her* son, and Madam Wang consented to the match. Princess Ch'ang, angered at Lady Li's refusal, took every opportunity to talk viciously of her shortcomings to the emperor. "Whenever Lady Li meets any of the ladies of the inner palace who are more honored and favored than herself," she said, "she has her attendants utter curses and magic spells and spit behind their backs. She is prac-

[6] In Chinese dream interpretation, the sun is a symbol of the ruler.

ticing sorcery in an attempt to win your affections!" As a result of such talk Emperor Ching came to hate Lady Li. He had always been uneasy about his health and his mind was never at peace. He had entrusted his sons, whom he had made kings, to the care of Lady Li, telling her, "When my hundred years of life are ended, I hope you will look after them," but Lady Li in her resentment had refused to acknowledge his request, and when she did speak her words were lacking in humility. Emperor Ching was enraged, but he hid his anger and for the time did nothing.

Princess Ch'ang daily praised the beauty of Madam Wang's son, and Emperor Ching also regarded him as a boy of unusual worth. In addition there had been the auspicious sign of the sun which Madam Wang had seen in her dream. But as yet the emperor had no definite plans for making him heir apparent in place of Lady Li's son.

Madam Wang knew that the emperor was annoyed with Lady Li and that his anger was not yet appeased, so she secretly sent someone to urge the high ministers to set up Lady Li as empress. When the grand messenger had finished reporting on other matters to the throne one day, he said, "A son is honored because of his mother, and a mother because of her son. Now the mother of the heir apparent has no title. It is fitting that Lady Li be given the title of empress."

"What business have you to make such a proposal?" replied the emperor in a rage. Eventually he had the grand messenger investigated and punished,[7] and deposed the heir apparent Liu Jung, appointing him king of Lin-chiang instead. Lady Li's resentment grew more bitter than ever, but she was never again allowed to see the emperor and died of grief. In the end Madam Wang was set up as empress and her son became heir apparent. Her older brother Wang Hsin was enfeoffed as marquis of Kai.

When Emperor Ching passed away the heir apparent succeeded to the throne. He honored his mother's mother Tsang Erh with the title of "Mistress of P'ing-yüan," enfeoffed his uncle T'ien Fen as marquis of Wu-an, and his uncle T'ien Sheng as marquis of Chou-yang.

---

[7] The emperor no doubt suspected that Lady Li was conspiring with the grand messenger and had persuaded him to make the proposal. This was, of course, precisely the effect Madam Wang had hoped to achieve.

Emperor Ching had fourteen sons,[8] one of whom became Emperor Wu, while the other thirteen were all made kings. Wang Erh-hsü, Madam Wang's younger sister, died young, but her four sons all became kings. Madam Wang's oldest daughter was given the title of Princess P'ing-yang, her second daughter that of Princess Nan-kung, and her third daughter that of Princess Lin-lü. The marquis of Kai, Wang Hsin, was very fond of drinking. T'ien Fen and his brother T'ien Sheng were greedy men and very clever with words. Madam Wang's father Wang Chung died early and was buried at Huai-li. He was given the posthumous title of Kung or "Respectful Marquis" and a park and village of two hundred families set up for him. When Madam Wang's mother Tsang Erh, the mistress of P'ing-yüan, died, she was buried with the members of the T'ien family at Ch'ang-ling, and a park set up for her like that of Wang Chung. Empress Dowager Wang outlived her husband Emperor Ching by sixteen years, passing away in the fourth year of the era *yüan-so* [125 B.C.]. She was buried with Emperor Ching at Yang-ling. Of the clan of Empress Dowager Wang three men in all became marquises.

Empress Wei, Consort of Emperor Wu

Empress Wei's name was Tzu-fu. She was of very humble birth. Her family bore the name of Wei and came from the village of the marquis of P'ing-yang, the husband of Princess P'ing-yang.[9] Tzu-fu was a singing girl in the household of Princess P'ing-yang. After Emperor Wu ascended the throne several years passed and he was still without a son. Princess P'ing-yang, his elder sister, had sought out ten or more girls of good family whom she dressed in fine clothes and kept in her house, and when Emperor Wu was returning from a sacrifice at Pa-shang and stopped to pay a visit with her the princess showed him the beautiful young ladies she had gathered together to serve in her house. The emperor, however, was not impressed by any

---

[8] The text says "thirteen sons" but, as shown by *Shih chi* 59 below, this is an error.

[9] Her mother was a lady in waiting to the marquis of P'ing-yang. It is nowhere made clear who her father was, or whether Wei was the family name of her father or her mother. Her younger half brother was an illegitimate child, and it is possible that she also was illegitimate.

of them. After wine had been served the singing girls came forward to perform. Looking them over, the emperor found only Wei Tzu-fu to his liking. In the course of the day, when he rose and left the hall to change his clothes, Tzu-fu went along to wait on him and assist him with his robes, and in the passageway he bestowed his favor on her. The emperor returned to his seat, looking exceedingly pleased, and presented the princess with a thousand catties of gold. The princess accordingly offered him Tzu-fu, and it was arranged that she should be sent to live in the palace.

When Tzu-fu was about to climb into the carriage Princess P'ing-yang patted her on the back and said, "Go! Eat well and take care of yourself. If you should become honored, do not forget me!"

Tzu-fu remained in the palace over a year, but was never in that time favored by the emperor. The emperor in the meantime had decided to select those ladies in waiting who were performing no useful function and dismiss them and send them home and, when Wei Tzu-fu was granted an audience with him, she wept and begged to be sent away with the group. But the emperor felt sorry for her and favored her once more. In time she became pregnant and the honor and privilege which she enjoyed increased daily. Her older brother Wei Ch'ang-chün and her younger brother Wei Ch'ing were summoned and made palace attendants. After this Tzu-fu enjoyed extraordinary favor with the emperor. She bore him three daughters and a son, the last named Liu Chü.

While the emperor was still heir apparent he had taken Princess Ch'ang's daughter, whose surname was Ch'en, as his consort, and when he became emperor she was made empress. She had no children. The fact that the emperor had been named successor to the throne was largely due to the efforts of her mother, Princess Ch'ang, and for this reason Empress Ch'en was very haughty and gave herself airs of grandeur. When she heard that Wei Tzu-fu had won such great favor with the emperor she became so enraged that she was several times on the point of death. The emperor came to dislike her more and more. Empress Ch'en finally resorted to the black arts of female sorcery in an effort to win his affection. The whole affair came to light, and as a result Empress Ch'en was deposed and Wei Tzu-fu set up as empress in her place.

Families Related to the Emperors

Empress Ch'en's mother Princess Ch'ang, the emperor's aunt, several times complained to the emperor's older sister Princess P'ing-yang of what had happened, saying, "If it had not been for me, the emperor would never have succeeded to the throne. Yet, now that he is set up, he throws away my daughter! Indeed! What is this but turning one's back upon basic obligations for the sake of mere self-indulgence?"

"It is only because she has no children that she has been deposed," replied Princess P'ing-yang. Empress Ch'en tried very hard to have a son, paying out as much as ninety million cash to various doctors, but to the end she remained childless.

Before Wei Tzu-fu was made empress her older brother Wei Ch'ang-chün died. Her younger brother Wei Ch'ing was made a general and, winning merit in attacks on the barbarians, was enfeoffed as marquis of Ch'ang-p'ing. Wei Ch'ing's three sons were all enfeoffed as marquises while they were still in swaddling clothes. There was also a woman named Shao-erh who was said to be Empress Wei's elder sister. Shao-erh had a son named Ho Ch'ü-ping who, because of his military achievement, was enfeoffed as marquis of Kuan-chün. He was given the title of "General of Swift Cavalry," while Wei Ch'ing was given that of general in chief. Empress Wei's son Liu Chü was made heir apparent. Various branches of the Wei family achieved eminence because of their military achievements, so that five of them became marquises.

After Empress Wei's beauty had faded a Madam Wang of Chao enjoyed favor with the emperor. She had a son who became king of Ch'i. Madam Wang died young and was succeeded in the imperial favor by Madam Li of Chung-shan. She had one son who became king of Ch'ang-i, but she too died young. Her older brother Li Yen-nien won prominence at court because of his knowledge of music and was given the title of "Harmonizer of the Tunes." He had originally been a singer. All of the Li brothers were tried on charges of immorality and condemned to death, along with their families. At this time the oldest brother Li Kuang-li, the "Sutrishna General," [10] was conducting an attack upon Ferghana, and so escaped execution. When he returned to the capital the emperor had already wiped out the Li family. Later

---

[10] So called because he captured the city of Erh-shih or Sutrishna, the capital of Ferghana.

the emperor took pity upon his family and enfeoffed Li Kuang-li as marquis of Hai-hsi.

There were two sons of the emperor by other consorts who became the kings of Yen and Kuang-ling respectively, but their mothers did not enjoy the emperor's affections and they died of grief. After the death of Madam Li there were others such as Lady Yin who, one after the other, engaged the emperor's attentions. But all of these attracted the emperor's notice only because they were singers. None of them were daughters of nobles or landowners, and hence they were quite unfit to become the consort of the ruler of men.[11]

[11] Because Ssu-ma Ch'ien has already made his general remarks at the beginning of the chapter, he does not close with the customary section introduced by the words "The Grand Historian remarks." The present text of the chapter concludes with a long addition by Ch'u Shao-sun, carrying the narrative down to the time of Emperor Shao, which has been omitted in translation.

Part IX
THE GREAT FAMILIES

Shih chi 50: The Hereditary House of King Yüan of Ch'u

After Kao-tsu had effected his scheme of deception and taken Han Hsin prisoner at Ch'en, because the lands of Yüeh and Ching were fickle and untrustworthy, he enfeoffed his younger brother Liu Chiao as king of Ch'u, ruling from the city of P'eng-ch'eng, so that he might strengthen the regions of the Huai and Ssu rivers and act as a bastion to the house of Han. Liu Mou fell into evil ways, but Liu Li was called to carry on the line. In recognition of the aid which Liu Chiao rendered to Kao-tsu, I made The Hereditary House of King Yüan of Ch'u.

Liu Chiao

Liu Chiao, King Yüan or the "First King" of Ch'u, was a younger brother of Kao-tsu by the same mother. His polite name was Yu. Kao-tsu was one of four brothers. His oldest brother Liu Po died early. When Kao-tsu was still a commoner he was for a while in hiding from the officials and from time to time used to go with his friends to visit Liu Po's wife for a meal. His brother's wife disliked Kao-tsu and, whenever he arrived with his guests, she would rattle the soup ladle around the kettle and pretend that there was no more soup left. The guests would accordingly take their leave, but afterwards, when Kao-tsu would look in the kettle, there would still be soup in it. Because of this Kao-tsu came to hate his sister-in-law.

After Kao-tsu became emperor he enfeoffed all his brothers, but Liu Po's son was given no fief. When Kao-tsu's father, the Grand Supreme Emperor, asked him about this, Kao-tsu replied, "It is not that I forgot to enfeoff him. It is only that his mother is not a very high-minded person." With this, he proceeded to enfeoff Liu Po's son Liu Hsin as "Marquis Soup Rattle." His second eldest brother, Liu Chung, he made king of the region of Tai.

In the sixth year of his reign, after Kao-tsu had taken Han Hsin, the king of Ch'u, prisoner at Ch'en, he made his younger brother Liu Chiao the new king of Ch'u with his capital at P'eng-ch'eng.

In the twenty-third year of his rule Liu Chiao died and was succeeded by his son Liu Ying, posthumously known as King I. Liu Ying died after four years of rule and was succeeded by his son Liu Mou.

In the twentieth year of his rule [155 B.C.] Liu Mou was convicted of having illicit intercourse while in mourning for Empress Dowager Po and was deprived of the province of Tung-hai.

In the spring Liu Mou joined with the king of Wu, Liu P'i, in plotting a revolt. His prime minister Chang Shang and his grand tutor Chao I-wu both counseled him against the move, but he refused to heed their advice and eventually murdered them. Then he raised his troops and joined with Wu in marching west to attack Liang. After capturing Chi-pi they marched to the south of Ch'ang-i, where they joined in battle with the Han general Chou Ya-fu. The Han forces cut off the Wu and Ch'u supply roads so that their soldiers starved. Liu P'i fled, Liu Mou committed suicide, and their armies surrendered to the Han forces.

After peace had been restored to Wu and Ch'u, Emperor Ching wanted to set up the son of Liu P'i, Marquis Te, to carry on the line of Wu, and Liu Li, the son of Liu Chiao, to carry on the line of Ch'u, but Empress Dowager Tou objected. "The king of Wu was an old man. He should have been compliant and helpful to the imperial family, to which he belonged, but instead of that he headed the seven kingdoms in raising a revolt and throwing the empire into turmoil. Why should his line be carried on?"

So she would not permit the establishment of an heir in Wu, but only of one in Ch'u. At this time Liu Li, who was director of the imperial clan, was made king of Ch'u so that he might serve the ancestral temple of his great-grandfather King Yüan of Ch'u. He is posthumously known as King Wen of Ch'u.

In the third year of his rule King Wen died and was succeeded by his son Liu Tao, posthumously titled King An. King An died in the twenty-second year of his rule and was succeeded by his son Liu Chu, King Hsiang. King Hsiang died in the fourteenth year of his rule and was succeeded by his son Liu Shun. (After Liu Shun was set up, in the second year of the era *ti-chieh* [68 B.C.], someone in his palace sent a report to the throne saying that the king of Ch'u was plotting revolt. The king committed suicide, and his kingdom was taken away from his family and placed under the central court, being made into the province of P'eng-ch'eng.) [1]

Liu Sui, the King of Chao

Liu Sui, the king of Chao, was the son of Liu Yu, Kao-tsu's sixth son, whose posthumous title was King Yu, the "Somber King." He was given this title because he died of grief.[2]

After his death Empress Lü made Lü Lu the king of Chao, but a year later she passed away and the great ministers overthrew Lü Lu and the rest of the Lü family and set up Liu Yu's son Liu Sui as king of Chao.

The second year after he came to the throne Emperor Wen separated the province of Ho-chien from the kingdom of Chao and set up Liu Sui's younger brother Liu Pi-ch'iang as king of Ho-chien. He is posthumously known as King Wen. He died in the thirteenth year of his rule and was succeeded by his son Liu Fu, known as King Ai. Liu Fu died in the first year of his rule and, because he left no heir, the line was discontinued and his kingdom abolished, and the region of Ho-chien was placed under the jurisdiction of the central court.

Liu Sui ruled as king of Chao for twenty-six years, but in the time of Emperor Ching he was accused of some fault by Ch'ao Ts'o and deprived of the rulership of the province of Ch'ang-shan. When the kingdoms of Wu and Ch'u revolted Liu Sui joined with them in plotting to raise troops. His prime minister Chien Te and his internal secretary Wang Han both advised him against this, but he refused to listen to them and finally had them burned to death. Then he called out his troops and stationed them on his western border, intending to wait for the troops of Wu and proceed with them westward. He also

---

[1] The section in parentheses, dealing with events after the death of Ssu-ma Ch'ien, is a later interpolation.

[2] The word *yu* which I have translated as "somber" carries the meaning both of darkness and melancholy, and of confinement, and so it is particularly appropriate to Liu Yu, who was confined to his quarters by Empress Lü and starved to death.

sent envoys north to the Hsiung-nu to conclude an alliance with them and induce them to attack the Han.

The Han court sent Li Chi, the marquis of Ch'ü-chou, to attack Liu Sui, who retreated and took up a position in the city of Han-tan, where the two armies remained in stalemate for seven months. In the meantime the armies of Wu and Ch'u were defeated in Liang and were unable to march west, and the Hsiung-nu, hearing of this, halted their preparations and refused to cross the border into Han territory.

After the Han general Lüan Pu had defeated the rebel armies in Ch'i and was on his way back to the capital he joined his forces with those of Li Chi and, leading in water from the river, flooded the city of Han-tan. The city walls collapsed and the king of Chao committed suicide. Thus Han-tan finally capitulated and the line of the Somber King came to an end.

The Grand Historian remarks: When a state is about to rise to glory there will always be good omens and signs: wise men will find a place in office and small-minded men will be put aside. But when a state is about to perish worthy men will retire and rebellious ministers command honor. If Liu Mou, the king of Ch'u, had not punished Master Shen but had followed his advice, and if the king of Chao had employed Master Fang Yü,[3] how would they ever have conceived their treasonous schemes and become the archcriminals of the world? Worthy men, worthy men, people say, but if one does not have worth within himself, how can he make use of the worth of others? It is well said that safety and peril hinge upon the issuing of orders, and survival and defeat upon the men one puts in office. How true that is!

[3] Though these two men are not mentioned in the narrative above, they seem to be scholar-advisers who cautioned the kings not to join the revolt but whose good advice was ignored.

Shih chi 51: The Hereditary Houses of Ching and Yen

When Kao-tsu raised his mighty army Liu Chia joined with him, but later he was attacked by Ch'ing Pu and lost the regions of Ching and Wu. Liu Tse, by intimidating Empress Lü, became king of Lang-ya but, enticed by Chu Wu, he trusted the king of Ch'i and went to him, and was never allowed to return to his kingdom.[1] Eventually he marched west and entered the Pass and, when Emperor Wen came to the throne, was able to become a king once more, this time in Yen. Before the empire had been fully brought under control both Liu Chia and Liu Tse, because of their kinship with the imperial family, were made feudal protectors of the Han. Thus I made The Hereditary Houses of Ching and Yen.

Liu Chia, the King of Ching

Liu Chia, the king of Ching, was a member of the Liu clan, though it is not known just how he was related to Kao-tsu or when he got his start. In the first year of the Han, when Kao-tsu, then the king of Han, returned from his territory and conquered the three kingdoms of Ch'in, Liu Chia was made a general and conquered the region of Sai. Later he accompanied Kao-tsu east in his attack on Hsiang Yü. In the fourth year Kao-tsu, having suffered defeat at Ch'eng-kao, crossed the Yellow River to the north, took command of the armies of Chang Erh and Han Hsin, and made his camp at Hsiu-wu, deepening the moats and raising high fortifications. At that time he dispatched Liu Chia with a force of twenty thousand soldiers and several hundred cavalry to cross back over the Yellow River at White Horse Ford and invade the region of Ch'u. Liu Chia succeeded in burning Ch'u's stores of supplies and destroying its productive activities so that it became impossible for Hsiang Yü's armies to secure provisions. Eventually Liu Chia was attacked by the Ch'u forces, but he fortified

---

[1] The explanation of this statement will be found not in this chapter but in the following chapter on the king of Ch'i.

his camp and refused to engage in battle. He and P'eng Yüeh, by aiding each other, together managed to maintain their positions in the region.

In the fifth year, when Kao-tsu pursued Hsiang Yü as far as Ku-ling, he sent Liu Chia south across the Huai River to lay siege to the city of Shou-ch'un. When Liu Chia was about to return from this mission Kao-tsu secretly sent someone to invite the grand marshal of Ch'u, Chou Yin, to join him. Chou Yin turned against Hsiang Yü and came to the aid of Liu Chia, raising the troops of Chiu-chiang and joining the forces of Ch'ing Pu, the king of Wu. They all met at Kai-hsia and together attacked Hsiang Yü.

Following this Kao-tsu dispatched Liu Chia with the forces of Chiu-chiang and sent him with the grand commandant Lu Wan to march to the southwest and attack Kung Wei, the king of Lin-chiang. After Kung Wei had been killed Kao-tsu made the kingdom of Lin-chiang into the province of Nan.

In the sixth year of Han, when Kao-tsu met with the feudal lords at Ch'en, he deposed Han Hsin, the king of Ch'u, and took him prisoner, dividing his territory into two kingdoms. At this time Kao-tsu's sons were still very young, and his brothers few and undistinguished. Yet he wished to set up kings of his own surname in order to strengthen his hold on the empire, so he issued an edict saying, "Liu Chia has achieved merit as a general. In addition to him, let some other sons and brothers of the Liu family be selected who may be made kings."

His ministers all replied, "Liu Chia should be made king of Ching, ruling the fifty-two cities east of the Huai River." Kao-tsu's younger brother Liu Chiao was made king of Ch'u, ruling the thirty-six cities west of the Huai, and following this Kao-tsu's son Liu Fei was set up as king of Ch'i. This was the first time that the sons and brothers of the Liu family were made kings.

In the autumn of the eleventh year of Kao-tsu's reign Ch'ing Pu, the king of Huai-nan, revolted and marched east to attack Ching. Liu Chia, the king of Ching, engaged him in battle but, failing to win a victory, fled to Fu-ling, where he was killed by Ch'ing Pu's army. Kao-tsu went in person to attack and defeat Ch'ing Pu, and in the twelfth year set up Liu P'i, the marquis of P'ei, as king of Wu to rule the territory which had formerly been called Ching.

Liu Tse, the King of Yen

Liu Tse, the king of Yen, was a member of the Liu clan and distantly related to the emperor. In the third year of Kao-tsu's reign he became a palace attendant. In the eleventh year he led an army in the attack on Ch'en Hsi and captured Ch'en Hsi's general Wang Huang, for which he was made marquis of Ying-ling.

During the time of Empress Lü, Master T'ien, a man of Ch'i who was traveling about the empire in very reduced circumstances, managed by some device to obtain an audience with Liu Tse in the capital. Liu Tse took a great liking to him and presented him with two hundred catties of gold as a birthday gift. After he received the money, Master T'ien went back home to Ch'i. Two years later Liu Tse sent someone to inform Master T'ien that he no longer considered him a friend.[2]

Master T'ien journeyed again to Ch'ang-an, but did not come to see Liu Tse. Instead he rented a large house and sent his son to seek employment with Chang Ch'ing, the palace master of guests, who enjoyed great favor with Empress Lü.

After a few months Master T'ien's son asked Chang Ch'ing if he would do him the honor of coming to his house for a quiet party which his father was giving. Chang Ch'ing accepted the invitation and, when he arrived, was astonished by the gorgeous hangings and vessels of Master T'ien's house, which were like those of the residence of a marquis. When the party was at its height Master T'ien dismissed the attendants and began to talk to Chang Ch'ing. "Here in the capital," he said, "I have seen the homes of a hundred or more marquises and kings, all of them faithful followers of Kao-tsu who won outstanding merit. We must keep in mind, however, that the members of the Lü family as well did a great deal from the very first to boost Kao-tsu to power and help him win control of the empire, and their merit also is very great. Among the imperial relatives Empress Dowa-

[2] Because he had made no move to repay Liu Tse's generosity.

ger Lü naturally occupies a position of high honor. But the empress dowager is well along in years and the other members of the Lü family are very weak. The empress dowager would like to make Lü Ch'an the king of Lü to rule over the region of Tai,[3] but she has hesitated to bring up the matter because she is afraid that the high officials will not hear of such a thing. Now you enjoy great favor with her and are respected by the officials. Why don't you hint to them that they should listen to the empress dowager's suggestion? The empress dowager would surely be pleased, and with the Lüs set up as kings, a marquisate of ten thousand households could certainly be yours! You know the empress dowager's secret desires and, as one who attends her within the palace, if you do not quickly make them known to others, then I fear that some misfortune may come to you!"

Chang Ch'ing approved of this idea and dropped a hint to the high officials that they should broach the subject before the empress dowager. When the empress dowager was holding court, therefore, they inquired about her wishes, and she requested them to set up Lü Ch'an as king of Lü. She also presented Chang Ch'ing with a thousand catties of gold, half of which he wished to give to Master T'ien. Master T'ien, however, refused to accept it, but instead said, "Lü Ch'an has become a king, but the high officials are by no means resigned to the move. As it happens, Liu Tse, the marquis of Ying-ling, is a member of the Liu family and an outstanding general, and yet he has been greatly disappointed in his lot. Now if you could persuade the empress dowager to set aside ten or so districts somewhere and make him ruler of them, then he could become a king and would leave the capital completely satisfied, and thus the position of the Lü kings would be stronger than ever."

Chang Ch'ing took up the matter with the empress dowager, who gave her approval, so that Liu Tse was made king of Lang-ya. Liu Tse set out for his new kingdom accompanied by Master T'ien, who urged him to hasten on his way without delay. After they had gone beyond the Pass the empress dowager, as Master T'ien had foreseen, sent a

---

[3] This is the only place where we hear of the empress dowager's desire to make Lü Ch'an the ruler of Tai, and the word "Tai" may well be an error.

messenger after them to tell them to halt, but when he found that they had already gone on, he returned to the capital.

After the empress dowager passed away Liu Tse raised his forces and, announcing that "the new emperor is young and all power of government is in the hands of the Lü family, so that the Liu clan stands alone and weak," joined with the king of Ch'i in laying plans to march west and overthrow the Lüs. He had gotten as far as Liang when he received news that the Han court had dispatched Kuan Ying with an army, which was camped at Jung-yang, whereupon he led his troops back to defend the western border of his territory. Finally he marched by forced stages to Ch'ang-an and, when the king of Tai arrived from his territory, joined with the other generals and ministers in setting him up as the new Son of Heaven. The emperor transferred Liu Tse to the position of king of Yen and gave the region of Lang-ya back to the state of Ch'i, of which it had formerly been a part.

In the second year of his rule Liu Tse, the king of Yen, died and was given the posthumous title of King Ching. His kingdom passed to his son Liu Chia, King K'ang, and eventually to his grandson Liu Ting-kuo. Liu Ting-kuo had illicit intercourse with his father's concubine, who bore him a son; he seized his younger brother's wife and made her his concubine; and he had intercourse with her three daughters. Liu Ting-kuo was looking for some excuse to execute some of his ministers, among them the magistrate of Fei-ju, Ying-jen. Ying-jen and some of the others reported the king's misdoings to the Han court, but Liu Ting-kuo sent his master of guests to arrest Ying-jen on other grounds and had him beaten to death in order to silence him. In the first year of the era *yüan-so* [128 B.C.], however, Ying-jen's brothers once again sent a report to the throne revealing the full extent of the king's secret doings, so that the whole affair came to light. The emperor referred the case to the high officials, who unanimously pronounced that "Liu Ting-kuo has conducted himself like a beast, violating the laws of human relations and offending against Heaven. He should be executed." The emperor approved their verdict, whereupon Liu Ting-kuo committed suicide and his kingdom was abolished and the territory made into a province.

The Grand Historian remarks: Liu Chia's appointment as king of Ching came when Kao-tsu had just conquered the empire and it was not yet firmly in his control. Therefore, although Liu Chia was only a distant relative, Kao-tsu, for reasons of policy, made him a king in order to stabilize the area between the Huai and Yangtze rivers. Liu Tse became a king by opportunely encouraging the ambitions of the Lü clan; yet in the end he and his heirs managed to face south and call themselves sovereign rulers for three generations. Although the circumstances in both their cases were rather complex, there is no doubt that they were extraordinary men.

Shih chi 52: The Hereditary House of King Tao-hui of Ch'i

Though Kao-tsu had few close relatives, the most distinguished among them was his son Liu Fei, King Tao-hui, who, after Kao-tsu had won control of the empire, restored law and order to the eastern regions. King Ai arbitrarily called out his troops because of his hatred for the Lü family but, since his uncle Ssu Chün was so vicious a man, the court would not permit King Ai to become emperor. Chu-fu Yen brought calamity to King Li. In recognition of the service which Liu Fei rendered to the Han, I made The Hereditary House of King Tao-hui of Ch'i.

Liu Fei, posthumously known as King Tao-hui of Ch'i, was the eldest son of Kao-tsu. His mother was not Empress Lü, however, but a concubine of the emperor who belonged to the Ts'ao family. In the sixth year of his reign Kao-tsu set up Liu Fei as king of Ch'i with the revenue from seventy cities; all the people who could speak the dialect of Ch'i were assigned to his jurisdiction.

As the oldest son, Liu Fei was an elder brother of Emperor Hui, and in the second year of Emperor Hui's reign, when Liu Fei journeyed to the court, Emperor Hui gave a banquet for him at which he dispensed with the customary etiquette between ruler and subject and treated Liu Fei as an older brother. Empress Dowager Lü was furious at this and was about to do away with Liu Fei when the latter, fearful that he would be unable to escape from the capital in safety, followed a suggestion made by his internal secretary, Shih,[1] and donated the province of Ch'eng-yang to Empress Lü's daughter, Princess Yüan of Lu, to be her "bath-town." Empress Lu was pleased with this, and Liu Fei was thereby able to leave the capital without harm and return to his kingdom.

In the sixth year of Emperor Hui's reign, thirteen years after he

[1] The text here gives his name as Hsün but I have followed the reading given in "The Annals of Empress Lü."

became king of Ch'i, Liu Fei died and was given the posthumous title of Tao-hui, the "Compassionate King Who Died Young." He was succeeded by his son Liu Hsiang, posthumously known as King Ai. In the first year of King Ai's rule Emperor Hui passed away. Empress Dowager Lü began to issue decrees in the manner of an emperor and all affairs pertaining to the rule of the empire were subject to her decision.

In the second year of her reign Empress Lü set up Lü T'ai, the marquis of Li, the son of her elder brother, as king of Lü, stripping the province of Chi-nan from the territory of the king of Ch'i and assigning it to the new king of Lü to supply him with revenue.

In the third year of King Ai's rule his younger brother Liu Chang journeyed to Ch'ang-an to take up residence as a guardian of the Han court. Empress Lü enfeoffed him as marquis of Chu-hsü and gave him the daughter of Lü Ch'an for a wife. Four years later she enfeoffed his younger brother Liu Hsing-chü as marquis of Tung-mou. Both brothers continued to live in Ch'ang-an as guardians of the court.

In the eighth year of King Ai's rule Empress Lü detached the province of Lang-ya from the territory of Ch'i and set up Liu Tse, the marquis of Ying-ling, as king of Lang-ya.

The following year Liu Yu, the king of Chao, journeyed to court and died in confinement at the state residence of Chao. After his death Liu Hui became king of Chao but committed suicide. Thus three kings of Chao in succession vacated the position.[2] Meanwhile Empress Lü made kings of three of her own clan, setting up Lü T'ung as king of Yen, Lü Lu as king of Chao, and Lü Ch'an as king of Liang. The Lüs managed the government in any way they pleased.

Liu Chang, the marquis of Chu-hsü, was twenty years old and a man of great spirit and strength. He was embittered at the fact that the members of the Liu family could no longer attain important positions at court. Once, when there was a banquet in the palace and Liu Chang was attending Empress Lü, the empress appointed him to act as her master of wine for the evening. "I have a request to make,"

[2] The first, Liu Ju-i, was poisoned by the empress; the second, Liu Yu, died in confinement; and the third, Liu Hui, committed suicide. All were sons of Kao-tsu by concubines. The narrative at this point is very much abbreviated and has been expanded somewhat in translation.

said Liu Chang. "Since I come from a family of generals, I would like to direct the dispensing of the wine in accordance with the rules of the army."

"That is quite all right," replied the empress.

When the banquet had reached its height Liu Chang came forward, poured wine for the empress, and performed a song and dance. After this was over he said, "Now, if I may, I would like to recite a ploughing song for the empress dowager."

The empress, who regarded him as a mere child, laughed and said, "Only your father knew anything about the work of the fields. You were born a prince! What do you know about such things?"

"I know a little," replied Liu Chang.

"Then try telling me about the fields!" said the empress, and Liu Chang began to recite:

> Deep we plough and thick we sow the seed;
> We set out the little plants where they will have room to grow.
> Whatever comes up that is not from our seed,
> We hoe it out and throw it away![3]

Empress Lü was silent.

After a while a man of the Lü family who had become drunk rose and slipped away from the party. Liu Chang went after him and, drawing his sword, cut the man down. Then he returned and reported to the gathering, "Some man tried to desert the banquet! In accordance with army regulations I have duly carried out the penalty of execution!"

Empress Lü and those about her were completely dumfounded but, since she had already given Liu Chang permission to follow military regulations, she could accuse him of no fault, but instead declared the banquet at an end. From this time on the members of the Lü family stood in awe of Liu Chang and even the high officials relied on him for support, so that because of him the Liu family began to regain power.

The following year Empress Lü passed away. Lü Lu, the king of Chao, acted as supreme commander of the army and Lü Ch'an, the king of Lü, as prime minister. Both of them resided in Ch'ang-an,

---

[3] The political import of the song is too obvious to require explanation.

where they massed a force of troops with which to intimidate the high officials, planning to start a revolt. Liu Chang's wife was a daughter of Lü Lu, and Liu Chang therefore was aware of their plot. Accordingly he sent someone in secret to report to his older brother, the king of Ch'i, asking him to send his troops west, in which case Liu Chang and his brother Liu Hsing-chü would cooperate from within the capital and together they would overthrow the Lü family and set up the king of Ch'i as emperor. When the king of Ch'i received word of this suggestion he began to plot in secret with his mother's brother Ssu Chün, his chief of palace attendants Chu Wu, and his military commander Wei P'o on how to go about dispatching his troops.

Shao P'ing, the prime minister of Ch'i, heard of their plans and forthwith called out the troops and surrounded the king's palace.[4] Wei P'o went to Shao P'ing and deceived him by saying, "Even though the king wants to send out the troops, he does not have the tiger seals of the Han court which would give him the authority to do so. I beg you to allow me to take command of the troops for you and keep the king under guard!"

Shao P'ing, believing that Wei P'o was on his side, put him in charge of the troops surrounding the king's palace, but after he had taken command, Wei P'o instead dispatched them to surround the prime minister's office. "Alas!" said Shao P'ing. "The Taoists have a saying,

> Strike when the hour comes,
> Or suffer the ruin that follows!

This, then, is what they mean!" He committed suicide.

With this, the king of Ch'i appointed Ssu Chün as his new prime minister, Wei P'o as commander of the army, and Chu Wu as internal secretary, and called out all the troops in the kingdom. He sent Chu Wu east to deceive Liu Tse, the king of Lang-ya, by saying, "The members of the Lü family have started a revolt and the king of Ch'i has called out his troops and intends to send them west to punish the evildoers. But the king considers himself a mere child who has no ex-

---

[4] The prime ministers of the feudal kingdoms were appointed by the central court to keep an eye on the local kings and, since they had possession of the Han seals, had the power to call out the troops.

perience in matters of warfare. He wishes therefore to entrust the troops which he has levied to Your Majesty's command, since you have been a general since the time of Emperor Kao-tsu and are practiced in military affairs. The king of Ch'i, however, does not dare to leave his troops, and so he has sent me to make this request of you. He hopes that you will be good enough to journey to Lin-tzu, where you may meet with him and plan your strategy, and then, with the combined armies of Ch'i, march west and put down the rebellion in the area within the Pass."

The king of Lang-ya trusted Chu Wu and, considering his request reasonable, hastened west to meet the king of Ch'i. The king of Ch'i, acting with Wei P'o and the others, forcibly detained the king of Lang-ya, and sent Chu Wu to call out all the troops of the kingdom of Lang-ya and combine them with the forces already under his command.

When the king of Lang-ya saw that he had been deceived and could not return to his kingdom, he said to the king of Ch'i, "King Tao-hui of Ch'i was the eldest son of Emperor Kao-tsu, so that from the point of view of lineage you are Emperor Kao-tsu's oldest grandson in the legitimate line of descent and should by rights become ruler. Now the high officials are hesitating and have not yet chosen a new emperor. Since I am the oldest member of the Liu clan, they will surely wait for my arrival before deciding on any plan. There is no point in your detaining me here. It would be better to let me go to the capital and take part in their deliberations."

The king of Ch'i agreed with this and, providing him with ample carriages and fittings, sent him off to the capital. After the king of Lang-ya had left, the king of Ch'i raised his troops and marched west to attack the state of the king of Lü in Chi-nan. At this time he sent a letter to the other feudal lords and kings saying:

When Emperor Kao-tsu conquered the empire he made kings of his sons and younger brothers. Among these was King Tao-hui, who was made king of Ch'i. After King Tao-hui died Emperor Hui sent Chang Liang to establish me as king of Ch'i. When Emperor Hui passed away the empress took over the management of the government, but she was far along in years and, heeding the advice of the members of the Lü family, arbitrarily deposed the emperor and put another in his place.[5] In addition she killed three kings of Chao in succession, wiped out the royal families of Liang, Yen, and Chao, made kings of the members of the Lü clan, and divided the territory of Ch'i into four kingdoms. Although the loyal ministers advised her against these moves, she refused in her delusion to heed them. Now the empress has passed away and the emperor, being young in years, is incapable of governing the empire, but must rely solely upon the aid of the officials and lords. The members of the Lü family have therefore proceeded to help themselves to official posts, have massed soldiers to consolidate their power, have terrorized the marquises and loyal officials, and are forging imperial decrees and issuing orders to the empire. Such actions imperil the ancestral temples of the dynasty. I have therefore led forth my troops and shall enter the capital to punish all those who have unrightfully assumed the title of king!

When the Han court received news that the king of Ch'i had called out his troops and was marching west, the prime minister Lü Ch'an dispatched General Kuan Ying to march east to attack him. After he had gotten as far as Jung-yang, Kuan Ying began to consider what to do. "The Lü family have seized control of the troops in the area within the Pass and are imperiling the Liu clan, intending to make themselves rulers," he said to himself. "Now if I defeat the forces of Ch'i and return to the court to report my success, this will only increase the power of the Lüs." He therefore halted and made camp at Jung-yang, sending envoys to the king of Ch'i and the other nobles asking them to join with him in peaceful alliance and wait and, if the Lü clan should attempt to overthrow the government, to unite in wiping them out. When the king of Ch'i received word of this he proceeded west to recover control of the province of Chi-nan, which had formerly been part of his territory, and then stationed his troops on the western border of Ch'i to await further developments in accordance with the agreement.

Lü Lu and Lü Ch'an were about to start their revolt in the area within the Pass, but Liu Chang, along with the grand commandant Chou P'o, the chancellor Ch'en P'ing, and the others, overthrew them, Liu Chang leading the way by cutting down Lü Ch'an. Thus Chou P'o and the rest were finally able to wipe out the Lü clan. The king of Lang-ya in the meantime arrived in Ch'ang-an from Ch'i, and the

[5] Following the reading in "The Annals of Empress Lü."

great ministers began to discuss whether or not to set up the king of Ch'i as emperor. But the king of Lang-ya and the great ministers pointed out that "the king of Ch'i's mother belongs to the same family as Ssu Chün, an evil and rebellious man who is no better than a tiger with a hat on. The whole empire was brought almost to ruin because of the Lü family but, if we set up the king of Ch'i as ruler, we will have another Lü family all over again. The king of Tai's mother, on the other hand, belongs to the Po clan, a well-bred and distinguished family. Moreover, the king of Tai is an actual son of Emperor Kao-tsu and the oldest among his sons who are still living. As a son he is obviously the next in line of succession, and since he is a good man the high officials can rest easy under him."

With this, the great ministers proceeded with their plans to bring the king of Tai to the capital and set him up as emperor, dispatching Liu Chang to report the overthrow of the Lü clan to the king of Ch'i and order him to disperse his troops.

Kuan Ying, who was in Jung-yang, found out that Wei P'o had been the one who originally counseled the king of Ch'i to raise his troops against the central government and, after the Lü clan had been overthrown and the troops of Ch'i dispersed, he sent a messenger to summon Wei P'o and began to berate him.[6] "When the house is on fire," said Wei P'o, "is one supposed to take time to report to the master first before trying to put out the blaze?" Then he withdrew and stood at a distance, his legs shaking with fright, too terrified to say anything more. Kuan Ying stared intently at Wei P'o for a while and then began to laugh. "People told me that Wei P'o was a brave man, but he is nothing but a common fool! What could a fellow like this ever do?" he said, and dismissed Wei P'o and sent him away.

(Wei P'o's father was a very skillful zither player and had appeared before the First Emperor of the Ch'in. When Wei P'o was young he wished to meet the prime minister of Ch'i, Ts'ao Ts'an, but his family was very poor and he had no way to arrange for an interview. So he made a habit of going alone early each morning and sweeping out-

[6] The king of Ch'i and his ministers were technically guilty of treason in calling out their troops against the central government, though their action was excused on grounds that the Lü clan had in fact usurped the power of the government.

side the gate of the home of one of the prime minister's retainers. The retainer grew suspicious and, thinking it might be some kind of phantom, went out to investigate, whereupon he discovered Wei P'o. "I would like to meet the prime minister," said Wei P'o, "but I have no way to arrange it. So I thought if I swept your gate for you, you might introduce me to him."

The retainer took Wei P'o in to see Ts'ao Ts'an, who made him a retainer. One time when he was driving Ts'ao Ts'an's carriage for him, Wei P'o had a chance to talk with the prime minister about various affairs, and Ts'ao Ts'an, impressed by his wisdom, mentioned him to King Tao-hui of Ch'i. King Tao-hui sent for Wei P'o to come to see him and made him his internal secretary. After he entered the service of King Tao-hui he advanced as high as a position paying two thousand piculs of grain. When King Tao-hui died and was succeeded by his son King Ai, Wei P'o handled all the affairs of government and became more powerful than the prime minister of Ch'i.)

To resume, after the king of Ch'i had disbanded his troops and returned to his kingdom, the king of Tai arrived in the capital and was made emperor. He is posthumously known as Emperor Wen the Filial.

In the first year of his reign Emperor Wen restored to the kingdom of Ch'i the provinces of Ch'eng-yang, Lang-ya, and Chi-nan, all of which had been detached from Ch'i during the time of Empress Lü. The king of Lang-ya he transferred to the position of king of Yen, and increased the fiefs of Liu Chang, the marquis of Chu-hsü, and his brother Liu Hsing-chü, the marquis of Tung-mou, by two thousand households each. In this year King Ai of Ch'i died and was succeeded by the crown prince, Liu Ts'e, who is posthumously known as King Wen.

In the first year of King Wen's rule the Han government took the province of Ch'eng-yang away from Ch'i and set up Liu Chang as king of Ch'eng-yang, and took away the province of Chi-pei and set up Liu Hsing-chü as king of Chi-pei.

In the second year of Emperor Wen's reign Liu Hsing-chü, the king of Chi-pei, revolted. He was killed by the Han forces and his territory taken over by the central government. Two years later Emperor Wen enfeoffed Liu Pa-chün and the other sons of King Tao-hui of Ch'i, seven men in all, as marquises. Fourteen years after he ascended the throne of Ch'i, King Wen died. Since he left no heir, his kingdom was abolished and the territory taken over by the Han government. The following year Emperor Wen divided up all the former provinces of Ch'i and made kings of the sons of King Tao-hui whom he had previously enfeoffed as marquises. The marquis of Yang-hsü, Liu Chiang-lü, was made king of Ch'i, and is posthumously known as King Hsiao of Ch'i. Liu Chih became king of Chi-pei, Liu Pi-kuang became king of Chi-nan, Liu Hsien became king of Tzu-ch'uan, Liu Ang became king of Chiao-hsi, and Liu Hsiung-ch'ü became king of Chiao-tung. These, along with Liu Chang, the king of Ch'eng-yang, made seven kings in the region of Ch'i.

In the eleventh year of the rule of King Hsiao of Ch'i, Liu P'i, the king of Wu, and Liu Mou, the king of Ch'u, revolted and, raising their troops, marched west, announcing to the other feudal lords that they were "going to punish the traitorous minister of the Han, Ch'ao Ts'o, in order to bring peace to the dynastic altars!" The kings of Chiao-hsi, Chiao-tung, Tzu-ch'uan, and Chi-nan all ordered out their troops to respond to the call from Wu and Ch'u, and wanted the king of Ch'i to join with them. But the king of Ch'i hesitated and, guarding his capital of Lin-tzu, refused to listen to their suggestions, whereupon the troops of the four other kingdoms [7] surrounded the king of Ch'i.

The king of Ch'i dispatched his minister Lu to report to the emperor, who sent Lu back with the message, "Hold fast to your city! Even now my troops are defeating Wu and Ch'u!" When Lu returned, however, he found the armies of the four kingdoms surrounding the city of Lin-tzu several layers deep so that he could not get through their lines to deliver the message.

The generals of the four kingdoms seized Lu and forced him to promise that he would report falsely to the king of Ch'i. "You will tell him that the Han forces have been defeated and that if Ch'i does not surrender to us at once, the whole population of the city will be slaughtered!" they demanded. Lu agreed to do as they said but, when

---

[7] The text here and following reads "three kingdoms," but this seems inconsistent with what has gone before.

he reached the foot of the city walls and looked up and saw the king of Ch'i, he shouted, "The Han court has already dispatched a force of a million men, and the grand commandant Chou Ya-fu has attacked and defeated Wu and Ch'u. Even now he is leading his men to rescue Ch'i. Ch'i must hold fast to the city and not surrender!" The generals of the four kingdoms executed the minister Lu for his betrayal.

When the king of Ch'i was first surrounded and besieged by the armies of the four kingdoms he secretly began negotiations to join their plot but, before he had concluded the alliance, he heard to his joy that Lu was on his way back from the Han court. In addition his high ministers urged him not to surrender to the four kingdoms. Before any time had passed, the Han generals Lüan Pu, Ts'ao Chi, the marquis of P'ing-yang, and the others arrived in Ch'i with their forces, attacked and defeated the armies of the four kingdoms, and raised the siege. After they had withdrawn the Han generals discovered that the king of Ch'i had originally been plotting with the four kingdoms, and they were about to move their troops back into the area and attack Ch'i, but the king of Ch'i, becoming alarmed, drank poison and died.

When Emperor Ching heard what had happened he decided that the king of Ch'i had in the beginning been loyal, but had been coerced into plotting with the others, for which he should not be held guilty, and so he set up the king's son, the crown prince Liu Shou, as king of Ch'i. He is posthumously known as King I, and carried on the line of Ch'i. The kings of Chiao-hsi, Chiao-tung, Chi-nan, and Tzu-ch'uan were all wiped out and their territories taken over by the Han court. Liu Chih, the king of Chi-pei, was transferred to the position of king of Tzu-ch'uan.

King I of Ch'i died in the twenty-second year of his rule and was succeeded by his son Liu Tzu-ching, who is posthumously known as King Li.

King Li's mother was Queen Dowager Chi. Queen Chi had given the daughter of her younger brother to King Li to be his consort, but the king had no love for the girl. The queen, hoping to increase the favor and influence of her family, ordered her eldest daughter, Princess Chi, to enter the king's household and take charge of the women's quarters, and not to allow any of the concubines to approach the king. In this way she hoped to make the king fall in love with her niece of the Chi family, but instead the king took advantage of the opportunity to have incestuous relations with his sister, Princess Chi.

It happened that there was a man of Ch'i named Hsü Shen who had become a eunuch and gone to the capital to enter the service of Empress Dowager Wang, the mother of Emperor Wu. The empress dowager had a daughter called Lady Hsiu-ch'eng whom she loved dearly but who was not of the Liu family.[8] The empress dowager felt very sorry for her and hoped to marry Lady Hsiu-ch'eng's daughter, E, to one of the feudal princes. The eunuch Hsü Shen therefore asked the empress dowager to send him to Ch'i, promising that he would without fail persuade the king of Ch'i to send a letter to the court asking for her granddaughter E to be his queen. The empress dowager was delighted with this idea and dispatched Hsü Shen to Ch'i.

At this time there was a man of Ch'i named Chu-fu Yen who found out that Hsü Shen had come to Ch'i to arrange the king of Ch'i's marriage to a new consort, and he said to Hsü Shen, "If the matter should be settled satisfactorily, I hope you will do me the favor of speaking for my daughter as well. I would like to have her accepted as one of the ladies of the palace."

After Hsü Shen arrived at the court of Ch'i he began to hint at these two matters, whereupon Queen Dowager Chi became furious. "The king of Ch'i already has a consort and his palace is fully supplied with ladies in waiting!" she said. "This Hsü Shen is some poor man of Ch'i who was so pressed by poverty that he allowed himself to be made a eunuch. He entered the service of the Han court, but since he was not able to get anywhere there he has come here and is trying to upset the family of my son the king! As for Chu-fu Yen, who does he think he is that he should try to have his daughter made a lady in waiting?"

Hsü Shen's plans were completely frustrated, and he returned to the capital to report to the empress dowager. "The king of Ch'i expressed a desire to marry your granddaughter E, but there is a certain grave objection. Under the circumstances you might better have married

---

[8] Lady Hsiu-ch'eng was a daughter by Empress Dowager Wang's earlier marriage to a man of the Chin family.

her to the king of Yen." (The king of Yen had had illicit relations with his brother's children and had just been tried and condemned to death and his kingdom abolished. Therefore Hsü Shen mentioned the king of Yen in order to warn the empress dowager of the danger.)

"Say nothing more about this matter of marrying my granddaughter to the king of Ch'i," she replied. "Let the matter drop out of sight, or it may come to the hearing of the emperor."

Because of this affair Chu-fu Yen bore a grudge against the court of Ch'i. Shortly afterwards he gained favor with the emperor and was given a position in the government, and he took advantage of this to point out to the emperor that Lin-tzu, the capital of Ch'i, had a population of a hundred thousand households and that the taxes from its markets amounted to a thousand catties of gold a day, so that in wealth and size it was greater even than the city of Ch'ang-an. "No one but a trusted brother or favorite son of Your Majesty should be allowed to rule such a territory," he said, "and yet in recent years the kings of Ch'i have grown increasingly distant from the imperial family." In the course of the conversation he mentioned that, in the reign of Empress Lü, the state of Ch'i had intended to revolt, and had come near to making trouble again at the time of the rebellion of Wu and Ch'u. "And now," he concluded, "I have heard that the king of Ch'i has behaved immorally with his own sister!"

With this, the emperor appointed Chu-fu Yen to the position of prime minister of Ch'i and sent him to clear up the matter. As soon as he reached Ch'i, Chu-fu Yen at once seized the ladies of the palace and eunuchs who had acted as go-betweens for the king and his sister, Princess Chi, and subjected them to examination, seeing to it that their confessions all implicated the king. The king was still young and, fearing that he would be accused of a capital crime and seized and executed by the law officials, he drank poison and died. He left no heir.

Liu P'eng-tsu, the king of Chao and a brother of the emperor, began to be afraid that Chu-fu Yen, having already destroyed the royal family in Ch'i, would go on until little by little he had created enmity between the emperor and all the rest of his relatives as well, and so he sent a report to the throne accusing Chu-fu Yen of having accepted gifts of money and used his authority unjustly. The emperor accordingly had

King Tao-hui of Ch'i

Chu-fu Yen put in prison. The prime minister Kung-sun Hung stated that, since the king of Ch'i had died of grief and left no heir, his territory should be taken over by the Han government. He also suggested that unless Chu-fu Yen were executed there would be no way of stilling the resentment of the empire over what he had done. Eventually Chu-fu Yen was executed. King Li of Ch'i died in the fifth year of his rule and, as he left no heir, his territory became a part of the central government.

Of the territories ruled by the descendants of King Tao-hui of Ch'i two still remained, the kingdoms of Ch'eng-yang and Tzu-ch'uan. The emperor took pity on the royal family of Ch'i and, since the territory of Tzu-ch'uan adjoined that of Ch'i, he detached the eastern part of Lin-tzu, the province where the grave and funerary park of King Tao-hui of Ch'i were situated, and gave it, along with the towns surrounding the grave, to Liu Chih, the king of Tzu-ch'uan, so that he could offer sacrifices there to the spirit of his father King Tao-hui.

Liu Chang, King Ching of Ch'eng-yang, was also a son of King Tao-hui of Ch'i. When he was still marquis of Chu-hsü he joined with the great ministers in overthrowing the Lü family, leading the way in person by cutting down the prime minister Lü Ch'an in the Eternal Palace. After Emperor Wen came to the throne he increased Liu Chang's fief by two thousand households and awarded him a thousand catties of gold. In the second year of his reign Emperor Wen made Liu Chang the king of Ch'eng-yang, ruling the province of Ch'eng-yang, which had previously been a part of Ch'i. The second year after he became king Liu Chang died and was succeeded by his son Liu Hsi, who is posthumously known as King Kung. In the eighth year of his rule he was moved to the position of king of Huai-nan, but four years later was returned to the position of king of Ch'eng-yang. In all he ruled for thirty-three years and, after his death, was succeeded by his son Liu Chien-yen, who is posthumously known as King Ch'ing. King Ch'ing died in the twenty-eighth year of his rule and was succeeded by his son Liu I, who is known as King Ching. King Ching died in the ninth year of his rule and was succeeded by his son Liu Wu (known as King Hui. King Hui died in the eleventh year of his rule and was succeeded by his son Liu Shun, known as King Huang. King

Huang died in the forty-sixth year of his rule and was succeeded by his son Liu Hui, known as King Tai. King Tai died in the eighth year of his rule and was succeeded by his son Liu Ching. Liu Ching died in the third year of the era *chien-shih* [30 B.C.] at the age of fifteen).[9]

Liu Hsing-chü, the king of Chi-pei, was a son of King Tao-hui of Ch'i. As marquis of Tung-mou he aided the great ministers in overthrowing the Lü family, though he did little to distinguish himself. When the king of Tai arrived from his kingdom Liu Hsing-chü announced, "I beg to go with the master of carriage Lord T'eng to prepare the palace for Your Majesty's arrival and depose the young emperor." Later he joined with the great ministers in setting up the king of Tai as emperor. In the second year of his reign, at the same time that he set up the king of Ch'eng-yang, Emperor Wen set up Liu Hsing-chü as king of Chi-pei, ruling the province of Chi-pei which had formerly been a part of Ch'i. In the second year of his rule Liu Hsing-chü revolted.

Originally, at the time when the great ministers overthrew the Lü family, Liu Chang achieved the highest distinction, and the ministers agreed to make him king of the entire territory of Chao and to make Liu Hsing-chü king of the territory of Liang. After Emperor Wen ascended the throne, however, he discovered that Liu Chang and Liu Hsing-chü had originally wanted to set up their older brother, the king of Ch'i, as emperor, and so he did all he could to disparage their achievements. In the second year, when he enfeoffed the sons of King Tao-hui of Ch'i, he took two provinces from the territory of Ch'i and appointed Liu Chang and Liu Hsing-chü to rule them, but Liu Chang and his brother continued to feel that they had been deprived of their rightful positions and robbed of the reward due their achievements.

After Liu Chang died Liu Hsing-chü received news that the Hsiung-nu had invaded the empire in great force and that the Han government had dispatched a large number of troops under the command of the chancellor Kuan Ying to attack them. Since Emperor Wen had himself journeyed north to T'ai-yüan, Liu Hsing-chü supposed

---

[9] The section in parentheses deals with events after Ssu-ma Ch'ien's death and is a later interpolation.

that the emperor was going to lead the attack on the barbarians in person, and so he eventually called out his forces and started a revolt in Chi-pei. When the emperor received news of this he dismissed Kuan Ying and the forces that had been dispatched to attack the Hsiung-nu and sent them back to Ch'ang-an, at the same time ordering the marquis of Chi-p'u, General Ch'ai Wu,[10] to attack the king of Chi-pei. The king was defeated and taken prisoner. He committed suicide, and his territory was taken over by the central government and made into a province.

Thirteen years later, in the sixteenth year of his reign, Emperor Wen set up another of King Tao-hui's sons, Liu Chih, the marquis of An-tu, as king of Chi-pei. In the eleventh year of his rule, when the kingdoms of Wu and Ch'u raised their revolt, Liu Chih held fast to his kingdom and refused to join with the other feudal lords in their plot against the government. After the rebellion of Wu and Ch'u had been put down Liu Chih was transferred to the position of king of Tzu-ch'uan.

Liu Pi-kuang, the king of Chi-nan, was also a son of King Tao-hui of Ch'i. In the sixteenth year of Emperor Wen's reign he was advanced from the position of marquis of Li to that of king of Chi-nan. In the eleventh year of his rule he joined with Wu and Ch'u in revolt, but he was attacked and killed by the Han forces. His kingdom of Chi-nan was taken over by the central government and made into a province.

Liu Hsien, the king of Tzu-ch'uan, also a son of King Tao-hui, was advanced from the position of marquis of Wu-ch'eng in the sixteenth year of Emperor Wen's reign and made king of Tzu-ch'uan. In his eleventh year of rule he joined the revolt of Wu and Ch'u and was killed by the Han forces. The emperor accordingly moved Liu Chih, the king of Chi-pei, to the position of king of Tzu-ch'uan. (Liu Chih was a son of King Tao-hui, who had been advanced from the position of marquis of An-tu to that of king of Chi-pei. Since the king of Tzu-ch'uan revolted and left no heir, the king of Chi-pei was transferred to his position.) [11]

Liu Chih died in the thirty-fifth year of his rule and was given the

[10] Elsewhere his name is given as Ch'en Wu.
[11] The text becomes so repetitious at this point that we must suppose that it is corrupt.

posthumous title of King I. His son Liu Chien succeeded him and is known as King Ching. He died in his twentieth year of rule and was succeeded by his son Liu I (posthumously known as King Ch'ing. He died in the thirty-sixth year of his rule and was succeeded by his son Liu Chung-ku, known as King Ssu. King Ssu died in the twenty-eighth year of his rule and was succeeded by his son Liu Shang, known as King Hsiao. King Hsiao died in his fifth year and was succeeded by his son Liu Heng. He died in the third year of the era *chien-shih* [30 B.C.] at the age of eleven).[12]

Liu Ang, the king of Chiao-hsi, was a son of King Tao-hui and in the sixteenth year of Emperor Wen was advanced from the position of marquis of Ch'ang-p'ing to that of king of Chiao-hsi. In his eleventh year of rule he joined the revolt of Wu and Ch'u and was attacked and killed by the Han forces. His territory was taken over by the central government and made into the province of Chiao-hsi.

Liu Hsiung-ch'ü, the king of Chiao-tung, was a son of King Tao-hui. Formerly marquis of Po-shih, he was made king of Chiao-tung in the sixteenth year of Emperor Wen. In his eleventh year of rule he joined the revolt of Wu and Ch'u and was attacked and killed by the Han forces. His territory was taken over and made into the province of Chiao-tung.

The Grand Historian remarks: Among the great kingdoms of the feudal lords, none surpassed that of King Tao-hui of Ch'i. Kao-tsu had few sons and younger brothers but, after he had brought peace to the land within the four seas, he was outraged that the Ch'in before him had refused to dole out so much as a foot of territory in fiefs, and so he granted generous territories to the members of his clan in order to set the hearts of the common people at peace. Later the kingdom of Ch'i was split up, but this was of course done for a reason.

---

[12] The section in parentheses is a later interpolation.

Shih chi 54 (excerpt): The Hereditary House of Prime Minister Ts'ao

With Han Hsin he conquered the region of Wei, defeated Chao and Ch'i, and broke the power of the Ch'u leader Hsiang Yü. He succeeded Hsiao Ho as prime minister of the Han court, taking care not to change old ways, and the people found peace. In recognition of the fact that he did not boast of his military achievements nor brag of his ability, I made The Hereditary House of Prime Minister Ts'ao.

[Ts'ao Ts'an was a native of P'ei, the birthplace of Kao-tsu, founder of the Han. Under the Ch'in dynasty he served as police chief of P'ei and, when Kao-tsu became governor of P'ei and began his uprising, Ts'ao Ts'an became one of his most trusted followers. He served Kao-tsu faithfully and distinguished himself repeatedly in the battles against the Ch'in armies, and later against Kao-tsu's rival Hsiang Yü. In 202 B.C., when Kao-tsu finally won control of the empire and assumed the title of Supreme Emperor, he enfeoffed Ts'ao Ts'an as marquis of P'ing-yang and appointed him prime minister to his eldest son Liu Fei, the king of Ch'i, posthumously known as King Tao-hui of Ch'i.

The entire first part of Ssu-ma Ch'ien's chapter on Ts'ao Ts'an consists of no more than a dry recital of the campaigns in which Ts'ao Ts'an participated and the military achievements he won, copied by the historian, it would seem, from official records preserved at court. In the translation I have omitted this first section, which would be of little interest to the reader, and begun at the point when, after serving as general in the campaign against the rebel Ch'en Hsi, Ts'ao Ts'an is once more appointed prime minister of the state of Ch'i—*Trans.*]

In the first year of his reign [194 B.C.] Emperor Hui changed the title of the post of prime minister in the various feudal kingdoms and renamed it chancellor. He ordered Ts'ao Ts'an to resume his position as chancellor to Ch'i. Earlier, when Ts'ao Ts'an was first appointed prime minister to Ch'i, a great state of some seventy cities, order had just been restored to the empire and King Tao-hui of Ch'i was still a young man. Upon his arrival in Ch'i, Ts'ao Ts'an summoned all the elders and scholars of the state and inquired of them how he should go about bringing peace and stability to the people. But there were hundreds of Confucian scholars making their home in Ch'i, and each of them told him something different. Ts'ao Ts'an had not made up his mind which advice to follow, when he heard that in the region of Chiao-hsi there was a Master Kai who was versed in the teachings of the Yellow Emperor and Lao Tzu. He sent someone with generous gifts to invite Master Kai to court. Master Kai responded and in an interview with Ts'ao Ts'an advised him that the way to govern was through purity and stillness, so the people of themselves would find peace.[1] He elaborated this theory with arguments and examples, and Ts'ao Ts'an was so impressed that he relinquished his own place of authority in the main hall to Master Kai. In governing the state of Ch'i, Ts'ao Ts'an on the whole followed Taoist teachings, and as a result the state enjoyed peace and stability during his nine years as prime minister and Ts'ao Ts'an gained a reputation as a worthy minister.

In the second year of Emperor Hui's reign [193 B.C.] Hsiao Ho, the prime minister of the Han court, died. When Ts'ao Ts'an received the news he told his servants, "Hurry and make ready for the journey, for I will be going to the capital to become the new prime minister!" Shortly afterwards an envoy arrived from Ch'ang-an and, as Ts'ao Ts'an had predicted, summoned him to the post of prime minister.

When Ts'ao Ts'an was about to leave for his new post he admonished the official who was to succeed him as chancellor of Ch'i, saying, "I am entrusting you with the supervision of the jails and markets. Be careful and see that you do not stir them up!"

"But is there nothing more important in governing than just this?" asked his successor.

"Oh, yes," said Ts'ao Ts'an. "It is only that the jails and markets harbor all sorts of people, good and bad. If you stir up the markets and empty out the jails, then evil men will have no place to stay and

---

[1] The typical Taoist theory of laissez-faire government.

will make trouble for you elsewhere. That is why I mentioned this matter first of all." [2]

In the old days, when Ts'ao was still a humble official, he was a good friend of Hsiao Ho but, after he became a general and Hsiao Ho was appointed prime minister at the central court, they had a falling out. When Hsiao Ho lay on his death bed, however, he recommended Ts'ao Ts'an as the only man worthy to succeed him. Ts'ao Ts'an accordingly replaced Hsiao Ho as prime minister, but he made no changes whatsoever in the management of affairs, conducting everything exactly in accordance with the rules that Hsiao Ho had laid down. From among the officials in the feudal and provincial governments he purposely selected those who were clumsy and inept in the use of words but who were known for their loyal and generous conduct, and summoned them to the capital to join his staff. If he discovered that any of his subordinates was attempting to make a name for himself by applying the letter of the law with undue severity, he would summarily dismiss the man.

Ts'ao Ts'an spent his time day and night drinking strong wine. It became apparent to all, from the highest officials down to Ts'ao Ts'an's own clerks and retainers, that he was not attending to his duties, and everyone who came to his office attempted to speak to him on the matter. It was his custom at such times, however, to bring out his strong wine and immediately pour his visitor a drink. After an interval had passed, when the visitor once more tried to say what he had on his mind, Ts'ao Ts'an would pour him another drink, so that in the end the visitor would go away drunk, having been unable to find any opportunity to deliver his advice. The garden back of the prime minister's quarters was situated next to the dormitory where the clerks of the ministry lived. The clerks in the dormitory spent their time every day drinking, singing, and shouting and, though Ts'ao Ts'an's valet was much annoyed, he could do nothing to quiet them. The valet

---

[2] It was an assumption among Han officials and intellectuals that most, if not all, men engaged in trade were swindlers. Confucian thinkers usually favored strong measures to suppress the merchant class. Ts'ao Ts'an, a follower of Taoist principles, is here recommending that the merchants be left alone so that their pernicious ways will not spread to other areas of society.

accordingly invited Ts'ao Ts'an to take a stroll in the gardens, hoping that, when he heard the singing and shouting of the drunken clerks, he would send for them and reprimand them. Contrary to his expectations, however, Ts'ao Ts'an ordered wine brought and, spreading a mat in the garden, sat down to drink too, and before long was singing and shouting back and forth in time with the clerks.

Whenever Ts'ao Ts'an discovered that someone had been guilty of a minor fault, he did his best to cover up for the man and keep the affair quiet instead of initiating an investigation, so that his office had practically no business to attend to.

Ts'ao Ts'an's son Ts'ao Chü was a palace counselor. Emperor Hui was puzzled by the fact that Ts'ao Ts'an paid no attention to his duties as prime minister, and felt that Ts'ao Ts'an was contemptuous of his ability as a ruler. The emperor therefore said to Ts'ao Chü, "When you return home next time, I want you to wait until some time when you are alone with your father and then say to him, 'Emperor Kao-tsu has only lately departed from the host of officials,[3] and the new emperor is still young. And yet, although you are prime minister, you spend your days drinking and do not attend to your duties. Have you no care for the welfare of the empire?' But you must not tell him that I instructed you to say this!"

Accordingly, when his next "bath and hair washing day" came and he returned home, Ts'ao Chü waited until an opportunity presented itself and reprimanded his father as though of his own volition. Ts'ao Ts'an was furious and gave his son two hundred blows of the rod. "Go back to court at once and tend to your business!" he said. "You have no right to speak about the affairs of the empire!"

The next time the officials were gathered at court Emperor Hui began to upbraid Ts'ao Ts'an. "Why did you beat your son Chü?" he asked. "It was I who sent him to reprimand you the other day."

Ts'ao Ts'an removed his cap and apologized, saying, "In wisdom and military prowess, whom does Your Majesty consider superior, yourself or Emperor Kao-tsu?"

"How would I dare hope to equal my father the former emperor?" replied Emperor Hui.

[3] I.e., died.

"And who would you say had greater ability as a minister. Hsiao Ho or I?" asked Ts'ao Ts'an.

"You are no match for Hsiao Ho!"

"Your Majesty has spoken correctly," said Ts'ao Ts'an. "Emperor Kao-tsu and Hsiao Ho brought peace to the empire, and because of them the laws by which it should be governed have been made plain. Now if Your Majesty would be content to sit quietly upon the throne,[4] while I and the other officials guard our posts and endeavor to carry out the laws without error, would that not be sufficient?"

"You are quite right," said Emperor Hui. "You may go."

Ts'ao Ts'an died after serving as prime minister of the Han for some three years. He was given the posthumous title of I, the "Admirable Marquis." His son Ts'ao Chü succeeded to the marquisate. The common people composed a song that went:

> Hsiao Ho made us laws,
> As plain as the figure "one."
> Ts'ao Ts'an took his place
> And upheld them without fault.
> He governed with purity and stillness,
> And the people were at peace.

During the reign of Empress Lü, Ts'ao Chü, who had succeeded his father as marquis of P'ing-yang, rose to the position of imperial secretary, but when Emperor Wen came to the throne he retired from the post, retaining only the title of marquis. Twenty-nine years after he succeeded his father as marquis he died and was given the posthumous title of Ching or "Quiet Marquis." His son Ts'ao Chi succeeded to the marquisate and died seven years later; he was given the posthumous title of Chien, the "Sincere Marquis." His son Ts'ao Shih succeeded to the marquisate and married Princess Yang-hsin, Emperor Ching's daughter, who was henceforth known as Princess P'ing-yang. By her he had a son named Ts'ao Hsiang. Ts'ao Shih left the capital because of the plague and retired to his territory. Twenty-three years after he succeeded to the marquisate he died and was given the posthumous title of I, the "Peaceful Marquis." His son Ts'ao Hsiang

---

[4] Literally "dangle your robes and fold your hands," a conventional phrase for laissez-faire government.

succeeded to the marquisate and married Princess Wei, by whom he had a son named Ts'ao Tsung. Sixteen years later he died and was given the title of Kung, the "Respectful Marquis." His son Ts'ao Tsung succeeded to the marquisate. In the second year of the era *cheng-ho* [91 B.C.] Ts'ao Tsung was tried in connection with the revolt of the heir apparent and his territory abolished.

The Grand Historian remarks: The reason Ts'ao Ts'an was able to win the impressive number of achievements in sieges and battles which I have recorded was that he was fighting along with Han Hsin, the marquis of Huai-nan. After Han Hsin was executed, however, Ts'ao Ts'an was left alone to enjoy the highest place among the distinguished followers of Kao-tsu. As prime minister of the Han, he strove for the utmost purity and his words accorded with the Tao. At that time the common people had just escaped from the harsh rule of the Ch'in and they joined with Ts'ao Ts'an in finding rest in inaction. Therefore the world unanimously praised his worth.

Shih chi 57: The Hereditary House of Chou P'o, the Marquis of Chiang

The members of the Lü clan ruled with a wanton hand and plotted to weaken the defenses of the capital, but Chou P'o brought them to order and restored power to the proper authorities. Faced with the armies of Wu and Ch'u, Chou Ya-fu took up his position in the city of Ch'ang-i, inflicting injury on Ch'i and Chao but leaving Liang to its fate. Thus I made The Hereditary House of the Marquis of Chiang.

Chou P'o, the marquis of Chiang, was a native of P'ei. His ancestors came from Chüan, but had moved to P'ei. Chou P'o made a living by weaving racks for silkworms out of rushes; in addition he frequently assisted at funerals by playing the pipes. He was a member of the militia with the position of strong-puller crossbowman.[1]

When Kao-tsu became governor of P'ei and began his uprising Chou P'o followed as one of his pages and took part in the attack on Hu-ling and the capture of Fang-yü. When Fang-yü revolted, Kao-tsu and his men joined in battle again, drove back the enemy, and attacked Feng; after striking the Ch'in army east of Tang they returned to camp at Liu and Hsiao, then once more attacked Tang and captured it, along with Hsia-i. Chou P'o was commended for leading the way in battle and was awarded the rank of fifth lord.

When the army attacked and seized Meng and Yü and struck the carriage and cavalry of the Ch'in general Chang Han, Chou P'o was charged with guarding the rear. The governor of P'ei then brought the region of Wei under control, attacked and seized the area from

---

[1] See above "The Biography of Chang Ts'ang," note 6. The paragraphs which follow consist, as in the biographies of several other military leaders of the period, of a dull recital of all the engagements which Chou P'o took part in and the special merit which he achieved. Ssu-ma Ch'ien is apparently copying from military records preserved in the court archives.

Yüan-chi and Tung-min to Li, and attacked Nieh-sang. Chou P'o was again commended for leading the way in battle.

The governor of P'ei's men attacked the Ch'in army before the walls of Tung-a, and defeated and pursued it as far as P'u-yang; captured Chen-ch'eng, attacked Tu-kuan and Ting-t'ao, surprised and seized Yüan-ch'ü, and took prisoner the district magistrate of Tan-fu.

In the night they surprised and seized Lin-chi, attacked Chang, and advanced and defeated Chüan. When they attacked the army of the Ch'in general Li Yu before the walls of Yung-ch'iu, and marched on K'ai-feng, Chou P'o was the first to reach the city walls and thus achieved outstanding merit. Later, when Chang Han killed Hsiang Liang in battle, the governor of P'ei and Hsiang Yü led their troops back to Tang. A year and two months had passed from the time the governor first began his uprising in P'ei until he returned to Tang.

King Huai of Ch'u enfeoffed the governor of P'ei as marquis of Wu-an and made him head of Tang Province. The governor in turn appointed Chou P'o as magistrate of Hu-pi. In his position as magistrate Chou P'o again accompanied the governor of P'ei in bringing the region of Wei under control. They attacked the commander of Tung Province at Ch'eng-wu and routed him, and struck and defeated the army of the Ch'in general Wang Li. They attacked Ch'ang-she, and Chou P'o was commended for leading the way in battle. They attacked Ying-yang and Kou-shih, cut off the fords across the Yellow River, and struck the army of the Ch'in general Chao Pen north of Shih. Advancing south, they attacked I, the governor of Nan-yang Province, broke through the Wu and Yao passes, defeated the Ch'in army at Lan-t'ien and, marching to the capital city of Hsien-yang, overthrew the Ch'in dynasty. When Hsiang Yü arrived from the east he made the governor of P'ei king of Han, and the king in turn awarded Chou P'o the title of marquis of Wei-wu. Chou P'o accompanied the king to his territory in Han and was appointed a general of the army.

When the king of Han returned from his territory and won control of the three kingdoms of Ch'in and the old capital he awarded Chou P'o the revenue from the town of Huai-te. In the attacks on Huai-li and Hao-chih, Chou P'o achieved the highest distinction, and likewise in the attack on Chao Pen and Pao, the prefect of the capital. Turning north, they attacked Ch'i and struck the armies of Chang P'ing and Yao Ang; in the west they brought Ch'ien under control, returned to capture Mei and P'in-yang, surrounded Chang Han at Fei-ch'iu, defeated the assistant magistrate of Hsi, and struck and defeated the army of Chang Han's general Tao Pa. They attacked Shang-kuei, marched east to guard the Yao Pass, and then moved on to strike at Hsiang Yü, attacking Ch'ü-ni. Again Chou P'o achieved the most outstanding distinction. They returned to guard the Ao Granary and pursue the struggle against Hsiang Yü.

After Hsiang Yü's death the armies marched through the east, bringing order to the provinces of Ssu River and Tung-hai in the region of Ch'u, in all winning control of twenty-two districts. They then returned west to guard Lo-yang and Yüeh-yang. As a reward for his services Chou P'o was granted the revenue from the cities of Chung-li, which he was to share with Kuan Ying, the marquis of Ying-yin.

In his capacity as general he accompanied Emperor Kao-tsu in attacking and defeating Tsang Tu, the king of Yen, who had revolted, before the city of I. The troops under Chou P'o's command marched into the thick of battle and won outstanding glory. Chou P'o was rewarded with the rank of marquis and given the split tallies that entitled his heirs to hold the fief for generation after generation without end. He was granted the revenue from 8,180 households in Chiang and was made marquis of Chiang.

Again in his capacity as general he accompanied Emperor Kao-tsu in the expedition against Hsin, the king of Hann, who had raised a revolt in the region of Tai. After capturing Sha-jen they advanced as far as Wu-ch'üan, where they attacked the barbarian cavalry north of Wu-ch'üan and routed them. Then they turned and attacked Hann Hsin's army at T'ung-ti and routed it, and returned to capture six cities of T'ai-yüan. They struck the barbarian cavalry which was aiding Hann Hsin at Chin-yang, defeated it, and captured Chin-yang. After this they attacked Hann Hsin's army at Sha-shih and routed it, pursued the remnants for eighty *li* to the north, returned to attack three cities of Lou-fan, and from there struck at the barbarian cavalry before the walls of P'ing-ch'eng. Because the men under Chou P'o's command marched squarely into battle and won outstanding glory, he was transferred to the position of grand commandant.

They attacked Ch'en Hsi and massacred the inhabitants of the city of Ma-i, and the troops under Chou P'o's command cut down Ch'en Hsi's general Ch'eng-ma Ch'ih. They attacked and routed the armies of Hann Hsin, Ch'en Hsi, and Chao Li at Lou-fan, taking prisoner Ch'en Hsi's general Sung Tsui and the governor of Yen-men, Hun. From there they attacked Yün-chung and seized as prisoners the governor Su, the chancellor Chi Ssu, and General Hsün. They restored order to the seventeen districts of Yen-men Province and the twelve districts of Yün-chung Province. From there they attacked Ch'en Hsi at Ling-ch'iu, defeated his army, and killed him. They made prisoners of Ch'en Hsi's chancellor Ch'eng Tsung, his general Ch'en Wu, and a colonel named Kao Ssu, and brought nine districts of the province of Tai under control.[2]

When Lu Wan, the king of Yen, revolted, Chou P'o was made prime minister of Yen and sent to replace Fan K'uai. He led an attack on the city of Chi and captured it, took prisoner Lu Wan's commanding general Ti, his chancellor Yen, a governor named Hsing, his grand commandant Jo, and his palace secretary Shih. He massacred the inhabitants of the city of Hun-tu, routed Lu Wan's army at Shang-lan, struck and routed it again at Chü-yang, and pursued it as far as the Great Wall. He brought to order the twelve districts of Shang-ku, the sixteen districts of Yu-pei-p'ing, the twenty-nine districts of Liao-hsi and Liao-tung, and the twenty-two districts of Yü-yang. From the time that he first became a follower of Kao-tsu, Chou P'o achieved the following distinctions: he took prisoner one prime minister of a state, two chancellors, and three generals or officials of the rank of two thou-

[2] Throughout this long passage describing Chou P'o's military exploits, there is no subject expressed for the sentences. It is natural to assume that Chou P'o is the subject, and in some cases this is correct. But other sections of the *Shih chi* show that practically all of the operations mentioned here were actually led by Kao-tsu, Chou P'o being no more than one of his subordinates, so it is impossible to translate as though Chou P'o alone "attacked such-and-such," "captured so-and-so," etc. This omission of the subject is a trick of style which Ssu-ma Ch'ien often uses in recitals of military exploits, perhaps from a generous desire to make the hero of a particular chapter appear more distinguished than he actually was.

sand piculs; in addition he defeated two armies, captured three cities, and brought under control five provinces and seventy-nine districts; he also took prisoner one chancellor and one commanding general.

Chou P'o was a man of great honesty and warmth of feeling, and Kao-tsu considered him worthy to be entrusted with important duties of state. He had no fondness for learning and, whenever he called some scholar or rhetorician before him, he himself would take the seat of honor facing east and tell the man impatiently to "hurry up and come to the point of what you have to say to me!" This was the brusque, unaffected sort of manner he had in all matters.

By the time he returned from the campaign in Yen, Emperor Kao-tsu had already passed away and he served as a marquis at the court of Emperor Hui. In the sixth year of Emperor Hui's reign the office of grand commandant was established and Chou P'o appointed to fill it.

Ten years later Empress Lü passed away. At this time Lü Lu, the king of Chao, had been made supreme commander of the Han armies and Lu Ch'an, the king of Lü, had been made prime minister; together they wielded all the power in the Han court and were threatening the position of the Liu family. Chou P'o, although he was the grand commandant, could not gain entrance to the garrisons of the army, while the chancellor Ch'en P'ing was not permitted to manage the affairs of state. Accordingly the two of them plotted together and in the end succeeded in wiping out the Lü family and setting Emperor Wen on the throne. (A discussion of these events will be found in the chapters on Empress Lü and Emperor Wen.)

After Emperor Wen came to the throne he appointed Chou P'o as chancellor of the right and awarded him five thousand catties of gold and the revenue from a city of ten thousand households.

A month or so later someone said to Chou P'o, "Since you overthrew the Lü family and helped to set up the king of Tai as emperor, the whole empire stands in awe of you. You have received generous awards and acquired a position of great honor as the result of the favor you enjoy with the emperor. If you keep on like this I am afraid that some misfortune will befall you!" [3]

[3] Because too much good luck begets its opposite.

Chou P'o, alarmed by the man's words, began to believe that he was actually in danger, and so he asked to be allowed to relinquish the seals of the office of chancellor. The emperor gave his permission but a year or so later, when the chancellor of the left, Ch'en P'ing, died, the emperor recalled Chou P'o to the position of chancellor.

About ten months later the emperor said to Chou P'o, "Some time ago I issued an edict ordering the marquises to proceed to their territories, but there are still some of them who have not yet gone. Since you are one of my most trusted officials, I hope you will be good enough to lead the way for the rest." He then relieved Chou P'o of his duties as chancellor and sent him to his territory in Chiang.

A year or so later the military commander of the governor of Ho-tung province was making a tour of the districts in the province and arrived in the territory of Chiang. Chou P'o, the marquis of Chiang, terrified that he was going to be punished for some offense, wore armor wherever he went and ordered the men of his household to bring their weapons when he interviewed the commander. Some time later someone sent a report to the throne stating that Chou P'o was about to revolt. The emperor referred the matter to the commandant of justice. The commandant of justice in turn referred it to the officials in Ch'ang-an, who arrested Chou P'o and began to question him. Chou P'o was frightened and did not know how to explain away the charges. When the officials began to abuse and manhandle him Chou P'o offered the prison warden a thousand pieces of gold. The warden then wrote on the back of his wooden writing tablet: "Get the princess to vouch for you!" and held it up in such a way that Chou P'o could read the message. (The "princess" referred to was the daughter of Emperor Wen who had married Chou P'o's eldest son, Chou Sheng-chih. Therefore the warden instructed Chou P'o to get her to testify to his loyalty.)

Earlier, when Chou P'o's fief had been enlarged and he had received various gifts from the emperor, he had presented them all to Po Chao, the younger brother of Emperor Wen's mother, Empress Dowager Po. Accordingly, when Chou P'o was arrested and found himself in trouble, Po Chao spoke to Empress Dowager Po on his behalf. The empress dowager herself likewise believed that he was innocent of

Chou P'o, the Marquis of Chiang

the charge of disaffection. When Emperor Wen came to pay his respects to his mother she snatched up a shawl that lay at hand and, flinging it angrily in his face, exclaimed, "The marquis of Chiang once gripped the imperial seals themselves in his hands and commanded the soldiers of the northern garrison, and yet at that time he did not revolt! Now that he lives away in some little district, do you suppose he would suddenly decide to start a rebellion?"

Emperor Wen had already looked over the statements which Chou P'o made under examination in prison. "The officials are right now looking into the matter and will release him soon!" he replied, apologizing to his mother. He then sent a messenger bearing the imperial credentials to pardon Chou P'o and restore his title and lands to him.

After Chou P'o was released from prison he said, "I myself was once the commander of an army of a million men, but I never realized what a powerful person a prison warden is!"

Chou P'o returned to his territory and died in the eleventh year of Emperor Wen's reign [169 B.C.]. He was given the posthumous title of Wu, the "Military Marquis."

Chou P'o's son Chou Sheng-chih succeeded to the marquisate. He had been married to the daughter of Emperor Wen for six years, but they did not get along together. Chou Sheng-chih was tried on charges of murder and his fief was taken away from him but, after the marquisate had been discontinued for a year, Emperor Wen selected a more worthy son of Chou P'o, the governor of Ho-nei, Chou Ya-fu, and enfeoffed him as marquis of T'iao in order to carry on his father's title.

Once, in the time before he became governor of Ho-nei, Chou Ya-fu had had his fortune told by a certain Hsü Fu who was good at physiognomizing. "After three years you will become a marquis," said Hsü Fu. "Eight years after that you will become a general and statesman, grasping the reins of government and enjoying great honor and favor. Among all the emperor's subjects there will be none to compare with you. And nine years after that you will starve to death!"

Chou Ya-fu laughed and replied, "My older brother has already succeeded my father as marquis, and if he should happen to die his son would inherit the title. What talk is this about me becoming a marquis? And if I achieve all the honor that you tell me about, how can you say that I will starve to death afterward? Show me your proof!"

Hsü Fu pointed to Chou Ya-fu's mouth and said, "These vertical lines entering your mouth—they are the sign of death by starvation!"

Three years after this incident his older brother Chou Sheng-chih was convicted, and Emperor Wen began to look around for some more worthy son of Chou P'o to enfeoff. When everyone recommended Chou Ya-fu, the emperor enfeoffed him as marquis of T'iao to carry on his father's line.

In the sixth year of the latter part of Emperor Wen's reign [158 B.C.] the Hsiung-nu invaded the border in great force. In order to guard against the barbarians the emperor made Liu Li, the director of the imperial clan, a general and sent him to garrison Pa-shang; made the marquis of Chu-tzu, Hsü Li, a general and ordered him to Chi-men; and made Chou Ya-fu, at this time the governor of Ho-nei, a general and sent him to camp at Hsi-liu. To encourage his men the emperor journeyed in person to the encampments at Pa-shang and Chi-men. In both places the emperor galloped without ado straight into the camps, the generals and their subordinates coming out to greet him and see him off. Having finished at these places, he proceeded to Chou Ya-fu's encampment at Hsi-liu. Upon his arrival he found all the sentries in armor and bearing their swords and other weapons, their crossbows cocked and full of arrows. When the riders in the vanguard of his procession reached the camp they could not gain admittance. "The Son of Heaven is coming!" insisted the front riders, but the colonel in charge of the gate of the camp replied, "The general says that as long as we are in camp here we do not listen even to the edicts of the Son of Heaven. We take orders only from him!"

Before long the emperor himself arrived, but was likewise unable to gain admission. Thereupon he dispatched a messenger bearing the imperial credentials with word that he wished to enter the camp and talk to the men. Chou Ya-fu then sent word to open the gates of the battlements.

After the guards had opened the gates one of them told the cavalry and carriage drivers accompanying the emperor, "The general says there is to be no galloping within the camp!" The emperor accordingly

Chou P'o, the Marquis of Chiang

reined in the horses of his carriage and proceeded at a slow pace to the headquarters. General Chou Ya-fu appeared bearing his arms and bowed curtly. "Since a soldier in armor is not required to make the customary prostrations," he said, "I trust I may conduct the interview according to military etiquette."

The emperor, much impressed, straightened up in his carriage and bowed in return from the crossbar. Then he sent one of his men to report to the general that "the emperor respectfully wishes to thank the general for his pains."

After the ceremony was over and the emperor's party had taken leave and gone out of the garrison gate the officials accompanying him were all terrified of what his reaction would be, but Emperor Wen said, "Ah! Now there is a real general! Those other garrisons I visited at Pa-shang and Chi-men were nothing but child's play. Their generals could be attacked by surprise and taken prisoner in no time. But this Chou Ya-fu—you would never be able to trick him!" For a long time the emperor went on praising Chou Ya-fu.

After a month or so the three armies were recalled and Chou Ya-fu was appointed to the post of palace military commander. When Emperor Wen was on his deathbed he admonished his son, the heir apparent, saying, "If there is ever any trouble, Chou Ya-fu is the man best fitted to lead the troops!"

After Emperor Wen passed away Chou Ya-fu was promoted to the rank of general of carriage and cavalry. In the third year of Emperor Ching's reign [154 B.C.], when the states of Wu and Ch'u rebelled, Chou Ya-fu was promoted from palace military commander to grand commandant and ordered east to attack Wu and Ch'u. At this time he sent a request to the emperor stating, "The troops of Ch'u are swift and nimble and it will be difficult to make contact with them. I would like to be allowed to leave them the area of Liang and concentrate instead on cutting off their lines of supply. In that case I believe they can be brought under control." The emperor approved of this strategy.

After Chou Ya-fu had massed his troops in Jung-yang, Wu opened an assault on Liang. Liu Wu, the king of Liang and brother of Emperor Ching, sorely pressed by the attack, sent a request for aid. Chou

Ya-fu led his troops in a dash to the northeast to Ch'ang-i, where he deepened the moats and guarded his position. Messengers arrived daily from Liang begging Chou Ya-fu to come to the king's aid, but he held fast to his point of vantage and refused to go. The king of Liang then sent a report on the matter to Emperor Ching, who dispatched an envoy to Chou Ya-fu with an imperial order for him to go to the rescue of Liang. Chou Ya-fu refused to obey the order, but held fast behind his walls and would not march forth. He dispatched Han T'ui-tang, the marquis of Kung-kao, and others with a force of light cavalry to cut the supply lines in the rear of the Wu and Ch'u armies.

The troops of Wu were running out of provisions and, driven by hunger, repeatedly challenged Chou Ya-fu to battle, but he continued to stay within his walls. In the middle of the night an alarm was raised in his camp and it was found that attackers had entered the walls and thrown the camp into confusion,[4] penetrating as far as the tent of the commander Chou Ya-fu himself. But Chou Ya-fu stayed in bed and did not bother to get up, and eventually order was restored.

Later the besieging troops of Wu made a rush on the southeast corner of Chou Ya-fu's walls. Chou Ya-fu then ordered his men to the northwest corner to prepare for an attack and, as he had foreseen, Wu sent its best trained men to make a rush at the northwest corner, but they were unable to breach the walls.

After this the troops of Wu, in the throes of starvation, withdrew from the siege and marched away, whereupon Chou Ya-fu sent out his best men to pursue and attack them, inflicting a crushing defeat. Liu P'i, the king of Wu, abandoned his army and fled with several thousand of his younger soldiers to Chiang-nan, where he sought protection in the city of Tan-hsi. Taking advantage of their victories, the Han troops made prisoners of all the enemy leaders, received the surrender of their armies, and put a price of a thousand pieces of gold on the head of the king of Wu. After a month or so the people of Yüeh executed the king of Wu and sent his head to the authorities.

[4] The passage is obscure, and it may mean that a faction within Chou Ya-fu's camp, disgusted with his watch-and-wait tactics, attacked the guards and caused a commotion.

Chou Ya-fu had been attacked and besieged for three months in all, and in the end he succeeded in crushing Wu and Ch'u and bringing them under control again. After it was all over the other generals unanimously acknowledged that Chou Ya-fu's strategy had been correct but, because Chou Ya-fu had refused to come to his aid, King Hsiao of Liang came to hate him.

When he returned from the expedition Chou Ya-fu was reappointed to the post of grand commandant. Five years later he was transferred to the position of chancellor and enjoyed great favor with Emperor Ching.

When Emperor Ching removed Lady Li's son from the position of heir apparent Chou Ya-fu did all he could as chancellor to oppose the move, but his efforts were to no avail, and as a result of the affair he began to lose favor with Emperor Ching. In addition, whenever Liu Wu, the king of Liang, came to court, he assiduously pointed out all of Chou Ya-fu's shortcomings to the emperor's mother, Empress Dowager Tou.

"Wang Hsin, the older brother of your empress, ought to be made a marquis!" the empress dowager said to Emperor Ching, but he declined to follow her suggestion. "The marquis of Nan-p'i and the marquis of Chang-wu [5] were not given their titles by my father, the former emperor. It was only after I myself came to the throne that they were made marquises. Therefore it is not possible to make Wang Hsin a marquis at this time!"

"A ruler disposes of each affair at whatever time he thinks fit!" said the empress dowager. "I have always deeply regretted that my brother Tou Ch'ang-chün was never made a marquis during his lifetime. It was only after his death that his son Tou P'eng-tsu got to be a marquis. You must make Wang Hsin a marquis at once!"

"You will have to let me take it up with the chancellor first," replied the emperor.

[5] The marquis of Nan-p'i, Tou P'eng-tsu, was the son of Empress Dowager Tou's older brother Tou Ch'ang-chün. The marquis of Chang-wu was her younger brother Tou Shao-chün. The emperor's point is that it is not proper for the ruler to make marquises of the male relatives of his empress during his own lifetime.

When the emperor consulted the chancellor on the matter Chou Ya-fu replied, "Emperor Kao-tsu made an agreement with his followers that no one who was not of the Liu family should be made a king, and no one who had not achieved some outstanding merit should be made a marquis. If anyone violated this agreement, the empire was to unite in attacking him. Now although Wang Hsin is the older brother of the empress, he has won no particular merit. If he were made a marquis, it would be a violation of the agreement!" The emperor was forced to remain silent and abandon the idea.

Some time later, when Hsü Lu, a chieftain of the Hsiung-nu, and several other Hsiung-nu leaders, five men in all, surrendered to the Han court, Emperor Ching wanted to make them marquises in order to encourage others to desert, but the chancellor Chou Ya-fu objected. "These men have turned against their own sovereign and deserted to Your Majesty. If you honor them with the title of marquis, then how can you blame your own subjects if they do not stick loyally by their posts?"

"The opinions of the chancellor are not worth listening to!" exclaimed the emperor, and proceeded to enfeoff Hsü Lu and all the other Hsiung-nu leaders as marquises. Chou Ya-fu asked to be allowed to resign because of ill health, and in the third year of the middle period of Emperor Ching's reign [147 B.C.] he was relieved of his duties as chancellor.

Not long after this Emperor Ching invited Chou Ya-fu to join him at dinner in the private apartments of the palace. When the meal was served, however, only a large joint of meat was placed before Chou Ya-fu, with no smaller slices cut from it and no chopsticks to eat it with. Nervous and flustered, Chou Ya-fu turned to the chief waiter and said, "Bring me some chopsticks!"

Emperor Ching looked over at him and said with a laugh, "Is there something about the arrangements that does not meet with your satisfaction?"

Chou Ya-fu removed his cap and bowed in apology.

"Get up!" ordered the emperor,[6] and Chou Ya-fu rose and hurried from the room. As the emperor followed him with his eyes, he said,

---

[6] Following the reading in *Han shu* 40.

"This ill-contented wretch will never do as a minister for my son, the young lord!"

Not long after this Chou Ya-fu's son purchased five hundred sets of armor and shields from the emperor's own workshop to be used for his father's funeral. He hired a day laborer to help him but, after working the man very hard, refused to give him his wages. The laborer knew that Chou Ya-fu's son was guilty of having illegally obtained goods from the government workshops and, angered at the treatment he had received, he reported to the authorities on the son's irregular actions, implicating Chou Ya-fu in the affair as well. When the report came to the emperor's attention he referred the matter to the law officials. The officials prepared their list of charges and began to cross-examine Chou Ya-fu, but he refused to answer them. "I have no further use for the man!" exclaimed the emperor angrily and ordered him sent to the commandant of justice.

"Tell me, my lord, did you intend to revolt?" demanded the commandant of justice.

"The goods I bought were articles for a funeral!" replied Chou Ya-fu. "Why should anyone say I was going to revolt?"

"Then perhaps you did not intend to revolt in this world, but only in the world below?" said the constables, and pressed their examination with increasing fury.

When Chou Ya-fu was first arrested by the law officials he was about to commit suicide, but his wife begged him to desist, so that he missed the opportunity to die by his own hand. Finally, after he had been brought before the commandant of justice, he refused to eat for five days and eventually spat blood and died. His fief was abolished.

A year later Emperor Ching enfeoffed another of Chou P'o's sons, Chou Chien, as marquis of P'ing-ch'ü in order to carry on the title. Nineteen years later Chou Chien died and was given the posthumous title of Kung or "Respectful Marquis." His son Chou Chien-te succeeded to the marquisate and thirteen years later became grand tutor to the heir apparent. In the fifth year of the era *yüan-ting* [112 B.C.], however, he was accused of having sent in a poor grade of gold as his "wine tribute" money and because of this offense his territory was taken away from him.

Thus it was that Chou Ya-fu, the marquis of T'iao, did after all die of starvation. After his death Emperor Ching enfeoffed Wang Hsin as marquis of Kai.

The Grand Historian remarks: At first, when Chou P'o, the marquis of Chiang, was still a commoner, he was a simple rustic, in ability scarcely surpassing the ordinary run of men. Yet after he joined with Kao-tsu in conquering the world, he filled the positions of general and statesman. When the men of the Lü clan were plotting revolt, he rescued the state from peril and set it back upon its proper course. Even the great ministers of antiquity I Yin and the duke of Chou could have done no better!

In the use of arms Chou Ya-fu displayed a might and endurance which the famous general Jang-chü of old could hardly have surpassed. But he thought too well of himself and did not learn from the times; he was too unbending in the defense of his principles, until in the end, alas, he found himself in serious difficulty!

Shih chi 58: The Hereditary House of King Hsiao of Liang

When the seven kingdoms rose in revolt the king of Liang acted as a bastion and shield for the capital; he alone bore the brunt of the attack. But when he presumed too much upon the love of the emperor and made a show of his achievements he came near to inviting disaster. In recognition of his services in holding off the rebel armies of Wu and Ch'u, I made The Hereditary House of King Hsiao of Liang.

Liu Wu, posthumously titled "King Hsiao of Liang," was a son of Emperor Wen. His mother was Empress Dowager Tou, who was also the mother of Emperor Ching.

Emperor Wen had four sons. The eldest was the heir apparent, who later became Emperor Ching. The second was Liu Wu, the third Liu Ts'an, and the fourth Liu Sheng. In the second year after he came to the throne Emperor Wen made Liu Wu the king of Tai, Liu Ts'an the king of T'ai-yüan, and Liu Sheng the king of Liang. Two years later he transferred Liu Wu to the position of king of Huai-yang and turned over all of Liu Wu's former kingdom of Tai to Liu Ts'an, the king of T'ai-yüan, whom he retitled king of Tai. Seventeen years after he became king, in the second year of the latter part of Emperor Wen's reign [162 B.C.], Liu Ts'an died and was given the posthumous title of Hsiao or "Filial King of Tai." His son Liu Teng succeeded to the throne, and is posthumously known as King Kung. He died twenty-nine years later, in the second year of the era *yüan-kuang* [133 B.C.]. His son Liu I succeeded him as king of Tai. In the nineteenth year of his rule the Han court decided to enlarge the area within the Pass so that it would extend as far as the Ch'ang Mountains. The emperor accordingly moved Liu I from his position of king of Tai and made him king of Ch'ing-ho. This took place in the third year of the era *yüan-ting* [114 B.C.].

Ten years after Liu Wu became king of Huai-yang, Liu Sheng, the king of Liang, died, and was given the posthumous title of Huai or "Beloved King of Liang." (He was the youngest of Emperor Wen's sons, and his father loved and favored him above all his other sons.) The following year Liu Wu was transferred from the position of king of Huai-yang to that of king of Liang. (He became king of Liang in the twelfth year of Emperor Wen's reign [168 B.C.], but at this time had already held the title of king of other regions for eleven years.) In the fourteenth year of his rule he came to the central court to pay his respects, and again in the seventeenth and eighteenth years. After this last visit he remained in the capital and did not return to his kingdom until the following year. In the twenty-first year he again came to court. In the twenty-second year of his rule Emperor Wen passed away. Liu Wu came to court in the twenty-fourth year and again in the twenty-fifth year of his rule.

At this time Emperor Ching, who had succeeded Emperor Wen, had not yet designated an heir apparent. The emperor was one time feasting and drinking with his younger brother, the king of Liang, when he remarked in the course of the conversation, "After my days are ended, I shall pass on the throne to you!" The king of Liang declined to listen to such a suggestion but, although he knew that the emperor was not speaking seriously, he was secretly pleased by the idea, as was their mother, Empress Dowager Tou.[1]

In the spring of this year Wu, Ch'u, Ch'i, Chao, and several other states, seven in all, revolted. The armies of Wu and Ch'u led the attack by striking at Chi-pi in Liang, killing twenty or thirty thousand men. The king of Liang guarded his capital at Sui-yang and dispatched Han An-kuo, Chang Yü, and others of his ministers as generals to hold off the armies of Wu and Ch'u. The rebel armies were forced to halt in Liang and did not venture to advance any farther west. There they remained for three months, held in check by the grand commandant Chou Ya-fu and the others. After the revolt had been crushed it was found that, in the number of enemy killed and prisoners taken, the

---

[1] This question of passing the throne along to a younger brother had come up earlier in the reign of Emperor Wen, but it was opposed by the officials, who insisted that the only proper manner of succession was from father to son.

Liang armies had achieved virtually as much as the forces of the Han government.

The following year Emperor Ching appointed an heir apparent, but even after this the king of Liang enjoyed great distinction at court and continued to be on the most intimate terms with the emperor. His kingdom was of considerable size and occupied one of the richest regions of the empire, extending north to Mount T'ai and west as far as Kao-yang, and including over forty cities, all of which commanded important districts. Because he was her younger son, Empress Dowager Tou loved the king dearly and showered him with countless presents. The king proceeded to lay out for himself an "Eastern Park" measuring over three hundred *li* square, and enlarged his capital city of Sui-yang by seventy *li*. He built palaces and halls on a grand scale, and constructed an elevated walk running over thirty *li* from his palace to the Level Terrace. He had received as a gift from the court the flags and pennants of the Son of Heaven and, when he left the palace, his entourage included a thousand carriages and ten thousand riders. He went on hunting expeditions to the east and west in the manner of an emperor and, when he left the palace or returned, attendants preceded him crying, "Clear the way! Attention!" He invited famous men from all around to come to his court, and from the mountains east to the sea there was not a single wandering rhetorician who did not accept his invitation, including such men as Yang Sheng, Kung-sun Kuei, and Tsou Yang of Ch'i. Kung-sun Kuei was full of strange and dubious schemes. When he first came to visit the king, the latter awarded him a gift of a thousand pieces of gold and employed him in official positions as high as that of military commander, so that the people of Liang came to refer to him as "General Kung-sun." The kingdom of Liang manufactured weapons in great quantities, crossbows and spears to the number of several hundred thousand; its coffers contained close to a hundred million in gold and cash, and more jewels and precious objects than the capital itself.

In the twenty-ninth year of his rule, the tenth month [150 B.C.], the king of Liang went to attend the court of the emperor. Emperor Ching sent an envoy bearing the imperial credentials and a carriage drawn by four horses to meet the king at the Pass. After the king had made his report to the emperor he remained on at the capital because of the ties of affection between him and his mother, Empress Dowager Tou. Within the palace grounds he waited on Emperor Ching and accompanied him in his hand carriage, and when the emperor went out on hunting trips he rode in the same chariot, shooting birds and beasts with him in the Shang-lin Park. The palace attendants, master of guests, and other members of the king of Liang's party wrote their names in the roster of officials and went in and out of the emperor's gate of the palace in exactly the same way as the officials of the Han court.

In the eleventh month Emperor Ching removed his son by Lady Li from the position of heir apparent. Empress Dowager Tou personally hoped that he would designate the king of Liang as his successor, but the high officials and others such as Yüan Ang strongly advised him against such a move. Empress Dowager Tou was forced to abandon her scheme and after this never again brought up the matter of making the king of Liang the heir to the throne. The whole affair was handled in secret so that the people of the time knew nothing about it. Shortly afterwards the king of Liang took leave of the court and returned to his kingdom, and in the summer, the fourth month, Emperor Ching designated his son the king of Chiao-tung as heir apparent.

The king of Liang was embittered at Yüan Ang and the counselors of the court who had opposed the move to make him successor to the throne and, plotting with Yang Sheng, Kung-sun Kuei, and his other advisers, sent men in secret to assassinate Yüan Ang and ten or more of the counselors. A search was made for the assassins and, even before they were seized, the emperor began to suspect that the king of Liang was involved. After the assassins had been arrested and it became obvious that the king of Liang had in fact employed them the emperor dispatched a veritable stream of officials to Liang to investigate the matter and arrest Kung-sun Kuei and Yang Sheng, both of whom went into hiding in the women's quarters of the palace. When the emperor's envoys pressed their examination of the high officials of Liang and demanded action the prime minister Hsüan-ch'iu Pao and the palace secretary Han An-kuo came forward and reprimanded the king for his conduct in the affair. The king finally ordered Yang Sheng and

Kung-sun Kuei to commit suicide and had their bodies placed on view.

As a result of this affair the emperor was deeply angered with his brother. The king, fearful of the consequences, dispatched Han An-kuo to go to his sister, Princess Ch'ang, and ask her to intercede with their mother, Empress Dowager Tou, and beg forgiveness for his faults. Thus the affair was eventually settled and the emperor's anger somewhat appeased.

Sometime afterwards the king of Liang sent a letter to the emperor expressing his desire to come to court. When he reached the Pass he followed the advice of his minister Mao Lan and, changing to a plain carriage accompanied by only two riders, entered the capital incognito and hid in the garden of Princess Ch'ang's home. An envoy from the Han court arrived at the Pass to greet the king, but found only his carriages and attendants outside, ignorant of where the king had gone. When news of this reached the court, Empress Dowager Tou began to wail, "The emperor has killed my son!" and Emperor Ching himself was filled with fear and anxiety. Then the king appeared and prostrated himself before the palace gate, begging pardon for his crimes. The empress dowager and Emperor Ching greeted him with tears of joy, and all were once more united as before. Emperor Ching sent orders for the king's entourage to be brought in from the Pass, but he treated his brother with increasing coolness and no longer invited the king to ride with him in his carriage.

In the winter of the thirty-fifth year of his rule [144 B.C.] the king of Liang once more came to court and, after making his report to the emperor, expressed a desire to remain in the capital; the emperor refused permission. The king returned to his territory, but his mind was filled with uneasiness and he could find no pleasure in anything. When he went on a hunting trip north to Mount Liang someone presented him with a calf that had a foot growing out of the middle of its back. The king was filled with loathing at so fearful a prodigy. In the sixth month he fell ill of a fever, and on the sixth day he died. He was given the posthumous title of Hsiao, the "Filial King of Liang."

Liu Wu, the king of Liang, was an affectionate and filial son. Whenever he heard that his mother, Empress Dowager Tou, was ill he could hardly bring himself to eat and was unable to sleep at night for worry.

His constant desire was to remain in Ch'ang-an so that he might take care of his mother. Empress Dowager Tou for her part loved him dearly and, when she received the news of his death, she wailed and displayed the profoundest grief, refusing to eat. "The emperor has finally succeeded in killing my son!" she declared. Emperor Ching was filled with anxiety and did not know what to do but, after consulting with his sister Princess Ch'ang, he decided to divide the region of Liang into five parts and enfeoff all of Liu Wu's five sons as kings, and to award his five daughters the revenue from various "bath-towns." When he reported these moves to the empress dowager, she was appeased and consented for the sake of the emperor to take a little nourishment.

Liu Wu's eldest son Liu Mai became king of Liang, and is posthumously known as King Kung. His son Liu Ming became king of Chi-ch'uan; his son Liu P'eng-li became king of Chi-tung; his son Liu Ting became king of Shan-yang; and his son Liu Pu-shih became king of Chi-yin.

While Liu Wu was still alive his wealth reached enormous sums that defied computation, and even after his death the coffers of Liang still contained over four hundred thousand catties of yellow gold, with other treasures to match. In the third year of Liu Mai's rule Emperor Ching passed away. Seven years after he became king Liu Mai, King Kung of Liang, died, and was succeeded by his son Liu Hsiang, posthumously known as King P'ing.

In the fourteenth year of his rule the following incident occurred. Liu Hsiang's mother was known as Queen Dowager Ch'en; his grandmother, the mother of his father King Kung, was known as Queen Dowager Li, and his own consort, a daughter of the Jen family, was titled Queen Jen. Queen Jen enjoyed great favor with the king. Earlier, when King Hsiao was still alive, he had an ornamented wine goblet which was worth a thousand pieces of gold. King Hsiao warned his heirs that they must take good care of this wine goblet and under no circumstances give it to anyone else. When Queen Jen heard about the goblet, she decided that she must have it, but King P'ing's grandmother, Queen Dowager Li, told her, "The former king gave orders that the wine goblet was never to be given away. Any-

King Hsiao of Liang

thing else you wish, though it be worth a hundred million cash, you may have for the asking!"

But the queen continued to beg and beg, until King P'ing finally sent a man to open the storehouse and take out the ornamented wine goblet and present it to her.

Queen Dowager Li was furious and, when an envoy arrived from the Han court, she tried to report the affair to him, but King P'ing and Queen Jen pushed her into her room and slammed the door and, though she struggled to get out, she only succeeded in getting her fingers pinched in the door and was never able to see the envoy.

As it happened, Queen Dowager Li herself had been guilty of carrying on in secret in an irregular fashion with the chief steward, the palace attendant Yin Chi, and others of the court, and so the king and queen sent someone to intimate to her that she had better mind her own behavior. After this she gave up her wanton ways, and shortly afterwards fell ill and died. During her illness Queen Jen never once came to inquire how she was, and after her death the queen refused to put on mourning.

During the era *yüan-so* [128–123 B.C.] it happened that the father of a man named Lei-han Fan, who lived in Sui-yang, the capital of Liang, was insulted by someone. The man who had perpetrated the insult was riding one day in the same carriage with one of the retainers of the governor of Huai-yang and, after the retainer had stepped down from the carriage, Lei-han Fan leaped up, killed his father's enemy where he sat in the carriage, and fled. The governor of Huai-yang was enraged and complained to the high officials of Liang. They and their subordinates began a thorough search for Lei-han Fan, and arrested the other members of his family. Lei-han Fan happened to know all about the secret affairs of the kingdom, and so he sent a report to the throne on the irregular doings, describing in full the matter of the fight between the king and his grandmother over the wine goblet. He further asserted that, at the time, everyone from the prime minister on down was aware of the incident, hoping in this way to involve the chief officials of Liang in the trouble. When the report came to the emperor's attention, he referred the matter to the law officers for investigation, and it was found that the charges were true. The high officials suggested that Liu Hsiang be removed from his position as king and made a commoner, but the emperor said, "Queen Dowager Li was herself guilty of wanton acts, while Liu Hsiang had no worthy assistants to guide him, and it is for this reason that he fell into improper ways." He accordingly took away eight of Liang's cities, and had Queen Jen executed and her head exposed in the market place, but allowed the kingdom of Liang to retain some twenty or thirty cities.

In the thirty-ninth year of his rule Liu Hsiang died and was given the posthumous title of P'ing, the "Peaceful King." His son Liu Wu-shang succeeded him as king of Liang.

Liu Ming, the king of Chi-ch'uan, was a son of King Hsiao of Liang. In the sixth year of the middle period of Emperor Ching's reign he was promoted from the position of marquis of Huan-i to that of king of Chi-ch'uan. Seven years later he was tried on charges of having shot and killed his military commander. The Han officials requested that he be executed, but the emperor could not bear to inflict the death penalty and instead made him a commoner and banished him to Fang-ling. His kingdom was taken over by the Han government and made into a province.

Liu P'eng-li, another son of King Hsiao of Liang, was made king of Chi-tung in the sixth year of the middle period of Emperor Ching's reign. Liu P'eng-li was arrogant and cruel, and paid no attention to the etiquette demanded between ruler and subject. In the evenings he used to go out on marauding expeditions with twenty or thirty slaves or young men who were in hiding from the law, murdering people and seizing their belongings for sheer sport. When the affair came to light in the twenty-ninth year of his rule it was found that he had murdered at least a hundred or more persons. Everyone in the kingdom knew about his ways, so that the people were afraid to venture out of their houses at night. The son of one of his victims finally sent a report to the throne, and the Han officials requested that he be executed. The emperor could not bear to carry out their recommendation, but made him a commoner and banished him to Shang-yung. His territory was taken over by the Han government and made into the province of Ta-ho.

Liu Ting, posthumously known as King Ai of Shan-yang, another son of King Hsiao of Liang, was made king of Shan-yang in the same year that his brothers were made kings. He died nine years later and, since he left no heir, his kingdom was abolished and the territory taken over by the Han government and made into the province of Shan-yang.

The last son of King Hsiao, Liu Pu-shih, posthumously titled King Ai of Chi-yin, was made king of Chi-yin in the same year. A year later he died and, as he left no heir, his kingdom was abolished and the territory made into the province of Chi-yin.

The Grand Historian remarks: Although King Hsiao of Liang, because he was a brother of Emperor Ching and a son of Empress Dowager Tou, was made ruler of what was a rich and fertile region to begin with, he also had the fortune to live at a time when the house of Han was at its height of glory and the people enjoyed great wealth, so that he was able to multiply his wealth, enlarge his palaces, and in his carriages and vestments imitate the splendor of the Son of Heaven himself. But in doing so he overstepped his station.

Shih chi 59: The Hereditary Houses of the Five Families

All the sons of Emperor Ching by his five concubines were enfeoffed as kings. Some fulfilled their duties, living in peace and harmony with their kin and, whether their domains were large or small, acting as bastions to the imperial house. But others overstepped their positions, and little by little their power declined and faded away. Thus I made The Hereditary Houses of the Five Families.

Thirteen of Emperor Ching's sons became kings.[1] They were the offspring of five of his concubines, and I have therefore treated the sons of the same mother as one family. Liu Jung, Liu Te, and Liu O-yü were sons of the emperor by Lady Li; Liu Yü, Liu Fei, and Liu Tuan were sons by Lady Ch'eng; Liu P'eng-tsu and Liu Sheng were sons by Madam Chia; Liu Fa was the son of Lady T'ang; and Liu Yüeh, Liu Chi, Liu Sheng, and Liu Shun were sons of Madam Wang Erh-hsü, the younger sister of Emperor Ching's consort, Empress Wang.

The Sons of Lady Li

Liu Te, King Hsien of Ho-chien, because he was a son of the emperor, was appointed king of Ho-chien in the second year of the former part of Emperor Ching's reign [155 B.C.]. He was very fond of Confucian learning, and in dress and action was invariably guided by its dictates, so that many of the Confucian scholars from the region east of the mountains flocked to his court. Twenty-six years after he became a king he died and was succeeded by his son Liu Pu-hai, King Kung. King Kung died in the fourth year of his rule and was succeeded by his son Liu Chi, King Kang. He died in his twelfth year of rule and was succeeded by his son Liu Shou (King Ch'ing).[2]

[1] Emperor Ching's other son Liu Ch'e became Emperor Wu and is hence not mentioned here.
[2] Since Ssu-ma Ch'ien mentions no successor to Liu Shou, it is apparent that

Liu O-yü, King Ai of Lin-chiang, being a son of the emperor, was appointed king of Lin-chiang in the second year of Emperor Ching's reign. He died three years later and, since he left no heir, his kingdom was abolished and the area made into a province.

Liu Jung, King Min of Lin-chiang, was appointed heir apparent to Emperor Ching in the fourth year of the former part of Emperor Ching's reign [153 B.C.]. Four years later, however, he was removed from this position. Because he had formerly been heir apparent he was appointed king of Lin-chiang, the position lately occupied by his younger brother Liu O-yü. Four years after this he was accused of having torn down the outer wall of one of the ancestral temples of the dynasty in order to use the land for his palace. Emperor Ching summoned him to court to answer the charges, and Liu Jung set out on his way, stopping at the northern gate of his capital city of Chiang-ling to sacrifice to the god of the road. He had no sooner mounted his carriage than the axle broke and the carriage was rendered unfit for the journey. The elders of Chiang-ling standing by began to weep, whispering to each other, "Our king will never return!" When he reached the capital he proceeded to the office of the military commander to answer the charges brought against him. There the military commander of the capital, Chih Tu, began to cross-examine him severely until the king, fearful of the outcome, committed suicide. He was buried in Lan-t'ien, and after his burial countless flocks of swallows came bearing earth in their beaks and built a mound over his grave. The common people were deeply moved by his fate. Liu Jung was actually the oldest son of Emperor Ching, though I have mentioned him after his brothers. He left no heirs, and with his death his kingdom was abolished and the territory taken over by the Han government and made into the province of Nan. The kings first enfeoffed in the three kingdoms treated above were all sons of Emperor Ching by Lady Li.

The Sons of Lady Ch'eng

Liu Yü, King Kung of Lu, was appointed king of Huai-yang in the second year of Emperor Ching's reign [155 B.C.] because of his royal

---

Liu Shou was still alive when he was writing. The mention of Liu Shou's posthumous title "King Ch'ing" must therefore be a later interpolation.

birth. In the second year of his rule, after Wu and Ch'u had raised their revolt and been defeated, he was moved to the position of king of Lu; this was in the third year of Emperor Ching's reign. He was fond of building palaces and gardens, and raising dogs and horses. In his later years he developed a taste for music, but he had no interest in literature and rhetoric; from childhood he was afflicted with a stutter. He died in his twenty-sixth year of rule and was succeeded by his son Liu Kuang. As a young man Liu Kuang shared his father's liking for music, carriages, and horses, but in his old age he grew miserly and spent all his time worrying about whether he had enough money to live on.

Liu Fei, King I of Chiang-tu, was appointed king of Ju-nan in the same year in which his brother Liu Yü was made king of Huai-yang. At the time of the revolt of Wu and Ch'u, though he was only fifteen, he was a sturdy and spirited youth, and he sent a letter to the emperor asking to be allowed to take part in the attack on Wu. Emperor Ching granted him the seals of a general and ordered him to attack the Wu armies. Two years after the defeat of Wu he was transferred to the position of king of Chiang-tu and sent to make his capital in the former kingdom of Wu. In recognition of his military achievements during the revolt he was awarded the flags and pennants of the Son of Heaven. In the fifth year of the era *yüan-kuang* [130 B.C.], when the Hsiung-nu were invading and plundering Han territory in great numbers, he sent a letter to Emperor Wu asking that he be allowed to attack them, but the emperor refused permission. Liu Fei admired daring and physical prowess. He built palaces and observation towers, and invited to his court all the local heroes and strong men from everywhere around. His way of life was marked by extreme arrogance and luxury; he died in the twenty-sixth year of his rule.

He was succeeded by his son Liu Chien, who committed suicide seven years later. This came about as follows. When the kings of Huai-nan and Heng-shan were laying their plans for revolt [3] Liu Chien happened to hear all about their plot and, because his kingdom adjoined

---

[3] This plot by two disaffected kings, which ended with their suicides in 122 B.C., is described in full in biographies of the kings, *Shih chi* 118, translated in Volume II.

that of Huai-nan, he began to fear that if they should actually call out their troops in open rebellion, he himself would inevitably be swept up in the revolt. He therefore set about manufacturing weapons in secret, and from time to time would ride about in a carriage decorated with the pennants of the Son of Heaven and wearing at his girdle the general's seals which Emperor Ching had presented to his father. He had also developed a great liking for his father's favorite concubine, Lady Nao; after his father died, but before the funeral had even taken place, he sent someone at night to fetch Lady Nao and had relations with her in the mourning quarters where he was staying. When the king of Huai-nan's plot came to light and an investigation was made to determine who his accomplices were, all the evidence seemed to implicate Liu Chien, the king of Chiang-tu. Liu Chien was terrified and dispatched men with large sums of money in an attempt to buy his way out of the difficulty. He also put great faith in shamans and priests and set men to praying for him and concocting supernatural proofs of his innocence. Among his other crimes was the fact that he had committed incest with all of his sisters.[4] After the whole affair had come to light the Han high officials requested that he be arrested and brought to the capital for trial, but Emperor Wu could not bear to take such measures and instead sent one of his ministers to Liu Chien's residence to cross-examine him there. Liu Chien confessed his crimes and eventually committed suicide. His kingdom was abolished and the territory taken over by the Han government and made into the province of Kuang-ling.

Liu Tuan, King Yü of Chiao-hsi, was enfeoffed as king of Chiao-hsi in the third year of Emperor Ching's reign [154 B.C.], after the revolt of the Seven Kingdoms, led by Wu and Ch'u, had been put down. Liu Tuan was of a violent and recalcitrant nature. He was sexually impotent, and any attempt to have relations with a woman would make him ill for several months. Instead he had a young man whom he treated with great affection and favor and appointed as a palace at-

[4] In the corresponding chapter in the *Han shu* (53), Pan Ku gives a much more elaborate description of Liu Chien's various crimes. Whether Ssu-ma Ch'ien was unaware of the whole story, or whether he deliberately chose to omit the more lurid and revolting details of Liu Chien's career, it is impossible to say.

tendant, but when he later discovered that the youth had been carrying on a secret affair with one of the palace ladies, he had him arrested and executed, and even murdered the woman, and the child that had been born from their union. Liu Tuan committed a number of violations of the law, and the Han officials several times requested that he be punished, but Emperor Wu was always reluctant to take action against his own brothers, so that Liu Tuan only grew increasingly lawless in his ways. The officials then requested that his kingdom be reduced in size, and he was deprived of over half of his domain. He nursed his anger in secret and before long had ceased to pay any attention to the management of his kingdom. His storehouses began to leak and fall into ruin, and the goods in them, valued at millions of cash, rotted away until they could not even be moved from the spot. He ordered his officials to cease the collection of taxes, dismissed his guards, and sealed up all the gates of the palace, leaving only one gate to come and go by. He frequently assumed a false name and traveled to other states and provinces disguised as a commoner. When chancellors and officials of the two thousand picul class arrived in his kingdom with orders from the Han court to uphold the law and clear up the situation, he would hastily seek for someone to lay the blame on and, if he could find no one willing to confess, he would bring false charges against others and force the victims to drink poison. He tried every deception, exhausted every device; as the saying has it, his strength of will was fit only for rejecting reprimand, and his wisdom served only to ornament his wickedness. The chancellors and two thousand picul officials would no sooner attempt to bring charges against him than they would find that they themselves had become entangled in the Han laws. Thus, although Chiao-hsi was a small kingdom, it saw the death and undoing of an astonishing number of high officials. Forty-seven years after Liu Tuan became king of Chiao-hsi he died and, since he had never sired any sons to succeed him, his kingdom was abolished and the territory taken over by the Han government and made into the province of Chiao-hsi. The kings first enfeoffed in the three kingdoms treated above were all sons of Emperor Ching by Lady Ch'eng.

The Sons of Madam Chia

Liu P'eng-tsu, the king of Chao, because of his royal birth was enfeoffed as king of Kuang-ch'uan in the second year of Emperor Ching's reign. Four years later he was transferred to the position of king of Chao to replace Liu Sui, the former king of Chao, who had taken part in the unsuccessful revolt against the central government. In the fifteenth year of his rule Emperor Ching passed away. Liu P'eng-tsu was by nature an artful flatterer, given to shows of humility and elaborate respect for others, but at heart he was stern and cruel. He had a passion for legal affairs and loved to bring others to ruin with his cunning arguments. Included in his household were a number of concubines whom he favored with his attentions, and his offspring by them. He was aware that if the chancellors and the two thousand picul officials from the central court should attempt to enforce the Han laws and make him conform to them, it would mean only trouble for him and his household and so, whenever any of these officials arrived in his kingdom, he would don the black robes of a menial and go in person to greet them, sweeping the path for them as they entered the official lodging house. These and numerous other peculiar actions he indulged in in order to confuse the officials and make them as ill at ease as possible. Whenever any of the two thousand picul officials happened by a slip of the tongue to violate some taboo,[5] he would instantly make a record of the incident and use it later to intimidate the officials if they attempted to bring him to order; if they refused to heed his threats he would submit a report to the throne on them, or even set about to blacken their reputations by accusing them of misusing their authority for personal profit. Thus, although Liu P'eng-tsu ruled for over fifty years, not one of the chancellors or two thousand picul officials sent to his kingdom was able to hold his position for the space of two years before the king had tripped him up on some offense and had him summarily dismissed; those accused of more serious crimes were executed, while those under lighter accusation suffered other punishments. As a result the officials never dared to call the king to account

[5] There were strict taboos against mentioning the personal names of emperors or other members of the ruling family; since many of the names were common words, it was easy to make a slip.

for his misbehavior, and he was able to wield authority in a completely arbitrary manner. He dispatched his officials to the districts in his domain to levy tolls on all the transactions of the merchants, and the income from this source was so great that it exceeded the regular income from taxes. In this way the king amassed a considerable fortune, though he gave it all away in gifts to his concubines and their children. He managed to bring to his court Lady Nao, the favorite concubine of Liu Fei, the former king of Chiang-tu, with whom Liu Chien, Liu Fei's son, had had secret relations, and made her his own concubine, treating her with great affection. He had no interest in building palaces or praying to the gods for good luck, but was extremely fond of playing the part of a law official. He sent a letter to the throne asking that he be put in personal charge of the suppression of robbers within his kingdom, and every night he would go out accompanied by a band of attendants to patrol the streets and byways of his capital, Han-tan. Because of such perverse and alarming habits, things reached the point where envoys from the central government and visitors to the state no longer dared to stay in Han-tan. The crown prince Liu Tan had committed incest with his younger half sister, and even with an older sister who had the same mother as himself. Later, when he had a falling out with one of his retainers named Chiang Ch'ung, the latter sent a report to the throne on his misdoings. As a result Liu Tan was removed from the position of crown prince and another heir was appointed for the throne of Chao.

Liu Sheng, King Ching of Chung-shan, was appointed king of that state in the third year of Emperor Ching's reign. In the fourteenth year of his rule Emperor Ching passed away. Liu Sheng loved to drink and was very fond of women so that, with all his offspring and their families, his household numbered over a hundred and twenty persons. He was always criticizing his older brother, the king of Chao, saying, "Although my brother is a king, he spends all his time doing the work of his own clerks and officials. A true king should pass his days listening to music and delighting himself with beautiful sights and sounds." The king of Chao replied with criticisms of his own, declaring, "The king of Chung-shan fritters away his days in sensual gratification instead of assisting the Son of Heaven to bring order to the common people. How can someone like that be called a 'bastion of the throne'?" After forty-two years of rule Liu Sheng died and was succeeded by his son Liu Ch'ang, posthumously known as King Ai. He died in his first year of rule and his son Liu K'un-ch'ih succeeded him as king of Chung-shan. The kings first enfeoffed in the two kingdoms treated above were both sons of Emperor Ching by Madam Chia.

The Son of Lady T'ang

Liu Fa, King Ting of Ch'ang-sha, was the son of Emperor Ching by Lady T'ang. Lady T'ang was originally a waiting woman of Lady Ch'eng. Once Emperor Ching sent word for Lady Ch'eng to come to his chamber but, because of the time of the month, she was unable to answer the summons. Instead she dressed up her maid Miss T'ang and sent her in the night to join the emperor. The emperor, who was intoxicated at the time, did not notice the difference and, assuming that it was Lady Ch'eng, bestowed his favor on her. Later, when she became pregnant, he discovered that it had not been Lady Ch'eng at all, and after she bore a son the emperor accordingly instructed that the boy be named Fa, which means "Discovery." Because of his royal birth he was made king of Ch'ang-sha in the second year of Emperor Ching's reign. His mother was of low position and did not enjoy favor with the emperor, and that was the reason he was enfeoffed with such a poor domain as Ch'ang-sha, situated in a low, swampy region. Twenty-seven years after he became king he died and was succeeded by his son Liu K'ang, King Yung. Liu K'ang died in the twenty-eighth year of his rule and his son Liu Fu-chü succeeded him as king of Ch'ang-sha. The king first enfeoffed in the kingdom treated above was a son of Emperor Ching by Lady T'ang.

The Sons of Madam Wang

Liu Yüeh, King Hui of Kuang-ch'uan, was made king of Kuang-ch'uan in the second year of the middle period of Emperor Ching's reign [148 B.C.]. He died twelve years later and was succeeded by his son Liu Ch'i. Liu Ch'i had a trusted minister named Sang Chü. Later he discovered that Sang Chü had committed some crime and was about to execute him when Sang Chü fled from the kingdom. The king then seized the members of Sang Chü's family. Enraged at this, Sang Chü sent a report to the throne accusing the king of having committed incest with his sisters. From this time on the king frequently sent reports to the throne bringing accusations against high officials of the Han court, Emperor Wu's favorite minister So Chung, and others.[6]

Liu Chi, King K'ang of Chiao-tung, was made king of that region in the second year of the middle period of Emperor Ching's reign and died twenty-eight years later. When the king of Huai-nan was laying plans for a revolt Liu Chi heard rumors of the affair and set about secretly constructing wheeled observation towers, manufacturing barbed arrows, and making other preparations for battle, waiting for the day when the king of Huai-nan would call out his troops. When the Han officials arrived in Huai-nan to clear up the affair, their investigations brought these facts to light. Among Emperor Ching's sons, Liu Chi was most closely related to the present emperor,[7] and he was so grieved at his own misconduct that he grew ill and died. He did not dare to appoint an heir to succeed him. After his death the emperor made inquiries and found that the mother of his oldest son, whose name was Liu Hsien, had not enjoyed favor with the king; all of Liu Chi's affections had been reserved for the mother of his younger son, Liu Ch'ing, and the king had always hoped to make this son his heir but, because the boy was not in line for succession, and because he himself had been guilty of misconduct, he had died without making his wishes known to the emperor. The emperor took pity on him and, leaving Liu Hsien to rule Chiao-tung and carry on the line of his father, King K'ang, he enfeoffed Liu Ch'ing with the territory that had formerly comprised the kingdom of Heng-shan, giving him the title of king of Liu-an. Liu Hsien died in the fourteenth year of his rule and was given the posthumous title of King Ai. He was succeeded by

[6] The passage ends abruptly and it would seem that, at the time of writing, Ssu-ma Ch'ien was still waiting to see how the affair would end.
[7] Liu Chi was the oldest son of Madam Wang Erh-hsü, the younger sister of Empress Wang, who was the mother of Emperor Wu, the "present emperor."

his son Liu T'ung-p'ing.[8] Liu Ch'ing was appointed king of Liu-an in the first year of the era *yüan-so* [122 B.C.].

Liu Sheng, King Ai of Ch'ing-ho, was appointed king of that region in the third year of the middle period of Emperor Ching's reign and died twelve years later. Since he left no heir, his kingdom was abolished and the territory taken over by the Han government and made into the province of Ch'ing-ho.

Liu Shun, King Hsien of Ch'ang-shan, because of his royal birth, was made king of Ch'ang-shan in the fifth year of the middle period of Emperor Ching's reign [145 B.C.]. Being a son of Madam Wang, he was closely related to the present emperor, and in addition was the youngest of Emperor Ching's sons so that, although he was arrogant, lazy, and given to sensual indulgence, and had committed frequent violations of the law, the emperor always treated him with leniency and let him off without punishment. He died in his thirty-second year of rule, and the crown prince Liu P'o succeeded him as king.

King Hsien's oldest son was Liu Cho, whose mother was a concubine for whom the king felt no particular affection; as a result her son likewise did not enjoy favor with the king. The crown prince Liu P'o was the son of King Hsien's consort, Queen Hsiu. In addition the king kept a number of other concubines, by whom he had two other sons, Liu P'ing and Liu Shang. Queen Hsiu rarely enjoyed his attentions. When the king became seriously ill his favorite concubines attended him constantly, but Queen Hsiu, jealous of the other women, refused to stay by the king but, having made a visit, would return at once to her own quarters. When the doctors came with medicine the crown prince Liu P'o failed to taste it before giving it to his father,[9] nor would he spend the night by his father's bed or tend him while he was ailing. Only after the king died did the queen and the crown prince appear at his bedside.

[8] The text gives his name as Liu Ch'ing, but it is unlikely that he would have the same name as his uncle, the king of Liu-an; *Han shu* 53, which gives his name as Liu T'ung-p'ing, seems to be correct.

[9] Sons were expected to taste all medicine before giving it to their parents to make certain it contained no harmful ingredients, and failure to do so was regarded as the most serious kind of criminal neglect.

King Hsien had always regarded his oldest son Liu Cho as completely worthless, and in his will he left no share of his wealth or property to the boy. Some of the palace attendants advised the crown prince and Queen Hsiu that they would do well to divide the king's estate with Liu Cho and the king's other sons, but they paid no attention. Even after the crown prince became ruler he made no provisions whatsoever for his older brother's welfare, and as a result Liu Cho came to hate him and his mother, Queen Hsiu. When an envoy arrived from the Han court to attend King Hsien's funeral Liu Cho therefore reported to him how the queen and the crown prince had failed to attend the king when he was ill, and had left their mourning quarters only six days after his death. He also stated that the crown prince indulged in lecherous acts in secret and spent his days drinking, gambling, and strumming the lute; and that he would often take his women friends along in his carriage and go galloping about the city, visiting the market places or entering the jails and gaping at the prisoners. The emperor dispatched the grand messenger Chang Ch'ien to investigate the charges against Queen Hsiu and the crown prince and arrest those who had been accomplices with the prince in his lechery. The prince attempted to hide the witnesses to his crimes but, when Chang Ch'ien's men began to search for them and press for their arrest, the prince in desperation sent men to flog and manhandle the Han officials, in the meantime arbitrarily allowing the suspects to escape from the kingdom. The officials of the central court requested that Queen Hsiu and the crown prince be executed for their crimes, but the emperor was of the opinion that Queen Hsiu had not been guilty of any very serious misconduct, but had only become entangled in the affair because of Liu Cho's reports, while the crown prince had fallen into evil ways because he lacked worthy tutors, and he therefore could not bear to pronounce the death penalty. The officials then requested that the queen and her son be deprived of their positions and sent with the members of their family to live as commoners in Fang-ling, to which the emperor gave his approval. Thus the crown prince Liu P'o had acted as king for no more than a few months when he was exiled to Fang-ling.

The Five Families

A month or so after the kingdom had been abolished, because Liu Shun, its first king, had been so closely related to him, the emperor issued an edict to the officials stating: "King Hsien of Ch'ang-shan died an untimely death and, because of the lack of harmony between his queen and his concubines, and the mutual slanders and quarrels of his heir and his other son, the family fell into unrighteous ways and his kingdom has been wiped out. This grieves me deeply. Let King Hsien's son Liu P'ing be enfeoffed with thirty thousand households as king of Chen-ting, and let his brother Liu Shang be enfeoffed with an equal number as king of Ssu-shui."

Because he was a son of King Hsien, Liu P'ing was hence enfeoffed as king of Chen-ting in the fourth year of the era *yüan-ting* [113 B.C.]. Liu Shang, King Ssu of Ssu-shui, was enfeoffed in the same year. He died eleven years later and was succeeded by his son Liu An-shih, King Ai of Ssu-shui, who died eleven years later, leaving no heir. The emperor was distressed that the line of the king of Ssu-shui should thus come to an end, and so he enfeoffed Liu An-shih's younger brother Liu Chia as king of Ssu-shui. The kings first enfeoffed in the four kingdoms treated above were all sons of Emperor Ching by Madam Wang Erh-hsü. The Han government later enfeoffed two others among their descendants, creating the kings of Liu-an and of Ssu-shui, so that at present there are six kings who are descended from Madam Wang.

The Grand Historian remarks: In the time of Emperor Kao-tsu the feudal lords not only received all the taxes from their domains, but were allowed to appoint and dismiss their own internal secretaries; only their prime ministers were selected for them by the Han court and given gold seals to indicate their authority. In addition the feudal lords were permitted to appoint palace secretaries, commandants of justice, and erudits, in imitation of the court of the Son of Heaven. After the revolt of Wu and Ch'u, however, the Han court appointed officials of the two thousand picul rank to the courts of the kings, such as those of the five families described above, changed the title of prime minister to chancellor, and granted these officials only silver seals. The feudal lords were permitted nothing more than the tax revenue from their lands, while the rest of their prerogatives were all taken away. In later years some of them grew so poor that they were obliged to ride about in ox carts.[10]

[10] Since horses were relatively rare in Han China, their use was confined to the military and such nobles, officials, and merchants as could afford to buy them. The common people used oxen to pull their carts.

Part X
THE LEADER OF THE REVOLT

Shih chi 106: The Biography of Liu P'i, the King of Wu.[1]

Because his father, Liu Chung, was deprived of the kingdom of Tai, Liu P'i happened to become the ruler of Wu. In the early days of the Han, when peace had just been restored, he brought order to the region between the Yangtze and the Huai rivers. Thus I made The Biography of Liu P'i, the King of Wu.

Liu P'i, the king of Wu, was the son of Kao-tsu's elder brother Liu Chung. After Kao-tsu had won control of the empire, in the seventh year of his reign [200 B.C.], he set up his brother Liu Chung as king of Tai. When the Hsiung-nu attacked Tai, however, Liu Chung was unable to defend his position but abandoned his kingdom and fled in secret to Lo-yang, where he threw himself on the mercy of the emperor. Because Liu Chung was his own brother, Kao-tsu could not bear to inflict the penalty prescribed by law in such cases, but instead deprived his brother of his position as king of Tai and made him marquis of Ho-yang.

In the autumn of the eleventh year of Kao-tsu's reign [196 B.C.] Ch'ing Pu, the king of Huai-nan, revolted. He seized the region of Ching [i.e., Wu] to the east and, forcing its soldiers to join him, crossed west over the Huai River and attacked Ch'u. Emperor Kao-tsu in person led a force to punish the rebels. Liu Chung's son Liu P'i, at that time marquis of P'ei, though only twenty years old, displayed great bravery, joining the emperor's forces as a cavalry general and taking part in the defeat of Ch'ing Pu's army at Kuei-chui west of Ch'i, at which Ch'ing Pu was put to flight.

Liu Chia, the king of Ching, had been killed by Ch'ing Pu's forces

---

[1] Because Liu P'i revolted against his sovereign, Ssu-ma Ch'ien has "censured" him by placing his biography after those of all the other important men of the period, i.e., in Chapter 106. To help the reader to follow the account of the revolt, I have rearranged the order of the chapters in translation.

and had left no heir. Kao-tsu was concerned that there was no vigorous young ruler who could insure the loyalty of the reckless and untrustworthy regions of Wu and K'uai-chi. His own sons were too young for the task, and so, while Kao-tsu was visiting P'ei, he appointed Liu P'i as king of Wu to rule the three provinces and thirteen cities of Wu.

After Kao-tsu had conferred this title on Liu P'i and presented him with the seals of enfeoffment he summoned him to his side and examined his countenance. "Your face bears the marks of one who will revolt!" said the emperor, and he was secretly sorry that he had chosen Liu P'i. But the appointment had already been made, and so he patted Liu P'i on the back and said, "If within the next fifty years an uprising against the Han should break out in the southeast, I imagine it will be your doing. But remember that the empire belongs to the Liu clan, and that we are all of the same family. Better to be cautious and not revolt!"

Liu P'i bowed his head and replied, "I would not dare to do such a thing!"

During the reigns of Emperor Hui and Empress Lü peace had just been restored to the empire and the feudal lords in the various provinces and kingdoms were busy putting their people in order. The territory of Wu possessed mountains rich in copper in the province of Yü-chang. Liu P'i set about inviting fugitives from all over the empire to come to his kingdom, minted cash from the copper ore in ever-increasing quantities, and boiled the sea water to extract salt, so that he was able to dispense with the poll tax, and his kingdom enjoyed great wealth and prosperity.

During the reign of Emperor Wen, Liu P'i's son, the crown prince of Wu, journeyed to court to pay his respects to the emperor and, while there, was granted the honor of joining the heir apparent, the future Emperor Ching, in drinking and playing chess. The tutors of the crown prince were all men of Ch'u, reckless and untrustworthy,[2] while the crown prince himself was by nature inclined to be overbearing. In the course of their game the prince of Wu forgot his manners and began

---

[2] Ssu-ma Ch'ien here and elsewhere uses the terms Ch'u, Wu, and Ching more or less interchangeably to refer to the southeast corner of the empire. He repeatedly characterizes the people of this region as restless, fickle, rash, etc.

to argue with the heir apparent over the proper way to play chess, whereupon the heir apparent picked up the chessboard, hit the prince of Wu over the head, and killed him. The body was sent home for burial but, when the cortege reached Wu, the boy's father declared angrily, "The whole empire belongs to the same Liu clan! If one of our family dies in Ch'ang-an, he should be buried in Ch'ang-an. What reason is there to bring him here for burial?" He thereupon sent the body back to Ch'ang-an, where it was buried.

After this incident Liu P'i began gradually to disregard the etiquette proper to a vassal minister. Declaring that he was ill, he no longer came to court to pay his respects. People in the capital knew that it was only because of the death of his son that he was pleading illness and refusing to appear at court and, when investigation was made, it was found that he was in fact not ill at all. Whenever envoys arrived in the capital from Wu, they were immediately imprisoned and subjected to severe cross-examination. Alarmed at this situation, Liu P'i began to plot with greater urgency. Later he sent someone in his place to convey his respects to the emperor at the autumn assembly of the feudal lords, but Emperor Wen once more seized the Wu envoy and cross-examined him. "The king is not really ill," the envoy admitted. "It was only because the Han imprisoned and cross-examined so many of the previous envoys from Wu that he finally pleaded ill and refused to come. It is bad luck, they say, to peer too closely at the fish swimming in the depths.[3] The king originally lied by saying that he was ill. But now that the falsehood has been discovered and his envoys are being severely pressed, his position grows more and more desperate. He fears that Your Majesty will punish him, and can think of no way to escape from his dilemma. The only hope is for Your Majesty to forget what has happened in the past and make a new beginning with him!"

Emperor Wen accordingly pardoned the Wu envoy and sent him home, and at the same time presented the king of Wu with an armrest and a cane, indicating that he was too old to journey to court. Thus Liu P'i escaped punishment for his faults, and bit by bit relaxed his plans to take drastic action. At the same time, because his kingdom produced

---

[3] I.e., a ruler should not pry too assiduously into the faults of his vassals or they may be driven to some desperate action.

copper and salt, he was able to dispense with the poll tax on his subjects. Whenever men hired themselves out for *corvée* labor in place of others, he saw to it that they were paid a fair wage.[4] At certain times each year he sent officials to search for men of outstanding ability, and presented awards and gifts to deserving people in the towns and villages. If officials from other provinces or kingdoms came and attempted to arrest fugitives from their jurisdiction, he would insure refuge to the fugitives and refuse to hand them over to the authorities. This was the way he conducted the affairs of his kingdom during the forty-odd years of his reign, and thus he was able to win the support of his people.

When Ch'ao Ts'o became steward to the heir apparent and won his confidence he took advantage of his position to remark to the prince from time to time that the king of Wu ought to be punished for his irregular actions by having his territory reduced in size. Ch'ao Ts'o also submitted several memorials to Emperor Wen urging such action, but Emperor Wen was of a lenient nature and could not bear to inflict punishment. Thus the king of Wu daily grew more willful in his ways.

When the heir apparent ascended the throne Ch'ao Ts'o was made imperial secretary. He addressed the new ruler, Emperor Ching, saying "In the early days of the dynasty, when Emperor Kao-tsu first restored peace to the empire, he had few brothers and his sons were still very young, and he therefore granted fiefs of exceptional size to the men of his own clan. Thus Liu Fei, his son by a concubine, became King Tao-hui of Ch'i, ruling seventy-odd cities of Ch'i; his younger brother Liu Chiao became King Yüan of Ch'u, ruling forty-odd cities; and Liu P'i, the son of his older brother, was made king of some fifty cities of Wu. He granted half of the entire area of the empire in fiefs to these three men of his family. Because the king of Wu was embittered over the death of his son some years ago, he feigned illness and refused to

---

[4] By law all able-bodied men were required to spend a certain amount of time each year garrisoning the borders of the empire. It was customary, however, for men of means to hire others to serve in their place. According to the interpretation of the sentence which I have followed, the king of Wu won favor with his subjects by seeing to it that the wages for such hire were adjusted to the actual value of money at any given time rather than being arbitrarily set at a fixed amount.

come to court. According to the old laws he should have been executed, but Emperor Wen could not bear to take action and instead granted him an armrest and a cane, treating him with the utmost generosity. It was only proper that after this the king should have mended his faults and made a new start. On the contrary, however, he has grown increasingly insubordinate, minting cash from the ore in the mountains of his kingdom, boiling sea water to extract salt, and inviting fugitives from all over the empire to join him so that he may plot an uprising. Now, whether you reduce his territory or not, he is bound to revolt. If you take away part of his territory, the revolt will come quickly and its effect will be slight. But if you do not reduce his territory, then the revolt will be delayed until later and will be a much more serious affair!"

In the winter of the third year of Emperor Ching's reign [155 B.C.] Liu Mou, the king of Ch'u, came to court to pay his respects. Ch'ao Ts'o took advantage of the occasion to accuse the king of having had illicit intercourse the previous year when, as a member of the imperial family, he was supposed to be living in mourning quarters because of the death of Empress Dowager Po. Ch'ao Ts'o recommended that he be executed.[5] The emperor, however pardoned him, but as a punishment deprived him of the province of Tung-hai. At the same time he deprived the king of Wu of the provinces of Yü-chang and K'uai-chi. The previous year Liu Sui, the king of Chao, had been convicted of some offense and deprived of the province of Ch'ang-shan,[6] and Liu Ang, the king of Chiao-hsi, had been deprived of six districts because of irregular sale of noble titles. It was at this time that the Han court officials began seriously to discuss the question of reducing the size of the kingdom of Wu. Liu P'i, fearful that there was to be no end to the deprivations of territory, began to make concrete plans for a general revolt. He was concerned that so few of the other feudal lords seemed worthy to join him in the plot, but he had heard that Liu Ang, the king of Chiao-hsi, was a brave and spirited man who was fond of

---

[5] During periods of deep mourning one was required to live in special quarters. Sexual irregularities during such periods were offenses of the gravest nature.

[6] The text erroneously reads "the province of Ho-chien."

warfare and was feared by all the other kingdoms of Ch'i.[7] He therefore sent his palace counselor Ying Kao to invite the king of Chiao-hsi to join the conspiracy. Liu P'i did not entrust his message to writing, but instructed Ying Kao to say, "The king of Wu, unworthy as he is, has long been beset by worries. He does not dare to leave his territory himself, but has sent me to convey to you his kind intentions."

"And what message would he send me?" asked the king of Chiao-hsi.

"At present," replied Ying Kao, "the emperor, swayed by evil men and imposed upon by false ministers, thinks only of petty profit and gives ear to slanderers. He arbitrarily alters the laws of the empire and seizes the lands of the feudal lords; day by day his demands become greater and his punishments of innocent men more frequent. People have a saying that 'after the husk has been licked away, the kernel will be eaten up.'[8] You and my master, the rulers of Wu and Chiao-hsi, are among the most renowned of the feudal lords, but if some day you are subjected to investigation, it is unlikely that you will escape with impunity. The king of Wu is suffering from an infirmity and for over twenty years has been unable to journey to the capital to appear at court. He has long been concerned that such a failure might arouse suspicion and he would have no opportunity to justify himself, and with the present state of affairs he is all but prostrate with anxiety that he will not be forgiven. Rumors have reached him that Your Majesty has been punished for some affair involving noble titles. In this and in other cases which he has heard about where feudal lords have been deprived of territory, the offense has not been of sufficient gravity to justify such action. He is fearful that the situation may not end with mere seizure of territory!"

"The rumors your king heard of my punishment were correct," replied the king. "And what do you suggest we do about it?"

"They say," said Ying Kao, "that those with the same hates help each other, those with the same loves aid each other, those with the

[7] Emperor Wen, it will be recalled, had divided up the kingdom of King Tao-hui of Ch'i among his sons, creating six kingdoms: Ch'i, Chi-pei, Chi-nan, Tzu-ch'uan, Chiao-hsi, and Chiao-nan.

[8] That is, after the emperor has stripped the feudal kingdoms of their outer provinces, he will end by abolishing them entirely.

same thoughts bolster each other, those with the same hopes work for each other, and those with the same aims die for each other. Now the king of Wu believes that he shares the same griefs with Your Majesty. His desire is to seize this opportunity to enforce justice, to set aside thoughts of his own welfare in order to rid the empire of harm! Is his intent not a worthy one?"

The king of Chiao-hsi drew back in amazement. "How would I dare such a thing?" he exclaimed. "No matter how the emperor may afflict me, I have no choice but to die! What can I do but be loyal to him?"

"The imperial secretary Ch'ao Ts'o is misleading the emperor and seizing the lands of the feudal lords, forcing loyal ministers into the shade and stifling the counsels of worthy men, so that the court is filled with hatred for him and all the feudal lords entertain thoughts of revolt," said Ying Kao. "Human affairs have reached a crisis, while a comet has appeared in the sky and locusts have several times swarmed over the land. This is an opportunity which comes only once in ten thousand generations, a time of grief and trouble which will bring forth a true sage. Therefore the king of Wu proposes to march upon the capital to rid the world of Ch'ao Ts'o, and in the provinces to follow after Your Majesty in sweeping across the empire. Whoever we confront will surrender, whoever we point our fingers at will submit, and throughout the world there will be none who dare to resist. If Your Majesty will be truly gracious enough to give one word of consent, then the king of Wu will lead the king of Ch'u in seizing the Han-ku Pass, guarding the stores of grain at Jung-yang and the Ao Granary, and blocking the advance of the Han soldiers; there he will halt, make his camp, and wait for you. If you are willing to join the enterprise, then the whole empire can be conquered. If it were then divided between the two of you, would that not be sufficient?"

"The plan is a good one," replied the king of Chiao-hsi.

Ying Kao returned and reported the king's answer to the king of Wu. But Liu P'i was still afraid that the king of Chiao-hsi might not join the conspiracy, and so he journeyed as his own envoy to Chiao-hsi and concluded the agreement with the king in person.

One of the ministers of the king of Chiao-hsi heard that the king was plotting a conspiracy and reprimanded him, saying, "There is no greater happiness than to serve a single emperor. Now Your Majesty proposes to join with the king of Wu in marching west upon the capital but, even if the undertaking is successful, strife will ensue between the two of you and your troubles will only have begun. The lands of the feudal lords comprise less than one fifth of the provinces of the Han empire. To raise a revolt and inflict anxiety upon your mother, the queen dowager, is surely not a wise idea!"

The king, however, refused to listen to his advice but dispatched envoys to conclude agreements with the kingdoms of Ch'i, Tzu-ch'uan, Chiao-tung, Chi-nan, and Chi-pei. All of them consented to join the conspiracy. "King Ching of Ch'eng-yang," he said, "is a man of unshakable loyalty, as he demonstrated at the time of the overthrow of the Lü family. He will not join us.[9] After affairs are settled, we will divide his lands among ourselves."

A number of the feudal lords had already been roused to fear by the punishments and deprivations of territory that had been inflicted upon them, and were enraged against Ch'ao Ts'o. When the order arrived from the court depriving Wu of the provinces of K'uai-chi and Yü-chang the king of Wu took the lead by calling out his troops. On the day *ping-wu* of the first month [Feb. 28, 154 B.C.] he and the king of Chiao-hsi executed all the Han officials of the rank of two thousand piculs and under in their territories, and the kingdoms of Chiao-tung, Tzu-ch'uan, Chi-nan, Ch'u, and Chao followed suit. The armies of the conspirators began their march west toward the capital.

The king of Ch'i, regretting what he had done, broke his promise to join the conspirators and drank poison and died. The king of Chi-pei was still engaged in repairing the fortifications of his capital and had not yet completed preparations for sending out his troops. His chief of palace attendants threatened him with violence and forced him to stay in his capital, so that Chi-pei was unable to dispatch its forces. The

[9] Either something is wrong with the text or Ssu-ma Ch'ien is nodding. King Ching, the posthumous title of Liu Chang, the first king of Ch'eng-yang, died in 177, some twenty-two years before this. At the time of the conspiracy his son Liu Hsi was king of Ch'eng-yang, so that the mention of Liu Chang's part in the overthrow of the Lü family makes little sense. The fact remains, however, that the kingdom of Ch'eng-yang refused to join the conspiracy. The parallel passage in *Han shu* 35 omits this speech.

king of Chiao-hsi assumed command of the forces in the region of Ch'i and, with the armies of Chiao-tung, Tzu-ch'uan, and Chi-nan, besieged Lin-tzu, the capital of the kingdom of Ch'i. The king of Chao also revolted and secretly plotted to join forces with the Hsiung-nu.

When Wu, Ch'u, Chiao-hsi, Chiao-tung, Tzu-ch'uan, Chi-nan, and Chao, the seven kingdoms of the conspiracy, dispatched their troops, the king of Wu called out all his soldiers, circulating an order through the kingdom stating: "I am sixty-two, and yet I shall lead my troops in person. My youngest son is fourteen, but he too will command the soldiers. Therefore let all men between the ages of myself and my youngest son be called into service!" In this way he raised a force of over two hundred thousand men. He sent envoys south to the barbarian states of Min-yüeh and Eastern Yüeh, the latter of which also dispatched troops to join his forces.

On the day *chia-tzu* of the first month of the third year of Emperor Ching's reign [154 B.C.] the king of Wu marched with his army out of his capital at Kuang-ling and crossed the Huai River to the west, where he joined with the forces of Ch'u. He dispatched envoys to the various feudal lords bearing a letter which read:

I, Liu P'i, the king of Wu, respectfully inquire of the kings of Chiao-hsi, Chiao-tung, Tzu-ch'uan, Chi-nan, Chao, Ch'u, Huai-nan, Heng-shan, and Lu-chiang, and the sons of the late king of Ch'ang-sha, if they will be kind enough to lend me their guidance. Because there are traitorous ministers in the Han court who, though they have done no service for the empire, unrightfully seize the lands of the feudal lords; who arrest and question our envoys and make it their sole concern to inflict insult and injury; who do not treat the feudal lords with the proper respect, although they are flesh and blood of the imperial clan of Liu, but thrust aside the ministers who have won merit under the former emperor and replace them with evil men, bringing chaos to the empire and endangering the sacred altars of the dynasty; and because the emperor, in ill health and intent upon his own well-being, is unable to perceive the true state of affairs, I propose to call out my troops to punish the evildoers. I therefore humbly request your guidance.

Although my kingdom is small, it embraces an area three thousand *li* square; although my people are few, I can supply five hundred thousand trained men. I have been on friendly terms with the barbarians of Southern Yüeh for over thirty years and the kings and chieftains of the area have unanimously agreed to send their troops to join me, so that from that source I can secure another three hundred thousand men or more.

Since the region of Ch'ang-sha adjoins the territory of Yüeh, I would ask the sons of the late king of Ch'ang-sha to take control from Ch'ang-sha north, and then march with all speed through Shu and Han-chung. The rulers of Eastern Yüeh and the kings of Ch'u, Huai-nan, Heng-shan, and Lu-chiang, I would ask to join me in marching west. The rulers of the various kingdoms of Ch'i and the king of Chao should gain control of the regions of Ho-chien and Ho-nei, and either proceed through the Lin-chin Pass or meet with me at Lo-yang. The kings of Yen and Chao have already concluded agreements with the Hsiung-nu ruler, so that the king of Yen should march north and bring under control the areas of Tai and Yün-chung and then, leading the hordes of the Hsiung-nu, enter the Su Pass and hasten to Ch'ang-an to correct the errors of the emperor and safeguard the ancestral temple of Emperor Kao-tsu.[10] I beg the kings to carry out my suggestions with diligence!

The present king of Ch'u, grandson of King Yüan of Ch'u, and the kings of Huai-nan, Heng-shan, and Lu-chiang have scarcely had the heart to bathe or wash their hair for over ten years, so consumed are they by anger; for long they have hoped for some chance to take their revenge.[11] I have as yet had no opportunity to hear the feelings of the other kings, nor have I ventured to inquire about them. But if the kings are truly willing to fight to preserve their perishing states and give new life to their dying families, to aid the weak and overthrow the violent in order to secure peace for the Liu family, they will be doing a service to the sacred altars of the dynasty.

Although my kingdom is poor, I have been occupied day and night for the past thirty years and more in economizing on the use of food and clothing, accumulating funds, preparing weapons and gathering stores of grain, all for the realization of this aim. I beg the other kings to make use of what I have prepared! Let us agree that anyone who kills or captures a general in chief shall be rewarded with five thousand catties of gold and a fief of

[10] Liu P'i is here proposing a step which brought grief to innumerable Chinese dynasties both before and after the Han: inviting non-Chinese peoples to invade the empire in order to take part in an internal struggle.

[11] The kings of Huai-nan, Heng-shan, and Lu-chiang, all sons of Liu Ch'ang, King Li of Huai-nan, had reason to be resentful of the Han ministers since, at the suggestion of the latter, Emperor Wen had removed their father from his position on charges of insubordination and ordered him banished to Shu; he refused to eat and starved to death on the way. There seems to be no particular reason, however, why Liu Mou, the king of Ch'u, should have been consumed by anger.

ten thousand households; for a ranking general, three thousand catties and a fief of five thousand households; for a lieutenant general, two thousand catties and two thousand households; for an official of the rank of two thousand piculs, a thousand catties and a thousand households; for an official of one thousand piculs, five hundred catties and five hundred households; all to be awarded the title of marquis. The capture of an army of ten thousand men or a city of ten thousand inhabitants shall be rewarded the same as the capture of a general in chief; an army or a city of five thousand the same as a ranking general; an army or city of three thousand the same as a lieutenant general; and an army or a city of one thousand the same as an official of two thousand picul rank. Those who capture lesser officials shall be rewarded with titles and gold in accordance with the rank of the captives. All other grants of fiefs and money shall likewise be twice those prescribed by the usual Han laws. Those who in the past have already received noble titles and fiefs shall be granted new awards regardless of their previous holdings. I beg the kings to make these rulings clearly known to their respective staffs, for I swear that there is no deception in them. I have stores of funds scattered here and there throughout the empire, so that grants of money need not necessarily come from Wu itself. The kings may make use of my funds day and night and there will still be no fear of exhausting them. Therefore, if there is anyone who deserves to be rewarded, let a report be made to me and I will send the money from wherever I happen to be. With due respect I make the above announcement.

When this letter on the revolt of the seven kingdoms was brought to the attention of Emperor Ching he dispatched Chou Ya-fu, the marquis of T'iao, at the head of an army of thirty-six generals to attack Wu and Ch'u. At the same time he dispatched Li Chi, the marquis of Ch'ü-chou, to attack Chao, General Lüan Pu to attack the region of Ch'i, and the general in chief Tou Ying to garrison Jung-yang and observe the movements of the troops of Chao and Ch'i.

When the letter announcing the revolt of Wu and Ch'u first came to the Emperor's attention, and before he had called out the troops or dispatched Tou Ying, he was informed that Yüan Ang, the former prime minister of the state of Wu, was living in retirement near the capital, and so he summoned Yüan Ang to an interview. When Yüan Ang appeared before him, the emperor was busy checking the strength of his forces and calculating the amount of provisions for the army with Ch'ao Ts'o. "You were formerly prime minister to the king of Wu," said the emperor. "What sort of man is the Wu general T'ien Lu-po? Now that Wu and Ch'u have revolted, what do you think will be the outcome?"

"The matter is not worth worrying about," replied Yüan Ang. "They will be defeated at once!"

"But the king of Wu has been minting cash from the ore in his territory, extracting salt from the sea water, and inviting worthy men from all over the empire, and now, though he is an old man, he has started a revolt. If he were not absolutely sure that his scheme would succeed, why would he dispatch his troops? What makes you think that he can do nothing against us?"

"As for the copper and salt in his kingdom," said Yüan Ang, "the king of Wu has undoubtedly profited from them, but it is impossible to believe that he has attracted worthy men to his court. If he had actually succeeded in attracting worthy men, they would have persuaded him to remain loyal and not to revolt. The only men the king of Wu has attracted are ruffians and their gangs, fugitives from justice and criminals engaged in the illegal minting of cash. This is why they have led him on to revolt!"

"Yüan Ang has given an excellent appraisal of the situation!" exclaimed Ch'ao Ts'o.

"What plan do you think I should adopt?" asked the emperor.

"I beg Your Majesty to dismiss your attendants so that we may speak in private," said Yüan Ang. The emperor ordered those about him to retire, leaving only Ch'ao Ts'o at his side. "What I have to say," said Yüan Ang, "is not for the ears of Your Majesty's ministers!" With this the emperor waved Ch'ao Ts'o away. Hastening from the audience room, Ch'ao Ts'o retired to the eastern corridor, overcome with rage.

The emperor then proceeded to question Yüan Ang, who replied, "The kings of Wu and Ch'u have distributed a letter calling for a revolt and claiming that, although Emperor Kao-tsu divided his lands among his sons and brothers, the traitorous official Ch'ao Ts'o is now accusing the feudal lords of various faults and unrightfully seizing their territories from them. Therefore they have declared their intention to revolt and march west to the capital together to punish Ch'ao Ts'o; when their lands have been restored to them, they will disband their forces. The best plan at this point is therefore simply to execute Ch'ao Ts'o, issue a pardon to the kings of Wu, Ch'u, and the other members of the conspiracy, and return the lands that have been taken away from them. In this way their troops can be turned back without recourse to bloodshed."

The emperor was silent for a long time, and then he said, "If your plan would really work, I would not hesitate to sacrifice a single man in order to appease the rest of the empire. . . ."

"I have nothing else to suggest," said Yüan Ang. "I beg Your Majesty to give it due consideration."

Emperor Ching appointed Yüan Ang as master of ritual and Liu T'ung, the son of the younger brother of the king of Wu, as director of the imperial clan. Yüan Ang set about getting his clothes and belongings ready for a journey. Some ten days later the emperor ordered the military commander to summon Ch'ao Ts'o and, pretending to drive him to the palace, to take him instead to the eastern market. There Ch'ao Ts'o, wearing the court robes he had donned for his trip to the palace, was cut in two at the waist. Then, with Yüan Ang appointed as master of ritual to uphold the service of the ancestral temples and Liu T'ung as director of the imperial clan to appeal to his own kinsmen, the emperor dispatched the two of them to report his action to the king of Wu in accordance with Yüan Ang's plan.

When the two men arrived in Wu the armies of Wu and Ch'u were already attacking the fortifications of Liang. As a kinsman, Liu T'ung was admitted first into the presence of the king of Wu and, explaining his mission, forced him to bow and receive the imperial orders. When the king of Wu heard that Yüan Ang had also come on the mission he knew that Yüan Ang would try to persuade him to desist, and he replied with a laugh, "I am already emperor of the east! What need have I to grant audience to anyone else?" He refused to see Yüan Ang, but ordered him to be detained in the midst of his camp and tried to force him to become a general on the side of Wu. When Yüan Ang refused, he sent men to surround and guard him, intending to murder him, but

Yüan Ang managed to escape from the camp at night and flee to the army of Liang. Eventually he returned to the capital and reported on his mission.

Chou Ya-fu, the commander of the Han forces, hurried with his retinue of six relay carriages and joined the army at Jung-yang. When he reached Lo-yang on the way he met Chü Meng [12] and exclaimed with delight, "Because of the revolt of the seven kingdoms, I hastened here by relay carriage, uncertain whether I would be able to get even this far. I supposed that the rebel lords would already have enlisted your aid, but now I find that you have made no move to join them. I will make Jung-yang my base of operations, and from there on east I see I will have nothing to worry about!"

When Chou Ya-fu reached Huai-yang he questioned Colonel Teng, who had formerly been a retainer of Chou Ya-fu's father Chou P'o, as to what strategy to adopt. Colonel Teng replied, "The troops of Wu have a very keen striking power; it would be difficult to meet them head on. Those of Ch'u are lightly equipped and will not be able to hold out for long. If I were to suggest a plan for you, I think you had best lead your forces northeast and build your fortifications at Ch'ang-i, abandoning the region of Liang to the armies of Wu. The king of Wu is sure to throw all his might against Liang, while you may simply deepen your moats and raise the height of your walls, sending out light troops at the same time to block the juncture of the Huai and Ssu rivers and cut off Wu's supply road. In this way Wu and Liang will wear each other out, and Wu's provisions will soon be exhausted. Then with your army at full strength you may fall upon your weary opponent, and victory over Wu will be certain."

"Excellent!" said Chou Ya-fu, and set about putting the plan into operation, building powerful fortifications south of Ch'ang-i and sending light troops to cut off Wu's supply road.

---

[12] Chü Meng, described in "The Biographies of the Wandering Knights," *Shih chi* 124, was the most influential of the unofficial "bosses" in the area of Lo-yang. Chou Ya-fu, in an effort to flatter Chü Meng, may deliberately be exaggerating the importance of Chü-Meng's loyalty, though such local "bosses" wielded considerable influence in the countryside and could have been a source of trouble to the Han cause.

When the king of Wu first called out his troops he appointed his minister T'ien Lu-po as general in chief. "We have massed our troops and are preparing to march west," said T'ien Lu-po, "but I fear that unless we resort to some unusual tactics we will have difficulty in winning success. I would like to be given a force of fifty thousand men to lead on a separate expedition up along the Huai and Yangtze rivers in order to seize control of Huai-nan and Ch'ang-sha. From there I can enter the Wu Pass and rejoin Your Majesty's forces. This would be one trick we could use."

The crown prince of Wu, however, advised his father against this plan. "You yourself have declared that you are in revolt, so that it is difficult to entrust your soldiers to others. If you entrust your men to others and then they in turn revolt against you, what will you do? In any event, if you arbitrarily split up your troops into expeditionary forces it is hard to judge what profit you may gain. More likely you will only damage your own position." The king of Wu accordingly refused T'ien Lu-po's request for troops.

One of the younger commanders of Wu, General Huan, advised the king of Wu, "Wu has a great many foot soldiers, which are employed to greatest advantage in mountainous terrain, while the Han has a large number of chariots and horsemen, which are most effective in the open plains. I would suggest therefore that, if Your Majesty encounters cities on your line of march which refuse to surrender, you let them go for the moment and hasten west with all speed so that you may make your base at the storehouses of Lo-yang, provision your troops from the Ao Granary, block the mountain defiles along the Yellow River, and from there issue your orders to the other feudal lords. In this way, though you do not even enter the Pass into the capital area, you will already have control of the empire. If Your Majesty proceeds slowly, stopping along the way to force the surrender of each city, then before we know it the chariots and horsemen of the Han armies will be upon us, swooping through the outskirts of the cities of Liang and Ch'u, and our cause will be lost!"

The king of Wu consulted with his older generals on this plan of action, but they replied, "Only a young man who thinks of nothing but dashing into the face of the enemy would suggest such a move! What does he know about over-all strategy?" The king of Wu therefore did not follow the suggestion of General Huan.

The king of Wu bent all his efforts toward gathering his forces into one army. Before he crossed the Huai River he appointed various of his retainers as generals, commanders, lieutenants, and marshals; only Chou Ch'iu was given no appointment. Chou Ch'iu was a native of Hsia-p'ei who, fleeing from the law in his own city, had come to Wu, where he made a living selling wine. He had done nothing to distinguish himself, and the king of Wu accordingly thought little of him and gave him no appointment. Chou Ch'iu went to visit the king and said, "Because of my lack of ability I have not been allowed the honor of taking part in the campaign. I would not venture to ask for the post of general, but if Your Majesty would give me one of the credentials used by the Han envoys, I promise to bring you a fitting reward." When the king of Wu accordingly handed over to him one of the Han credentials he took it and galloped by night to his home in Hsia-p'ei. The cities of Hsia-p'ei, hearing of the revolt in Wu, were at the time all tightly shut and guarded. When Chou Ch'iu reached the official lodging house he sent an order summoning the magistrate of the district. The magistrate had no sooner entered the door than Chou Ch'iu accused him of some crime and had his attendants cut the man in two. He then proceeded to summon the important officials, who were friends of his brothers, and addressed them as follows: "The rebel troops of Wu will soon be here and, when they arrive, the men of Hsia-p'ei will be massacred in no more time than it takes to gobble a meal. But if we take the lead in submitting to their cause before they arrive, then our homes will be saved from destruction and the ablest among us will even be enfeoffed as marquises!" The officials went out and reported his words throughout the district, whereupon the whole of Hsia-p'ei capitulated to the rebels. Thus in one night Chou Ch'iu secured thirty thousand men. He sent someone to report to the king of Wu what he had done, while he himself led the forces he had secured in pillaging the cities to the north. By the time he reached Ch'eng-yang he had an army of over a hundred thousand men. There he defeated the army of the military commander of Ch'eng-yang but,

Liu P'i, the King of Wu

hearing that the king of Wu had been defeated and was in flight, he decided that there was no more chance of winning success in the cause of Wu, and so he led his troops back toward Hsia-p'ei. Before he reached home, an ulcer broke out on his back and he died.

In the second month, after the forces of the king of Wu had already suffered defeat and were in flight, Emperor Ching issued an edict to his army which read:

It is said that Heaven rewards the doer of good with blessings and the doer of evil with misfortune. Emperor Kao-tsu in person bestowed marks of recognition on his worthy ministers and set up the various feudal lords. Later, when the kingdoms of Liu Yu, King Yu of Chao, and Liu Fei, King Tao-hui of Ch'i, were left without heirs, Emperor Wen took pity upon them and established Liu Yu's son Liu Sui as king of Chao, and Liu Ang and the other sons of Liu Fei as kings in the region of Ch'i, so that they might tend the mortuary temples of their ancestors, the former kings, and serve as bastion states to the court of Han. In so doing, his virtuous generosity rivaled that of heaven and earth, and his enlightenment matched the sun and the moon. And yet Liu P'i, the king of Wu, turned his back upon such generosity and betrayed his duty, inviting fugitives and criminals from all over the empire to come to his kingdom, debasing the currency of the empire by his minting of coins, and, on the grounds that he was ill, refusing for over twenty years to attend the court of the emperor. The officials repeatedly recommended that Liu P'i be called to account for his crimes, but Emperor Wen preferred to be lenient, hoping that in time he would mend his ways and do good. Now he has joined with the king of Ch'u, Liu Mou; the king of Chao, Liu Sui; the king of Chiao-hsi, Liu Ang; the king of Chi-nan, Liu Pi-kuang; the king of Tzu-ch'uan, Liu Hsien; and the king of Chiao-tung, Liu Hsiung-ch'ü, in an alliance of revolt, committing the most heinous treason. He has called out his troops to menace the ancestral temples of the dynasty; he has murdered the ministers and envoys of the Han, oppressed the commoners, slaughtered the innocent, and fired the homes of the people and dug up their grave mounds, spreading the utmost tyranny before him. Liu Ang and the others have added even greater outrages, burning down the temples of the dynasty and pillaging the sacred objects.[13] Deeply grieved by these acts, I have donned the white robes of mourning and retired from the hall of state. I call upon my generals to urge forward their officers and strike at the rebellious

[13] Mortuary temples dedicated to the founder of the dynasty had been set up in all the provinces and feudal kingdoms.

villains! In attacking the rebels, he who marches deepest into their territories and kills the largest number shall win the highest merit. In the question of whether to cut off the heads of captives or take them prisoner, let all those who are of the three hundred picul rank or above be killed on the spot without mercy. If anyone shall dare to question this edict or fail to obey it, he shall be cut in two at the waist!

When the king of Wu first crossed the Huai River he joined with the king of Ch'u in marching west and attacking and overcoming the city of Chi-pi. Taking advantage of this victory, they proceeded on their way, a force of formidable keenness. Liu Wu, King Hsiao of Liang, the brother of Emperor Ching, alarmed at the situation, dispatched six generals to attack the Wu forces, but Wu succeeded in defeating two of the generals and sending their men scurrying back to Liang. The king of Liang several times sent envoys to Chou Ya-fu begging for aid, but Chou Ya-fu refused to listen to their request. The king of Liang also dispatched envoys to criticize Chou Ya-fu's conduct to the emperor. The emperor sent one of his men to order Chou Ya-fu to go to the aid of Liang, but Chou Ya-fu, considering his own advantage, stayed where he was and still refused to go to Liang's rescue. The king of Liang then dispatched as generals Han An-kuo and Chang Yü, the younger brother of Chang Shang, the prime minister of Ch'u who had met death because he counseled the king of Ch'u against revolt; these two managed to inflict several defeats on the troops of Wu. The forces of Wu had hoped to march west but, with the cities of Liang firmly guarded, they did not dare to proceed in that direction, but instead raced toward the army of Chou Ya-fu, which they encountered at Hsia-i. They hoped to engage Chou Ya-fu in battle, but he stayed within his fortifications and refused to fight. The Wu army, its provisions exhausted and its men on the verge of starvation, repeatedly challenged him to battle. Finally they made a rush on the fortifications, causing great alarm at the southeast corner of the camp. Chou Ya-fu then ordered his men to prepare for an attack from the northwest and, as he had foreseen, the enemy attempted to penetrate from that direction. Eventually the Wu army suffered a crushing defeat, many of its men died of starvation, and the remainder turned their backs and fled.

The king of Wu, accompanied by several thousand able-bodied men from his command, escaped in the night, crossed the Yangtze, fled through Tan-t'u, and took up a position in the barbarian kingdom of Eastern Yüeh. Eastern Yüeh still had a force of over ten thousand soldiers, and the king of Wu sent out men to gather up the fleeing remnants of his own army. But the Han dispatched an envoy to entice the men of Eastern Yüeh with offers of gain until they agreed to trick the king of Wu. When the king came out of his headquarters to review the troops that he had gathered together, the men of Eastern Yüeh sent someone to run him through with a spear. Then they placed his head in a box and sent it by relay carriage to the capital. Liu Tzu-hua and Liu Tzu-chü, the sons of the king of Wu, fled to the region of Min-yüeh. After the king of Wu abandoned his forces and fled, his army gradually crumbled and the men bit by bit surrendered to Chou Ya-fu or to the army of Liang. The army of Liu Mou, the king of Ch'u, was also defeated, and the king committed suicide.

The kings of Chiao-hsi, Chiao-tung, and Tzu-ch'uan had besieged the king of Ch'i in the city of Lin-tzu, but after three months they were still unable to take the city. When the Han forces arrived the three kings withdrew their troops and returned to their own kingdoms.

Upon his return Liu Ang, the king of Chiao-hsi, spread a mat of straw and, seating himself upon it, bared his arms and feet and refused to take anything but water, begging forgiveness from his mother, the queen dowager, for his actions. His son, the crown prince Liu Te, said to his father, "The troops of Han have marched a long way and they appear to me to be already exhausted from the expedition. Now is the time to make a surprise attack! I beg to gather up the remnants of my father's troops and strike at them. If the attack is not successful, it will still not be too late to flee to the islands off the coast!"

"My forces have been completely crushed. It is impossible to call out the men again!" replied the king, but the crown prince refused to heed his father's words.

The Han general Han T'ui-tang, marquis of Kung-kao, sent a letter to the king of Chiao-hsi, saying, "I have been ordered by the emperor to punish those who have failed in their duty. Those who surrender will be pardoned for their crimes and treated as before;

those who fail to surrender will be wiped out! Which course will the king of Chiao-hsi choose? I will await your answer and act accordingly."

The king bared his arms and, knocking his head on the ground before the encampment of the Han army, requested an audience with General Han. "Because I have failed to honor the laws of the empire with sufficient care, I have brought alarm to the common people and burdened the general, causing him to journey this great distance to my worthless kingdom. For such crimes I deserve to be punished by having my flesh cut up and pickled."

General Han, bearing in his hands the gong and drum with which he signaled the advance or retreat of his troops, appeared before the king and said, "It is true that you have caused great trouble to the army. May I inquire the circumstances which impelled you to call out your troops?"

The king bowed his head and, crawling forward on his knees, replied, "In recent times Ch'ao Ts'o was one of the most trusted of the emperor's ministers, but he altered the laws which had been laid down by Emperor Kao-tsu and unrightfully seized the lands of the feudal lords. I and the others believed that such actions were unjust and we feared that he would bring ruin to the empire. Therefore seven of us called out the troops of our kingdoms, intending to punish him. Now that we have heard that he has already been punished, we have disbanded our forces and respectfully withdrawn to our own territories."

"If you really believed that Ch'ao Ts'o was acting wrongly," said General Han, "why did you not submit a report to the throne? Instead of that you did not even wait for an order from the emperor, but arbitrarily used the military credentials granted to you by the court to call out your troops and attack the loyal kingdom of Ch'i. From such actions as these it is apparent that your true intention was not really to punish Ch'ao Ts'o!" He then produced the imperial edict and read it to the king. When he had finished reading he said, "I leave you to decide what action to take!" "For someone such as I, even death cannot atone for my crimes," replied the king. Shortly thereafter he committed suicide, along with the queen dowager, his son the crown prince, and the other members of his family. The kings of Chiao-tung, Tzu-ch'uan, and Chi-nan likewise committed suicide. Their kingdoms were abolished and their territories taken over by the Han government.

The Han general Li Chi besieged the king of Chao in the city of Han-tan. After ten months [14] the city capitulated, and the king of Chao committed suicide. Liu Ching, the king of Chi-pei, because he had been forced into the revolt against his will, was not punished but was transferred to the position of king of Tzu-ch'uan.

Liu P'i, the king of Wu, first began the revolt, joining his forces with those of Ch'u and entering into an agreement with the armies of Chao and the kingdoms in the region of Ch'i. They called out their forces in the first month, and by the third month all had been defeated except Chao, which held out alone until the latter part of the year. Later Emperor Ching set up the marquis of P'ing-lu, Liu Li, a younger son of Liu Chiao, King Yüan of Ch'u, as king of Ch'u, in order to carry on the line of the royal family of Ch'u. Liu Fei, the king of Ju-nan, he made ruler of the region of Wu with the title of king of Chiang-tu.

The Grand Historian remarks: Liu P'i happened to be appointed king of Wu because his father was deprived of the kingdom of Tai. He was able to reduce taxes, use his people wisely, and at the same time take free advantage of the resources of the hills and sea. The seeds of rebellion first took root in his mind because of the untimely death of his son; the trouble which arose over a trivial game of chess finally destroyed his whole family. Liu P'i allied himself with the barbarians in Yüeh in plotting against his own clan, the rulers of the dynasty, and in the end met destruction. Ch'ao Ts'o adopted policies which he believed would benefit the state in the distant future, and yet in no time at all he met misfortune instead. Yüan Ang was one of the most influential advisers to the emperor but, though he enjoyed favor at first, he later suffered disgrace. Therefore in ancient times it was said that the territories of the feudal lords should not exceed a hundred *li* in size, and that they should not be allowed to make use of the

[14] But *Shih chi* 50, "The Hereditary House of King Yüan of Ch'u," translated above, says seven months, which seems more likely.

resources of the hills and seas. It was also said that one should never become friendly with the barbarians and thrust aside one's own kin. Such sayings were meant, no doubt, for men like the king of Wu. Do not take the lead in planning affairs, or you will suffer the consequences, people say. This applies, does it not, to Yüan Ang and Ch'ao Ts'o?

Some Remarks on the Han Peers: I[1]

Shih chi 17: The Chronological Table of the Feudal Lords from the Beginning of the Han, Introduction

During the hundred years from the founding of the Han down to the era t'ai-ch'u [206 to 104 B.C.] the various feudal lords were enfeoffed or removed from their positions and their territories were divided or taken away from them, but their records and genealogies are by no means clear and the officials have failed to mention why such changes were made in each generation. Thus I made The Chronological Table of the Feudal Lords from the Beginning of the Han.

The Grand Historian remarks: The Shang dynasty and the ages before it are too far away to say much about, but we know that the Chou dynasty granted five degrees of noble title: duke, marquis, earl, viscount, and baron. When the Chou dynasty enfeoffed Po-chin in Lu and K'ang-shu in Wei it granted them each a territory of four hundred square *li*. The size of their fiefs was unusually large because, as they were relatives of the royal family, it was proper to treat them with special deference and to reward them for their virtue. When the Chou enfeoffed the Grand Duke Lü Shang in Ch'i it granted him the combined territories of five marquises in order to honor him for his diligent labors. Outside of these, Kings Wu, Ch'eng, and K'ang of the Chou enfeoffed several hundred men, among them fifty-five members of their own clan, to act as guardians of the royal house. Of the fiefs they granted, the largest did not exceed a hundred *li* and the smallest was

[1] The Introductions to *Shih chi* 17, 18, and 19 are given here under a general title supplied by the translator.

thirty *li*. The feudal states of Kuan, Ts'ai, K'ang-shu, Ts'ao, and Cheng were in some cases larger than this and in some cases smaller.[2]

After the time of Kings Li and Yu [eighth and seventh centuries B.C.] the royal house lost its hold and the great states of the feudal lords rose to power. The Son of Heaven was too weak to be able to restore them to order. It was not that his virtue lacked purity, but that the circumstances rendered him helpless.

When the Han dynasty arose it awarded only the two noble ranks of king and marquis. In the latter years of his reign Emperor Kao-tsu made an agreement with his followers that if anyone not of the Liu family should become a king, and anyone who had not distinguished himself in battle or attained high position should become a marquis, the empire should unite in punishing him. Nine of Kao-tsu's sons and brothers of the Liu family were made kings of states. The only king who was not of the Liu family was Wu Jui, the king of Ch'ang-sha. Kao-tsu also enfeoffed over a hundred of his distinguished followers as marquises. From Yen-men and T'ai-yüan east to Liao-yang comprised the states of Yen and Tai. From the Ch'ang mountains south, and east from the T'ai-hsing mountains across the Yellow and Chi rivers and through A and Chen east to the sea, comprised the states of Ch'i and Chao. The region from Ch'en to the west, south to the Nine Peaks, and east along the Yangtze, Huai, Ku, and Ssu rivers as far as K'uai-chi, was divided into the kingdoms of Liang, Ch'u, Huai-nan and Ch'ang-sha. All of these states on their outer borders adjoined the lands of the northern and southern barbarians, while in the inner part of China the entire area east from the great mountain ranges of the north was in the hands of the various feudal lords. The largest territories consisted of as many as five or six provinces, comprising twenty or thirty cities, and their rulers set up various government offices and built palaces and towers in flagrant imitation of the Son of Heaven. The Han court retained possession only of the provinces of Tung, Ho-tung, Ho-nei, Ho-nan, Ying-ch'uan, and Nan-yang, and the region from Chiang-nan west to Shu, north from Yün-chung to Lung-hsi, and the capital area, fifteen provinces in all, and even within this

---

[2] The sentence is obscure and the inclusion of K'ang-shu, who has already been mentioned above, is probably an error.

area various princesses and marquises received revenue from many of the cities. The reason for this was that, when the empire was first brought under control, the emperor had few close relatives of his own clan and so he set up a number of his sons by concubines in powerful positions in order that they might bring peace and order to the realm and provide aid and protection for the Son of Heaven.

During the hundred years after the founding of the Han these various branches of the imperial family became increasingly estranged from the central court. Some among the feudal lords grew arrogant and extravagant, and were misled by the schemes of vicious ministers into evil and insubordination. The most powerful among them rebelled, while the lesser ones committed violations of the law, endangering their lives and bringing ruin upon themselves and their states. Later the Son of Heaven, imitating the ways of antiquity, graciously allowed the various feudal lords to share their blessings and to divide up their territories among their various sons and brothers.[3] Hence the state of Ch'i came to be divided into seven parts, Chao into six, Liang into five, and Huai-nan into three. The sons of the emperors by their concubines were made kings, and the sons of the kings by their concubines were made marquises, numbering over a hundred.

At the time of the revolt of the seven kingdoms led by Wu and Ch'u the territories of many of the feudal lords were reduced because of faults they had committed before or after the revolt. Hence the states of Yen and Tai lost their northern provinces, and those of Wu, Huai-nan and Ch'ang-sha their southern provinces, which bordered on the lands of the barbarians, while the outlying provinces and the important mountains, lakes, and seacoasts of Ch'i, Chao, Liang, and Ch'u were similarly all taken over by the Han court. Thus the domains of the feudal lords were bit by bit diminished in size until the largest states did not exceed ten cities or more, and the smallest of the marquisates were no more than twenty or thirty square *li*, sufficient only to render tribute and services to the central court, to provide for the sacrifices to the ancestors of the feudal lords, and to act as defenders

---

[3] Ssu-ma Ch'ien's wording is ironic. What the emperors were doing, of course, was forcing the feudal lords to divide their domains among all their sons in order to weaken their power.

of the capital. The Han court administered eighty or ninety provinces, disposed here and there among the domains of the feudal lords and interlocking with them like the teeth of a dog, and kept a hold on strategic defense points and particularly profitable lands. By means of this policy, known as "strengthening the root and weakening the branches," the distinction between exalted and humble was made clear to everyone and all affairs were disposed in the proper way.

Your servant Ch'ien [4] has respectfully prepared this record of the feudal lords from the time of Kao-tsu down to the era *t'ai-ch'u*, listing under the title of each lord the changes which took place in his fief through the succeeding generations, in order that later ages may see what the situation was. No matter how strong one's position may be, the important thing is that he should make benevolence and righteousness the basis of his conduct.

[4] This is the only place in the *Shih chi* where Ssu-ma Ch'ien refers to himself as "your servant Ch'ien." Commentators have suggested that in his original manuscript Ssu-ma Ch'ien used this phrase throughout, and that later editors, perhaps Ssu-ma Ch'ien's grandson Yang Yün who worked to publicize his grandfather's book, changed the wording to "the Grand Historian," overlooking only this passage.

Some Remarks on the Han Peers: II

Shih chi 18: The Chronological Table of the Distinguished Followers of Kao-tsu Who Became Marquises, Introduction

To these, his principal followers, who aided him like arms and legs, Kao-tsu granted the split tallies of enfeoffment and noble titles, and they in turn passed their blessings on to their descendants. But there were some who forgot the spirit tablets of their fathers and brought death to themselves and destruction to their domains. Thus I made The Chronological Table of the Distinguished Followers of Kao-tsu Who Became Marquises.

The Grand Historian remarks: In ancient times the subjects of a ruler were distinguished by five grades of merit. First were those who, by their virtue, established the ancestral temples of their families and maintained in their domains the altars of the soil and grain, and their merit was called "loyalty." Next were those who distinguished themselves by their sound advice, and their merit was called "exertion." Next were those who wielded their strength in battle, and their merit was called "achievement." Next were those who brought enlightenment to their ranks, and their merit was called "eminence." Finally there were those who held office for a long time, and their merit was called "longevity."

When the feudal lords received their titles they took an oath that, "though the Yellow River become no broader than a girdle, though Mount T'ai become no larger than a whetstone, in peace and harmony will I possess this domain and it shall be handed down to my descendants after me." In the beginning each hoped that the root he had thus planted would be firm and sound, and yet the branches and leaves which sprang from it in time withered and died away.

When I read the records of the distinguished followers of Kao-tsu who were enfeoffed as marquises, and observe the reasons for which their descendants were deprived of the fiefs of their fathers, I am struck by how different the situation is from what I have heard concerning ancient times.

The *Book of Documents,* speaking of Emperor Yao, says, "He brought harmony to the ten thousand states,"[1] and some of these states maintained their existence through the changes of the Hsia and Shang dynasties and lasted for several thousand years. In like manner the eight hundred fiefs granted by the early Chou rulers may still be seen, even after the times of Kings Yu and Li, in the pages of the *Spring and Autumn Annals.* The nobles who were descendants of Emperors Yao and Shun mentioned in the *Book of Documents* held their positions throughout the three dynasties of Hsia, Shang, and Chou, a period of over a thousand years, and fulfilled their duty as guardians of the Son of Heaven. Was it not because they were diligent in virtue and attendant to the laws of their superiors?

When the Han arose, over a hundred of the distinguished followers of Kao-tsu received fiefs. At that time peace had only just been restored to the world and the great towns and famous cities were deserted and in ruins, so that where before there had been ten households, only two or three could be found to enroll in the population registers. Thus the fiefs of the greatest marquises did not exceed ten thousand families, while the smallest comprised only five or six hundred households.

After a few decades, however, the people returned to their native towns and the number of households gradually increased, so that the fiefs of men like Hsiao Ho, Ts'ao Ts'an, Chou P'o, and Kuan Ying reached the number of forty thousand households, and those of the lesser marquises doubled in population. But in the midst of such affluence the descendants of these lords, giving themselves up to arrogance and luxurious living, and forgetting their duty to their fathers, fell into evil ways. By the time of the era *t'ai-ch'u* [104 B.C.], a hundred years after the founding of the dynasty, there were only five of these marquises left. All the rest had been tried for some offense, had lost their

[1] "Canon of Yao."

lives, or had been deprived of their domains. It is true that by this time the laws of the empire had become somewhat stricter and more exacting, and yet none of these men behaved with the slightest caution toward the restrictions of the times.

One who lives in the present age and considers the ways of the past has a mirror wherein he may see that the two are not necessarily alike. Emperors and kings all have different rites and different things which they consider important. If a man hopes to win success and establish a lasting family, he cannot afford to confuse past and present! Again, if one examines the ways in which men win position and favor and the reasons why they lose these and incur disgrace, he will have the key to success and failure in his own age. What need is there to consult the traditions of antiquity?

So I have with all diligence drawn up this chronological table and made a record of each fief from beginning to end. There are a number of places in which the listings are not complete. I have set down only what was certain, and in doubtful cases have left a blank. If scholars later on wish to surmise further and fill out the record, they will at least be able to peruse what I have written.

Some Remarks on the Han Peers: III

Shih chi 19: The Chronological Table of the Marquises during the Reigns of Emperors Hui to Ching, Introduction

For the period of the reign of Emperor Hui to that of Emperor Ching, I have set forth a record of the distinguished ministers and relatives of the imperial family who were granted titles and fiefs, making The Chronological Table of the Marquises during the Reigns of Emperors Hui to Ching.

When, as Grand Historian, I have occasion to read over the records of enfeoffment and come to the case of Wu Ch'ien, the marquis of Pien, I say to myself, "Yes, there was good reason for this!" His father, Wu Jui, was enfeoffed as king of Ch'ang-sha by special order of the government in recognition of his loyalty to Emperor Kao-tsu. In the early days of the dynasty, when Kao-tsu first brought order to the world, he marked out a number of domains and enfeoffed eight of his distinguished followers who were not members of his own clan as kings of these states. But by the reign of Emperor Hui only one of these, the domain of Ch'ang-sha, had passed down safely through five generations of the Wu family, though eventually it was abolished because of the lack of an heir. Wu Jui and his successors remained to the end free from all error, fulfilling their duty as protectors of the imperial house, a model of fidelity. It was for this reason that Wu Jui was able to pass on his blessings to his descendants so that a number of them, though distinguished by no particular merit themselves, were able to become marquises.

During the fifty years from the reign of Emperor Hui to that of Emperor Ching over ninety fiefs were granted, some as belated rewards to followers who had distinguished themselves in the time of Kao-tsu, some to the ministers who accompanied Emperor Wen from his kingdom in Tai, some to those who achieved merit during the uprising of the states of Wu and Ch'u, some to the sons of marquises or to men related to the imperial family by marriage, and some to men who came from foreign countries and acknowledged fealty to the Han.[1] In the following table I have set forth a complete list of these from beginning to end, a record of the men who distinguished themselves during this age by their virtue and accomplishment.

[1] That is, the Hsiung-nu leaders who voluntarily surrendered to the Han court in 147 B.C.

Part XI
THE EMINENT OFFICIALS

Shih chi 84: The Biographies of Ch'ü Yüan and Master Chia[1]

In fine phrases he censured the actions of the king, and with examples and analogies argued for the right. Such is the nature of Ch'ü Yüan's poem, "Encountering Sorrow." Thus I made The Biographies of Ch'ü Yüan and Master Chia.

Ch'ü Yüan

Ch'ü Yüan, whose familiar name was Ch'ü P'ing, bore the same surname as one of the royal families of the state of Ch'u.[2] He acted as aide to King Huai of Ch'u [328–299 B.C.]. Possessed of wide learning and a strong will, he was wise in affairs of government and skilled in the use of words. In the inner palace he deliberated with the king on

[1] In this chapter Ssu-ma Ch'ien has coupled the lives of two statesmen-poets, Ch'ü Yüan (third century B.C.) and Chia I (201–169 B.C.). Because of the similarity of their lives and poetic works and the admiration which Chia I expressed for his great predecessor, the grouping seems justified, but in doing so Ssu-ma Ch'ien is forced to violate the chronological order of his biographical section. For the life of Ch'ü Yüan, therefore, the reader must go back in time to the period of the Warring States, before the empire had been unified under the Ch'in dynasty, when China was divided into a number of independent kingdoms engaged in an unending struggle for power and self-preservation. The biography of Ch'ü Yüan is rather disconnected in places and presents a number of problems of interpretation. Some commentators are of the opinion that sections of the narrative have been misplaced, and suggest possible rearrangements of the text. I am inclined to believe, however, that Ssu-ma Ch'ien was less interested in presenting the exact historical facts of Ch'ü Yüan's life (already difficult to determine in his own day because of the wealth of legend which surrounded the figure of the poet) than in expounding the tragic themes of injustice and mistaken judgment which the legends and poetic works attributed to Ch'ü Yüan so beautifully illustrate. Because his own experiences at the court of Emperor Wu were in many ways similar to what Ch'ü Yüan suffered, he is led time and again to break into the course of his narrative with discussions of these larger themes.

[2] The rulers of Ch'u bore the surname Mi, but the Ch'ü family claimed descent from one of the early kings of Ch'u and many of its members held important positions at the court of Ch'u.

national affairs and the issuing of orders, and in the outer court he received visitors and held audience with the feudal lords. The king put the greatest trust in him, and the chief minister, who was thus forced to share the same rank with Ch'ü Yüan, vied with him for the king's favor and was secretly disturbed by his great ability.

King Huai set Ch'ü Yüan the task of drawing up a code of laws. While Ch'ü Yüan was still working on the rough draft the chief minister got a glimpse of it and tried to get it away from Ch'ü Yüan so he could steal the ideas for himself, but Ch'ü Yüan refused to give it to him. Thereupon the minister began to slander Ch'ü Yüan, saying, "The king has given Ch'ü Yüan the task of drawing up laws, the sort of thing that anyone could do and yet, when each new law is finished, he goes about boasting of his achievement and saying that 'in my opinion no one but myself could have done this!'"

The king, angered by these reports, grew cold toward Ch'ü Yüan. Ch'ü Yüan grieved that the king should be so deceived in what he heard and that his understanding should be clouded by idle slander, that petty evil should be allowed to injure the public good and justice should be without a hearing. Plunged into melancholy thought because of the affair, he composed his poem entitled "Li Sao," which means "encountering sorrow."

Heaven is the beginning of man, and father and mother the root from which he springs. When a man finds his way blocked he will turn again to the source of his being. Therefore, when he is troubled and weary, he will always cry to Heaven, and when he is grieved and in pain, he will call upon his father and mother. Ch'ü Yüan conducted himself with justice and forthrightness, displaying the utmost loyalty and exhausting his wisdom in the service of his lord, and yet libelous men came between them. This is indeed what it means to find one's way blocked. To be faithful and yet doubted, to be loyal and yet suffer slander—can one bear this without anger? Ch'ü Yüan's composition of the "Li Sao" sprang, I am sure, from this very anger. The "Airs from the States" in the *Book of Odes* sing of romantic love but are never lewd; the "Lesser Odes" in the same work are full of anger and censure, but never of insubordination. A work like the "Li Sao," however, may be said to combine the best qualities of both of these. In it the poet praises the Sage Emperor K'u of ancient times, relates the deeds of Kings T'ang and Wu of a later age and, coming to more recent times, describes Duke Huan of Ch'i, in order to censure his own age and make clear the worth of virtue and the form and principles of good government, leaving no point untouched. His phrases are brief and his words subtle; his will is pure and his conduct virtuous. Though he appears to speak of small matters, his meaning is profound; though he chooses examples from close at hand, he uses them to illustrate far-reaching principles. Since his will is pure, he speaks often of fragrant plants and trees; and because his conduct was virtuous, he chose to die rather than seek a place in the world. He took himself off from the stagnant pools and fens; like a cicada slipping from its shell, he shook off the filth that surrounded him and soared far beyond its defilement. He would not allow himself to be soiled by the dust of the world but, shining pure amidst its mire, kept himself free from stain. Such a will as his is fit to vie for brilliance with the very sun and moon themselves!

Sometime after Ch'ü Yüan had lost his position at court the state of Ch'in began to make plans to attack the state of Ch'i. But Ch'i and Ch'u were both members of the Vertical Alliance,[3] and King Hui, the king of Ch'in, was afraid that if he attacked Ch'i, Ch'u would come to its aid. He therefore ordered his minister Chang I to leave Ch'in and, bearing lavish gifts, to visit the king of Ch'u and attempt to deceive him by saying, "Ch'in bears a deep hatred for Ch'i, but Ch'i and Ch'u are joined in an alliance of friendship. If you are willing, however, to break off relations with Ch'i, then Ch'in will be happy to present you with the cities of Shang and Wu and their surrounding territories of six hundred *li*." King Huai of Ch'u was greedy for land and trusted Chang I's words, and so he broke off his alliance with Ch'i and sent an envoy to Ch'in to receive the title to the lands. But when the envoy from Ch'u appeared before Chang I the latter falsely denied his promise, saying, "I agreed to give the king of Ch'u six *li*. I have no recollection of any talk of six hundred *li!*"

The Ch'u envoy left Ch'in in great anger and returned to report to

[3] The alliance of states in the east formed to prevent Ch'in from expanding in that direction.

King Huai what had happened. King Huai was furious and raised a huge army to attack Ch'in. Ch'in sent out its troops to meet the attack and inflicted a severe defeat on the Ch'u army between the Tan and Hsi rivers, cutting off eighty thousand heads and capturing the Ch'u general Ch'ü Kai. The Ch'in troops proceeded to seize the Ch'u territory of Han-chung.

King Huai then called up all the troops in the state of Ch'u and marched deep into the state of Ch'in, engaging the Ch'in forces at Lan-t'ien. When the state of Wei heard of the expedition, it launched a surprise attack on Ch'u, invading it as far as Teng. The Ch'u forces, afraid for the safety of their own land, withdrew from Ch'in, and Ch'i, angered at Ch'u's behavior, refused to come to its aid, so that Ch'u found itself in grave difficulties.

The following year Ch'in offered to divide the region of Han-chung and return part of it to Ch'u in order to bring peace between the two states, but the king of Ch'u replied, "I do not want land. I only want Chang I so that I may have my revenge on him!"

When this was reported to Chang I he said, "If I alone am worth as much to the king of Ch'u as the region of Han-chung, then I beg to be sent to Ch'u!" Chang I once more journeyed to Ch'u and, bringing lavish gifts for the king's trusted minister Chin Shang, had him plead by artful means with the king's favorite concubine, Cheng Hsiu, for her intervention.[4] King Huai eventually gave in to Cheng Hsiu's requests and pardoned Chang I and allowed him to return to Ch'in.

At this time Ch'ü Yüan, already out of favor, had not been restored to his former position but had instead been sent as an envoy to Ch'i. When he returned to Ch'u he admonished King Huai, saying, "Why did you not kill Chang I?" King Huai began to regret that he had let Chang I go free, and sent men to pursue him, but they were unable to overtake him in time. After this a number of the feudal lords joined

[4] The "artful means" which Chin Shang used to persuade the concubine to intervene on Chang I's behalf consisted of telling her that, if Chang I were not quickly pardoned, the king of Ch'in would undoubtedly send a present of a number of beautiful women to the king of Ch'u in an attempt to ransom him. With this prospect before her, the lady exerted all her efforts to get Chang I pardoned and released from prison, where the king had confined him. The fuller account is found in "The Biography of Chang I," *Shih chi* 70.

in attacking Ch'u, inflicting a severe defeat and killing the Ch'u general T'ang Mei.

At this time King Chao, who had succeeded King Hui as king of Ch'in and allied himself with Ch'u by marriage, asked King Huai to come to Ch'in to meet with him. King Huai was about to depart for Ch'in when Ch'ü Yüan advised him that "Ch'in is a nation of tigers and wolves and cannot be trusted. It would be better not to make the journey!" But King Huai's youngest son Tzu-lan encouraged his father to go, saying that it would not do to disrupt the friendly relations which had been established between Ch'u and Ch'in. King Huai accordingly set out but, after he had entered the Wu Pass, the Ch'in soldiers ambushed his party and, blocking their escape, detained the king, demanding that he cede part of his territory to Ch'in. King Huai was infuriated and refused to listen to their demands. He fled to the border of the state of Chao, but Chao refused to admit him and he was forced to return to Ch'in. Eventually he died in Ch'in and his body was returned to Ch'u for burial.

King Huai's eldest son, posthumously known as King Ch'ing-hsiang, ascended the throne of Ch'u and appointed his younger brother Tzu-lan as prime minister. The people of Ch'u blamed Tzu-lan for encouraging his father to make the journey to Ch'in from which he never returned.

Ch'ü Yüan had always disliked Tzu-lan and, though he had fallen from favor and been sent to Ch'i, he had anxiously watched the proceedings in Ch'u and had been gravely concerned for King Huai, never forgetting his desire to awaken the king to the danger that faced him. He hoped to be fortunate enough eventually to enlighten his lord and reform the ways of the state. Repeatedly in his poems he expressed this desire to save the ruler and aid his country, but in the end his wishes proved vain. He was unable to remedy the situation and eventually it became apparent that King Huai would never wake to the danger that awaited him if he journeyed to Ch'in.[5]

Any ruler, whether he be wise or foolish, worthy or unworthy, will

[5] The text of this passage and its relation to the rest of the narrative are far from clear. Here and elsewhere in the biography of Ch'ü Yüan I am much indebted to the translation and study by David Hawkes in his *Ch'u Tz'u: The Songs of the South,* Oxford University Press, 1959.

invariably seek for loyal men to aid him, and wise men to be his assistants. And yet the fact that we see endless examples of kingdoms lost and ruling families ruined, while generation after generation passes without showing us a sage ruler who can bring order to his country, is simply because the so-called loyal men are not really loyal, and the so-called wise ones are not wise. It was because King Huai could not distinguish the truly loyal that he was misled by his own concubine Cheng Hsiu and deceived in foreign affairs by Chang I, that he drove Ch'ü Yüan from the court and trusted his chief minister and his son Tzu-lan instead, that his soldiers were driven back and his territory seized, and that he lost six provinces to his enemies and died a stranger's death in Ch'in, the mockery of the world! This is the fate of those who do not know how to judge men! The *Book of Changes* says:

> Though the well is pure, men do not drink;
> My heart is filled with grief at it.
> If the king is wise and will dip up the water,
> We will all share his blessings![6]

But if the king is not wise, how can he be worthy to receive blessings?

When the prime minister Tzu-lan heard of Ch'ü Yüan's opposition to him he was very angry and eventually persuaded the chief minister to criticize Ch'ü Yüan to King Ch'ing-hsiang. The king was incensed and banished Ch'ü Yüan to the south.

When Ch'ü Yüan reached the banks of the Yangtze he was one day wandering along the river embankment lost in thought, his hair unbound, his face haggard with care, his figure lean and emaciated, when a fisherman happened to see him and asked, "Are you not the high minister of the royal family? What has brought you to this?"[7]

"All the world is muddied with confusion," replied Ch'ü Yüan.

[6] From the explanation of the hexagram *ching* or "well." Ssu-ma Ch'ien is likening the wise and loyal minister to the pure water of the well.

[7] This description of the meeting between Ch'ü Yüan and the fisherman, believed in later times to be an imaginary dialogue composed by Ch'ü Yüan himself and included as a separate work in the *Ch'u Tz'u* or *Elegies of Ch'u*, the collected works of Ch'ü Yüan and his imitators, uses a number of rhymed lines in the style of a *fu* or rhyme-prose.

"Only I am pure! All men are drunk, and I alone am sober! For this I have been banished!"

"A true sage does not stick at mere things, but changes with the times," said the fisherman. "If all the world is a muddy turbulence, why do you not follow its current and rise upon its waves? If all men are drunk, why do you not drain their dregs and swill their thin wine with them? Why must you cling so tightly to this jewel of virtue and bring banishment upon yourself?"

Ch'ü Yüan replied, "I have heard it said that he who has newly washed his hair should dust off his cap, and he who has just bathed his body should shake out his robes. What man can bear to soil the cleanness of his person with the filth you call 'mere things'? Better to plunge into this never-ending current beside us and find an end in some river fish's belly! Why should radiant whiteness be clouded by the world's vile darkness?"

Then he composed a poem in the rhyme-prose style entitled "Embracing the Sands":[8]

> Warm, bright days of early summer,
> When shrubs and trees grow rich with green,
> And I, in anguish and endless sorrow,
> Hasten on my way to a southern land.
> My eyes are dazed by darkness,
> Deep stillness lies all around me;
> Bound by injustice, grieved by wrong,
> I bear the long torment of this pain.
> I still my heart and follow my will;
> Bowing before injustice, I humble myself.
> They would round the corners of my squareness,
> But I will not change my constant form.
> To abandon the course he has set out upon:
> This is a disgrace to a worthy man.
> As a builder with his line, I have laid out my plan,

[8] The rhyme-prose or *fu* style probably derives from the religious songs of the state of Ch'u. Because it employs a longer and freer line than the style of poetry used in the *Book of Odes*, it is particularly suited to narrative and rhapsody.

I will not alter my former course.
To be forthright in nature and of loyal heart:
This is the pride of a great man.
If the skilled carpenter never carves,
Who can tell how true he cuts?
Dark patterns in a hidden place
The ill of sight call a formless nothing;
The subtle glance of the keen-eyed Li Lou
The ignorant mistake for blindness.
They have changed white into black,
Toppled "up" and made it "down."
Phoenixes they pen in cages,
While common fowl soar aloft;
Jewels and stones they mix together,
And weigh them in the same balance.
The men in power, with their petty envies,
Cannot recognize my worth.
I could bear high office and bring glory to the world,
Yet I am plunged to the depths and deprived of success.
So I must embrace this jewel of virtue
And to the end share it with no one.
As the packs of village dogs bark,
So they bark at what is strange;
To censure greatness and doubt the unusual,
Such is the nature of the herd.
Though ability and refinement combine in me,
The world does not know my excellence.
Though I have abundance of talent,
No one acknowledges my possessions.
I have honored benevolence and upheld duty,
Been diligent and faithful in full degree;
Yet, since I cannot meet Emperor Shun of old,
Who is there to appreciate my actions?
Many men have been born in an ill age,
But I cannot tell the reason.
The sages T'ang and Yü have long departed;
Though I yearn for them, they are far away.
I will calm my wrath and mend my anger,
Still my heart, and be strong.

>   Though I meet darkness, I will not falter;
>   Let my determination serve as a model to men!
>   I walk the road to my lodge in the north; [9]
>   The day grows dark; night is falling.
>   I will cast off sorrow and delight in woe,
>   For all will have an end in the Great Affair of death.

Reprise:
>   Broad flow the waters of the Yüan and the Hsiang;
>   Their two streams roar on to the Yangtze.
>   Long is the road and hidden in shadow;
>   The way I go is vast and far.
>   I sing to myself of my constant sorrow,
>   Lost in lamentation.
>   In the world no one knows me;
>   There is none to tell my heart to.
>   I must embrace my thoughts, hold fast my worth;
>   I am alone and without a mate.
>   Po Lo, judge of fine steeds, has long passed away;
>   Who now can tell the worth of a thoroughbred? [10]
>   Man at his birth receives his fate,
>   And by it each life must be disposed.
>   I will calm my heart and pluck up my will;
>   What more have I to fear? [11]
>   I know that death cannot be refused;
>   May I love life no longer!
>   This I proclaim to all worthy men:
>   I will be an example for you!

With this he grasped a stone in his arms and, casting himself into the Mi-lo River, drowned.

After the death of Ch'ü Yüan there were a number of his followers such as Sung Yü, T'ang Le, and Ching Ch'a, who were fond of fine writing and won fame by their compositions in the rhyme-prose style. But although they all imitated Ch'ü Yüan's actions and fine phrases,

---

[9] North is the direction of winter and death.

[10] The thoroughbred steed is often used in Chinese rhetoric as a metaphor for the man of superior worth.

[11] I have omitted four lines of the original, a slightly different version of lines five to eight of the reprise above, which commentators believe have erroneously been copied into the text at this point.

none of them dared to remonstrate openly with the king. The state of Ch'u continued to lose territory day by day until, some twenty or thirty years later, it was finally destroyed by Ch'in.

Chia I

A hundred years or so after Ch'ü Yüan threw himself into the Mi-lo there was a scholar of the Han named Master Chia who, being appointed as grand tutor to the king of Ch'ang-sha, visited the Hsiang River and cast into its waters a copy of his work, "A Lament for Ch'ü Yüan."

Master Chia, whose familiar name was Chia I, was a native of Lo-yang. By the age of eighteen he was already renowned in his province for his ability to recite the *Book of Odes* and compose works of literature. The commandant of justice Wu, who was at this time governor of the province of Ho-nan, hearing of his outstanding ability, invited him to be one of his retainers and treated him with great affection.

When Emperor Wen first came to the throne he heard that Lord Wu, the governor of Ho-nan, was one of the most skilled administrators in the empire and, being from the same city as the famous Ch'in minister Li Ssu, had once studied under Li Ssu.[12] He therefore summoned Lord Wu to court and made him commandant of justice. Lord Wu in turn recommended Chia I who, though still young, he said, had already mastered the writings of the hundred schools of philosophy. Emperor Wen accordingly summoned Chia I and made him an erudit. Chia I, only a little over twenty years old, was the youngest among the court scholars, but whenever the draft of some edict or ordinance was referred to the scholars for discussion, though the older masters were unable to say a word, Chia I would in their place give a full reply to the emperor's inquiries, expressing what each of the others would like to have said but could not put into words. The other scholars soon

[12] Li Ssu, one time prime minister to the First Emperor of the Ch'in, was an exponent of Legalist philosophy and largely responsible for many of the policies of the First Emperor, including the infamous "burning of the books" and the persecution of Confucian scholars. This is a good example of how the Han rulers, while professing Confucian principles and condemning all that the First Emperor had done, in actual practice often took advantage of the Ch'in's legacy. Note that the post Lord Wu was appointed to was that of commandant of justice, the head of criminal investigation and prosecution, a position for which a man of hard-headed Legalist convictions would be most suitable.

came to feel that they were no match for Chia I in ability. Emperor Wen was highly pleased with Chia I and advanced him with unusual rapidity, so that in the space of a year Chia I reached the position of palace counselor.

Chia I believed that, since by the reign of Emperor Wen the Han had already been in power for over twenty years and the empire was at peace, it was time for the dynasty to alter the month upon which the year began, change the color of the vestments, put its administrative code in order, fix the titles of officials, and encourage the spread of rites and music.[13] He therefore drew up a draft of his proposals on the proper ceremonies and regulations to be followed, maintaining that the dynasty should honor the color yellow and the number five, and should invent new official titles instead of following the practices used by the Ch'in. But Emperor Wen had just come to the throne and he modestly declined any ability or leisure to put into effect such far-reaching measures. He did, however, direct revisions in the pitch pipes and in the statutes and order the marquises to leave the capital and reside in their own territories, both of which measures originated from suggestions made by Chia I. Emperor Wen then consulted with his ministers, asking whether they did not think that Chia I was worthy of promotion to a top position in the government. Chou P'o, Kuan Ying, Chang Hsiang-ju, Feng Ching, and the rest of their group, however, all opposed such a move and disparaged Chia I, saying, "This fellow from Lo-yang is still young and has just begun his studies, and yet he is trying to seize all the authority in the government and throw everything into confusion!"

After this the emperor grew cool toward Chia I and ceased to listen to his proposals, but instead appointed him as grand tutor to Wu Ch'a, the king of Ch'ang-sha.

When Chia I had taken leave of the court and set out on his way he heard that the region of Ch'ang-sha was low-lying and damp, and he feared that in such a climate he would not live for long.[14] Also he was aware that he was being sent away as a reprimand, and he was deeply

[13] According to the scholars of the time such measures were necessary to demonstrate to the world that the Han was a new dynasty, entirely independent of the dynasties which preceded it.

[14] The northern Chinese of this time had a horror of the warm, damp climate of the Yangtze valley, where Ch'ang-sha was situated.

disturbed. When he crossed the Hsiang River he composed a poem in the rhyme-prose style, entitled "A Lament for Ch'ü Yüan," which read:

> With awe I receive the imperial blessing,
> And await chastisement at Ch'ang-sha.
> I have heard men tell of Ch'ü Yüan,
> And how he drowned himself in the Mi-lo.
> I have come, and to Hsiang's flowing waters
> With reverence entrust this lament for the Master.[15]
> You met with the evil ones of the world
> And they have destroyed this body.
> Pitiful, alas,
> That you should fall upon such days.
> Hidden are the phoenixes from sight,
> While kites and owls flap abroad.
> Now the dullard gains favor and fame;
> The slanderer and the toady have their way.
> The wise and sage they turn aside;
> The righteous they have toppled over.
> Now the world calls Po-i greedy
> And speaks of the purity of Robber Chih;
> The blade Mu-yeh, they say, is dull,
> And praise for keenness knives of lead.[16]
> (Alas, Master, I am dumb—
> You, who were without fault!)
> Cast aside are the cauldrons of Chou;
> Pots of clay are what men hold precious now.
> Wearied oxen draw the carriages;
> To the chariot the lame nag is harnessed up,
> While the fine-blooded stallion droops his ears
> And plods before a wagon of salt.
> The caps of state are trod underfoot—
> Confusion cannot be far off!

[15] Hsiang was the name of the upper part of the Mi-lo River. In what follows Chia I, while relating the misfortunes of Ch'ü Yüan, is at the same time lamenting his own fall from favor.

[16] Po-i, who gave away his kingdom to his younger brother, is the symbol of purity and unselfishness, as Robber Chih is that of evil and violence. Mu-yeh is a famous sword of ancient times.

Ah, bitter, my Master,
That you met with this sorrow!

Reprise:
"It is over.
There is none in the kingdom who knows me!" [17]
Alone in my woe,
To whom shall I speak?
Lightly the phoenix soars aloft;
Far off he withdraws, he departs.
The holy dragons of the nine-fold depths
Conceal their rareness in fathomless tides;
Deep their iridescence hide
Where leech and mudworm cannot bore.[18]
The shining virtue of the sage
Must shut itself far from the filth of the world.
If the unicorn be leashed,
How does he differ from dog or ram?
Hesitation brought you to this fate;
Was this not the sin of my lord?
Roaming the nine lands to save your prince,
Must you yet long for the capital?
To the rarest heights the phoenix soars;
Alights where the light of virtue shines.
Spying the snares of petty goodness,
He beats his wings and flies away.
How in this shallow, mud-clogged fen
Should swim the giants of the sea?
The whale, stranded on the river shoals,
Ants and crickets feed upon!

Three years after Chia I became grand tutor to the king of Ch'ang-sha a hoot-owl one day flew into his lodge and perched on the corner of his mat. The people of the south call this type of owl a *fu*. Chia I had been disgraced and sent to live in Ch'ang-sha, a damp, low-lying region, and he believed that he did not have long to live. He was filled

[17] A quotation from Ch'ü Yüan's poem the "Li Sao" or "Encountering Sorrow."

[18] Worms, ants, and other insects, as well as owls and kites, are symbols of petty-minded slanderers, as phoenixes, unicorns, dragons, and whales are those of the pure and virtuous.

with horror and grief at the appearance of the bird and, to console himself, composed a poem in the rhyme-prose style which read:

> In the year of *tan-o*,
> Fourth month, first month of summer [June, 174 B.C.],
> On the day *kuei-tzu*, when the sun was low in the west,
> An owl came to my lodge
> And perched on the corner of my mat,
> Phlegmatic and fearless.
> Secretly wondering the reason
> The strange thing had come to roost,
> I sought a book to divine it,
> And the oracle told me its secret:
> > "Wild bird enters the hall;
> > The master will soon depart."
> I asked and importuned the owl,
> "Where is it I must go?
> Do you bring good luck? Then tell me!
> Misfortune? Relate what disaster!
> Must I depart so swiftly?
> Then speak to me of the hour!"
> The owl breathed a sigh,
> Raised its head, and beat its wings.
> Its beak could utter no word,
> But let me tell you what it sought to say: [19]
> All things alter and change;
> Never a moment of ceasing.
> Revolving, whirling, and rolling away;
> Driven far off and returning again;
> Form and breath passing onward,
> Like the mutations of a cicada.
> Profound, subtle, and illimitable,
> Who can finish describing it?
> Good luck must be followed by bad;
> Bad in turn bow to good.
> Sorrow and joy throng the gate;
> Weal and woe in the same land.

[19] The passage which follows contains many ideas and phrases taken from the works of the famous Taoist philosopher Chuang Tzu, and is one of the best-known expressions of early Han Taoist thought.

Wu was powerful and great;
Under Fu-ch'a it sank in defeat.
Yüeh was crushed at K'uai-chi,
But Kou-chien made it an overlord.
Li Ssu, who went forth to greatness, at last
Suffered the five mutilations.
Fu Yüeh was sent into bondage,
Yet Wu-ting made him his aide.[20]
Thus fortune and disaster
Entwine like the strands of a rope.
Fate cannot be told of,
For who shall know its ending?
Water, troubled, runs wild;
The arrow, quick-sped, flies far.
All things, whirling and driving,
Compelling and pushing each other, roll on.
The clouds rise up, the rains come down,
In confusion inextricably joined.
The Great Potter fashions all creatures,
Infinite, boundless, limit unknown.
There is no reckoning Heaven,
Nor divining beforehand the Tao.
The span of life is fated;
Man cannot guess its ending.
Heaven and Earth are the furnace,
The workman, the Creator;
His coal is the yin and the yang,
His copper, all things of creation.
Joining, scattering, ebbing and flowing,
Where is there persistence or rule?
A thousand, a myriad mutations,
Lacking an end's beginning.
Suddenly they form a man:

[20] Wu and Yüeh were rival states in the southeast during pre-Ch'in times, and Fu-ch'a and Kou-chien the rulers who led them to defeat and glory respectively. Li Ssu, prime minister to the First Emperor of the Ch'in, was later overthrown by a rival at court and executed. Wu-ting was a king of the ancient Shang dynasty who dreamed of a worthy minister and later discovered the man of his dream in an ex-convict laborer, Fu Yüeh.

How is this worth taking thought of?
They are transformed again in death:
Should this perplex you?
The witless takes pride in his being,
Scorning others, a lover of self.
The man of wisdom [21] sees vastly
And knows that all things will do.
The covetous run after riches,
The impassioned pursue a fair name;
The proud die struggling for power,
While the people long only to live.
Each drawn and driven onward,
They hurry east and west.
The great man is without bent;
A million changes are as one to him.
The stupid man chained by custom
Suffers like a prisoner bound.
The sage abandons things
And joins himself to the Tao alone,
While the multitudes in delusion
With desire and hate load their hearts.
Limpid and still, the true man
Finds his peace in the Tao alone.
Transcendent, destroying self,
Vast and empty, swift and wild,
He soars on wings of the Tao.
Borne on the flood he sails forth;
He rests on the river islets.
Freeing his body to Fate,
Unpartaking of self,
His life is a floating,
His death a rest.
In stillness like the stillness of deep springs,
Like an unmoored boat drifting aimlessly,
Valuing not the breath of life,
He embraces and drifts with Nothing.
Comprehending Fate and free of sorrow,

---

[21] "Man of wisdom," "great man," "true man," and "man of virtue" are Taoist terms for the sage who has reached perfect understanding.

> The man of virtue heeds no bonds.
> Petty matters, weeds and thorns—
> What are they to me?

A year or so after this Chia I was summoned to the capital for an audience with the emperor. At the time of the audience Emperor Wen was seated in the Great Hall of the Eternal Palace receiving the remainders of the sacrificial meats from the various shrines, and his mind was accordingly filled with thoughts of the gods and spirits. He questioned Chia I about the nature of spiritual beings, and Chia I explained the matter to him in great detail, talking far into the night while the emperor leaned forward on his mat in rapt attention. After he had dismissed Chia I he said, "I have not seen Master Chia for a long time. I used to think I knew more than he, but now I see I am no match for him!"

Shortly afterwards he appointed Chia I to the post of grand tutor to Liu Chi, King Huai of Liang. King Huai of Liang was the youngest son of Emperor Wen. His father loved him dearly, and the boy himself was fond of literature, and it was for these reasons that the emperor selected Chia I to be his tutor.

Later, when Emperor Wen enfeoffed the four sons of Liu Ch'ang, King Li of Huai-nan, as marquises, Chia I remonstrated with him, fearing that trouble would arise from such a move. From time to time he sent memorials to the throne pointing out that some of the marquises held territories spreading over several adjoining provinces, a situation which was not in accord with the practices of antiquity, and suggesting that the size of their territories be somewhat reduced, but Emperor Wen took no heed of his proposals.

Several years after Chia I's appointment as tutor to King Huai of Liang the king was out riding one day and fell from his horse and was killed. He left no heir. Chia I blamed himself for having failed to carry out his duties as tutor properly, lamenting bitterly at the king's death, and in a year or so he himself died. He was then thirty-three years old. After Emperor Wen passed away, when Emperor Wu came to the throne,[22] he appointed Chia I's two grandsons as governors of

---

[22] The text reads as though Emperor Wu succeeded Emperor Wen, though in fact the reign of Emperor Ching intervened.

provinces. One of these, Chia Chia, is a man of great learning and is carrying on the traditions of the family. He has often exchanged letters with me. (In the time of Emperor Chao, Chia Chia became a high official.) [23]

The Grand Historian remarks: At first when I read Ch'ü Yüan's "Encountering Sorrow," "Heavenly Questions," "Summons of the Soul," and "Grieving for Ying," I was moved to pity by his determination, and at times when I visited Ch'ang-sha and viewed the deep waters where he had drowned himself, I could never keep from shedding tears and trying to imagine what sort of person he was. Later, when I read the lament which Chia I wrote for him, I began to wonder why a man with the ability of Ch'ü Yüan who, if he had chosen to serve some other lord, would have been welcomed anywhere, should have brought such an end upon himself! [24] Faced with the rhyme-prose on the owl, in which Chia I regards death as the same as life and makes light of all worldly success, I find myself utterly at a loss for words!

[23] Emperor Chao succeeded Emperor Wu in 87 B.C. It is highly unlikely that Ssu-ma Ch'ien was still alive at the time and the sentence in parentheses is almost certainly a later addition.

[24] The reader will recall that, in his "Lament for Ch'ü Yüan" above, Chia I censures Ch'ü Yüan for continuing his attempts to enlighten the king of Ch'u when it was apparent that his advice was not being heeded. One should also remember that Ssu-ma Ch'ien, when he was imprisoned by Emperor Wu, failed to take his own life, as was customary in such cases, preferring to suffer disgrace so that he could complete his history, and he is therefore very touchy on the subject of suicide.

Shih chi 101: The Biographies of Yüan Ang and Ch'ao Ts'o

For the sake of their duty to the ruler, they did not hesitate to speak out in the face of displeasure; they gave no thought to their own safety, but laid long-range plans for the state. Thus I made The Biographies of Yüan Ang and Ch'ao Ts'o.

Yüan Ang

Yüan Ang, whose polite name was Yüan Ssu, was a native of Ch'u. His father had at one time been a member of a robber band, but later moved to An-ling.[1] During the reign of Empress Lü, Yüan Ang became a retainer of Lü Lu, and after Emperor Wen came to the throne, on the recommendation of his older brother Yüan K'uai, he was made a palace attendant.

At this time Chou P'o, the marquis of Chiang, was acting as chancellor. As soon as court was over Chou P'o used to hurry out of the palace with an air of great importance and the emperor, who treated him with extreme deference, would always sit watching him until he had left the room.[2]

One day Yüan Ang stepped forward from his place and asked, "In Your Majesty's opinion, what sort of man is the chancellor?"

"He is a veritable guardian of the altars of the nation," replied the emperor.

"Chou P'o may indeed be termed a worthy minister," said Yüan Ang, "but he is no guardian of the nation. A true guardian of the nation will serve his lord while his lord lives, but if his lord should perish he will perish with him. In the time of Empress Lü the members

---

[1] Powerful provincial families or other elements in the population which threatened the security of the government were often forced to move to the towns near the capital established around the tombs of the emperors, where the officials could keep a closer watch on them. An-ling was the tomb town of Emperor Hui.

[2] Following the reading in *Han shu* 49.

of the Lü family wielded power in the government and arbitrarily made themselves kings and ministers, so that the life of the Liu dynasty hung by a thread. At that time Chou P'o was grand commandant and was in charge of the military, and yet he was not able to remedy the situation. After Empress Lü passed away, when the high officials plotted to overthrow the Lü clan, Chou P'o, because of his office as grand commandant, happened to win a measure of success. Therefore I say he may be termed a worthy minister, but hardly a guardian of the altars of the nation. He appears before his ruler with an arrogant air, while Your Majesty is polite and yielding, so that the proper etiquette between ruler and subject is turned upside down. For Your Majesty's sake may I make bold to suggest that such a situation is unacceptable."

After this the emperor behaved with greater austerity in court, and Chou P'o approached him with increasing awe. From this time on Chou P'o came to hate Yüan Ang. "Your brother and I are good friends, and yet now you are trying to destroy my reputation at court!" he complained, but Yüan Ang refused to offer any apology.

After Chou P'o retired from the position of chancellor and returned to his territory in Chiang one of the natives of the place sent a report to the throne that Chou P'o was planning to revolt. Chou P'o was summoned and brought in chains to the inquiry room, but not one of the court officials or members of the imperial family dared to speak a word in his defense. Only Yüan Ang pleaded for him and proved that he was not guilty. His eventual release was due entirely to the efforts of Yüan Ang, and after this the two became close friends.

When Liu Ch'ang, the king of Huai-nan and younger brother of Emperor Wen, came to the capital to pay his respects, he killed Shen I-chi, the marquis of Pi-yang, and conducted himself with the utmost arrogance. Yüan Ang warned the emperor, "If the feudal lords are allowed to become too arrogant, they will surely breed mischief. It would be well to punish him by depriving him of part of his territory."

But Emperor Wen refused to listen to this advice, and the king of Huai-nan became increasingly high-handed. Later, it was discovered that the heir of Ch'ai Wu,[3] the marquis of Chi-p'u, was plotting revolt; he was brought to trial, and investigation revealed that the king

[3] Elsewhere called Ch'en Wu.

of Huai-nan was implicated in the plot. The emperor summoned the king from his territory and ordered him exiled to Shu, imprisoning him in a caged cart and sending him by post relay.

Yüan Ang, who at this time was general of the palace attendants, admonished the emperor, saying, "Your Majesty originally encouraged the king of Huai-nan in his arrogant ways and made no attempt to curb him, until affairs reached this pass. Now with sudden severity you have struck him down. The king of Huai-nan is a man of implacable spirit. If, exposed to the cold and damp of the road, he should die along the way, it would appear that Your Majesty, with the vast expanse of the empire at your command, could not bear to grant him a single place of rest! What if you should incur the name of a fratricide?"

But the emperor refused to listen and sent the king of Huai-nan on his way. When the king reached Yung he fell ill and died. Informed of his death, the emperor refused to eat and gave himself up to the bitterest lamentations. Yüan Ang came before him and, bowing his head, begged pardon for not having urged his counsel more strongly.

"All of this happened because I did not listen to your words," said the emperor.

"Your Majesty must take heart," said Yüan Ang. "The thing has already happened. What good is there in regrets? Moreover, Your Majesty has on three occasions displayed conduct far above the standard of the age. This present affair is not important enough to efface the fair name you have earned in the past."

"And what are these three examples of outstanding conduct?" asked the emperor.

"When Your Majesty was still king of Tai your mother, the queen dowager, was ill for three years. During that time you did not shut your eyes in sleep, you did not doff your robes; no broth of herbs was presented to her until you in person had tasted it. Even Tseng Ts'an, the paragon of filial piety in ancient times, though only a commoner, could hardly have done as much. Yet you, a king, behaved in such a way, far surpassing the filial piety of Tseng Ts'an. Again, when the Lü family dominated the throne and the high ministers wielded power at their pleasure, Your Majesty journeyed to the capital from Tai in a party of only six relay carriages, hastening into what lair of dangers you knew not. Even the heroes of antiquity Meng Pen and Hsia Yü could not match such bravery. Finally, when you had reached the state residence of Tai you faced west and declined twice to accept the throne and, facing south, declined it three times again. Hsü Yu in ancient times declined such an offer once, we are told, but Your Majesty surpassed him by four times.

"When you exiled the king of Huai-nan to Shu it was your intention merely to humble his spirit and lead him to reform his ways. It was only because of the laxity of the officials who were guarding him that he fell ill and died."

His grief somewhat assuaged, the emperor asked, "What should I do now?"

"The king of Huai-nan left three sons," replied Yüan Ang. "Their fate is in Your Majesty's hands."

Emperor Wen proceeded to make kings of the three sons of Liu Ch'ang. Because of the incident, Yüan Ang's name commanded even greater respect at court.

Yüan Ang was a man of fierce loyalty and was motivated in all his conduct by the highest principles. It happened that there was a eunuch named Chao T'an who, because of his knowledge of numerology, had gained favor with Emperor Wen. This man took every opportunity to speak ill of Yüan Ang, until Yüan Ang began to fear that some misfortune would befall him. Yüan Chung, the son of Yüan Ang's elder brother, was a horseman in the emperor's retinue and used to bear the imperial credentials and accompany the emperor's carriage. He advised his uncle, saying, "You had best have an open conflict with Chao T'an and shame him before the court, so that the emperor will pay no more attention to his slander."[4] Accordingly, when Emperor Wen left the palace one day in his carriage accompanied by Chao T'an, Yüan Ang prostrated himself before the carriage and said, "I have always been told that only the most distinguished men of the empire are privileged to ride with the Son of Heaven in his six-foot carriage of

---

[4] That is, after such an incident the emperor will assume that any attacks Chao T'an might make on you are motivated by personal dislike and pay no further attention to them.

state. Now although the Han may be lacking in worthy men, I cannot imagine why Your Majesty would deign to ride in the same carriage with a man who is no more than a remnant of the knife and saw!"[5]

The emperor laughed and ordered Chao T'an to get down from the carriage. Weeping bitterly, Chao T'an descended.

Another time Emperor Wen had ridden in his carriage to the top of the hill at Pa-ling and was proposing to gallop down the steep slope to the west. Yüan Ang, accompanying the emperor on horseback, stood by the emperor's carriage, pulling at the reins of the emperor's horses. "What is the matter, General Yüan?" asked the emperor. "Are you afraid?"

"I have heard people say," replied Yüan Ang, "that the heir to an estate of a thousand pieces of gold should not sit on the edge of a porch for fear he might fall off; that the heir to an estate of a hundred gold pieces should not lean on the railings for fear they might break; and that the sacred ruler of the nation should not court danger in his carriage and trust all to mere good luck! Now Your Majesty proposes to gallop down a steep slope in a carriage drawn by six horses. If the horses should become frightened and the carriage upset, you may think what might happen to you of little importance, but what of your duty to the ancestral temple of your father and to your mother?" The emperor gave up the idea.

Emperor Wen was one time paying a visit to the Shang-lin Park, accompanied by the empress and his favorite concubine, Lady Shen. In the inner rooms of the palace it was customary for the empress and Lady Shen to sit side by side on the same mat as though they were equals and, when the party came to take their seats in the park, the official in charge of the arrangements spread the mats in the usual fashion. But Yüan Ang pulled Lady Shen's mat back a little way from that of the empress. Lady Shen was furious and refused to take her seat, and the emperor, also in a rage, got up and went back to the palace. When the opportunity presented itself Yüan Ang appeared before the emperor and said, "I have heard it said that only when the proper hierarchical distinctions are observed is there harmony between superiors and inferiors. Now Your Majesty has already chosen an em-

---

[5] A term of contempt for eunuchs.

press, while Lady Shen is no more than a concubine. How is it possible that a concubine and her mistress should sit side by side? Your Majesty is pleased with Lady Shen and naturally you wish to shower her with favors. But though you believe you are doing it for her sake, you may in fact be bringing disaster upon her. Has Your Majesty alone not seen the 'human pig'?" [6]

The emperor was pleased with his words and, summoning Lady Shen, explained the situation to her. She in turn rewarded Yüan Ang with a gift of fifty catties of gold. Yüan Ang continued to admonish the emperor from time to time in this outspoken fashion, however, so that he was not permitted to stay for long at court, but was transferred to the position of colonel of Lung-hsi province. He treated the soldiers under his command with great compassion, and there was not one who would have hesitated to die for him. He was transferred to the position of prime minister of Ch'i, and later to that of prime minister of Wu. When he was taking leave to go to this last appointment his nephew Yüan Chung said to him, "Liu P'i, the king of Wu, has for a long time grown more overbearing each day, and his kingdom is guilty of numerous irregularities. But if now you should attempt to expose him and bring order, he would either send some slanderous report to the emperor about you, or dispatch you at once with the point of a sword! The kingdom of Wu lies in the south, a damp and swampy region. You must take care to drink and eat your daily fill, and not worry yourself about other things. From time to time you may urge the king not to revolt, and that is all. If you do this, you may be fortunate enough to escape harm!"

Yüan Ang did as his nephew suggested, and was treated with favor by the king of Wu. After some time he was granted permission to return to the capital for a visit. In the street he happened to meet the chancellor, Shen-t'u Chia. Yüan Ang descended from his carriage and went over to greet the chancellor, but Shen-t'u Chia merely acknowledged the greeting without getting down from his own carriage. Yüan Ang returned to his company, filled with embarrassment at the insult he had suffered before the eyes of his own officials. He went at once to

---

[6] A reference to Lady Ch'i, the favorite concubine of Emperor Kao-tsu who, after the death of the emperor, was horribly mutilated by Empress Lü and contemptuously titled the "human pig." See "The Annals of Empress Lü" above.

the office of the chancellor, where he sent in his name card and requested an interview with Shen-t'u Chia. After keeping him waiting for a long time the chancellor granted him an interview. Yüan Ang knelt before the chancellor and said, "I would like to speak to you in private."

"If what you have to say concerns some public matter, you may go to the proper office and discuss it with my secretary or one of the clerks, and in due time I will present your report to the throne. But if you have come on private business, you should know that I do not discuss matters of a private nature!"

Still kneeling before him, Yüan Ang said, "Now that you have become chancellor, do you consider yourself the equal of your predecessors in office, Ch'en P'ing and Chou P'o?"

"Surely not," replied Shen-t'u Chia.

"Fine. So you admit you are not their equal. Ch'en P'ing and Chou P'o were both outstanding statesmen and generals. They assisted Emperor Kao-tsu in the conquest of the empire, and later overthrew the Lü clan and rescued the imperial family from peril. You began your career, I believe, as a crossbow man, and were transferred to the position of head of a battalion. Later, because of your services, you managed to become governor of Huai-yang, but I do not recall that you won any distinction for farsighted strategies or exploits on the field of battle.

"Since the present emperor arrived from Tai to take the throne, he has always listened to the reports of the various palace attendants and officials whenever he appeared in court. I have never known him to refuse to stop his carriage to listen to a word from one of them. If the suggestion is of no worth, he merely sets it aside; but if it proves to be sound, he always puts it into effect, and never fails to commend the person who gave it. Why is this? Because he hopes thereby to attract to the court the wisest and most worthy men of the empire. Each day that he hears something he had not heard before, or learns something that until then he was ignorant of, he increases his august wisdom. And yet now you would put a gag into the mouths of the empire, so that each day you grow more ignorant. If so wise a ruler were to reprimand so ignorant a minister, I fear disaster would not be long in coming to you!"

Shen-t'u Chia bowed to Yüan Ang several times. "I am a stupid man," he said. "I did not realize that you would be kind enough to teach me my errors." And he led Yüan Ang into his rooms and placed him in the seat of honor.

Yüan Ang had always been on bad terms with Ch'ao Ts'o. Whenever Ch'ao Ts'o came into a room and sat down Yüan Ang would get up and leave, and whenever Yüan Ang sat down Ch'ao Ts'o would leave; the two men would never sit talking in the same room together. After Emperor Wen passed away and Emperor Ching came to the throne Ch'ao Ts'o was made imperial secretary. He sent his officials to investigate charges that Yüan Ang had accepted bribes from the king of Wu, and had Yüan Ang convicted, but the emperor issued an edict pardoning him and demoting him to the rank of commoner.

When news came that the kings of Wu and Ch'u had revolted Ch'ao Ts'o summoned his clerks and secretaries and told them, "Yüan Ang accepted a number of gifts of money from the king of Wu and exerted all his efforts to cover up the king's evil doings, insisting that he had no thoughts of rebellion. Now, as it turns out, he has revolted. I want you to have Yüan Ang brought up for examination. He probably knows all about the plot to rebel."

But his clerks replied, "Before the revolt broke out, we might have been able to forestall it by examining Yüan Ang. But by now the rebel armies are already marching west toward the capital. What profit would there be now in an investigation? Anyway it is hardly likely that he had any part in the plot."

Ch'ao Ts'o hesitated and had not yet decided what course to take when someone reported the affair to Yüan Ang. Fearful of what might happen, Yüan Ang went at night to see Tou Ying, relating to him the causes of the revolt and begging him to appear before the emperor and explain the situation in person. Tou Ying went to the emperor and spoke to him as Yüan Ang had asked, whereupon the emperor sent for Yüan Ang to come to see him. Ch'ao Ts'o was with the emperor at the time but, when Yüan Ang requested that the others be sent away and he be granted a private interview, Ch'ao Ts'o, much to his anger, was forced to withdraw from the room. Yüan Ang then reported in full the reasons why the king of Wu had revolted, laying the blame entirely on Ch'ao Ts'o. "If only Ch'ao Ts'o were executed at once and apologies made to the king of Wu, then he would surely halt his armies," he concluded. (A fuller account will be found in the chapter on the king of Wu.)

The emperor appointed Yüan Ang as master of ritual and made Tou Ying a general in chief. The two men had long been friends, and now that the kingdom of Wu was in revolt, wealthy men from the various tomb towns around the capital, as well as distinguished officials of Ch'ang-an, flocked to join the two, so that the carriages in their train increased by several hundred each day.

After the emperor had executed Ch'ao Ts'o he sent Yüan Ang to the state of Wu as master of ritual. The king of Wu wanted to make Yüan Ang one of his generals but, when Yüan Ang refused to consent, he decided to kill him and sent one of his colonels with a body of five hundred men to surround Yüan Ang and keep him under guard in the midst of the army camp.

Some years before, when Yüan Ang was acting as prime minister of Wu, one of his subordinate officials was carrying on a secret affair with a maidservant of Yüan Ang's. Yüan Ang learned of the romance, but mentioned it to no one and continued to treat the official as before. Someone warned the man that his master knew all about his intrigue with the servant girl, whereupon he attempted to run away. But Yüan Ang galloped after him in person and later presented him with the girl and restored him to his official position. Now, when Yüan Ang was being held prisoner by the king of Wu, it happened that this same official was acting as marshal to the colonel who was in charge of guarding Yüan Ang. The marshal proceeded to trade all of his uniforms and possessions for two large measures of rich wine, which he passed out among the soldiers guarding the southwest sector of the camp. The weather was cold and the soldiers were tired and hungry, and it was not long before they all fell into a drunken sleep. Then, under cover of darkness, the marshal roused Yüan Ang and said, "Now is your chance to escape! The king of Wu has given orders to execute you tomorrow at dawn!"

"But who are you?" asked Yüan Ang incredulously.

"I am the official who used to serve under you and was carrying on a secret affair with your maid," replied the marshal.

Yüan Ang was astonished but declined to take the opportunity to escape. "Your parents, I trust, are still alive. I could not bear to have you and your family involved in trouble on my account."

"Just go!" said the marshal. "After you are gone I will run away too and see to it that my parents escape into hiding. What is there for you to worry about?" Then he took a knife and, cutting a hole in the tent, led Yüan Ang out past the drunken soldiers and directly out of the camp, where the two of them parted. Yüan Ang removed the oxtail pennant from his staff of office and hid it in his breast and, using the staff as a cane, walked along the road for seven or eight *li*. At dawn he met some riders from the loyal armies of Liang, who carried him off on their horses. Eventually he returned to the capital and reported on his mission.

After the rebellion of Wu and Ch'u had been put down the emperor set up Liu Li, the marquis of P'ing-lu and the son of Liu Chiao, King Yüan of Ch'u, as king of Ch'u, and appointed Yüan Ang to be his prime minister. Yüan Ang sent reports to the throne containing various recommendations, but his advice was never listened to and, because of illness, he was relieved of his post. After this he retired to his home in An-ling, where he mingled freely with the people of the neighborhood and joined them in cockfighting and dog racing. Chü Meng of Lo-yang [7] once came to visit him, and Yüan Ang received him with great courtesy. A certain rich man of An-ling remarked to Yüan Ang on this. "I have heard that Chü Meng is a gambler. I cannot imagine why a man like you, General Yüan, would have anything to do with him!"

"He may be a gambler," replied Yüan Ang, "but when his mother died the carriages of over a thousand guests appeared to attend her funeral. So he must be something more than an ordinary man. Moreover, everyone sooner or later finds himself in serious trouble. But if one morning you were to go with your troubles and knock on Chü Meng's gate, he would not put you off with excuses about responsibility to his parents, or try to avoid the issue because of the danger to himself. The only men you can really count on in the world today are

---

[7] One of the local "bosses" in the area of Lo-yang. See "The Biography of Liu P'i, the King of Wu," above.

Chi Hsin[8] and Chü Meng! Now you go about with a retinue of several horsemen, but if some day you find yourself in difficulty, do you think they will be any help to you?" So he railed at the rich man and refused to have anything further to do with him. When people heard of the incident they admired Yüan Ang more than ever.

Although Yüan Ang lived at home in retirement, Emperor Ching from time to time sent men to consult him on questions of government policy. Liu Wu, the king of Liang and younger brother of Emperor Ching, tried to have himself designated heir to the throne but, after Yüan Ang advised against it, all talk of such a move came to an end. Because of this the king of Liang bore Yüan Ang a deep hatred and even sent a man to assassinate him. When the assassin reached the area within the Pass and began to inquire about Yüan Ang, he found that everyone he asked praised Yüan Ang and could not say enough in his favor. Finally he went to see Yüan Ang himself and said, "I have received money from the king of Liang to come and kill you but, because you are a worthy man, I cannot bear to carry out my charge. There will be ten or twelve others coming after me, though, to see that the deed is done! You must be prepared!"

Yüan Ang grew very uneasy, and in addition to this all sorts of strange things began to happen in his house, until finally he went to the home of Master P'ei, a diviner, to inquire what the future held. On his way home the other assassins, who had come from Liang as the man had predicted, surrounded him and stabbed him to death outside the city gate of An-ling.

Ch'ao Ts'o

Ch'ao Ts'o was a native of Ying-ch'uan. He studied the Legalist doctrines of Shen Pu-hai and Shang Yang at the home of Master Chang Hui in Chih, where he was a fellow student of Sung Meng and Liu Li of Lo-yang. Because of his learning he was made a custodian of ancient affairs under the master of ritual. As a person Ch'ao Ts'o was always very severe and outspoken.

At this time, during the reign of Emperor Wen, there was no one

---

[8] Another well-known "boss" in the area within the Pass and younger brother of Chi Pu. See "The Biography of Chi Pu," above.

in the empire who knew much about the *Book of Documents*. Only one man, a Master Fu of Chi-nan, who had formerly been an erudit under the Ch'in dynasty, was said to have a thorough knowledge of the classic, but Master Fu was already over ninety and too old to summon to court. The emperor therefore ordered the master of ritual to send someone to receive instruction from the aged scholar. The master of ritual dispatched Ch'ao Ts'o, who went to the home of Master Fu and studied the *Book of Documents* with him. After his return to court Ch'ao Ts'o submitted a report to the throne recommending various improvements in the government, in which he quoted from the *Book of Documents* and praised the teachings of his master. The emperor appointed him as a retainer to the heir apparent, and in the course of time he rose to the position of gate keeper and eventually that of steward. He won great favor with the heir apparent because of his skill in discourse, and was referred to by the members of the prince's household as the "Wisdom Bag."

From time to time Ch'ao Ts'o submitted memorials to Emperor Wen urging that the territories of the feudal lords be reduced in size and the laws of the empire revised. In all he sent in over ten reports. Emperor Wen ignored the suggestions but, impressed by his ability, transferred him to the position of palace counselor. The heir apparent was strongly in favor of his ideas, but Yüan Ang and many of the other high officials disliked Ch'ao Ts'o.

When the heir apparent, Emperor Ching, ascended the throne, he made Ch'ao Ts'o the prefect of the capital. Ch'ao Ts'o often used to discuss matters of state with the emperor in private, and the emperor readily listened to his advice. Soon he enjoyed greater favor at court than the highest officials, and at his suggestion many changes were made in the laws of the empire.

The chancellor Shen-t'u Chia was deeply resentful of Ch'ao Ts'o, but did not have the means to strike back at him. It happened that the office of the prefect of the capital was situated within the outer wall of the mortuary temple of Kao-tsu's father, the Grand Supreme Emperor. There was a gate to the east but, because it was inconvenient to use, Ch'ao Ts'o had a second gate constructed on the south side, cutting a hole in the outer wall of the mortuary temple. When Shen-t'u Chia heard of this he was furious and decided to use the incident to trip up his enemy and to submit a petition to the emperor for Ch'ao Ts'o's execution. Ch'ao Ts'o got word of his plans and, visiting the emperor in private at night, explained his actions in full. Shen-t'u Chia in due time submitted his petition, accusing Ch'ao Ts'o of "piercing the wall of a mortuary temple in order to make a gate," and requesting that he be turned over to the commandant of justice for execution, but the emperor replied, "The wall in question is not the actual wall of the temple, but an outer wall separated from it by an open space. There has been no infringement of the law."

Shen-t'u Chia apologized for bringing up the matter and, when court was over, remarked angrily to his chief secretary, "I should have executed him first and reported the matter afterward. Instead I was mistaken enough to request permission, and gave the little upstart a chance to trick me!" Shortly afterwards Shen-t'u Chia fell ill and died.

After this Ch'ao Ts'o commanded even greater honor, and was transferred to the position of imperial secretary. He began to submit reports to Emperor Ching accusing the feudal lords of various crimes and recommending that their territories be reduced and the outlying provinces taken over by the central government. The emperor brought his recommendations before the high officials and the members of the aristocracy and imperial house for discussion, but none of them dared to express any opposition. Only Tou Ying spoke out against them, and because of this Ch'ao Ts'o and Tou Ying became enemies.

Ch'ao Ts'o succeeded in having thirty new statutes added to the laws, though the feudal lords, who hated Ch'ao Ts'o, unanimously opposed all of them. Ch'ao Ts'o's father, hearing of this, journeyed from Ying-ch'uan to the capital and spoke to his son. "Since the present emperor came to the throne, you have wielded great power in the government, but you have used it to trespass upon the feudal lords and deprive them of territory, bringing dissension between the ruler and his own kin. All men speak against you, and you have aroused bitter resentment in many quarters! Why do you persist in such a course?"

"What you say is quite true," replied Ch'ao Ts'o. "But if I did not take these measures the Son of Heaven would not receive the proper respect and the ancestral temples of the Liu family would be imperiled!"

"The Liu family is safe enough," said his father. "It is the Ch'ao family that is in peril! I will leave you now and go home."[9] Shortly after this he swallowed poison and died, declaring, "I cannot bear to sit by until disaster comes to me as well!"

Some ten days after his death, as the old man had feared, Wu, Ch'u, and the other states, seven in all, rose in revolt, their objective, they declared, being to force the execution of Ch'ao Ts'o. At the urging of Tou Ying and Yüan Ang, the emperor ordered Ch'ao Ts'o to put on his court robes and had him cut in two in the eastern market of the capital.

After the death of Ch'ao Ts'o there was a man named Lord Teng, the chief master of guests, who was sent as a commander to attack the armies of Wu and Ch'u. At the request of his superior general he returned to the capital to report to Emperor Ching on the progress of the campaign. When he appeared in audience the emperor said, "You have just come from the battle area. Now that the news of Ch'ao Ts'o's death has gone around, have the armies of Wu and Ch'u begun to retreat?"

"The king of Wu has been plotting revolt for twenty or thirty years," replied Lord Teng. "He was enraged over being deprived of territory and used the execution of Ch'ao Ts'o as an excuse for taking action. But it was not really Ch'ao Ts'o that he was concerned about. Moreover, with what has happened now, I fear that people in the empire will clamp their lips shut and no one will ever dare to speak out again!"

"Why do you say that?" asked the emperor.

"Ch'ao Ts'o was afraid that the feudal lords would become so powerful that they could no longer be held in check. Therefore he requested that their territories be diminished in size in order to increase the prestige of the central court. He was thinking of what benefits such a policy would bring in long years to come. But he had no sooner begun to put his plans into effect than he suddenly found himself the

---

[9] The word *kuei* in the original means both "to go home" and "to go to one's destination," i.e., to die.

victim of the direst penalty. Your Majesty is gagging the mouths of your own ministers in order to allay the hatreds of the feudal lords. Such a policy, if I may say so, is hardly to Your Majesty's benefit."

Emperor Ching was silent, and then after a long time he said, "You have spoken well. I regret what I did." He honored Lord Teng with the post of military commander of Ch'eng-yang.

Lord Teng was a native of Ch'eng-ku and was noted for his wealth of unusual ideas and schemes. During the era *chien-yüan* [140–135 B.C.], when Emperor Wu sent out a call for worthy men to take positions in the government, the high officials all recommended Lord Teng. Although Lord Teng had already retired from official life, he left his home and reentered government service, holding one of the most important posts. After a year he pleaded illness and once more returned to a life of retirement. His son Teng Hsiu was well known among the gentlemen of the time as a devotee of the teachings of the Yellow Emperor and Lao Tzu.

The Grand Historian remarks: Although Yüan Ang had no fondness for learning, he was clever at getting his point across. At heart he was a kind man, outspoken in his loyalty and devoted to the cause of duty. He was fortunate enough to serve during the time of Emperor Wen, when his talents were most suited to the age. But the following reign saw changes that were, for him, less fortunate, and though he made one recommendation at the time of the revolt of Wu and Ch'u, and it was carried out, it failed to have the desired effect of halting the rebellion. He was too fond of fame and boastful of his own worth, so that in the end his reputation suffered.

From the period when Ch'ao Ts'o was steward in the household of the heir apparent, he began from time to time to submit recommendations to the throne, though his suggestions were never followed. After he became able to wield power at will in the government he instituted a great many changes and innovations. The feudal lords vehemently opposed him, but instead of bending every effort to correct the situation and quiet the discord, he gave himself up to personal vindictiveness, so that in the end destruction fell upon himself. The proverb has it that:

> He who changes old ways
> Or meddles with custom
> Will suffer banishment
> If not death itself!

It refers, no doubt, to men like Ch'ao Ts'o.

Shih chi 102: The Biographies of Chang Shih-chih and Feng T'ang

They upheld the law without doing violence to larger principles; they discoursed on the worthy men of antiquity and increased the understanding of the ruler. Thus I made The Biographies of Chang Shih-chih and Feng T'ang.

Chang Shih-chih

The commandant of justice Chang Shih-chih, whose polite name was Chang Chi, was a native of Tu-yang. He lived at home with his elder brother Chang Chung. Because of the wealth of his family he was made a palace horseman [1] and served under Emperor Wen. In ten years of service, however, he failed to win any promotion and remained completely unknown. "I have been in government service for a long time and used up all of my brother's wealth, but I have accomplished nothing," he said and requested that he be relieved of his post so that he could return home. But the general of palace attendants Yüan Ang knew that he was a worthy man and hated to see him leave, so he arranged for him to be transferred to the post of master of guests.

After Chang Shih-chih had made his appearance in court and the usual ceremonies were over he stepped forward and began to speak to the emperor on matters of government policy. "I find your discourse somewhat too lofty," said Emperor Wen. "Would you mind lowering the tone and confining yourself to practical suggestions which can be put into effect at once?"

Chang Shih-chih accordingly began to speak of events of the Ch'in and Han, explaining at great length why the Ch'in dynasty failed and the Han was able to come to power. The emperor was pleased with

[1] Commentators disagree as to whether Chang Shih-chih actually used his wealth to purchase a position in the government, or whether the fact that he came from a wealthy family entitled him to such a post.

his words and rewarded him with the position of chief master of guests.

Chang Shih-chih once accompanied Emperor Wen on a visit to the Tiger Fold, the imperial zoo in the Shang-lin Park. The emperor questioned the keeper of the park about the list of birds and beasts that were housed in the zoo, asking some ten or twelve questions, but the keeper only looked about helplessly at his assistants, and no one was able to make any reply. At this point one of the workmen in the zoo who happened to be standing by began to speak in place of the keeper, answering all the emperor's inquiries about the animals. Making every effort to show off his ability, he replied promptly and with complete ease to each question the emperor put to him. "This is the way an official ought to be, is it not? The keeper is unfit for his post!" the emperor declared and ordered Chang Shih-chih to see to it that the workman was appointed director of the Shang-lin Park.

After some time Chang Shih-chih stepped forward and asked, "What does Your Majesty think of the marquis of Chiang, Chou P'o?"

"He is an excellent man," replied the emperor.

"And the marquis of Tung-yang, Chang Hsiang-ju?"

"He too is an excellent man."

"You have said that these two are excellent men, and yet both of them, when questioned on some matter, are frequently unable to give an immediate reply. Would you have them imitate this chattering workman with his glib tongue and ready answers? The First Emperor of the Ch'in entrusted his government to a lot of petty clerks, who outdid each other in enforcing the letter of the law and spying on people in order to enhance their own reputations. Their fault was that they cared only for outward appearances and had no real compassion for the people. As a result the emperor was never informed of his faults, and the situation continued to deteriorate until, in the time of the Second Emperor, the dynasty collapsed and its empire fell to pieces. Now if Your Majesty were suddenly to select this workman for an official position because of his clever talk, I am afraid that the world would be quick to see which way the wind is blowing and people would begin outdoing each other in glib chatter that has nothing to do with reality. The governed respond to the influence of their governors as swiftly as shadows or echoes. One must therefore be very careful in this matter of selecting men for office!"

"You are quite right," said the emperor, and canceled his order to make the workman an official. When the emperor returned to his carriage he invited Chang Shih-chih to ride with him and, as they drove slowly back to the palace, the emperor questioned him about the failings of the Ch'in dynasty. He was impressed with the good sense of Chang Shih-chih's words and, after they had returned to the palace, promoted him to the position of master of the public carriage.

Sometime after Chang Shih-chih's appointment to this post the heir apparent was visiting the court with his brother Liu Wu, the king of Liang. When they drove through the marshal's gate, the main gate of the palace, they failed to alight from their carriage. Chang Shih-chih, who was in charge of the gate, ran after them, halted their carriage, and refused to allow them to enter the inner gate to the reception hall. He promptly submitted a report to the throne accusing the two of lack of reverence because they had failed to alight from their carriage at the main gate. When word of the incident reached the emperor's mother, Empress Dowager Po, the emperor was obliged to visit his mother and, doffing his hat, apologize for the incident. "It is my fault," he said, "for failing to instruct my boys properly." The empress dowager then sent a messenger to receive an order from the emperor pardoning the heir apparent and his brother, and after this they were permitted to enter the court. Emperor Wen was much impressed by Chang Shih-chih's action and promoted him to the position of palace counselor. After some time Chang Shih-chih was advanced to the post of general of palace attendants.

Chang Shih-chih was one time accompanying the emperor on a visit to the hill at Pa-ling, which the emperor had selected as the site of his tomb. The emperor was seated on the northern slope of the hill, gazing out over the countryside, when he turned to his concubine, Lady Shen, who was attending him, and, pointing to the Hsin-feng road, said, "That is the road that goes to your native city of Han-tan!" Then, asking Lady Shen to play on the zither, he began to sing. His voice was sad and full of longing. Turning to his courtiers, he said, "Ah! if I could get some of the stones from those northern mountains to make my sarcophagus, and then fill up the seams with silk waste and seal it all with lacquer, I would have a coffin that no thief could break into!"[2]

"An excellent idea!" exclaimed the emperor's attendants, but Chang Shih-chih came forward and, pointing to the south, said, "If there are things in the tomb that men covet, then, although you were to seal up the whole of those southern mountains with iron, the thieves would still find some crack to enter by. But if you do not place such things inside the tomb, then you may dispense even with the stone coffin and there will be no danger of vandals." Emperor Wen was impressed by his words and later promoted him to the position of commandant of justice.

One time Emperor Wen had gone out on an excursion and was passing over the middle of the three bridges that span the Wei River, when a man suddenly ran out from under the bridge, startling the horses in the emperor's party. The emperor ordered his outriders to seize the man and hand him over to Chang Shih-chih, the commandant of justice. When Chang Shih-chih questioned him the man replied, "I come from the district around here and I was on my way to the capital when I heard the order to clear the road for the emperor, so I hid under the bridge. After a long while I supposed that the emperor had already passed over and I came out. Then I saw the carriages and horsemen and I started to run, that was all."

Chang Shih-chih sent a report to the emperor stating that the man was guilty of having violated the order to clear the roads and should be fined. "But this man actually startled my horses!" the emperor objected in a rage. "Fortunately my horses are very docile and even-natured, but if it had been any other horses, they might very well have upset the carriage and injured me! And yet you propose to let the fellow off with nothing but a fine?"

"The law must be upheld by the Son of Heaven and by everyone in the empire alike," replied Chang Shih-chih, "and that is the penalty the law prescribes. If I were to impose a heavier penalty in special cases,

---

[2] Grave robbing was a lucrative enterprise in ancient China and the emperor was concerned that his own tomb should not suffer this fate.

then the people would cease to have any faith in the laws. If at the time the incident occurred Your Majesty had ordered the man executed on the spot, then that would have been the end of the affair. But now the case has already been referred to me and, as commandant of justice, it is my responsibility to see that everyone in the empire is treated with absolute fairness. Should I once deviate from that standard of fairness, then the entire legal system of the empire would lose its impartiality and the people would be at a loss to know how to conduct themselves. May I ask Your Majesty to consider these consequences?"

After a long time the emperor replied, "The sentence which you propose is quite correct."

Some time after this a man was arrested for stealing one of the jade rings from the front of the seat in the mortuary temple of Emperor Kao-tsu. Emperor Wen was enraged and ordered the man hauled before the commandant of justice for trial. Chang Shih-chih looked up the statutes, charged the man with stealing the furnishings of a mortuary temple of the dynasty, and recommended that he be executed and his corpse exposed in the market place. "In stealing objects from the temple of the former emperor, this man is guilty of the most heinous offense!" said the emperor angrily. "I sent him to you expecting that you would recommend the death penalty for him and all the members of his family, but instead you recommend only the sentence prescribed by the statutes. This is hardly my idea of the proper respect to show for the ancestral temples of the dynasty!"

Chang Shih-chih removed his hat, bowed his head, and replied, "The sentence prescribed by the law is sufficient, I believe. Though actions such as these are all crimes, there are different degrees in the sacrilege of the offense. Now if Your Majesty were to execute this man and his family for having stolen objects from a funerary temple, then supposing by chance some ignorant person were to commit the even greater sacrilege of removing a handful of earth from the funeral mound of Emperor Kao-tsu at Ch'ang-ling?[3] There would in that case be no harsher penalty left to impose upon such an offender." Emperor

---

[3] The phrase "removing a handful of earth" is not to be taken literally, but is a euphemism for actual plundering of the grave.

Wen considered the matter for some time and, after discussing it with his mother, the empress dowager, decided to let Chang Shih-chih's recommendation stand.

At this time the marquis of T'iao, Chou Ya-fu, and the prime minister of Liang, the marquis of Shan-tu, Wang T'ien-k'ai, impressed with the fair way in which Chang Shih-chih administered justice, became friends with him, and it was not long before Chang Shih-chih's fame was known throughout the empire.

After Emperor Wen passed away and Emperor Ching came to the throne Chang Shih-chih, fearful of the consequences, pleaded illness, hoping that he would be relieved of his position. He was worried that he would be severely punished for the way he had reprimanded Emperor Ching when the latter was still heir apparent; he wanted to see the emperor in order to apologize in person, but did not know how to go about securing an audience. Eventually, using a plan suggested by Master Wang, he obtained an interview and made his apologies, and Emperor Ching took no action against him.

Master Wang was a devotee of the teachings of the Yellow Emperor and Lao Tzu, who lived in retirement. He was once summoned to court and, because he was a very old man, was allowed to sit down while the chancellor and the other high officials all stood about him. "My shoe is untied," he announced and, turning to Chang Shih-chih, the commandant of justice, said, "Tie my shoe for me, will you?" Chang Shih-chih knelt down and tied his shoe. After court was over someone asked Master Wang, "Why in the world did you humiliate the commandant of justice in front of the whole court by making him kneel down and tie your shoe?"

"I am an old man and in very humble circumstances," he replied, "and I doubt that there is anything I can ever do to help Chang Shih-chih. But Chang Shih-chih is now one of the most renowned officials in the empire, and so I thought that if I deliberately caused him a little humiliation by making him kneel and tie my shoe, then men would respect him even more." When they heard of the incident the people of the time admired Master Wang's wisdom and respected Chang Shih-chih for his humility.

Chang Shih-chih served Emperor Ching as commandant of justice but, after a year or so, was transferred to the position of prime minister to the king of Huai-nan. The emperor, it seems, was still annoyed with him for his former behavior. After some time Chang Shih-chih died.

His son was named Chang Chih or Chang Ch'ang-kung. He was given a post in the government and advanced as high as counselor, but he was dismissed because he could not accommodate himself to the ways of the time, and for the rest of his life held no official position.

Feng T'ang

Feng T'ang's grandfather was a native of the state of Chao. His father moved to Tai and later, after the Han dynasty came to power, moved again to the tomb town of An-ling. Because of his reputation for filial piety Feng T'ang was chosen to serve under Emperor Wen as head of the office of palace attendants. Emperor Wen was one day passing through the palace grounds in his palanquin when he stopped Feng T'ang and asked, "How did an old man like you happen to become a palace attendant? Where is your family from?"

When Feng T'ang told him all about his father and grandfather and how they had come from Chao the emperor said, "When I was still living in Tai my chief waiter Kao Ch'ü often used to tell me about what a fine man the Chao general Li Ch'i was, and describe to me the battle at Chü-lu.[4] Now I never sit down to a meal without thinking of that battle. Did your father know General Li Ch'i?"

"As a general Li Ch'i cannot be compared to Lien P'o and Li Mu,"[5] replied Feng T'ang.

"What makes you say that?" asked the emperor.

"When my grandfather lived in Chao he was a division general and was friendly with Li Mu, and later on when my father served as prime minister of Tai he was on close terms with Li Ch'i. So they had an opportunity to learn what sort of men both of them were."

The emperor had in the past often heard about what fine men Lien

---

[4] The great battle at Chü-lu, the capital of the state of Chao, between the Ch'in armies and the forces of Hsiang Yü and the other rebellious nobles. See above, "The Annals of Hsiang Yü."

[5] Two famous generals of the state of Chao in late Chou times whose biographies are recorded in *Shih chi* 81.

P'o and Li Mu had been and, slapping his thigh in delight at Feng T'ang's words, he cried, "Ah! If only I could find men like those two to be my generals now, I would have nothing more to worry about from the Hsiung-nu!"

"If I may say so," replied Feng T'ang, "though Your Majesty were to have Lien P'o and Li Mu themselves, you would not know how to use them properly."

The emperor was furious and hurried off at once to the inner palace. After some time he summoned Feng T'ang and upbraided him. "Why did you have to shame me in front of my attendants?" he asked. "Could you not wait until some time when there was no one around?"

"I am a worthless man," replied Feng T'ang, apologizing, "and I have no knowledge of the proper restraints to be observed."

At this time the Hsiung-nu had just made a new assault on the district of Ch'ao-na, invading with great force and killing Sun Ang, the military commander of Pei-ti Province, so that Emperor Wen had this problem of the barbarian invaders on his mind. After a while he began to question Feng T'ang again. "How do you know that I would not be able to make proper use of men like Lien P'o and Li Mu?" he asked.

"I have heard," said Feng T'ang, "that when the kings of ancient times sent off their generals to war, they knelt and, pushing the hub of their war chariots, said, 'The affairs within the threshold of the palace I shall direct, but anything beyond the threshold I leave to my generals!' The degree of merit which the fighters had achieved in battle, the titles and rewards they were to receive, were all decided by the generals in the field, and when they returned to court, they simply submitted a memorial to the king to this effect. And this is no mere empty tale of antiquity. My grandfather used to tell me that, when Li Mu was general of Chao and was camped on the border, the taxes from the markets set up in the army camp all went to secure provisions for his soldiers. Rewards were decided by the men in the field without interference from the court. The king of Chao entrusted full power to his general and held him responsible for the success of his mission, so that Li Mu was able to exercise to the full his wisdom and ability. The court supplied him with a picked force of thirteen hundred chariots, thirteen thousand horseman archers, and a hundred thousand of the bravest soldiers. With these he was able to drive out the Hsiung-nu ruler in the north, conquer the Eastern Barbarians, and destroy the Tan-lin tribes; in the west he succeeded in turning back the powerful forces of Ch'in and in the south held off the armies of Han and Wei, so that in his time the state of Chao came near to being one of the great powers of China. But later King Ch'ien, whose mother was a dancing girl, came to the throne of Chao. Heeding the slanders of his minister Kuo K'ai, he finally executed Li Mu and appointed Yen Chü in his place. As a result the soldiers on the northern border were defeated and the state was overrun and destroyed by Ch'in.

"Now I have happened to hear stories that Wei Shang, the governor of Yün-chung, uses all the taxes from his camp markets for the support of his men, and that he even lays out money from his private funds, slaughtering an ox once every five days to provide meat for his officers and men. This is the reason why the Hsiung-nu stay away from Yün-chung and do not dare to approach its borders. If any of them are so foolish as to invade the region, Wei Shang leads his horsemen in attacking and killing them in great numbers. But his men all come from peasant families, and were recruited into the army directly from the fields, so of course they know nothing about the proper forms for submitting battle reports. At the end of a day of hard fighting they report to headquarters the number of enemy heads cut off and prisoners taken; but if there is the slightest irregularity in the form of their reports, then the civil clerks claim that they are not following regulations and in the end, instead of the soldiers receiving their rewards, the clerks are upheld in the enforcement of the letter of the law. It is my humble opinion that Your Majesty's laws are too detailed, your rewards too meager, and your penalties too heavy. This same Wei Shang who was governor of Yün-chung has been reprimanded because of a discrepancy of six persons in his report on the number of enemy dead and prisoners. Your Majesty has had him tried before the law officials, and they have not only deprived him of his titles, but have imposed a penalty on him as well. That is the reason I say that, although Your Majesty were to have Lien P'o and Li Mu themselves as your generals, you would not know how to use them. However, I am a thoroughly ignorant man and am undoubtedly deserving of death for speaking out with such impertinence."

Emperor Wen was pleased with Feng T'ang's words and on the same day sent him with the imperial credentials to pardon Wei Shang and restore him to his post as governor of Yün-chung. He appointed Feng T'ang as a colonel of carriage and cavalry and put him in charge of the carriage fighters of the military commanders and of the provinces and kingdoms.

Seven years later Emperor Ching came to the throne and appointed Feng T'ang as prime minister of Ch'u. He was later relieved of the post. When Emperor Wu took the throne he sent out a call for worthy men and Feng T'ang was recommended, but by this time he was over ninety and could not again assume the duties of office, so the emperor instead selected his son Feng Sui to be a palace attendant. Feng Sui, whose polite name was Feng Wang-sun, was a man of unusual ability and a close friend of mine.

The Grand Historian remarks: Chang Shih-chih knew how to define a worthy man and to uphold the law without toadying to the will of the emperor, while Feng T'ang's discussions of the way to be a general—ah! they too have a flavor about them! The proverb says, "If you do not know a man, look at his friends." The sayings of these two men are worthy to be inscribed upon the walls of the court. In the *Book of Documents* it says, "Neither partial nor partisan, but broad and fair is the way of the king; neither partisan nor partial, but level and true is his way!" [6] Chang Shih-chih and Feng T'ang came near to this ideal.

[6] Found in the "Hung-fan" section of the *Book of Documents,* where the wording is slightly different.

Shih chi 103: The Biographies of Lord Wan-shih and Chang Shu

Loyal and noble, loving to their children and filial to their parents, slow in speech but earnest in conduct, serving with a becoming humility, they were true and worthy gentlemen. Thus I made The Biographies of Lord Wan-shih and Chang Shu.

Lord Wan-shih

The real name of Wan-shih-chün or Lord Ten Thousand Piculs was Shih Fen. His father was a native of Chao, but after the state of Chao was destroyed by the Ch'in dynasty, he moved to Wen. When Kao-tsu marched east to attack Hsiang Yü he passed through the region of Ho-nei where the Shih family was living, and Shih Fen, then only a lad of fifteen, became a minor official in the service of the future emperor. Kao-tsu questioned the boy and was much taken with his respectful manner. "How many are there in your family?" he asked, to which Shih Fen replied, "Of my parents, only my mother is living, and she, alas, is blind. Our family is very poor, but I have an older sister who is good at playing the zither!"

"Do you think you can become one of my followers?" asked Kao-tsu.

"If I may have the chance, I will do my best!" replied the boy. Kao-tsu then summoned his sister and made her a lady in waiting, and appointed Shih Fen as his page with the task of handling letters and visitors' name cards. Later the family moved to Ch'ang-an and lived in the quarter set aside for the families of the palace ladies. This was because Shih Fen's sister was a lady in waiting to Kao-tsu.

By the time of Emperor Wen, Shih Fen had advanced to the position of palace counselor because of his long and worthy service. He had no knowledge of literature, but in respectfulness of manner and circumspection he was unmatched by any in the court. During the reign of Emperor Wen the marquis of Tung-yang, Chang Hsiang-ju, who had been acting as grand tutor to the heir apparent, was relieved of his post, and the question arose of a suitable replacement. On the unanimous recommendation of the court, Shih Fen was appointed as the new tutor to the heir apparent. When the heir apparent, Emperor Ching, came to the throne, he advanced Shih Fen to one of the highest ministerial posts, but he soon found it irksome to have his former tutor so close at hand and transferred him to the post of prime minister to one of the feudal lords.

Shih Fen's eldest son was named Chien, his second son *chia,* his third son *i,*[1] and his fourth son Ch'ing. All were distinguished for their respectful manner and filial behavior, and they all advanced to positions in the government paying salaries of two thousand piculs of grain. Commenting on this, Emperor Ching remarked that "Lord Shih and his four sons all hold positions of the two thousand picul rank. The highest honors that a minister can enjoy have flocked to his gate!", and he gave Shih Fen the nickname of Wan-shih-chün or "Lord Ten Thousand Piculs."

During the latter years of Emperor Ching's reign Shih Fen retired on his salary as a high official and spent the remainder of his days at home, only attending court at certain times of the year to pay his respects. Whenever he passed the gate of the palace, he would always dismount from his carriage and hurry along on foot and, if he met the imperial equipage in the street, he always bowed from his carriage. When any of his sons or grandsons who were minor officials came home from court to pay a visit he would put on his court robes to receive them and would never address them by their familiar names. If his sons or grandsons had committed any fault, he would not scold them; instead he would retire to his own rooms and, when his meals were served, would sit in front of the table and refuse to eat until his other sons had upbraided the offenders and persuaded them to go with the eldest son and, baring their arms, apologize respectfully for their faults. If they corrected their faults, he always forgave them. If he was with any of his sons or grandsons who were old enough to wear

---

[1] Ssu-ma Ch'ien evidently did not know the names of the two middle sons and so has been obliged to call them simply *chia* and *i,* or, as we should say, "A" and "B."

the cap of manhood, although it might be an informal occasion, he would always put on his own cap.[2] His manner was relaxed, and with his servants he was pleasant and cheerful, but at all times circumspect. Whenever the emperor sent a gift of food to his family he would always bow his head respectfully before beginning to eat, as though he were actually in the presence of the emperor. At funerals he displayed a profound grief. His sons and grandsons honored his teachings and conducted themselves in the same way, so that his family was famous as far as the provinces for respectful and filial behavior. Even the Confucian scholars of Ch'i and Lu, who prided themselves on their conduct, all admitted that they were no match for the family of Lord Wan-shih.[3]

In the second year of the era *chien-yüan* [139 B.C.] the chief of palace attendants Wang Tsang was accused of some fault because of his literary activities.[4] Emperor Wu's grandmother, Grand Empress Dowager Tou, was of the opinion that Confucian scholars like Wang Tsang were strong on words but made a poor showing in actual conduct, whereas a family like that of Lord Wan-shih did little talking but put their moral principles into actual practice. On her advice the emperor appointed Lord Wan-shih's eldest son Shih Chien as chief of palace attendants. Lord Wan-shih's youngest son Shih Ch'ing he made prefect of the capital. Although by this time Shih Chien was old and white-haired, his father Lord Wan-shih was still in good health. Every five days, when his rest day came around, Shih Chien would leave the palace and return home to visit his father. At such times he would

[2] At the age of twenty, Chinese boys were "capped," a ceremony indicating that they had reached manhood.

[3] In this passage, and elsewhere in the chapter, Ssu-ma Ch'ien uses a number of phrases reminiscent of the descriptions of Confucius' conduct in the *Analects* to indicate how closely Shih Fen and his sons followed the example of the Master.

[4] Wang Tsang was a student of the *Book of Odes* and had been a tutor to Emperor Wu while he was still heir apparent. When Emperor Wu came to the throne in 140 B.C. Wang Tsang advised him to set up a *ming-t'ang* or "Bright Hall," the audience hall supposedly used by the rulers of antiquity. But the emperor's grandmother, Grand Empress Dowager Tou, was a devotee of Taoist teachings and used her influence to thwart the efforts of Wang Tsang and the emperor's other Confucian advisers.

always go to his own rooms and, summoning one of the servants in private, would have his father's undergarments brought to him. These he would wash out in person and then return them to the servant, instructing the servant not to inform his father of the matter. While he was acting as chief of palace attendants, if he felt that there was some matter which should be brought to the emperor's attention, he would dismiss the others from the room and speak very openly and sharply to the emperor, but when he appeared with the other ministers before the emperor in court, he seemed to be unable to say a word. For this reason the emperor treated him with warmth and respect.

Lord Wan-shih later moved his residence to another neighborhood of the capital, called Ling-li. His youngest son, Shih Ch'ing, who was prefect of the capital, came home drunk one time and failed to dismount from his carriage at the gate of the neighborhood. When Lord Wan-shih heard of this he refused to eat and, although Shih Ch'ing went to him in great fear and, baring his arms, begged forgiveness, his father would not accept his apologies. Finally all the members of the family, including his oldest brother Shih Chien, went and bared their arms in apology. "To be prefect of the capital is such an exalted position!" said their father, upbraiding them sarcastically. "When he comes in the gate, it is quite proper, I suppose, that the elders of the neighborhood should scurry out of his way, while the prefect rides at ease in his carriage!" After this he accepted their apologies and dismissed Shih Ch'ing. From then on, whenever Shih Ch'ing or any of the others of the family came through the gate of the neighborhood, they always dismounted and hurried to the house on foot.

Lord Wan-shih died in the fifth year of the era *yüan-so* [124 B.C.]. His eldest son Shih Chien, the chief of palace attendants, lamented bitterly and was so overcome with grief that he was barely able to walk with the aid of a staff. After a year or so Shih Chien also died. All of the sons and grandsons of Lord Wan-shih were noted for their filial conduct, but among them Shih Chien was the most exemplary, surpassing even Lord Wan-shih himself.

Once when Shih Chien was chief of palace attendants he had occasion to submit a report to the emperor. Later, after the report had been returned to him, he was reading it over, when he exclaimed in great alarm, "A mistake in writing! The character for 'horse' should have five lines for the feet and tail, but this has only four lines.⁵ One of the feet is missing! The emperor might have had me put to death for such an error!" He was just as cautious and meticulous as this in whatever he did.

Lord Wan-shih's youngest son Shih Ch'ing served for a while as master of carriage and was coachman for the emperor when he went out for drives. Once the emperor, seated in his carriage, asked Shih Ch'ing how many horses were pulling it. Shih Ch'ing carefully counted each horse with his whip, and only then did he hold up his fingers and reply, "Six horses." Shih Ch'ing was the most easygoing of all Lord Wan-shih's sons, but even he was as meticulous as this. Later, when he became prime minister of Ch'i, the people of Ch'i were so impressed by his family's reputation for fine conduct that he did not have to give any orders at all and the whole state was perfectly governed; the people of Ch'i even set up in his honor an altar called the Shrine of Prime Minister Shih.

In the first year of the era *yüan-shou* [122 B.C.] Emperor Wu designated an heir apparent and asked his officials who would be suitable to appoint as the boy's tutor. On their recommendation Shih Ch'ing was summoned from his post as governor of P'ei and made grand tutor to the heir apparent. Seven years later he was transferred to the post of imperial secretary. In the fifth year of the era *yüan-ting* [112 B.C.] the chancellor Chao Chou was accused of some fault and removed from his post. The emperor sent an order to Shih Ch'ing saying, "Lord Wan-shih enjoyed the esteem of the former emperor, and his sons and grandsons have distinguished themselves for their filial behavior. Therefore let the imperial secretary Shih Ch'ing be promoted to the position of chancellor and enfeoffed as marquis of Mu-ch'iu."

At this time the Han armies were engaged in an expedition against the two kingdoms of Yüeh in the south, were attacking Korea in the east, driving back the Hsiung-nu in the north, and in the west striking at Ta-yüan [Ferghana], so that China was involved in a great number

⁵ It is not certain just what style of writing was used in reports to the emperor, but it would seem from extant Han documents that the character for "horse" was written much the same as it is today: 馬

of military undertakings. The emperor made frequent hunts and progresses about the empire, reestablishing the shrines of ancient times, carrying out the Feng and Shan sacrifices, and working to encourage the revival of rites and music, so that the public treasuries were depleted. Men like Sang Hung-yang schemed to augment the national wealth by government monopolies, Wang Wen-shu and his group increased the severity of the laws, Erh K'uan and others were advanced to the highest ministerial posts because of their literary achievements, and all of them were coming forward with one new proposal after another. As chancellor, Shih Ch'ing no longer had any say in affairs of government, but conducted himself with care and circumspection. Though he occupied the post for nine years, he was never able to do anything to correct the situation. At one time he attempted to bring charges against So Chung, one of the emperor's intimate advisers, and another high minister named Chien Hsüan, but he was not able to carry the case through; on the contrary, he was accused of misconduct himself and forced to pay a fine.

During the fourth year of the era *yüan-feng* [107 B.C.] it was reported that there were two million people east of the Pass who had wandered from their homes and another million and four hundred thousand whose homes were not even registered.[6] The high officials discussed what measures should be taken, and Shih Ch'ing suggested that the vagrants be deported to the border regions as a punishment for deserting their homes. The emperor considered that Shih Ch'ing was too old and cautious to be of any help in the deliberations, and so he granted him leave to return to his home and referred the question instead to the imperial secretary and the other junior officials and interested parties for discussion. Shih Ch'ing was deeply hurt at the implication that he was not fit for his position, and sent a letter to the emperor, saying, "I have graciously been allowed to fill the post of chancellor and, with my poor abilities, to aid in the government of the empire. Now the cities are deserted and the granaries empty, and many of the people are wandering about homeless. As a responsible official

[6] As the parallel passage in *Han shu* 46 makes clear, the people had been forced to leave their homes because of floods resulting from a break in the dikes of the Yellow River.

I deserve to die beneath the executioner's axe for such a situation. If Your Majesty cannot bear to carry out the penalty, I beg to return the seals which were granted to me as chancellor and marquis and to be allowed to retire to private life so that I may make way for more worthy men."

To this the emperor wrote in reply, "The granaries are already empty and the people destitute and homeless, and yet you wish to deport them to the border! You would stir them to even greater unrest, increase the gravity of the situation, and then retire from your post! And on whom do you propose to shift the blame for what follows?"

Shih Ch'ing was deeply chagrined at the severity of the emperor's reprimand, and once more resumed his duties as chancellor. He fulfilled the letter of the law and conducted his affairs with thoughtfulness and care, but after this he brought forward no more large-scale proposals for the disposition of the people. Some three years later, during the second year of the era *t'ai-ch'u* [103 B.C.], Shih Ch'ing died in office and was given the posthumous title of T'ien, the "Quiet Marquis."

Shih Ch'ing showed particular favor for his second son, Shih Te, and the emperor accordingly recognized Shih Te as his heir and allowed him to succeed to the marquisate. Shih Te later became master of ritual, but was tried for some offense and sentenced to death. On payment of a fine he was released from prison and made a commoner. While Shih Ch'ing held the post of chancellor a number of his sons and grandsons became officials, and thirteen of them eventually reached positions paying two thousand piculs. After his death, however, many of them were accused of crimes and removed from their posts, and the family's reputation for filial conduct and circumspection gradually declined.

Wei Wan

The marquis of Chien-ling, Wei Wan, was a native of Ta-ling in Tai. Because of his ability to do stunt riding in a carriage he was made a palace attendant and served at the court of Emperor Wen. After discharging his duties satisfactorily for the requisite number of years he was promoted to the position of general of palace attendants.

He devoted great care and energy to his post and took no thought for anything else.

Once when Emperor Ching was still heir apparent he summoned some of his father's attendants to join him in drinking, but Wei Wan pleaded illness and declined the invitation. When Emperor Wen lay on his deathbed, he charged his son, saying, "Wei Wan is a worthy man—see that you treat him well!" But after Emperor Wen passed away and Emperor Ching came to the throne a year or so went by and the emperor never questioned Wei Wan on any affair. Wei Wan for his part continued to go about his duties each day with care and diligence. Once Emperor Ching made a visit to the Shang-lin Park, and ordered Wei Wan to ride with him in his carriage. On the way back to the palace the emperor asked, "Do you know why you were summoned to ride with me?"

"I began my career as a carriage attendant and, because of length of service, I have graciously been allowed to advance to the post of general of palace attendants. But I do not know why I have been honored today."

"When I was still heir apparent, I invited you once to a party, but you refused to come. Why was that?" asked the emperor.

"If it please Your Majesty, I was actually ill!" replied Wei Wan. The emperor then presented him with a sword, but Wei Wan declined, saying, "The former emperor was kind enough to give me several swords—six, in fact. I could not possibly accept another one."

"But everybody gives swords away or exchanges them for something else. You don't mean that you still have all six of them today?"

"They are all in my possession," replied Wei Wan, and when the emperor sent someone to look at the six swords, he found that they were all still in their scabbards and had never been worn.

Whenever one of Wei Wan's subordinates was guilty of some fault he would always accept the blame himself. He did not vie with the other generals but, if he had won some merit, always gave the credit to someone else. Emperor Ching valued him for his modesty, loyalty, and unselfish devotion to duty, and honored him with the position of grand tutor to his son Liu Te, the king of Ho-chien.

When the states of Wu and Ch'u revolted, Emperor Ching made

Wei Wan a general and sent him to lead the troops of Ho-chien against the rebels. He won merit in the campaign and was promoted to the post of palace military commander. Three years later, in the sixth year of the former part of Emperor Ching's reign [144 B.C.], he was enfeoffed as marquis of Chien-ling because of his military achievements. The following year the emperor decided to depose the heir apparent and wipe out Li Ch'ing and the other maternal relatives of the prince. But he knew that Wei Wan, being a worthy man, could not bear to carry out so harsh a duty, and so he allowed Wei Wan to leave his post and return home, charging Chih Tu instead with the arrest and prosecution of the Li family. Later, when he had designated the king of Chiao-tung as his new heir, he summoned Wei Wan once more and made him grand tutor to the heir apparent.

After some time Wei Wan was advanced to the post of imperial secretary, and five years later he replaced the marquis of T'ao, Liu She, as chancellor. He reported to the emperor on the execution of his assigned duties at the regular sessions of the court, but during all his official career from palace attendant to chancellor he never came forward with any unusual proposal. Nevertheless Emperor Ching esteemed him for his honest and loyal nature and believed he would be an excellent aide for his young son when he became ruler, and he therefore treated Wei Wan with great favor and showered him with gifts.

Three years after Wei Wan became chancellor Emperor Ching passed away and Emperor Wu came to the throne. In the first years of his reign the new emperor dismissed Wei Wan from the post of chancellor. "When Emperor Ching was ailing and could no longer attend to public affairs," he said, "a number of officials were imprisoned and tried for offenses of which they were not guilty, and yet you failed to carry out your duty as chancellor to see that justice was done!" Some time afterwards Wei Wan died and his son Wei Hsin succeeded to the marquisate, but he was accused of some irregularity in the tribute money he presented to the throne and deprived of his title.

Chih Pu-i

Chih Pu-i, the marquis of Sai, a native of Nan-yang, became a palace attendant under Emperor Wen. Once one of the officials who lived in the same dormitory with Chih Pu-i was going home on vacation and mistakenly picked up someone else's money and went off with it. When the owner of the money discovered his loss he accused Chih Pu-i, who confessed to the theft and, apologizing, procured the sum and reimbursed the owner. Later, when the other man came back from his vacation and returned the actual money, the owner was deeply chagrined at his mistake and Chih Pu-i received wide praise for his worthy action. Emperor Wen thought highly of him and gradually advanced him to the position of palace counselor.

One time when the officials were gathered in court someone tried to slander him by saying, "Chih Pu-i is certainly good looking, but what can you do with a man who carries on in secret with his older brother's wife?" When Chih Pu-i heard of the remark he said, "As a matter of fact, I have no older brother," but he was unwilling to go to any further trouble to clear himself of the charge.

At the time of the revolt of Wu and Ch'u, Chih Pu-i, in his capacity as an official of two thousand piculs, led a force of troops against the rebel armies. In the first year of the latter part of Emperor Ching's reign [143 B.C.] he was advanced to the post of imperial secretary and, when the emperor got around to rewarding those who had distinguished themselves at the time of the revolt, he was enfeoffed as marquis of Sai. During the first years of Emperor Wu's reign he was accused of some fault at the same time as the chancellor Wei Wan and relieved of his post.

He was a student of the teachings of Lao Tzu and, whatever post he occupied, he sought to do only as much as his predecessor in office and no more; he had a horror that people would take too much notice of his official actions. He disliked any sort of striving for fame, and yet, because of this, he was renowned as a worthy man. After his death his son Chih Hsiang-ju succeeded to the marquisate, but his grandson Chih Wang was accused of some irregularity in tribute money and lost the title.

Chou Jen

The ancestors of the chief of palace attendants Chou Wen, whose familiar name was Chou Jen, came originally from Jen-ch'eng. Because of his knowledge of medicine Chou Jen was employed at court and, while Emperor Ching was still heir apparent, was appointed as one of the prince's retainers. After a number of years of service he gradually advanced and, while Emperor Wen was still reigning, reached the position of palace counselor. When Emperor Ching came to the throne he promoted Chou Jen to the post of chief of palace attendants.

Chou Jen was very silent and reserved, and never repeated what he heard. He always went about in a worn and patched robe and urine-stained trousers, purposely presenting a dirty and unattractive appearance. For this reason Emperor Ching favored him and allowed him to go in and out of his private chambers; whenever there were secret revels in the women's quarters Chou Jen was always present.[7]

Chou Jen remained chief of palace attendants up to the time that Emperor Ching passed away, but he never spoke out on any matter. Once the Emperor questioned him about someone's character, but Chou Jen replied, "Your Majesty will have to judge the man for yourself." He never made any attempt to slander others. Because of this Emperor Ching twice made personal visits to his home, and moved his family to Yang-ling, where the emperor had constructed his mausoleum. The emperor offered him many gifts, but Chou Jen always declined them, and he likewise refused to accept bribes and gifts from the feudal lords and other officials.

After Emperor Wu came to the throne he treated Chou Jen with respect because he had been a servant of his father, the former emperor. Chou Jen retired from his post because of illness and, with a salary of two thousand piculs, returned home to spend the rest of his days. His sons and grandsons all advanced to important positions in the government.

[7] Perhaps the emperor felt that, because of his unattractive appearance, none of the palace ladies would be tempted to misbehave with Chou Jen; or perhaps Ssu-ma Ch'ien is implying something more unsavory about the relationship between Chou Jen and the emperor.

Chang Shu

The imperial secretary Chang Shu, whose familiar name was Chang Ou, was a son by a concubine of Chang Yüeh, the marquis of An-ch'iu. During the reign of Emperor Wen he was given a position with the household of the heir apparent because of his knowledge of the Legalist teachings on functions and titles.[8] But although a student of this branch of Legalism, he was at the same time a worthy man. Emperor Ching esteemed him greatly and always employed him in some high ministerial position. In the fourth year of the era *yüan-so* of Emperor Wu's reign [125 B.C.] Han An-kuo was removed from the post of imperial secretary and Chang Shu appointed to replace him. From the time he first became an official he never attempted to bring charges against anyone, but devoted all his efforts to the worthy execution of his duties. His subordinates, knowing that he was a worthy man, likewise did not dare to commit any deception. Whenever they brought some criminal case before him for action, if he felt that the charges could be dismissed, he would dismiss them; but if the case was so serious that it had to be referred to the emperor, he would turn his face aside and, with tears in his eyes, reluctantly place his seal on the document. Such was his compassion for others.

When he grew old and was seriously ill he asked to be relieved of his post. The emperor presented him with a special letter of dismissal and allowed him to return to his home to live out his days with the salary of a high official. His home was in Yang-ling. His sons and grandsons all advanced to important positions in the government.

The Grand Historian remarks: Confucius once said that "a gentleman endeavors to be slow in speech but earnest in conduct."[9] Would this not apply to Lord Wan-shih, Wei Wan, and Chang Shu? They were not severe in teaching others, and yet they accomplished their

---

[8] A branch of Legalism derived from the teachings of Shen Pu-hai, which specialized in questions of personnel control. The particular problem facing Emperor Wen and his son was how to control the feudal lords and keep them from becoming too powerful.

[9] *Analects* IV, 24.

objective; they were not harsh, and yet they achieved order. Chih Pu-i was subtle and artful, while Chou Jen used dubious means to gain intimacy with the emperor, so that gentlemen may be inclined to dismiss both of them as hardly more than servile flatterers. And yet they too in their way can be called gentlemen of faithful conduct.

Shih chi 104: The Biography of T'ien Shu

With directness and honesty he carried out his duty; in his support of right he is worthy to be called pure, and his actions are an inspiration to wisdom. Entrusted with heavy responsibilities, he refused to compromise his principles. Thus I made The Biography of T'ien Shu.

T'ien Shu was a native of Ching-ch'eng in Chao. His ancestors were descendants of the T'ien family of the state of Ch'i. T'ien Shu was very fond of swordsmanship and studied the doctrines of the Yellow Emperor and Lao Tzu at the home of Master Lo Chü. As a person he took great pride in scrupulous honesty and enjoyed making friends with the worthwhile people of his time. The men of Chao recommended him to Chao Wu, the prime minister of Chao, who in turn spoke about him to Chang Ao, the king of Chao. The king made him a palace attendant, and for several years he executed his duties with fairness and candor. But, although the king admired his worth, he did not promote him to a higher position.

In the seventh year of Han, Ch'en Hsi raised his revolt in the region of Tai and Emperor Kao-tsu marched north to punish the rebels. On his way back he visited the state of Chao. The king of Chao, Chang Ao, served the emperor his meals in person and treated him with the utmost courtesy and respect, but Kao-tsu for his part merely sprawled about on his mat and abused the king. At this time the prime minister Chao Wu, Kuan Kao,[1] and a number of the other ministers, infuriated by the emperor's behavior, said to the king, "You have waited on the emperor with the greatest courtesy, and yet he treats you like this! We beg you to allow us to raise a revolt!"

The king bit his finger until he drew blood and replied, "When

---

[1] The name of Kuan Kao, one of the chief conspirators, has evidently dropped out of the text at this point. In the account of this incident in "The Biographies of Chang Erh and Ch'en Yü," above, Kuan Kao, not Chao Wu, is mentioned as prime minister of Chao.

my father Chang Erh lost his kingdom, if it had not been for the aid of His Majesty, we would all have died a beggar's death in the fields. How can you speak of such a thing? I beg you, say no more of this!"

"Our king is a worthy man and will not betray a debt of gratitude," said Kuan Kao and the other ministers, but in the end they secretly plotted together to assassinate Emperor Kao-tsu. The affair came to light and the emperor sent an order for the arrest of the king of Chao and all of his ministers who were guilty of taking part in the plot. Chao Wu and the others committed suicide, but Kuan Kao alone allowed himself to be taken prisoner. At this time the emperor issued an edict warning that any of the king's men who dared to follow him to the capital would be executed along with their families. In spite of this, however, Meng Shu, T'ien Shu, and some ten others shaved their heads, donned the red clothes and manacles of convicts, and, pretending to be slaves of the king's household, accompanied him on his journey. After the king reached Ch'ang-an, Kuan Kao's testimony proved that the king was not involved in the plot and he was cleared of suspicion. He was removed from his position and made marquis of Hsüan-p'ing, at which time he spoke to the emperor on behalf of T'ien Shu and the others who had accompanied him. The emperor summoned them all to an audience and talked with them. He was favorably impressed and, declaring that there were no finer ministers in the Han court itself, appointed them all as governors of provinces or prime ministers to the feudal lords. T'ien Shu was made governor of Han-chung, a post which he held for over ten years.

Following this, Empress Lü passed away, and the Lü family plotted to seize power. The high ministers overthrew them and set up Emperor Wen. After he came to the throne Emperor Wen summoned T'ien Shu to court and asked, "Do you know who the worthiest men of the empire are?"

"How would a person like myself know such a thing?" he replied.

"Since you yourself are a worthy man, you ought to know."

T'ien Shu bowed his head and replied, "Meng Shu, the former governor of Yün-chung, is a worthy man." At this time the Hsiung-nu had crossed the northern border and invaded and plundered in great numbers, committing the worst damage in the province of Yün-chung, and as a result Meng Shu had been tried and removed from his post as governor of that province.

"The former emperor appointed Meng Shu as governor of Yün-chung, a post which he held for over ten years," said Emperor Wen. "And yet when the barbarians invaded his territory, he was not only unable to guard his fortifications but, for no reason at all, he sent out several hundred of his soldiers to die in battle. Does a worthy man have to murder his men in this fashion? How can you call him worthy?"

T'ien Shu bowed his head to the ground and replied, "It is precisely this incident which proves that he is worthy. When Kuan Kao and the others were plotting revolt, and Emperor Kao-tsu issued an edict threatening death to any man and his family who dared to accompany the king of Chao to the capital, Meng Shu shaved his head, put a manacle about his neck, and followed the king wherever he went. His only thought was to sacrifice himself, for of course he had no way of knowing that such action would bring him the governorship of Yün-chung. The soldiers of the empire were exhausted by the long struggle between the forces of Han and Ch'u, and the Hsiung-nu ruler, Mo-tun, having newly conquered the barbarian tribes on his north, came to menace our borders. Meng Shu knew that his men were weary, and he could not bear to order them out to battle. And yet the soldiers vied with each other in mounting the walls and struggling to the death with the enemy. They were like sons fighting for a father, or younger brothers fighting for an elder brother, and so it happened that several hundred of them were killed. It was certainly not a case of Meng Shu driving them into battle! This is why I say that he is a worthy man."

"Perhaps, as you say, he is a worthy man after all," agreed the emperor, and he recalled Meng Shu and restored him to his position as governor of Yün-chung.

Several years later T'ien Shu was accused of some offense and removed from his position. At this time it happened that Liu Wu, the king of Liang, sent assassins to murder the former prime minister of Wu, Yüan Ang. Emperor Ching summoned T'ien Shu and sent him to Liang to investigate the matter. After uncovering the full details of the plot T'ien Shu returned to the capital and made his report to the emperor. "Was my brother the king of Liang actually involved in the plot?" asked Emperor Ching.

"I am very sorry to have to report that he was," replied T'ien Shu.

"In what way?"

"For Your Majesty's sake I beg you to inquire no further about the affair." [2]

"Why do you say that?" asked the emperor.

"If the affair is brought to light, then your brother will have to be punished or the laws of the dynasty will not be upheld. But if your brother should be punished according to the law, then your mother the empress dowager would be so distressed that she could not eat or sleep, and this would cause Your Majesty great worry, I fear."

Emperor Ching was impressed with T'ien Shu's wisdom in handling the matter and appointed him as prime minister to the state of Lu. When he first arrived in Lu some hundred or so people of the kingdom came to him with complaints that the king of Lu had seized their goods and property, begging him to see that justice was done. T'ien Shu had the leaders of the group punished with fifty strokes of the rod, and the rest of the petitioners with twenty strokes each. "The king is your sovereign lord, is he not?" he declared angrily. "How dare you speak against your lord!" When the king of Lu heard of the incident he was filled with shame and, opening his storehouses, handed over the goods he had taken to T'ien Shu to be restored to the proper owners. But T'ien Shu objected, saying, "It was the king himself who seized the goods. Now if he gives them to me, his prime minister, to return, it will appear that the king is doing evil and his prime minister is doing good. I cannot accept the goods!" With this, the king himself returned all the things he had seized.

The king of Lu was very fond of hunting and T'ien Shu as prime minister invariably accompanied him to the royal hunting park. "You may go back to your office now," the king would say, but T'ien Shu always insisted upon sitting down in the open outside the park and waiting for the king. The king would send messengers from time to time urging him to go home, but he refused to move. "While my king is still exposed to the open air in the park, how would I dare to return

---

[2] Following the reading in *Han shu* 37.

to my quarters alone?" he protested. As a result the king of Lu found it impossible to go out hunting very often.³

After several years T'ien Shu died in office. The people of Lu took up a collection and offered a hundred pieces of gold to his family to pay for sacrifices to his spirit, but his youngest son T'ien Jen refused to accept the money. "I would not want a matter of a hundred pieces of gold to reflect upon my father's reputation for honesty!"

T'ien Jen, a vigorous youth, became a retainer of General Wei Ch'ing and under his command made several attacks on the Hsiung-nu. On General Wei's recommendation he was made a palace attendant and after several years was promoted to the post of chief secretary to the prime minister, a position paying a salary of two thousand piculs. He lost this post but was later appointed inspector of the three provinces of Ho-nan, Ho-tung, and Ho-nei. When the emperor made a tour of the east T'ien Jen submitted a report on his investigations. The emperor was pleased with him and made him a colonel of the capital district, and, a month or so later, promoted him to the position of director of justice. Several years later he was involved in the revolt of the heir apparent Prince Li. When the heir apparent raised his rebellion in the capital the chancellor of the left Liu Ch'ü-li led the troops against him in person and gave orders to T'ien Jen to shut the gates of the city and see to it that the prince did not escape. After the prince succeeded in slipping out anyway T'ien Jen was tried on charges of having deliberately allowed him to escape, and he and the members of his family were executed.⁴

The Grand Historian remarks: It was said of Confucius that "whatever state he visited, he never failed to learn about its government." ⁵

³ Because they considered hunting a dangerous and time-consuming pastime Chinese officials tried various methods to persuade their rulers to spend as little time at it as possible. T'ien Shu's method is one of the more ingenious ones.

⁴ The text of this paragraph is obviously corrupt. I have omitted a few brief sentences and translated the rest in the light of the parallel passages in *Han shu* 37. In 91 B.C., in the latter days of Emperor Wu's reign, Prince Li and his mother, Empress Wei, were accused of attempting to kill the emperor by sorcery. On the unsuccessful revolt of the heir apparent Prince Li, which took place in 91 B.C., see *Ssu-ma Ch'ien: Grand Historian of China,* Appendix B, pp. 194-98.

⁵ *Analects* I, 10.

The same might apply to T'ien Shu. He fulfilled his duties and did not forget other men of worth; he worked to enhance the reputation of his sovereign and to save him from error. His son T'ien Jen was a friend of mine and so I have added at the end a few remarks on his life.

FINDING LIST OF CHAPTERS OF THE *SHIH CHI*

Basic Annals (SC 1–12):
SC 1–6   Omitted
SC 7   Vol. I, Part II
SC 8   Vol. I, Part III
SC 9   Vol. I, Part VII
SC 10   Vol. I, Part VII
SC 11   Vol. I, Part VII
SC 12   Vol. I, Part VII

Chronological Tables, Introductions (SC 13–22):
SC 13–15 Omitted
SC 16   Vol. I, Part III
SC 17   Vol. I, Part X
SC 18   Vol. I, Part X
SC 19   Vol. I, Part X
SC 20   Vol. II, Part II
SC 21–22 Omitted

Treatises (SC 23–30):
SC 23–27 Omitted
SC 28   Vol. II, Part I
SC 29   Vol. II, Part I
SC 30   Vol. II, Part I

Hereditary Houses (SC 31–60):
SC 31–47 Omitted
SC 48   Vol. I, Part I
SC 49   Vol. I, Part VIII
SC 50   Vol. I, Part IX
SC 51   Vol. I, Part IX
SC 52   Vol. I, Part IX
SC 53   Vol. I, Part IV
SC 54   Vol. I, Part IX
SC 55   Vol. I, Part IV
SC 56   Vol. I, Part IV
SC 57   Vol. I, Part IX
SC 58   Vol. I, Part IX
SC 59   Vol. I, Part IX
SC 60   Omitted

Biographies and Accounts of Foreign Peoples (SC 61–130):
SC 61–83 Omitted
SC 84   Vol. I, Part XI
SC 85–88 Omitted
SC 89   Vol. I, Part V
SC 90   Vol. I, Part V
SC 91   Vol. I, Part V
SC 92   Vol. I, Part V
SC 93   Vol. I, Part V
SC 94   Vol. I, Part V
SC 95   Vol. I, Part VI
SC 96   Vol. I, Part VI
SC 97   Vol. I, Part VI
SC 98   Vol. I, Part VI
SC 99   Vol. I, Part VI
SC 100   Vol. I, Part VI
SC 101   Vol. I, Part XI
SC 102   Vol. I, Part XI

Biographies and Accounts of Foreign Peoples (SC 61–130) *Cont.:*

SC 103	Vol. I, Part XI	SC 116	Vol. II, Part II
SC 104	Vol. I, Part XI	SC 117	Vol. II, Part II
SC 105	Omitted	SC 118	Vol. II, Part III
SC 106	Vol. I, Part X	SC 119	Vol. II, Part IV
SC 107	Vol. II, Part II	SC 120	Vol. II, Part II
SC 108	Vol. II, Part II	SC 121	Vol. II, Part IV
SC 109	Vol. II, Part II	SC 122	Vol. II, Part IV
SC 110	Vol. II, Part II	SC 123	Vol. II, Part II
SC 111	Vol. II, Part II	SC 124	Vol. II, Part IV
SC 112	Vol. II, Part II	SC 125	Vol. II, Part IV
SC 113	Vol. II, Part II	SC 126	Omitted
SC 114	Vol. II, Part II	SC 127	Vol. II, Part IV
SC 115	Vol. II, Part II	SC 128	Omitted
		SC 129	Vol. II, Part IV
		SC 130	Omitted